Oxford
Primary
Spanish
Dictionary

Editor Michael Janes
Consultants Martyn Ellis
 Rosa Martín

OXFORD
UNIVERSITY PRESS

Great Clarendon Street, Oxford OX2 6DP

Oxford University Press is a department of the University of Oxford.
It furthers the University's objective of excellence in research, scholarship,
and education by publishing worldwide in

Oxford New York

Auckland Cape Town Dar es Salaam Hong Kong Karachi
Kuala Lumpur Madrid Melbourne Mexico City Nairobi
New Delhi Shanghai Taipei Toronto

with offices in

Argentina Austria Brazil Chile Czech Republic France Greece
Guatemala Hungary Italy Japan Poland Portugal Singapore
South Korea Switzerland Thailand Turkey Ukraine Vietnam

Oxford is a registered trade mark of Oxford University Press
in the UK and in certain other countries

© Oxford University Press 2007

Database right Oxford University Press (maker)

First published 2007

British Library cataloguing in Publication Data

Data available

ISBN: 978-0-19-911524-2

10 9 8 7 6 5 4 3 2 1

Typeset in OUP Argo Infant and OUP Swift Infant

Printed in Singapore by KHL Printing Co. Pte Ltd.

Contents

Introduction

The *Oxford Primary Spanish Dictionary* is a completely new dictionary written for primary schoolchildren between the ages of 7 and 11.

This dictionary is much more than a basic resource for looking up translations: it also helps children to see patterns in the way Spanish is used and structured and identify relationships between similar-looking Spanish and English words. It provides an understanding of the basic concepts of grammar and also includes age-appropriate and interesting cultural information.

A selection of the most important Latin American words are included. There are lots of differences between European and Latin American Spanish. For example, the words **tú** and **ustedes** (the familiar word for 'you' in the singular and plural) are not usually used in Latin America – **vos** and **vosotros/vosotras** are used instead.

The layout is modern and clear with Spanish picked out in green and English picked out in blue. Child-friendly example sentences and phrases illustrate common usage and constructions, and feature panels present information in a simple graphic way.

The illustrated thematic centre section of the dictionary is a further opportunity to develop key vocabulary skills with its topic-based phrases and sentences. The central verb table section provides a simple first step into using and understanding verb tenses.

The *Oxford Primary Spanish Dictionary* makes learning another language enjoyable, fun, and easy. It is a vital and effective tool that will enable children to start using Spanish confidently.

The publishers and editor are indebted to all the advisors, consultants, teachers, and readers who were involved in planning and compiling this dictionary. Special thanks go to Martyn Ellis and Rosa Martín.

MJ

Get to know your dictionary

The dictionary is divided into two halves, the *Spanish-English* side and the *English-Spanish* side. These are separated by a picture section and verb tables in the middle.

Spanish **English**

- **Where do I find the English translation of a Spanish word?**
- Look in the *Spanish-English* half which comes first.

English **Spanish**

- **Where do I find the Spanish translation of an English word?**
- Look in the *English-Spanish* half towards the back of the book.

- **How do I find a word quickly?**
- Use the alphabet on the edge of each page to find the first letter of the word you need.

carroza ➡ castañuelas

- Then use the guidewords highlighted on the top of the page. They are the first and last words on the page. Think of the order of letters in your word to make sure you are on the right page.

 For example, what does **casi** mean in English?

- Look in the *Spanish-English* half.

- Find where **c** is highlighted in the alphabet on the edge of the page.

- Look at the two words at the top of a page. Find the words beginning with **ca**, then **cas**, until you get to **casi**.

culture panel

guide words

cafetería ➡ conductora

la cafetería noun fem.
 cafe

🌐 **CULTURE**
In Spain cafes sell alcohol as well as coffee.

headword — **caminar** verb
 to walk

la camisa noun fem. — word class
 shirt

Canadá noun masc.
 Canada
 Vamos a Canadá. We're going to Canada.

gender — **canadiense** adjective masc. & fem.
 Canadian
 Es canadiense. He's Canadian.

el or la canadiense noun masc. & fem.
 Canadian

el canal noun masc.
signpost — **1** (on TV) **channel**
 Cambia de canal. Change the channel.
 2 canal
 el Canal de Panamá the Panama Canal
 el Canal de la Mancha the English Channel

la cancha noun fem.
 1 (for tennis, squash, etc.) **court**
 2 (for football, rugby, etc.) **pitch**

translation — **el capítulo** noun masc.
 chapter

la capucha noun fem.
 hood

la cara noun fem.
 1 face
 Voy a lavarme la cara. I'm going to wash my face.
numbered — **2** (when throwing a coin) **¡Cara!** Heads!
meanings **¿Cara o cruz?** Heads or tails?
 3 nerve
 ¡Tienes mucha cara! You've got a nerve!

cocinar verb
 to cook

el cocinero noun masc., **la cocinera** fem.
 cook
 Soy muy buen cocinero. I'm a good cook.

comer verb
 1 to eat
 ¿Quieres comer algo? Do you want something to eat?
 2 (at lunchtime) **to have lunch**

el or la comerciante noun masc. & fem.
 shopkeeper

la cometa noun fem.
 kite

♂ **LANGUAGE**
Do you think a kite looks like a comet? The Spanish words for both are the same but the genders are different – 'comet' is masculine: **el cometa.**

la comida noun fem.
 1 food
 No hay suficiente comida. There isn't enough food.
 2 meal
 Hago tres comidas al día. I have three meals a day.
 3 (at lunchtime) **lunch**

la comisaría noun fem.
 police station

el conductor noun masc., **la conductora** fem.
 driver

⚠ **FALSE FRIEND**
un conductor = a driver (not a conductor)

a
b
c
d
e
f
g
h
i
j
k
l
m
n
o
p
q
r
s
t
u
v
w
x
y
z

Spanish / English — language tab

alphabet tab

language panel

example

• Use **el** and **uno** for masculine words and **la** and **una** for feminine words.

footnote

false friend panel

vi

headwords
These are the words you look up. The Spanish headwords are in green. The English headwords are in blue.

word classes
Most headwords in the dictionary are nouns, verbs, or adjectives. Sometimes a word can be more than one word class: for example, 'phone' can be a noun (He's on the phone) or a verb (Phone me tomorrow). For nouns, the dictionary gives the Spanish word for 'the', e.g. el autocar, la barca, los espaguetis, las gafas.

gender
Spanish nouns and adjectives are either masculine (*masc.*) or feminine (*fem.*). Nouns and adjectives can be singular (just one) or plural (more than one).

translations
These are the headwords translated in English or Spanish.

examples
Examples show you how to use the headword in a typical way.

numbered meanings
If a headword has more than one translation, numbers separate each translation.

signposts
These point you to the right translation, usually when there is more than one meaning of the word you are looking up, e.g. a 'picture' can be a (*drawing*), and the Spanish is debujo, or a picture you see (*on TV*) and then the Spanish is imagen.

language panels
Vital information about how to use the headwords correctly is shown in the key language panels.

false friend panels
These are important warnings to stop you from using a Spanish word which looks like an English one but which has a completely different meaning!

culture panels
Interesting facts about Spanish culture are shown in these panels.

alphabet tab
To help you navigate your way through the dictionary, the letter you are on is highlighted on the alphabet strip on every page.

language tab
This shows which side of the dictionary you are on.

guide words
These help you to find the word you are looking for easily. They show you the first and last word on the page.

footnotes
These give you useful general language reminders.

Aa

a preposition

> **🔑 LANGUAGE**
> a + el = al

1 to
 a la biblioteca to the library
 a España to Spain
 Voy al médico. I'm going to the doctor.
 He aprendido a leer. I've learnt to read.

2 (*with words of giving, sending, etc.*) **to**
 Doy un regalo a mi amigo. I am giving my friend a present.

3 at
 a las siete at seven o'clock
 a medianoche at midnight
 Llego a casa a las cuatro. I arrive home at four.

4 on
 a la derecha on the right
 Voy a pie. I go on foot.
 Subí al tren. I got on the train.

5 in
 a lápiz in pencil
 al sol in the sun
 Me tiré al agua. I jumped in the water.

6 (*in the distance*) **away**
 Está a cinco kilómetros de aquí. It's five kilometres away.

7 (*with dates*)
 Estamos a diez de marzo. It's the tenth of March.

8 (*when saying how many times*) **a**
 dos veces al día twice a day

9 (*not translated, with a person or a pet*)

> **🔑 LANGUAGE**
> A is used after verbs in front of nouns for people or pets.

 ¿Has visto a Rafael? Have you seen Rafael?

 Conozco a tu padre. I know your dad.
 Lavo a mi perro. I wash my dog.

abajo adverb
1 down
 arriba y abajo up and down
 No mires abajo. Don't look down.
2 downstairs
 Estoy abajo en el salón. I'm downstairs in the living room.
3 de abajo below
 el piso de abajo the flat below
4 (*talking about the lowest one*)
 de abajo bottom
 en el estante de abajo on the bottom shelf

el **abanico** noun *masc.*
 fan

el **abecedario** noun *masc.*
 alphabet

la **abeja** noun *fem.*
 bee

abierto adjective *masc.*,
abierta *fem.*
1 open
 La puerta está abierta. The door's open.
2 on
 El grifo está abierto. The tap's on.

el **abogado** noun *masc.*,
la **abogada** *fem.*
 lawyer
 She's a lawyer. Es abogada.

el **abrazo** noun *masc.*
 hug
 Un abrazo, Antonio. (*in a letter*) With best wishes, Antonio.

el **abrigo** noun *masc.*
 coat

• Languages and nationalities do not take a capital letter in Spanish.

abril noun masc.
April
en abril in April
Mi cumpleaños es en abril.
My birthday's in April.

abrir verb
1 to open
Abre la puerta. Open the door.
¿A qué hora abre el
supermercado? What time does
the supermarket open?
2 to turn on
abrir el grifo to turn on the tap

abrochar verb
to do up
Abróchate la chaqueta. Do up
your jacket.

el **abuelo** noun masc.,
la **abuela** fem.
grandfather, grandmother
mis abuelos my grandparents

aburrido adjective masc.,
aburrida fem.
1 boring
Es aburrido. It's boring.
2 bored
Estoy aburrido. I'm bored.

aburrirse verb
to get bored
Me aburro. I get bored.

acabar verb
1 to finish
He acabado mis deberes. I've
finished my homework.
2 acabar de hacer algo to have just
done something
Acabo de llegar. I've just arrived.

> 🔑 **LANGUAGE**
> Use **acabar de** with the infinitive when
> you want to say you've done something a
> short time ago/just now.

acampar verb
to camp

acariciar verb
to stroke
Me gusta acariciar al gato. I like
stroking the cat.

el **accidente** noun masc.
accident
Mi amigo tuvo un accidente de
coche. My friend had a car
accident.

la **acción** noun fem.
action
una película con mucha acción
a film with lots of action

el **aceite** noun masc.
oil
el aceite de oliva olive oil

la **aceituna** noun fem.
olive

el **acento** noun masc.
accent
'Fútbol' lleva acento en la 'u'.
'Fútbol' has an accent on the 'u'.
María tiene acento español. Maria
has a Spanish accent.

aceptar verb
to accept

la **acera** noun fem.
pavement

acercarse verb
to get closer
Acércate a la ventana. Get closer
to the window.

acertar verb
acertar algo to get something
right
¿Acertaste? Did you get it right?

acompañar verb
to go with, to come with
¿Me acompañas? Are you coming
with me?

acordarse verb
to remember
No me acuerdo. I don't remember.

• The months of the year and days of the week do not take a capital letter in Spanish.

acordarse de algo to remember something
Me acuerdo del número. I remember the number.
¿Te acuerdas de mí? Do you remember me?

acostarse verb
to go to bed
Me acuesto a las ocho. I go to bed at eight.

el or la **acróbata** noun *masc. & fem.*
acrobat

la **actividad** noun *fem.*
activity

activo adjective *masc.*, **activa** *fem.*
active

el **actor** noun *masc.*
actor

la **actriz** noun *fem.* (plural las **actrices**)
actress

actuar verb
(*in a play, film, etc.*) **to act**

el **acuerdo** noun *masc.*
estar de acuerdo to agree
Estoy de acuerdo contigo. I agree with you.

acusar verb
to accuse

el or la **acusica** noun *masc. & fem.*
telltale

adelantar verb
1 (*in a car*) **to overtake**
2 (*in a game*) **to move forward**
Adelanta una casilla. Move to the next square.

adelante adverb
forward
más adelante further on
¡Adelante! Come in! (*entering a room*); Go on! (*telling somebody to do something*)

además adverb
as well, **besides**

Es inteligente y además trabajador. He's intelligent and hard-working as well.
Es caro y además es feo. It's expensive and it's ugly besides.

adentro adverb
inside
Pasa adentro. Come inside.

el **adhesivo** noun *masc.*
sticker

adiós exclamation
goodbye

adivinar verb
to guess

el **adjetivo** noun *masc.*
adjective

el or la **adolescente** noun *masc. & fem.*
teenager

adónde adverb
where
¿Adónde vas? Where are you going?

los **adornos** plural noun *masc.*
decorations
los adornos de Navidad the Christmas decorations

adrede adverb
on purpose
Lo has hecho adrede. You did it on purpose.

el **adulto** noun *masc.*, la **adulta** *fem.*
adult

el **adverbio** noun *masc.*
adverb

advertir verb
to warn
¡Te lo advierto! I'm warning you!

el **aeropuerto** noun *masc.*
airport

• *See the centre section for verb tables.*

a
b
c
d
e
f
g
h
i
j
k
l
m
n
o
p
q
r
s
t
u
v
w
x
y
z

a
b
c
d
e
f
g
h
i
j
k
l
m
n
o
p
q
r
s
t
u
v
w
x
y
z

la **afición** noun *fem.*
hobby
¿Qué aficiones tienes? What hobbies do you have?

aficionado adjective *masc.*,
aficionada *fem.*
ser aficionado a algo to be a fan of something
Es aficionado al fútbol. He's a football fan.

África noun *fem.*
Africa

africano adjective *masc.*,
africana *fem.*
African

el **africano** noun *masc.*,
la **africana** *fem.*
African
los africanos Africans

afuera adverb
outside
Vete afuera. Go outside.

agacharse verb
to bend down, **to crouch down**
¡Agáchate! Bend down!, Crouch down!

agarrar verb
to get hold of
Me agarró del brazo. He got hold of my arm.

agarrarse verb
to hold on
¡Agárrate!, que te caes. Hold on or you'll fall down.

la **agencia de viajes** noun *fem.*
travel agent's

la **agenda** noun *fem.*
diary
la agenda del colegio the school diary

⚠ **FALSE FRIEND**
una agenda = a diary (*not* an agenda)

agosto noun *masc.*
August
el ocho de agosto the eighth of August
Me voy de vacaciones en agosto. I'm going on holiday in August.

agradable adjective *masc. & fem.*
pleasant

agradecer verb
agradecer algo a alguien to thank somebody for something
Le he agradecido el regalo. I've thanked him for the present.

el **agricultor** noun *masc.*,
la **agricultora** *fem.*
farmer

agrio adjective *masc.*, **agria** *fem.*
sour
La naranja está agria. The orange is sour.

el **agua** noun *fem.*
water
¿Quieres agua? Do you want some water?
el agua mineral mineral water

🔑 **LANGUAGE**
Be careful: you use **el** with **agua** but it is not a masculine noun.

el or la **aguafiestas** noun *masc. & fem.* (plural los or las **aguafiestas**)
spoilsport

aguantar verb
to stand, **to tolerate**
No aguanto este ruido. I can't stand this noise.

el **águila** noun *fem.*
eagle

🔑 **LANGUAGE**
Be careful: you use **el** with **águila** but it is not a masculine noun.

la **aguja** noun *fem.*
needle

• *Use* el *and* uno *for masculine words and* la *and* una *for feminine words.*

las agujas del reloj the hands of the clock

el **agujero** noun *masc.*
hole

ahí adverb
there
¡Ahí está! There she is!
ahí abajo down there
buscar por ahí to look around there
Ve por ahí. Go that way.
¿Adónde vas? – Me voy por ahí.
Where are you going? – I'm going that way.

la **ahijada** noun *fem.*
goddaughter

el **ahijado** noun *masc.*
godson

ahogarse verb
to drown
Se ahogó en el mar. He drowned in the sea.

ahora adverb
now
Ahora estoy en casa. I'm at home now.
ahora mismo right now

ahorrar verb
to save
Tienes que ahorrar dinero.
You have to save money.

el **aire** noun *masc.*
air
Tiré el balón al aire. I threw the ball into the air.
el aire condicionado air conditioning

el **ajedrez** noun *masc.*
1 chess
¿Quieres jugar al ajedrez? Do you want to play chess?
2 chess set

el **ajo** noun *masc.*
garlic

ajustado adjective *masc.*,
ajustada *fem.*
tight
unos vaqueros ajustados tight jeans

al preposition

> **LANGUAGE**
> a + el = al

to the
ir al cine to go to the cinema

> **LANGUAGE**
> For more examples of al look at a.

el **ala** noun *fem.*
wing

> **LANGUAGE**
> Be careful: you use el with ala but it is not a masculine noun.

la **alarma** noun *fem.*
alarm
una alarma contra incendios a fire alarm

el **albañil** noun *masc.*
builder

el **albergue juvenil** noun *masc.*
youth hostel

el **álbum** noun *masc.*
album
un álbum de fotos a photo album

el **alcalde** *masc.*,
la **alcaldesa** noun *fem.*
mayor

alcanzar verb
1 to catch up with
Corre si quieres alcanzarlo. Run if you want to catch up with him.
2 to reach
¿Alcanzas al techo? Can you reach the ceiling?

el **alcohol** noun *masc.*
alcohol

a b c d e f g h i j k l m n o p q r s t u v w x y z

• Languages and nationalities do not take a capital letter in Spanish.

a
b
c
d
e
f
g
h
i
j
k
l
m
n
o
p
q
r
s
t
u
v
w
x
y
z

alegrarse verb
to be happy
Me alegro de verte. I'm pleased to see you.

alegre adjective *masc. & fem.*
happy
Estás muy alegre hoy. You're looking very happy today.

la **alegría** noun *fem.*
joy

el **alemán** noun *masc.*
(*the language*) **German**
¿Hablas alemán? Do you speak German?

alemán adjective *masc.*,
alemana *fem.*
German
Frank es alemán. Frank is German.

el **alemán** noun *masc.*,
la **alemana** *fem.*
German
los alemanes the Germans

Alemania noun *fem.*
Germany

la **alergia** noun *fem.*
allergy
Tengo alergia a la penicilina. I'm allergic to penicillin.

alérgico adjective *masc.*,
alérgica *fem.*
allergic

alfabético adjective *masc.*
en orden alfabético in alphabetical order

el **alfabeto** noun *masc.*
alphabet

la **alfombra** noun *fem.*
rug

algo pronoun
1 something
¿Buscas algo? Are you looking for something?
algo interesante something interesting
2 anything
¿Algo más? Anything else?

el **algodón** noun *masc.*
cotton
unos calcetines de algodón cotton socks

alguien pronoun
1 somebody
Alguien ha llamado. Somebody phoned.
2 anybody
¿Alguien ha visto mi libro? Has anybody seen my book?

alguno adjective & pronoun *masc.*,
alguna *fem.*

LANGUAGE
The masculine singular **alguno** becomes **algún** when it is used before a noun.

1 some
Algunos niños tienen bicicletas. Some children have bicycles.
alguna vez sometimes
en alguna parte somewhere
Sólo me gustan algunos. I only like some.
2 any
¿Tocas algún instrumento? Do you play any instrument?
Tengo muchos caramelos. ¿Quieres alguno? I've got lots of sweets. Do you want any?

la **alimentación** noun *fem.*
diet
una alimentación sana a healthy diet

allá adverb
over there
La farmacia está más allá. The chemist is further away.

• *The months of the year and days of the week do not take a capital letter in Spanish.*

allí adverb
there
Siéntate allí. Sit there.

el **almacén** noun *masc.*
warehouse
unos grandes almacenes
a department store

la **almendra** noun *fem.*
almond

la **almohada** noun *fem.*
pillow

almorzar verb
1 to have lunch
2 to have a mid-morning snack

el **almuerzo** noun *masc.*
1 lunch
2 mid-morning snack

alojarse verb
(*in a hotel etc.*) **to stay**

alquilar verb
1 to rent
Hemos alquilado un apartamento.
We've rented a flat.
2 to hire
Alquilé una bici. I hired a bike.

alrededor adverb
alrededor de around
alrededor de la mesa around the
table
Me acuesto alrededor de las
nueve. I go to bed around nine.

el **altavoz** noun *masc.* (plural los
altavoces)
(*for sound and music*) **speaker**

alto adverb
loud
Habla más alto. Speak louder.

alto adjective *masc.*, **alta** *fem.*
1 tall
Soy alto. I'm tall.
2 high
Aquella montaña es muy alta.
That mountain's very high.
3 loud

• *See the centre section for verb tables.*

La radio está muy alta. The radio's
very loud.
4 en lo alto de at the top of

la **alubia** noun *fem.*
bean

el **alumno** noun *masc.*,
la **alumna** *fem.*
pupil

amable adjective *masc. & fem.*
kind
Es muy amable. She's very kind.

amanecer verb
to get light
Amanece a las seis. It gets light at
six.

amargo adjective *masc.*,
amarga *fem.*
bitter
La naranja está amarga.
The orange is bitter.

amarillo adjective *masc.*,
amarilla *fem.*
yellow
una blusa amarilla a yellow
blouse

el **amarillo** noun *masc.*
yellow
Prefiero el amarillo. I prefer
yellow.

ambos adjective & plural pronoun *masc.*,
ambas *fem.*
both
Me gustan ambos. I like both of
them.

la **ambulancia** noun *fem.*
ambulance

amenazar verb
to threaten

América noun *fem.*
America
América Central Central America
América del Sur South America
América Latina Latin America

a
b
c
d
e
f
g
h
i
j
k
l
m
n
o
p
q
r
s
t
u
v
w
x
y
z

7

americano adjective *masc.*,
americana *fem.*
American

el **americano** noun *masc.*,
la **americana** *fem.*
American
los americanos the Americans

el **amigo** noun *masc.*,
la **amiga** *fem.*
friend
mi mejor amigo my best friend
Somos muy amigas. We're good
friends.

el **amor** noun *masc.*
love

ancho adjective *masc.*, **ancha** *fem.*
1 wide
una calle ancha a wide street
2 loose
Me gusta la ropa ancha. I like
loose clothes.

anciano adjective *masc.*,
anciana *fem.*
old
Mi abuela es muy anciana.
My grandmother is very old.

LANGUAGE
This is a polite way of saying 'old' in
Spanish.

el **anciano** noun *masc.*,
la **anciana** *fem.*
old man, **old lady**
los ancianos old people

LANGUAGE
This is a polite way of talking about old
people in Spanish.

Andalucía noun *fem.*
Andalusia

andar verb
to walk
Voy andando a la escuela. I walk
to school.

el **andén** noun *masc.* (plural los
andenes)
(*in a station*) **platform**

los **Andes** plural noun *masc.*
the Andes

el **ángel** noun *masc.*
angel

las **anginas** plural noun *fem.*
tonsils
Tengo anginas. I've got tonsillitis.

el **anillo** noun *masc.*
ring

animado adjective *masc.*,
animada *fem.*
lively
una fiesta animada a lively party

el **animal** noun *masc.*
animal

animar verb
to cheer on
Hay que animar al equipo.
We must cheer on the team.

ánimo exclamation
1 come on!
¡Ánimo, que vas a ganar! Come on,
you're going to win!
2 cheer up!

el **aniversario** noun *masc.*
anniversary

anoche adverb
last night

anteayer adverb
the day before yesterday

la **antena** noun *fem.*
aerial
una antena parabólica a satellite
dish

los **anteojos** plural noun *masc.*
(*Latin America*) **glasses**

• Use el and uno for masculine words and la and una for feminine words.

8

anterior adjective *masc. & fem.*
 before
 el día anterior the day before

antes adverb
 1 before
 He terminado antes. I finished before.
 2 antes de before
 Hago los deberes antes de salir. I do my homework before going out.

el **antibiótico** noun *masc.*
 antibiotic

anticuado adjective *masc.*,
 anticuada *fem.*
 old-fashioned
 Mi padre es muy anticuado.
 My dad's very old-fashioned.

antiguo adjective *masc.*,
 antigua *fem.*
 old
 un libro antiguo an old book
 mi antiguo colegio my old school

las **Antillas** plural noun *fem.*
 West Indies

antipático adjective *masc.*,
 antipática *fem.*
 very unfriendly

el **anuncio** noun *masc.*
 1 advert
 Hay muchos anuncios de juguetes.
 There are lots of adverts for toys.
 2 announcement

añadir verb
 to add

el **año** noun *masc.*
 1 year
 el año pasado last year
 el año que viene next year
 el Año Nuevo the New Year
 2 (*when saying how old somebody is*)
 ¿Cuántos años tienes? How old are you?
 Tengo diez años. I'm ten.

apagado adjective *masc.*,
 apagada *fem.*
 1 off
 La tele está apagada. The TV is off.
 2 out
 El fuego está apagado. The fire is out.

apagar verb
 1 to switch off
 Apaga la luz. Switch off the light.
 2 to put out
 Han apagado el incendio. They've put out the fire.

el **aparato** noun *masc.*
 (*for teeth*) **brace**

el **aparcamiento** noun *masc.*
 car park

aparcar verb
 to park
 'Prohibido aparcar' 'No parking'

aparecer verb
 to appear

el **apartamento** noun *masc.*
 apartment

aparte adverb
 1 to one side
 poner algo aparte to put something to one side
 2 separately

el **apellido** noun *masc.*
 surname

apenas adverb
 hardly
 Apenas salen. They hardly go out.

apetecer verb
 ¿Te apetece un helado? Do you feel like an ice cream?
 Me apetece ir al cine. I feel like going to the cinema.

• *Languages and nationalities do not take a capital letter in Spanish.*

9

a
b
c
d
e
f
g
h
i
j
k
l
m
n
o
p
q
r
s
t
u
v
w
x
y
z

el **apetito** noun *masc.*
appetite

aplaudir verb
to clap, **to applaud**

el **apodo** noun *masc.*
nickname

apoyar verb
to lean
Apoyé la bici en la pared. I leaned
my bike against the wall.

aprender verb
to learn
Aprendemos español. We learn
Spanish.
Quiero aprender a nadar. I want to
learn to swim.

apretar verb
to press
Aprieta el botón. Press the button.
Me aprietan los zapatos. My shoes
are tight.

aprobar verb
to pass
Aprobé el examen. I passed the
exam.

el **aprobado** noun *masc.*
pass mark
Tengo un aprobado. I got a pass.

aprovechar verb
¡Que aproveche! Enjoy your meal!

apuntar verb
1 to write down
Apúntalo en la agenda. Write it
down in your diary.
2 to point

los **apuntes** plural noun *masc.*
notes
Tengo mis apuntes de español.
I have my Spanish notes.

apurarse verb
(*Latin American*) **to hurry**

aquel adjective *masc.*, **aquella** *fem.*
that
aquel coche that car
aquella casa that house

aquél pronoun *masc.*, **aquélla** *fem.*
1 that one
Quiero aquél. I want that one.
¿Quieres aquélla? Do you want
that one?
2 that
Aquélla es mi maestra. That's my
teacher.

LANGUAGE
The accent goes on **aquél** and **aquélla** to
show clearly you're using the pronoun.

aquello pronoun
that
¿Qué es aquello? What's that?

aquellos adjective *masc.*,
aquellas *fem.*
those
aquellos edificios those buildings
aquellas niñas those girls

aquellos, (or **aquéllos**) pronoun
masc., **aquellas**,
(or **aquéllas**) *fem.*
those
Quiero aquellos. I want those.
¿Quieres aquellas? Do you want
those?

LANGUAGE
The accent can go on **aquéllos** and
aquéllas if you want to show clearly
you're using the pronoun.

aquí adverb
here
¡Aquí está! Here he is!
¡Ven aquí! Come here!
Aquí tienes el libro. Here's the
book.
¿Hay una farmacia por aquí?
Is there a chemist around here?
Pasa por aquí. Come this way.

• The months of the year and days of the week do not take a capital letter in Spanish.

árabe adjective *masc. & fem.*
Arab
los países árabes the Arab
countries

el **árabe** noun *masc.*
Arabic
Yasmina habla árabe. Yasmina
speaks Arabic.

el or la **árabe** noun *masc. & fem.*
Arab

Aragón noun *masc.*
Aragon

la **araña** noun *fem.*
spider

arañar verb
(*animals, fingernails, etc.*) **to scratch**
Mi gato me araña. My cat
scratches me.

el **árbitro** noun *masc.*,
la **árbitra** *fem.*
1 (*in football etc.*) **referee**
2 (*in cricket, tennis, etc.*) **umpire**

el **árbol** noun *masc.*
tree
un árbol de Navidad a Christmas
tree

el **arbusto** noun *masc.*
bush

el **archivo** noun *masc.*
(*on a computer*) **file**

el **arco** noun *masc.*
bow
arcos y flechas bows and arrows

el **arco iris** noun *masc.*
rainbow

la **ardilla** noun *fem.*
squirrel

la **arena** noun *fem.*
sand

Argentina noun *fem.*
Argentina

argentino adjective *masc.*,
argentina *fem.*
Argentinian

el **argentino** *masc.*,
la **argentina** noun *fem.*
Argentinian
los argentinos the Argentinians

el **armario** noun *masc.*
1 wardrobe
Mis camisas están en el armario.
My shirts are in the wardrobe.
2 cupboard
un armario de cocina a kitchen
cupboard

arrancar verb
1 to pull out
arrancar las páginas de un libro to
pull the pages out of a book
2 (*talking about a car*) **to start**
El coche no arranca. The car won't
start.

arreglado adjective *masc.*,
arreglada *fem.*
tidy
una casa muy arreglada a very
tidy house

arreglar verb
1 to fix
Han arreglado la bici. They've
fixed the bike.
2 to tidy
Arregla tu habitación. Tidy your
room.

arreglarse verb
to get ready
¡Arréglate! Get ready!

arriba adverb
1 up
arriba y abajo up and down
aquí arriba up here
¡Mira hacia arriba! Look up!
2 upstairs
Estoy arriba. I'm upstairs.
3 de arriba above
el piso de arriba the flat above

a
b
c
d
e
f
g
h
i
j
k
l
m
n
o
p
q
r
s
t
u
v
w
x
y
z

• *See the centre section for verb tables.*

4 (talking about the highest one)
de arriba top
en el cajón de arriba in the top drawer

la **arroba** noun fem.
(in email addresses) **the @ symbol**

arrodillarse verb
to kneel down
¡Arrodíllate! Kneel down!

el **arroyo** noun masc.
stream

el **arroz** noun masc.
rice

el **arte** noun masc.
art
el arte español Spanish art

el **artículo** noun masc.
article

> **LANGUAGE**
> In Spanish grammar the article is a word such as **el**, **la**, **los**, **lss** (the); or **un**, **una** (a/an).

el or la **artista** noun masc. & fem.
artist
Es artista. He's an artist.

el **asa** noun fem.
handle

> **LANGUAGE**
> Be careful: you use **el** with **asa** but it is not a masculine noun.

asaltar verb
to rob
asaltar un banco to rob a bank

el **ascensor** noun masc.
lift

los **aseos** plural noun masc.
toilets

asesinar verb
to murder

el **asesinato** noun masc.
murder

el **asesino** noun masc.,
la **asesina** fem.
murderer

así adverb
1 like this
Hazlo así. Do it like this.
2 like that
Dijo algo así. He said something like that.

Asia noun fem.
Asia

el **asiento** noun masc.
seat
el asiento delantero the front seat

la **asignatura** noun fem.
subject
mi asignatura favorita
my favourite subject

asistir verb
to attend
asistir a clase to attend a class

el **asma** noun fem.
asthma
Tengo asma. I have asthma.

> **LANGUAGE**
> Be careful: you use **el** with **asma** but it is not a masculine noun.

asomar verb
asomar la cabeza por la ventana
to lean your head out of the window
No te asomes a la ventana.
Don't lean out of the window.
¡Asómate! Put your head out of the window!

la **aspiradora** noun fem.
vacuum cleaner, Hoover®
No me gusta pasar la aspiradora.
I don't like hoovering.

asqueroso adjective masc.,
asquerosa fem.
disgusting

• Use el and uno for masculine words and la and una for feminine words.

el or **la astronauta** noun *masc. & fem.*
astronaut

asustar verb
to scare
¡No me asustes! Don't scare me!

atacar verb
to attack

el atajo noun *masc.*
short cut

el ataque noun *masc.*
attack
un ataque de asma an asthma attack

atar verb
to tie
Ata el paquete. Tie up the parcel.
Átate los cordones. Tie your laces.

el atasco noun *masc.*
traffic jam

la atención noun *fem.*
attention
Julia no presta atención. Julia doesn't pay attention.
¡Pon más atención! Pay more attention!

atender verb
to pay attention
Los niños tienen que atender en clase. The children have to pay attention in class.

aterrizar verb
to land
¿Ha aterrizado el avión? Has the plane landed?

el Atlántico noun *masc.*
Atlantic

el atlas noun *masc.* (plural los **atlas**)
atlas

el or **la atleta** noun *masc. & fem.*
athlete

el atletismo noun *masc.*
athletics

la atmósfera noun *fem.*
atmosphere

atrás adverb
1 back
Da un paso atrás. Take one step back.
2 behind
Me quedé atrás. I stayed behind.
3 at the back
Los niños se sientan atrás. The children sit at the back.
4 de atrás back
la puerta de atrás the back door

atrevido adjective *masc.*,
atrevida *fem.*
daring

atropellar verb
to run over

el atún noun
tuna

el aula noun *fem.*
classroom

⚷ **LANGUAGE**
Be careful: you use **el** with **aula** but it is not a masculine noun.

aumentar verb
to increase

aún adverb
1 still
¿Aún vives en Londres? Do you still live in London?
2 yet
Aún no he comido. I haven't eaten yet.

aunque conjunction
although

los auriculares plural noun *masc.*
headphones

ausente adjective *masc. & fem.*
absent
Juan está ausente hoy. Juan is absent today.

• *Languages and nationalities do not take a capital letter in Spanish.*

a
b
c
d
e
f
g
h
i
j
k
l
m
n
o
p
q
r
s
t
u
v
w
x
y
z

Australia noun *fem.*
 Australia

australiano adjective *masc.*,
 australiana *fem.*
 Australian

el **australiano** noun *masc.*,
 la **australiana** *fem.*
 Australian
 los australianos the Australians

Austria noun *fem.*
 Austria

el **autobús** noun *masc.* (plural los
 autobuses)
 bus
 en autobús by bus

el **autocar** noun *masc.*
 coach
 en autocar by coach

la **autopista** noun *fem.*
 motorway

el **autor** noun *masc.*, la **autora** *fem.*
 author

avanzar verb
 1 to move forward
 2 to make progress
 Has avanzado en tu español.
 You've made progress in your
 Spanish.

el **ave** noun *fem.*
 bird

> 🔑 **LANGUAGE**
> Be careful: you use **el** with **ave** but it is not
> a masculine noun.

la **avenida** noun *fem.*
 avenue

la **aventura** noun *fem.*
 adventure

> 🔑 **LANGUAGE**
> Spanish = a**ventura**
> English = a**dventure**

el **avión** noun *masc.* (plural los
 aviones)
 plane
 ir en avión to go by plane
 mandar algo por avión to send
 something by airmail

avisar verb
 to warn

el **aviso** noun *masc.*
 warning

la **avispa** noun *fem.*
 wasp

ay exclamation
 1 ouch!
 ¡Ay, me haces daño! Ouch, you're
 hurting me!
 2 oh!
 ¡Ay, qué susto! Oh, what a fright
 you gave me!

ayer adverb
 yesterday
 ayer por la mañana yesterday
 morning
 ayer por la noche yesterday night

la **ayuda** noun *fem.*
 help

ayudar verb
 to help
 Ayúdame a lavar el coche.
 Help me wash the car.

el **ayuntamiento** noun *masc.*
 town hall

el **azúcar** noun *masc.* 🔑
 sugar
 Echo azúcar en los cereales.
 I put sugar on my cereal.

azul adjective *masc. & fem.*
 blue
 Tengo los ojos azules. I have blue
 eyes.

el **azul** noun *masc.*
 blue
 Me encanta el azul. I love blue.

• *The months of the year and days of the week do not take a capital letter in Spanish.*

Bb

el **bacalao** noun *masc.*
cod

el **bachillerato** noun *masc.*

 CULTURE
El bachillerato is a course taken in the last two years of school for students who want to go to university.

bailar verb
to dance
Me gusta bailar. I like to dance.

el **bailarín** noun *masc.*,
la **bailarina** *fem.*
dancer

🔑 **LANGUAGE**
The plural of **bailarín** is **bailarines**.

el **baile** noun *masc.*
1 dance
Voy a clase de baile. I go to dance classes.
2 dancing

bajar verb
1 to go down
Baja al sótano. Go down to the basement.
Bajó en el ascensor. He went down in the lift.
2 to come down
¡Ya bajo! I'm coming down!
Bajé las escaleras. I came down the stairs.
3 to get off
¡Baja de la bici! Get off your bike!
4 to get down
¿Me puedes bajar ese libro? Can you get that book down for me?
5 to put down
Baja la persiana. Put the blind down.

6 to turn down
¿Puedes bajar la tele, por favor? Can you turn down the TV, please?
7 to download
He bajado una canción de Internet. I've downloaded a song from the Internet.

bajarse verb
1 to get off
Me bajé del autobús en el centro. I got off the bus in the centre.
2 to get out
Dave se bajó del coche. Dave got out of the car.
3 to get down
¡Bájate del árbol! Get down from the tree!

bajo adverb
quietly
Habla más bajo. Speak more quietly.

bajo preposition
below
tres grados bajo cero three degrees below zero

bajo adjective *masc.*, **baja** *fem.*
1 short
Soy muy bajo. I'm very short.
2 low
Sus notas son muy bajas. His marks are very low.

el **balancín** noun *masc.* (plural los **balancines**)
seesaw

• See the centre section for verb tables.

el **balcón** noun *masc.* (plural los **balcones**)
balcony

las **Baleares** plural noun *fem.*
the Balearic Islands

la **ballena** noun *fem.*
whale

el **balón** noun *masc.* (plural los **balones**)
ball
un balón de fútbol a football

⚠ **FALSE FRIEND**
un balón = a ball (*not* a balloon)

el **baloncesto** noun *masc.*
basketball
jugar al baloncesto to play basketball

el **banco** noun *masc.*
1 (*for sitting on*) **bench**
2 (*for money*) **bank**
3 un banco de datos a database

la **banda** noun *fem.*
1 (*of criminals*) **gang**
2 (*playing music*) **band**

la **bandeja** noun *fem.*
tray

la **bandera** noun *fem.*
flag

la **banqueta** noun *fem.*
stool

el **bañador** noun *masc.*
1 (*for girls*) **swimming costume**
2 (*for boys*) **swimming trunks**

bañarse verb
1 **to have a bath**
2 **to have a swim**
Me bañé en el mar. I had a swim in the sea.

la **bañera** noun *fem.*
bath
Hay mucha agua en la bañera.
There's a lot of water in the bath.

el **baño** noun *masc.*
1 **bath**
Quiero darme un baño. I want to have a bath.
2 **swim**
Me doy un baño en la piscina.
I go for a swim in the pool.
3 **bathroom**

el **bar** noun *masc.*
bar

barato adjective *masc.*, **barata** *fem.*
cheap

la **barba** noun *fem.*
beard
Mi abuelo tiene barba.
My grandfather has a beard.

la **barbacoa** noun *fem.*
barbecue
hacer una barbacoa to have a barbecue

la **barbilla** noun *fem.*
chin

la **barca** noun *fem.*
boat

el **barco** noun *masc.*
1 **boat**
en barco by boat
un barco de vela a sailing boat
2 **ship**

la **barra** noun *fem.*
1 (*for drinks*) **bar**
2 (*of metal*) **bar**
una barra de hierro an iron bar
3 una barra de pan a loaf of bread

la **barriga** noun *fem.*
tummy, stomach
Me duele la barriga. I have a tummy ache.

borracho *masc.* adjective, **borracha** *fem.*
drunk
Está borracho. He's drunk.

• Use *el* and *uno* for masculine words and *la* and *una* for feminine words.

el **barrio** noun *masc.*
area
Vivo en el barrio. I live in the area.

el **barro** noun *masc.*
mud
lleno de barro covered in mud

basta exclamation
that's enough!

bastante adverb & pronoun
1 enough
Tengo bastante. I have enough.
2 quite
Hablo español bastante bien.
I speak Spanish quite well.
un libro bastante bueno quite a
good book
3 quite a lot
El maestro me ayuda bastante.
The teacher helps me quite a lot.

bastante adjective *masc. & fem.*
1 enough
¿Tienes bastante dinero? Do you
have enough money?
2 quite a lot of
Hay bastantes coches. There are
quite a lot of cars.

el **bastón** noun *masc.* (plural los
bastones)
walking stick

la **basura** noun *fem.*
rubbish
sacar la basura to put out the
rubbish
tirar algo a la basura to throw
something into the rubbish bin

la **bata** noun *fem.*
1 dressing gown
2 (*of a doctor etc.*) **white coat**
3 (*of a schoolboy or girl*) **overall**

la **batalla** noun *fem.*
battle

la **batería** noun *fem.*
1 (*in a car*) **battery**
2 drums
tocar la batería to play the drums

el **batido** noun *masc.*
milk shake

batir verb
batir un récord to break a record

el **bebé** noun *masc.*
baby

beber verb
to drink
Estoy bebiendo agua. I'm drinking
some water.

la **bebida** noun *fem.*
drink
una bebida caliente a hot drink

el **béisbol** noun *masc.*
baseball
jugar al béisbol to play baseball

belga adjective *masc. & fem.*
Belgian

el or la **belga** noun *masc. & fem.*
Belgian

Bélgica noun *fem.*
Belgium

besar verb
to kiss

el **beso** noun *masc.*
kiss
Dame un beso. Give me a kiss.

la **Biblia** noun *fem.*
Bible

la **biblioteca** noun *fem.*
library

el **bicho** noun *masc.*
insect

la **bici** noun *fem.*
bike

la **bicicleta** noun *fem.*
bicycle
ir en bicicleta to go by bicycle
Yo sé montar en bicicleta. I can
ride a bicycle.

a
b
c
d
e
f
g
h
i
j
k
l
m
n
o
p
q
r
s
t
u
v
w
x
y
z

• *Languages and nationalities do not take a capital letter in Spanish.*

bien adverb & adjective
1 well
Hablo español muy bien. I speak Spanish very well.
No me encuentro bien. I don't feel well.
¿Cómo estás? – Bien. How are you? – Fine.
2 all right, **okay**
¿Estás bien? Are you all right?
Esta película está bien. This film's okay.
3 nice
Huele bien. It smells nice.
4 right
No lo estás haciendo bien. You're not doing it right.

bienvenido adjective masc., **bienvenida** fem.
welcome
¡Bienvenido a España! Welcome to Spain!

el **bigote** noun masc.
moustache

el **bikini** noun masc.
bikini

bilingüe adjective masc. & fem.
bilingual

el **billete** noun masc.
1 ticket
un billete de autobús a bus ticket
sacar un billete to get a ticket
2 (money) **note**
un billete de veinte euros a twenty-euro note

la **biología** noun fem.
biology

el **biquini** noun masc.
bikini

el **bistec** noun masc.
steak

blanco adjective masc., **blanca** fem.
white
una camisa blanca a white shirt

el **blanco** noun masc.
white
Me gusta el blanco. I like white.

blando adjective masc., **blanda** fem.
soft
Esta cama es muy blanda. This bed's very soft.

el **bloc** noun masc. (plural los **blocs**)
writing pad

el **bloque** noun masc.
un bloque de pisos a block of flats

la **blusa** noun fem.
blouse

bobo adjective masc., **boba** fem.
silly
Eres boba. You're silly.

la **boca** noun fem.
mouth
Abre la boca. Open your mouth.
Duermo boca arriba. I sleep on my back.
Duermo boca abajo. I sleep face down.

LANGUAGE
Word for word **boca arriba** means 'with your mouth up', and **boca abajo** 'with your mouth down'.

el **bocadillo** noun masc.
sandwich
un bocadillo de queso a cheese sandwich

CULTURE
A **bocadillo** is made from French bread.

la **bocina** noun fem.
(on a car) **horn**

la **boda** noun fem.
wedding

la **bodega** noun fem.
(for wines etc.) **cellar**

• The months of the year and days of the week do not take a capital letter in Spanish.

18

la **bola** noun *fem.*
ball
una bola de nieve a snowball

la **bolera** noun *fem.*
bowling alley

el **boleto** noun *masc.*
(*Latin America*) **ticket**

el **boli** noun *masc.*
pen

⚷ **LANGUAGE**
Boli is short for **bolígrafo**.

el **bolígrafo** noun *masc.*
ballpoint pen

Bolivia noun *fem.*
Bolivia

el **bollo** noun *masc.*
bun
un bollo de chocolate a chocolate
bun

los **bolos** plural noun *masc.*
tenpin bowling
jugar a los bolos to go bowling

la **bolsa** noun *fem.*
bag
una bolsa de plástico a plastic bag

el **bolsillo** noun *masc.*
pocket
Tengo el pañuelo en el bolsillo.
I've got my handkerchief in my
pocket.

el **bolso** noun *masc.*
handbag
La mujer ha perdido el bolso.
The woman has lost her bag.

la **bomba** noun *fem.*
1 **bomb**
Estalló una bomba. A bomb went
off.
2 **pump**
una bomba de bicicleta a bicycle
pump
3 ¡Me lo pasé bomba! I had a great
time!

el **bombero** noun *masc.*,
la **bombera** *fem.*
fireman, **firefighter**
Mi padre es bombero. My dad's a
fireman.
llamar a los bomberos to call the
fire brigade

⚷ **LANGUAGE**
Bombero comes from the **bomba** (pump)
for pumping water on to fires.

la **bombilla** noun *fem.*
light bulb

el **bombón** noun *masc.* (plural los
bombones)
chocolate
¿Quieres un bombón? Do you want
a chocolate?

bonito adjective *masc.*, **bonita** *fem.*
pretty
un vestido muy bonito a very
pretty dress

el **bonobús** noun *masc.* (plural
los **bonobuses**)
bus pass

borrar verb
1 **to rub out**
Borra esta palabra. Rub this word
out.
2 **to delete**
He borrado ese fichero. I've
deleted that file.

el **bosque** noun *masc.*
1 (*big*) **forest**
2 (*small*) **wood**
Hay un bosque aquí. There's a
wood here.
Se perdió en el bosque. He got lost
in the woods.

bostezar verb
to yawn

la **bota** noun *fem.*
boot
las botas de fútbol football boots
las botas de goma wellingtons

• See the centre section for verb tables.

19

botar verb
to bounce
Esta pelota no bota. This ball doesn't bounce.

el **bote** noun *masc.*
1 tin
un bote de pintura a tin of paint
2 jar
un bote de mermelada a jar of jam
3 boat
un bote de remos a rowing boat
un bote salvavidas a lifeboat

la **botella** noun *fem.*
bottle

el **botiquín** noun *masc.* (plural los **botiquines**)
first-aid box

el **botón** noun *masc.* (plural los **botones**)
button

el **boxeo** noun *masc.*
boxing

las **bragas** plural noun *fem.*
knickers

Brasil noun *masc.*
Brazil

bravo exclamation
well done!

el **brazo** noun *masc.*
arm

brillante adjective *masc. & fem.*
1 (*metal, hair, etc.*) **shiny**
2 (*light, sun*) **bright**
3 (*student*) **brilliant**

brillar verb
to shine
El sol brilla. The sun is shining.

la **brisa** noun *fem.*
breeze

británico adjective *masc.*, **británica** *fem.*
British
Soy británico. I'm British.

el **británico** noun *masc.*, la **británica** *fem.*
British man, **British woman**
los británicos the British

la **broma** noun *fem.*
joke
¡Es una broma! It's a joke!

bromear verb
to joke

el **bronceado** noun *masc.*
suntan

broncearse verb
to get a suntan

la **bruja** noun *fem.*
witch

la **brújula** noun *fem.*
compass

bruto adjective *masc.*, **bruta** *fem.*
rough
¡Qué bruto! You're so rough!

bucear verb
to dive
Nos vamos a bucear. We're going diving.

budista adjective *masc. & fem.*
Buddhist

bueno adjective *masc.*, **buena** *fem.*

> **LANGUAGE**
> The masculine singular **bueno** becomes **buen** when it is used before a noun.

1 good
Este libro es muy bueno. This book is very good.
Es un buen libro. It's a good book.
2 (*when wishing somebody something*)
¡Buenos días! Good morning!
¡Buenas tardes! Good afternoon!
¡Buenas noches! Good night!
¡Buen viaje! Have a good trip!
3 (*as exclamation*) **all right!**, **OK!**
¿Vienes conmigo? – ¡Bueno! Are you coming with me? – All right!

• Use el and uno for masculine words and la and una for feminine words.

el **búho** noun *masc.*
owl

la **burbuja** noun *fem.*
bubble

el **burro** noun *masc.*
donkey

burro adjective *masc.*,
burra *fem.*
stupid
¡Qué burro! You're so stupid!

buscar verb
1 **to look for**
Estoy buscando mi boli.
I'm looking for my pen.
2 **to look**
¿Has buscado en el salón?
Have you looked in the living room?
3 **to look up**

Cc

la **cabalgata** noun *fem.*
parade

 CULTURE
La cabalgata de Reyes (the parade of the Three Wise Men) takes place on 5th January, the day before Spanish children usually receive their Christmas presents.

el **caballero** noun *masc.*
gentleman
'caballeros' (*sign on toilet*) 'gents'

los **caballitos** plural noun *masc.*
merry-go-round

el **caballo** noun *masc.*
horse
montar a caballo to ride a horse

caber verb
caber en algo to fit into something
Esto no cabe en la caja. This doesn't fit into the box.

Búscalo en el diccionario. Look it up in the dictionary.
4 **ir a buscar** to get
Voy a buscar tus gafas. I'll get your glasses.
Te voy a buscar al colegio.
I'll come and get you at school.

la **butaca** noun *fem.*
1 **armchair**
2 (*in a cinema or theatre*) **seat in the stalls**

el **buzón** noun *masc.* (plural los **buzones**)
1 (*for posting letters*) **postbox**
2 (*at the house*) **letter box**
3 (*for getting email*) **mailbox**

 CULTURE
In Spain postboxes are usually yellow.

la **cabeza** noun *fem.*
head
Me di un golpe en la cabeza. I hit my head.

los **cabezudos** plural noun *masc.*

 CULTURE
In many Spanish festivals **cabezudos** are people in fancy dress with big heads (**cabeza** is 'head').

la **cabina** noun *fem.*
1 una cabina telefónica a phone box
2 (*in a plane*) **cockpit**

el **cable** noun *masc.*
1 (*of TV, phone, etc.*) **wire**
2 **cable**
la televisión por cable cable television

la **cabra** noun *fem.*
goat

el **cacahuete** noun *masc.*
peanut

• Languages and nationalities do not take a capital letter in Spanish.

a
b
c
d
e
f
g
h
i
j
k
l
m
n
o
p
q
r
s
t
u
v
w
x
y
z

a
b
c
d
e
f
g
h
i
j
k
l
m
n
o
p
q
r
s
t
u
v
w
x
y
z

el **cacao** noun *masc.*
cocoa

la **cacerola** noun *fem.*
saucepan

el **cachorro** noun *masc.*,
la **cachorra** *fem.*
puppy

cada adjective *masc. & fem.*
1 each
Cada alumno tiene su propio ordenador. Each pupil has his own computer.
cada uno each one
cada uno de nosotros each of us
2 every
cada vez every time
cada cinco días every five days

la **cadena** noun *fem.*
1 chain
una cadena de plata a silver chain
2 channel
una cadena de televisión a television channel

la **cadera** noun *fem.*
hip

caer verb
(*talking about rain, snow, bombs, etc.*) **to fall**
Ha caído una bomba. A bomb fell.

caerse verb
to fall
Me caí de la silla. I fell off the chair.
Luisa se cayó por la escalera. Luisa fell down the stairs.
Corrí y me caí. I ran and fell over.
Se ha caído un botón. A button has fallen off.

el **café** noun *masc.*
coffee
¿Vas a tomar un café? Are you going to have a coffee?
un café con leche a white coffee
un café solo a black coffee

la **cafetería** noun *fem.*
cafe

el **caimán** noun *masc.* (plural los caimanes)
alligator

la **caja** noun *fem.*
1 box
una caja de cartón a cardboard box
2 (*in a supermarket*) **checkout**
No me gusta hacer cola en la caja. I don't like queueing at the checkout.
3 (*in a shop*) **till**
4 una caja fuerte a safe

el **cajero** noun *masc.*, la **cajera** *fem.*
1 cashier
2 (*in a supermarket*) **checkout assistant**
3 un cajero automático a cash machine

el **cajón** noun *masc.* (plural los cajones)
drawer

el **calabacín** noun *masc.* (plural los calabacines)
courgette

la **calabaza** noun *fem.*
pumpkin
Me han dado calabazas en matemáticas. I've failed maths.

🔑 **LANGUAGE**
Dar calabazas means to fail somebody in an exam; word for word it means 'to give pumpkins'.

el **calamar** noun *masc.*
squid

el **calambre** noun *masc.*
cramp

calcar verb
to trace
calcar un dibujo to trace a picture

el **calcetín** noun *masc.* (plural los calcetines)
sock

• *The months of the year and days of the week do not take a capital letter in Spanish.*

la **calculadora** noun fem.
calculator

calcular verb
to calculate

la **calefacción** noun fem.
heating
la calefacción central central heating

el **calendario** noun masc.
calendar

la **calidad** noun fem.
quality
un vestido de buena calidad a dress of good quality

caliente adjective masc. & fem.
1 hot
Esta sopa está muy caliente. This soup is very hot.
2 warm
Este jersey es muy caliente. This sweater is very warm.

callar verb
to be quiet, **to shut up**
¡Todos a callar! Everybody shut up!

callarse verb
to be quiet, **to shut up**
¡Cállate! Be quiet!

la **calle** noun fem.
street
al otro lado de la calle on the other side of the street

> **LANGUAGE**
> You can also say 'road' in English, e.g. **cruzar la calle** ('to cross the road').

calmarse verb
to calm down
¡Cálmate! Calm down!

el **calor** noun masc.
1 heat
No me gusta este calor. I don't like this heat.

2 tener calor to be hot
Tengo calor. I'm hot.

> **LANGUAGE**
> Spanish = **tener** calor Tengo calor.
> English = **to be** hot I'm hot.

3 Hace calor. It's hot.
¡Qué calor hace! It's so hot!

calvo adjective masc., **calva** fem.
bald
Mi padre es calvo. My dad's bald.

los **calzoncillos** plural noun masc.
underpants

la **cama** noun fem.
bed
Estoy en la cama. I'm in bed.
Me voy a la cama. I'm going to bed.

la **cámara** noun fem.
camera
una cámara digital a digital camera

el **camarero** noun masc., la **camarera** fem.
waiter, **waitress**

cambiar verb
1 to change
cambiar la fecha to change the date
No has cambiado mucho. You haven't changed much.
2 cambiar de algo to change something
cambiar de autobús to change buses
¿Quieres cambiar de sitio? Do you want to change places?

> **LANGUAGE**
> You use **cambiar de** when you mean to change one thing for another.

3 to swap
Te cambio mi compacto por tu libro. I'll swap my CD for your book.

• *See the centre section for verb tables.*

a
b
c
d
e
f
g
h
i
j
k
l
m
n
o
p
q
r
s
t
u
v
w
x
y
z

cambiarse verb
1 to get changed
Me voy a cambiar. I'm going to get changed.
2 cambiarse de algo to change something
Me voy a cambiar de calcetines. I'm going to change my socks.
cambiarse de casa to move house

el **cambio** noun masc.
change
¿Tienes cambio para la máquina? Do you have change for the machine?
un cambio de planes a change of plan

el **camello** noun masc.
camel

caminar verb
to walk

el **camino** noun masc.
1 road
Tomé el camino más corto. I took the shortest road.
2 path
un camino por el bosque a path through the forest
3 way
Yo no sé el camino. I don't know the way.

el **camión** noun masc. (plural los **camiones**)
lorry
un camión de bomberos a fire engine

el **camionero** noun masc., la **camionera** fem.
lorry driver

la **camioneta** noun fem.
van

la **camisa** noun fem.
shirt

la **camiseta** noun fem.
1 T-shirt
2 (under a shirt) **vest**
3 (for football, rugby) **shirt**
una camiseta de fútbol a football shirt

el **camisón** noun masc. (plural los **camisones**)
nightdress

el **campamento** noun masc.
camp
un campamento de verano a summer camp

la **campana** noun fem.
bell
la campana de la iglesia the church bell

el **campeón** noun masc., la **campeona** fem.
champion

LANGUAGE
The plural of **campeón** is **campeones**.

el **campesino** noun masc., la **campesina** fem.
country person
los campesinos country people

el **camping** noun masc. (plural los **campings**)
1 camping
ir de camping to go camping
2 campsite

el **campo** noun masc.
1 country
una casa en el campo a house in the country
2 countryside
El campo está muy bonito. The countryside looks very pretty.
3 (for growing food) **field**
4 pitch
un campo de fútbol a football pitch
un campo de deportes a sports ground

• Use el and uno for masculine words and la and una for feminine words.

24

Canadá noun *masc.*
Canada
Vamos a Canadá. We're going to Canada.

canadiense adjective *masc. & fem.*
Canadian
Es canadiense. He's Canadian.

el or la **canadiense** noun *masc. & fem.*
Canadian

el **canal** noun *masc.*
1 (*on TV*) **channel**
Cambia de canal. Change the channel.
2 canal
el Canal de Panamá the Panama Canal
el Canal de la Mancha the English Channel

el **canario** noun *masc.*
canary

cancelar verb
to cancel

el **cáncer** noun *masc.*
cancer
Tiene cáncer. She has cancer.

la **cancha** noun *fem.*
1 (*for tennis, squash, etc.*) **court**
2 (*for football, rugby, etc.*) **pitch**

la **canción** noun *fem.* (plural las **canciones**)
song

el **cangrejo** noun *masc.*
crab

el **canguro** noun *masc.*
kangaroo

el or la **canguro** noun *masc. & fem.*
babysitter

la **canoa** noun *fem.*
canoe

cansado adjective *masc.*,
cansada *fem.*
tired
Estoy cansado. I'm tired.

cansarse verb
to get tired
Me cansé mucho en la excursión. I got very tired on the trip.

el or la **cantante** noun *masc. & fem.*
singer

cantar verb
to sing

la **cantidad** noun *fem.*
1 amount
una gran cantidad de dinero a large amount of money
cantidad de lots of
Tengo cantidad de amigos. I've got lots of friends.
2 quantity

la **caña de pescar** noun *fem.*
fishing rod

la **capital** noun *fem.*
capital
Madrid es la capital de España. Madrid is the capital of Spain.

el **capitán** *masc.*,
la **capitana** noun *fem.*
captain

🔑 **LANGUAGE**
The plural of **capitán** is **capitanes**.

el **capítulo** noun *masc.*
chapter

la **capucha** noun *fem.*
hood

la **cara** noun *fem.*
1 face
Voy a lavarme la cara. I'm going to wash my face.
2 (*when throwing a coin*) ¡Cara! Heads!
¿Cara o cruz? Heads or tails?
3 nerve
¡Tienes mucha cara! You've got a nerve!

• Languages and nationalities do not take a capital letter in Spanish.

a b c d e f g h i j k l m n o p q r s t u v w x y z

Spanish English

a
b
c
d
e
f
g
h
i
j
k
l
m
n
o
p
q
r
s
t
u
v
w
x
y
z

el **caracol** noun *masc.*
snail

el **carácter** noun *masc.*
character

el **caramelo** noun *masc.*
sweet
Me encantan los caramelos. I love sweets.

⚠ **FALSE FRIEND**
un caramelo = a sweet (*not* a caramel)

la **caravana** noun *fem.*
1 (*traffic jam*) **tailback**
2 caravan

el **carbón** noun *masc.*
coal

la **cárcel** noun *fem.*
prison
Están en la cárcel. They're in prison.

el **Caribe** noun *masc.*
el Caribe the Caribbean

caribeño adjective *masc.*,
caribeña *fem.*
Caribbean

el **cariño** noun *masc.*
1 love
Siento cariño por mi gato. I'm very fond of my cat.
2 (*when calling somebody*)
¡cariño! darling!

cariñoso adjective *masc.*,
cariñosa *fem.*
affectionate

el **carnaval** noun *masc.*
carnival

🌎 **CULTURE**
Spanish people celebrate the festival known as **carnaval** in the second week of February just before Christian Lent. They put on fancy dress, play music, and dance. Two famous **carnavales** are those of Tenerife and Cadiz.

la **carne** noun *fem.*
meat
la carne picada minced meat
la carne de vaca beef

el **carné**, **carnet** noun *masc.*
card
el carné de identidad identity card
el carné de conducir driving licence

la **carnicería** noun *fem.*
butcher's shop

el **carnicero** noun *masc.*,
la **carnicera** *fem.*
butcher

caro adjective *masc.*, **cara** *fem.*
expensive
Es demasiado caro. It's too expensive.

la **carpeta** noun *fem.*
(*for papers, and on a computer*) **folder**

el **carpintero** noun *masc.*,
la **carpintera** *fem.*
carpenter

la **carrera** noun *fem.*
race
Te echo una carrera. I'll have a race with you.
una carrera universitaria a university course

la **carretera** noun *fem.*
road
la carretera de Valencia the road to Valencia

el **carril** noun *masc.*
(*part of a road*) **lane**
un carril bus a bus lane
un carril bici a cycle path

el **carrito** noun *masc.*
(*for shopping etc.*) **trolley**

el **carro** noun *masc.*
1 cart
2 (*Latin America*) **car**

• *The months of the year and days of the week do not take a capital letter in Spanish.*

26

la **carroza** noun *fem.*
(*in a Spanish carnival*) **float**

la **carta** noun *fem.*
1 letter
Escribo una carta. I am writing a letter.
2 card
jugar a las cartas to play cards
3 (*in a restaurant*) **menu**

el **cartel** noun *masc.*
1 poster
2 sign
un cartel de 'se vende' a 'for sale' sign

la **cartera** noun *fem.*
1 (*for money*) **wallet**
2 (*for papers*) **document case**
3 (*for schoolbooks*) **schoolbag**

el **cartero** noun *masc.*,
la **cartera** *fem.*
postman, **postwoman**

el **cartón** noun *masc.*
cardboard
una caja de cartón a cardboard box

la **casa** noun *fem.*
1 house
una casa pequeña a small house
Estoy en casa de Aurelio. I'm in Aurelio's house.
2 home
Estoy en casa. I'm at home.
Me fui a casa. I went home.

casado adjective *masc.*,
casada *fem.*
married
Está casada con un inglés. She's married to an Englishman.

casarse verb
to get married
casarse con alguien to get married to somebody

la **cascada** noun *fem.*
waterfall

la **cáscara** noun *fem.*
(*of an egg or nut*) **shell**

el **casco** noun *masc.*
helmet

los **cascos** plural noun *masc.*
headphones

la **caseta** noun *fem.*
1 (*for a dog*) **kennel**
2 hut, **shed**

el or la **casete** noun *masc. & fem.*
cassette

casi adverb
1 almost
Son casi las nueve. It's almost nine o'clock.
2 (*in negative sentences*) **hardly**
casi nunca hardly ever
casi nada hardly anything

la **casilla** noun *fem.*
1 (*on forms, worksheets, etc.*) **box**
2 (*in crosswords etc.*) **square**

el **caso** noun *masc.*
hacer caso a alguien to take notice of somebody
No me haces caso. You don't take any notice of me.

la **castaña** noun *fem.*
chestnut

castaño adjective *masc.*,
castaña *fem.*
(*hair, eyes*) **brown**
Tengo el pelo castaño. I have brown hair.

las **castañuelas** plural noun *fem.*
castanets

CULTURE
Castanets are held in the hand and make clicking sounds in flamenco dancing.

• *See the centre section for verb tables.*

a
b
c
d
e
f
g
h
i
j
k
l
m
n
o
p
q
r
s
t
u
v
w
x
y
z

Spanish English

a b c d e f g h i j k l m n o p q r s t u v w x y z

el **castellano** noun *masc.*
Spanish
Hablo castellano. I speak Spanish.

🌏 **CULTURE**
Spanish is known as **español** or **castellano**. Other languages in Spain are **catalán** (Catalan), **gallego** (Galician), and **vasco** (Basque).

castigar verb
to punish
Mi padre me ha castigado. My dad has punished me.
El maestro lo dejó castigado. The teacher gave him a detention.

el **castigo** noun *masc.*
punishment

Castilla noun *fem.*
Castile

el **castillo** noun *masc.*
castle
un castillo de arena a sand castle

la **casualidad** noun *fem.*
coincidence
¡Qué casualidad! What a coincidence!
por casualidad by chance

el **catalán** noun *masc.*
Catalan
¿Hablas catalán? Do you speak Catalan?

Cataluña noun *fem.*
Catalonia

la **catarata** noun *fem.*
waterfall

el **catarro** noun *masc.*
cold
Tengo un catarro. I have a cold.

la **catedral** noun *fem.*
cathedral

católico adjective *masc.*,
católica *fem.*
Catholic
Soy católica. I'm a Catholic.

catorce number
1 fourteen
Mi prima tiene catorce años. My cousin is fourteen.
2 (*with dates*) **fourteenth**
el catorce de agosto the fourteenth of August

cavar verb
to dig

el **cazo** noun *masc.*
saucepan

el **CD** noun *masc.* (plural los **CDs**)
CD
un reproductor CD a CD player

la **cebolla** noun *fem.*
onion

la **cebra** noun *fem.*
zebra

la **ceja** noun *fem.*
eyebrow

celebrar verb
to celebrate
celebrar un cumpleaños to celebrate a birthday
¡Vamos a celebrarlo! Let's celebrate!

el **celo** noun *masc.*
Sellotape®

celoso adjective *masc.*, **celosa** *fem.*
jealous

el **celular** noun *masc.*
(*Latin America*) **mobile phone**

el **cementerio** noun *masc.*
cemetery

la **cena** noun *fem.*
dinner
¿Qué hay de cena? What's for dinner?

cenar verb
to have dinner

el **centavo** noun *masc.*
cent

• Use **el** and **uno** for masculine words and **la** and **una** for feminine words.

centígrado adjective *masc.*,
 centígrada *fem.*
 centigrade
 ocho grados centígrados eight
 degrees centigrade

el **centímetro** noun *masc.*
 centimetre

el **céntimo** noun *masc.*
 (*part of a euro*) **cent**

central adjective *masc. & fem.*
 central

céntrico adjective *masc.*,
 céntrica *fem.*
 central
 Vivo en un barrio céntrico. I live in
 a central part of town.

el **centro** noun *masc.*
 centre
 el centro de la ciudad the town
 centre
 ir al centro to go into town
 un centro comercial a shopping
 centre

cepillar verb
 to brush

el **cepillo** noun *masc.*
 brush
 un cepillo de dientes a toothbrush

cerca adverb
 1 near
 Mi escuela está muy cerca. My
 school is very near.
 2 nearby
 La piscina está cerca. The
 swimming pool is nearby.
 3 (*with nouns and pronouns*)
 cerca de near
 cerca de la ventana near the
 window
 cerca de mí near me

el **cerdo** noun *masc.*
 1 pig
 2 pork
 No como cerdo. I don't eat pork.

los **cereales** plural noun *masc.*
 cereal
 Siempre desayunamos cereales.
 We always have cereal for
 breakfast.

> 🔑 **LANGUAGE**
> Spanish = **los cereales** is plural
> English = **cereal** is singular

el **cerebro** noun *masc.*
 brain

la **cereza** noun *fem.*
 cherry

la **cerilla** noun *fem.*
 match
 una caja de cerillas a box of
 matches

el **cero** noun *masc.*
 1 zero
 2 nil
 El equipo ha ganado dos a cero.
 The team won two nil.

cerrado adjective *masc.*,
 cerrada *fem.*
 1 closed
 La puerta está cerrada. The door's
 closed.
 2 off
 El grifo está cerrado. The tap's off.

cerrar verb
 1 to close
 Cierra la ventana. Close the
 window.
 El museo cierra a las seis. The
 museum closes at six.
 2 to turn off
 Cierra el grifo. Turn off the tap.

el **certificado** noun *masc.*
 certificate

la **cerveza** noun *fem.*
 beer

la **cesta** noun *fem.*
 basket

a
b
c
d
e
f
g
h
i
j
k
l
m
n
o
p
q
r
s
t
u
v
w
x
y
z

• *Languages and nationalities do not take a capital letter in Spanish.*

el **chalet** noun *masc.*
house

el **champiñón** noun *masc.* (plural los **champiñones**)
mushroom

el **champú** noun *masc.*
shampoo

el **chándal** noun *masc.*
tracksuit

la **chancleta** noun *fem.*
flip-flop

chao exclamation
(*Latin American*) **bye**, **bye-bye**

la **chapa** noun *fem.*
badge
una chapa de policía a police badge

el **chaparrón** noun *masc.* (plural los **chaparrones**)
downpour

la **chaqueta** noun *fem.*
1 **jacket**
2 **cardigan**

el **charco** noun *masc.*
puddle

charlar verb
to chat

el **chat** noun *masc.*
chatroom

el **cheque** noun *masc.*
cheque

chévere adjective
(*Latin American*) **great**, **fantastic**

la **chica** noun *fem.*
girl
una chica de diez años a girl of ten

el **chichón** noun *masc.*
(*on your head*) **bump**

el **chicle** noun *masc.*
chewing gum

el **chico** noun *masc.*
boy
un chico de dieciséis años a boy of sixteen

Chile noun *masc.*
Chile

chileno adjective *masc.*, **chilena** *fem.*
Chilean

el **chileno** noun *masc.*, la **chilena** *fem.*
Chilean

chillar verb
to scream, **to shout**

la **chimenea** noun *fem.*
1 **chimney**
2 **fireplace**
Hay una chimenea en el salón. There's a fireplace in the lounge.

China noun *fem.*
China

la **chincheta** noun *fem.*
drawing pin

el **chino** noun *masc.*
Chinese
¿Hablas chino? Do you speak Chinese?

chino adjective *masc.*, **china** *fem.*
Chinese
Es china. She's Chinese.

el **chino** noun *masc.*, la **china** *fem.*
Chinese man, **Chinese woman**
los chinos the Chinese

el **chiste** noun *masc.*
1 **joke**
contar un chiste to tell a joke
2 (*funny drawing*) **cartoon**
los chistes del periódico the newspaper cartoons

el **chivato** noun *masc.*, la **chivata** *fem.*
telltale

• *The months of the year and days of the week do not take a capital letter in Spanish.*

chocar verb
chocar con to crash into
El coche chocó con un árbol.
The car crashed into a tree.

> 🔑 **LANGUAGE**
> You can say **chocar contra** as well as
> **chocar con.**

el **chocolate** noun *masc.*
chocolate
un helado de chocolate
a chocolate ice cream

la **chocolatina** noun *fem.*
bar of chocolate

el **choque** noun *masc.*
(*between cars, trains, etc.*) **crash**
los autos or **los coches de choque**
the dodgems

el **chorizo** noun *masc.*
spicy pork sausage

la **chuleta** noun *fem.*
1 chop
una chuleta de cerdo a pork chop
2 (*for cheating at exams*) **crib sheet**

el **chupachups**® noun *masc.*
lollipop

el **chupete** noun *masc.*
dummy

el **churro** noun *masc.*

> **CULTURE**
> **Churros** are like long thin doughnuts that
> people eat hot with thick hot chocolate.

el **cibercafé** noun *masc.*
Internet cafe

la **cicatriz** noun *fem.* (plural las
cicatrices)
scar

el **ciclismo** noun *masc.*
cycling

el or la **ciclista** noun *masc. & fem.*
cyclist

ciego adjective *masc.*, **ciega** *fem.*
blind
Es ciega. She's blind.

el **ciego** *masc.*, la **ciega** noun *fem.*
blind man, **blind woman**

el **cielo** noun *masc.*
1 sky
2 heaven
3 angel
Eres un cielo. You're an angel.

el **ciempiés** noun *masc.* (plural los
ciempiés)
centipede

cien number
hundred
cien euros a hundred euros

la **ciencia** noun *fem.*
science
Me encantan las ciencias. I love
science.

> 🔑 **LANGUAGE**
> **Ciencias** is used in the plural for the
> school subject.

el **científico** noun *masc.*,
la **científica** *fem.*
scientist

ciento number
hundred
ciento cincuenta a hundred and
fifty
cientos de personas hundreds of
people

cierto adjective *masc.*, **cierta** *fem.*
true
No es cierto. It's not true.

el **ciervo** noun *masc.*
deer

la **cifra** noun *fem.*
figure
Se escribe en cifras. It is written in
figures.

a
b
c
d
e
f
g
h
i
j
k
l
m
n
o
p
q
r
s
t
u
v
w
x
y
z

• *See the centre section for verb tables.*

la **cima** noun *fem.*
 top
 la cima de la montaña the top of
 the mountain

cinco number
 1 five
 Mi hermano tiene cinco años.
 My brother is five.
 Son las cinco. It's five o'clock.
 Son las nueve menos cinco. It's five
 to nine.
 Son las diez y cinco. It's five past
 ten.
 2 (*with dates*) **fifth**
 el cinco de junio the fifth of June

cincuenta number
 fifty
 Mi abuela tiene cincuenta años.
 My grandma is fifty.

el **cine** noun *masc.*
 cinema
 Fui al cine. I went to the cinema.

la **cinta** noun *fem.*
 1 ribbon
 2 tape
 Tengo una cinta para grabar la
 película. I have a tape to record
 the film.
 la cinta adhesiva sticky tape

la **cintura** noun *fem.*
 waist

el **cinturón** noun *masc.* (plural los
 cinturones)
 belt
 un cinturón de seguridad
 a seatbelt

el **circo** noun *masc.*
 circus

el **círculo** noun *masc.*
 circle
 sentarse en círculo to sit in a circle

la **ciruela** noun *fem.*
 plum

el **cisne** noun *masc.*
 swan

la **cita** noun *fem.*
 1 appointment
 2 date
 Tiene una cita con su novia. He has
 a date with his girlfriend.

la **ciudad** noun *fem.*
 1 city
 Madrid es una gran ciudad.
 Madrid is a big city.
 2 town
 ir a la ciudad to go into town

el **clarinete** noun *masc.*
 clarinet
 Yo toco el clarinete. I play the
 clarinet.

claro adverb
 1 clearly
 No oigo muy claro. I can't hear
 very clearly.
 2 of course
 ¡Claro que sí! Yes, of course!
 ¡Claro que no! Of course not!

claro adjective *masc.*, **clara** *fem.*
 1 clear
 una explicación clara a clear
 explanation
 Está claro. That's clear.
 2 light
 los colores claros light colours
 blusas azul claro light blue
 blouses

⚷ **LANGUAGE**
When **claro** follows the name of a colour
(e.g. **verde**, **azul**), use **claro** and the
colour word in the masculine singular
form only.

la **clase** noun *fem.*
 1 class
 Hassan está en mi clase. Hassan is
 in my class.
 Hoy tenemos clase de español.
 We have a Spanish class today.
 2 classroom
 3 kind
 libros de todas clases books of all
 kinds

• *Use* el *and* uno *for masculine words and* la *and* una *for feminine words.*

la **clave** noun *fem.*
code
un mensaje en clave a message in code

el **clavo** noun *masc.*
nail

el **clic** noun *masc.*
click
hacer clic en algo to click on something

el **cliente** noun *masc.*,
la **clienta** *fem.*
1 (*in a shop etc.*) **customer**
2 (*in a hotel*) **guest**

el **clima** noun *masc.*
climate

> 🔑 **LANGUAGE**
> Be careful: **clima** ends in an **-a** but it is not a feminine noun.

climatizado adjective *masc.*,
climatizada *fem.*
air-conditioned

el **clip** noun *masc.* (plural los **clips**)
1 **paperclip**
2 **music video**

el **club** noun *masc.* (plural los **clubs**)
club
un club de fútbol a football club

el or la **cobaya** noun *masc. & fem.*
guinea pig

la **Coca-Cola**® noun *fem.*
Coke®

el **coche** noun *masc.*
1 **car**
Me gusta ir en coche. I like to go by car.
un coche de carreras a racing car
un coche de bomberos a fire engine
2 (*of a train*) **carriage**

el **cochecito** noun *masc.*
baby buggy

el **cocido** noun *masc.*
stew (*made of meat, vegetables, and chickpeas*)

la **cocina** noun *fem.*
1 **kitchen**
en la cocina in the kitchen
2 **cooker**
una cocina de gas a gas cooker
3 **cooking**
la cocina española Spanish cooking
un libro de cocina a cookery book

cocinar verb
to cook

el **cocinero** noun *masc.*,
la **cocinera** *fem.*
cook
Soy muy buen cocinero. I'm a good cook.

el **coco** noun *masc.*
coconut

el **cocodrilo** noun *masc.*
crocodile

> 🔑 **LANGUAGE**
> Spanish = cocodrilo
> English = crocodile

el **cocotero** noun *masc.*
coconut tree

el **código** noun *masc.*
code
el código postal the postcode

el **codo** noun *masc.*
elbow

coger verb
1 **to take**
Coge un bombón. Take a chocolate.
coger el autobús to take the bus
2 **to catch**
Cogí un resfriado. I caught a cold.
Coge la pelota. Catch the ball.

a
b
c
d
e
f
g
h
i
j
k
l
m
n
o
p
q
r
s
t
u
v
w
x
y
z

• *Languages and nationalities do not take a capital letter in Spanish.*

a
b
c
d
e
f
g
h
i
j
k
l
m
n
o
p
q
r
s
t
u
v
w
x
y
z

Han cogido al ladrón. They've caught the thief.

3 to get
coger los billetes to get the tickets

CULTURE
Coger is used especially in Spain; in Latin America use **tomar** instead.

el **cohete** noun *masc.*
rocket

el **cojín** noun *masc.* (plural los **cojines**)
cushion

la **col** noun *fem.*
cabbage

la **cola** noun *fem.*
1 tail
El perro está moviendo la cola. The dog's wagging its tail.
2 queue
Hay cola. There's a queue.
hacer cola to queue up
3 glue
4 una cola de caballo a ponytail

el **colchón** noun *masc.* (plural los **colchones**)
mattress

el **cole** noun *masc.*
school

🔑 **LANGUAGE**
Cole is short for **colegio**.

la **colección** noun *fem.* (plural las **colecciones**)
collection

coleccionar verb
to collect
Colecciono sellos. I collect stamps.

el **colegial** noun *masc.*,
la **colegiala** *fem.*
schoolboy, schoolgirl
los colegiales schoolchildren

el **colegio** noun *masc.*
school
en el colegio at school
ir al colegio to go to school

🔑 **LANGUAGE**
Colegio is related to 'college'.

la **coleta** noun *fem.*
ponytail

colgar verb
to hang
Cuelga el abrigo de la percha. Hang your coat on the hook.

la **coliflor** noun *fem.*
cauliflower

la **colina** noun *fem.*
hill

el **collar** noun *masc.*
1 necklace
2 (*on a dog or cat*) **collar**

colocar verb
to put

Colombia noun *fem.*
Colombia

la **colonia** noun *fem.*
summer camp
pasar el mes de agosto en las colonias to spend August in a summer camp

el **color** noun *masc.*
colour
¿De qué color es? What colour is it?

colorado adjective *masc.*,
colorada *fem.*
red
ponerse colorado to go red, to blush

colorear verb
to colour in
colorear un dibujo to colour in a picture

• *The months of the year and days of the week do not take a capital letter in Spanish.*

la **columna** noun *fem.*
column

columpiar verb
to push (*on a swing*)

el **columpio** noun *masc.*
swing

la **coma** noun *fem.*
1 comma
2 decimal point
tres coma cinco three point five

la **comba** noun *fem.*
skipping rope
jugar a la comba to skip

el **comedor** noun *masc.*
1 (*in a house*) **dining room**
2 (*in a factory, school, etc.*) **canteen**

comenzar verb
to begin
La clase comienza a las nueve.
The class begins at nine.

comer verb
1 to eat
¿Quieres comer algo? Do you want
something to eat?
2 (*at lunchtime*) **to have lunch**

el or la **comerciante** noun *masc. &*
fem.
shopkeeper

la **cometa** noun *fem.*
kite

LANGUAGE
Do you think a kite looks like a comet? The
Spanish words for both are the same but
the genders are different – 'comet' is
masculine: **el cometa**.

el **cómic** noun *masc.*
comic
Me gusta leer cómics. I like
reading comics.

cómico adjective *masc.*,
cómica *fem.*
funny

• See the centre section for verb tables.

la **comida** noun *fem.*
1 food
No hay suficiente comida. There
isn't enough food.
2 meal
Hago tres comidas al día. I have
three meals a day.
3 (*at lunchtime*) **lunch**

la **comisaría** noun *fem.*
police station

como preposition & conjunction
1 like
Soy como mi padre. I'm like my
father.
2 as
Hazlo como te he dicho. Do it as I
told you to.
3 (*when comparing*)
tan ... como as ... as
Soy tan inteligente como tú. I'm as
clever as you.

cómo adverb
1 how
¿Cómo estás? How are you?
¿Cómo se dice 'sky' en español?
How do you say 'sky' in Spanish?
2 what
¿Cómo es? What's it like?
¿Cómo es tu hermana? What's
your sister like?
¿Cómo has dicho? What did you
say?
¡Cómo! What!

la **cómoda** noun *fem.*
chest of drawers

cómodo adjective *masc.*,
cómoda *fem.*
(*chair, shoes, etc.*) **comfortable**

el **compacto** noun *masc.*
CD

el **compañero** *masc.*,
la **compañera** noun *fem.*
1 (*in school*) **school friend**
2 (*boyfriend, girlfriend*) **partner**

Spanish English

la **compañia** noun *fem.*
company
Mi padre trabaja en una compañia irlandesa. My dad works for an Irish company.

comparar verb
to compare

compartir verb
to share

el **compás** noun *masc.* (plural los compases)
pair of compasses

la **competición** noun *fem.*
competition
una competición de natación a swimming competition

completamente adverb
completely

completar verb
to complete

completo adjective *masc.*, **completa** *fem.*
1 (*sentence, list, etc.*) **complete**
2 (*hotel, plane, etc.*) **full**

complicado adjective *masc.*, **complicada** *fem.*
complicated

el **comportamiento** noun *masc.*
behaviour

la **compra** noun *fem.*
shopping
hacer la compra to do the shopping
ir de compras to go shopping
una bolsa de la compra a shopping bag
una lista de la compra a shopping list

comprar verb
to buy
Quiero comprar un libro. I want to buy a book.
¿Me compras un helado? Can you buy me an ice cream?

comprender verb
to understand

comprobar verb
to check

el **computador** noun *masc.*, la **computadora** *fem.* (*Latin America*) **computer**

común adjective *masc. & fem.*
common
en común in common
Tenemos muchas cosas en común. We have a lot in common.

comunicar verb
(*talking about the phone*) **to be engaged**
Está comunicando. It's engaged.

con preposition
1 **with**
beber con una pajita to drink with a straw
con mis amigas with my friends
Son tres euros con cinco. That's three euros and five cents.
2 **to**
Soy malo con mi hermano. I'm mean to my brother.
hablar con alguien to speak to somebody

concentrarse verb
to concentrate

la **concha** noun *fem.*
shell

el **concierto** noun *masc.*
concert
un concierto de rock a rock concert

el **concurso** noun *masc.*
1 **competition**
un concurso de fotografía a photo competition
2 **quiz**
un programa concurso a quiz show

conducir verb
to drive
conducir un coche to drive a car

• *Use el and uno for masculine words and la and una for feminine words.*

36

el **conductor** noun *masc.*,
la **conductora** *fem.*
driver

⚠ **FALSE FRIEND**
un conductor = a driver (*not* a conductor)

conectarse verb
conectarse a Internet to connect to the Internet
Estamos conectados a Internet. We're connected to the Internet.

el **conejo** noun *masc.*
rabbit

confortable adjective *masc. & fem.*
comfortable

confundir verb
to confuse
Me confundí en el examen. I got confused in the exam.

congelado adjective *masc.*,
congelada *fem.*
frozen

el **congelador** noun *masc.*
freezer

congelar verb
(*in a freezer*) **to freeze**

la **conjugación** noun *fem.* (plural las **conjugaciones**)
conjugation

la **conjunción** noun *fem.* (plural las **conjunciones**)
conjunction

conmigo pronoun
1 with me
Ven conmigo. Come with me.
2 to me
¿Quieres hablar conmigo? Do you want to speak to me?

conocer verb
1 to know
Conozco a tu primo. I know your cousin.

¿Conoces Madrid? Do you know Madrid?
2 to meet
Conocí a una chica en la playa. I met a girl at the beach.
Nos conocimos en la escuela. We met at school.

los **conocimientos** plural noun *masc.*
(*of Spanish, maths, etc.*) **knowledge**

el or la **conserje** noun *masc. & fem.*
(*in a school*) **caretaker**

la **consigna** noun *fem.*
left-luggage office

la **consola** noun *fem.*
(*for games*) **console**

la **consonante** noun *fem.*
consonant

constipado adjective *masc.*,
constipada *fem.*
estar constipado to have a cold

⚠ **FALSE FRIEND**
estar constipado = to have a cold (*not* to be constipated)

construir verb
to build

el or la **contable** noun *masc. & fem.*
accountant

🔑 **LANGUAGE**
Contable comes from contar (to count).

contar verb
1 to count
Cuenta hasta veinte. Count up to twenty.
2 to tell
Cuéntame un cuento. Tell me a story.

contento adjective *masc.*,
contenta *fem.*
happy
Estoy muy contento. I'm very happy.

• Languages and nationalities do not take a capital letter in Spanish.

a
b
c
d
e
f
g
h
i
j
k
l
m
n
o
p
q
r
s
t
u
v
w
x
y
z

contestar verb
to answer
No contesta. He isn't answering.
Contesté a la pregunta. I answered the question.

contigo pronoun
1 with you
¿Puedo ir contigo? Can I go with you?
2 to you
Quiero hablar contigo. I want to speak to you.

el **continente** noun masc.
continent

continuar verb
to continue
Continúa leyendo. Continue reading.

contra preposition
against
contra la pared against the wall

contrario adjective masc.,
contraria fem.
1 opposite
la dirección contraria the opposite direction
¿Qué es lo contrario de 'largo'? What's the opposite of 'long'?
2 opposing
el equipo contrario the opposing team

la **contraseña** noun fem.
password

el **control** noun masc.
1 control
2 check
el control de pasaportes passport check

controlar verb
1 to control
¡Contrólate! Control yourself!
2 (passports etc.) **to check**

la **conversación** noun fem. (plural las **conversaciones**)
conversation

convertirse verb
to turn into
¡El príncipe se convirtió en rana! The prince turned into a frog!

la **copa** noun fem.
1 glass
una copa de vino a glass of wine
2 drink
tomar una copa to have a drink
3 (prize) **cup**
la Copa del Mundo the World Cup

la **copia** noun fem.
copy

copiar verb
to copy

el **Corán** noun masc.
Koran

el **corazón** noun masc. (plural los **corazones**)
heart

la **corbata** noun fem.
tie
Llevo corbata. I'm wearing a tie.

el **cordero** noun masc.
lamb
una chuleta de cordero a lamb chop

el **cordón** noun masc.
(for shoes) **lace**
¿Puedes atarme los cordones? Can you do up my laces?

el **coro** noun masc.
choir
cantar en el coro to sing in the choir

la **corona** noun fem.
crown

el **corral** noun masc.
(for chickens etc.) **farmyard**

• The months of the year and days of the week do not take a capital letter in Spanish.

la **correa** noun *fem.*
(*on a watch, handbag, etc.*) **strap**

correcto adjective *masc.*,
correcta *fem.*
correct
Mis respuestas son correctas.
My answers are correct.

el **corredor** noun *masc.*,
la **corredora** *fem.*
runner

corregir verb
1 (*mistakes etc.*) **to correct**
2 (*exercises, homework, etc.*) **to mark**

el **correo** noun *masc.*
post
mandar algo por correo to send
something by post
por correo aéreo by airmail
correo electrónico email

Correos noun *masc.*
post office
Voy a Correos. I'm going to the
post office.

LANGUAGE
Be careful: **Correos** is spelt with a capital
'C' and ends with an 's'. Never use **el** with
it.

correr verb
1 **to run**
Rafael corre muy rápido. Rafael
runs very fast.
2 **to hurry**
¡Corre, cierra la puerta! Hurry,
close the door!

corresponder verb
to match
Esta palabra corresponde a ese
dibujo. This word matches that
drawing.

la **corrida** noun *fem.*
bullfight

• See the centre section for verb tables.

corriente adjective *masc. & fem.*
common
un problema muy corriente a very
common problem

la **corriente** noun *fem.*
1 **draught**
Hay corriente. There's a draught.
2 **electricity**
No hay corriente en la casa.
There's no electricity in the house.

cortar verb
to cut
Corta el pan. Cut the bread.
Me he cortado el dedo. I've cut my
finger.
Me he cortado el pelo. I've had my
hair cut.

el **corte** noun *masc.*
cut
Tengo un corte en el dedo. I have a
cut on my finger.
un corte de pelo a haircut

la **cortina** noun *fem.*
curtain

corto adjective *masc.*, **corta** *fem.*
short
Tengo el pelo corto. I have short
hair.

la **cosa** noun *fem.*
thing
Tengo muchas cosas que hacer.
I have lots of things to do.
Quiero otra cosa. I want
something else.
¿Quieres otra cosa? Do you want
anything else?

coser verb
to sew

las **cosquillas** plural noun *fem.*
Tengo cosquillas. I'm ticklish.

la **costa** noun *fem.*
coast
en la costa on the coast

costar verb
1 to cost
¿Cuánto cuesta? How much does it cost?
Cuesta mucho. It costs a lot.
2 (*talking about time*) **to take**
¿Cuánto cuesta llegar? How long does it take to get there?

la **costilla** noun *fem.*
rib

la **costumbre** noun *fem.*
1 habit
una mala costumbre a bad habit
2 custom
una costumbre española
a Spanish custom

crear verb
to create

crecer verb
to grow
He crecido mucho. I've grown a lot.

creer verb
1 to think
Creo que está en la cocina. I think he's in the kitchen.
Creo que sí. I think so.
Creo que no. I don't think so.
2 to believe
Te creo. I believe you.

la **crema** noun *fem.*
cream

la **cremallera** noun *fem.*
zip
subir la cremallera to do up the zip

el **crimen** noun *masc.* (plural los **crímenes**)
1 murder
2 (serious) crime

el or la **criminal** noun *masc. & fem.*
criminal

el **cristal** noun *masc.*
1 glass
Es de cristal. It's made of glass.

una botella de cristal a glass bottle
cristales rotos broken glass
2 window
Has roto el cristal. You've broken the window.

cristiano adjective *masc.*, **cristiana** *fem.*
Christian

criticar verb
to criticize

el **cruce** noun *masc.*
1 crossroads
en el cruce at the crossroads
2 crossing
un cruce de peatones a pedestrian crossing

el **crucigrama** noun *masc.*
crossword

LANGUAGE
Be careful: **crucigrama** ends in an -a but it is not a feminine noun.

crudo adjective *masc.*, **cruda** *fem.*
raw
una zanahoria cruda a raw carrot

cruel adjective *masc. & fem.*
cruel
un hombre cruel a cruel man

la **cruz** noun *fem.* (plural las **cruces**)
1 cross
2 (*when throwing a coin*) ¡Cruz! Tails!
¿Cara o cruz? Heads or tails?

cruzar verb
to cross
cruzar la calle to cross the road
cruzar los brazos to cross your arms

el **cuaderno** noun *masc.*
exercise book
mi cuaderno de español my Spanish exercise book

la **cuadra** noun *fem.*
stable

• Use el and uno for masculine words and la and una for feminine words.

40

el **cuadrado** noun *masc.*
square

cuadrado adjective *masc.*,
cuadrada *fem.*
square
una caja cuadrada a square box

el **cuadro** noun *masc.*
1 picture
Hay un cuadro en la pared. There's a picture on the wall.
2 painting
un cuadro de Dalí a painting by Dali

cuál pronoun *masc. & fem.*
1 what
¿Cuál es tu número de teléfono? What's your phone number?
¿Cuáles son tus colores favoritos? What are your favourite colours?
2 which
Tengo dos libros. ¿Cuál quieres? I have two books. Which do you want?
3 which one
¿Cuál quieres? Which one do you want?
¿Cuáles quieres? Which ones do you want?

la **cualidad** noun *fem.*
quality
El niño tiene muchas cualidades. The boy has many qualities.

cuando conjunction
when
Voy a ir a casa cuando termine. I'm going home when I finish.

cuándo adverb
(*in questions*) **when**
¿Cuándo vas a venir? When are you coming?

🔑 **LANGUAGE**
Remember to put the accent on **cuándo** in questions.

cuánto adjective & pronoun *masc.*,
cuánta *fem.*
1 how much
¿Cuánto dinero tienes? How much money do you have?
¿Cuánta agua? How much water?
¿Cuánto cuesta? How much does it cost?
¿Cuánto tiempo llevas aquí? How long have you been here?
2 how many
¿Cuántos bombones quieres? How many chocolates do you want?
¿Cuántas niñas hay en tu clase? How many girls are there in your class?
¿Cuántos años tienes? How old are you?

cuarenta number
forty
Mi padre tiene cuarenta años. My dad is forty.

el **cuarto** noun *masc.*
1 room
el cuarto de baño the bathroom
2 quarter
un cuarto de hora a quarter of an hour
Son las tres y cuarto. It's a quarter past three.
a las ocho menos cuarto at a quarter to eight

cuarto adjective *masc.*,
cuarta *fem.*
fourth
en el cuarto piso on the fourth floor

cuatro number
1 four
Mi primo tiene cuatro años. My cousin is four.
Son las cuatro. It's four o'clock.
2 (*with dates*) **fourth**
el cuatro de septiembre the fourth of September

a
b
c
d
e
f
g
h
i
j
k
l
m
n
o
p
q
r
s
t
u
v
w
x
y
z

• *Languages and nationalities do not take a capital letter in Spanish.*

a
b
c
d
e
f
g
h
i
j
k
l
m
n
o
p
q
r
s
t
u
v
w
x
y
z

cuatrocientos number *masc.*,
 cuatrocientas *fem.*
 four hundred

Cuba noun *fem.*
 Cuba

cubano adjective *masc.*,
 cubana *fem.*
 Cuban

los **cubiertos** plural noun *masc.*
 cutlery

el **cubito de hielo** noun *masc.*
 ice cube

el **cubo** noun *masc.*
 1 bucket
 un cubo de agua a bucket of water
 2 cube
 3 un cubo de basura a dustbin

cubrir verb
 to cover

la **cucaracha** noun *fem.*
 cockroach

la **cuchara** noun *fem.*
 spoon

la **cucharilla** noun *fem.*
 teaspoon

🔑 **LANGUAGE**
You can also say **la cucharita** in Spanish.

el **cuchillo** noun *masc.*
 knife

el **cuello** noun
 1 neck
 2 collar
 el cuello de mi camisa my shirt
 collar

la **cuenta** noun *fem.*
 1 bill
 ¡La cuenta, por favor! The bill,
 please!
 2 darse cuenta de algo to realize
 something
 No me di cuenta. I didn't realize.

el **cuento** noun *masc.*
 1 story
 Cuéntame un cuento. Tell me a
 story.
 2 tale
 un cuento de hadas a fairy tale

la **cuerda** noun *fem.*
 1 rope
 2 string
 Ata el paquete con una cuerda.
 Tie the parcel with string.
 3 saltar a la cuerda to skip

el **cuero** noun *masc.*
 leather
 una chaqueta de cuero a leather
 jacket

el **cuerpo** noun *masc.*
 body

la **cuesta** noun *fem.*
 1 hill
 Tienes que subir la cuesta.
 You have to go up the hill.
 2 slope

la **cueva** noun *fem.*
 cave

el **cuidado** noun *masc.*
 care
 con cuidado carefully
 tener cuidado to be careful
 ¡Cuidado con el escalón! Be careful
 of the step!

cuidar verb
 to look after
 cuidar a alguien to look after
 somebody
 Yo cuido a los niños. I look after
 the children.

la **culpa** noun *fem.*
 fault
 No es mi culpa. It's not my fault.
 Tú tienes la culpa. It's your
 fault.

• *The months of the year and days of the week do not take a capital letter in Spanish.*

culpable adjective *masc. & fem.*
guilty

el **cumpleaños** noun *masc.*
birthday
Ayer fue mi cumpleaños.
My birthday was yesterday.
¡Feliz cumpleaños! Happy
birthday!
una fiesta de cumpleaños
a birthday party

cumplir verb
Mañana cumplo ocho años.
Tomorrow I'll be eight.

la **cuna** noun *fem.*
cot

el **cura** noun *masc.*
priest

curioso adjective *masc.*,
curiosa *fem.*
curious

el **curso** noun *masc.*
1 **year**
¿En qué curso estás? What year
are you in?
2 **course**
un curso de español a Spanish
course

el **cursor** noun *masc.*
cursor

la **curva** noun
1 (*in the road*) **bend**
2 **curve**
dibujar una curva to draw a curve

curvo adjective *masc.*, **curva** *fem.*
curved
una línea curva a curved line

Dd

el **dado** noun *masc.*
dice
Tira los dados. Throw the dice.

la **dama** noun *fem.*
1 **lady**
2 **las damas** draughts
jugar a la damas to play draughts

el **daño** noun *masc.*
hacer daño a alguien to hurt
somebody
Me he hecho daño. I've hurt
myself.

los **daños** plural noun *masc.*
damage

> 🔑 **LANGUAGE**
> Spanish = **los daños** is plural
> English = **damage** is singular

dar verb
1 **to give**
Dame el libro. Give me the book.
Ricardo le dio el dinero a su padre.
Ricardo gave the money to his
dad.
2 **to go for**
dar un paseo to go for a walk
dar una vuelta en coche to go for a
drive
3 **to make**
Me da sed. It makes me thirsty.
Me da sueño. It makes me sleepy.
Me dio miedo. It scared me.
4 **to put on**
¿Qué dan en la tele? What's
on TV?
Dan una película. They're putting
on a film.

• See the centre section for verb tables.

a
b
c
d
e
f
g
h
i
j
k
l
m
n
o
p
q
r
s
t
u
v
w
x
y
z

darse verb
to have
darse un baño to have a bath
Me he dado una ducha. I've had a shower.
Me di un golpe en la cabeza.
I bumped my head.

de preposition

🔑 **LANGUAGE**
de + el = del

1 of
un vaso de agua a glass of water
una niña de ocho años a girl of eight
dos páginas del libro two pages of the book
2 (talking about belonging to somebody, being made of something, etc.)
los calcetines de Alberto Alberto's socks
la casa de mis padres my parents' house
la puerta de la cocina the kitchen door
una bolsa de plástico a plastic bag

🔑 **LANGUAGE**
In English you usually use -'s or -s', and you can leave out 'of' completely.

3 from
Soy de Bilbao. I come from Bilbao.
4 by
un cuadro de Picasso a painting by Picasso
5 about
hablar de algo to talk about something
6 in
el mejor alumno de la clase the best student in the class
a las seis de la mañana at six in the morning

debajo adverb
1 underneath
Está debajo. It's underneath.
2 debajo de under
debajo de la silla under the chair

deber verb
1 must
Debo ir al colegio. I must go to school.
2 should
Deberías hacerlo. You should do it.
3 to owe
Te debo cinco euros. I owe you five euros.

los deberes plural noun masc.
homework
mis deberes de español my Spanish homework

🔑 **LANGUAGE**
Spanish = los deberes is plural
English = homework is singular

débil adjective masc. & fem.
weak

decidir verb
to decide
He decidido venir contigo. I've decided to come with you.
¡Decídete! Make up your mind!

décimo adjective masc., décima fem.
tenth
en el décimo piso on the tenth floor

decir verb
1 to say
No he dicho nada. I haven't said anything.
Dice que no quiere venir. He says he doesn't want to come.
¿Cómo se dice 'coche' en inglés? How do you say 'coche' in English?
2 to tell
decir algo a alguien to tell somebody something
Te he dicho la verdad. I've told you the truth.
3 (when answering the phone)
¡Diga! Hello?

• Use el and uno for masculine words and la and una for feminine words.

44

la **decisión** noun *fem.* (plural las **decisiones**)
decision
tomar una decisión to make a decision

decorar verb
to decorate

el **dedo** noun *masc.*
1 finger
2 el dedo del pie the toe
el dedo gordo del pie the big toe

defender verb
to defend

dejar verb
1 to leave
Déjalo aquí. Leave it here.
¡Déjame en paz! Leave me alone!
2 to let
No me dejan salir. They don't let me go out.
3 to lend
¿Me dejas tu bici? Can you lend me your bike?
4 dejar de hacer algo to stop doing something
¡Deja de molestarme! Stop annoying me!

del preposition

🔑 **LANGUAGE**
de + el = del

1 of the
una página del libro a page of the book
la hermana del panadero the baker's sister
2 from the
Vengo del hotel. I've come from the hotel.

el **delantal** noun *masc.*
apron

delante adverb
1 in front
Ve delante. Go in front.
2 delante de in front of

delante de la biblioteca in front of the library
3 pasar por delante de to go past
El autobús pasa por delante de la escuela. The bus goes past the school.

delantero adjective *masc.*, **delantera** *fem.*
front
el asiento delantero the front seat

deletrear verb
to spell
¿Me lo deletreas? Can you spell it?

el **delfín** noun *masc.* (plural los **delfines**)
dolphin

delgado adjective *masc.*, **delgada** *fem.*
thin
Soy delgada. I'm thin.

delicioso adjective *masc.*, **deliciosa** *fem.*
delicious
Está delicioso. It's delicious.

el or la **delincuente** noun *masc. & fem.*
criminal

demás adjective & pronoun
1 other
los demás niños the other children
2 lo demás the rest
los demás the others
¿Dónde están los demás? Where are the others?

demasiado adverb
1 too
Es demasiado pequeño. It's too small.
2 too much
Comes demasiado. You eat too much.

a b c d e f g h i j k l m n o p q r s t u v w x y z

• *Languages and nationalities do not take a capital letter in Spanish.*

45

a
b
c
d
e
f
g
h
i
j
k
l
m
n
o
p
q
r
s
t
u
v
w
x
y
z

demasiado adjective & pronoun *masc.*,
demasiada *fem.*
1 too much
demasiado dinero too much money
Tengo demasiados deberes.
I've got too much homework.
2 too many
demasiadas veces too many times
¿Hay demasiados? Are there too many?

el or la **dentista** noun *masc. & fem.*
dentist
ir al dentista to go to the dentist

dentro adverb
1 inside
Está dentro. It's inside.
aquí dentro in here
dentro de algo inside something
dentro del edificio inside the building
2 dentro de una semana within a week

el **departamento** noun *masc.*
1 department
2 (*Latin America*) **apartment, flat**

depender verb
to depend
depender de algo to depend on something
Depende. It all depends.

el **dependiente** noun *masc.*,
la **dependienta** *fem.*
shop assistant

el **deporte** noun *masc.*
sport
mi deporte favorito my favourite sport
hacer deporte to play sports

deportista adjective *masc. & fem.*
sporty

el or la **deportista** noun *masc. & fem.*
sportsman, sportswoman

deportivo adjective *masc.*,
deportiva *fem.*
sports
un coche deportivo a sports car
ropa deportiva sports clothes

deprisa adverb
quickly
Lo he hecho deprisa. I did it quickly.

la **derecha** noun *fem.*
right
Está a la derecha. It's on the right.
Gira a la derecha. Turn right.
conducir por la derecha to drive on the right

derecho adverb
straight
Siga derecho. Go straight on.

derecho adjective *masc.*,
derecha *fem.*
1 right
Escribo con la mano derecha.
I write with my right hand.
2 (*talking about pictures, hats, etc.*) **straight**
No está derecho. It isn't straight.
Siéntate derecho. Sit up straight.

derramar verb
to spill

desabrochar verb
to undo
Desabróchate la chaqueta.
Undo your jacket.

desagradable adjective *masc. & fem.*
unpleasant

desaparecer verb
1 to disappear
2 (*talking about people*) **to go missing**

el **desastre** noun *masc.*
disaster

desatar verb
to untie

• *The months of the year and days of the week do not take a capital letter in Spanish.*

Spanish English

desayunar verb
to have breakfast

el **desayuno** noun masc.
breakfast

descalzo adjective masc.,
descalza fem.
in bare feet
correr descalzo to run in bare feet

descansar verb
to rest
Tengo que descansar. I have to have a rest.

el **descanso** noun masc.
rest
Necesito un descanso. I need a rest.

descarado adjective masc.,
descarada fem.
cheeky

descargar verb
1 to download
He descargado un programa de Internet. I've downloaded a program from the Internet.
2 to unload

desconectar verb
1 (a computer, lamp, etc.) **to unplug**
2 to disconnect

el **desconocido** noun masc.,
la **desconocida** fem.
stranger

describir verb
to describe

la **descripción** noun fem. (plural las **descripciones**)
description

el **descubrimiento** noun masc.
discovery

descubrir verb
to discover

descuidado adjective masc.,
descuidada fem.
careless

desde preposition
1 from
desde Londres from London
desde ahora from now on
2 since
No le he visto desde ayer. I haven't seen him since yesterday.
Vivo aquí desde el año pasado. I've been living here since last year.
3 desde hace **for**
Vivo aquí desde hace dos años. I've been living here for two years.

desear verb
1 to wish
Te deseo buena suerte. I wish you good luck.
2 (used for saying 'would like')
¿Qué desea, señor? What would you like, sir?

desenchufar verb
to unplug

el **deseo** noun masc.
wish
pedir un deseo to make a wish

el **desfile** noun masc.
parade

deshacer verb
1 to unpack
deshacer las maletas to unpack the cases
2 to undo
deshacer un nudo to undo a knot

el **desierto** noun masc.
desert

deslizarse verb
to slide

desmayarse verb
to faint

desnudarse verb
to get undressed

• See the centre section for verb tables.

47

desnudo adjective *masc.*,
desnuda *fem.*
1 **naked**
2 **bare**
con los brazos desnudos with bare arms

desobedecer verb
to disobey

desobediente adjective *masc. & fem.*
disobedient

el **desorden** noun *masc.*
mess
¡Qué desorden! What a mess!

desordenado adjective *masc.*,
desordenada *fem.*
untidy

desordenar verb
to mess up

el **despacho** noun *masc.*
office

despacio adverb
slowly

despegar verb
to take off
El avión ha despegado. The plane has taken off.

el **despegue** noun *masc.*
(*of a plane*) **take-off**

el **despertador** noun *masc.*
alarm clock
¿Has puesto el despertador? Have you set the alarm?

despertar verb
to wake up
¿Me puedes despertar a las ocho? Can you wake me up at eight?

despertarse verb
to wake up
Me despierto a las seis. I wake up at six.

despierto adjective *masc.*,
despierta *fem.*
awake
Está despierta. She's awake.

después adverb
1 **afterwards**
poco después soon afterwards
2 **later**
dos años después two years later
3 (*with nouns*)
después de after
después de las vacaciones after the holidays
Llegó después que yo. He arrived after me.

el **destino** noun *masc.*
destination

destruir verb
to destroy

el **detalle** noun *masc.*
detail
con todo detalle in detail

el or la **detective** noun *masc. & fem.*
detective

detener verb
1 **to stop**
detener el coche to stop the car
2 **to arrest**
Han detenido al ladrón They've arrested the thief

detrás adverb
1 **behind**
Ponte detrás. Stand behind.
2 (*with nouns and pronouns*)
detrás de behind
detrás del árbol behind the tree
detrás de mí behind me

devolver verb
1 **to take back**
devolver un libro a la biblioteca to take a book back to the library
2 **to give back**

• Use el and uno for masculine words and la and una for feminine words.

¿Puedes devolverme la bici mañana? Can you give me back my bike tomorrow?
3 to throw up
Voy a devolver. I'm going to throw up.

el **día** noun *masc.*
day
¿Qué día es hoy? What day is it today?
todos los días every day
todo el día all day
Es de día. It's light outside.
un día de fiesta a holiday
el día de la Madre Mother's Day
el día del Padre Father's Day

> ⚷ **LANGUAGE**
> Be careful: **día** ends in an -a but it is not a feminine noun.

el **diablo** noun *masc.*
devil

el **diagrama** noun *masc.*
diagram

> ⚷ **LANGUAGE**
> Be careful: **diagrama** ends in an -a but it is not a feminine noun.

el **diamante** noun *masc.*
diamond
un anillo de diamantes a diamond ring

el **diario** noun *masc.*
1 diary
Escribo en mi diario. I write in my diary.
2 newspaper

diario adjective *masc.*, **diaria** *fem.*
daily

dibujar verb
to draw
Dibujé un caballo. I drew a horse.

el **dibujo** noun *masc.*
1 drawing
hacer un dibujo to do a drawing, to draw a picture
2 los dibujos animados cartoons

el **diccionario** noun *masc.*
dictionary
buscar una palabra en el diccionario to look up a word in the dictionary

diciembre noun *masc.*
December
Mi cumpleaños fue en diciembre. My birthday was in December.
Se van el diez de diciembre. They leave on the tenth of December.

diecinueve number
1 nineteen
Mi hermana tiene diecinueve años. My sister is nineteen.
2 *(with dates)* **nineteenth**
el diecinueve de mayo the nineteenth of May

dieciséis number
1 sixteen
Mi hermano tiene dieciséis años. My brother is sixteen.
2 *(with dates)* **sixteenth**
el dieciséis de abril the sixteenth of April

diecisiete number
1 seventeen
Mi primo tiene diecisiete años. My cousin is seventeen.
2 *(with dates)* **seventeenth**
el diecisiete de octubre the seventeenth of October

dieciocho number
1 eighteen
Mi prima tiene dieciocho años. My cousin is eighteen.
2 *(with dates)* **eighteenth**
el dieciocho de julio the eighteenth of July

a b c d e f g h i j k l m n o p q r s t u v w x y z

• *Languages and nationalities do not take a capital letter in Spanish.*

a
b
c
d
e
f
g
h
i
j
k
l
m
n
o
p
q
r
s
t
u
v
w
x
y
z

el **diente** noun *masc.*
tooth
Me estoy lavando los dientes.
I'm brushing my teeth.

🔑 **LANGUAGE**
Diente is related to 'dentist'.

la **dieta** noun *fem.*
diet

diez number
1 ten
Tengo diez años. I'm ten.
Son las diez. It's ten o'clock.
Son las tres menos diez. It's ten to three.
Son las siete y diez. It's ten past seven.
2 (*with dates*) **tenth**
el diez de febrero the tenth of February

la **diferencia** noun *fem.*
difference

diferente adjective *masc. & fem.*
different
Son muy diferentes. They're very different.

difícil adjective *masc. & fem.*
difficult
un problema difícil a difficult problem

la **dificultad** noun *fem.*
difficulty

digital adjective *masc. & fem.*
digital
una cámara digital a digital camera

el **dinero** noun *masc.*
money
No tengo dinero. I haven't got any money.

el **dinosaurio** noun *masc.*
dinosaur

Dios noun *masc.*
God

la **dirección** noun *fem.* (plural las **direcciones**)
1 address
¿Cuál es tu dirección? What's your address?
2 direction
¿En qué dirección se fue? What direction did she go in?

directamente adverb
straight, **directly**
Fuimos directamente a Madrid.
We went straight to Madrid.

directo adjective *masc.*,
directa *fem.*
1 direct
un vuelo directo a direct flight
2 straight
Fui directo a casa. I went straight home.

el **director** noun *masc.*,
la **directora** *fem.*
1 headmaster, **headmistress**
2 (*of a company*) **manager**
3 (*of an orchestra*) **conductor**

el **disco** noun *masc.*
1 disk
Graba los archivos en un disco.
Copy the files onto a disk.
un disco compacto a CD, a compact disc
2 record
un disco viejo an old record

la **discoteca** noun *fem.*
disco

la **disculpa** noun *fem.*
apology
Tienes que pedir disculpas.
You have to apologize.

disculparse verb
to apologize

el **discurso** noun *masc.*
speech

• *The months of the year and days of the week do not take a capital letter in Spanish.*

la **discusión** noun *fem.*
1 argument
tener una discusión to have an
argument
2 discussion

discutir verb
1 to argue
discutir con alguien to argue with
somebody
2 to discuss

diseñar verb
to design

el **diseño** noun *masc.*
design

el **disfraz** noun *masc.* (plural los
disfraces)
costume, **fancy dress**
un disfraz de pirata a pirate
costume
una fiesta de disfraces a fancy
dress party

disfrazarse verb
to dress up
Me disfracé de pirata. I dressed up
as a pirate.

disléxico adjective *masc.*,
disléxica *fem.*
dyslexic
Soy disléxica. I'm dyslexic.

la **distancia** noun *fem.*
distance
una distancia de cien metros
a distance of a hundred metres
¿A qué distancia está la biblioteca?
How far is the library?

distinto adjective *masc.*,
distinta *fem.*
different
Soy muy distinto a mi hermano.
I'm very different from my brother.

divertido adjective *masc.*,
divertida *fem.*
1 funny
Mis amigos son muy divertidos.
My friends are very funny.

2 enjoyable
La fiesta fue divertida. The party
was enjoyable.
¡Qué divertido! What fun!

divertirse verb
to have fun
Me divertí mucho. I had a lot of
fun.

dividir verb
to divide
Doce dividido por dos son seis.
Twelve divided by two is six.

divorciado adjective *masc.*,
divorciada *fem.*
divorced
Mis padres están divorciados.
My parents are divorced.

doblar verb
1 to fold
doblar algo por la mitad to fold
something in half
2 to bend
doblar el brazo to bend your arm
3 to turn
Dobla a la derecha. Turn right.
4 to double

doble adjective *masc. & fem.*
double
una habitación doble a double
room

el **doble** noun *masc.*
twice as much
Este vestido cuesta el doble.
This dress costs twice as much.

doce number
1 twelve
Mi hermana tiene doce años.
My sister is twelve (years old).
Son las doce. It's twelve o'clock.
2 (with dates) **twelfth**
el doce de marzo the twelfth of
March

• See the centre section for verb tables.

a
b
c
d
e
f
g
h
i
j
k
l
m
n
o
p
q
r
s
t
u
v
w
x
y
z

a
b
c
d
e
f
g
h
i
j
k
l
m
n
o
p
q
r
s
t
u
v
w
x
y
z

la **docena** noun *fem.*
dozen
una docena de huevos a dozen eggs
dos docenas two dozen

el **doctor** noun *masc.*,
la **doctora** *fem.*
doctor

el **dólar** noun *masc.*
dollar

doler verb
to hurt
Me duele la pierna. My leg hurts.
Me duele mucho. It hurts a lot.
Me duele la cabeza. I have a headache.

el **dolor** noun *masc.*
1 pain
Siento mucho dolor. I'm in a lot of pain.
2 ache
Tengo dolor de cabeza. I have a headache.
Tengo dolor de muelas. I have a toothache.

el **domingo** noun *masc.*
Sunday
Hoy es domingo. It's Sunday today.
el domingo on Sunday
Te veo el domingo. I'll see you on Sunday.
los domingos on Sundays
Voy a la piscina los domingos. I go swimming on Sundays.

> **LANGUAGE**
> Remember the difference between **el domingo** (one Sunday only) and **los domingos** (every Sunday).

el **dominó** noun *masc.*
dominoes
jugar al dominó to play dominoes

donde adverb
where
Es la ciudad donde nací. It's the town where I was born.

dónde adverb
(*in questions*) **where**
¿Dónde estás? Where are you?
¿Dónde vas? Where are you going?
¿De dónde eres? Where are you from?
¿por dónde? which way?

> **LANGUAGE**
> Remember to put the accent on **dónde** in questions.

dorado adjective *masc.*,
dorada *fem.*
golden

dormir verb
to sleep
Están durmiendo. They're sleeping.
estar medio dormido to be half asleep

dormirse verb
to fall asleep
Me dormí. I fell asleep.

el **dormitorio** noun *masc.*
1 bedroom
2 (*in a school etc.*) **dormitory**

> **LANGUAGE**
> Both **dormitorio** and 'dormitory' are related to **dormir** (to sleep) because you sleep there.

dos number
1 two
Mi hermano tiene dos años. My brother is two.
Son las dos. It's two o'clock.
2 (*with dates*) **second**
el dos de agosto the second of August
3 both
Están cansados los dos. They're both tired.

• Use **el** and **uno** for masculine words and **la** and **una** for feminine words.

doscientos number *masc.*,
 doscientas *fem.*
 two hundred

el **dragón** noun *masc.* (plural los
 dragones)
 dragon

la **ducha** noun *fem.*
 shower
 La ducha no funciona. The shower
 doesn't work.
 darse una ducha to have a
 shower

ducharse verb
 to have a shower
 Me estoy duchando. I'm having a
 shower.

la **duda** noun *fem.*
 doubt

dudar verb
 to doubt
 Lo dudo. I doubt it.

dulce adjective *masc. & fem.*
 sweet
 una manzana muy dulce a very
 sweet apple

el **dulce** noun *masc.*
 sweet
 Me gustan los dulces. I like sweets.

durante preposition
 1 during
 durante la noche during the night
 2 for
 Me quedé en casa durante una
 semana. I stayed at home for a
 week.

durar verb
 to last
 Las vacaciones duran un mes.
 The holidays last for a month.
 ¿Cuánto tiempo dura la película?
 How long is the film?
 La película dura dos horas.
 The film is two hours long.

duro adjective *masc.*, **dura** *fem.*
 1 hard
 Las patatas están duras.
 The potatoes are hard.
 2 strict
 La maestra es muy dura.
 The teacher is very strict.

el **DVD** noun *masc.* (plural los **DVDs**)
 DVD
 un reproductor DVD a DVD player

Ee

e conjunction
 and
 español e inglés Spanish and
 English
 padre e hijo father and son

> **LANGUAGE**
> In Spanish you use **e** instead of the normal
> **y** before words beginning with **i** or **hi**, but
> not before **hie**.

echar verb
 1 to throw
 echar algo a la basura to throw
 something into the bin
 Me eché al agua. I jumped into the
 water.
 2 to put
 echar gasolina al coche to put
 petrol in the car
 3 to put on
 Echan una buena película. They're
 putting on a good film.
 4 echar de menos to miss
 Te echo de menos. I miss you.
 Echo de menos a mis padres. I miss
 my parents.

• *Languages and nationalities do not take a capital letter in Spanish.*

echarse verb
(*on a bed, sofa, etc.*) **to lie down**
Échate en la cama. Lie down on the bed.

Ecuador noun *masc.*
Ecuador

la **edad** noun *fem.*
age
a la edad de ocho años at the age of eight
¿Qué edad tienes? How old are you?

el **edificio** noun *masc.*
building

Edimburgo noun *masc.*
Edinburgh

la **educación** noun *fem.*
1 education
2 manners
Eso es de mala educación. That's bad manners.

educado adjective *masc.*,
educada *fem.*
polite
una niña bien educada a polite girl
un niño mal educado a rude boy

egoísta adjective *masc. & fem.*
selfish

el **ejemplo** noun *masc.*
example
por ejemplo for example

el **ejercicio** noun *masc.*
exercise
un ejercicio de español a Spanish exercise
Hago mucho ejercicio. I do a lot of exercise.

el **ejército** noun *masc.*
army

el determiner *masc.*
1 (*before masculine singular nouns*) **the**
el niño the boy
el tren the train

2 (*before feminine singular nouns beginning with a stressed 'a' sound*) **the**
el agua the water
el hada the fairy
3 (*no translation*)
Me gusta el chocolate. I like chocolate.
Tengo el pelo largo. I have long hair.
4 (*with adjectives used as nouns*) **the**
el rojo the red one
el pequeño the small one
5 (*with parts of the body, clothes, etc.*)
my, your, his (*etc.*)
Me he cortado el dedo. I've cut my finger.
Ponte el sombrero. Put your hat on.
Le han robado el móvil. Someone has stolen his mobile.

él pronoun *masc.*
1 he
Él lee libros pero su hermano prefiere ver la tele. He reads books but his brother prefers to watch TV.

LANGUAGE
Él is used for giving special importance to the word 'he'.

2 (*after a preposition etc.*) **him**
con él with him
Soy más alta que él. I'm taller than him.
Es él. It's him.
él mismo himself

la **elección** noun *fem.*
choice
una buena elección a good choice

la **electricidad** noun *fem.*
electricity

el or la **electricista** noun *masc. & fem.*
electrician
Mi tío es electricista. My uncle is an electrician.

eléctrico adjective *masc.*,
eléctrica *fem.*
electric

• *The months of the year and days of the week do not take a capital letter in Spanish.*

electrónico adjective *masc.*,
electrónica *fem.*
electronic
un correo electrónico an email
por correo electrónico by email

el **elefante** noun *masc.*
elephant

elegante adjective *masc. & fem.*
smart
Estás muy elegante. You look very smart.

elegir verb
to choose

ella pronoun *fem.*
1 she
Ella ha venido pero los otros no. She has come but the others haven't.

> **LANGUAGE**
> **Élla** is used for giving special importance to the word 'she'.

2 (*after a preposition etc.*) **her**
con ella with her
Juego mejor que ella. I play better than her.
Es ella. It's her.
ella misma herself

ellas pronoun *fem.*
1 they
Ellas van al parque pero yo no. They're going to the park but I'm not.

> **LANGUAGE**
> **Éllas** is used for giving special importance to the word 'they'.

2 (*after a preposition etc.*) **them**
con ellas with them
Somos más inteligentes que ellas. We're cleverer than them.
Son ellas. It's them.
ellas mismas themselves

• *See the centre section for verb tables.*

ellos pronoun *masc.*
1 they
Ellos vienen a la fiesta pero nosotros no. They're coming to the party but we are not.

> **LANGUAGE**
> **Éllos** is used for giving special importance to the word 'they'.

2 (*after a preposition etc.*) **them**
con ellos with them
Soy más alto que ellos. I'm taller than them.
Son ellos. It's them.
ellos mismos themselves

embarazada adjective *fem.*
pregnant
Está embarazada de seis meses. She's six months pregnant.

la **emergencia** noun *fem.*
emergency
una salida de emergencia an emergency exit

emocionante adjective *masc. & fem.*
exciting
una película emocionante an exciting film

la **empanadilla** noun *fem.*
pastie

empatar verb
(*talking about teams*) **to draw**

el **empate** noun *masc.*
(*in a match*) **draw**

empezar verb
to start
La película empieza a las dos. The film starts at two.
Hemos empezado a aprender español. We've started to learn Spanish.

a
b
c
d
e
f
g
h
i
j
k
l
m
n
o
p
q
r
s
t
u
v
w
x
y
z

el **empleado** noun *masc.*,
la **empleada** *fem.*
1 office worker
2 (*in a bank*) **bank worker**

el **empleo** noun *masc.*
job
buscar empleo to look for a job

la **empresa** noun *fem.*
company

empujar verb
to push
¡No me empujes! Don't push me!

en preposition
1 in
en la caja in the box
en Escocia in Scotland
en inglés in English
2 into
Entré en la cocina. I went into the kitchen.
3 on
en la mesa on the table
en la tele on TV
4 by
en autobús by bus
5 at
en la estación at the station
en casa at home

enamorado adjective *masc.*,
enamorada *fem.*
in love
estar enamorado de alguien to be in love with somebody

enamorarse verb
to fall in love

el **enano** noun *masc.*, la **enana** *fem.*
dwarf

encantado adjective *masc.*,
encantada *fem.*
pleased
Encantado de conocerte. Pleased to meet you.
Estoy encantada con los regalos. I'm very pleased with the presents.

encantador adjective *masc.*,
encantadora *fem.*
lovely

encantar verb
to love
Me encanta el fútbol. I love football.
Me encantan las películas. I love films.
A Zafir le encanta leer. Zafir loves to read.

🔑 **LANGUAGE**
Encantar means 'to please very much' so the order of the words in the Spanish sentence is different, e.g. **Me encanta el fútbol** is, word for word, 'Football pleases me very much'.

el **encargado** noun *masc.*,
la **encargada** *fem.*
manager, person in charge

encender verb
1 to light
encender una vela to light a candle
2 to switch on
encender la luz to switch on the light

encendido adjective *masc.*,
encendida *fem.*
1 (*light, computer, etc.*) **on**
La tele está encendida. The TV is on.
2 burning
El fuego está encendido. The fire is burning.

enchufar verb
to plug in

la **enciclopedia** noun *fem.*
encyclopedia

• *Use* **el** *and* **uno** *for masculine words and* **la** *and* **una** *for feminine words.*

encima adverb
1 on top
Pon el libro aquí encima. Put the book here on top.
2 encima de on top of
encima del armario on top of the wardrobe
3 por encima de over
El balón pasó por encima de la portería. The ball went over the goal.

🔑 **LANGUAGE**
Use **por encima de** with verbs of movement like **pasar** (go) or **saltar** (jump).

encontrar verb
to find
No encuentro mi reloj. I can't find my watch.

encontrarse verb
1 to meet
Nos encontramos en la calle.
We met in the street.
encontrarse con alguien to meet somebody
2 to feel
No me encuentro bien. I don't feel well.

el **enemigo** noun masc.,
la **enemiga** fem.
enemy

la **energía** noun fem.
energy

enero noun masc.
January
Ven a mi fiesta en enero. Come to my party in January.
el seis de enero on the sixth of January

enfadado adjective masc.,
enfadada fem.
angry
¿Estás enfadada conmigo?
Are you angry with me?

enfadarse verb
to get angry

la **enfermedad** noun fem.
illness

el **enfermero** noun masc.,
la **enfermera** fem.
nurse
Mi madre es enfermera.
My mother's a nurse.

enfermo adjective masc.,
enferma fem.
ill
Estoy enferma. I'm ill.
ponerse enfermo to get ill

el **enfermo** noun masc.,
la **enferma** fem.
1 sick person
los enfermos sick people
2 (in a hospital etc.) **patient**

enfrente adverb
1 opposite
Siéntate enfrente. Sit down opposite.
2 (with nouns and pronouns)
enfrente de opposite
enfrente de la estación opposite the station
Gabriel está sentado enfrente de mí. Gabriel is sitting opposite me.
3 de enfrente opposite
la casa de enfrente the opposite house

enhorabuena exclamation
congratulations!

el **enlace** noun masc.
(on a web page) **link**
Sigue el enlace. Follow the link.

enorme adjective masc. & fem.
huge, enormous

la **ensalada** noun fem.
salad
una ensalada de frutas a fruit salad

a b c d e f g h i j k l m n o p q r s t u v w x y z

• Languages and nationalities do not take a capital letter in Spanish.

a
b
c
d
e
f
g
h
i
j
k
l
m
n
o
p
q
r
s
t
u
v
w
x
y
z

la **ensaladilla** noun *fem.*
Russian salad

 CULTURE
A Russian salad is made with boiled potatoes, carrots, hard-boiled eggs, peas, etc. mixed with mayonnaise.

el **ensayo** noun *masc.*
rehearsal
Tenemos ensayo. We have a rehearsal.

enseguida adverb
straight away
Enseguida vuelvo. I'm coming straight back.

la **enseñanza** noun *fem.*
education
la enseñanza primaria primary education

enseñar verb
1 to teach
La señora Campbell enseña inglés. Mrs Campbell teaches English.
Mi madre me enseñó a leer. My mum taught me to read.
2 to show
Enséñame el cuaderno. Show me the exercise book.

entender verb
to understand
Entiendo el español. I understand Spanish.
¿Entiendes? Do you understand?

entenderse verb
to get on
Nos entendemos bien. We get on well.

entero adjective *masc.*, **entera** *fem.*
whole
una semana entera a whole week

entonces adverb
1 then
Entonces no había coches. There were no cars then.
desde entonces since then

2 so, then
Entonces, ¿qué vas a hacer? So, what are you going to do?, What are you going to do, then?

la **entrada** noun *fem.*
1 entrance
¿Dónde está la entrada? Where's the entrance?
2 (*for the cinema, museum, etc.*) **ticket**

entrar verb
1 to go in
Entra tú, yo te espero. You go in, and I'll wait for you.
Entré en la tienda. I went into the shop.
2 to come in
¿Puedo entrar? Can I come in?
3 (*used for saying you're starting to get hungry, cold, etc.*)
Me está entrando hambre. I'm getting hungry.

entre preposition
1 between
entre la escuela y la estación. between the school and the station.
2 entre todos **together**
Decoramos la clase entre todos. We decorated the classroom all together.

entregar verb
1 to deliver
entregar un paquete to deliver a parcel
2 to hand in
entregar los deberes to hand in the homework

el **entrenamiento** noun *masc.*
training

entrenar verb
(*for football etc.*) **to train**

la **entrevista** noun *fem.*
interview

entusiasmado adjective *masc.*, **entusiasmada** *fem.*
excited

• *The months of the year and days of the week do not take a capital letter in Spanish.*

Spanish English

enviar verb
to send

envidioso adjective *masc.*,
envidiosa *fem.*
jealous, **envious**

envolver verb
to wrap up
envolver un regalo to wrap up a present

el **episodio** noun *masc.*
episode

la **época** noun *fem.*
time
esta época del año this time of the year

el **equilibrio** noun *masc.*
balance
Perdí el equilibrio. I lost my balance.

el **equipaje** noun *masc.*
luggage

el **equipo** noun *masc.*
1 team
un equipo de fútbol a football team
2 equipment
el equipo de camping the camping equipment
un equipo de música a stereo

la **equitación** noun *fem.*
horse riding
hacer equitación to go riding

equivocado adjective *masc.*,
equivocada *fem.*
wrong
Estás equivocado. You're wrong.
la respuesta equivocada the wrong answer

equivocarse verb
1 to be wrong
Te equivocas. You're wrong.
Me he equivocado de autobús. I got on the wrong bus.

2 to make a mistake
Lo siento, me he equivocado. Sorry, I made a mistake.

era verb SEE **ser**
was
Era cierto. It was true.

eran verb SEE **ser**
were
Mis amigos eran españoles. My friends were Spanish.

eres verb SEE **ser**
are
Eres mi mejor amiga. You're my best friend.

el **error** noun *masc.*
mistake
cometer un error to make a mistake

es verb SEE **ser**
is
Es inglesa. She's English.
No es difícil. It isn't hard.

esa, **ésa** adjective & pronoun *fem.*
SEE **ese, ése** adjective & pronoun
that, **that one**

esas, **ésas** adjective & pronoun *fem.*
SEE **esos, ésos** adjective & pronoun
those

la **escalera** noun *fem.*
1 staircase
2 stairs
bajar la escalera to go down the stairs

LANGUAGE
You can also say **las escaleras** in the plural in Spanish.

3 ladder
subirse a una escalera to climb a ladder
una escalera de mano a ladder
4 una escalera mecánica an escalator

• *See the centre section for verb tables.*

a b c d e f g h i j k l m n o p q r s t u v w x y z

el escalón noun masc. (plural los **escalones**)
step
¡Cuidado con el escalón! Mind the step!

el escáner noun masc.
scanner

el escaparate noun masc.
shop window

escaparse verb
1 to escape
2 to run away
Se escapó de la escuela. He ran away from school.

el escarabajo noun masc.
beetle

la escayola noun fem.
plaster (for broken bones)

escayolado adjective masc., **escayolada** fem.
in plaster
Tengo la pierna escayolada. I've got my leg in plaster.

la escoba noun fem.
broom

escocés adjective masc., **escocesa** fem.
Scottish

LANGUAGE
The plural of escocés is escoceses.

el escocés masc., **la escocesa** noun fem.
Scot

LANGUAGE
The plural of escocés is escoceses.

Escocia noun fem.
Scotland

escoger verb
to choose
He escogido el verde. I've chosen the green one.

escolar adjective masc. & fem.
school
un autobús escolar a school bus
las vacaciones escolares the school holidays

el or la escolar noun masc. & fem.
schoolboy, **schoolgirl**
los escolares schoolchildren

esconder verb
to hide
Esconde los regalos. Hide the presents.

esconderse verb
to hide
Me escondí detrás de la puerta. I hid behind the door.

escondido adjective masc., **escondida** fem.
hidden
Está escondido allí. It's hidden there.

el escondite noun masc.
hiding place
jugar al escondite to play hide-and-seek

escribir verb
1 to write
Escribe las palabras en tu cuaderno. Write the words in your exercise book.
Nos escribimos. We write to each other.
2 to spell
Lo has escrito mal. You've spelled it wrong.
¿Cómo se escribe tu nombre? How do you spell your name?

el escritor noun masc., **la escritora** fem.
writer

el escritorio noun masc.
desk

• Use el and uno for masculine words and la and una for feminine words.

60

escuchar verb
to listen, to listen to
¡Escucha! Listen!
Me gusta escuchar música. I like to listen to music.

> 🔑 **LANGUAGE**
> Spanish = **escuchar** algo/a alguien
> English = **to listen to** something/ somebody

el **escudo** noun *masc.*
shield

la **escuela** noun *fem.*
school
en la escuela at school
ir a la escuela to go to school

escupir verb
to spit

ese adjective *masc.*, **esa** *fem.*
that
ese niño that boy
esa bicicleta that bicycle

ése pronoun *masc.*, **ésa** *fem.*
1 that one
Me gusta ése. I like that one.
Toma ésa. Take that one.
2 that
¿Quién es ésa? Who's that?

> 🔑 **LANGUAGE**
> The accent goes on **ése** and **ésa** to show clearly you're using the pronoun.

el **esfuerzo** noun *masc.*
effort
hacer un esfuerzo to make an effort

el **esguince** noun *masc.*
sprain
Tengo un esguince en el tobillo. I've sprained my ankle.

el **esmalte** noun *masc.*
el esmalte de uñas nail varnish

eso pronoun
that
¿Qué es eso? What's that?
¡Eso es! That's it!

esos adjective *masc.*, **esas** *fem.*
those
esos libros those books
esas sillas those chairs

ésos pronoun *masc.*, **ésas** *fem.*
those
Quiero ésos. I want those.
Ésas son mejores. Those are better.

> 🔑 **LANGUAGE**
> The accent goes on **ésos** and **ésas** to show clearly you're using the pronoun.

espacial adjective *masc. & fem.*
space
una estación espacial a space station
una nave espacial a spaceship

el **espacio** noun *masc.*
1 room, space
No hay suficiente espacio. There isn't enough room.
2 space
Deja un espacio. Leave a space.
un viaje en el espacio a journey into space

la **espada** noun *fem.*
sword

los **espaguetis** plural noun *masc.*
spaghetti

> 🔑 **LANGUAGE**
> Spanish = **los espaguetis** is plural
> English = **spaghetti** is singular

la **espalda** noun *fem.*
back
Me duele la espalda. My back hurts.

España noun *fem.*
Spain
Estamos en España. We're in Spain.
Quiero ir a España. I want to go to Spain.

• *Languages and nationalities do not take a capital letter in Spanish.*

a b c d e f g h i j k l m n o p q r s t u v w x y z

a
b
c
d
e
f
g
h
i
j
k
l
m
n
o
p
q
r
s
t
u
v
w
x
y
z

el **español** noun *masc.*
Spanish
Hablo español. I speak Spanish.

español adjective *masc.*,
española *fem.*
Spanish
Soy español. I'm Spanish.

el **español** noun *masc.*,
la **española** *fem.*
Spaniard
los españoles the Spanish

especial adjective *masc. & fem.*
special

especialmente adverb
especially

espectacular adjective *masc. & fem.*
spectacular

el **espectáculo** noun *masc.*
(*with actors, musicians, etc.*) **show**

el **espejo** noun *masc.*
mirror
en el espejo in the mirror

la **espera** noun *fem.*
wait
una larga espera a long wait
una sala de espera a waiting room

esperar verb
1 to wait, **to wait for**
Espera aquí. Wait here.
Espérame. Wait for me.

LANGUAGE
Spanish = **esperar** a alguien
English = **to wait for** somebody

2 to hope
Espero tener buen tiempo. I hope I
have good weather.
Espero que sí. I hope so.
3 to expect
Te espero a las cinco. I'll expect
you at five.
Está esperando un niño. She's
expecting a baby.

espeso adjective *masc.*, **espesa** *fem.*
thick

las **espinacas** plural noun *fem.*
spinach

LANGUAGE
Spanish = **las espinacas** is plural
English = **spinach** is singular

la **esponja** noun *fem.*
sponge

la **esposa** noun *fem.*
wife

el **esposo** noun *masc.*
husband

el **esqueleto** noun *masc.*
skeleton

el **esquí** noun *masc.*
1 ski
un par de esquís a pair of skis
una pista de esquí a ski slope
2 skiing
Me encanta el esquí. I love skiing.

esquiar verb
to ski

la **esquina** noun *fem.*
corner
doblar la esquina to turn the
corner

esta, **ésta** adjective & pronoun *fem.*
SEE **este, éste** adjective & pronoun
this, **this one**

está verb SEE **estar**
is
La puerta está abierta. The door's
open.
Papá está en el jardín. Dad's in the
garden.

estaba verb SEE **estar**
was
Estaba en Toledo. He was in
Toledo.

• *The months of the year and days of the week do not take a capital letter in Spanish.*

estaban verb SEE **estar**
were
Estaban en la escuela. They were in school.

la **estación** noun *fem.* (plural las **estaciones**)
1 station
en la estación at the station
una estación de autobuses a bus station
2 season
la estación de las lluvias the rainy season

estacionar verb
to park
'Prohibido estacionar'
'No parking'

el **estadio** noun *masc.*
stadium

el **estado** noun *masc.*
condition
en buen estado in good condition

Estados Unidos noun *masc.*
United States
Voy a Estados Unidos. I'm going to the United States.

LANGUAGE
Estados Unidos is usually singular, and **los** (the) is not usually given.

estadounidense adjective *masc. & fem.*
American

estáis verb SEE **estar**
are
Tomás y Rafael, ¿dónde estáis? Tomás and Rafael, where are you?

estallar verb
to explode
Una bomba estalló. A bomb exploded.

estamos verb SEE **estar**
are

Estamos en la cocina. We're in the kitchen.

están verb SEE **estar**
are
Están cansados. They're tired.
Están en la playa. They're on the beach.

la **estancia** noun *fem.*
stay
mi estancia en Barcelona my stay in Barcelona

el **estanco** noun *masc.*
tobacconist's shop

CULTURE
In Spain a tobacconist also sells stamps and postcards. In Britain newsagents usually sell these things.

el **estanque** noun *masc.*
pond

el **estante** noun *masc.*
shelf

la **estantería** noun *fem.*
bookcase

estar verb
1 to be
Estoy en mi habitación. I'm in my room.
¿Dónde está mi libro? Where's my book?
Tu hermano no está. Your brother isn't here.
¿Cómo estás? How are you?
¿Estáis cansadas? Are you tired?
Estamos jugando. We're playing.
¿Qué están haciendo? What are they doing?
Han estado de vacaciones. They've been on holiday.
2 (*with dates*)
¿A cuántos estamos? What's the date?

• *See the centre section for verb tables.*

a
b
c
d
e
f
g
h
i
j
k
l
m
n
o
p
q
r
s
t
u
v
w
x
y
z

Spanish English

a
b
c
d
e
f
g
h
i
j
k
l
m
n
o
p
q
r
s
t
u
v
w
x
y
z

Estamos a cinco de junio. It's the fifth of June.

> 🔑 **LANGUAGE**
> There are two main verbs for saying 'to be': **estar** and **ser**. Use **estar** when you're talking about where something is or about something that normally lasts only a short time e.g. **Estoy cansado** (I'm tired). Use it also with verbs ending in **-ando** or **-iendo** ('-ing' in English), e.g. **Estoy cantando** (I'm singing), **Está escribiendo** (He's writing).

estas, **éstas** adjective & pronoun *fem.*
SEE **estos, éstos** adjective & pronoun
these

estás verb SEE **estar**
are
¿Dónde estás, Maite? Where are you, Maite?

la **estatua** noun *fem.*
statue

la **estatura** noun *fem.*
height

este noun *masc.* & adjective
east
en el este in the east
la costa este the east coast

este adjective *masc.*, **esta** *fem.*
this
este coche this car
esta niña this girl

éste pronoun *masc.*, **ésta** *fem.*
1 this one
Me gusta éste. I like this one.
Mira ésta. Look at this one.
2 this
¿Quién es ésta? Who's this?

> 🔑 **LANGUAGE**
> The accent goes on **éste** and **ésta** to show clearly you're using the pronoun.

estirar verb
to stretch
Estira las piernas. Stretch your legs.

estirarse verb
(*after waking up etc.*) **to stretch**

esto pronoun
this
¿Qué es esto? What's this?

el **estofado** noun *masc.*
stew

el **estómago** noun *masc.*
stomach
Me duele el estómago. I have a stomach ache.

estornudar verb
to sneeze

> **CULTURE**
> In Spain people say **¡Jesús!** (Jesus) when somebody sneezes.

estos adjective *masc.*, **estas** *fem.*
these
estos compactos these CDs
estas cajas these boxes

éstos *masc.*, **éstas** *fem.*pronoun
these
Quiero éstos. I want these.
Éstas son más grandes. These are bigger.

> 🔑 **LANGUAGE**
> The accent goes on **éstos** and **éstas** to show clearly you're using the pronoun.

estoy verb SEE **estar**
am
Estoy triste. I'm sad.
Estoy en mi habitación. I'm in my room.

estrecho adjective *masc.*,
estrecha *fem.*
1 narrow
una calle estrecha a narrow street
2 tight

• *Use* **el** *and* **uno** *for masculine words and* **la** *and* **una** *for feminine words.*

La falda está estrecha. The skirt is too tight.

la **estrella** noun *fem.*
star
una estrella de cine a film star

estresado adjective *masc.*,
estresada *fem.*
stressed out

estricto adjective *masc.*,
estricta *fem.*
strict

estropear verb
1 (*a toy, the TV, etc.*) **to break**
2 (*clothes, holidays, etc.*) **to ruin**

estropearse verb
to break down
Se ha estropeado el coche. The car has broken down.

el **estuche** noun *masc.*
case
un estuche para lápices a pencil case

el or la **estudiante** noun *masc. & fem.*
student
Mi hermano es estudiante. My brother is a student.

estudiar verb
to study

el **estudio** noun *masc.*
1 **studio**
un estudio de televisión a TV studio
2 **studio flat**

los **estudios** plural noun *masc.*
(*in school*) **studies**

estupendo adjective *masc.*,
estupenda *fem.*
great
¡Estupendo! Great!

estúpido adjective *masc.*,
estúpida *fem.*
stupid

la **etiqueta** noun *fem.*
label

el **euro** noun *masc.*
euro

Europa noun *fem.*
Europe

europeo adjective *masc.*,
europea *fem.*
European
la Unión Europea the European Union

el **europeo** noun *masc.*,
la **europea** *fem.*
European

Euskadi noun
the Basque Country

el **euskera** noun *masc.*
Basque (*the language*)

evitar verb
to avoid

exacto adjective *masc.*,
exacta *fem.*
exact

exagerar verb
to exaggerate

el **examen** noun *masc.* (plural los **exámenes**)
exam
un examen de español a Spanish exam

excelente adjective *masc. & fem.*
excellent

excepto preposition
except
todos excepto yo everybody except me

a
b
c
d
e
f
g
h
i
j
k
l
m
n
o
p
q
r
s
t
u
v
w
x
y
z

• Languages and nationalities do not take a capital letter in Spanish.

la **excursión** noun *fem.* (plural las **excursiones**)
trip
Voy de excursión al campo.
I'm going on a trip to the country.

la **excusa** noun *fem.*
excuse

existir verb
to exist

el **éxito** noun *masc.*
success

⚠ **FALSE FRIEND**
el éxito = success (*not* exit)

la **experiencia** noun *fem.*
experience

el **experimento** noun *masc.*
experiment

el **experto** noun *masc.*,
la **experta** *fem.*
expert

la **explicación** noun *fem.* (plural las **explicaciones**)
explanation

explicar verb
to explain
¿Puede explicarme esto? Can you explain this to me?

explorar verb
to explore

la **explosión** noun *fem.* (plural las **explosiones**)
explosion

la **exposición** noun *fem.* (plural las **exposiciones**)
exhibition

la **expresión** noun *fem.* (plural las **expresiones**)
expression

extender verb
1 (*butter, glue, etc.*) **to spread**
Extiende el pegamento. Spread the glue.

2 to stretch
extender la mano to stretch out your hand

el **exterior** noun *masc.*
outside
el exterior de la casa the outside of the house

el **extranjero** noun *masc.*
1 en el extranjero abroad
vivir en el extranjero to live abroad
2 (*with verbs showing movement*)
al extranjero abroad
ir al extranjero to go abroad

extranjero adjective *masc.*,
extranjera *fem.*
foreign

el **extranjero** noun *masc.*,
la **extranjera** *fem.*
foreigner
Soy extranjera. I'm a foreigner.

extraño adjective *masc.*,
extraña *fem.*
strange

extraordinario adjective *masc.*,
extraordinaria *fem.*
1 unusual
2 (*success, beauty, etc.*) **outstanding**

el or la **extraterrestre** noun *masc. & fem.*
extraterrestrial

el **extremo** noun *masc.*
end
Ponte al otro extremo de la fila.
Go to the other end of the line.
al otro extremo de la ciudad at the other end of town

• *The months of the year and days of the week do not take a capital letter in Spanish.*

Ff

la **fábrica** noun *fem.*
factory

fabricar verb
to make
'Fabricado en España.' 'Made in Spain.'

fácil adjective *masc. & fem.*
easy
Es fácil de entender. It's easy to understand.

fácilmente adverb
easily

la **factura** noun *fem.*
(*for gas, phone, etc.*) **bill**

la **falda** noun *fem.*
skirt

las **Fallas** plural noun *fem.*
the festival of San José (Saint Joseph) in Valencia

CULTURE
Every March the people of Valencia make **fallas**: cardboard figures of famous people that they display in the streets. The most important part of the festival is the burning of the **fallas** on 19th March.

falso adjective *masc.*, **falsa** *fem.*
false
¿Verdadero o falso? True or false?

la **falta** noun *fem.*
1 mistake
hacer una falta de ortografía to make a spelling mistake
2 (*in sport*) **foul**

faltar verb
to be missing
Falta una página. There's a page missing.
¿Quién falta? Who's missing?

• *See the centre section for verb tables.*

la **familia** noun *fem.*
family
en familia with the family
una familia numerosa a big family

famoso adjective *masc.*, **famosa** *fem.*
famous

el **fantasma** noun *masc.*
ghost

LANGUAGE
Be careful: **fantasma** ends in an **-a** but it is not a feminine noun.

fantástico adjective *masc.*, **fantástica** *fem.*
fantastic

el **farmacéutico** *masc.*, la **farmacéutica** noun *fem.*
chemist

la **farmacia** noun *fem.*
chemist's, pharmacy

el **faro** noun *masc.*
1 (*on the coast*) **lighthouse**
2 (*of a car*) **headlamp**

la **farola** noun *fem.*
1 lamp-post
chocar contra una farola to crash into a lamp-post
2 streetlight

fatal adjective *masc. & fem.*
1 fatal
un accidente fatal a fatal accident
2 really awful
Me siento fatal. I feel really awful.

fatal adverb
really badly
Lo has hecho fatal. You've done it really badly.

el **favor** noun masc.
favour
¿Me haces un favor? Can you do me a favour?
por favor please
Apaga la luz, por favor. Turn the light off, please.

favorito adjective masc.,
favorita fem.
favourite

febrero noun masc.
February
Mi cumpleaños es en febrero. My birthday is in February.
el tres de febrero on the third of February

la **fecha** noun fem.
date
mi fecha de nacimiento my date of birth
¿A qué fecha estamos hoy? What's the date today?

la **felicidad** noun fem.
1 happiness
2 ¡Felicidades! Congratulations!
¿Es tu cumpleaños? – ¡Felicidades! Is it your birthday? – Happy birthday!

feliz adjective masc. & fem. (plural **felices**)
happy
Soy muy feliz aquí. I'm very happy here.
¡Feliz cumpleaños! Happy birthday!
¡Feliz Año Nuevo! Happy New Year!
¡Feliz Navidad! Happy Christmas!

femenino adjective masc.,
femenina fem.
1 (in grammar) **feminine**
el género femenino the feminine gender

2 women's
el equipo femenino the women's team

🔑 **LANGUAGE**
Spanish = femenino
English = feminine

fenomenal adjective masc. & fem.
fantastic

feo adjective masc., **fea** fem.
ugly

la **feria** noun fem.
fair

feroz adjective masc. & fem. (plural **feroces**)
fierce

el **ferrocarril** noun masc.
railway
una línea de ferrocarril a railway line

festivo adjective masc.
un día festivo a holiday

la **ficha** noun fem.
1 (in a game) **counter**
2 card

el **fichero** noun masc.
(on a computer) **file**

los **fideos** plural noun masc.
noodles

la **fiebre** noun fem.
1 temperature
tener fiebre to have a temperature
2 fever
Tengo fiebre del heno. I have hay fever.

la **fiesta** noun fem.
1 party
Van a dar una fiesta. They're going to have a party.
una fiesta de cumpleaños a birthday party
2 holiday
El martes es fiesta. Tuesday is a holiday.

• Use el and uno for masculine words and la and una for feminine words.

un día de fiesta a holiday

la **fila** noun *fem.*
1 line
 ponerse en fila to get into line
 en fila india in single file
2 (*in the cinema etc.*) **row**
 en la primera fila in the front row

el **fin** noun *masc.*
1 end
 el fin del año escolar the end of the school year
 la fiesta de fin de curso the end-of-year party
 el fin de semana the weekend
2 ¡por fin! at last!

el **final** noun *masc.*
1 end
 al final de ha calle at the end of the street
 al final in the end
 a finales de agosto at the end of August
2 (*of a book, film, or play*) **ending**
 un final feliz a happy ending

la **final** noun *fem.*
final
 Nuestro equipo la ganado la final. Our team has won the final.

fino adjective *masc.*, **fina** *fem.*
thin
 una rebanada fina a thin slice

la **firma** noun *fem.*
signature

firmar verb
to sign

físico adjective *masc.*, **física** *fem.*
physical

flaco adjective *masc.*, **flaca** *fem.*
skinny

el **flamenco** noun *masc.*
flamenco

CULTURE
Flamenco is a type of popular music with dancing, singing, and guitar playing that started in Andalusia in the south of Spain.

la **flauta** noun *fem.*
flute
 Joaquín toca la flauta. Joaquín plays the flute.
 la flauta dulce the recorder

LANGUAGE
Word for word **flauta dulce** means 'sweet flute'.

la **flecha** noun *fem.*
arrow

el **flequillo** noun *masc.*
fringe
 Llevo flequillo. I have a fringe.

flojo adjective *masc.*, **floja** *fem.*
1 (*knot, wire, etc.*) **loose**
2 weak
 Está flojo. He's weak.

la **flor** noun *fem.*
flower
 un ramo de flores a bunch of flowers

el **florero** noun *masc.*
vase

el or la **florista** noun *masc. & fem.*
florist

la **floristería** noun *fem.*
florist's

flotar verb
to float

la **foca** noun *fem.*
seal

el **fondo** noun *masc.*
1 bottom
 en el fondo del mar at the bottom of the sea

• *Languages and nationalities do not take a capital letter in Spanish.*

2 end
al fondo del pasillo at the end of the corridor
3 back
al fondo de la clase at the back of the class

el **fontanero** noun *masc.*,
la **fontanera** *fem.*
plumber
Mi padre es fontanero. My dad's a plumber.

el **footing** noun *masc.*
jogging
hacer footing to go jogging

la **forma** noun *fem.*
1 shape
en forma de cruz in the shape of a cross
2 en forma fit
Carlos está en forma. Carlos is fit.

formar verb
1 to form
formar un círculo to form a circle
Han formado un grupo. They've formed a band.
¡Formad parejas! Get into pairs!
2 to make up
El equipo está formado por niños y niñas. The team is made up of boys and girls.

el **formulario** noun *masc.*
form
rellenar un formulario to fill in a form

la **foto** noun *fem.*
photo
He hecho una foto de mi casa.
I've taken a photo of my house.
¿Puede hacernos una foto? Could you take a photo of us?

la **fotocopia** noun *fem.*
photocopy

la **fotocopiadora** noun *fem.*
photocopier

fotocopiar verb
to photocopy

la **fotografía** noun *fem.*
photograph
hacer una fotografía to take a photograph

el **fotógrafo** noun *masc.*,
la **fotógrafa** *fem.*
photographer

la **frambuesa** noun *fem.*
raspberry
la mermelada de frambuesa raspberry jam

el **francés** noun *masc.*
French
¿Hablas francés? Do you speak French?

francés adjective *masc.*,
francesa *fem.*
French
Alain es francés. Alain is French.

🔑 **LANGUAGE**
The plural of **francés** is **franceses**.

el **francés** noun *masc.*,
la **francesa** *fem.*
Frenchman, Frenchwoman
los franceses the French

Francia noun *fem.*
France

la **frase** noun *fem.*
1 sentence
Esta frase tiene dos verbos.
This sentence has two verbs.
2 phrase
una frase hecha a set phrase

frecuente adjective *masc. & fem.*
1 common
un error frecuente a common mistake
2 frequent

frecuentemente adverb
frequently

• *The months of the year and days of the week do not take a capital letter in Spanish.*

el **fregadero** noun *masc.*
(*in the kitchen*) **sink**

fregar verb
to wash
fregar los platos to wash the dishes

frenar verb
to put on the brakes

el **freno** noun *masc.*
brake

la **frente** noun *fem.*
forehead

frente a preposition
opposite
frente al colegio opposite the school

la **fresa** noun *fem.*
strawberry
la mermelada de fresa strawberry jam

fresco adjective *masc.*, **fresca** *fem.*
1 cool
una bebida fresca a cool drink
Hace fresco. The weather's cool.
2 fresh
huevos frescos fresh eggs

el **frigorífico** noun *masc.*
fridge

el **frío** noun *masc.*
1 cold
No me gusta el frío. I don't like the cold.
2 tener frío to be cold
Tengo frío. I'm cold.

🔑 **LANGUAGE**
Spanish = **tener** frío **Tengo frío.**
English = **to be** cold **I'm cold.**

3 Hace frío. It's cold.
¡Qué frío hace! It's so cold!

frío adjective *masc.*, **fría** *fem.*
cold
La sopa está fría. The soup's cold.

• *See the centre section for verb tables.*

frito adjective *masc.*, **frita** *fem.*
fried
un huevo frito a fried egg

la **frontera** noun *fem.*
border

la **fruta** noun *fem.*
fruit
Me gusta la fruta. I like fruit.
un zumo de fruta a fruit juice

la **frutería** noun *fem.*
fruit shop

fue verb
1 went SEE **ir**
Fue a casa. He went home.
2 was SEE **ser**
Ayer fue mi cumpleaños.
Yesterday was my birthday.

el **fuego** noun *masc.*
fire
encender el fuego to light the fire
los fuegos artificiales fireworks

la **fuente** noun *fem.*
1 fountain
2 serving dish

fuera adverb
1 out
Estoy aquí fuera. I'm out here.
Mi madre está fuera del país.
My mum's out of the country.
2 outside
Están jugando fuera. They're playing outside.
fuera de nuestra casa outside our house
3 away
Javier está fuera hasta el domingo.
Javier is away until Sunday.

fueron verb
1 went SEE **ir**
Fueron al supermercado. They went to the supermarket.
2 were SEE **ser**
Las vacaciones fueron muy buenas. The holidays were very good.

a
b
c
d
e
f
g
h
i
j
k
l
m
n
o
p
q
r
s
t
u
v
w
x
y
z

fuerte adjective *masc. & fem.*
1 strong
Soy fuerte. I'm strong.
2 loud
La música está muy fuerte. The music's very loud.
hablar más fuerte to speak louder
3 bad
un dolor fuerte a bad pain
un resfriado muy fuerte a very bad cold

la **fuerza** noun *fem.*
strength

LANGUAGE
Fuerza is related to 'force', another word for 'strength'.

fui verb
1 went SEE **ir**
Fui al colegio. I went to school.
2 was SEE **ser**
Fui la primera en llegar. I was the first to arrive.

funcionar verb
to work
El ordenador no funciona. The computer isn't working.

la **funda** noun *fem.*
1 (*for glasses, guitar, etc.*) **case**
2 (*for cushion, sofa, etc.*) **cover**

el **funeral** noun *masc.*
funeral

la **furgoneta** noun *fem.*
van

furioso adjective *masc.,*
furiosa *fem.*
furious
Estoy furioso contigo. I'm furious with you.

el **fútbol** noun *masc.*
football
Me gusta jugar al fútbol. I like to play football.
un balón de fútbol a football

el or la **futbolista** noun *masc. & fem.*
footballer
Quiero ser futbolista. I want to be a footballer.

el **futuro** noun *masc.*
future
en el futuro in the future

Gg

las **gafas** plural noun *fem.*
Llevo gafas. I wear glasses.
las gafas de sol sunglasses

la **galería** noun *fem.*
una galería comercial a shopping mall

Gales noun *masc.*
Wales
el País de Gales Wales

el **galés** noun *masc.*
Welsh
David habla galés. David speaks Welsh.

galés adjective *masc.,*
galesa *fem.*
Welsh

LANGUAGE
The plural of galés is galeses.

el **galés** noun *masc.,*
la **galesa** *fem.*
Welshman, Welshwoman
los galeses the Welsh

Galicia noun *fem.*
Galicia

• Use el and uno for masculine words and la and una for feminine words.

el gallego noun *masc.*
Galician
¿Hablas gallego? Do you speak Galician?

la galleta noun *fem.*
biscuit

la gallina noun *fem.*
1 hen
2 chicken
darles de comer a las gallinas to feed the chickens

el gallo noun *masc.*
cockerel, rooster

la gamba noun *fem.*
prawn

la gana noun *fem.*
tener ganas de hacer algo to feel like doing something
No me da la gana. I don't feel like it.

el ganador noun *masc.*,
la ganadora *fem.*
winner

ganar verb
1 to win
ganar una carrera to win a race
2 to beat
Les ganamos tres a cero. We beat them three nil.
3 to earn
ganar mucho dinero to earn lots of money

el gancho noun *masc.*
hook

el ganso noun *masc.*, **la gansa** *fem.*
goose

el garaje noun *masc.*
garage

LANGUAGE
Spanish = garaje
English = garage

la garganta noun *fem.*
throat

Me duele la garganta. I have a sore throat.

el gas noun *masc.*
gas
una cocina de gas a gas cooker
agua con gas fizzy water

la gaseosa noun *fem.*
lemonade

la gasolina noun *fem.*
petrol
echar gasolina to fill up with petrol

la gasolinera noun *fem.*
petrol station

gastar verb
1 to spend
He gastado mucho dinero. I've spent a lot of money.
2 to use
¿Has gastado toda el agua? Have you used all the water?

el gato noun *masc.*, **la gata** *fem.*
cat

el gazpacho noun *masc.*
gazpacho

CULTURE
Gazpacho is a cold soup made from tomatoes and other vegetables. It's especially common in Andalusia in the south of Spain.

la gelatina noun *fem.*
jelly

el gemelo noun *masc.*,
la gemela *fem.*
identical twin

los gemelos plural noun *masc.*
binoculars

general adjective *masc. & fem.*
general
en general generally

generalmente adverb
generally

a b c d e f g h i j k l m n o p q r s t u v w x y z

• Languages and nationalities do not take a capital letter in Spanish.

73

a
b
c
d
e
f
g
h
i
j
k
l
m
n
o
p
q
r
s
t
u
v
w
x
y
z

el **género** noun masc.
gender
'Cristal' es del género masculino.
'Cristal' is masculine.

generoso adjective masc.,
generosa fem.
generous

genial adjective masc. & fem.
brilliant
¡Es genial! It's brilliant!

el **genio** noun masc.
1 genius
Rosa es un genio. Rosa is a
genius.
2 temper
José tiene mal genio. José has a
bad temper.
3 genie

la **gente** noun fem.
people
Hay mucha gente aquí. There are a
lot of people here.
No hay gente en la playa.
There isn't anybody on the
beach.

> **LANGUAGE**
> Gente is a singular noun.

la **geografía** noun fem.
geography

gigante adjective masc. & fem.
giant
una pantalla gigante a giant
screen

el **gigante** noun masc.,
la **giganta** fem.
giant

> **CULTURE**
> Los gigantes y cabezudos are giant
> carnival figures with big heads that you
> see in many Spanish festivals.

la **gimnasia** noun fem.
1 exercise
hacer gimnasia to do exercise

2 (in school) **PE**
Hoy tenemos gimnasia. Today we
have PE.
3 gymnastics

el **gimnasio** noun masc.
gym

girar verb
1 to turn
Gira a la izquierda. Turn left.
girar el volante to turn the
steering wheel
2 to go round
La tierra gira alrededor del sol.
The earth goes round the sun.

el **girasol** noun masc.
sunflower

> **LANGUAGE**
> The Spanish means 'turns towards the
> sun'.

el **gitano** noun masc., la **gitana** fem.
gypsy

el **globo** noun masc.
1 balloon
inflar un globo to blow up a
balloon
2 globe

glotón adjective masc.,
glotona fem.
greedy

> **LANGUAGE**
> The plural of glotón is glotones.

el **gol** noun masc.
goal
marcar un gol to score a goal

el **golf** noun masc.
golf
Mi hermano juega al golf.
My brother plays golf.

la **golosina** noun fem.
sweet
una tienda de golosinas a sweet
shop

• The months of the year and days of the week do not take a capital letter in Spanish.

el **golpe** noun *masc.*
knock
Recibió un golpe en la cabeza.
He got a hit on the head.
Me he dado un golpe en la rodilla.
I've knocked my knee.
Beatriz me ha dado un golpe.
Beatriz has hit me.

golpear verb
1 to hit
La pelota me golpeó en la cara.
The ball hit me in the face.
2 to bang
Están golpeando la mesa. They're
banging the table.

la **goma** noun *fem.*
1 rubber
¿Me prestas la goma? Can you
lend me your rubber?
2 elastic band

el **gordo** noun *masc.*
first prize in the Spanish lottery

gordo adjective *masc.*, **gorda** *fem.*
fat
Estoy gordo. I'm fat.

el **gorila** noun *masc.*
gorilla

> 🔑 **LANGUAGE**
> Be careful: **gorila** ends in an **-a** but it is not
> a feminine noun.

la **gorra** noun *fem.*
cap

el **gorro** noun *masc.*
hat
un gorro de lana a woolly hat

la **gota** noun *fem.*
drop
una gota de agua a drop of water

grabar verb
1 to record
¿Has grabado la película? Have
you recorded the film?
2 to save
Graba el archivo. Save the file.

gracias exclamation
thank you!
¡Muchas gracias! Thank you very
much!

las **gracias** plural noun *fem.*
dar las gracias a alguien to thank
somebody

gracioso adjective *masc.*,
graciosa *fem.*
funny

el **grado** noun *masc.*
(*of temperature*) **degree**
Estamos a veinte grados.
It's twenty degrees.

la **gramática** noun *fem.*
grammar

el **gramo** noun *masc.*
gram

Gran Bretaña noun *fem.*
Great Britain
Vivimos en Gran Bretaña. We live
in Great Britain.

grande adjective *masc. & fem.*

> 🔑 **LANGUAGE**
> **Grande** becomes **gran** when it is used
> before a singular noun.

big
una casa grande a big house
un gran incendio a big fire

los **grandes almacenes** plural
noun *masc.*
department store

granizar verb
to hail
Está granizando. It's hailing.

el **granizo** noun *masc.*
hail

la **granja** noun *fem.*
farm

el **granjero** noun *masc.*,
la **granjera** *fem.*
farmer

a
b
c
d
e
f
g
h
i
j
k
l
m
n
o
p
q
r
s
t
u
v
w
x
y
z

• *The months of the year and days of the week do not take a capital letter in Spanish.*

el **grano** noun *masc.*
 1 spot
 Tengo muchos granos. I've got lots of spots.
 2 (*of salt, sand, etc.*) **grain**

la **grapa** noun *fem.*
 staple

la **grapadora** noun *fem.*
 stapler

gratis adjective & adverb
 free
 Es gratis. It's free.
 dos entradas gratis two free tickets
 Entré gratis. I got in free.

grave adjective *masc. & fem.*
 serious
 un problema grave a serious problem
 El abuelo está grave. Grandfather is seriously ill.

gravemente adverb
 seriously
 gravemente herido seriously injured

Grecia noun *fem.*
 Greece

griego adjective *masc.*, **griega** *fem.*
 Greek

el **griego** noun *masc.*, la **griega** *fem.*
 Greek
 los griegos the Greeks

el **grifo** noun *masc.*
 tap
 abrir el grifo to turn on the tap

la **gripe** noun *fem.*
 flu
 Tengo gripe. I have the flu.

gris adjective *masc. & fem.*
 grey
 una camisa gris a grey shirt

el **gris** noun *masc.*
 grey
 No me gusta el gris. I don't like grey.

gritar verb
 1 to shout
 No me grites. Don't shout at me.
 2 (*with pain etc.*) **to scream**

el **grito** noun *masc.*
 1 shout
 2 scream

grueso adjective *masc.*, **gruesa** *fem.*
 1 (*wall, slice, etc.*) **thick**
 2 (*person*) **fat**

gruñón adjective *masc.*, **gruñona** *fem.*
 grumpy

LANGUAGE
The masculine plural of **gruñón** is **gruñones**.

el **grupo** noun *masc.*
 group

el **guante** noun *masc.*
 glove

guapo adjective *masc.*, **guapa** *fem.*
 1 pretty
 una niña muy guapa a very pretty girl
 2 good-looking
 Carlos es muy guapo. Carlos is very good-looking.

guardar verb
 1 to keep
 Guarda el billete. Keep the ticket.
 2 to put away
 Guarda los juguetes. Put the toys away.
 3 to save
 ¿Me guardas el sitio? Can you save my place?
 He guardado el archivo. I've saved the file.

• *See the centre section for verb tables.*

el **guardarropa** noun *masc.*
cloakroom

> 🔑 **LANGUAGE**
> Be careful: **guardarropa** ends in an **-a** but it is not a feminine noun.

la **guardería** noun *fem.*
nursery

el or la **guardia** noun *masc. & fem.*
policeman, policewoman

guay adjective *masc. & fem.*
cool
¡Qué película más guay! What a cool film!

la **guayaba** noun *fem.*
guava

la **guerra** noun *fem.*
war

la **guía** noun *fem.*
(*book*) **guide**
una guía de Madrid a guide to Madrid
la guía telefónica the phone book

el or la **guía** noun *masc. & fem.*
(*person*) **guide**

guiar verb
to guide

el **guión** noun *masc.* (plural los **guiones**)
hyphen

Se escribe con un guión. It's spelled with a hyphen.

el **guisante** noun *masc.*
pea

la **guitarra** noun *fem.*
guitar
Toco la guitarra. I play the guitar.

el **gusano** noun *masc.*
worm

gustar verb
to like
Me gusta el chocolate. I like chocolate.
Me gusta. I like it.
Me gustan los perros. I like dogs.
A Raúl le gusta leer. Raúl likes to read.
¿Te gusta la música? Do you like music?

> 🔑 **LANGUAGE**
> **Gustar** means 'to please' so the order of the words in the Spanish is different, e.g. **Me gusta el chocolate** is 'Chocolate pleases me'.

el **gusto** noun *masc.*
(*when being introduced to somebody*)
¡Mucho gusto! Pleased to meet you!

Hh

ha verb
1 has
¿Ha llegado Javier? Has Javier arrived?
2 have SEE **haber**
Usted no ha dicho nada. You haven't said anything.

habéis verb SEE **haber**
have

Niños, ¿habéis leído el libro? Have you read the book, children?

haber verb
(*used for making past tenses*) **to have**
He visto la película. I've seen the film.
Ha hecho sus deberes. He has done his homework.
Han cerrado la puerta. They've closed the door.

• Use **el** and **uno** for masculine words and **la** and **una** for feminine words.

a
b
c
d
e
f
g
h
i
j
k
l
m
n
o
p
q
r
s
t
u
v
w
x
y
z

había verb
1 there was
Había un libro en la mesa. There was a book on the table.
2 there were SEE **hay**
Había dos libros en la mesa. There were two books on the table.

la **habitación** noun *fem.* (plural las **habitaciones**)
room
La casa tiene cinco habitaciones. The house has five rooms.

el or la **habitante** noun *masc. & fem.*
inhabitant

habitual adjective *masc. & fem.*
usual

hablador adjective *masc.*, **habladora** *fem.*
talkative

hablar verb
1 to speak
¿Hablas español? Do you speak Spanish?
'Se habla inglés.' 'English spoken.'
2 to talk
Gabriel habla demasiado. Gabriel talks too much.
Estoy hablando con mis amigas. I'm talking to my friends.

hacer verb
1 to do
¿Qué estás haciendo? What are you doing?
No hago nada. I'm not doing anything.
Hace mucho deporte. He does a lot of sport.
2 to make
Hacen mucho ruido. They're making a lot of noise.
Me hace reír. He makes me laugh.
He hecho un pastel. I've made a cake.
3 to be
Hace frío. It's cold.

Hace buen tiempo. It's a lovely day.

> **LANGUAGE**
> With the weather **hace** = **it is**

4 ago
Se fue hace una semana. She left a week ago.

> **LANGUAGE**
> **Hace** goes before the amount of time but **ago** goes after.

5 for
Hace un mes que estudio español. I've been studying Spanish for a month.

hacerse verb
to become
hacerse famoso to become famous
Nos hicimos amigos. We became friends.

hacia preposition
1 towards
hacia la puerta towards the door
2 around
hacia las nueve de la mañana around nine in the morning
3 hacia arriba up
hacia abajo down
hacia atrás backwards

el **hada** noun *fem.*
fairy
un cuento de hadas a fairy tale

> **LANGUAGE**
> Be careful: you use **el** with **hada** but it is not a masculine noun.

hago verb SEE **hacer**
1 do
Hago mis deberes. I do my homework.
2 make
Hago mucho ruido. I make a lot of noise.

la **hamaca** noun *fem.*
(*on the beach*) **deckchair**

• *Languages and nationalities do not take a capital letter in Spanish.*

el **hambre** noun *fem.*
hunger
tener hambre to be hungry
Tengo mucha hambre. I'm very hungry.

> 🔑 **LANGUAGE**
> Spanish = **tener** hambre **Tengo hambre.**
> English = **to be** hungry **I'm hungry.**

> 🔑 **LANGUAGE**
> Be careful: you use **el** with **hambre** but it is not a masculine noun.

la **hamburguesa** noun *fem.*
hamburger

el **hámster** noun *masc.*
hamster

han verb SEE **haber**
have
Los chicos han llegado. The boys have arrived.

la **harina** noun *fem.*
flour

harto adjective *masc.*, **harta** *fem.*
fed up
Estoy harto de ti. I'm fed up with you.

has verb SEE **haber**
have
¿Has terminado los deberes? Have you finished your homework?

hasta preposition
1 until
Está abierto hasta las seis. It's open until six.
2 up to
Cuenta hasta diez. Count up to ten.
hasta ahora up to now
3 (*in greetings*)
¡Hasta mañana! See you tomorrow!
¡Hasta las nueve! See you at nine!
¡Hasta luego! See you!

hay verb
1 there is

Hay una biblioteca muy cerca. There's a library nearby.
No hay pan. There isn't any bread.
2 there are
Hay juguetes en el suelo. There are toys on the floor.
3 (*for saying 'must'*)
Hay que esperar. We must wait.

> 🔑 **LANGUAGE**
> **Hay** is a special form of the verb **haber** (to have).

he verb SEE **haber**
have
He comprado una bici. I've bought a bike.

el **hechizo** noun *masc.*
magic spell

el **hecho** noun *masc.*
fact

hecho adjective *masc.*, **hecha** *fem.*
1 made
Está bien hecho. It's well made.
hecho a mano made by hand
2 done
¡Bien hecho! Well done!

la **helada** noun *fem.*
frost

el **helado** noun *masc.*
ice cream
un helado de chocolate a chocolate ice cream

helado adjective *masc.*,
helada *fem.*
1 frozen
El río está helado. The river is frozen.
2 freezing
La habitación está helada. The room is freezing.
¡Estoy helado! I'm freezing!

helar verb
to be frosty
Esta noche ha helado. It was frosty last night.

a
b
c
d
e
f
g
h
i
j
k
l
m
n
o
p
q
r
s
t
u
v
w
x
y
z

• *The months of the year and days of the week do not take a capital letter in Spanish.*

helarse verb
to freeze
El agua se ha helado. The water
has frozen.

el **helicóptero** noun *masc.*
helicopter

la **hembra** noun *fem.*
female
un elefante hembra a female
elephant

hemos verb SEE **haber**
have
Hemos terminado el ejercicio.
We've finished the exercise.

la **herida** noun *fem.*
injury

herido adjective *masc.*, **herida** *fem.*
injured
Está herida. She's injured.

la **hermana** noun *fem.*
sister

la **hermanastra** noun *fem.*
stepsister

el **hermanastro** noun *masc.*
stepbrother

el **hermano** noun *masc.*
brother
mi hermano mayor my big brother
¿Tienes hermanos? Do you have
any brothers or sisters?

hermoso adjective *masc.*,
hermosa *fem.*
beautiful

el **héroe** noun *masc.*
hero

la **heroína** noun *fem.*
heroine

las **herramientas** plural noun *fem.*
tools

hervir verb
to boil
hervir la leche to boil the milk
estar hirviendo to be boiling

el **hielo** noun *masc.*
ice
un cubito de hielo an ice cube

la **hierba** noun *fem.*
1 grass
2 herb

el **hierro** noun *masc.*
iron

la **hija** noun *fem.*
daughter

la **hijastra** noun *fem.*
stepdaughter

el **hijastro** noun *masc.*
stepson

el **hijo** noun *masc.*
1 son
Tienen un hijo. They have a son.
2 hijos children
¿Cuántos hijos tienen? How many
children do they have?

LANGUAGE
Hijos is the Spanish for 'sons' but can also
mean children – either boys or girls.

el **himno** noun *masc.*
hymn
el himno nacional the national
anthem

el or la **hincha** noun *masc. & fem.*
fan
un hincha del fútbol a football
fan

hinchado adjective *masc.*,
hinchada *fem.*
swollen

hindú adjective *masc. & fem.* (plural
hindúes)
Hindu

el **hipermercado** noun *masc.*
superstore

el **hipo** noun *masc.*
tener hipo to have hiccups

• *See the centre section for verb tables.*

80

la **historia** noun *fem.*
1 story
El libro cuenta la historia de ...
The book tells the story of ...
2 history
la historia de Inglaterra English
history

el **hogar** noun *masc.*
home

la **hoguera** noun *fem.*
bonfire

la **hoja** noun *fem.*
1 leaf
las hojas del árbol the leaves of
the tree
2 sheet
una hoja de papel a sheet of paper
3 page
las hojas del libro the pages of the
book

hola exclamation
hello!

Holanda noun *fem.*
Holland

el **holandés** noun *masc.*
Dutch
hablar holandés to speak Dutch

holandés adjective *masc.*,
holandesa *fem.*
Dutch

🔑 **LANGUAGE**
The plural of **holandés** is **holandeses**.

el **holandés** noun *masc.*,
la **holandesa** *fem.*
Dutchman, **Dutchwoman**
los holandeses the Dutch

el **hombre** noun *masc.*
man
un hombre y una mujer a man and
a woman

el **hombro** noun *masc.*
shoulder

hondo adjective *masc.*, **honda** *fem.*
deep

la **hora** noun *fem.*
1 hour
media hora half an hour
un cuarto de hora a quarter of an
hour
una hora y cuarto an hour and a
quarter
la hora punta the rush hour
2 time
¿Qué hora es? What time is it?
¿Tienes hora? Do you have the
time?
¿a qué hora ...? what time ...?
Es hora de ir a la escuela. It's time
to go to school.
mis horas libres my free time
llegar a la hora to arrive on time
3 (*with a doctor etc.*) **appointment**
pedir hora to make an
appointment

el **horario** noun *masc.*
timetable
el horario de clases the school
timetable

la **hormiga** noun *fem.*
ant

el **horno** noun *masc.*
oven
un horno microondas a microwave
oven

horrible adjective *masc. & fem.*
horrible

el **horror** noun *masc.*
horror
¡Qué horror! That's horrible!

el **hospital** noun *masc.*
hospital
estar en el hospital to be in
hospital

a b c d e f g h i j k l m n o p q r s t u v w x y z

• *Use el and uno for masculine words and la and una for feminine words.*

a
b
c
d
e
f
g
h
i
j
k
l
m
n
o
p
q
r
s
t
u
v
w
x
y
z

el **hotel** noun *masc.*
hotel

hoy adverb
today
Hoy es mi cumpleaños. Today is my birthday.
¿A qué fecha estamos hoy? What's the date today?

hubo verb
1 there was
Hubo un accidente. There was an accident.
2 there were
Hubo dos accidentes. There were two accidents.

> **LANGUAGE**
> **Hubo** is the past tense of **hay**.

la **hucha** noun *fem.*
money box

el **hueco** noun *masc.*
1 space
Aquí hay un hueco. There's a space here.
2 (*in a timetable, fence, etc.*) **gap**

la **huella** noun *fem.*
footprint
una huella dactilar a fingerprint

el **huérfano** noun *masc.*,
la **huérfana** *fem.*
orphan

el **hueso** noun *masc.*
bone

el or la **huésped** noun *masc. & fem.*
guest

el **huevo** noun *masc.*
egg
un huevo duro a hard-boiled egg
un huevo pasado por agua a soft-boiled egg
huevos revueltos scrambled eggs

huir verb
1 to run away
2 to escape
El ladrón huyó en una moto. The thief escaped on a motorbike.

humano adjective *masc.*,
humana *fem.*
human
un ser humano a human being

húmedo adjective *masc.*,
húmeda *fem.*
damp

el **humo** noun *masc.*
smoke

el **humor** noun *masc.*
mood
estar de buen humor to be in a good mood
tener sentido del humor to have a sense of humour

hundirse verb
to sink
El barco se hundió. The boat sank.

el **huracán** noun *masc.* (plural los **huracanes**)
hurricane

Ii

el **icono** noun *masc.*
icon
Haz clic en el icono. Click on the icon.

la **ida** noun *fem.*
un billete de ida a single ticket
un billete de ida y vuelta a return ticket

• *Languages and nationalities do not take a capital letter in Spanish.*

82

la **idea** noun *fem.*
idea
Tengo una idea. I have an idea.
cambiar de idea to change your mind

idéntico adjective *masc.*, **idéntica** *fem.*
identical

la **identidad** noun *fem.*
identity
el carné de identidad identity card

el **idioma** noun *masc.*
language
Hablo dos idiomas. I speak two languages.

⚷ **LANGUAGE**
Be careful: **idioma** ends in an -a but it is not a feminine noun.

idiota adjective *masc. & fem.*
stupid

el or la **idiota** noun *masc. & fem.*
idiot

la **iglesia** noun *fem.*
church
ir a la iglesia to go to church

igual adjective *masc. & fem.* & adverb
1 **equal**
dos grupos iguales two equal groups
2 **the same**
Estos colores son iguales. These colours are the same.
Se escriben igual. They're spelled the same.
Eres igual a tu hermana. You're the same as your sister.
Me da igual. I don't mind.

la **imagen** noun *fem.*
(*on TV screen*) **picture**

la **imaginación** noun *fem.* (plural las **imaginaciones**)
imagination

imaginar verb
to imagine

imaginarse verb
to imagine
¡Imagínate! Imagine that!

imaginario adjective *masc.*, **imaginaria** *fem.*
imaginary
un amigo imaginario an imaginary friend

el **imán** noun *masc.* (plural los **imanes**)
magnet

imbécil adjective *masc. & fem.*
stupid
¡Qué imbécil eres! You're so stupid!

el or la **imbécil** noun *masc. & fem.*
idiot

imitar verb
to imitate

impaciente adjective *masc. & fem.*
impatient

impar adjective *masc.*
un número impar an odd number

el **impermeable** noun *masc.*
raincoat

la **importancia** noun *fem.*
importance
Tiene mucha importancia. It's very important.

importante adjective *masc. & fem.*
important
una persona importante an important person

importar verb
1 **to matter**
No importa. It doesn't matter.
2 **to mind**
¿le importa ...? do you mind ...?
¿Le importa si me siento aquí? Do you mind if I sit here?
No me importa. I don't mind.

imposible adjective *masc. & fem.*
impossible

a b c d e f g h i j k l m n o p q r s t u v w x y z

• *The months of the year and days of the week do not take a capital letter in Spanish.*

impresionante ➡ infantil

impresionante adjective *masc. & fem.*
amazing, impressive

la **impresora** noun *fem.*
printer

imprimir verb
(*on a computer etc.*) **to print**

incapaz adjective *masc. & fem.* (plural **incapaces**)
ser incapaz de hacer algo to be unable to do something

el **incendio** noun *masc.*
fire
apagar el incendio to put out the fire

inclinarse verb
1 **to bend down**
inclinarse para recoger algo to bend down to pick something up
2 **to lean over**
Inclínate hacia delante. Lean forward.

incluido adjective *masc.*, **incluida** *fem.*
included
El servicio está incluido. The service is included.

incluir verb
to include
todos, incluyendo a mi hermana everybody, including my sister

incluso adverb
even
Incluso yo puedo hacerlo. Even I can do it.

incómodo adjective *masc.*, **incómoda** *fem.*
uncomfortable

• *See the centre section for verb tables.*

incorrecto adjective *masc.*, **incorrecta** *fem.*
incorrect

increíble adjective *masc. & fem.*
incredible

independiente adjective *masc. & fem.*
independent

la **India** noun *fem.*
India

las **indicaciones** plural noun *fem.*
instructions
seguir las indicaciones to follow the instructions

indicar verb
to show
indicar el camino to show the way

indio adjective *masc.*, **india** *fem.*
Indian
una lengua india an Indian language

CULTURE
In Latin America **indio** means American Indian, not from India.

el **indio** noun *masc.*, la **india** *fem.*
Indian

individual adjective *masc. & fem.*
1 (*bed, portion, etc.*) **single**
una habitación individual a single room
2 **individual**

inesperado adjective *masc.*, **inesperada** *fem.*
unexpected

infantil adjective *masc. & fem.*
1 **children's**
un cuento infantil a children's story
2 **childish**
Eres muy infantil. You're very childish.

la **infección** noun *fem.* (plural las **infecciones**)
infection

el **infinitivo** noun *masc.*
infinitive

inflar verb
to blow up
inflar un globo to blow up a balloon

la **información** noun *fem.*
1 information
buscar información to look for information
2 (*on TV or in the newspaper*) **news**

la **informática** noun *fem.*
IT, **computing**

informático adjective *masc.*, **informática** *fem.*
computer
un programa informático a computer program

el **ingeniero** noun *masc.*, la **ingeniera** *fem.*
engineer

Inglaterra noun *fem.*
England
Vivo en Inglaterra. I live in England.
¿Quieres venir a Inglaterra? Do you want to come to England?

el **inglés** noun *masc.*
English
¿Hablas inglés? Do you speak English?

inglés adjective *masc.*, **inglesa** *fem.*
English
Soy inglesa. I'm English.

LANGUAGE
The plural of **inglés** is **ingleses**.

el **inglés** noun *masc.*, la **inglesa** *fem.*
Englishman, **Englishwoman**
los ingleses the English

el **ingrediente** noun *masc.*
ingredient

las **iniciales** plural noun *fem.*
initials

el **inicio** noun *masc.*
(*on a web page*) **home**
la página de inicio the home page

injusto adjective *masc.*, **injusta** *fem.*
unfair

inmediatamente adverb
immediately

LANGUAGE
Spanish = **inmediatamente**
English = **immediately**

inmenso adjective *masc.*, **inmensa** *fem.*
huge, **immense**

LANGUAGE
Spanish = **inmenso**
English = **immense**

inocente adjective *masc. & fem.*
innocent

inquieto adjective *masc.*, **inquieta** *fem.*
worried

el **insecto** noun *masc.*
insect

insolente adjective *masc. & fem.*
cheeky

instalar verb
to install
instalar un programa to install a program

el **instante** noun *masc.*
moment
hace un instante a moment ago

• Use **el** and **uno** for masculine words and **la** and **una** for feminine words.

el **instituto** noun masc.
(secondary) school

las **instrucciones** plural noun fem.
instructions

el **instrumento** noun masc.
instrument
tocar un instrumento to play an
instrument

inteligente adjective masc. & fem.
intelligent

intentar verb
to try
intentar hacer algo to try to do
something
Inténtalo otra vez. Try again.

interesante adjective masc. & fem.
interesting

interesar verb
to interest
Me interesan los idiomas.
I'm interested in languages.
No me interesa. I'm not
interested.

el **interior** noun masc.
inside
el interior de la caja the inside of
the box

el **intermedio** noun masc.
interval

internacional adjective masc. & fem.
international

el **internado** noun masc.
boarding school

el or la **internauta** noun masc. & fem.
Internet user

Internet noun masc. & fem.
Internet
en Internet on the Internet

> **LANGUAGE**
> **El** or **la** are not used with **Internet**.

interrumpir verb
to interrupt
¡No me interrumpas! Don't
interrupt!

el **interruptor** noun masc.
switch

la **inundación** noun fem. (plural las
inundaciones)
flood

inútil adjective masc. & fem.
useless

inventar verb
to invent

el **invento** noun masc.
invention

el **invierno** noun masc.
winter
en invierno in the winter

invisible adjective masc. & fem.
invisible

la **invitación** noun fem. (plural las
invitaciones)
invitation

el **invitado** noun masc.,
la **invitada** fem.
guest

invitar verb
to invite
**Isabel me ha invitado a una
fiesta.** Isabel has invited me
to a party.

la **inyección** noun fem. (plural las
inyecciones)
injection
**La enfermera me ha puesto una
inyección.** The nurse has given me
an injection.

ir verb
1 to go
Voy al colegio en autobús. I go to
school by bus.
¿Adónde vas? Where are you
going?

• Languages and nationalities do not take a capital letter in Spanish.

Ha ido al parque. He's gone to the park.
Fueron de compras. They went shopping.
2 (*used with another verb when talking about the future*)
ir a ... to be going to ...
¿Qué vas a hacer? What are you going to do?
Voy a ver la tele. I'm going to watch TV.
3 (*used for making suggestions*)
Vamos a ... Let's ...
Vamos a jugar. Let's play.
¡Vamos a ver! Let's see!
Vamos. Let's go.
4 to come
¡Ya voy! I'm coming!
¡Vamos! ¡Ayúdame! Come on! Help me!
5 to suit
El verde te va bien. Green suits you.

irse verb
1 to leave
Tengo que irme. I have to leave.
Me voy el lunes. I'm leaving on Monday.
Se ha ido del hotel. She has left the hotel.
2 to go away
¡Vete! Go away!
¡Vámonos! Let's go!

Irlanda noun *fem.*
Ireland

el **irlandés** noun *masc.*
Irish
Hablan irlandés. They speak Irish.

irlandés adjective *masc.*,
irlandesa *fem.*
Irish

LANGUAGE
The plural of **irlandés** is **irlandeses**.

el **irlandés** *masc.*,
la **irlandesa** noun *fem.*
Irishman, **Irishwoman**
los irlandeses the Irish

la **isla** noun *fem.*
island
las Islas Baleares the Balearic Islands
las Islas Británicas the British Isles

islámico adjective *masc.*,
islámica *fem.*
Islamic

Italia noun *fem.*
Italy

el **italiano** noun *masc.*
Italian
¿Hablas italiano? Do you speak Italian?

italiano adjective *masc.*,
italiana *fem.*
Italian
Son italianos. They're Italian.

el **italiano** noun *masc.*,
la **italiana** *fem.*
Italian

la **izquierda** noun *fem.*
left
Está a la izquierda. It's on the left.
girar a la izquierda to turn left
conducir por la izquierda to drive on the left

izquierdo adjective *masc.*,
izquierda *fem.*
left
Escribo con la mano izquierda. I write with my left hand.

• *The months of the year and days of the week do not take a capital letter in Spanish.*

Jj

el **jabón** noun masc.
soap
una pastilla de jabón a bar of soap

jamás adverb
never
¡Jamás he visto eso! I've never seen that!
nunca jamás never ever

el **jamón** noun masc.
ham
un bocadillo de jamón a ham sandwich

> **LANGUAGE**
> The plural of **jamón** is **jamones**.

Japón noun masc.
Japan

el **japonés** noun masc.
Japanese
hablar japonés to speak Japanese

japonés adjective masc.,
japonesa fem.
Japanese
Es japonés. He's Japanese.

el **japonés** noun masc.,
la **japonesa** fem.
Japanese man, Japanese woman
los japoneses the Japanese

el **jardín** noun masc.
garden
Nuestra casa tiene jardín.
Our house has a garden.
el jardín de infancia nursery school

> **LANGUAGE**
> The plural of **jardín** is **jardines**.

el **jardinero** noun masc.,
la **jardinera** fem.
gardener

la **jarra** noun fem.
jug

el **jarrón** noun masc. (plural los **jarrons**)
vase

la **jaula** noun fem.
cage

el **jefe** noun masc., la **jefa** fem.
1 boss
2 (of a group or gang) **leader**
3 (of a department) **head**

el **jersey** noun masc. (plural los **jerseys** or los **jerséis**)
sweater

Jesús exclamation
(when somebody sneezes) **Bless you!**

la **jirafa** noun fem.
giraffe

joven adjective masc. & fem.
young
Eres más joven que yo. You're younger than me.

el or la **joven** noun masc. & fem.
young man, young woman
los jóvenes young people

la **joya** noun fem.
jewel

la **joyería** noun fem.
jewellery shop

jubilado adjective masc.,
jubilada fem.
retired

la **judía** noun fem.
bean
las judías verdes green beans

judío adjective masc., la **judía** fem.
Jewish

• See the centre section for verb tables.

el **judo** noun *masc.*
judo
hacer judo to do judo

el **juego** noun *masc.*
game
un juego de mesa a board game
los Juegos Olímpicos the Olympic Games

el **jueves** noun *masc.*
Thursday
Hoy es jueves. It's Thursday today.
el jueves on Thursday
¡Hasta el jueves! See you on Thursday!
los jueves on Thursdays
Voy a la biblioteca los jueves. I go to the library on Thursdays.

> 🔑 **LANGUAGE**
> Remember the difference between **el jueves** (one Thursday only) and **los jueves** (every Thursday)

el or la **juez** noun *masc. & fem.*
judge

el **jugador** noun *masc.*,
la **jugadora** *fem.*
player
una jugadora de tenis a tennis player

jugar verb
to play
Estamos jugando en el jardín. We're playing in the garden.
jugar al fútbol to play football
jugar a la pelota to play ball

> 🔑 **LANGUAGE**
> Use **jugar** + **a** with games and sports.

el **jugo** noun *masc.*
juice

el **juguete** noun *masc.*
toy

> 🔑 **LANGUAGE**
> **Juguete** comes from **jugar** (to play).

la **juguetería** noun *fem.*
toy shop

julio noun *masc.*
July
en julio in July
Vamos a Barcelona en julio. We're going to Barcelona in July.
Nací el tres de julio. I was born on the third of July.

la **jungla** noun *fem.*
jungle

junio noun *masc.*
June
Mi cumpleaños es en junio. My birthday is in June.
Dan una fiesta el lunes nueve de junio. They're having a party on Monday, the ninth of June.

junto a preposition
next to
La silla está junto a la ventana. The chair is next to the window.

juntos adjective *masc. plural*,
juntas *fem. plural*
together
Han llegado juntos. They've arrived together.
Las mesas están demasiado juntas. The tables are too close together.

justo adverb
just
Viven justo al lado. They live just next door.
justo a tiempo just in time

justo adjective *masc.*, **justa** *fem.*
1 fair
¡No es justo! It's not fair!
2 tight
Estos vaqueros me quedan justos. These jeans are too tight.

juzgar verb
to judge

a
b
c
d
e
f
g
h
i
j
k
l
m
n
o
p
q
r
s
t
u
v
w
x
y
z

• *Use* el *and* uno *for masculine words and* la *and* una *for feminine words.*

Kk

el **kárate** noun *masc.*
karate
hacer kárate to do karate

el **kilo** noun *masc.*
kilo
tres euros el kilo three euros a kilo

el **kilómetro** noun *masc.*
kilometre
Está a diez kilómetros de aquí.
It's ten kilometres away.

el **kiosco** noun *masc.*
1 (*for newspapers*) **news-stand**
2 (*for flowers, ice creams, etc.*) **kiosk**

Ll

la determiner *fem.*
1 (*before feminine singular nouns*) **the**
la silla the chair
la mujer the woman
2 (*no translation*)
No me gusta la leche. I don't like milk.
Me voy a la cama. I'm going to bed.
la hermana de Julio Julio's sister
3 (*with adjectives used as nouns*) **the**
la verde the green one
la grande the big one
4 (*with parts of the body, clothes, etc.*)
my, **your**, **his** (*etc.*)
Me he roto la pierna. I've broken my leg.
Ponte la camisa. Put your shirt on.
Levantó la mano. He put up his hand.

la pronoun *fem.*
1 **her**
La conozco. I know her.
Quiero ayudarla. I want to help her.
2 **it**
¿Dónde está mi chaqueta? – No la veo. Where's my jacket? – I can't see it.
3 **you**
La acompaño, señora López. I'll go with you, Mrs López.

el **laberinto** noun *masc.*
maze

el **labio** noun *masc.*
lip

el **lado** noun *masc.*
1 **side**
al otro lado de la calle on the other side of the road
2 **al lado de** next to
Siéntate al lado de Carlos. Sit next to Carlos.
a mi lado next to me
al lado next door
Viven al lado. They live next door.
3 **por todos lados** everywhere
por ningún lado nowhere

ladrar verb
to bark

el **ladrillo** noun *masc.*
brick

el **ladrón** noun *masc.*,
la **ladrona** *fem.*
1 **thief**
2 **burglar**

⚷ LANGUAGE
The plural of **ladrón** is **ladrones**.

el **lagarto** noun *masc.*
lizard

• *Languages and nationalities do not take a capital letter in Spanish.*

a b c d e f g h i j **k** **l** m n o p q r s t u v w x y z

el **lago** noun *masc.*
 lake

la **lágrima** noun *fem.*
 tear

la **lámpara** noun *fem.*
 lamp

la **lana** noun *fem.*
 wool
 una bufanda de lana a woolly scarf

la **langosta** noun *fem.*
 lobster

lanzar verb
 to throw
 Lánzame la pelota. Throw the ball to me.
 Me han lanzado una piedra. They've thrown a stone at me.

el **lápiz** noun *masc.* (plural los **lápices**)
 pencil
 a lápiz in pencil

largo adjective *masc.*, **larga** *fem.*
 long
 Tengo el pelo largo. I have long hair.

⚠ FALSE FRIEND
largo = **long** (*not* large)

las determiner *fem. plural*
 1 (*before feminine plural nouns*) **the**
 las casas the houses
 las hermanas the sisters
 2 (*no translation*)
 Odio las naranjas.
 I hate oranges.
 las amigas de María María's friends
 3 (*with adjectives used as nouns*) **the**
 las azules the blue ones
 las largas the long ones
 4 (*with parts of the body, clothes, etc.*)
 my, **your**, **his** (*etc.*)
 Me he lavado las manos.
 I've washed my hands.

Ponte las gafas. Put your glasses on.
Se quitó las botas. He took his boots off.

las pronoun *fem. plural*
 1 them
 Las conozco. I know them.
 Dámelas. Give them to me.
 2 you
 Las esperan, señoras. They're waiting for you, ladies.

la **lástima** noun *fem.*
 pity
 ¡Qué lástima! What a pity!

la **lata** noun *fem.*
 1 tin
 una lata de tomates a tin of tomatoes
 2 can
 una lata de cerveza a can of beer

Latinoamérica noun *fem.*
 Latin America

latinoamericano adjective *masc.*, **latinoamericana** *fem.*
 Latin American
 Soy latinoamericano. I'm a Latin American.

el **latinoamericano** *masc.*, la **latinoamericana** noun *fem.*
 Latin American

el **lavabo** noun *masc.*
 1 sink
 Lávate las manos en el lavabo. Wash your hands in the sink.
 2 toilet
 Voy al lavabo. I'm going to the toilet.

la **lavadora** noun *fem.*
 washing machine

el **lavaplatos** noun *masc.* (plural los **lavaplatos**)
 dishwasher

• *The months of the year and days of the week do not take a capital letter in Spanish.*

lavar verb
to wash
lavar la ropa to wash the clothes

lavarse verb
to wash
Me estoy lavando. I'm washing.
Me he lavado las manos. I've washed my hands.
Se está lavando los dientes. She's cleaning her teeth.

el **lavavajillas** noun *masc.* (plural los **lavavajillas**)
dishwasher

Le pronoun *masc. & fem.*
1 **him**, **to him**
Le he mandado una carta. I've sent him a letter., I've sent a letter to him.
Dale el disco compacto. Give him the CD.
2 **her**, **to her**
Le he dado el dinero. I've given her the money., I've given the money to her.
Quiero decirle algo. I want to tell her something.
3 **you**, **to you**
Voy a decirle la verdad, señor. I'm going to tell you the truth, sir.
Le doy esto a usted. I'm giving this to you.

la **lección** noun *fem.* (plural las **lecciones**)
lesson

la **leche** noun *fem.*
milk

la **lechuga** noun *fem.*
lettuce

leer verb
to read
Yo sé leer. I know how to read.
Me gusta leer. I like reading.

• *See the centre section for verb tables.*

las **legumbres** plural noun *fem.*
pulses

🔑 **LANGUAGE**
Pulses are vegetables like beans and peas.

lejos adverb
far
¿Está lejos? Is it far?
No está muy lejos. It's not very far.
Montevideo está lejos. Montevideo is a long way away.
Está un poco más lejos. It's a bit further.

la **lengua** noun *fem.*
1 **tongue**
2 **language**
Hablo dos lenguas. I speak two languages.

lento adverb
slowly

lento adjective *masc.*, **lenta** *fem.*
slow
Soy muy lento. I'm very slow.

el **león** noun *masc.* (plural los **leones**)
lion

el **leopardo** noun *masc.*
leopard

les pronoun *masc. & fem.*
1 **them**, **to them**
Les he mandado un regalo. I've sent them a present., I've sent a present to them.
Dales los libros. Give them the books.
2 **you**, **to you**
Les doy esto a ustedes. I'm giving this to you.

la **lesión** noun *fem.* (plural las **lesiones**)
(*in sports etc.*) **injury**

la **letra** noun *fem.*
1 (*of the alphabet*) **letter**
la letra Q the letter Q

2 handwriting
Tengo muy buena letra. I've got very good handwriting.
3 la letra de una canción the words of a song

el **letrero** noun *masc.*
sign

levantar verb
1 to lift
Levanta esta maleta. Lift up this case.
2 to put up
Levantad la mano. Put your hands up.

levantarse verb
1 to get up
Me levanto a las siete. I get up at seven.
2 to stand up, **to get up**
Levántate. Stand up., Get up.

la **libertad** noun *fem.*
freedom

la **libra** noun *fem.*
(*money and weight*) **pound**

libre adjective *masc. & fem.*
free
Este asiento está libre. This seat is free.
un día libre a day off

la **librería** noun *fem.*
1 bookshop
La librería está cerrada. The bookshop's closed.
2 bookcase

⚠ **FALSE FRIEND**
una librería = a bookshop (*not* a library)

el **libro** noun *masc.*
book
He leído este libro. I've read this book.
un libro de bolsillo a paperback

el or la **líder** noun *masc. & fem.*
leader

ligero adjective *masc.*, **ligera** *fem.*
1 light
un paquete ligero a light parcel
2 slight
un ligero acento francés a slight French accent

el **limón** noun *masc.* (plural los **limones**)
lemon

la **limonada** noun *fem.*
lemon drink (*with fresh lemons and lemonade*)

limpiar verb
to clean
limpiar la casa to clean the house

la **limpieza** noun *fem.*
cleaning
hacer la limpieza to do the cleaning

limpio adjective *masc.*, **limpia** *fem.*
clean
una casa limpia a clean house

la **línea** noun *fem.*
line
una línea recta a straight line
en línea online

la **linterna** noun *fem.*
torch

el **líquido** noun *masc.*
liquid

liso adjective *masc.*, **lisa** *fem.*
smooth
tener la piel lisa to have smooth skin
tener el pelo liso to have straight hair

la **lista** noun *fem.*
1 list
una lista de la compra a shopping list
2 register
pasar lista to take the register

a b c d e f g h i j k **l** m n o p q r s t u v w x y z

• *Use* **el** *and* **uno** *for masculine words and* **la** *and* **una** *for feminine words.*

listo adjective *masc.*, **lista** *fem.*
1 smart
un chico muy listo a very smart boy
2 ready
Estamos listas. We're ready.

la **litera** noun *fem.*
bunk bed
Dormimos en una litera. We sleep in bunk beds.

la **literatura** noun *fem.*
literature

el **litro** noun *masc.*
litre

la **llama** noun *fem.*
flame

la **llamada** noun *fem.*
call
hacer una llamada to make a phone call

llamar verb
1 to call
Tu padre te llama. Your father is calling you.
llamar al médico to call the doctor
2 to phone
Te llamo mañana. I'll phone you tomorrow.
3 Están llamando a la puerta.
There's somebody at the door.

llamarse verb
to be called
¿Cómo se llama el libro? What's the book called?
¿Cómo te llamas? What's your name?
Me llamo Miguel. My name's Miguel.
Se llama Yasmina. Her name is Yasmina.

llano adjective *masc.*, **llana** *fem.*
flat
un país llano a flat country

la **llave** noun *fem.*
1 key
2 (*Latin America*) **tap**

la **llegada** noun *fem.*
1 arrival
2 (*in a race*) **finish**

llegar verb
1 to arrive
Llegan a las ocho. They arrive at eight.
2 llegar tarde to be late
Siempre llegas tarde. You're always late.
3 to reach
No llego a la lámpara. I can't reach the lamp.
4 llegar a ser to become
Más tarde llegó a ser famosa. She later became famous.

llenar verb
to fill
llenar una bañera de agua to fill a bath with water

lleno adjective *masc.*, **llena** *fem.*
full
El cubo está lleno de agua. The bucket's full of water.

llevar verb
1 to take
Mi madre me lleva al colegio. My mum takes me to school.
Lleva el cuaderno a la maestra. Take the exercise book to the teacher.
2 to wear
Llevo vaqueros. I'm wearing jeans.
3 to carry
Lleva una maleta. He's carrying a suitcase.
4 (*talking about time*) **to be**
¿Cuánto tiempo llevas aquí? How long have you been here?
Llevo una hora esperando. I've been waiting for an hour.

llevarse verb
1 to take

• *Languages and nationalities do not take a capital letter in Spanish.*

a
b
c
d
e
f
g
h
i
j
k
l
m
n
o
p
q
r
s
t
u
v
w
x
y
z

¿Quién se ha llevado mi boli?
Who's taken my pen?
2 llevarse bien con alguien to get on
with somebody
Me llevo bien con mi hermana.
I get on well with my sister.

llorar verb
to cry
¿Por qué lloras? Why are you
crying?

llover verb
to rain
Está lloviendo. It's raining.

la **lluvia** noun *fem.*
rain
Me gusta la lluvia. I like rain.

lo determiner *masc.*
1 (*used with adjectives*) **the ... thing**
lo bueno the good thing
lo mejor the best thing
2 lo que what
Dime lo que quieres. Tell me what
you want.

lo pronoun *masc.*
1 him
Lo conozco. I know him.
No quiero verlo. I don't want to see
him.
2 it
Lo he leído. I've read it.
3 you
Lo acompaño, señor Gallego.
I'll go with you, Mr Gallego.

el **lobo** noun *masc.*
wolf
el lobo feroz the big bad wolf

loco adjective *masc.*, **loca** *fem.*
mad
¡Estás loca! You're mad!

la **locomotora** noun *fem.*
(*of a train*) **engine**

el **lomo** noun *masc.*
back
el lomo de un caballo the back of
a horse

la **loncha** noun *fem.*
slice

Londres noun *masc.*
London

la **longitud** noun *fem.*
length

el **loro** noun *masc.*
parrot

los determiner *masc. plural*
1 (*before masculine plural nouns*) **the**
los jardines the gardens
los niños the children
2 (*no translation*)
Me gustan los tomates. I love
tomatoes.
los libros de mi hermana my
sister's books
3 (*with adjectives used as nouns*) **the**
los rojos the red ones
los pequeños the small ones
4 (*with parts of the body, clothes, etc.*)
my, **your**, **his**, etc.
Me pongo los calcetines. I put my
socks on.
¿Te duelen los pies? Do your feet
hurt?
Se quitaron los zapatos. They took
off their shoes.

los pronoun *masc. plural*
1 them
Los veo. I can see them.
¿Puedo comerlos? Can I eat them?
2 you
Los han llamado a ustedes.
They've called you.

la **lotería** noun *fem.*
lottery
jugar a la lotería to play the
lottery
Me ha tocado la lotería. I've won
the lottery.

• *The months of the year and days of the week do not take a capital letter in Spanish.*

luego adverb
1 then
Primero está Juan y luego yo. Juan is first and then it's me.
2 later
Mi padre viene luego. My dad's coming later.
¡Hasta luego! See you later!

el **lujo** noun masc.
luxury
un hotel de lujo a luxury hotel

la **luna** noun fem.
moon

el **lunes** noun masc.
Monday
Hoy es lunes. Today is Monday.
el lunes on Monday

Voy a la piscina el lunes. I'm going swimming on Monday.
los lunes on Mondays
Los lunes tenemos clase de gimnasia. On Mondays we have PE.

LANGUAGE
Remember the difference between el lunes (one Monday only) and los lunes (every Monday).

la **lupa** noun fem.
magnifying glass

la **luz** noun fem.
1 light
encender la luz to turn on the light
apagar la luz to turn off the light
2 electricity
No hay luz en la casa. There's no electricity in the house.

Mm

los **macarrones** plural noun masc.
macaroni

LANGUAGE
Spanish = los macarrones is plural
English = macaroni is singular

la **maceta** noun fem.
flowerpot

el **macho** masc.
male
un cachorro macho a male puppy

la **madera** noun fem.
wood
Es de madera. It's made of wood.
un juguete de madera a wooden toy

la **madrastra** noun fem.
stepmother

la **madre** noun fem.
mother, **mum**

Mi madre es maestra. My mother's a teacher.

Madrid noun masc.
Madrid
Estoy en Madrid. I'm in Madrid.
Voy a Madrid. I'm going to Madrid.

madrileño adjective masc.,
madrileña fem.
from Madrid
Soy madrileño. I'm from Madrid.

la **madrina** noun fem.
godmother

la **madrugada** noun fem.
1 dawn
de madrugada at dawn
2 (between midnight and dawn) **morning**
las tres de la madrugada three o'clock in the morning
de madrugada early in the morning

• See the centre section for verb tables.

a b c d e f g h i j k l m n o p q r s t u v w x y z

maduro adjective *masc.,*
 madura *fem.*
 ripe
 un tomate maduro a ripe tomato

el **maestro** *masc.,*
 la **maestra** noun *fem.*
 teacher
 Mi maestra se llama Antonia.
 My teacher's name is Antonia.

la **magia** noun *fem.*
 magic
 un truco de magia a magic trick

mágico adjective *masc.,*
 mágica *fem.*
 magic
 una varita mágica a magic wand

el **magnetófono** noun *masc.*
 tape recorder

magnífico adjective *masc.,*
 magnífica *fem.*
 superb

el **mago** noun *masc.,* la **maga** *fem.*
 1 magician
 2 (*in stories*) **wizard**

el **maíz** noun *masc.*
 sweetcorn

mal adjective *masc. & fem.*
 1 bad
 un mal ejemplo a bad example
 No está mal. It isn't bad.
 2 wrong
 La fecha está mal. The date's
 wrong.
 3 ill
 Me siento mal. I feel ill.

LANGUAGE
Mal is used instead of malo before a
masculine singular noun, e.g. mal
ejemplo instead of ejemplo malo.

mal adverb
 1 badly
 Canto muy mal. I sing very
 badly.

2 wrong
 Lo has escrito mal. You've spelled
 it wrong.
 3 bad
 Huele mal. It smells bad.

la **malanga** noun *fem.*
 eddo (*a vegetable*)

maleducado adjective *masc.,*
 maleducada *fem.*
 rude

la **maleta** noun *fem.*
 suitcase
 He hecho la maleta. I've packed
 my case.

Mallorca noun *fem.*
 Majorca

malo adjective *masc.,* **mala** *fem.*

LANGUAGE
The masculine singular malo becomes
mal when it is used before a noun.

 1 bad
 un hotel malo a bad hotel
 La película es muy mala. The
 film's very bad.
 un mal ejemplo a bad example
 Hace mal tiempo. The weather's
 bad.
 2 naughty
 un niño malo a naughty boy
 3 ill
 Papá está malo. Dad's ill.

la **mamá** noun *fem.*
 mum
 Sí, mamá. Yes, mum.

la **mancha** noun *fem.*
 stain
 una mancha de chocolate
 a chocolate stain

mandar verb
 1 to send
 mandar una carta a alguien
 to send somebody a letter
 2 to be in charge
 ¡Aquí mando yo! I'm in charge
 here!

• *Use* el *and* uno *for masculine words and* la *and* una *for feminine words.*

97

la **mandarina** noun *fem.*
mandarin orange

el **mando a distancia** noun *masc.*
remote control

la **manecilla** noun *fem.*
hand
las manecillas del reloj the hands of the clock

la **manera** noun *fem.*
way
Hazlo de esta manera. Do it this way.
Lo hago a mi manera. I'll do it my way.

la **manga** noun *fem.*
sleeve
una camisa de manga corta a shirt with short sleeves

el **mango** noun *masc.*
handle
el mango de la sartén the handle of the frying pan

el **manillar** noun *masc.*
handlebars

LANGUAGE
Spanish = **el manillar** is singular
English = **handlebars** is plural

la **mano** noun *fem.*
hand
¿Tienes algo en la mano? Have you got anything in your hand?
levantar la mano to put your hand up
dar la mano a alguien to shake hands with somebody
Se dan la mano. They shake hands.

la **manta** noun *fem.*
blanket

el **mantel** noun *masc.*
tablecloth

mantener verb
to keep
mantenerse en forma to keep fit

la **mantequilla** noun *fem.*
butter

la **manzana** noun *fem.*
apple
zumo de manzana apple juice

el **manzano** noun *masc.*
apple tree

mañana adverb
tomorrow
pasado mañana the day after tomorrow
mañana por la mañana tomorrow morning
mañana por la noche tomorrow night

la **mañana** noun *fem.*
morning
por la mañana in the morning
ayer por la mañana yesterday morning
a las siete de la mañana at seven in the morning

el **mapa** noun *masc.*
map

LANGUAGE
Be careful: **mapa** ends in an **-a** but it is not a feminine noun.

el **maquillaje** noun *masc.*
make-up

maquillarse verb
to put your make-up on

la **máquina** noun *fem.*
machine
una máquina de afeitar a razor, a shaver

el **mar** noun *masc.*
sea

el or la **maratón** noun *masc. & fem.*
(plural los **maratones**)
marathon

maravilloso adjective *masc.*,
maravillosa *fem.*
wonderful, **marvellous**

• *Languages and nationalities do not take a capital letter in Spanish.*

la **marca** noun *fem.*
1 mark
dejar una marca to leave a mark
2 make
¿De qué marca es tu ordenador?
What make is your computer?

marcar verb
1 to mark
2 to dial
marcar un número to dial a
number
3 to score
marcar un gol to score a goal

la **marcha** noun *fem.*
(*in a car*)
dar marcha atrás to reverse

el **marciano** noun *masc.*,
la **marciana** *fem.*
Martian

la **marea** noun *fem.*
tide
La marea está alta. The tide's in.
La marea está baja. The tide's out.

mareado adjective *masc.*,
mareada *fem.*
1 sick
Estoy mareado. I feel sick.
2 (*in a boat*) **seasick**
3 (*losing your balance etc.*) **dizzy**

marearse verb
1 to get sick
2 to get seasick
Me mareo en los barcos. I get sick
on boats.
3 to get dizzy

la **margarina** noun *fem.*
margarine

el **margen** noun *masc.*
margin
No escribas en el margen.
Don't write in the margin.

el **marido** noun *masc.*
husband

el **marinero** noun *masc.*
sailor

la **mariposa** noun *fem.*
butterfly

la **mariquita** noun *fem.*
ladybird

el **marisco** noun *masc.*
seafood

marrón adjective *masc. & fem.*
brown
una falda marrón a brown skirt

> 🔑 **LANGUAGE**
> The singular form **marrón** is the same in
> the masculine and feminine, and the
> plural is **marrones**.

el **marrón** noun *masc.*
brown
Me gusta el marrón. I like brown.

el **martes** noun *masc.*
Tuesday
Hoy es martes. Today is Tuesday.
el martes on Tuesday
Es mi cumpleaños el martes.
It's my birthday on Tuesday.
los martes on Tuesdays
Los martes jugamos al fútbol.
On Tuesdays we play football.

> 🔑 **LANGUAGE**
> Remember the difference between **el
> martes** (one Tuesday only) and **los
> martes** (every Tuesday).

el **martillo** noun *masc.*
hammer

marzo noun *masc.*
March
Nací en marzo. I was born in
March.
El avión sale de Londres el tres de
marzo. The plane leaves London
on the third of March.

a
b
c
d
e
f
g
h
i
j
k
l
m
n
o
p
q
r
s
t
u
v
w
x
y
z

• *The months of the year and days of the week do not take a capital letter in Spanish.*

Spanish English

a
b
c
d
e
f
g
h
i
j
k
l
m
n
o
p
q
r
s
t
u
v
w
x
y
z

más adverb, adjective & pronoun
1 more
Comes más que yo. You eat more than me.
Eres más alta que él. You're taller than him.
¿Quieres más azúcar? Do you want any more sugar?
Quiero más. I want some more.
2 (talking about numbers)
más de more than
más de cinco manzanas more than five apples
3 else
nadie más nobody else
nada más nothing else
4 most
Es el que más me gusta. It's the one I like most.
la niña más inteligente the most intelligent girl
el edificio más alto the tallest building
el más pequeño de todos the smallest of them all
5 plus
Cinco más dos son siete. Five plus two is seven.

la **máscara** noun fem.
mask

masculino adjective masc.,
masculina fem.
1 (in grammar) **masculine**
el género masculino the masculine gender
2 men's
el equipo masculino the men's team

masticar verb
to chew

matar verb
to kill

las **matemáticas** plural noun fem.
maths

el **matrimonio** noun masc.
marriage

maullar verb
to miaow

el **máximo** noun masc.
maximum

máximo adjective masc.,
máxima fem.
maximum

mayo noun masc.
May
Llovió mucho en mayo. It rained a lot in May.
Es mi cumpleaños el domingo ocho de mayo. It's my birthday on Sunday, the eighth of May

la **mayonesa** noun fem.
mayonnaise

mayor adjective masc. & fem.
1 older
Eres mayor que yo. You're older than me.
mi hermano mayor my older brother
2 eldest
la hija mayor the eldest daughter
3 bigger
un tamaño mayor a bigger size
4 biggest
el mayor edificio del pueblo the biggest building in the village
la mayor parte de ... most of ...
5 grown-up
Ya eres mayor. You're grown-up now.

el or la **mayor** noun masc. & fem.
1 oldest
la mayor de las hermanas the oldest of the sisters
2 grown-up
una película para mayores a film for grown-ups

• See the centre section for verb tables.

la **mayoría** noun fem.
la mayoría de ... most of ...
la mayoría de los niños most of the
children

la **mayúscula** noun fem.
capital letter
en mayúsculas in capital letters
Se escribe con S mayúscula.
It's written with a capital S.

me pronoun
1 me
¿Me conoces? Do you know me?
Llámame mañana. Call me
tomorrow.
Me ha dado el compacto.
She's given me the CD.
2 to me
Me lo ha mandado. He has sent it
to me.
Dámela. Give it to me.
3 myself
Me estoy lavando. I'm washing
myself.
4 (with parts of the body, clothes, etc.) **my**
Me he roto el brazo. I've broken
my arm.
Me pongo la camisa. I'm putting
my shirt on.

el **mecánico** noun masc.,
la **mecánica** fem.
mechanic

la **medalla** noun fem.
medal
una medalla de plata a silver
medal

la **media** noun fem.
1 (talking about time) **half**
a las ocho y media at half past
eight
dos horas y media two and a half
hours
2 (Latin America) **sock**

mediano adjective masc.,
mediana fem.
medium

de tamaño mediano of medium
size

la **medianoche** noun fem.
midnight
a medianoche at midnight

las **medias** plural noun fem.
tights

el **medicamento** noun masc.
medicine

la **medicina** noun fem.
medicine

el **médico** noun masc.,
la **médica** fem.
doctor
Mi padre es médico. My dad's a
doctor.
ir al médico to go to the doctor

medio adverb
half
Está medio dormido. He's half
asleep.

el **medio** noun masc.
middle
Ponlo en el medio. Put it in the
middle.
en medio de in the middle of

el **medio ambiente** noun masc.
environment

medio adjective masc., **media** fem.
half
medio litro half a litre
media hora half an hour
siete y medio seven and a half
una hora y media an hour and a
half
Son las cuatro y media. It's half
past four.

el **mediodía** noun masc.
midday
a mediodía at midday

medir verb
to measure
medir una habitación to measure a
room

• Use **el** and **uno** for masculine words and **la** and **una** for feminine words.

a
b
c
d
e
f
g
h
i
j
k
l
m
n
o
p
q
r
s
t
u
v
w
x
y
z

¿**Cuánto mides?** How tall are you?
Mido un metro cincuenta. I'm one
metre fifty.

el **Mediterráneo** noun *masc.*
Mediterranean

la **mejilla** noun *fem.*
cheek

mejor adjective *masc. & fem.*
1 **better**
Mi casa es mejor que la tuya.
My house is better than yours.
Me encuentro mejor. I'm feeling
better.
2 **best**
mi mejor amigo my best friend
**uno de los mejores alumnos de la
clase** one of the best pupils in the
class

mejor adverb
1 **better**
Juegas al fútbol mejor que yo.
You play football better than me.
2 **best**
¿Quién lo ha hecho mejor?
Who's done it best?
3 **a lo mejor** maybe

el or la **mejor** noun *masc. & fem.*
best
Esta bici es la mejor. This bike is
the best.
Elige los mejores. Pick the best
ones.

mejorar verb
1 **to get better**
El tiempo está mejorando.
The weather's getting better.
¡Que te mejores! Get well soon!
2 **to improve**
Quiero mejorar mi español. I want
to improve my Spanish.

el **mellizo** noun *masc.*,
la **melliza** *fem.*
twin
Son mellizos. They're twins.

el **melocotón** noun *masc.* (plural los
melocotones)
peach

la **melodía** noun *fem.*
tune

el **melón** noun *masc.* (plural los
melones)
melon

la **memoria** noun *fem.*
memory
Tengo buena memoria. I've got a
good memory.
aprender algo de memoria
to learn something by heart

menor adjective *masc. & fem.*
1 **younger**
Soy menor que tú. I'm younger
than you.
mi hermana menor my younger
sister
2 **youngest**
el hijo menor the youngest son

el or la **menor** noun *masc. & fem.*
youngest
el menor de los hermanos
the youngest of the brothers

menos adverb, adjective, pronoun &
preposition
1 **less**
Hablo menos que tú. I talk less
than you.
**Esta película es menos
interesante.** This film is less
interesting.
Tengo menos dinero que ella.
I have less money than her.
2 **not as**
Eres menos alto que yo. You're not
as tall as me.
3 **not as many**, **fewer**
**Tengo menos amigos que mi
hermano.** I don't have as many
friends as my brother., I have
fewer friends than my brother.
4 (*talking about numbers*)
menos de less than

• *Languages and nationalities do not take a capital letter in Spanish.*

menos de cinco euros less than five euros

5 least
Es la que menos me gusta. It's the one I like least.
el libro menos interesante the least interesting book
los menos caros the least expensive ones
por lo menos at least

6 minus
Nueve menos tres son seis. Nine minus three is six.

7 except
todos menos Javier everybody except Javier

8 (when telling the time) **to**
Son las seis menos cinco. It's five to six.

el **mensaje** noun masc.
message
un mensaje de texto a text message

la **menta** noun fem.
mint
un caramelo de menta a mint

mentir verb
to lie
No miento. I'm not lying.

la **mentira** noun fem.
lie
decir mentiras to tell lies
¿Verdad o mentira? True or false?

el **mentiroso** noun masc.,
la **mentirosa** fem.
liar

el **menú** noun masc. (plural los **menús**)
menu

a **menudo** adverb
often
La veo a menudo. I see her often.

el **mercado** noun masc.
market

merecer verb
to deserve

merendar verb
to have an afternoon snack

la **merienda** noun fem.
(late) afternoon snack

la **mermelada** noun fem.
1 jam
la mermelada de fresa strawberry jam
2 marmalade

el **mes** noun masc.
month
el mes pasado last month
el mes que viene next month

la **mesa** noun fem.
table
en la mesa on the table
poner la mesa to lay the table
quitar la mesa to clear the table

el **metal** noun masc.
metal
una caja de metal a metal box

el **mesero** noun masc.,
la **mesera** fem.
(Latin America) **waiter**, **waitress**

meter verb
to put
Mete la carta en el sobre. Put the letter in the envelope.

meterse verb
meterse en to get into
Me metí en el agua. I got into the water.

el **metro** noun masc.
1 metre
2 underground
en metro by underground
coger el metro to take the underground

México noun masc.
Mexico

• The months of the year and days of the week do not take a capital letter in Spanish.

a
b
c
d
e
f
g
h
i
j
k
l
m
n
o
p
q
r
s
t
u
v
w
x
y
z

mexicano adjective *masc.*,
mexicana *fem.*
Mexican

el **mexicano** noun *masc.*,
la **mexicana** *fem.*
Mexican

la **mezcla** noun *fem.*
mixture

mezclar verb
to mix

la **mezquita** noun *fem.*
mosque

mi adjective *masc. & fem.*
my
mi casa my house
mis libros my books

mí pronoun
me
para mí for me
detrás de mí behind me
A mí me gusta. I like it.

los **microbios** plural noun *masc.*
germs

el **micrófono** noun *masc.*
microphone

el **microondas** noun *masc.* (plural
los **microondas**)
microwave

el **microscopio** noun *masc.*
microscope

el **miedo** noun *masc.*
fear
tener miedo to be afraid
Tengo miedo a la oscuridad.
I'm afraid of the dark.
Tengo miedo de caerme. I'm afraid
of falling.

el **miembro** noun *masc.*
member

mientras conjunction
while
Espera aquí mientras me visto.
Wait here while I get dressed.

el **miércoles** noun *masc.*
Wednesday
Hoy es miércoles. Today is
Wednesday.
el miércoles on Wednesday
Voy al cine el miércoles. I'm going
to the cinema on Wednesday.
los miércoles on Wednesdays
Hago deportes los miércoles.
I do sports on Wednesdays.

las **migas** plural noun *fem.*
crumbs

mil number
thousand
mil personas a thousand people
dos mil personas two thousand
people
miles de euros thousands of euros

el **milagro** noun *masc.*
miracle

el **millón** noun *masc.*
million
un millón de personas a million
people
dos millones two million

• *See the centre section for verb tables.*

el **millonario** noun *masc.*,
la **millonaria** *fem.*
millionaire

mineral adjective *masc. & fem.*
mineral
el agua mineral mineral water

la **minifalda** noun *fem.*
miniskirt

el **mínimo** noun *masc.*
minimum

mínimo adjective *masc.*,
mínima *fem.*
minimum

la **minúscula** noun *fem.*
small letter
Se escribe con minúscula.
It's written with a small letter.

minusválido adjective *masc.*,
minusválida *fem.*
disabled

el **minusválido** noun *masc.*,
la **minusválida** *fem.*
disabled man, **disabled woman**

el **minuto** noun *masc.*
minute
Espera un minuto. Wait a minute.

mío adjective *masc.*, **mía** *fem.*
mine
Este libro es mío. This book is
mine.
Estas bicis son mías. These bikes
are mine.
un amigo mío a friend of mine

el **mío** pronoun *masc.*, la **mía** *fem.*
mine
tu hermano y el mío your brother
and mine
Tu casa es más grande que la mía.
Your house is bigger than mine.

mirar verb
to look, **to look at**
mirar por la ventana to look out of
the window

¡Mira! Look!
Estoy mirando las fotos.
I'm looking at the photos.

⚷ **LANGUAGE**
Spanish = **mirar** algo/a alguien
English = **to look at** something/
somebody

la **misa** noun *fem.*
mass
ir a misa to go to mass

mismo adverb
right
ahora mismo right now
aquí mismo right here

mismo adjective *masc.*, **misma** *fem.*
1 same
Tienes la misma blusa que yo.
You have the same blouse as me.
al mismo tiempo at the same time
2 ...self (plural **...selves**)
yo mismo myself
ella misma herself
nosotros mismos ourselves

el **mismo** pronoun *masc.*,
la **misma** *fem.*
1 same one
Tengo el mismo. I've got the same
one.
2 lo mismo the same thing
Siempre dice lo mismo. She always
says the same thing.

el **misterio** noun *masc.*
mystery

misterioso adjective *masc.*,
misteriosa *fem.*
mysterious

la **mitad** noun *fem.*
half
la mitad de los alumnos half the
pupils
Corta el pastel por la mitad.
Cut the cake in half.
a mitad de camino halfway

a
b
c
d
e
f
g
h
i
j
k
l
m
n
o
p
q
r
s
t
u
v
w
x
y
z

• *Use* el *and* uno *for masculine words and* la *and* una *for feminine words.*

la **mochila** noun *fem.*
1 backpack
2 schoolbag

🔑 **LANGUAGE**
Schoolchildren carry a **mochila** on their backs.

los **mocos** plural noun *masc.*
tener mocos to have a runny nose

la **moda** noun *fem.*
fashion
una revista de modas a fashion magazine
estar de moda to be fashionable

los **modales** plural noun *masc.*
manners
buenos modales good manners

el **modelo** noun *masc.*
model
el último modelo the latest model

el or la **modelo** noun *masc. & fem.*
model
Es una modelo española. She's a Spanish model.

moderno adjective *masc.*,
moderna *fem.*
modern

mojado adjective *masc.*,
mojada *fem.*
wet
una toalla mojada a wet towel

mojarse verb
to get wet
Me he mojado con la lluvia. I got wet in the rain.

molestar verb
1 to bother
Siento molestarle. I'm sorry to bother you.
¿Le molesta si abro la ventana? Will it bother you if I open the window?
2 to annoy
Mi hermano me molesta. My brother annoys me.

el **momento** noun *masc.*
moment
¡Un momento! Just a moment!
en este momento at the moment

la **moneda** noun *fem.*
coin
una moneda de dos euros a two euro coin

el **monedero** noun *masc.*
purse

el **monitor** noun *masc.*
(*computer screen*) **monitor**

el **monitor** noun *masc.*,
la **monitora** *fem.*
instructor
un monitor de esquí a ski instructor

la **monja** noun *fem.*
nun

mono adjective *masc.*, **mona** *fem.*
lovely
un niño mono a lovely baby

el **mono** noun *masc.*, la **mona** *fem.*
monkey

el **monopatín** noun *masc.* (plural los **monopatines**)
skateboard

el **monstruo** noun *masc.*
monster

la **montaña** noun *fem.*
mountain
en la montaña in the mountains
la montaña rusa the roller coaster
una bicicleta de montaña a mountain bike

montar verb
1 to ride
montar en bici to ride a bike
montar a caballo to ride a horse
2 montar una tienda to put up a tent

• *Languages and nationalities do not take a capital letter in Spanish.*

el **montón** noun *masc.* (plural los **montones**)

1 pile
un montón de libros a pile of books

2 un montón de loads of
Hay un montón de niños. There are loads of children.

el **monumento** noun *masc.*
historic building

la **moqueta** noun *fem.*
(fitted) carpet

la **mora** noun *fem.*
blackberry

morado adjective *masc.*, **morada** *fem.*
purple
una camisa morada a purple shirt

el **morado** noun *masc.*
purple
Prefiero el morado. I prefer purple.

morder verb
to bite
Me muerdo las uñas. I bite my nails.

moreno adjective *masc.*, **morena** *fem.*

1 dark
Tengo el pelo moreno. I've got dark hair.

2 brown, **tanned**
Estoy muy moreno. I'm very brown., I'm very tanned.

morir verb
to die
Mi gato murió ayer. My cat died yesterday.
¡Me muero de hambre! I'm starving!

la **mosca** noun *fem.*
fly

el **mosquito** noun *masc.*
mosquito

la **mostaza** noun *fem.*
mustard

el **mostrador** noun *masc.*
1 (*in a shop*) **counter**
2 (*at an airport*) **check-in desk**

mostrar verb
to show

el **motivo** noun *masc.*
reason
el motivo de algo the reason for something

la **moto** noun *fem.*
motorbike

la **motocicleta** noun *fem.*
motorcycle

el **motor** noun *masc.*
(*of a car*) **engine**

el or la **motorista** noun *masc. & fem.*
motorcyclist

⚠️ **FALSE FRIEND**
motorista = motorcyclist (*not* motorist)

mover verb
to move
He movido la silla. I've moved the chair.

moverse verb
to move
No puedo moverme. I can't move.
No te muevas. Don't move.

el **móvil** noun *masc.*
mobile phone
Llámame al móvil. Call me on my mobile.

el **movimiento** noun *masc.*
movement

la **muchacha** noun *fem.*
girl

el **muchacho** noun *masc.*
boy

a b c d e f g h i j k l **m** n o p q r s t u v w x y z

• *The months of the year and days of the week do not take a capital letter in Spanish.*

a
b
c
d
e
f
g
h
i
j
k
l
m
n
o
p
q
r
s
t
u
v
w
x
y
z

mucho adverb
1 a lot
Leo mucho. I read a lot.
mucho más grande a lot bigger
2 much
No leo mucho. I don't read much.
No me gusta mucho. I don't like it
very much.
mucho más grande much bigger

mucho adjective & pronoun *masc.*,
mucha *fem.*
1 a lot of
mucho dinero a lot of money
muchos coches a lot of cars
Me has dado mucho. You've given
me a lot.
hace mucho tiempo a long time
ago
2 much
No tengo mucho dinero. I don't
have much money.
No tengo mucho. I don't have
much.
3 many
No hay muchas casas. There aren't
many houses.
¿Tienes muchos? Do you have
many?
Muchas gracias. Many thanks.
4 very
Hace mucho calor. It's very hot.
Tengo mucha hambre. I'm very
hungry.

mudarse verb
to move house
Se mudan mañana. They're
moving tomorrow.

el **mueble** noun *masc.*
los muebles furniture
un mueble a piece of furniture

la **muela** noun *fem.*
back tooth
Tengo dolor de muelas. I have a
toothache.

la **muerte** noun *fem.*
death

muerto adjective *masc.*,
muerta *fem.*
dead
Está muerta. She's dead.
Hay muchos muertos. Lots of
people have been killed.

la **mujer** noun *fem.*
1 woman
un hombre y una mujer a man and
a woman
2 wife
la mujer de mi primo my cousin's
wife

la **muleta** noun *fem.*
crutch
Anda con muletas. He's on
crutches.

multiplicar verb
to multiply
Multiplica ocho por cinco.
Multiply eight by five.
las tablas de multiplicar the times
tables

el **Mundial** noun *masc.*
(*in football*) **the World Cup**

el **mundo** noun *masc.*
1 world
el mejor del mundo the best in the
world
2 todo el mundo everybody
Todo el mundo ha leído este libro.
Everybody has read this book.

la **muñeca** noun *fem.*
1 doll
una casa de muñecas a doll's
house
2 wrist

el **muñeco de nieve** noun *masc.*
snowman

el **murciélago** noun *masc.*
bat

el **muro** noun *masc.*
wall

• *See the centre section for verb tables.*

108

el **músculo** noun *masc.*
muscle

el **museo** noun *masc.*
1 museum
2 (*for paintings*) **art gallery**

la **música** noun *fem.*
music

el **músico** noun *masc.*,
la **música** *fem.*
musician

el **muslo** noun *masc.*
un muslo de pollo a chicken leg

musulmán adjective *masc.*,
musulmana *fem.*
Muslim

⚷ **LANGUAGE**
The plural of **musulmán** is **musulmanes**.

muy adverb
very
muy bueno very good
muy bien very well

Nn

nacer verb
to be born
Nací en Madrid. I was born in Madrid.

el **nacimiento** noun *masc.*
birth
mi fecha de nacimiento my date of birth

nacional adjective *masc. & fem.*
national

la **nacionalidad** noun *fem.*
nationality

nada pronoun & adverb
1 nothing
¿Qué haces? – Nada. What are you doing? – Nothing.
nada más nothing else
2 anything
No he dicho nada. I haven't said anything.
No quiero nada más. I don't want anything else.

⚷ **LANGUAGE**
No + *verb* + **nada**, for example: **No quiero nada.**

3 at all
No me gusta nada. I don't like it at all.

4 de nada you're welcome
¡Gracias! – De nada. Thank you! – You're welcome.

nadar verb
to swim

nadie pronoun
1 nobody
No hay nadie en la cocina. There's nobody in the kitchen.
2 anybody
No conozco a nadie. I don't know anybody.

⚷ **LANGUAGE**
No + *verb* + **nadie**, for example: **No hay nadie.**

naranja adjective *masc. & fem.*
orange
calcetines naranja orange socks

⚷ **LANGUAGE**
Naranja is the same in the masculine, feminine, and plural.

el **naranja** noun *masc.*
(*colour*) **orange**
El naranja te queda bien. Orange looks good on you.

• Use **el** and **uno** for masculine words and **la** and **una** for feminine words.

la **naranja** noun *fem.*
 orange
 un zumo de naranja an orange juice

la **nariz** noun *fem.* (plural las **narices**)
 nose

la **nata** noun *fem.*
 cream
 fresas con nata strawberries and cream

la **natación** noun *fem.*
 swimming

natural adjective *masc. & fem.*
 natural

la **naturaleza** noun *fem.*
 nature

la **navaja** noun *fem.*
 penknife

la **nave** noun *fem.*
 ship
 una nave espacial a spaceship

navegar verb
 1 navegar en Internet to surf the Internet
 2 to sail

la **Navidad** noun *fem.*
 Christmas
 en Navidad at Christmas
 ¡Feliz Navidad! Happy Christmas!
 el día de Navidad Christmas Day

necesario adjective *masc.*,
necesaria *fem.*
 necessary

necesitar verb
 to need
 Necesito un libro nuevo. I need a new book.

la **nectarina** noun *fem.*
 nectarine

el **negativo** noun *masc.*
 (*in grammar*) **negative**

los **negocios** plural noun *masc.*
 business
 estar en un viaje de negocios to be on a business trip

negro adjective *masc.*, **negra** *fem.*
 black
 un traje negro a black suit

el **negro** noun *masc.*
 black
 Yo prefiero el negro. I prefer black.

el **nervio** noun *masc.*
 nerve
 un ataque de nervios an attack of nerves

nervioso adjective *masc.*,
nerviosa *fem.*
 nervous
 Estoy nerviosa. I'm nervous.

el **neumático** noun *masc.*
 tyre

la **nevada** noun *fem.*
 snowfall

nevar verb
 to snow
 Está nevando. It's snowing.

la **nevera** noun *fem.*
 fridge

ni conjunction
 1 or
 No sabes leer ni escribir. You can't read or write.
 2 nor
 Isabel no viene. – Ni yo tampoco. Isabel isn't coming. – Nor am I.
 3 ni ... ni not either ... or
 No quiero ni pescado ni carne. I don't want either fish or meat.
 4 ni ... ni neither ... nor
 ni María ni su hermano neither María nor her brother

el **nido** noun *masc.*
 nest

• *Languages and nationalities do not take a capital letter in Spanish.*

la **niebla** noun *fem.*
fog
Hay niebla. It's foggy.

la **nieta** noun *fem.*
granddaughter

el **nieto** noun *masc.*
grandson
los nietos grandchildren

la **nieve** noun *fem.*
snow

ninguno adjective & pronoun *masc.*,
ninguna *fem.*

LANGUAGE
The masculine singular **ninguno**
becomes **ningún** when it is used before a
noun.

1 not any
No toco ningún instrumento.
I don't play any instrument.
No he comprado ninguno.
I haven't bought any.

2 neither, not either
¿Quieres la bici negra o la roja? –
Ninguna. Do you want the black
bike or the red one? – Neither.
No me gusta ninguno de los dos.
I don't like either of them.

3 none
¿Cuántos libros tienes? – Ninguno.
How many books do you have? –
None.
ninguno de los niños none of the
children

la **niña** noun *fem.*
1 girl
Mi hermana tiene una niña de dos
años. My sister has a little girl of
two.

2 child
Es una niña tímida. She's a shy
child.

3 baby
Mi prima espera una niña.
My cousin is expecting a baby girl.

la **niñera** noun *fem.*
nanny

el **niño** noun *masc.*
1 boy
Mi prima tiene un niño de cuatro
años. My cousin has a little boy of
four.

2 child
Es un niño tímido. He's a shy child.

3 los niños children, boys and girls
Hay veinte niños en la clase. There
are twenty children in the class.

4 baby
Ha tenido un niño. She's had a
baby boy.

el **nivel** noun *masc.*
level

no adverb
1 no
¿Has visto esta película? - No.
Have you seen this film? - No.
No, gracias. No thanks.

2 not
No soy alta. I'm not tall.
No me gusta. I don't like it.
todavía no not yet
no mucho not much

3 (with negatives such as nunca, nada)
No hace nunca los deberes. He
never does his homework.
No tengo nada. I don't have
anything.

4 (in questions)
Vas a la biblioteca, ¿no? You're
going to the library, aren't you?
Es inglés, ¿no? He's English, isn't
he?

LANGUAGE
English uses questions such as 'aren't
you?', 'isn't he?' but Spanish simply puts
¿no? at the end.

la **noche** noun *fem.*
1 night
por la noche at night
ayer por la noche yesterday night

• *The months of the year and days of the week do not take a capital letter in Spanish.*

a
b
c
d
e
f
g
h
i
j
k
l
m
n
o
p
q
r
s
t
u
v
w
x
y
z

a las diez de la noche at ten o'clock at night
esta noche tonight
¡Buenas noches! Good night!
Es de noche. It's dark.
2 evening
por la noche in the evening
a las ocho de la noche at eight o'clock in the evening
¡Buenas noches! Good evening!

la **Nochebuena** noun fem.
Christmas Eve

CULTURE
In Spain the main Christmas meal is on **Nochebuena**, and it is eaten before Midnight Mass.

la **Nochevieja** noun fem.
New Year's Eve

nocturno adjective masc.,
nocturna fem.
1 night
el tren nocturno the night train
2 evening
una clase nocturna an evening class

el **nombre** noun masc.
1 name
No sé su nombre. I don't know her name.
2 noun
'Mesa' y 'silla' son nombres. 'Table' and 'chair' are nouns.

normal adjective masc. & fem.
normal

normalmente adverb
normally

norte noun masculine & adjective
north
en el norte in the north
la costa norte the north coast
el Mar del Norte the North Sea

Norteamérica noun fem.
North America

norteamericano adjective masc.,
norteamericana fem.
American
Es norteamericana. She's American.

el **norteamericano** noun masc.,
la **norteamericana** fem.
American

nos pronoun
1 us
Nos han visto. They've seen us.
Quiere vernos. He wants to see us.
2 to us
Nos ha dicho algo. He said something to us.
3 ourselves
Nos estamos lavando. We're washing ourselves.
4 (with parts of the body, clothes, etc.) **our**
Nos quitamos los zapatos. We took our shoes off.
5 each other
Nos escribimos. We write to each other.

nosotros pronoun masc.,
nosotras fem.
1 we
Nosotros hemos venido pero nuestros padres no. We've come but our parents haven't.

LANGUAGE
Nosotros/nosotras is used for giving special importance to the word 'we'.

2 (after a preposition etc.) **us**
con nosotros with us
Somos nosotras. It's us.
nosotros mismos ourselves

la **nota** noun fem.
1 mark
He sacado buenas notas. I've got good marks.
2 note
Escribe una nota. Write a note.

• See the centre section for verb tables.

112

notar verb
to notice

la **noticia** noun *fem.*
1 news
Tengo una buena noticia. I have some good news.
No tenemos noticias de Raúl. We don't have any news of Raúl.

🔑 **LANGUAGE**
las noticias = more than one piece of news

2 las noticias the news (*on TV or the radio*)
las noticias de las nueve the nine o'clock news

la **novela** noun *fem.*
novel

noveno adjective *masc.*,
novena *fem.*
ninth
en el noveno piso on the ninth floor

noventa number
ninety

la **novia** noun *fem.*
1 girlfriend
Mi hermano tiene novia. My brother has a girlfriend.
2 bride

noviembre noun *masc.*
November
Es mi cumpleaños en noviembre. It's my birthday in November.
Voy a Madrid el cinco de noviembre. I'm going to Madrid on the fifth of November.

el **novio** noun *masc.*
1 boyfriend
Mi hermana tiene novio. My sister has a boyfriend.
2 bridegroom
los novios the bride and groom

la **nube** noun *fem.*
cloud

nublado adjective *masc.*,
nublada *fem.*
cloudy
Está nublado. It's cloudy.

el **nudo** noun *masc.*
knot
hacer un nudo to tie a knot

nuestro adjective *masc.*,
nuestra *fem.*
1 our
nuestra escuela our school
nuestros padres our parents
2 ours
Este ordenador es nuestro. This computer is ours.
Estos libros son nuestros. These books are ours.
un amigo nuestro a friend of ours

🔑 **LANGUAGE**
Nuestros/nuestras is used with a plural noun.

el **nuestro** pronoun *masc.*,
la **nuestra** *fem.*
ours
Su piscina es mejor que la nuestra. His pool is better than ours.
tus libros y los nuestros your books and ours

Nueva Zelanda noun *fem.*
New Zealand

nueve number
1 nine
Tengo nueve años. I'm nine.
Son las nueve. It's nine o'clock.
2 (*with dates*) **ninth**
el nueve de diciembre the ninth of December

a
b
c
d
e
f
g
h
i
j
k
l
m
n
o
p
q
r
s
t
u
v
w
x
y
z

• *Use* el *and* uno *for masculine words and* la *and* una *for feminine words.*

a
b
c
d
e
f
g
h
i
j
k
l
m
n
o
p
q
r
s
t
u
v
w
x
y
z

nuevo adjective *masc.*, **nueva** *fem.*
new
una bicicleta nueva a new bicycle
mis nuevos amigos my new friends
el Año Nuevo the New Year

la **nuez** noun *fem.* (plural las **nueces**)
walnut

el **número** noun *masc.*
number
¿Cuál es tu número de teléfono?
What's your phone number?
un gran número de a large number of

nunca adverb
1 never
No llego tarde nunca. I never arrive late.
Nunca salgo sola. I never go out by myself.
2 ever
No salgo casi nunca. I hardly ever go out.
más que nunca more than ever

> **LANGUAGE**
> no + *verb* + **nunca**, for example: **No** salgo **nunca**.

Oo

o conjunction
or
hoy o mañana today or tomorrow
¿Vienes o no? Are you coming or not?

obedecer verb
to obey
Ese niño no obedece al maestro.
That child doesn't obey the teacher.

el **objeto** noun *masc.*
object

obligar verb
to make, **to force**
Lo han obligado a salir. They've made him leave.

la **obra** noun *fem.*
play
hacer una obra to put on a play

las **obras** plural noun *fem.*
roadworks

el **obrero** noun *masc.*,
la **obrera** *fem.*
worker

obtener verb
to get
He obtenido el primer premio.
I got the first prize.

la **ocasión** noun *fem.*
1 opportunity
una buena ocasión a good opportunity
2 occasion
en varias ocasiones on several occasions

el **océano** noun *masc.*
ocean

ochenta number
eighty

ocho number
1 eight
Tengo ocho años. I'm eight.
Son las ocho. It's eight o'clock.
2 (with dates) **eighth**
el ocho de mayo the eighth of May

el **ócorro** noun *masc.*
okra

octavo *masc.*, **octava** adjective *fem.*
eighth

• Languages and nationalities do not take a capital letter in Spanish.

octubre noun masc.
October
Mis abuelos llegan en octubre.
My grandparents are coming in
October.
¿Qué haces el dos de octubre?
What are you doing on the second
of October?

 CULTURE
On 12th October people in Spain and Latin
America celebrate the finding of America
by Christopher Columbus. In Spain this is
called **el día de la Hispanidad.**

ocupado masc.,
ocupada adjective fem.
1 busy
Estoy ocupada. I'm busy.
2 (talking about a toilet etc.) **engaged**
3 taken
Este asiento está ocupado.
This seat is taken.

ocurrir verb
to happen

LANGUAGE
Ocurrir is similar to the English 'occur'.

odiar verb
to hate
Odio el pescado. I hate fish.

oeste noun masc. & adjective
west
en el oeste in the west
la costa oeste the west coast

la oficina noun fem.
office
la oficina de correos the post office
la oficina de turismo the tourist
office

ofrecer verb
to offer
ofrecer algo a alguien to offer
somebody something

el oído noun masc.
ear

oír verb
to hear
No te oigo. I can't hear you.
¡Oiga, por favor! Excuse me!

el ojo noun masc.
eye
Tengo los ojos verdes. I have green
eyes.

la ola noun fem.
wave

oler verb
to smell
oler las flores to smell the flowers
oler a algo to smell of something
Huele a pescado. It smells of fish.
Huele bien. It smells nice.

olímpico adjective masc.,
olímpica fem.
Olympic
los Juegos Olímpicos the Olympic
Games

el olor noun masc.
smell
Hay olor a gas. There's a smell of
gas.

olvidar verb
to forget

olvidarse verb
to forget
Me olvido de todo. I forget
everything.
Se me ha olvidado tu dirección.
I've forgotten your address.
¡Se me olvidó! I forgot!

once number
1 eleven
Tengo once años. I'm eleven.
Son las once. It's eleven o'clock.
2 (with dates) **eleventh**
el once de enero the eleventh of
January

a b c d e f g h i j k l m n **o** p q r s t u v w x y z

• *The months of the year and days of the week do not take a capital letter in Spanish.*

a
b
c
d
e
f
g
h
i
j
k
l
m
n
o
p
q
r
s
t
u
v
w
x
y
z

ondulado adjective *masc.*, **ondulada** *fem.*
wavy
Tengo el pelo ondulado. I've got wavy hair.

operar verb
to operate on
Van a operarme. I'm going to have an operation.
Me han operado del hombro. I've had an operation on my shoulder.

operarse verb
to have an operation
Tiene que operarse del brazo. He has to have an operation on his arm.

la **opinión** noun *fem.* (plural las **opiniones**)
opinion
en mi opinión in my opinion
He cambiado de opinión. I've changed my mind.

la **oportunidad** noun *fem.*
chance, opportunity
una segunda oportunidad a second chance

la **óptica** noun *fem.*
optician's
ir a la óptica to go to the optician's

optimista adjective *masc. & fem.*
optimistic

opuesto adjective *masc.*, **opuesta** *fem.*
opposite
en direcciones opuestas in opposite directions

la **oración** noun *fem.* (plural las **oraciones**)
1 (*in grammar*) **sentence**
2 **prayer**

el **orden** noun *masc.*
order
en orden alfabético in alphabetical order
La habitación está en orden. The room's tidy.

ordenado adjective *masc.*, **ordenada** *fem.*
tidy

el **ordenador** noun *masc.*
computer
un ordenador portátil a laptop

ordenar verb
to tidy

la **oreja** noun *fem.*
ear

organizar verb
to organize

orgulloso adjective *masc.*, **orgullosa** *fem.*
proud
Estoy muy orgullosa de ti. I'm very proud of you.

original adjective *masc. & fem.*
original

la **orilla** noun *fem.*
bank
sentarse a la orilla del río to sit down on the river bank
la orilla del mar the seashore

el **oro** noun *masc.*
gold
una medalla de oro a gold medal

la **orquesta** noun *fem.*
1 (*playing dance music etc.*) **band**
2 **orchestra**

la **ortografía** noun *fem.*
spelling
una falta de ortografía a spelling mistake

• See the centre section for verb tables.

116

la **oruga** noun *fem.*
caterpillar

os pronoun
1 you
Os conozco. I know you.
Queremos ayudaros. We want to help you.
2 to you
Os ha escrito. He has written to you.
3 yourselves
¿Os habéis cortado? Have you cut yourselves?
4 *(with parts of the body, clothes, etc.)* **your**
Os podéis lavar las manos. You can wash your hands.
¡Lavaos las manos! Wash your hands!
5 each other
¿Os conocéis? Do you know each other?

> **LANGUAGE**
> Use os when you are talking to two or more friends, people in your family, or people your own age.

la **oscuridad** noun *fem.*
dark
Está sentado en la oscuridad. He's sitting in the dark.

oscuro adjective *masc.*, **oscura** *fem.*
dark
Aquí está oscuro. It's dark here.
faldas verde oscuro dark green skirts

> **LANGUAGE**
> When oscuro follows the name of a colour (e.g. verde, azul), use the colour word in the masculine singular form only.

el **osito de peluche** noun *masc.*
teddy bear

el **oso** noun *masc.*
bear

el **otoño** noun *masc.*
autumn
en otoño in the autumn

otro adjective & pronoun *masc.*, **otra** *fem.*
1 another
Quiero otro libro. I want another book.
Tengo otro. I have another one.
2 other
el otro día the other day
las otras niñas the other girls
Tengo otros. I have others.
3 otra cosa something else
Dame otra cosa. Give me something else.
4 otra vez again
¿Puedo leerlo otra vez? Can I read it again?

el **otro** pronoun *masc.*, la **otra** *fem.*
the other one
¿Dónde está el otro? Where is the other one?
Las otras están en la mesa. The others are on the table.

la **oveja** noun *fem.*
sheep

el **OVNI** noun *masc.*
UFO

> **LANGUAGE**
> The Spanish stands for **objeto volador no identificado**, matching the English 'unidentified flying object'.

oxidado *masc.*, **oxidada** adjective *fem.*
rusty

el **oxígeno** noun *masc.*
oxygen

a
b
c
d
e
f
g
h
i
j
k
l
m
n
o
p
q
r
s
t
u
v
w
x
y
z

• Use el and uno for masculine words and la and una for feminine words.

Pp

la **paciencia** noun *fem.*
patience
tener paciencia to be patient

el or la **paciente** noun *masc. & fem.*
(*of a doctor*) **patient**

el **Pacífico** noun *masc.*
Pacific

el **padrastro** noun *masc.*
stepfather

el **padre** noun *masc.*
father, **dad**
Mi padre es fontanero. My father's
a plumber., My dad's a plumber.
mis padres my parents

> ⚠ **FALSE FRIEND**
> mis padres = my parents (*not* my
> fathers)

el **padrino** noun *masc.*
godfather
mis padrinos my godparents

la **paella** noun *fem.*
paella

> **CULTURE**
> **Paella** is made from rice, cooked with
> chicken, vegetables, and shellfish.

la **paga** noun *fem.*
1 pay
2 (*for children*) **pocket money**

pagar verb
1 to pay
Pagué diez euros. I paid ten euros.
2 to pay for
¿Has pagado la entrada? Have you
paid for the ticket?

la **página** noun *fem.*
page
en la página siete on page seven

el **país** noun *masc.*
1 country
un país extranjero a foreign
country
2 el País de Gales Wales
los Países Bajos the Netherlands
el País Vasco the Basque Country

el **paisaje** noun *masc.*
scenery, **landscape**
Mira el paisaje. Look at the
scenery.

la **paja** noun *fem.*
straw
un sombrero de paja a straw hat

el **pájaro** noun *masc.*
bird

la **pajita** noun *fem.*
(*for drinking*) **straw**
beber con una pajita to drink with
a straw

la **pala** noun *fem.*
1 shovel
2 spade
un cubo y una pala a bucket and
spade
3 (*for table tennis*) **bat**

el **palacio** noun *masc.*
palace

pálido adjective *masc.*,
pálida *fem.*
pale
Estás muy pálido. You look very
pale.

• *Languages and nationalities do not take a capital letter in Spanish.*

los **palillos** plural noun *masc.*
chopsticks

la **palmera** noun *fem.*
palm tree

el **palo** noun *masc.*
stick
Me ha pegado con un palo. He hit me with a stick.

la **paloma** noun *fem.*
pigeon

las **palomitas** plural noun *fem.*
popcorn

🔑 **LANGUAGE**
Spanish = **las palomitas** is plural
English = **popcorn** is singular

el **pan** noun *masc.*
1 bread
¿Quieres pan con mantequilla? Do you want some bread and butter?
el pan tostado toast
una barra de pan a loaf of bread
2 loaf
un pan a loaf of bread

la **panadería** noun *fem.*
baker's shop

Panamá noun *masc.*
Panama

el **panda** noun *masc.*
panda
un oso panda a panda

🔑 **LANGUAGE**
Be careful: **panda** ends in an -**a** but it is not a feminine noun.

la **pandilla** noun *fem.*
gang

el **panecillo** noun *masc.*
bread roll

la **pantalla** noun *fem.*
screen
la pantalla del ordenador the computer screen

los **pantalones** plural noun *masc.*
trousers
unos pantalones a pair of trousers

el **pañal** noun *masc.*
nappy

el **paño** noun *masc.*
cloth

el **pañuelo** noun *masc.*
1 handkerchief
2 scarf
un pañuelo de seda a silk scarf

la **papa** noun *fem.*
(*Latin America*) **potato**

el **Papa** noun *masc.*
Pope

🔑 **LANGUAGE**
Be careful: **Papa** ends in an -**a** but it is not a feminine noun.

el **papá** noun *masc.*
dad
Gracias, papá Thanks, dad
mis papás my mum and dad
Papá Noel Father Christmas

la **papaya** noun *fem.*
pawpaw

el **papel** noun *masc.*
1 paper
una bolsa de papel a paper bag
el papel higiénico toilet paper
el papel pintado wallpaper
el papel de aluminio tinfoil
2 piece of paper
Escribe tu nombre en un papel. Write your name on a piece of paper.
3 (*in a play or film*) **part**
Hace el papel del mago. He plays the part of the wizard.

la **papelera** noun *fem.*
1 wastepaper basket
2 (*in the street*) **litter bin**

a
b
c
d
e
f
g
h
i
j
k
l
m
n
o
p
q
r
s
t
u
v
w
x
y
z

• The months of the year and days of the week do not take a capital letter in Spanish.

la **papelería** noun fem.
stationery shop

las **paperas** plural noun fem.
mumps

el **paquete** noun masc.
1 packet
un paquete de galletas a packet of biscuits
2 parcel

Paquistán noun masc.
Pakistan

par adjective masc. & fem.
un número par an even number

el **par** noun masc.
1 pair
un par de zapatos a pair of shoes
2 un par de a couple of
un par de veces a couple of times

para preposition
1 for
Es para mí. It's for me.
¿Para qué? What for?
para siempre for ever
2 to
el próximo vuelo para Barcelona the next flight to Barcelona
Dame dinero para comprar un helado. Give me some money to buy an ice cream.

la **parada** noun fem.
stop
bajar en la próxima parada to get off at the next stop
una parada de autobús a bus stop

el **paracaídas** noun masc. (plural los **paracaídas**)
parachute

parado adjective masc.,
parada fem.
unemployed

el **paraguas** noun masc. (plural los **paraguas**)
umbrella

Paraguay noun masc.
Paraguay

parar verb
1 to stop
¿Puedes parar el coche? Can you stop the car?
El autobús para delante del colegio. The bus stops in front of the school.
2 (Latin America) **to stand up**

pararse verb
to stop
Mi reloj se ha parado. My watch has stopped.

parecer verb
1 to look
Parecen iguales. They look the same.
Parece que va a llover. It looks like rain.
2 to think
¿Qué te parece el libro? What do you think of the book?
Me parece difícil. I think it's difficult.
Me parece que sí. I think so.

parecerse verb
to look like
Te pareces a tu prima. You look like your cousin.
Las dos hermanas se parecen. The two sisters look alike.

parecido adjective masc.,
parecida fem.
similar
Tus pantalones son parecidos a los míos. Your trousers are similar to mine.

la **pared** noun fem.
wall
en la pared on the wall

• See the centre section for verb tables.

la **pareja** noun *fem.*
1 pair
trabajar en parejas to work in pairs
2 couple
una pareja de casados a married couple
3 (*in a game, school play, etc.*) **partner**

el or la **pariente** noun *masc. & fem.*
relative

⚠ **FALSE FRIEND**
los parientes = relatives (*not* parents)

el **párpado** noun *masc.*
eyelid

el **parque** noun *masc.*
park
un parque de atracciones an amusement park

el **párrafo** noun *masc.*
paragraph

la **parte** noun *fem.*
1 part
la primera parte de la película the first part of the film
en parte partly
2 la mayor parte de most of
la mayor parte del día most of the day
3 (*for saying 'somewhere' etc.*)
estar en alguna parte to be somewhere
ir a alguna parte to go somewhere
No vamos a ninguna parte. We're going nowhere.
por todas partes everywhere

participar verb
to take part
participar en algo to take part in something

particular adjective *masc. & fem.*
private
clases particulares private lessons

la **partida** noun *fem.*
game

una partida de ajedrez a game of chess

el **partido** noun *masc.*
match
un partido de fútbol a football match

la **pasa** noun *fem.*
raisin

el **pasado** noun *masc.*
1 past
en el pasado in the past
2 (*in grammar*) **past tense**

pasado adjective *masc.*,
pasada *fem.*
last
la semana pasada last week
el jueves pasado last Thursday

el **pasajero** noun *masc.*,
la **pasajera** *fem.*
passenger

el **pasaporte** noun *masc.*
passport

pasar verb
1 to pass
¿Me pasas el azúcar, por favor? Can you pass me the sugar, please?
2 to go past
El autobús pasa por el colegio. The bus goes past the school.
3 to go through
pasar por un túnel to go through a tunnel
¡Déjame pasar! Let me go through!
4 to come
Pasaré mañana. I'll come tomorrow.
¿Puedo pasar? Can I come in?
5 to happen
¿Qué pasa? What's happening?
No pasó nada. Nothing happened.
6 to be the matter
¿Qué pasa? What's the matter?
¿Qué te pasa? What's the matter with you?

• *Use* el *and* uno *for masculine words and* la *and* una *for feminine words.*

a
b
c
d
e
f
g
h
i
j
k
l
m
n
o
p
q
r
s
t
u
v
w
x
y
z

7 to spend
He pasado una semana en Bilbao.
I've spent a week in Bilbao.
pasar las vacaciones en ...
to spend the holidays in ...
8 pasarlo bien to have a good time
Lo pasé muy bien. I had a very
good time.

el **pasatiempo** noun masc.
hobby

la **Pascua** noun fem.
Easter
un huevo de Pascua an Easter egg

pasear verb
1 to walk
Me gusta pasear por el parque.
I like walking in the park.
ir a pasear to go for a walk
2 (by bike, car, etc.) **to ride**
Fui a pasear en bici. I went for a
ride on my bike.

el **paseo** noun masc.
1 walk
ir a dar un paseo to go for a walk
2 (by car, bike, etc.) **ride**
ir a dar un paseo en coche to go for
a ride in the car

el **pasillo** noun masc.
corridor
al final del pasillo at the end of the
corridor

el **paso** noun masc.
1 step
Da un paso hacia adelante.
Take one step forward.
oír pasos to hear footsteps
2 way
cerrar el paso to block the way
un paso subterráneo a subway
un paso de peatones a pedestrian
crossing

la **pasta** noun fem.
pasta
Me gusta la pasta. I like pasta.
la pasta de dientes toothpaste

el **pastel** noun masc.
1 cake
Me gustan los pasteles. I like
cakes.
2 pie
un pastel de manzana an apple
pie

la **pastelería** noun fem.
cake shop

la **pastilla** noun fem.
tablet
tomar una pastilla to take a tablet
una pastilla de jabón a bar of soap

el **pasto** noun masc.
(Latin America) **grass**

la **pata** noun fem.
leg
la pata del perro the dog's leg

la **patada** noun fem.
kick
dar una patada a algo to kick
something
Me dio una patada. He kicked me.

la **patata** noun fem.
potato
patatas asadas baked potatoes
patatas fritas chips
una bolsa de patatas fritas
a bag of crisps

LANGUAGE
Word for word **patatas fritas** means
'fried potatoes'. This is the Spanish for
'chips' as well as 'crisps'.

el **patinaje** noun masc.
skating
el patinaje sobre hielo ice skating
el patinaje sobre ruedas
rollerskating

patinar verb
to skate

los **patines** plural noun masc.
skates
los patines de ruedas roller skates
los patines en línea rollerblades

• Languages and nationalities do not take a capital letter in Spanish.

el **patinete** noun *masc.*
scooter

el **patio** noun *masc.*
1 playground
el patio de la escuela the school playground
2 (*between houses*) **courtyard**

el **pato** noun *masc.*
duck

el **pavo** noun *masc.*
turkey
un pavo real a peacock

el **payaso** noun *masc.*,
la **payasa** *fem.*
clown

la **paz** noun *fem.*
peace
vivir en paz to live in peace
¡Déjame en paz! Leave me alone!

el **peatón** noun *masc.* (plural los **peatones**)
pedestrian

las **pecas** plural noun *fem.*
freckles

la **pecera** noun *fem.*
fish tank

el **pecho** noun *masc.*
chest

el **pedal** noun *masc.*
pedal

el **pedazo** noun *masc.*
piece
un pedazo de pan a piece of bread

pedir verb
1 to ask for
He pedido otro plato. I asked for another plate.
2 to ask
pedir un favor to ask a favour
3 (*in a restaurant*) **to order**
Hemos pedido pollo. We've ordered chicken.
4 pedir perdón to apologize

5 pedir prestado to ask to borrow
Pedí prestado un boli. I asked to borrow a pen.
Le pedí un libro. I asked to borrow a book from him., I borrowed a book from him.

pegajoso adjective *masc.*,
pegajosa *fem.*
sticky

el **pegamento** noun *masc.*
glue

pegar verb
1 to stick
He pegado la foto con celo. I stuck the photo with Sellotape.
2 to hit
Me han pegado. They hit me.
3 to give
Me pegó una patada. She gave me a kick.

la **pegatina** noun *fem.*
sticker

el **peinado** noun *masc.*
hairstyle

peinarse verb
1 to comb your hair
2 to brush your hair

el **peine** noun *masc.*
comb

p. ej. abbreviation
e.g.

> **LANGUAGE**
> **p. ej.** is short for **por ejemplo** ('for example').

pelar verb
to peel
pelar una manzana to peel an apple

la **pelea** noun *fem.*
1 fight
2 argument
tener una pelea con alguien to have an argument with somebody

a b c d e f g h i j k l m n o **p** q r s t u v w x y z

• The months of the year and days of the week do not take a capital letter in Spanish.

pelearse verb
1 to fight
José y Gabriel se están peleando. José and Gabriel are fighting.
2 to argue
Sus padres siempre se pelean. His parents are always arguing.

la **película** noun *fem.*
film
¿A qué hora es la película? What time is the film on?

el **peligro** noun *masc.*
danger

peligroso *masc.*,
peligrosa adjective *fem.*
dangerous

pelirrojo adjective *masc.*,
pelirroja *fem.*
ser pelirrojo to have red hair
Soy pelirroja. I have red hair.

el **pelo** noun *masc.*
1 hair
Tengo el pelo rubio. I have fair hair.
2 (*of an animal*) **fur**
el pelo del gato the cat's fur
pelos de gato cat hairs

la **pelota** noun *fem.*
ball
jugar a la pelota to play ball

peludo adjective *masc.*,
peluda *fem.*
hairy

la **peluquería** noun *fem.*
hairdresser's
ir a la peluquería to go to the hairdresser's

el **peluquero** noun *masc.*,
la **peluquera** *fem.*
hairdresser

la **pena** noun *fem.*
1 shame
¡Qué pena! What a shame!

2 *Vale la pena.* It's worth it.
No vale la pena hacerlo. It's not worth doing it.

el **pendiente** noun *masc.*
earring

pensar verb
1 to think
¿Qué piensas? What do you think?
Estoy pensando en ti. I'm thinking about you.
2 *pensar hacer algo* to intend to do something

peor adjective *masc. & fem.*
1 worse
Este libro es peor que el otro. This book is worse than the other one.
Me siento peor. I feel worse.
2 worst
el peor alumno de la clase the worst pupil in the class

peor adverb
1 worse
Yo juego peor que tú. I play worse than you.
2 worst
¿Quién escribe peor? Who writes the worst?

el or la **peor** noun *masc. & fem.*
worst, worst one
Eres el peor del equipo. You're the worst in the team., You're the worst one in the team.

el **pepino** noun *masc.*
cucumber

pequeño adjective *masc.*,
pequeña *fem.*
1 small
una casa pequeña a small house
Soy más pequeño que tú. I'm smaller than you.
2 little
mi hermano pequeño my little brother

• *See the centre section for verb tables.*

124

el **pequeño** noun *masc.*,
 la **pequeña** *fem.*
 1 little boy, **little girl**
 los pequeños little children
 2 youngest
 Es la pequeña de la familia. She's
 the youngest in the family.

la **pera** noun *fem.*
 pear

la **percha** noun *fem.*
 1 coat hanger
 2 coat peg

perder verb
 1 to lose
 He perdido el cuaderno. I've lost
 my exercise book.
 2 to miss
 He perdido el autobús. I've missed
 the bus.
 3 to waste
 perder el tiempo to waste time

perderse verb
 1 to get lost
 Nos perdimos. We got lost.
 2 to miss
 Te has perdido la fiesta. You've
 missed the party.

la **pérdida** noun *fem.*
 Es una pérdida de tiempo. It's a
 waste of time.

perdido adjective *masc.*,
 perdida *fem.*
 lost
 Estoy perdido. I'm lost.
 los objetos perdidos lost property

perdón exclamation
 1 sorry
 Perdón, no te vi. Sorry, I didn't see
 you.
 2 excuse me
 Perdón, ¿dónde está la estación?
 Excuse me, where is the station?

el **perdón** noun *masc.*
 pedir perdón to apologize

perdonar verb
 to forgive
 Te perdono. I forgive you.
 ¡Perdona! Sorry!
 ¡Perdona! ¿Tienes hora? Excuse
 me, do you have the time?

perezoso adjective *masc.*,
 perezosa *fem.*
 lazy
 Es perezosa. She's lazy.

perfeccionar verb
 to improve
 Necesito perfeccionar mi español.
 I need to improve my Spanish.

perfectamente adverb
 perfectly

perfecto adjective *masc.*,
 perfecta *fem.*
 perfect

el **perfume** noun *masc.*
 perfume

el **periódico** noun *masc.*
 newspaper

el **periodo** noun *masc.*
 period

el **periquito** noun *masc.*
 budgie

permanecer verb
 to stay

el **permiso** noun *masc.*
 permission
 tener permiso para hacer algo to
 have permission to do something
 un permiso de conducir a driving
 licence

permitir verb
 to allow

pero conjunction
 but
 Quiero salir, pero está lloviendo.
 I want to go out but it's raining.

a
b
c
d
e
f
g
h
i
j
k
l
m
n
o
p
q
r
s
t
u
v
w
x
y
z

• Use **el** and **uno** for masculine words and **la** and **una** for feminine words.

el **perrito** noun *masc.*
1 puppy
2 un perrito caliente a hot dog

el **perro** noun *masc.*, la **perra** *fem.*
dog

perseguir verb
to chase

la **persiana** noun *fem.*
blind
bajar las persianas to pull down the blinds

la **persona** noun *fem.*
person
una persona inteligente an intelligent person
las personas people
veinte personas twenty people

el **personaje** noun *masc.*
character
los personajes del libro the characters in the book

la **personalidad** noun *fem.*
personality

pertenecer verb
to belong
Esta casa pertenece a mi tío. This house belongs to my uncle.

Perú noun *masc.*
Peru

peruano adjective *masc.*,
peruana *fem.*
Peruvian

el **peruano** noun *masc.*,
la **peruana** *fem.*
Peruvian (*the person*)

la **pesadilla** noun *fem.*
nightmare

pesado adjective *masc.*,
pesada *fem.*
1 heavy
Es muy pesado. It's very heavy.
2 ¡Qué pesado eres! You're a real pest!

pesar verb
1 to weigh
Peso treinta kilos. I weigh thirty kilos.
2 to be heavy
Esta mochila pesa mucho. This schoolbag is heavy.

la **pescadería** noun *fem.*
fishmonger's

el **pescado** noun *masc.*
fish
Me gusta el pescado. I like fish.

el **pescador** noun *masc.*
fisherman

pescar verb
to fish
ir a pescar to go fishing

pesimista adjective *masc. & fem.*
pessimistic

el **peso** noun *masc.*
1 weight
perder peso to lose weight
2 peso

CULTURE
The **peso** is the money used in many Latin American countries.

el **pez** noun *masc.* (plural los **peces**)
fish
Hay muchos peces en el río. There are lots of fish in the river.
un pez de colores a goldfish

el or la **pianista** noun *masc. & fem.*
pianist

el **piano** noun *masc.*
piano
tocar el piano to play the piano

la **picadura** noun *fem.*
1 sting
una picadura de abeja a bee sting
2 bite
una picadura de mosquito a mosquito bite

• *Languages and nationalities do not take a capital letter in Spanish.*

picar verb
1 to sting
Me ha picado una avispa. I've been stung by a wasp.
2 to bite
Me ha picado un mosquito. I've been bitten by a mosquito.
3 to itch
Me pica la pierna. My leg itches.

el **pico** noun *masc.*
beak
Tiene un pico muy largo. It has a very long beak.

el **pie** noun *masc.*
foot
a pie on foot
estar de pie to be standing
ponerse de pie to stand up

la **piedra** noun *fem.*
stone
Me están tirando piedras. They're throwing stones at me.

la **piel** noun *fem.*
1 skin
la piel suave soft skin
2 leather
un bolso de piel a leather bag
3 (*of an apple etc.*) **peel**

la **pierna** noun *fem.*
leg

la **pieza** noun *fem.*
piece
las piezas del rompecabezas the pieces of the jigsaw puzzle

el **pijama** noun *masc.*
pyjamas
Estoy en pijama. I'm in pyjamas.
un pijama a pair of pyjamas

LANGUAGE
Spanish = el pijama is singular
English = pyjamas is plural

LANGUAGE
Be careful: pijama ends in an -a but it is not a feminine noun.

la **pila** noun *fem.*
1 battery
Funciona con pilas. It works on batteries.
2 pile
una pila de libros a pile of books

la **píldora** noun *fem.*
pill

pillar verb
to catch
¡A que no me pillas! I bet you can't catch me!

el or la **piloto** noun *masc. & fem.*
pilot

la **pimienta** noun *fem.*
pepper
¿Quieres sal o pimienta? Would you like salt or pepper?

el **pimiento** noun *masc.*
pepper
un pimiento rojo a red pepper

el **pincel** noun *masc.*
paintbrush

el **ping-pong** noun *masc.*
ping-pong
jugar al ping-pong to play ping-pong

el **pingüino** noun *masc.*
penguin

el **pino** noun *masc.*
pine tree

el **pintalabios** noun *masc.* (plural los **pintalabios**)
lipstick

pintar verb
to paint
Pinta esto en verde. Paint this green.

pintarse verb
to put on make-up
Mi hermana se pinta los labios. My sister wears lipstick.

a b c d e f g h i j k l m n o p q r s t u v w x y z

• The months of the year and days of the week do not take a capital letter in Spanish.

el **pintor** noun masc.,
la **pintora** fem.
 painter

la **pintura** noun fem.
1 paint
 un bote de pintura a tin of paint
2 painting
 una pintura de ... a painting by ...

la **piña** noun fem.
 pineapple

la **pirámide** noun fem.
 pyramid

el or la **pirata** noun masc. & fem.
 pirate

los **Pirineos** plural noun masc.
 Pyrenees

pisar verb
 to tread on
 pisar las flores to tread on the
 flowers
 pisar a alguien to tread on
 somebody's foot

la **piscina** noun fem.
 swimming pool

el **piso** noun masc.
1 floor
 en el segundo piso on the second
 floor
2 flat
 Tenemos un piso en Toledo.
 We have a flat in Toledo.

la **pista** noun fem.
1 (for races) **track**
 una pista de esquí a ski slope
 una pista de hielo an ice rink
 una pista de tenis a tennis court
2 clue
 Dame una pista. Give me a clue.

la **pistola** noun fem.
 gun

el **pito** noun masc.
 whistle

la **pizarra** noun fem.
 blackboard
 escribir algo en la pizarra
 to write something on the
 board

la **pizza** noun fem.
 pizza

el **plan** noun masc.
 plan
 No tengo planes para mañana.
 I don't have any plans for
 tomorrow.

la **plancha** noun fem.
 iron
 No necesita plancha. It doesn't
 need ironing.

planchar verb
 to iron
 planchar una falda to iron a
 skirt

planear verb
 to plan

el **planeta** noun masc.
 planet

⚬⌐ LANGUAGE
Be careful: **planeta** ends in an **-a** but it is
not a feminine noun.

el **plano** noun masc.
1 map
 un plano de Londres a map of
 London
 un plano del metro an
 underground map
2 plan
 el plano de la casa the plan of the
 house

• See the centre section for verb tables.

a b c d e f g h i j k l m n o p q r s t u v w x y z

plano adjective *masc.,*
 plana *fem.*
 flat
 zapatos planos flat shoes

la **planta** noun *fem.*
 1 plant
 regar las plantas to water the plants
 2 floor
 la planta baja the ground floor

plantar verb
 to plant

el **plástico** noun *masc.*
 plastic
 una bolsa de plástico a plastic bag

la **plastilina**® noun *fem.*
 Plasticine®

la **plata** noun *fem.*
 1 silver
 una medalla de plata a silver medal
 2 (*Latin America*) **money**

el **plátano** noun *masc.*
 banana

platicar verb
 (*Latin America*) **to talk**

el **platillo** noun *masc.*
 saucer
 un platillo volante a flying saucer

el **plato** noun *masc.*
 1 plate
 Pásame tu plato. Pass me your plate.
 2 dish
 lavar los platos to wash the dishes
 el plato del día today's special
 3 (*part of a meal*) **course**
 el primer plato the first course

la **playa** noun *fem.*
 beach

la **plaza** noun *fem.*
 1 (*in a town or village*) **square**
 la plaza mayor the main square
 2 (*on a bus, in a car, etc.*) **place**

la **pluma** noun *fem.*
 1 feather
 2 pen, fountain pen

el **plural** noun *masc.*
 plural
 en plural in the plural

pobre adjective *masc. & fem.*
 poor
 una familia pobre a poor family
 ¡Pobre Isabel! Poor Isabel!
 los pobres the poor

LANGUAGE
Use **pobre** after the noun when it means the opposite of 'rich', and before the noun when you feel sad about somebody.

poco adverb
 1 not much
 Hablo muy poco. I don't talk very much.
 poco después soon after
 2 not very
 muy poco conocido not very well known
 3 un poco a bit
 Estoy un poco cansada. I'm a bit tired.
 un poco de pastel a bit of cake
 ¿Quieres un poco de agua? Do you want some water?

poco adjective & pronoun *masc.,*
 poca *fem.*
 1 not much
 Tenemos poco dinero. We don't have much money.
 Comió poco. He didn't eat much.
 2 not many
 Tiene pocas amigas. She doesn't have many friends.
 3 few
 Cuesta unos pocos euros. It costs a few euros.

a b c d e f g h i j k l m n o p q r s t u v w x y z

• *Use* **el** *and* **uno** *for masculine words and* **la** *and* **una** *for feminine words.*

poder verb
can
Puedo hacerlo ahora. I can do it now.
¿Puedo ir al cine? Can I go to the cinema?
Puedes esperar aquí. You can wait here.
¿Puedes ayudarme? – Sí, puedo. Can you help me? – Yes, I can.
¡No puede ser! It can't be true!
Puede ser. Maybe.

podrido adjective *masc.*, **podrida** *fem.*
rotten

el **poema** noun *masc.*
poem

🔑 **LANGUAGE**
Be careful: **poema** ends in an -a but it is not a feminine noun.

el or la **poeta** noun *masc. & fem.*
poet

polar adjective *masc. & fem.*
polar
un oso polar a polar bear

el **policía** noun *masc.*
policeman

la **policía** noun *fem.*
1 police
llamar a la policía to call the police
2 policewoman

el **polideportivo** noun *masc.*
sports centre

el **pollito** noun *masc.*
chick

el **pollo** noun *masc.*
chicken

el **polo** noun *masc.*
ice lolly

el **Polo** noun *masc.*
el Polo Norte the North Pole
el Polo Sur the South Pole

Polonia noun *fem.*
Poland

el **polvo** noun *masc.*
dust
lleno de polvo full of dust
quitar el polvo to do the dusting

el **pomelo** noun *masc.*
grapefruit

el **pomo** noun *masc.*
handle

poner verb
1 to put
¿Dónde pongo mi mochila? Where shall I put my schoolbag?
Ponla aquí. Put it here.
2 (*music, the radio, etc.*) **to put on**
¿Puedo poner la tele? Can I put the TV on?
Ponen una película esta noche. They're putting on a film tonight.
3 to get
poner gasolina to get petrol
4 to set
poner la mesa to set the table
Hay que poner el despertador. We have to set the alarm clock.
5 to make
Eso me pone nervioso. This makes me nervous.

ponerse verb
1 to put on
Me pongo los zapatos. I'm putting my shoes on.
2 to wear
¿Qué te vas a poner? What are you going to wear?
3 to stand
Ponte ahí. Stand over there.
Poneos en fila. Stand in line.
Todo el mundo se puso de pie. Everybody stood up.
4 (*with adjectives*) **to get**
ponerse nervioso to get nervous
5 to set
El sol se pone a las ocho. The sun sets at eight.

• Languages and nationalities do not take a capital letter in Spanish.

el **poni** noun *masc.*
pony

popular adjective *masc. & fem.*
popular

por preposition
1 through
pasar por un túnel to go through a tunnel
por la ventana through the window
2 for
Vendo este libro por diez euros. I'm selling this book for ten euros.
por ejemplo for example
3 by
por correo by post
un libro escrito por ... a book written by ...
4 because of
por el mal tiempo because of the bad weather
5 (*saying where*)
viajar por España to travel around Spain
andar por la calle to walk along the street
6 (*saying when*)
por la mañana in the morning
por la noche at night
7 (*with numbers*)
Tres por tres son nueve. Three times three is nine.
cinco por ciento five per cent
8 ¿por qué? why?
No sé por qué. I don't know why.

porque conjunction
because
Lo hago porque me gusta. I do it because I like it.

portarse verb
to behave
Los niños se portan muy bien. The children behave very well.

portátil adjective *masc. & fem.*
portable

el **portátil** noun *masc.*
laptop

el **portazo** noun *masc.*
dar un portazo to slam the door

la **portería** noun *fem.*
goal

el **portero** noun *masc.*,
la **portera** *fem.*
1 goalkeeper
2 (*in a building*) **caretaker**

Portugal noun *masc.*
Portugal

el **portugués** noun *masc.*
Portuguese
¿Hablas portugués? Do you speak Portuguese?

portugués adjective *masc.*,
portuguesa *fem.*
Portuguese
Fernando es portugués. Fernando is Portuguese.

> **LANGUAGE**
> The plural of **portugués** is **portugueses**.

el **portugués** noun *masc.*,
la **portuguesa** *fem.*
Portuguese man, **Portuguese woman**
los portugueses the Portuguese

la **posibilidad** noun *fem.*
1 chance
tener posibilidades de hacer algo to have a good chance of doing something
2 possibility

posible adjective *masc. & fem.*
possible
Es posible. It's possible.

la **posición** noun *fem.* (plural las **posiciones**)
position

a b c d e f g h i j k l m n o **p** q r s t u v w x y z

• *The months of the year and days of the week do not take a capital letter in Spanish.*

la **postal** noun fem.
postcard

el **póster** noun masc. (plural los **pósters**)
poster

el **postre** noun masc.
dessert
¿Qué hay de postre? What's for dessert?

el **pozo** noun masc.
well
El agua del pozo es buena. The water from the well is good.

practicar verb
to practise
Tienes que practicar tu inglés. You have to practise your English.

práctico adjective masc., **práctica** fem.
1 handy
El móvil es muy práctico. The mobile is very handy.
2 practical
una falda muy práctica a very practical skirt

el **precio** noun masc.
price

precioso adjective masc., **preciosa** fem.
beautiful

el **precipicio** noun masc.
cliff

preferir verb
to prefer
Prefiero el pescado a la carne. I prefer fish to meat.
Prefiero ver la tele. I prefer to watch TV.

la **pregunta** noun fem.
question
hacer una pregunta to ask a question

preguntar verb
to ask
Pregúntale a tu padre. Ask your dad.
Le pregunté la hora. I asked him the time.

preguntarse verb
to wonder
Me pregunto por qué has hecho eso. I wonder why you did that.

prehistórico adjective masc., **prehistórica** fem.
prehistoric

el **premio** noun masc.
prize
ganar un premio to win a prize

prender verb
1 prender fuego a algo to set fire to something
2 (Latin America) **to turn on** (the radio, the lights, etc.)

preocupado adjective masc., **preocupada** fem.
worried
Estoy preocupada por mi hermana. I'm worried about my sister.

preocupar verb
to worry
¿Qué te preocupa? What are you worried about?
preocuparse por algo to worry about something
¡No te preocupes! Don't worry!

preparado adjective masc., **preparada** fem.
ready
Estoy preparado. I'm ready.

preparar verb
1 to get ready
Me estoy preparando para salir. I'm getting ready to go out.

• *See the centre section for verb tables.*

2 to make
Papá está preparando la comida.
Dad's making lunch.
3 to prepare
preparar la clase to prepare the
lesson

la **preposición** noun *fem.* (plural las
preposiciones)
preposition

presentar verb
1 to introduce
Te presento a mi hermano. Can I
introduce you to my brother?
2 to present
presentar un programa to present
a programme
presentarse a un concurso to enter
a competition

presente adjective *masc. & fem.*
present
¿Está presente Javier? Is Javier
present?
¡Presente! Here!

el **presente** noun *masc.*
1 present
el presente y el pasado the present
and the past
2 (*in grammar*) **present tense**

el **presidente** noun *masc.*,
la **presidenta** *fem.*
president

el **preso** noun *masc.*, la **presa** *fem.*
prisoner

prestado adjective *masc.*,
prestada *fem.*
Me ha dejado la bici prestada.
He's lent me his bike.
Pedí dinero prestado. I borrowed
some money.

prestar verb
to lend
¿Me prestas el libro? Can you lend
me the book?

primaria adjective *fem.*
la escuela primaria primary
school

CULTURE
La escuela primaria is for children from 6
to 12.

la **primavera** noun *fem.*
spring
en primavera in the spring

primero adverb
first
Primero cojo el autobús. First I
take the bus.

primero adjective *masc.*,
primera *fem.*

LANGUAGE
The masculine singular **primero** becomes
primer when it is used before a noun.

1 first
la primera página the first page
el primer día the first day
Quedé primero en la carrera.
I came first in the race.
los primeros auxilios first aid
2 el primer ministro the Prime
Minister

el **primero** pronoun *masc.*,
la **primera** *fem.*
first, **first one**
Soy el primero. I'm the first.,
I'm the first one.

el **primo** noun *masc.*, la **prima** *fem.*
cousin

la **princesa** noun *fem.*
princess

principal adjective *masc. & fem.*
main
la calle principal the main street

el **príncipe** noun *masc.*
prince

a b c d e f g h i j k l m n o p q r s t u v w x y z

• *Use* el *and* uno *for masculine words and* la *and* una *for feminine words.*

133

Spanish English

a b c d e f g h i j k l m n o **P** q r s t u v w x y z

el or la **principiante** noun masc. & fem.
beginner

el **principio** noun masc.
beginning
el principio del libro the beginning of the book
a principios de junio at the beginning of June
al principio at first

la **prisa** noun fem.
tener prisa to be in a hurry
Tengo prisa. I'm in a hurry.
¡Date prisa! Hurry up!

los **prismáticos** plural noun masc.
binoculars

privado adjective masc.,
privada fem.
private
una escuela privada a private school

probable adjective masc. & fem.
likely

probablemente adverb
probably

el **probador** noun masc.
changing room

probar verb
(food, machine, etc.) **to try**
Prueba este pastel. – ¿Te gusta?
Try this cake. – Do you like it?

probarse verb
to try on
Quiero probarme estos vaqueros.
I want to try on these jeans.

el **problema** noun masc.
problem

LANGUAGE
Be careful: **problema** ends in an **-a** but it is not a feminine noun.

producir verb
to produce

el or la **profe** noun masc. & fem.
teacher

LANGUAGE
Profe is short for **profesor**.

la **profesión** noun fem. (plural las **profesiones**)
profession

el **profesor** noun masc.,
la **profesora** fem.
teacher
Es profesor de español. He's a Spanish teacher.

⚠ **FALSE FRIEND**
un profesor = a teacher (not a professor)

profundo adjective masc.,
profunda fem.
deep

el **programa** noun masc.
1 programme
un programa de televisión
a TV programme
2 program
He bajado un programa de Internet. I've downloaded a program from the Internet.

LANGUAGE
Be careful: **programa** ends in an **-a** but it is not a feminine noun.

prohibir verb
to forbid
Está prohibido fumar. Smoking is forbidden.
'Prohibido fumar.' 'No smoking.'

la **promesa** noun fem.
promise
cumplir una promesa to keep a promise

prometer verb
to promise
Te lo prometo. I promise.
Ha prometido trabajar más.
He has promised to work harder.

• Languages and nationalities do not take a capital letter in Spanish.

el **pronombre** noun *masc.*
pronoun

el **pronóstico** noun *masc.*
forecast
el pronóstico del tiempo
the weather forecast

pronto adverb
1 soon
lo más pronto posible as soon as
possible
¡Hasta pronto! See you soon!
2 early
Has llegado pronto. You've
arrived early.

la **pronunciación** noun *fem.*
pronunciation

pronunciar verb
to pronounce
¿Cómo se pronuncia este nombre?
How do you pronounce this name?

propio adjective *masc.*, **propia** *fem.*
own
mi propia habitación my own
room

a **propósito** adverb
on purpose
hacer algo a propósito to do
something on purpose

el **protagonista** noun *masc.*
main character
el protagonista de la película
the main character in the film

proteger verb
to protect

protestante adjective *masc. & fem.*
Protestant

protestar verb
to complain
¡No protestes! Don't complain!

el **proverbio** noun *masc.*
proverb

próximo adjective *masc.*,
próxima *fem.*
next
la próxima vez next time
la próxima semana next week

la **prueba** noun *fem.*
test
una prueba de ortografía
a spelling test

el **público** noun *masc.*
1 public
Está abierto al público. It's open to
the public.
2 audience

público adjective *masc.*,
pública *fem.*
public
una biblioteca pública a public
library

el **pueblo** noun *masc.*
1 village
2 small town

el **puente** noun *masc.*
bridge

la **puerta** noun *fem.*
1 door
Llaman a la puerta. There's
somebody at the door.
2 gate
la puerta del jardín the garden
gate

el **puerto** noun *masc.*
port

pues adverb
1 well
¡Pues mira! Well, look!
¡Pues claro! Well, of course!
2 then
Estoy cansado. – Pues vete a la
cama. I'm tired. – Then go to bed.

el **pulgar** noun *masc.*
thumb

a
b
c
d
e
f
g
h
i
j
k
l
m
n
o
p
q
r
s
t
u
v
w
x
y
z

• *The months of the year and days of the week do not take a capital letter in Spanish.*

el **pulmón** noun *masc.* (plural los **pulmones**)
lung

el **pulpo** noun *masc.*
octopus

pulsar verb
to press
Pulsa el botón. Press the button.

la **pulsera** noun *fem.*
bracelet

la **punta** noun *fem.*
1 (*of a pencil, knife, etc.*) **point**
sacar punta a un lápiz to sharpen a pencil
2 **tip**
la punta de la nariz the tip of my nose

de **puntillas** adverb
on tiptoe

el **punto** noun *masc.*
1 **point**
sacar un punto to score a point
2 (*in a sentence*) **full stop**
punto y aparte full stop, new paragraph
3 **dot**
el punto sobre la 'i' the dot on the 'i'
4 **stitch**
El médico me puso tres puntos. The doctor gave me three stitches.
5 **knitting**
hacer punto to knit
una chaqueta de punto a knitted cardigan
6 estar a punto de hacer algo to be about to do something

la **puntuación** noun *fem.*
punctuation

> 🔑 **LANGUAGE**
> Spanish = **puntuación**
> English = **punctuation**

puntual adjective *masc. & fem.*
punctual
Es muy puntual. He's very punctual.

> 🔑 **LANGUAGE**
> Spanish = **puntual**
> English = **punctual**

el **puñetazo** noun *masc.*
punch
dar un puñetazo a alguien to punch somebody
Me ha dado un puñetazo. He punched me.

el **puño** noun *masc.*
fist

puro adjective *masc.*, **pura** *fem.*
pure

Qq

que pronoun
1 **who**
mi amigo que tiene el pelo largo my friend who has long hair
2 **that**, **which**
los libros que están en la mesa the books that are on the table, the books which are on the table
los animales que tengo the animals (that) I have

que conjunction
1 **that**
Creo que está lloviendo. I think (that) it's raining.
2 (*when comparing*) **than**
Soy más alta que tú. I'm taller than you.

• *See the centre section for verb tables.*

qué pronoun & adjective

1 (*in questions*) **what**

¿Qué estás haciendo? What are you doing?

¿Qué es? What is it?

¿Qué? What?

¿Qué hora es? What time is it?

¿Qué tal? How are you doing?

2 which, what

¿Qué libro quieres leer? Which book do you want to read?, What book do you want to read?

¿Qué coche es? Which car is it?

3 (*in exclamations*) **what**

¡Qué lástima! What a pity!

¡Qué vestidos tan bonitos! What pretty dresses!

qué adverb

¡Qué bonito! It's really pretty!

¡Qué difícil! It's really difficult!

quedar verb

1 to be left

Quedan tres manzanas. There are three apples left.

Me quedan diez euros. I have ten euros left.

2 to suit

El azul te queda bien. Blue suits you.

3 to meet, to plan to meet

He quedado con una amiga. I'm meeting a friend., I've planned to meet a friend.

¿Dónde quedamos? Where shall we meet?

quedarse verb

1 to stay

Me quedé en casa. I stayed at home.

Me quedé dormido. I fell asleep.

2 quedarse con algo to keep something

Quédate con el libro. You can keep the book.

quejarse verb

to complain

Se queja de todo. He complains about everything.

quemar verb

to burn

Quemó la basura. He burned the rubbish.

quemarse verb

1 to burn

Se está quemando algo. Something's burning.

Se ha quemado la casa. The house has burnt down.

2 to burn yourself

Se quemó. He burned himself.

Me he quemado el dedo. I've burnt my finger.

querer verb

1 to want

¿Qué quieres? What do you want?

Quiero ir al cine. I want to go to the cinema.

2 to love

María quiere a Juan. María loves Juan.

3 (*in polite questions*)

¿Quieres ...? Would you like ...?

¿Quieres beber algo? Would you like something to drink?

4 (*when asking for something*) Quisiera ... I would like ...

Quisiera hablar con la maestra. I would like to speak to the teacher.

5 querer decir to mean

¿Qué quiere decir esta palabra? What does this word mean?

querido adjective *masc.*, **querida** *fem.*

dear

Querido Pedro ... Dear Pedro ...

el **queso** noun *masc.*

cheese

• *Use* el *and* uno *for masculine words and* la *and* una *for feminine words.*

Spanish English

a
b
c
d
e
f
g
h
i
j
k
l
m
n
o
p
q
r
s
t
u
v
w
x
y
z

quién pronoun
1 (*in questions*) **who**
¿Quién es? Who is it?
¿Quiénes son? Who are they?
2 ¿de quién? **whose?**
¿De quién es? Whose is it?
¿De quién son estos calcetines?
Whose socks are these?

quieto adjective *masc.*, **quieta** *fem.*
still
Estate quieta. Keep still.

quince number
1 fifteen
Mi primo tiene quince años.
My cousin is fifteen.
2 (*with dates*) **fifteenth**
el quince de mayo the fifteenth of
May

quinientos number *masc.*,
quinientas *fem.*
five hundred

quinto adjective *masc.*, **quinta** *fem.*
fifth
en el quinto piso on the fifth floor

el **quiosco** noun *masc.*
1 (*for newspapers*) **news-stand**
2 (*for flowers, ice creams, etc.*) **kiosk**

quisiera verb SEE **querer**
would like
Quisiera una taza de té. I would
like a cup of tea.

quitar verb
1 to take away
Quita tus libros de aquí. Take your
books away from here.
2 to take off
¿Puedes quitarte los zapatos?
Can you take your shoes off?
3 to take
¿Quién me ha quitado la mochila?
Who's taken my bag?

quizá, **quizás** adverb
maybe, **perhaps**

Rr

el **rabo** noun *masc.*
tail

la **ración** noun *fem.* (plural las
raciones)
portion
una ración de patatas fritas
a portion of chips

el **radiador** noun *masc.*
radiator

⚷ LANGUAGE
Spanish = radiador
English = radiator

la **radio** noun *fem.*
radio
Lo oí por la radio. I heard it on the
radio.

la **radiografía** noun *fem.*
X-ray
Me han hecho una radiografía.
I've had an X-ray.

la **raíz** noun *fem.* (plural las **raíces**)
root

la **rama** noun *fem.*
branch

el **ramo** noun *masc.*
bunch
un ramo de flores a bunch of
flowers

la **rana** noun *fem.*
frog

rápidamente adverb
quickly

• *Languages and nationalities do not take a capital letter in Spanish.*

rápido adverb
fast
Hablas muy rápido. You speak too fast.
¡Rápido! Quick!

rápido adjective *masc.*, **rápida** *fem.*
1 quick
una respuesta rápida a quick reply
2 fast
un coche rápido a fast car

la **raqueta** noun *fem.*
racket
una raqueta de tenis a tennis racket

raro adjective *masc.*, **rara** *fem.*
strange
Aurelia es un poco rara. Aurelia is a bit strange.

el **rascacielos** noun *masc.* (plural los **rascacielos**)
skyscraper

rascarse verb
to scratch
Me rasco la nariz. I scratch my nose.

la **rata** noun *fem.*
rat

el **rato** noun *masc.*
while
quedarse un rato to stay a while

el **ratón** noun *masc.* (plural los **ratones**)
mouse
una alfombrilla de ratón a mouse mat

LANGUAGE
As in English, a **ratón** is an animal *and* a part of your computer.

 FALSE FRIEND
un ratón = a mouse (*not* a rat)

el **ratoncito** noun *masc.*
little mouse
el ratoncito Pérez the tooth fairy

 CULTURE
Spanish children leave their tooth under the pillow at bedtime and in the morning find some money or a present there instead. It's not a fairy but a little mouse (**ratoncito**) that comes to take the tooth away.

la **raya** noun *fem.*
1 stripe
una camisa con rayas azules a shirt with blue stripes
2 (*in your hair*) **parting**

el **rayo** noun *masc.*
lightning
los rayos lightning

la **raza** noun *fem.*
1 (*of dog, cat, etc.*) **breed**
2 race
la raza humana the human race

la **razón** noun *fem.*
1 reason
¿Por qué razón? For what reason?
2 tener razón to be right
Tengo razón. I'm right.
No tienes razón. You're wrong.

LANGUAGE
Spanish = **tener** razón **Tengo razón.**
English = **to be right** **I'm right.**

real adjective *masc. & fem.*
1 real
la vida real real life
2 royal
la familia real the royal family

la **realidad** noun *fem.*
reality
en realidad actually

• *The months of the year and days of the week do not take a capital letter in Spanish.*

a
b
c
d
e
f
g
h
i
j
k
l
m
n
o
p
q
r
s
t
u
v
w
x
y
z

las **rebajas** plural noun *fem.*
sales
¿Cuándo empiezan las rebajas?
When do the sales start?

la **rebanada** noun *fem.*
slice
una rebanada de pan a slice of
bread

rebobinar verb
to rewind
rebobinar un vídeo to rewind a
video

la **recepción** noun *fem.*
(*desk in a hotel*) **reception**

el or la **recepcionista** noun *masc.* &
fem.
receptionist

la **receta** noun *fem.*
recipe
la receta de un pastel the recipe
for a cake

recibir verb
to get, to receive
¿Has recibido mi carta? Have you
got my letter?

el **recibo** noun *masc.*
1 bill
el recibo del teléfono the phone
bill
2 receipt

recién adverb
just
Está recién pintado. It's just been
painted.

reciente adjective *masc.* & *fem.*
recent

recientemente adverb
recently

recoger verb
1 to pick up
Recoge estos libros del suelo.
Pick up these books from the floor.
¿Me puedes recoger a las dos?
Can you pick me up at two?

2 to tidy up
recoger la habitación to tidy up
the room
3 to pick
recoger flores to pick flowers

recomendar verb
to recommend

la **recompensa** noun *fem.*
reward

reconocer verb
to recognize

el **récord** noun *masc.* (plural los
récords)
record
batir el récord mundial to beat the
world record

recordar verb
1 to remember
No recuerdo su nombre. I don't
remember his name.
2 to remind
Recuérdame cómo se llama.
Remind me what his name is.
Me recuerdas a mi hermana.
You remind me of my sister.

recortar verb
to cut out
recortar una foto to cut out a
picture

el **recreo** noun *masc.*
playtime
Salimos al recreo a las dos.
We have playtime at two.

el **rectángulo** noun *masc.*
rectangle

recto adverb
seguir todo recto to go straight
ahead

recto adjective *masc.*, **recta** *fem.*
straight
una línea recta a straight line

• *See the centre section for verb tables.*

el **recuerdo** noun *masc.*
1 memory
 tener buenos recuerdos de algo
 to have good memories of
 something
2 souvenir
 Tráeme un recuerdo de tu
 viaje. Bring me a souvenir of your
 trip.
 una tienda de recuerdos a souvenir
 shop
3 recuerdos best wishes
 Recuerdos a tu mamá. Best wishes
 to your mum.

la **red** noun *fem.*
1 net
 La pelota ha tocado la red.
 The ball has touched the net.
2 la Red the Net
 navegar por la Red to surf the Net

redondo adjective *masc.*,
 redonda *fem.*
round
 una mesa redonda a round table

reducir verb
 to reduce

reflexivo *masc.* adjective
 (*in grammar*)
 un verbo reflexivo
 a reflexive verb

> ⚲ **LANGUAGE**
> A **verbo reflexivo** is a verb that is used
> with a pronoun, e.g. **despertarse** (to
> wake up): **me despierto** is 'I wake up',
> **te despiertas** is 'you wake up', etc.

el **refrán** noun *masc.* (plural los
 refranes)
 saying

el **refresco** noun *masc.*
 soft drink

regalar verb
 to give (*as a present*)
 Me han regalado una bici para mi
 cumpleaños. They've given me a
 bike for my birthday.

el **regalo** noun *masc.*
 present
 hacer un regalo a alguien to give
 somebody a present
 un regalo de cumpleaños
 a birthday present

regañar verb
 to tell off

regar verb
 to water

la **región** noun *fem.* (plural las
 regiones)
 region

la **regla** noun *fem.*
1 ruler
2 rule
 las reglas del juego the rules of the
 game

el **reglamento** noun *masc.*
 rules
 el reglamento del colegio the
 school rules

regular adjective *masc. & fem.*
1 regular
 un verbo regular a regular verb
2 not very good
 Es una película regular. It's not a
 very good film.
3 not too bad
 ¿Cómo estás? – Regular. How are
 you? – Not too bad.

la **reina** noun *fem.*
 queen

el **reino** noun *masc.*
 kingdom
 el Reino Unido the United Kingdom

reír verb
 to laugh
 Me ha hecho reír. He made me
 laugh.

reírse verb
 to laugh
 Me río con mis amigos. I laugh a
 lot with my friends.

a b c d e f g h i j k l m n o p q r s t u v w x y z

• *Use* **el** *and* **uno** *for masculine words and* **la** *and* **una** *for feminine words.*

Spanish English

relajar verb
to relax
Me relaja. It relaxes me.
Voy a relajarme. I'm going to relax.

el **relámpago** noun *masc.*
flash of lightning
los relámpagos lightning

la **religión** noun *fem.* (plural las religiones)
religion

religioso adjective *masc.*, **religiosa** *fem.*
religious

rellenar verb
to fill in
rellenar un formulario to fill in a form

el **reloj** noun *masc.*
1 clock
un reloj de pared a wall clock
2 watch
mi reloj digital my digital watch

remar verb
to row

el **remedio** noun *masc.*
No hay más remedio. There's no other choice.

el **renacuajo** noun *masc.*
tadpole

el **reno** noun *masc.*
reindeer

reñir verb
1 to tell off
Me ha reñido. She told me off.
2 to have a fight
He reñido con mi hermano. I had a fight with my brother.

reparar verb
to repair

repartir verb
1 to hand out
Reparte los libros. Hand out the books.
2 to deliver
repartir el correo to deliver the mail
3 to share

repasar verb
to revise
Tengo que repasar. I have to revise.

el **repaso** noun *masc.*
revision
un ejercicio de repaso a revision exercise

de **repente** adverb
suddenly

repetir verb
1 to repeat
¿Puedes repetir la pregunta? Can you repeat the question?
2 to say again
Repite, por favor. Can you say that again, please?

representar verb
1 to put on
representar una obra to put on a play
2 to show
¿Qué representa este dibujo? What does this picture show?

el **reproductor** noun *masc.*
player
un reproductor CD a CD player
un reproductor MP3 an MP3 player

el **reptil** noun *masc.*
reptile

resbalarse verb
to slip
resbalarse en el suelo to slip on the floor

a b c d e f g h i j k l m n o p q r s t u v w x y z

• *Languages and nationalities do not take a capital letter in Spanish.*

reservar verb
to reserve
Esta mesa está reservada.
This table is reserved.

el **resfriado** noun *masc.*
cold
Tengo un resfriado. I have a cold.

resfriado adjective *masc.*,
resfriada *fem.*
estar resfriado to have a cold

resolver verb
to solve

respetar verb
to obey
respetar las reglas to obey the
rules

respirar verb
to breathe

responder verb
to answer
No responde. He's not answering.
responder a una pregunta
to answer a question

responsable adjective *masc. & fem.*
responsible
Es un niño muy responsable.
He's a very responsible boy.

LANGUAGE
Spanish = responsable
English = responsible

el or la **responsable** noun *masc. &*
fem.
1 person responsible
2 person in charge
¿Quién es el responsable?
Who's the person in charge?

la **respuesta** noun *fem.*
answer
la respuesta correcta the right
answer

el **restaurante** noun *masc.*
restaurant

el **resto** noun *masc.*
rest
el resto del libro the rest of the
book

el **resultado** noun *masc.*
1 result
los resultados de los exámenes
the exam results
2 score
El resultado fue tres a dos.
The score was three two.

el **retraso** noun *masc.*
delay
llegar con retraso to arrive late
El tren lleva retraso. The train is
late.

el **retrato** noun *masc.*
portrait

la **reunión** noun *fem.* (plural las
reuniones)
meeting

reunirse verb
1 to gather
Los alumnos se reúnen delante del
colegio. The pupils gather in front
of the school.
2 to get together
La familia se reúne los domingos.
The family gets together on
Sundays.

revelar verb
to develop
revelar las fotos to develop the
photos

reventar verb
to burst
Reventó el globo. She burst the
balloon.

el **revés** adverb
1 inside out
Tus calcetines están al revés.
Your socks are inside out.
2 upside down
El cuadro está al revés. The picture
is upside down.

a b c d e f g h i j k l m n o p q r s t u v w x y z

• *The months of the year and days of the week do not take a capital letter in Spanish.*

143

a
b
c
d
e
f
g
h
i
j
k
l
m
n
o
p
q
r
s
t
u
v
w
x
y
z

3 back to front
Llevas el jersey al revés. You're wearing your sweater back to front.

la **revista** noun *fem.*
magazine

el **rey** noun *masc.*
king
los reyes de España the King and Queen of Spain
los Reyes Magos the Three Wise Men

 CULTURE
In Spain the 6th January is known as **el día de Reyes** (the day of the Three Wise Men) and is the day Spanish children usually receive their Christmas presents. They put out their shoes for the Wise Men to leave the presents in.

rezar verb
to pray

rico adjective *masc.*, **rica** *fem.*
1 rich
Es rica. She's rich.
2 delicious
La paella está muy rica. The paella is really delicious.

el **rico** noun *masc.*, la **rica** *fem.*
rich man, **rich woman**

ridículo adjective *masc.*,
ridícula *fem.*
ridiculous

la **rima** noun *fem.*
rhyme

el **rincón** noun *masc.* (plural los **rincones**)
corner

el **rinoceronte** noun *masc.*
rhinoceros

el **río** noun *masc.*
river

la **risa** noun *fem.*
laugh

el **ritmo** noun *masc.*
rhythm

rizado adjective *masc.*, **rizada** *fem.*
curly
tener el pelo rizado to have curly hair

robar verb
1 to steal
robar dinero a alguien to steal money from somebody
Me han robado la mochila. Somebody has stolen my schoolbag.
2 to rob
Nos han robado. We've been robbed.

el **robo** noun *masc.*
1 robbery
2 (*of money, things*) **theft**

el **robot** noun *masc.* (plural los **robots**)
robot

la **roca** noun *fem.*
rock

rodar verb
to roll
La pelota está rodando. The ball is rolling.

rodear verb
to surround
rodeado de amigos surrounded by friends

la **rodilla** noun *fem.*
knee
ponerse de rodillas to kneel down
Está de rodillas. He's kneeling down.

rojo adjective *masc.*, **roja** *fem.*
red
una camisa roja a red shirt

el **rojo** noun *masc.*
red
El rojo te queda bien. Red looks good on you.

• *See the centre section for verb tables.*

el **rollo** noun *masc.*
1 roll
un rollo de papel a roll of paper
2 ¡Qué rollo! How boring!

el **rompecabezas** noun *masc.*
(plural los **rompecabezas**)
jigsaw puzzle

> ⚷ **LANGUAGE**
> The Spanish comes from **rompe** (it breaks) and **cabezas** (heads)!

romper verb
1 to break
He roto una taza. I've broken a cup.
2 to tear
Rompí la página. I tore the page.

romperse verb
1 to break
La lámpara se ha roto. The lamp has broken.
Se rompió la pierna. He broke his leg.
2 to get torn
La camisa se ha roto. The shirt has got torn.

la **ropa** noun *fem.*
clothes
La ropa está en el armario.
The clothes are in the wardrobe.
la ropa interior underwear

> ⚷ **LANGUAGE**
> Spanish = **la ropa** is singular
> English = **clothes** is plural

rosa adjective *masc. & fem.*
pink
calcetines rosa pink socks

> ⚷ **LANGUAGE**
> The adjective **rosa** is the same in the masculine, feminine, and plural.

el **rosa** noun *masc.*
pink
No me gusta el rosa. I don't like pink.

la **rosa** noun *fem.*
rose

roto adjective *masc.*, **rota** *fem.*
1 broken
una taza rota a broken cup
2 torn
una camisa rota a torn shirt

la **rotonda** noun *fem.*
(*for traffic*) **roundabout**

rubio adjective *masc.*, **rubia** *fem.*
blond
tener el pelo rubio to have blond hair
una niña rubia a blonde girl

la **rueda** noun *fem.*
1 wheel
la rueda delantera the front wheel
2 tyre

el **rugby** noun *masc.*
rugby
jugar al rugby to play rugby

rugir verb
to roar
El león ruge. The lion roars.

el **ruido** noun *masc.*
noise
hacer ruido to make a noise

las **ruinas** plural noun *fem.*
(*of a castle etc.*) **ruins**
las ruinas del castillo the ruins of the castle

Rusia noun *fem.*
Russia

el **ruso** noun *masc.*
Russian
hablar ruso to speak Russian

ruso adjective *masc.*, **rusa** *fem.*
Russian
Es ruso. He's Russian.

el **ruso** noun *masc.*, la **rusa** *fem.*
Russian

a b c d e f g h i j k l m n o p q r s t u v w x y z

• Use **el** and **uno** for masculine words and **la** and **una** for feminine words.

Ss

a
b
c
d
e
f
g
h
i
j
k
l
m
n
o
p
q
r
s
t
u
v
w
x
y
z

el **sábado** noun *masc.*
Saturday
Hoy es sábado. Today is Saturday.
el sábado on Saturday
Mis abuelos llegan el sábado.
My grandparents arrive on
Saturday.
los sábados on Saturdays
Los sábados vamos a la biblioteca.
On Saturdays we go to the library.

🔑 **LANGUAGE**
Remember the difference between **el**
sábado (one Saturday only) and **los**
sábados (every Saturday).

la **sábana** noun *fem.*
sheet

saber verb
1 to know
¿Sabes dónde están? Do you know
where they are?
Ya lo sé. I know.
No lo sé. I don't know.
2 can, know how to
¿Sabes montar en bicicleta?
Can you ride a bike?
Pedro y Juan saben leer. Pedro and
Juan can read.
3 to taste
Sabe a fresa. It tastes of
strawberry.

sabio adjective *masc.*, **sabia** *fem.*
wise

el **sabor** noun *masc.*
1 taste
Tiene un sabor amargo. It has a
bitter taste.
2 flavour
cuatro sabores diferentes
four different flavours

el **sacapuntas** noun *masc.* (plural
los **sacapuntas**)
pencil sharpener

sacar verb
1 to take out
sacar algo del bolsillo to take
something out of your pocket
sacar la lengua to stick out your
tongue
2 to get
¿Has sacado los billetes? Have you
got the tickets?
Siempre saco buenas notas.
I always get good marks.
3 to take
sacar fotos to take photos
He sacado una foto de mi clase.
I've taken a photo of my class.
4 sacar punta a un lápiz to sharpen a
pencil

el **sacerdote** noun *masc.*
priest

el **saco** noun *masc.*
1 sack
un saco de patatas a sack of
potatoes
un saco de dormir a sleeping bag
2 (*Latin America*) **sweater**

sacudir verb
to shake

sagrado adjective *masc.*,
sagrada *fem.*
holy
una ciudad sagrada a holy city

la **sal** noun *fem.*
salt

la **sala** noun *fem.*
1 room
una sala de espera a waiting room
la sala de estar the living room
la sala de profesores the staff
room
2 hall
una sala de conciertos a concert
hall

• *Languages and nationalities do not take a capital letter in Spanish.*

salado adjective *masc.*, **salada** *fem.*
salty
Está muy salado. It's very salty.

la **salchicha** noun *fem.*
sausage

la **salida** noun *fem.*
1 exit
una salida de emergencia an emergency exit
2 departure
la hora de salida the departure time
3 start
la salida de la carrera the start of the race

salir verb
1 to go out
Ha salido al jardín. He's gone out into the garden.
María sale con mi hermano. María's going out with my brother.
2 to come out
¿A qué hora sales del colegio? What time do you come out of school?
3 to leave
El avión sale a las ocho. The plane leaves at eight.
Salgo de casa a las seis. I leave the house at six.
4 (*from a computer program*) **to log off**

el **salón** noun *masc.* (plural los **salones**)
living room

la **salsa** noun *fem.*
sauce

saltar verb
to jump
¡Salta! Jump!
saltar el arroyo to jump over the stream
saltar a la cuerda to skip

el **salto** noun *masc.*
jump
dar un salto to jump

la **salud** noun *fem.*
health

saludar verb
1 to say hello
Saluda a la profesora. Say hello to the teacher.
2 to wave
Me saludó con la mano. He waved to me.

el **saludo** noun *masc.*
greeting
Te manda un saludo. He sends you his best wishes.
Saludos de Álex. (*in a letter*) With best wishes, Álex.

salvaje adjective *masc. & fem.*
wild
animales salvajes wild animals

el **salvavidas** noun *masc.* (plural los **salvavidas**)
lifebelt

San adjective *masc.*
Saint
San Pablo Saint Paul

⚷ LANGUAGE
San is short for **Santo**.

la **sandalia** noun *fem.*
sandal

la **sandía** noun *fem.*
watermelon

el **sándwich** noun *masc.* (plural los **sándwiches**)
sandwich
un sándwich de queso a cheese sandwich

los **Sanfermines** plural noun *masc.*

 CULTURE
This is a festival in honour of St. Fermin that people celebrate in Pamplona every July when they let bulls run through the streets of the town.

• *The months of the year and days of the week do not take a capital letter in Spanish.*

Spanish English

a b c d e f g h i j k l m n o p q r s t u v w x y z

sangrar verb
to bleed

la **sangre** noun *fem.*
blood

sano adjective *masc.*, **sana** *fem.*
healthy
una vida sana a healthy life
sano y salvo safe and sound

santo adjective *masc.*, **santa** *fem.*
holy

el **santo** noun *masc.*, la **santa** *fem.*
1 saint
Es un santo. He's a saint.
el día de Todos los Santos
All Saints' Day
2 name day
Hoy es mi santo. Today it's my name day.

CULTURE
In Spain every day of the year has its own saint. If somebody has the same name as the saint whose day it is, they often celebrate their special 'name day'.

el **sapo** noun *masc.*
toad

el **sarampión** noun *masc.*
measles

la **sardina** noun *fem.*
sardine

el **sarpullido** noun *masc.*
rash

la **sartén** noun *fem.* (plural las **sartenes**)
frying pan

el **satélite** noun *masc.*
satellite
la televisión vía satélite satellite television

el **saxofón** noun *masc.* (plural los **saxofones**)
saxophone
tocar el saxofón to play the saxophone

se pronoun
1 (*talking about a boy or man*) **himself**
Se está lavando. He's washing himself.
2 (*talking about a girl or woman*) **herself**
Se ha hecho daño. She has hurt herself.
3 (*talking about a thing or animal*)
itself
El perro se ha cortado. The dog has cut itself.
4 themselves
Se miran al espejo. They look at themselves in the mirror.
5 (*polite form*) **yourself** (plural **yourselves**)
¿Se ha hecho daño, señor? Have you hurt yourself, sir?
6 each other
Se conocen. They know each other.
7 (*no translation*)
Se sentó. He sat down.
No se acuerdan. They don't remember.
8 (*with parts of the body, clothes, etc.*)
his, her, its, their, your
Se ha roto la pierna. He's broken his leg.
Se pone la chaqueta. He puts on his jacket.
Se lavan las manos. They wash their hands.

LANGUAGE
Se is used instead of **le** and **les** when there is another pronoun, e.g. **se lo** instead of **le lo**.

9 to him, him
Di a Javier que se lo he mandado. Tell Javier that I've sent it to him.
No se lo digas. Don't tell him.
10 to her, her
Isabel lo quiere y su hermana se lo ha dado. Isabel wants it and her sister gave it to her.
Dáselo. Give it to her.

• *See the centre section for verb tables.*

11 to them, **them**
Les gusta mi libro. ¿Puedo dárselo? They like my book. Can I give it to them?
Se lo he preguntado. I've asked them.

12 (*polite form*) **to you**, **you**
Se la han mandado, señorita. They've sent it to you, miss.
Se lo dije a usted. I told you.

13 (*in third person phrases*)
Se puede comprar esto en el supermercado. You can buy this in the supermarket.
'Se habla inglés'. 'English is spoken'.

el **secador de pelo** noun *masc.*
hairdryer

secar verb
to dry
secar los platos to dry the dishes
Me estoy secando el pelo. I'm drying my hair.

la **sección** noun *fem.* (plural las **secciones**)
section, **department**
¿Dónde está la sección de juguetes? Where is the toy section?, Where is the toy department?

seco adjective *masc.*, **seca** *fem.*
dry
La pintura está seca. The paint is dry.

el **secretario** noun *masc.*, la **secretaria** *fem.*
secretary
Mi hermana es secretaria. My sister's a secretary.

el **secreto** noun *masc.*
secret
guardar un secreto to keep a secret

secreto adjective *masc.*, **secreta** *fem.*
secret

la **sed** noun *fem.*
thirst
tener sed to be thirsty
Tengo mucha sed. I'm very thirsty.

🗝 **LANGUAGE**
Spanish = **tener** sed Tengo sed.
English = **to be** thirsty I'm thirsty.

la **seda** noun *fem.*
silk

en seguida adverb
straight away
Voy en seguida. I'm coming straight away.

seguir verb
1 to follow
Sígueme. Follow me.
2 to carry on
seguir haciendo algo to carry on doing something
Quiero seguir leyendo. I want to carry on reading.
3 (*used for saying something is still going on*) Sigue lloviendo. It's still raining.
¿Siguen en clase? Are they still in class?

según preposition
according to

el **segundo** noun *masc.*
second
un minuto y veinte segundos one minute and twenty seconds

segundo adjective *masc.*, **segunda** *fem.*
second
por segunda vez for the second time
Quedé segunda en la carrera. I came second in the race.

la **seguridad** noun *fem.*
safety

a
b
c
d
e
f
g
h
i
j
k
l
m
n
o
p
q
r
s
t
u
v
w
x
y
z

• Use **el** and **uno** for masculine words and **la** and **una** for feminine words.

Spanish English

a
b
c
d
e
f
g
h
i
j
k
l
m
n
o
p
q
r
s
t
u
v
w
x
y
z

seguro adjective *masc.*,
segura *fem.*
1 safe
Aquí estoy seguro. I'm safe here.
2 sure
No estoy segura. I'm not sure.
3 certain
Puedo venir pero no es seguro.
I can come but it's not certain.

seis number
1 six
Tengo seis años. I'm six.
Son las seis. It's six o'clock.
2 (*with dates*) **sixth**
el seis de abril the sixth of April

seleccionar verb
to select

el **sello** noun *masc.*
stamp
¿Coleccionas sellos? Do you
collect stamps?

la **selva** noun *fem.*
1 forest
una selva tropical a tropical rain
forest
2 jungle

el **semáforo** noun *masc.*
traffic lights
El semáforo está en rojo.
The traffic lights are red.

la **semana** noun *fem.*
1 week
la semana pasada last week
la semana que viene next week
entre semana during the week
2 la Semana Santa Holy Week
en Semana Santa at Easter

 CULTURE
Semana Santa means the whole Easter
period and can often be translated by
'Easter'. Spanish people take part in
religious processions, such as the famous
one in Seville.

el **semicírculo** noun *masc.*
semicircle

la **semifinal** noun *fem.*
semifinal

la **semilla** noun *fem.*
seed

sencillo adjective *masc.*,
sencilla *fem.*
simple
Es muy sencillo. It's very simple.

sensato adjective *masc.*,
sensata *fem.*
sensible
un niño sensato a sensible boy

sensible adjective *masc. & fem.*
sensitive
Raúl es muy sensible. Raúl is very
sensitive.

⚠️ **FALSE FRIEND**
sensible = sensitive (*not* sensible)

sentado adjective *masc.*,
sentada *fem.*
sitting
Estoy sentado en la silla.
I'm sitting on the chair.

sentarse verb
1 to sit down
Me senté en el sillón. I sat down on
the armchair.
¡Siéntate, Rosa! Sit down, Rosa!
¡Niños, sentaos! Sit down,
children!
2 to sit
¿Dónde puedo sentarme? Where
can I sit?

el **sentido** noun *masc.*
sense
No tiene sentido. It doesn't make
sense.
tener sentido del humor to have a
sense of humour

sentir verb
1 to feel
sentir un dolor en el brazo to feel a
pain in your arm

• *Languages and nationalities do not take a capital letter in Spanish.*

2 to be sorry
Lo siento. I'm sorry.
Siento mucho llegar tarde. I'm very sorry I'm late.

sentirse verb
to feel
No me siento bien. I don't feel well.
¿Te sientes mal? Do you feel ill?

la **seña** noun *fem.*
sign
hacer una seña to make a sign

la **señal** noun *fem.*
sign
una buena señal a good sign
una señal de tráfico a road sign

señalar verb
1 (*with your finger*) **to point**
Señala tu colegio con el dedo.
Point to your school.
2 to mark
Señala con una cruz. Mark with a cross.

las **señas** plural noun *fem.*
address
Dame tus señas. Give me your address.

el **señor** noun *masc.*
1 man
¿Qué quiere ese señor? What does that man want?
2 ¡Buenos días, señor! Good morning!

🔑 **LANGUAGE**
Used when talking to a man in a polite way and not usually translated, though 'sir' is sometimes used in English, especially at school, e.g. Sí, señor (Yes, sir).

3 Mr
el señor Lorca Mr Lorca

🔑 **LANGUAGE**
Señor is usually written on an envelope as Sr., e.g. Sr. Lorca.

la **señora** noun *fem.*
1 lady
Esa señora es mi tía. That lady is my aunt.
2 ¡Adiós, señora! Goodbye!

🔑 **LANGUAGE**
Used when talking to a woman in a polite way and not usually translated, though 'madam' is sometimes used in English.

3 Mrs
la señora González Mrs González

🔑 **LANGUAGE**
Señora is usually written on an envelope as Sra., e.g. Sra. González.

la **señorita** noun *fem.*
1 young lady
Te busca una señorita. A young lady is looking for you.
2 ¡Buenas tardes, señorita! Good afternoon!

🔑 **LANGUAGE**
Used when talking to a young woman in a polite way and not usually translated, though 'miss' is sometimes used in English, especially at school, e.g. Sí, señorita (Yes, miss).

3 Miss
la señorita Almenar
Miss Almenar

🔑 **LANGUAGE**
Señorita is usually written on an envelope as Srta., e.g. Srta. Almenar.

separado adjective *masc.*,
separada *fem.*
separated
Mis padres están separados.
My parents are separated.

separar verb
to separate

• *The months of the year and days of the week do not take a capital letter in Spanish.*

a
b
c
d
e
f
g
h
i
j
k
l
m
n
o
p
q
r
s
t
u
v
w
x
y
z

septiembre noun masc.
September
Nací en septiembre. I was born in
September.
Es mi cumpleaños el martes cinco
de septiembre. It's my birthday on
Tuesday, the fifth of September.

séptimo adjective masc.,
séptima fem.
seventh

ser verb
to be
Soy inglés. I'm English.
Eres mi amiga. You're my friend.
Mi hermana es enfermera.
My sister's a nurse.
¿Quién es? Who is it?
Es de Javier. It's Javier's.
Somos veinte en la clase. There are
twenty of us in the class.
¿Sois de Londres? Are you from
London?
Son muy pequeños. They're very
small.
Son las tres. It's three o'clock.
Ayer fue mi cumpleaños.
Yesterday was my birthday.

LANGUAGE
There are two main verbs for saying 'to
be': ser and estar. Use ser for saying how
something or somebody always is, what
job people do, or where they are from. Use
it also to talk about times and dates.

el **ser** noun masc.
being
un ser humano a human being

la **serie** noun fem.
series
une serie de televisión a TV series

serio adjective masc., **seria** fem.
serious
Hoy estás muy serio. You look very
serious today.

la **serpiente** noun fem.
snake

el **servicio** noun masc.
1 service
un buen servicio a good service
2 toilet
¿Dónde están los servicios? Where
are the toilets?

la **servilleta** noun fem.
napkin

servir verb
1 to serve
¿Te sirvo más sopa? Can I serve
you more soup?
2 to be useful
Este ordenador no sirve para nada.
This computer is useless.
¿Para qué sirve esto? What's this
for?

servirse verb
servirse algo to help yourself to
something
¡Sírvete! Help yourself!

sesenta number
sixty
Mi abuela tiene sesenta años.
My grandmother is sixty (years
old).

la **seta** noun fem.
mushroom

setenta number
seventy
Mi abuelo tiene setenta años.
My grandfather is seventy.

sexto adjective masc., **sexta** fem.
sixth
en el sexto piso on the sixth floor

si conjunction
if
Dime si puedes hacerlo. Tell me if
you can do it.
si no if not

sí adverb
yes
¿Sabes leer? – Sí Can you read? –
Yes

• See the centre section for verb tables.

siempre adverb
always
Siempre dices lo mismo. You always say the same thing.
como siempre as usual
para siempre forever

la **siesta** noun *fem.*
nap
echarse una siesta to have a nap

siete number
1 seven
Tengo siete años. I'm seven.
Son las siete. It's seven o'clock.
2 (*with dates*) **seventh**
el siete de julio the seventh of July

el **siglo** noun *masc.*
century
en el siglo veintiuno in the twenty-first century

el **significado** noun *masc.*
meaning

significar verb
to mean
¿Qué significa? What does it mean?

el **signo** noun *masc.*
1 sign
el lenguaje de signos sign language
2 mark
un signo de admiración an exclamation mark
un signo de interrogación a question mark

siguiente adjective *masc. & fem.*
next
en la página siguiente on the next page

sij adjective *masc. & fem.*
Sikh

la **sílaba** noun *fem.*
syllable

silbar verb
to whistle

el **silbato** noun *masc.*
whistle

el **silencio** noun *masc.*
silence
¡Silencio, por favor! Quiet, please!

silencioso adjective *masc.*,
silenciosa *fem.*
1 quiet
un coche silencioso a quiet car
2 silent

la **silla** noun *fem.*
chair
sentarse en una silla to sit down on a chair
una silla de montar a saddle
una silla de ruedas a wheelchair

el **sillín** noun *masc.* (plural los **sillines**)
(*on a bicycle*) **saddle**

la **sillita** noun *fem.*
buggy

el **sillón** noun *masc.* (plural los **sillones**)
armchair

el **símbolo** noun *masc.*
symbol

simpático adjective *masc.*,
simpática *fem.*
nice
Tu hermana es muy simpática. Your sister is very nice.

sin preposition
without
sin paraguas without an umbrella
sin decir nada without saying anything

la **sinagoga** noun *fem.*
synagogue

el **singular** noun *masc.*
singular
en singular in the singular

a
b
c
d
e
f
g
h
i
j
k
l
m
n
o
p
q
r
s
t
u
v
w
x
y
z

• *Use* el *and* uno *for masculine words and* la *and* una *for feminine words.*

a
b
c
d
e
f
g
h
i
j
k
l
m
n
o
p
q
r
s
t
u
v
w
x
y
z

sino conjunction
but
No es jueves, sino viernes. It's not Thursday, but Friday.

la **sirena** noun *fem.*
mermaid

el **sistema** noun *masc.*
system

🔑 **LANGUAGE**
Be careful: **sistema** ends in an **-a** but it is not a feminine noun.

el **sitio** noun *masc.*
1 place
un sitio seguro a safe place
¿Me guardas el sitio? Can you keep my place?
2 room
No hay sitio. There isn't any room.
Hazme sitio. Make room for me.
3 (*for saying 'somewhere' etc.*)
estar en algún sitio to be somewhere
en ningún sitio nowhere

el **sitio web** noun *masc.*
website

la **situación** noun *fem.* (plural las **situaciones**)
situation

el **SMS** noun *masc.*
text message
Te he enviado un SMS. I've sent you a text.

sobre preposition
1 on
sobre la cama on the bed
2 over
un puente sobre el río a bridge over the river
3 about
una película sobre los animales a film about animals
4 sobre todo especially

el **sobre** noun *masc.*
envelope

la **sobrina** noun *fem.*
niece

el **sobrino** noun *masc.*
nephew
Mis padres tienen muchos sobrinos. My parents have lots of nieces and nephews.

el **socio** noun *masc.*, la **socia** *fem.*
member
Soy socia del club de tenis. I'm a member of the tennis club.

el **socorro** noun *masc.*
help
¡Socorro! Help!

el **sofá** noun *masc.*
sofa

sois verb SEE **ser**
are
Isabel y Carlos, sois muy inteligentes. Isabel and Carlos, you're very clever.

el **sol** noun *masc.*
sun
al sol in the sun
Hace sol. It's sunny.
tomar el sol to sunbathe

solamente adverb
only

el or la **soldado** noun *masc. & fem.*
soldier

solo adjective *masc.*, **sola** *fem.*
1 alone
Estoy solo. I'm alone.
2 lonely
Me siento sola. I feel lonely.
3 by yourself
Lo he hecho solo. I've done it by myself.

• *Languages and nationalities do not take a capital letter in Spanish.*

sólo adverb
only
Sólo tengo diez euros. I only have ten euros.

> 🔑 **LANGUAGE**
> Remember to put the accent on **sólo** when it means 'only'.

soltar verb
to let go of
¡Suéltame! Let go of me!

la sombra noun *fem.*
1 shade
Aquí hay mucha sombra. There's a lot of shade here.
2 shadow
Vi una sombra en la pared. I saw a shadow on the wall.

el sombrero noun *masc.*
hat

la sombrilla noun *fem.*
sunshade

somos verb SEE ser
are
Somos amigos. We're friends.

son verb SEE ser
are
Mis abuelos son de Bilbao. My grandparents are from Bilbao.

sonar verb
1 to ring
El teléfono está sonando. The phone's ringing.
2 to sound
Tu nombre suena francés. Your name sounds French.

sonarse verb
sonarse la nariz to blow your nose
Suénate. Blow your nose.

el sonido noun *masc.*
sound

sonreír verb
to smile
¡Sonríe! Smile!

la sonrisa noun *fem.*
smile

soñar verb
to dream
soñar con alguien to dream about somebody

la sopa noun *fem.*
soup

soplar verb
1 to blow
Hoy sopla el viento. The wind is blowing today.
2 to blow out
soplar las velas to blow out the candles

soportar verb
to stand
No soporto a Maite. I can't stand Maite.

sordo adjective *masc.*, sorda *fem.*
deaf
Es sorda. She's deaf.

sorprender verb
to surprise
Me sorprende. It surprises me.

la sorpresa noun *fem.*
surprise
¡Qué sorpresa! What a surprise!

soso adjective *masc.*, sosa *fem.*
1 tasteless
La sopa está sosa. The soup is tasteless.
2 dull
Juan es muy soso. Juan is very dull.

sostener verb
to hold
¿Me sostienes la escalera? Can you hold the ladder?

el sótano noun *masc.*
basement
en el sótano in the basement

soy verb SEE ser
am
Soy delgado. I'm thin.

The months of the year and days of the week do not take a capital letter in Spanish.

Sr. abbreviation
Mr

> **LANGUAGE**
> Sr. is short for **Señor**.

Sra. abbreviation
Mrs

> **LANGUAGE**
> Sra. is short for **Señora**.

Sres. abbreviation
Mr & Mrs

> **LANGUAGE**
> Sres. is short for **Señores**.

Srta. abbreviation
Miss

> **LANGUAGE**
> Srta. is short for **Señorita**.

su adjective
1 (*talking about a boy or man*) **his**
 su hermana his sister
 sus juguetes his toys
2 (*talking about a girl or woman*) **her**
 su hermana her sister
 sus juguetes her toys
3 (*talking about a thing or animal*) **its**
 El perro está en su caseta.
 The dog's in its kennel.
 la ciudad y sus habitantes
 the town and its inhabitants
4 **their**
 Van al cine con su hermano.
 They're going to the cinema with
 their brother.
 Han traído sus libros. They've
 brought their books.
5 (*polite form*) **your**
 Aquí tiene su paraguas, señorita.
 Here's your umbrella, miss.
 ¿Me dicen sus nombres? Would
 you tell me your names?

> **LANGUAGE**
> Sus is used before a plural noun.

suave adjective *masc. & fem.*
1 **soft**
 la piel suave soft skin
2 **smooth**
 una superficie suave a smooth
 surface

subir verb
1 **to go up**
 Sube al primer piso. Go up to the
 first floor.
 Subió la escalera. He went up the
 stairs.
2 **to come up**
 ¡Ya subo! I'm coming up!
 ¡Sube! Come up!
3 **to get on**
 ¿Quieres subir al columpio?
 Do you want to get on the
 swing?
4 **to get in**
 Sube al coche. Get in the car.
5 **to take up**
 Ayúdame a subir la maleta.
 Help me take up the suitcase.
6 **to bring up**
 Súbeme una taza de té. Bring me
 up a cup of tea.
7 **to pull up**
 Sube la ventanilla. Pull the
 window up.
8 **to turn up**
 Sube la tele, por favor. Turn up the
 TV, please.

subirse verb
1 **to get on**
 subirse al tren to get on the
 train
2 **to get in**
 subirse al coche to get in the car
3 **to climb**
 subirse a un muro to climb a wall

el **submarino** noun *masc.*
 submarine

subrayar verb
 to underline

• *See the centre section for verb tables.*

156

subterráneo adjective masc., **subterránea** fem.
underground
un paso subterráneo a subway

los **subtítulos** plural noun masc.
subtitles

sucio adjective masc., **sucia** fem.
dirty
Mis calcetines están sucios.
My socks are dirty.

Sudáfrica noun fem.
South Africa

Sudamérica noun fem.
South America

sudamericano adjective masc., **sudamericana** fem.
South American
Es sudamericano. He's South American.

el **sudamericano** noun masc., la **sudamericana** fem.
South American

sudar verb
to sweat

el **suelo** noun masc.
1 floor
en el suelo on the floor
2 ground
Encontré un billete de diez euros en el suelo. I found a ten-euro note on the ground.
caerse al suelo to fall down

el **sueño** noun masc.
1 dream
tener un sueño to have a dream
2 sleep
nueve horas de sueño nine hours' sleep
tener sueño to be sleepy

> **LANGUAGE**
> Spanish = **tener** sueño **Tengo sueño.**
> English = **to be** sleepy **I'm sleepy.**

la **suerte** noun fem.
luck
Me trae suerte. It brings me luck.
¡Buena suerte! Good luck!
tener suerte to be lucky

> **LANGUAGE**
> Spanish = **tener** suerte **Tengo suerte.**
> English = **to be** lucky **I'm lucky.**

el **suéter** noun masc.
sweater

suficiente adjective & pronoun masc. & fem.
enough
No hay suficiente espacio. There isn't enough room.
¿Tienes suficientes pasteles? Do you have enough cakes?
No hay suficientes. There aren't enough.

sufrir verb
to suffer

Suiza noun fem.
Switzerland

suizo adjective masc., **suiza** fem.
Swiss

el **suizo** noun masc., la **suiza** fem.
Swiss man, **Swiss woman**
los suizos the Swiss

el **sujetador** noun masc.
bra

la **suma** noun fem.
sum
hacer sumas to do sums

súper, **super** adjective masc. & fem. & adverb
super

la **superficie** noun fem.
surface

el **supermercado** noun masc.
supermarket

a
b
c
d
e
f
g
h
i
j
k
l
m
n
o
p
q
r
s
t
u
v
w
x
y
z

• Use el and uno for masculine words and la and una for feminine words.

el **suplemento** noun *masc.*
extra charge
pagar un suplemento to pay an extra charge

suponer verb
to suppose
Supongo que sí. I suppose so.

por supuesto adverb
of course
¡Por supuesto que no! Of course not!

sur noun masculine & adjective
south
en el sur in the south
la costa sur the south coast

suspender verb
1 to fail
Ha suspendido el examen. He's failed the exam.
2 to call off
Han suspendido el partido. They've called off the match.

el **sustantivo** noun *masc.*
noun

sustituir verb
to replace

el **susto** noun *masc.*
fright
¡Qué susto! What a fright!

suyo adjective *masc.*, **suya** *fem.*
1 (*talking about a boy or man*) **his**

Este ordenador es suyo. This computer is his.
Estas fotos son suyas. These photos are his.
2 (*talking about a girl or woman*) **hers**
Este libro es suyo. This book is hers.
unas amigas suyas friends of hers
3 theirs
Esta casa es suya. This house is theirs.
4 (*polite form*) **yours**
Este abrigo es suyo, señorita. This coat is yours, miss.

el **suyo** pronoun *masc.*, la **suya** *fem.*
1 his
mi hermana y la suya my sister and his
Nuestro ordenador es más viejo que el suyo. Our computer is older than his.
2 hers
mi hermana y la suya my sister and hers
Vuestra casa es más pequeña que la suya. Your house is smaller than hers.
3 theirs
mis padres y los suyos my parents and theirs
4 (*polite form*) **yours**
Este paraguas es el suyo, señor. This umbrella is yours.

Tt

la **tabla** noun *fem.*
1 board
una tabla de planchar an ironing board
2 table
las tablas de multiplicar the times tables
la tabla del diez the ten-times table

el **tablero** noun *masc.*
(*for chess, notices, etc.*)
board

la **tableta** noun *fem.*
bar
una tableta de chocolate a bar of chocolate

• *Languages and nationalities do not take a capital letter in Spanish.*

el **tablón** noun *masc.* (plural los **tablones**)
board
un tablón de anuncios a notice board

el **taburete** noun *masc.*
stool

tacaño adjective *masc.*, **tacaña** *fem.*
mean
Es muy tacaña. She's very mean.

tachar verb
to cross out

el **tacón** noun *masc.* (plural los **tacones**)
(*of a shoe*) **heel**

tal adverb
1 ¿Qué tal? How are things?
¿Qué tal está tu hermana? How's your sister?
¿Qué tal es tu maestra? What's your teacher like?
¿Qué tal las vacaciones? What were your holidays like?
2 tal vez maybe

la **talla** noun *fem.*
size
¿Qué talla usas? What size do you take?

el **taller** noun *masc.*
1 workshop
2 (*for car repairs*) **garage**

el **talón** noun *masc.* (plural los **talones**)
heel

el **tamaño** noun *masc.*
size
¿De qué tamaño es? What size is it?

también adverb
too
Voy al cine hoy y mañana también. I'm going to the cinema today and tomorrow too.
Estoy cansada. – Yo también. I'm tired. – Me too.

el **tambor** noun *masc.*
drum
tocar un tambor to play a drum

el **Támesis** noun *masc.*
Thames

tampoco adverb
1 not ... either
Yo tampoco quiero ir. I don't want to go either.
No sabe nadar tampoco. He can't swim either.
2 neither
No tengo dinero. – Yo tampoco. I don't have any money. – Neither do I.

tan adverb
1 so
No es tan alto. He isn't so tall.
2 such
Es un chico tan inteligente. He's such a clever boy.
chicos tan inteligentes such clever boys
3 (*when comparing*)
tan ... como as ... as
Mi casa no es tan grande como la tuya. My house isn't as big as yours.

tanto adverb
so much
Tengo que estudiar tanto. I have to study so much.

• *The months of the year and days of the week do not take a capital letter in Spanish.*

159

Spanish English

a b c d e f g h i j k l m n o p q r s t u v w x y z

tanto adjective & pronoun *masc.*,
tanta *fem.*
1 so much
 tanto dinero so much money
 No quiero tanto. I don't want so much.
2 so many
 tantas cosas so many things
 No queremos tantos. We don't want so many.
3 as much
 No tengo tanto trabajo como tú. I don't have as much work as you.
 Hoy no hace tanto calor. Today it's not as hot.
4 as many
 No hay tantos coches como ayer. There aren't as many cars as yesterday.

la tapa noun *fem.*
1 lid
 la tapa de la caja the lid of the box
2 cover
 la tapa del libro the cover of the book
3 bar snack

CULTURE
Tapas are small amounts of food served with drinks in a bar or cafe.

la taquilla noun *fem.*
 ticket office

tardar verb
1 to take a long time
 Tardas mucho. You're taking a long time.
 No tardo mucho. I won't be long.
2 to take
 Tardé dos días en terminar. I took two days to finish.

tarde adverb
 late
 llegar tarde to be late, to arrive late
 Es tarde. It's late.
 más tarde later

la tarde noun *fem.*
1 afternoon
 por la tarde in the afternoon
 ayer por la tarde yesterday afternoon
 ¡Buenas tardes! Good afternoon!
2 evening
 por la tarde in the evening
 a las siete de la tarde at seven in the evening
 ¡Buenas tardes! Good evening!

la tarjeta noun *fem.*
 card
 una tarjeta de cumpleaños a birthday card
 una tarjeta de Navidad a Christmas card
 una tarjeta postal a postcard

el tarro noun *masc.*
 jar
 un tarro de mermelada a jar of jam

la tarta noun *fem.*
1 cake
 una tarta de cumpleaños a birthday cake
2 tart
 una tarta de fresa a strawberry tart

el tatuaje noun *masc.*
 tattoo

el taxi noun *masc.*
 taxi
 en taxi by taxi

el or **la taxista** noun *masc. & fem.*
 taxi driver

la taza noun *fem.*
 cup
 una taza de café a cup of coffee

el tazón noun *masc.* (plural los **tazones**)
 bowl, big cup

• *See the centre section for verb tables.*

temblar verb
1 to shake
Te tiemblan las manos. Your hands are shaking.
2 to shiver
Tiemblo de frío. I'm shivering.

la **temperatura** noun *fem.*
temperature

la **tempestad** noun *fem.*
storm

el **templo** noun *masc.*
temple
un templo sij a Sikh temple

la **temporada** noun *fem.*
season
la temporada de esquí the ski season

temprano adverb
early
He llegado temprano. I've arrived early.

tender verb
to hang out
Tiende la ropa. Hang out the cothes to dry.

el **tendedero** noun *masc.*
clothes line

el **tenedor** noun *masc.*
fork

tener verb
1 to have, to have got
Tengo un regalo para ti. I have a gift for you.
¿Qué tienes en la mano? What have you got in your hand?
Álex tiene los ojos azules. Álex has blue eyes.
No tenemos dinero. We haven't got any money.
2 to be
Tengo calor. I'm hot.
Rosa tiene diez años. Rosa is ten.

Tenemos suerte. We're lucky.

> **LANGUAGE**
> Spanish = **Tengo** calor/frío/hambre/ sed/miedo/10 años.
> English = **I am** hot/cold/hungry/thirsty/ scared/10 years old.

3 tener que hacer algo to have to do something
Tengo que ir al médico. I have to go to the doctor.
Tienes que trabajar más. You've got to work harder.

el **tenis** noun *masc.*
tennis
Juego al tenis. I play tennis.
el tenis de mesa table tennis

tercero *masc.*,
tercera adjective *fem.*

> **LANGUAGE**
> The masculine singular **tercero** becomes **tercer** when it is used before a noun.

third
en el tercer piso on the third floor
Quedé tercero en la carrera. I came third in the race.
una tercera parte a third

terco adjective *masc.*, **terca** *fem.*
stubborn

terminar verb
to finish
No he terminado. I haven't finished.

el **termo** noun *masc.*
flask

el **termómetro** noun *masc.*
thermometer

el **ternero** noun *masc.*,
la **ternera** *fem.*
calf

la **terraza** noun *fem.*
1 balcony
2 (*outside a cafe etc.*) **terrace**

• *Languages and nationalities do not take a capital letter in Spanish.*

a
b
c
d
e
f
g
h
i
j
k
l
m
n
o
p
q
r
s
t
u
v
w
x
y
z

el **terremoto** noun masc.
earthquake

el **terreno** noun masc.
1 land
2 (for sports) **field**

terrible adjective masc. & fem.
terrible

el **tesoro** noun masc.
treasure

> **LANGUAGE**
> Spanish = tesero
> English = treasure

la **tetera** noun fem.
1 teapot
2 kettle

el **texto** noun masc.
text
un libro de texto a textbook

ti pronoun
you
para ti for you
delante de ti in front of you
¿A ti te gusta? Do you like it?

> **LANGUAGE**
> Be careful: **ti** is not written with an accent like **mí**.

> **LANGUAGE**
> You use **ti** when you are talking to a friend, somebody in your family, or someone your own age.

la **tía** noun fem.
aunt

el **tiburón** noun masc. (plural los **tiburones**)
shark

el **tiempo** noun masc.
1 time
No tengo tiempo. I don't have time.
al mismo tiempo at the same time
mucho tiempo a long time

Hace mucho tiempo que no lo veo. I haven't seen him for a long time.
2 ¿cuánto tiempo? how long?
¿Cuánto tiempo dura? How long does it last?
3 weather
¿Qué tiempo hace? What's the weather like?
Hace buen tiempo. The weather's nice.

la **tienda** noun fem.
1 shop
una tienda de ropa a clothes shop
una tienda de comestibles a grocer's
2 tent
una tienda de campaña a tent

la **tierra** noun fem.
1 land
La tierra es seca. The land is dry.
2 earth
Está cubierto de tierra. It's covered with earth.

el **tigre** noun masc.
tiger

las **tijeras** plural noun fem.
scissors
unas tijeras a pair of scissors

el **timbre** noun masc.
bell
Sonó el timbre. The bell rang.

tímido adjective masc., **tímida** fem.
shy

la **tina** noun fem.
(Latin America) **bathtub**

la **tinta** noun fem.
ink
escribir con tinta to write in ink

tinto adjective masc.
un vino tinto a red wine

a b c d e f g h i j k l m n o p q r s t u v w x y z

• The months of the year and days of the week do not take a capital letter in Spanish.

el **tío** noun *masc.*
1 uncle
Es mi tío. He's my uncle.
mis tíos my uncle and aunt
2 guy
¡Vamos, tíos! Let's go, guys!

el **tiovivo** noun *masc.*
merry-go-round

el **tipo** noun *masc.*
1 type
¿Qué tipo de música es? What type of music is it?
2 guy
un tipo simpático a nice guy

el **tirante** noun *masc.*
1 strap
los tirantes del vestido the straps on the dress
2 los tirantes braces (*on trousers*)

tirar verb
1 to throw
Tírame la pelota. Throw me the ball.
Me tiró una piedra. He threw a stone at me.
Me tiré al agua. I jumped into the water.
2 to throw away
Tira estos papeles. Throw these papers away.
3 to knock over
No tires el vaso. Don't knock the glass over.
4 to pull
No me tires del pelo. Don't pull my hair.

la **tirita** noun *fem.*
(*for a cut, burn, etc.*) **plaster**

el **títere** noun *masc.*
puppet

el **título** noun *masc.*
1 title
el título del libro the title of the book
2 certificate

la **tiza** noun *fem.*
chalk
una tiza a piece of chalk

la **toalla** noun *fem.*
towel

el **tobillo** noun *masc.*
ankle

el **tobogán** noun *masc.* (plural los **toboganes**)
(*in a playground*) **slide**

tocar verb
1 to touch
No toques la pantalla. Don't touch the screen.
2 (*a musical instrument*) **to play**
¿Sabes tocar el piano? Can you play the piano?
3 to ring
tocar el timbre to ring the bell
4 ¿A quién le toca? Whose turn is it?
Me toca a mí. It's my turn.

el **tocino** noun *masc.*
bacon

todavía adverb
1 still
Todavía está durmiendo. He's still asleep.
2 yet
todavía no not yet
Todavía no ha llegado. She hasn't arrived yet.
3 even
todavía más difícil even more difficult

todo adjective *masc.*, **toda** *fem.*
1 all
todos los libros all the books
todas mis amigas all my friends
2 whole, all
todo el pastel the whole cake, all the cake
toda la mañana the whole morning, all morning
3 every
todos los días every day
todo el mundo everybody

• *See the centre section for verb tables.*

Spanish English

a b c d e f g h i j k l m n o p q r s t u v w x y z

todo pronoun *masc.*, **toda** *fem.*
1 everything
Todo está listo. Everything's ready.
2 all
Eso es todo. That's all.
Me lo he comido todo. I've eaten it all.
Las he comprado todas. I've bought them all.
3 everybody
Todos han venido. Everybody has come.

tomar verb
1 to take
Toma el autobús. Take the bus.
¿Has tomado la pastilla? Have you taken the tablet?
Toma, cómete esto. Here, eat this.
2 to have
Vamos a tomar el desayuno. We're going to have breakfast.
¿Qué quieres tomar? What do you want to have?
3 tomar el sol to sunbathe
tomar el aire to get some fresh air

el **tomate** noun *masc.*
tomato
una salsa de tomate a tomato sauce

la **tontería** noun *fem.*
1 stupid thing
hacer una tontería to do a stupid thing
2 nonsense
¡Qué tontería! What nonsense!
decir tonterías to talk nonsense

tonto adjective *masc.*, **tonta** *fem.*
stupid, silly

torcer verb
1 to twist
Me he torcido el tobillo. I've twisted my ankle.
2 to turn
Tuerce a la izquierda. Turn left.

torcido adjective *masc.*, **torcida** *fem.*
1 crooked
El cuadro está torcido. The picture's crooked.
2 twisted

el **torero** noun *masc.*, la **torera** *fem.*
bullfighter

la **tormenta** noun *fem.*
storm

el **toro** noun *masc.*
bull

la **torre** noun *fem.*
tower

la **torta** noun *fem.*
flat, round cake

la **tortilla** noun *fem.*
1 omelette
2 (*Mexico*) **tortilla** (*made of corn flour*)

la **tortuga** noun *fem.*
1 tortoise
2 turtle
una tortuga de mar a turtle

la **tos** noun *fem.*
cough
Tengo mucha tos. I have a bad cough.

toser verb
to cough

la **tostada** noun *fem.*
una tostada a piece of toast
¿Quieres tostadas? Do you want some toast?

tostado adjective *masc.*
el pan tostado toasted bread

el **total** noun *masc.*
total

trabajador adjective *masc.*, **trabajadora** *fem.*
hard-working

a b c d e f g h i j k l m n o p q r s t u v w x y z

• *Use* el *and* uno *for masculine words and* la *and* una *for feminine words.*

a
b
c
d
e
f
g
h
i
j
k
l
m
n
o
p
q
r
s
t
u
v
w
x
y
z

el **trabajador** noun *masc.*,
la **trabajadora** *fem.*
worker

trabajar verb
to work
Mi padre trabaja en una oficina.
My dad works in an office.

el **trabajo** noun *masc.*
1 work
Tengo mucho trabajo. I've got lots
of work.
ir al trabajo to go to work
2 job
encontrar trabajo to find a job

el **tractor** noun *masc.*
tractor

la **traducción** noun *fem.* (plural las
traducciones)
translation

traducir verb
to translate
Tradúcelo del español al inglés.
Translate it from Spanish into
English.

traer verb
to bring
Traigo un regalo para ti. I've
brought a present for you.

el **tráfico** noun *masc.*
traffic
Hay mucho tráfico. There's a lot of
traffic.

tragar verb
to swallow

el **traje** noun *masc.*
1 suit
Javier lleva un traje negro. Javier
is wearing a black suit.
un traje de chaqueta (*for a woman*) a
suit
un traje de baño (*for a man*)
swimming trunks; (*for a
woman*) swimsuit
2 costume
el traje regional regional costume

la **trampa** noun *fem.*
1 trap
2 hacer trampa to cheat

tramposo noun *masc.*,
tramposa *fem.*
cheat

tranquilo adjective *masc.*,
tranquila *fem.*
1 quiet
un sitio tranquilo a quiet place
2 calm
Tienes que estar tranquila. You
have to be calm.

el **transbordador** noun *masc.*
el transbordador espacial the
space shuttle

el **transporte** noun *masc.*
el transporte público public
transport

el **tranvía** noun *masc.*
tram

LANGUAGE
Be careful: **tranvía** ends in an -**a** but it is
not a feminine noun.

el **trapo** noun *masc.*
cloth
un trapo de cocina a tea towel

trasero adjective *masc.*,
trasera *fem.*
back
el asiento trasero the back seat

tratar verb
1 to treat
Trato muy bien a mi perro. I treat
my dog very well.
2 tratar de hacer algo to try to do
something
3 tratar de algo to be about
something
¿De qué trata el libro? What's the
book about?

• *Languages and nationalities do not take a capital letter in Spanish.*

a través de preposition
through
a través del cristal through the window

trece number
1 thirteen
Mi hermano tiene trece años.
My brother is thirteen (years old).
2 (with dates) **thirteenth**
el trece de octubre the thirteenth of October

treinta number
1 thirty
Mi madre tiene treinta años.
My mum is thirty (years old).
2 (with dates) **thirtieth**
el treinta de marzo the thirtieth of March

el **tren** noun masc.
train
en tren by train
cambiar de tren to change trains

las **trenzas** plural noun fem.
plaits

trepar verb
to climb
trepar a un árbol to climb a tree

tres number
1 three
Mi hermana tiene tres años.
My sister is three (years old).
Son las tres. It's three o'clock.
2 (with dates) **third**
el tres de junio the third of June

trescientos number masc.,
trescientas fem.
three hundred

el **triángulo** noun masc.
triangle

el **trigo** noun masc.
wheat

el **trimestre** noun masc.
term
el primer trimestre del año the first term of the year

el **trineo** noun masc.
sledge

el **triple** noun masc.
three times
Cuesta el triple. It costs three times as much.

la **tripulación** noun fem.
crew

triste adjective masc. & fem.
1 sad
¿Estás triste? Are you sad?
2 gloomy
un día triste a gloomy day

la **tristeza** noun fem.
sadness

el **triunfo** noun masc.
victory

la **trompa** noun fem.
trunk
la trompa del elefante the elephant's trunk

la **trompeta** noun fem.
trumpet
Raúl toca la trompeta. Raúl plays the trumpet.

el **tronco** noun masc.
trunk
el tronco del árbol the trunk of the tree

el **trono** noun masc.
throne

tropezar verb
to trip

el **trozo** noun masc.
piece
¿Quieres un trozo de tarta? Do you want a piece of cake?

el **truco** noun masc.
trick
un truco de magia a magic trick

el **trueno** noun masc.
thunder
Hubo truenos. There was thunder.

a b c d e f g h i j k l m n o p q r s t u v w x y z

• *The months of the year and days of the week do not take a capital letter in Spanish.*

Spanish English

a
b
c
d
e
f
g
h
i
j
k
l
m
n
o
p
q
r
s
t
u
v
w
x
y
z

tu adjective *masc. & fem.*
your
tu hermana your sister
tus dibujos your drawings

> **LANGUAGE**
> Tus is used before a plural noun.

> **LANGUAGE**
> Use tu when you are talking to a friend, somebody in your family, or someone your own age.

tú pronoun
1 (*for giving special importance to the word in the sentence*) **you**
Tú lo sabes pero las otras no. You know but the others don't.
¿Quieres venir tú? Do you want to come?
2 (*with 'que', 'ser', etc.*) **you**
Soy más alto que tú. I'm taller than you.
¿Eres tú? Is that you?
tú mismo yourself

> **LANGUAGE**
> Use tú when you are talking to a friend, somebody in your family, or someone your own age.

el **tubo** noun *masc.*
tube

tumbarse verb
to lie down

la **tumbona** noun *fem.*
deckchair

el **túnel** noun *masc.*
tunnel
Pasamos por el túnel. We went through the tunnel.

el **turismo** noun *masc.*
hacer turismo to go sightseeing
una oficina de turismo a tourist office

el or la **turista** noun *masc. & fem.*
tourist

• *See the centre section for verb tables.*

el **turno** noun *masc.*
turn
Es tu turno. It's your turn.

el **turrón** noun *masc.*
nougat

> **CULTURE**
> Turrón is a kind of nougat that Spanish people eat at Christmas.

tuve verb SEE **tener**
had
Tuve un problema. I had a problem.

tuvieron verb SEE **tener**
had
Tuvieron una discusión. They had an argument.

tuvo verb SEE **tener**
had
Tuvo un buen viaje. She had a good trip.

tuyo adjective *masc.*, **tuya** *fem.*
yours
Este paraguas es tuyo. This umbrella is yours.
Estas cajas son tuyas. These boxes are yours.
una amiga tuya a friend of yours

> **LANGUAGE**
> You use tuyo/tuya when you are talking to a friend, somebody in your family, or someone your own age.

el **tuyo** pronoun *masc.*, la **tuya** *fem.*
yours
mi hermano y el tuyo my brother and yours
Mi casa es más pequeña que la tuya. My house is smaller than yours.

> **LANGUAGE**
> Use el tuyo/la tuya when you are talking to a friend, somebody in your family, or someone your own age.

Uu

u conjunction
or
siete u ocho seven or eight

> 🔑 **LANGUAGE**
> The usual word for 'or' is **o** but **u** is used in front of a word starting with **o** or **ho**.

Ud. abbreviation
you

> 🔑 **LANGUAGE**
> **Ud.** is short for **usted** in the singular.

Uds. abbreviation
you

> 🔑 **LANGUAGE**
> **Uds.** is short for **ustedes** in the plural.

la **UE** noun *fem.*
EU (*European Union*)

últimamente adverb
lately

último adjective *masc.*,
última *fem.*
1 last
 la última vez the last time
 Quedé último en la carrera. I came last in the race.
2 latest
 las últimas noticias the latest news
3 top
 en el último piso on the top floor
4 back
 en la última fila in the back row

el **último** pronoun *masc.*,
la **última** *fem.*
last one, **last**
 ¿Eres la última? Are you the last one?
 Es el último de la clase. He's bottom of the class.

un determiner *masc.*, **una** *fem.*
1 a
 un coche a car
 una mesa a table
 un ala a wing
 un hada a fairy

> 🔑 **LANGUAGE**
> **Un** is used instead of **una** before feminine nouns (like **ala** or **hada**) beginning with a stressed 'a' sound.

2 an
 un elefante an elephant
 una manzana an apple

un number *masc.*, **una** *fem.*
one
 ¿Cuesta un euro o dos? Does it cost one euro or two?
 Es la una. It's one o'clock.
 Mi hermano tiene un año. My brother is one.

único adjective *masc.*,
única *fem.*
only
 Es el único vestido que me gusta. It's the only dress I like.
 Isabel es hija única. Isabel is an only child.

el **único** noun *masc.*,
la **única** *fem.*
only one
 Es el único que tengo. It's the only one I have.

el **uniforme** noun *masc.*
uniform

> **CULTURE**
> In Spain schoolchildren don't usually wear uniforms.

• *Use* **el** *and* **uno** *for masculine words and* **la** *and* **una** *for feminine words.*

a
b
c
d
e
f
g
h
i
j
k
l
m
n
o
p
q
r
s
t
u
v
w
x
y
z

la **Unión Europea** noun *fem.*
European Union

unir verb
to match
Une las dos palabras. Match the two words.

a
b
la **universidad** noun *fem.*
university
ir a la universidad to go to
c university

d el **universo** noun *masc.*
universe
e

f **uno** number & pronoun *masc.*,
una *fem.*
g **1 one**
el número uno number one
h Quiero sólo uno. I only want
i one.
uno de ellos, una de ellas one of
j them
k Es la una. It's one o'clock.
2 (*in dates*) **first**
l el uno de marzo the first of
m March

n **unos** adjective & pronoun *masc. plural*,
unas *fem. plural*
o **1 some**
p He comprado unos vaqueros.
I've bought some jeans.
q Unos quieren venir, otros no. Some
r want to come, others don't.
s **2 a few**
Voy a invitar a unos amigos.
t I'm going to invite a few
u friends.
3 about
v unos veinte niños about twenty
w children

x la **uña** noun *fem.*
nail
y una uña del dedo del pie a toe
z nail

la **urgencia** noun *fem.*
emergency
en caso de urgencia in an
emergency

urgente adjective *masc. & fem.*
urgent

Uruguay noun *masc.*
Uruguay

usar verb
1 to use
Usa una calculadora. Use a
calculator.
2 to take
¿Qué talla usas? What size do you
take?

usted pronoun
you
¿Cómo está usted? How are
you?
Esto es para usted. This is for
you.

LANGUAGE
You use **usted** when talking in a polite way to a grown-up or a stranger.

ustedes plural pronoun
you
¿Cómo están ustedes? How are
you?
Esto es para ustedes. This is for
you.

LANGUAGE
You use **ustedes** when talking in a polite way to two or more grown-ups or strangers.

útil adjective *masc. & fem.*
useful

utilizar verb
to use

la **uva** noun *fem.*
grape

• *Languages and nationalities do not take a capital letter in Spanish.*

Vv

va verb SEE **ir**
Va al cine. He goes to the cinema.
¿Qué va a hacer? What's she going to do?

la **vaca** noun *fem.*
cow

las **vacaciones** plural noun *fem.*
holiday, holidays
Estamos de vacaciones. We're on holiday.
Me voy de vacaciones en julio. I'm going on holiday in July.
las vacaciones de Navidad the Christmas holidays
las vacaciones de verano the summer holidays

vaciar verb
to empty

vacío adjective *masc.*, **vacía** *fem.*
empty
El vaso está vacío. The glass is empty.

vago adjective *masc.*, **vaga** *fem.*
lazy

el **vagón** noun *masc.* (plural los **vagones**)
(*on a train*) **carriage**

la **vainilla** noun *fem.*
vanilla
un helado de vainilla a vanilla ice cream

🔑 **LANGUAGE**
Spanish = vainilla
English = vanilla

la **vajilla** noun *fem.*
dishes
lavar la vajilla to wash the dishes

vale exclamation
okay
¿Quieres ir a la piscina? – ¡Vale! Do you want to go to the pool? – Okay!

el **vale** noun *masc.*
voucher
un vale de regalo a gift voucher

valer verb
1 to cost
¿Cuánto vale? How much does it cost?
2 to be worth
La bici vale mucho dinero. The bike is worth a lot of money.
3 valer la pena to be worth it
No vale la pena. It's not worth it.

valiente adjective *masc. & fem.*
brave

la **valla** noun *fem.*
fence

el **valle** noun *masc.*
valley

el **valor** noun *masc.*
value
un anillo de gran valor a very valuable ring

vamos verb SEE **ir**
Vamos al cole. We go to school.
¿Qué vamos a hacer? What are we going to do?
Vamos a ver la tele. Let's watch TV.

van verb SEE **ir**
Van en bici. They go by bike.
Van a comprar vaqueros. They're going to buy jeans.

el **vapor** noun *masc.*
steam

a
b
c
d
e
f
g
h
i
j
k
l
m
n
o
p
q
r
s
t
u
v
w
x
y
z

• *The months of the year and days of the week do not take a capital letter in Spanish.*

vaquero adjective *masc.*,
vaquera *fem.*
denim
una camisa vaquera a denim shirt

el **vaquero** noun *masc.*
cowboy
una película de vaqueros
a western

los **vaqueros** plural noun *masc.*
jeans
unos vaqueros a pair of jeans

la **varicela** noun *fem.*
chickenpox
Tengo la varicela. I have
chickenpox.

varios adjective *masc. plural*,
varias *fem. plural*
several
varios días several days

la **varita** noun *fem.*
wand
una varita mágica a magic wand

vas verb SEE **ir**
¿Adónde vas? Where are you
going?
¿Vas a ayudarme? Are you going
to help me?

el **vasco** noun *masc.*
(*the language*) **Basque**

vasco adjective *masc.*, **vasca** *fem.*
Basque
el País Vasco the Basque Country

el **vasco** noun *masc.*,
la **vasca** *fem.*
Basque
los vascos the Basques

el **vaso** noun *masc.*
glass
un vaso de agua a glass of water
un vaso de plástico a plastic cup

Vd. abbreviation
you

LANGUAGE
Vd. is short for **usted** in the singular.

Vds. abbreviation
you

LANGUAGE
Vds. is short for **ustedes** in the plural.

el **vecino** noun *masc.*, la **vecina** *fem.*
1 neighbour
Es mi vecina. She's my neighbour.
2 resident
los vecinos del pueblo the
residents of the village

vegetariano adjective *masc.*,
vegetariana *fem.*
vegetarian
Soy vegetariano. I'm vegetarian.

el **véhiculo** noun *masc.*
vehicle

veinte number
1 twenty
Mi primo tiene veinte años.
My cousin is twenty.
2 (*with dates*) **twentieth**
el veinte de septiembre the
twentieth of September

la **vela** noun *fem.*
1 candle
encender una vela to light a
candle
2 sailing
hacer vela to go sailing

la **velocidad** noun *fem.*
speed

vencer verb
1 to beat
vencer a un equipo to beat a team
2 to win

la **venda** noun *fem.*
bandage

• See the centre section for verb tables.

el **vendedor** noun *masc.*,
 la **vendedora** *fem.*
 sales person

vender verb
 to sell
 He vendido mi bici a mi amigo.
 I've sold my bike to my friend.
 'Se vende'. 'For sale'.

el **veneno** noun *masc.*
 poison

venenoso adjective *masc.*,
 venenosa *fem.*
 poisonous

Venezuela noun *fem.*
 Venezuela

venir verb
 1 to come
 ¿Quieres venir conmigo? Do you
 want to come with me?
 Vengo a verte. I'm coming to see
 you.
 Ya viene el autobús. Here comes
 the bus.
 Ven aquí. Come here.
 ¡Venga! Come on!
 Vine en coche. I came by car.
 2 que viene next
 la semana que viene next week

la **ventana** noun *fem.*
 window
 Abre la ventana. Open the
 window.

la **ventanilla** noun *fem.*
 (*of a car*) **window**
 Baja la ventanilla. Open the
 window.

el **ventilador** noun *masc.*
 fan

el **veo veo** noun *masc.*
 I spy
 jugar al veo veo to play I spy

ver verb
 1 to see
 ¿Has visto a mi hermana?
 Have you seen my sister?
 No la veo. I can't see her.
 Te vi en el supermercado.
 I saw you in the supermarket.
 A ver ... Let's see ...
 2 to watch
 ver la tele to watch TV

el **verano** noun *masc.*
 summer
 en verano in the summer

el **verbo** noun *masc.*
 verb

la **verdad** noun *fem.*
 1 truth
 ¿Me dices la verdad? Are you
 telling me the truth?
 Eso es verdad. That's true.
 2 (*in questions*)
 Hace calor, ¿verdad? It's hot, isn't
 it?
 Te gusta, ¿verdad? You like it,
 don't you?

LANGUAGE
¿Verdad? is often used to say 'isn't it?',
'don't you?', 'hasn't she?', etc.

verdadero adjective *masc.*,
 verdadera *fem.*
 1 real
 su verdadero nombre her real
 name
 2 true
 una historia verdadera
 a true story

verde adjective *masc. & fem.*
 green
 Tengo los ojos verdes. I have green
 eyes.

el **verde** noun *masc.*
 green
 El verde es mi color favorito.
 Green is my favourite colour.

• Use el and uno for masculine words and la and una for feminine words.

la **verdulería** noun *fem.*
greengrocer's

la **verdura** noun *fem.*
vegetable
sopa de verduras vegetable soup

la **vergüenza** noun *fem.*
1 shame
Me da vergüenza. I'm ashamed.
2 shyness
Tiene vergüenza. He's shy.

el **vestíbulo** noun *masc.*
1 (*in a house*) **hall**
2 (*in a hotel etc.*) **lobby**

el **vestido** noun *masc.*
dress
un vestido rojo a red dress

vestido adjective *masc.*,
vestida *fem.*
dressed
No estoy vestido. I'm not dressed.
Está vestida de azul. She's dressed
in blue.

vestir verb
to dress
Viste muy bien. He dresses very
well.

vestirse verb
1 to get dressed
Vístete. Get dressed.
2 to dress
Se viste de verde. She dresses in
green.
Se vistió de pirata. He dressed up
as a pirate.

el **vestuario** noun *masc.*
(*for sports*) **changing room**, **cubicle**

el **veterinario** noun *masc.*,
la **veterinaria** *fem.*
vet
Mi madre es veterinaria.
My mum's a vet.

la **vez** noun *fem.*
time
por primera vez for the first time
una vez once
dos veces al mes twice a month
a veces sometimes
otra vez again
tal vez maybe
en vez de instead of
'Érase una vez ...' (*in stories*) 'Once
upon a time there was ...'

la **vía** noun *fem.*
1 way, road
vías romanas Roman roads
2 (*for trains*) **platform**
3 la vía del tren the railway line
Se cayó a la vía. He fell onto the
line.

viajar verb
to travel
¿Te gusta viajar? Do you like
travelling?

el **viaje** noun *masc.*
1 trip
hacer un viaje to go on a trip
¡Buen viaje! Have a good trip!
2 journey
un viaje muy largo a very long
journey

el **viajero** noun *masc.*,
la **viajera** *fem.*
passenger

la **victoria** noun *fem.*
victory

la **vida** noun *fem.*
life
toda mi vida all my life

el **vídeo** noun *masc.*
video
Estamos viendo un vídeo.
We're watching a video.
en vídeo on video

• *Languages and nationalities do not take a capital letter in Spanish.*

a
b
c
d
e
f
g
h
i
j
k
l
m
n
o
p
q
r
s
t
u
v
w
x
y
z

videoconsola → viva

la **videoconsola** noun fem.
games console

el **videojuego** noun masc.
video game

el **vidrio** noun masc.
glass

viejo adjective masc., **vieja** fem.
old
Mi abuelo es muy viejo. My grandfather's very old.

el **viejo** noun masc., la **vieja** fem.
old man, old woman

el **viento** noun masc.
wind
Hace viento. It's windy.

la **viernes** noun masc.
Friday
Hoy es viernes. Today is Friday.
el viernes on Friday
Mis primos se van el viernes. My cousins are leaving on Friday.
los viernes on Fridays
Voy al parque los viernes. I go to the park on Fridays.

LANGUAGE
Remember the difference between **el viernes** (one Friday only) and **los viernes** (every Friday).

el **Viernes Santo** noun masc.
Good Friday

el **villancico** noun masc.
Christmas carol

el **vinagre** noun masc.
vinegar

el **vino** noun masc.
wine
el vino tinto red wine

violeta adjective masc. & fem.
violet
faldas violeta violet skirts

LANGUAGE
The form **violeta** is the same in the masculine, feminine, and plural.

el **violín** noun masc. (plural los **violines**)
violin
Toco el violín. I play the violin.

el **violonchelo** noun masc.
cello
Hakim toca el violonchelo. Hakim plays the cello.

la **Virgen** noun fem.
Virgin
la Virgen María the Virgin Mary

el **virus** noun masc. (plural los **virus**)
virus

la **visita** noun fem.
1 **visit**
la visita de mis primos my cousins' visit
2 **visitor**
Tenemos visitas. We have visitors.

el or la **visitante** noun masc. & fem.
visitor

visitar verb
to visit

la **vista** noun fem.
1 **view**
una vista maravillosa a wonderful view
¡Hasta la vista! See you!
2 **eyesight**

viva exclamation
hip hip hurrah!

• The months of the year and days of the week do not take a capital letter in Spanish.

Spanish English

a b c d e f g h i j k l m n o p q r s t u **v** w x y z

175

a
b
c
d
e
f
g
h
i
j
k
l
m
n
o
p
q
r
s
t
u
v
w
x
y
z

vivir verb
to live
¿Dónde vives? Where do you live?
Vivo en Toledo. I live in Toledo.

vivo adjective masc.,
viva fem.
alive
¿Está vivo? Is it alive?

el **vocabulario** noun masc.
vocabulary

la **vocal** noun fem.
vowel

el **volante** noun masc.
steering wheel

volar verb
1 to fly
Me gusta volar. I like to fly.
2 to blow up
Han volado un edificio. They've blown up a building.

el **volcán** noun masc. (plural los **volcanes**)
volcano

el **voleibol** noun masc.
volleyball
jugar al voleibol to play volleyball

el **volumen** noun masc.
volume
Sube el volumen. Turn up the volume.

el **voluntario** noun masc.,
la **voluntaria** fem.
volunteer

volver verb
1 to go back
Tengo que volver al colegio. I have to go back to school.
2 to come back
¿Cuándo vuelves de Madrid? When do you come back from Madrid?

3 to turn
Volví la cabeza. I turned my head.
4 (for saying 'again')
volver a hacer algo to do something again
Volveré a verlos mañana. I'll see them again tomorrow.

volverse verb
1 to turn round
Me volví a mirar. I turned round to look.
2 volver loco a alguien to drive somebody mad
La música me vuelve loco. The music is driving me mad.

vosotros pronoun masc.,
vosotras fem.
1 you
Vosotros podéis hacerlo. You can do it.

🔑 **LANGUAGE**
Vosotros/vosotras is used for giving special importance to the word 'you'.

2 (after a preposition etc.) **you**
con vosotros with you
Somos más altas que vosotras. We're taller than you.
vosotros mismos yourselves

🔑 **LANGUAGE**
Use **vosotros/vosotras** when you are talking to two or more friends, people in your family, or people your own age.

votar verb
to vote

voy verb SEE ir
Voy en coche. I go by car.
Voy a sentarme aquí. I'm going to sit here.

la **voz** noun fem. (plural las **voces**)
voice
Tiene una voz muy bonita. She has a lovely voice.

• *The months of the year and days of the week do not take a capital letter in Spanish.*

Lee esto en voz alta. Read this aloud.

Maite habla en voz baja. Maite speaks quietly.

el **vuelo** noun *masc.*
flight
El vuelo dura dos horas. The flight lasts two hours.

la **vuelta** noun *fem.*
1 return
la vuelta al colegio the return to school
2 change
Aquí tienes la vuelta. Here's your change.
3 walk
¿Quieres dar una vuelta? Do you want to go for a walk?
4 (*in a car, on a horse, etc.*) **ride**
Quiero dar una vuelta en bici. I want to go for a ride on my bike.
5 dar la vuelta a una página to turn a page
darse la vuelta to turn round
Me di la vuelta. I turned round.

vuestro adjective *masc.*,
vuestra *fem.*
1 your
vuestro colegio your school
vuestros juguetes your toys
2 yours
Este boli es vuestro. This pen is yours.
¿Son vuestros? Are they yours?
unas amigas vuestras some friends of yours

> **LANGUAGE**
> Use **vuestro/vuestra** when you are talking to two or more friends, people in your family, or people your own age.

el **vuestro** pronoun *masc.*,
la **vuestra** *fem.*
yours
Nuestro perro es más grande que el vuestro. Our dog is bigger than yours.
mis libros y los vuestros my books and yours

> **LANGUAGE**
> Use **el vuestro/la vuestra** when you are talking to two or more friends, people in your family, or people your own age.

Ww

la **web** noun *fem.*
web
una página web a web page
un sitio web a website

Xx

el **xilófono** noun *masc.*
xylophone
tocar el xilófono to play the xylophone

• *See the centre section for verb tables.*

Yy

y conjunction
and
rojo y verde red and green

ya adverb
1 already
Ya he comido. I've already eaten.
2 yet
¿Ya has terminado? Have you
finished yet?
3 now
Ya es hora de irnos. It's time to go
now.
4 ya no ... not ... any more
Ya no vivo en Londres. I don't live
in London any more.
5 (no translation)
Ya lo sé. I know.
¡Ya voy! I'm coming!

el **yate** noun masc.
yacht

Zz

la **zanahoria** noun fem.
carrot

la **zapatería** noun fem.
shoe shop

el **zapatero** noun masc.,
la **zapatera** fem.
1 shoemaker
2 shoe repairer's

la **zapatilla** noun fem.
slipper
Llevo zapatillas en casa. I wear
slippers at home.
zapatillas de deporte trainers

el **zapato** noun masc.
shoe
un par de zapatos a pair of shoes

la **yema** noun fem.
yolk

yo pronoun
1 (for giving special importance to the word in
the sentence) **I**
Yo soy inglesa pero las otras son
españolas. I'm English but the
others are Spanish.
Pedro y yo fuimos a casa. Pedro
and I went home.
2 (with que, ser, etc.) **me**
Eres más rápido que yo. You're
faster than me.
Soy yo. It's me.
yo mismo myself

el **yogur** noun masc.
yoghurt

el **yoyó** noun masc.
yo-yo

la **zarzamora** noun fem.
blackberry

la **zona** noun fem.
area
Vivo en una zona tranquila. I live
in a quiet area.

el **zoo** noun masc.
zoo

el **zoológico** noun masc.
zoo

el **zorro** noun masc.
fox

el **zumo** noun masc.
juice
zumo de naranja orange juice

zurdo adjective masc., **zurda** fem.
left-handed

• Use **el** and **uno** for masculine words and **la** and **una** for feminine words.

Animals
Clothes and colours
Calendar

Time
Body
Numbers

In the classroom
Friends
The weather

Shopping
Countries and places
Family

Healthy eating
Jobs
Where are you?

Feelings
A letter, a text, an email
Where I live

Sports
Hobbies
Story time

179

Los animales / Animals
¿Tienes un animal? / Do you have a pet?

No, no tengo animales.
No, I don't have any pets.

Sí, tengo …
Yes, I have …

un animal / animales	an animal / animals
un gato / gatos	a cat / cats
un perro / perros	a dog / dogs
un pájaro / pájaros	a bird / birds
un caballa / caballas	a horse / horses
un pez / peces	a fish / fish
un ratón / ratones	a mouse / mice
un hámster / hámsters	a hamster / hamsters
un cobaya / cobayas	a guinea pig / guinea pigs
un conejo / conejos	a rabbit / rabbits
una serpiente / serpientes	a snake / snakes
un camaleón / camaleones	a chameleon / chameleons

pío pío
tweet, tweet

guau guau
woof, woof

**Tengo un gato.
Es blanco y negro.**
I have a cat.
He is black and white.

No tengo caballo.
I don't have a horse.

miau
miaow

No tengo perro.
I don't have a dog.

La ropa y los colores / Clothes and colours

Mi color favorito es el azul.
My favourite colour is blue.

Odio el azul.
I hate blue.

la camisa
shirt

los zapatos
shoes

la camiseta
T-shirt

la sudadera
sweatshirt

los pantalones
trousers

Me encanta el rojo.
I love red.

s vaqueros
jeans

el suéter
sweater

la falda
skirt

el sombrero
hat

los calcetines
socks

¿De qué color es? / What colour is it?

blanco | blanca
white

rojo | roja
red

zul
lue

marrón
brown

negro | negra
black

amarillo | amarilla
yellow

rosa
pink

verde
green

gris
grey

naranja
orange

morado | morada
purple

El calendario / Calendar

Los días de la semana / Days of the week

lunes	Monday
martes	Tuesday
miércoles	Wednesday
jueves	Thursday
viernes	Friday
sábado	Saturday
domingo	Sunday

¿Qué día es hoy?
What day is it?

Hoy es lunes.
It is Monday.

Los meses / Months

enero	January
febrero	February
marzo	March
abril	April
mayo	May
junio	June
julio	July
agosto	August
septiembre	September
octubre	October
noviembre	November
diciembre	December
el día de Reyes	Twelfth Night (6th January)

¿Qué fecha es hoy?
What is today's date?

El 24 de enero.
24th January.

Days and months don't start with a capital letter in Spanish.

¡Feliz Navidad!
Happy Christmas!

los lunes
on Mondays

Las estaciones / Seasons

la primavera	spring
el verano	summer
el otoño	autumn
el invierno	winter

¡Feliz cumpleaños!
Happy birthday!

¡Feliz Año Nuevo!
Happy New Year!

182

La hora / Time

¿Qué hora es?
What time is it?

Es la una.
is one o'clock.

Son las tres.
It is three o'clock.

Son las cinco.
It is five o'clock.

Son las siete.
It is seven o'clock.

Son las dos.
It is two o'clock.

Son las cuatro.
It is four o'clock.

Son las seis.
It is six o'clock.

Son las ocho.
It is eight o'clock.

Son las diez.
It is ten o'clock.

Es mediodía.
It is noon / midday.

Son las nueve.
It is nine o'clock.

Son las once.
It is eleven o'clock.

Es medianoche.
It is midnight.

Es mediodía.	It is midday.	**Son las doce y media de la noche**	It is half past midnight.
Es la una.	It is one o'clock.	**Es la una y media.**	It is half past one.
Es la una y cuarto.	It is quarter past one.	**Es la una menos cuarto.**	It is quarter to one.

por la mañana
morning

por la tarde
in the afternoon / evening

por la noche
at night / in the evening

¿A qué hora es?
At what time is it?

El colegio empieza a las nueve menos cuarto.
School starts at 8.45.

Me acuesto a las ocho.
I go to bed at 8 o'clock.

Es a la una y veinticinco.
It is at 1.25.

Cenamos a las seis y media.
We eat at 6.30.

Salimos al recreo a las once.
Playtime is at 11.

Me levanto a las siete.
I get up at 7.

Salimos de clase a las cuatro y media.
School finishes at 4.30.

183

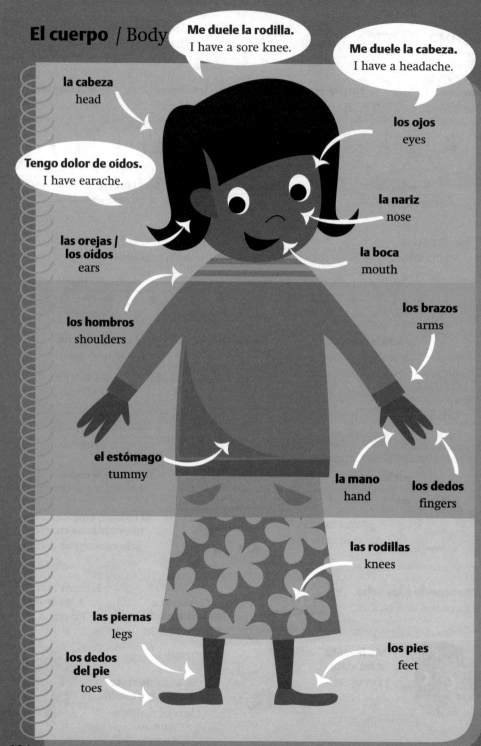

Los números / Numbers

cero	zero
uno, un/una	one
dos	two
tres	three
cuatro	four
cinco	five
seis	six
siete	seven
ocho	eight
nueve	nine
diez	ten

once	eleven
doce	twelve
trece	thirteen
catorce	fourteen
quince	fifteen
dieciséis	sixteen
diecisiete	seventeen
dieciocho	eighteen
diecinueve	nineteen
veinte	twenty

veintiuno, veintiún / veintiuna	twenty-one
treinta	thirty
cuarenta	forty
cincuenta	fifty
sesenta	sixty

1° / 1st
**primero,
primer / primera**

2°/ 2nd
segundo /segunda

3° / 3rd
tercero, tercer /tercera

más + add

Cinco más dos son siete.
Five plus two is seven.
5 + 2 = 7

menos - subtract

Seis menos dos son cuatro.
Six minus two is four.
6 - 2 = 4

por x multiplied by

Dos por cinco son diez.
Two times five is ten.
2 x 5 = 10

dividido entre ÷ divided by

**Doce dividido entre
dos son seis.**
Twelve divided by two is six.
12 ÷ 2 = 6

En la clase / In the classroom

¡Excelente!
¡Bien hecho!
Excellent!
Well done!

¿Qué es?
What is it?

¿Puedo ir al baño?
May I go to the toilet?

Tomad un lápiz.
Take a pencil.

un libro
a book

una goma
a rubber

un estuche
a pencil case

una mesa
a table

un maestro /
una maestra
a teacher

¡Silencio!
Silence!

¡Escribid!
Write!

¡Levantaos!
Stand up!

un lápiz
a pencil

¡Dámelo!
Give it to me!

¡Sentaos!
Sit down!

¡Mirad!
Look!

¡Miradme!
Watch me!

un bolígrafo
a pen

¡Escuchad!
Listen!

He perdido mi lápiz.
I've lost my pencil.

un alumno / una alumna
a pupil

Presente.
Here.

Ausente.
Absent.

un cuaderno
an exercise book

una silla
a chair

He terminado.
I've finished.

un sacapuntas
a pencil sharpener

un rotulador
a felt-tip pen

una cartera
a schoolbag

una regla
a ruler

Los amigos / Friends

¡Hola! Hello!	**¡Hola!** Hi!
¿Cómo te llamas? What is your name?	**Me llamo Felipe.** My name is Philip.
¿Cuántos años tienes? How old are you?	**Tengo ocho años.** I am eight.
¿Dónde vives? Where do you live?	**Vivo en York.** I live in York.
¡Adiós! Goodbye!	**¡Hasta pronto!** See you soon!

¿Cómo estás? How are you?	**Bien, gracias.** Fine, thanks.
	No muy bien. Not very well.
¿Hablas español? Do you speak Spanish?	**Sí, un poco.** Yes, a little.
	No muy bien. Not very well.

¿Cuándo es tu cumpleaños?
When is your birthday?

Es el diez de diciembre. ¿Y tú?
It's the tenth of December. And you?

Mi cumpleaños es el primero de abril.
My birthday is the first of April.

¡Feliz cumpleaños!
Happy birthday!

Voy al cine el sábado. ¿Quieres ir al cine el sábado?
I am going to the cinema on Saturday. Would you like to go to the cinema on Saturday?

Sí, gracias.
Yes, thanks.

¿Cuál es tu dirección de email?
What is your email address?

Es ...
It is ...

El tiempo / The weather

Hace viento.
It's windy.

Está nublado.
It's cloudy.

Está lloviendo.
It's raining.

Hay tormenta.
It's stormy.

Hace calor.
It's hot.

Hay niebla.
It's foggy.

Las compras / Shopping

¡Hola!
Hello!

una Coca-Cola
a Coke

¿Qué desea?
What would you like?

¿De qué sabor?
What flavour?

Cinco euros.
Five euros.

un zumo de naranja
an orange juice

¡Hola!
Hello!

Quiero un helado, por favor.
I would like an ice cream, please.

Aquí tiene. Gracias.
Here you are.
Thank you.

una taza de té
a cup of tea

un helado
an ice cream

una postal
a postcard

un sello
a stamp

un pan
some bread

un café
a coffee

Quiero ...
I would like ...

una limonada
a lemonade

una revista
a magazine

un pastel
a cake

la farmacia
chemist

un bocadillo de queso
a cheese sandwich

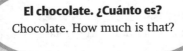

la panadería
baker

la pastelería
cake shop

El chocolate. ¿Cuánto es?
Chocolate. How much is that?

la tienda de periódicos
newsagent

... por favor
... please

Los países y los lugares / Countries and places

¿Qué país es?
What country is this?

Es ...
This is ...

Gales
Wales

Irlanda
Ireland

Francia
France

Reino Unido
United Kingdom

Escocia
Scotland

España
Spain

¿Dónde está ...?
Where is ...?

N

O

E

S

Está ...	**en el norte.**	**en el sur.**	**en el este.**	**en el oeste.**
It is ...	in the north.	in the south.	in the east.	in the west.
	el noreste	**el suroeste**	**el sureste**	**el noroeste**
	north-east	south-west	south-east	north-west

¿De qué nacionalidad eres?
What nationality are you?

Soy inglés / inglesa.	I am English.
Soy británico / británica.	I am British.
Soy galés / galesa.	I am Welsh.
Soy escocés / escocesa.	I am Scottish.
Soy irlandés / irlandesa.	I am Irish.

¿Qué idioma hablas?
What language do you speak?

Hablo inglés.	I speak English.
Hablo español.	I speak Spanish.
Hablo español, soy cubano.	I speak Spanish, I am Cuban.
Habla inglés, es norteamericana.	She speaks English, she is American.
Habla español, es mejicano.	He speaks Spanish, he is Mexican.
Habla español, es chileno.	He speaks Spanish, he is Chilean.
Hablo español, soy salvadoreña.	I speak Spanish, I am from El Salvador.
Habla español, es boliviana.	She speaks Spanish, she is Bolivian.
Habla español, es venezolano.	He speaks Spanish, he is Venezuelan.
Habla español, es peruana.	She speaks Spanish, she is Peruvian.
Habla español, es argentino.	He speaks Spanish, he is Argentinian.

La familia / Family

¿Tienes hermanos?
Do you have any brothers and sisters?

Soy hijo único / hija única.
I am an only child.

Tengo un hermano mayor / pequeño.
I have a big / little brother.

Tengo una hermana mayor / pequeña que se llama …
I have a big / little sister who is called …

No tengo hermano / hermana.
I don't have a brother / sister.

¿Quién es éste/ésta?
Who is this?

Te presento a …
This is …

mi madre / mi madrastra
my mother / stepmother

Soy yo.
This is me.

mi hermana / mi hermanastra
my sister / stepsister

mi padre / mi padrastro
my father / stepfather

mi abuelo
my grandfather

alto / alta
tall

pequeño / pequeña
small

grande
big

delgado / delgada
slim

moreno / morena
brown

mi abuela
my grandmother

rubio / rubia
blond / blonde

pelirrojo / pelirroja
red-haired

simpático / simpática
nice

difícil
difficult

Llevo / lleva gafas.
I wear / he / she
wears glasses.

**Llevo / lleva un aparato
en los dientes.**
I have / he /
she has a brace.

mi hermano / mi hermanastro
my brother / stepbrother

Una dieta sana / Healthy eating

Comer poco.
Eat a little.

Comer con moderación.
Eat in moderation.

Comer mucho.
Eat a lot.

la zanahoria
carrot

la manzana
apple

el tomate
tomato

el plátano
banana

el pollo
chicken

la lechuga
lettuce

las patatas
potatoes

el arroz
rice

la naranja
orange

el agua
water

el pan
bread

los espaguetis
spaghetti

el ajo
garlic

el queso
cheese

el helado
ice cream

el zumo de manzana
apple juice

los cereales
cereal

el yogur
yoghurt

los huevos
eggs

Me gustan los caramelos.
I like sweets.

No me gusta el café.
I don't like coffee.

la hamburguesa
burger

las patatas fritas
chips

el chocolate
chocolate

la mermelada
jam

el pastel
cake

la bebida
drink

el azúcar
sugar

las patatas fritas
crisps

199

El empleo / Jobs

Un día seré …
One day, I will be …

Mi padre es piloto.
My dad is a pilot.

Quisiera ser contable.
I would like to be an accountant.

**el maestro / la maestra,
el profesor / la profesora**
teacher

el / la astronauta
astronaut

el fotógrafo / la fotógrafa
photographer

**el bombero /
la bombera**
firefighter

el médico / la médica
doctor

el / la electricista
electrician

**el conductor / la conductora
de autobús**
bus driver

el / la policía
policeman / policewoman

¿Dónde estás? / Where are you?

y	o	pero	aunque
and	or	but	though
primero	**luego**	**finalmente**	**así que**
first	next	finally	so, therefore

¡Prohibido jugar a la pelota!
No ball games allowed!

¡Socorro!
Help!

en
on

por encima de
over

delante de
in front of

detrás de
behind

en
in

enfrente de
opposite

debajo de
below / under

Peligro
Danger

¡Cuidado con el perro!
Beware of the dog!

Agua no
potable.
Do not drink
the water.

¡Prohibida la entrada!
Keep out!

Sentimientos y sensaciones / Feelings

Es aburrido.
It's boring.

¡Es estupendo!
It's great!

Estoy triste.
I'm sad.

Gracias.
Thank you.

Tengo hambre.
I'm hungry.

¿Quieres …? Do you want …?	**Perdón.** Sorry.	**guay** cool	**No entiendo.** I don't understand.
Sí, por favor. Yes, please.	**Estoy cansado / cansada** I'm tired.	**fácil** easy	**No me importa.** I don't mind.
No, gracias. No, thank you.	**Lo siento.** I'm sorry.	**difícil** difficult	**¡Vale!** OK!
Quizás. Maybe.	**Gracias.** Thank you.	**gracioso / graciosa** funny	**No me apetece.** I don't feel like it.

Una carta / A letter

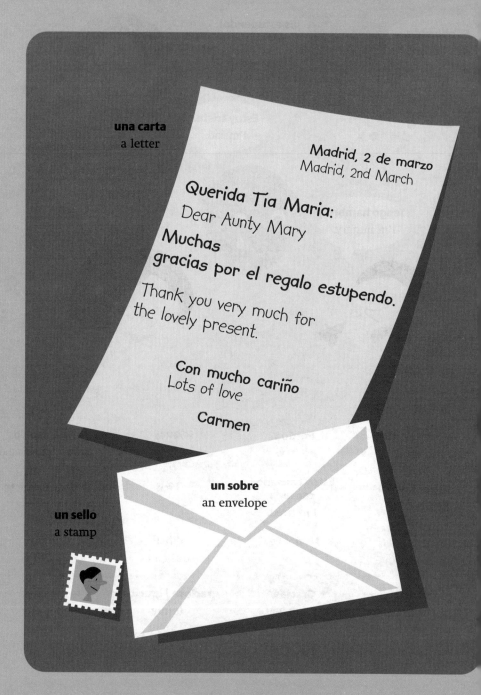

una carta
a letter

Madrid, 2 de marzo
Madrid, 2nd March

Querida Tía María:
Dear Aunty Mary

Muchas gracias por el regalo estupendo.
Thank you very much for the lovely present.

Con mucho cariño
Lots of love

Carmen

un sobre
an envelope

un sello
a stamp

Un SMS / A text

un móvil
a mobile

¡Hola!
Hi!

un SMS
a text message

bbtt. stas bn?
vams al cin o 1kf mñn?
Buenas tardes.
¿Estás bien?
¿Vamos al cine o a un
café mañana?

Hi. Are you OK?
Do you want to go to the
cinema or a cafe tomorrow?

Un correo electrónico / An email

un ordenador
a computer

A: Rosa
De: José

¿Quieres venir conmigo
al partido el sábado?
Do you want to come
to the match with
me on Saturday?

un email
an email

un ratón
a mouse

un teclado
a keyboard

El lugar donde vivo / Where I live

Vivo ...
I live ...

en una casa / un piso.
in a house / flat.

Vivo en Londres. Está en el sur de Inglaterra.
I live in London. It is in the south of England.

Hay ...
There is a ...

la oficina de correos
post office

el mercado
market

la oficina de turismo
tourist office

el parque
park

SUPER

el supermercado
supermarket

a pie / en autobús / en tren
on foot / by bus / by train

en el campo / en la ciudad
in the country / in the town

la piscina
pool

la mezquita
mosque

el colegio / la escuela
school

la estación de trenes
railway station

¡Perdón, señor!
Excuse me, sir!

el cine
cinema

¿Dónde está el / la ... por favor?
Where is the ... please?

iglesia
urch

Siga todo recto.
Go straight ahead.

Tome la primera / segunda a la derecha / izquierda.
Take the first / second right / left.

El deporte / Sports

¿Haces deporte?
Do you play sport?

Yo juego al rugby.
I play rugby.

¿Queréis jugar al fútbol?
Do you want to play football?

Mi deporte
favorito es ...
My favourite
sport is ...

el tenis
tennis

el fútbol
football

la equitación
horse-riding

la natación
swimming

el rugby
rugby

el bádminton
badminton

la gimnasia
gymnastics

el judo
judo

el baile
dancing

Los pasatiempos / Hobbies

el clarinete
clarinet

la flauta
flute

Toco el piano y la batería.
I play the piano and the drums.

Toco la guitarra.
I play the guitar.

Mi pasatiempo favorito es ...
My favourite hobby is…

el teclado
keyboard

la lectura
reading

la música
music

la televisión
television

el dibujo
drawing

los juegos de mesa
board games

la informática
computing

los videojuegos
computer games

Los cuentos / Story time

el sombrero
hat

la bruja mala
the wicked witch

el gato
cat

la escoba
broomstick

La Bella Durmiente
Sleeping Beauty

Pinocho
Pinocchio

la casa de pan de jengibre
gingerbread house

Cenicienta
Cinderella

Rumpelstiltskin
Rumpelstiltskin

Érase una vez ...
Once upon a time ...

un final feliz
happy ending

fueron felices y comieron perdices
they lived happily ever after

el cuento de hadas
fairy tale

la magia
magic

el mago bueno
the good wizard

Caperucita Roja
Little Red Riding Hood

la varita
wand

El Gato con Botas
Puss in Boots

210

Verb tables

In Spanish there are three main verb types, those ending in -ar (like hablar), -er (like comer), and -ir (like vivir).

You can use the ones on this page as models for other regular verbs as many follow the same patterns. Some verbs don't, so these verb tables also give you some common irregular verbs.

There are also verbs called reflexive verbs. Reflexive verbs are used with a pronoun (like me, te, se) for example, levantarse (to stand up): me levanto is 'I stand up', te levantas is 'you stand up', etc.

You can think of reflexive verbs as those that mean you do something to yourself rather than to someone else.

-ar hablar to talk, to speak

present tense

hablo	I talk
hablas	you talk
habla	he/she talks
hablamos	we talk
habláis	you talk
hablan	they talk

past tense

hablé	I talked
hablaste	you talked
habló	he/she talked
hablamos	we talked
hablasteis	you talked
hablaron	they talked

future tense

hablaré	I will talk
hablarás	you will talk
hablará	he/she will talk
hablaremos	we will talk
hablaréis	you will talk
hablarán	they will talk

-er comer to eat

present tense

como	I eat
comes	you eat
come	he/she eats
comemos	we eat
coméis	you eat
comen	they eat

past tense

comí	I ate
comiste	you ate
comió	he/she ate
comimos	we ate
comisteis	you ate
comieron	they ate

future tense

comeré	I will eat
comerás	you will eat
comerá	he/she will eat
comeremos	we will eat
comeréis	you will eat
comerán	they will eat

-ir vivir to live

present tense

vivo	I live
vives	you live
vive	he/she lives
vivimos	we live
vivís	you live
viven	they live

past tense

viví	I lived
viviste	you lived
vivió	he/she lived
vivimos	we lived
vivisteis	you lived
vivieron	they lived

future tense

viviré	I will live
vivirás	you will live
vivirá	he/she will live
viviremos	we will live
viviréis	you will live
vivirán	they will live

dar to give

present tense

doy	I give
das	you give
da	he/she gives
damos	we give
dais	you give
dan	they give

past tense

di	I gave
diste	you gave
dio	he/she gave
dimos	we gave
disteis	you gave
dieron	they gave

future tense

daré	I will give
darás	you will give
dará	he/she will give
daremos	we will give
daréis	you will give
darán	they will give

decir to say, to tell

present tense

digo	I say
dices	you say
dice	he/she says
decimos	we say
decís	you say
dicen	they say

past tense

dije	I said
dijiste	you said
dijo	he/she said
dijimos	we said
dijisteis	you said
dijeron	they said

future

diré	I will say
dirás	you will say
dirá	he/she will say
diremos	we will say
diréis	you will say
dirán	they will say

estar to be

present tense

estoy	I am
estás	you are
está	he/she is
estamos	we are
estáis	you are
están	they are

past tense

estuve	I was
estuviste	you were
estuvo	he/she was
estuvimos	we were
estuvisteis	you were
estuvieron	they were

future tense

estaré	I will be
estarás	you will be
estará	he/she will be
estaremos	we will be
estaréis	you will be
estarán	they will be

haber to have

present tense

he	I have
has	you have
ha	he/she has
hemos	we have
habéis	you have
han	they have

past tense

hube	I had
hubiste	you had
hubo	he/she had
hubimos	we had
hubisteis	you had
hubieron	they had

future tense

habré	I will have
habrás	you will have
habrá	he/she will have
habremos	we will have
habréis	you will have
habrán	they will have

hacer to do, to make

present tense

hago	I do
haces	you do
hace	he/she does
hacemos	we do
hacéis	you do
hacen	they do

past tense

hice	I did
hiciste	you did
hizo	he/she did
hicimos	we did
hicisteis	you did
hicieron	they did

future tense

haré	I will do
harás	you will do
hará	he/she will do
haremos	we will do
haréis	you will do
harán	they will do

ir to go

present tense

voy	I go
vas	you go
va	he/she goes
vamos	we go
vais	you go
van	they go

past tense

fui	I went
fuiste	you went
fue	he/she went
fuimos	we went
fuisteis	you went
fueron	they went

future tense

iré	I will go
irás	you will go
irá	he/she will go
iremos	we will go
iréis	you will go
irán	they will go

jugar to play

present tense

juego	I play
juegas	you play
juega	he/she plays
jugamos	we play
jugáis	you play
juegan	they play

past tense

jugué	I played
jugaste	you played
jugó	he/she played
jugamos	we played
jugasteis	you played
jugaron	they played

future tense

jugaré	I will play
jugarás	you will play
jugará	he/she will play
jugaremos	we will play
jugaréis	you will play
jugarán	they will play

oír to hear

present tense

oigo	I hear
oyes	you hear
oye	he/she hears
oímos	we hear
oís	you hear
oyen	they hear

past tense

oí	I heard
oíste	you heard
oyó	he/she heard
oímos	we heard
oísteis	you heard
oyeron	they heard

future tense

oiré	I will hear
oirás	you will hear
oirá	he/she will hear
oiremos	we will hear
oiréis	you will hear
oirán	they will hear

poder to be able

present tense

puedo	I can
puedes	you can
puede	he/she can
podemos	we can
podéis	you can
pueden	they can

past tense

pude	I could
pudiste	you could
pudo	he/she could
pudimos	we could
pudisteis	you could
pudieron	they could

future tense

podré	I will be able
podrás	you will be able
podrá	he/she will be able
podremos	we will be able
podréis	you will be able
podrán	they will be able

poner to put

present tense

pongo	I put
pones	you put
pone	he/she puts
ponemos	we put
ponéis	you put
ponen	they put

past tense

puse	I put
pusiste	you put
puso	he/she put
pusimos	we put
pusisteis	you put
pusieron	they put

future tense

pondré	I will put
pondrás	you will put
pondrá	he/she will put
pondremos	we will put
pondréis	you will put
pondrán	they will put

querer to want, to love

present tense

quiero	I want
quieres	you want
quiere	he/she wants
queremos	we want
queréis	you want
quieren	they want

past tense

quise	I wanted
quisiste	you wanted
quiso	he/she wanted
quisimos	we wanted
quisisteis	you wanted
quisieron	they wanted

future tense

querré	I will want
querrás	you will want
querrá	he/she will want
querremos	we will want
querréis	you will want
querrán	they will want

saber to know

present tense

sé	I know
sabes	you know
sabe	he/she knows
sabemos	we know
sabéis	you know
saben	they know

past tense

supe	I knew
supiste	you knew
supo	he/she knew
supimos	we knew
supisteis	you knew
supieron	they knew

future tense

sabré	I will know
sabrás	you will know
sabrá	he/she will know
sabremos	we will know
sabréis	you will know
sabrán	they will know

salir to go out

present tense

salgo	I go out
sales	you go out
sale	he/she goes out
salimos	we go out
salís	you go out
salen	they go out

future tense

saldré	I will go out
saldrás	you will go out
saldrá	he/she will go out
saldremos	we will go out
saldréis	you will go out
saldrán	they will go out

past tense

salí	I went out
saliste	you went out
salió	he/she went out
salimos	we went out
salisteis	you went out
salieron	they went out

sentir to feel

present tense

siento	I feel
sientes	you feel
siente	he/she feels
sentimos	we feel
sentís	you feel
sienten	they feel

past tense

sentí	I felt
sentiste	you felt
sintió	he/she felt
sentimos	we felt
sentisteis	you felt
sintieron	they felt

future tense

sentiré	I will feel
sentirás	you will feel
sentirá	he/she will feel
sentiremos	we will feel
sentiréis	you will feel
sentirán	they will feel

ser to be

present tense

soy	I am
eres	you are
es	he/she is
somos	we are
sois	you are
son	they are

past tense

fui	I was
fuiste	you were
fue	he/she was
fuimos	we were
fuisteis	you were
fueron	they were

future tense

seré	I will be
serás	you will be
será	he/she will be
seremos	we will be
seréis	you will be
serán	they will be

tener to have

present tense

tengo	I have
tienes	you have
tiene	he/she has
tenemos	we have
tenéis	you have
tienen	they have

past tense

tuve	I had
tuviste	you had
tuvo	he/she had
tuvimos	we had
tuvisteis	you had
tuvieron	they had

future tense

tendré	I will have
tendrás	you will have
tendrá	he/she will have
tendremos	we will have
tendréis	you will have
tendrán	they will have

venir to come

present tense

vengo	I come
vienes	you come
viene	he/she comes
venimos	we come
venís	you come
vienen	they come

past tense

vine	I came
viniste	you came
vino	he/she came
vinimos	we came
vinisteis	you came
vinieron	they came

future tense

vendré	I will come
vendrás	you will come
vendrá	he/she will come
vendremos	we will come
vendréis	you will come
vendrán	they will come

ver to see

present tense

veo	I see
ves	you see
ve	he/she sees
vemos	we see
veis	you see
ven	they see

past tense

vi	I saw
viste	you saw
vio	he/she saw
vimos	we saw
visteis	you saw
vieron	they saw

future tense

veré	I will see
verás	you will see
verá	he/she will see
veremos	we will see
veréis	you will see
verán	they will see

levantarse to stand up

present tense

me levanto	I stand up
te levantas	you stand up
se levanta	he/she stands up
nos levantamos	we stand up
os levantáis	you stand up
se levantan	they stand up

past tense

me levanté	I stood up
te levantaste	you stood up
se levantó	he/she stood up
nos levantamos	we stood up
os levantasteis	you stood up
se levantaron	they stood up

future tense

me levantaré	I will stand up
te levantarás	you will stand up
se levantará	he/she will stand up
nos levantaremos	we will stand up
os levantaréis	you will stand up
se levantarán	they will stand up

Aa

a determiner

🔑 **LANGUAGE**
Use **un** before a masculine noun (like **coche**), and **una** before a feminine noun (like **escuela**).

1 **un** *masc.*, **una** *fem.*
 a car un coche
 a school una escuela
 He's a very clever boy. Es un chico muy inteligente.
2 (*when saying how many times*) **al** *masc.*, **a la** *fem.*
 twice a day dos veces al día
 three times a week tres veces a la semana
3 (*no translation*)
 My dad's a doctor.
 Mi padre es médico.

🔑 **LANGUAGE**
In Spanish you don't use **un** or **una** when saying what somebody's job is.

able adjective
1 **David isn't able to come.** David no puede venir.
2 **Helen isn't able to swim.** Helen no sabe nadar.

🔑 **LANGUAGE**
Translate 'be able to' using the verb **poder** (can) but when it means 'know how to' use **saber**.

about adverb
1 (*with numbers*) **unos** *masc. plural*, **unas** *fem. plural*
 about fifteen boys unos quince chicos
 It costs about a hundred euros. Cuesta unos cien euros.
2 (*with time*) **alrededor de**
 We go to school at about eight. Vamos a la escuela alrededor de las ocho.

about preposition
1 (*on the subject of*) **sobre**
 a book about animals un libro sobre los animales
 What's the book about? ¿De qué trata el libro?
2 (*with 'talk'*) **de**
 to talk about something hablar de algo
3 (*with an infinitive*) **a punto de**
 We're about to go out. Estamos a punto de salir.

above preposition
1 **encima de**
 My grandparents live above a shop. Mis abuelos viven encima de una tienda.
2 (*with verbs showing movement*) **por encima de**
 The plane is flying above the town. El avión vuela por encima de la ciudad.

above adverb
arriba
 It's on the shelf above. Está en el estante de arriba.

abroad adverb
1 **en el extranjero**
 They live abroad. Viven en el extranjero.
2 (*with verbs showing movement*) **al extranjero**
 to go abroad ir al extranjero
 We always travel abroad. Viajamos siempre al extranjero.

absent adjective
ausente *masc. & fem.*
 Max is absent today. Max está ausente hoy.

accent noun
 el **acento** *masc.*

• *Languages and nationalities do not take a capital letter in Spanish.*

English Spanish

a b c d e f g h i j k l m n o p q r s t u v w x y z

Marie has a French accent. Marie tiene acento francés.

to **accept** verb
aceptar

accident noun
1 el accidente *masc.*
to have an accident tener un accidente
a car accident un accidente de coche
2 **by accident** sin querer
She did it by accident. Lo hizo sin querer.

accidentally adverb
sin querer
He accidentally knocked over the glass. Tiró el vaso al suelo sin querer.

to **accuse** verb
acusar
They accused me of breaking the window. Me acusaron de haber roto la ventana.

to **ache** verb
My arm aches. Me duele el brazo.
Do your legs ache? ¿Te duelen las piernas?

LANGUAGE
Use **duele** or **duelen** (from **doler** 'to hurt') followed by the name of the thing that aches.

acrobat noun
el or la acróbata *masc. & fem.*

across preposition & adverb
1 (*going from one side to the other*)
to go across cruzar
Richard went across the road. Richard cruzó la calle.
2 (*on the other side*) al otro lado de
They live across the street. Viven al otro lado de la calle.

to **act** verb
(*in a play or film*) actuar
He acts very well. Actúa muy bien.

action noun
la acción *fem.*

active adjective
activo *masc.*, activa *fem.*

activity noun
la actividad *fem.*

actor noun
el actor *masc.*

actress noun
la actriz *fem.* (plural las **actrices**)

actually adverb
en realidad
Actually, this isn't difficult. En realidad esto no es difícil.

to **add** verb
1 (*something extra*) añadir
We have to add more salt. Hay que añadir más sal.
2 (*using numbers*) sumar
Add up the three numbers. Suma los tres números.

address noun
la dirección *fem.* (plural las **direcciones**)
What's your address? ¿Cuál es tu dirección?

adjective noun
el adjetivo *masc.*

LANGUAGE
English = adj**e**ctive
Spanish = adj**e**tivo

adult noun
el adulto *masc.*, la adulta *fem.*

adventure noun
la aventura *fem.*

LANGUAGE
English = ad**v**enture
Spanish = a**v**entura

adverb noun
el adverbio *masc.*

• *The months of the year and days of the week do not take a capital letter in Spanish.*

advert noun
el **anuncio** *masc.*
There are lots of adverts for sweets. Hay muchos anuncios de caramelos.

advice noun
el **consejo** *masc.*
Can you give me some advice? ¿Puedes darme un consejo?

aerial noun
la **antena** *fem.*

aeroplane noun
el **avión** *masc.* (plural los **aviones**)
to travel on an aeroplane viajar en avión

to **afford** verb
tener dinero para comprar
We can't afford a computer. No tenemos dinero para comprarnos un ordenador.

afraid adjective
1 (*scared*)
I'm afraid. Tengo miedo.
to be afraid of tener miedo a
He's afraid of his brother. Le tiene miedo a su hermano.
I'm afraid to go out by myself. Me da miedo salir sola.
Don't be afraid! ¡No tengas miedo!

> **LANGUAGE**
> English = **I am** afraid.
> Spanish = **Tengo** miedo. (I have fear.)

2 (*sorry*)
I'm afraid she's ill. Lo siento pero está enferma.

> **LANGUAGE**
> Use **lo siento** to mean 'I'm afraid' when you are sorry about something.

Africa noun
África *fem.*

African adjective
africano *masc.*, **africana** *fem.*

• *See the centre section for verb tables.*

African noun
el **africano** *masc.*, la **africana** *fem.*

after preposition & conjunction
después de
after my birthday después de mi cumpleaños
after doing something después de hacer algo
After eating I want to watch TV. Después de comer quiero ver la tele.

after adverb
después
What are you doing after? ¿Qué vas a hacer después?

afternoon noun
la **tarde** *fem.*
in the afternoon por la tarde
at four o'clock in the afternoon a las cuatro de la tarde
this afternoon esta tarde
I'll see you on Sunday afternoon. Te veré el domingo por la tarde.
on Sunday afternoons los domingos por la tarde

afters noun
el **postre** *masc.*
What's for afters? ¿Qué hay de postre?

afterwards adverb
después
soon afterwards poco después

again adverb
1 otra vez
Are you crying again? ¿Otra vez estás llorando?
I'm going to read it again. Voy a leerlo otra vez.
2 (*using* **volver**)

> **LANGUAGE**
> In Spanish you can also use the verb **volver** (to come back) followed by **a** to say you're doing something again.

to do something again volver a hacer algo

a b c d e f g h i j k l m n o p q r s t u v w x y z

We'll see the film again tomorrow. Volveremos a ver la película mañana.

against preposition
contra
Madrid are playing against Barcelona. El Madrid juega contra el Barcelona.

age noun
la edad fem.
They're the same age. Tienen la misma edad.
at the age of ten a la edad de diez años
Helen is eight years of age. Helen tiene ocho años.

ago adverb
hace
I started a week ago. Empecé hace una semana.
a long time ago hace mucho tiempo
not very long ago no hace mucho tiempo

> 🔑 **LANGUAGE**
> Hace goes before the amount of time but 'ago' goes after.

to **agree** verb
estar de acuerdo
I agree. Estoy de acuerdo.
I don't agree with you. No estoy de acuerdo contigo.

ahead adverb
delante
I'll go ahead. Yo voy delante.
There's a river ahead. Hay un río delante de nosotros.
Walk straight ahead. Siga todo recto.

air noun
1 el aire masc.
in the open air al aire libre
2 **to travel by air** viajar en avión

air-conditioned adjective
climatizado masc.,
climatizada fem.

air conditioning noun masc.
el aire condicionado masc.

airmail noun
to send something by airmail mandar algo por avión

airport noun
el aeropuerto masc.

alarm noun
1 la alarma fem.
a fire alarm una alarma contra incendios
2 **an alarm clock** un despertador masc.

album noun
el álbum masc.
a photo album un álbum de fotos

A levels plural noun
los exámenes del final de la enseñanza secundaria masc. plural

> 🌍 **CULTURE**
> Students usually take A levels in the last two years before leaving school. In Spanish schools the last two years are known as **el bachillerato**, and students take an exam after this if they want to go on to university.

alien noun
el or la extraterrestre masc. & fem.

alike adjective
to look alike parecerse
My two brothers look alike. Mis dos hermanos se parecen.

alive adjective
vivo masc., viva fem.
Is it alive? ¿Está vivo?

all adjective
todo masc., toda fem.
all the cake todo el pastel
all the boys todos los chicos

• Use el and uno for masculine words and la and una for feminine words.

all the girls todas las chicas
all week toda la semana

all pronoun
1 (*everything*) **todo**
 That's all. Es todo.
 He's eaten it all. Se lo ha comido todo.
2 (*everyone*) **todos** *masc. plural*,
 todas *fem. plural*
 We're all going. Vamos a ir todos.
 All of them are very pretty. Son todas muy guapas.

all adverb
1 **todo**
 I'm all wet. Estoy todo mojado.
2 **completamente**
 all by myself completamente solo

allergic adjective
 alérgico *masc.*, **alérgica** *fem.*
 I'm allergic to milk. Soy alérgico a la leche.

alleyway noun
 el **callejón** *masc.* (plural los **callejones**)

alligator noun
 el **aligátor** *masc.*, el **caimán** *masc.* (plural los **caimanes**)

allowed adjective
1 **I'm allowed to watch TV.**
 Me dejan ver la tele.
 She's not allowed out. No la dejan salir.
2 **That's not allowed.** Está prohibido.

🔑 **LANGUAGE**
Use **dejar** (to let) for saying somebody is allowed to do something. Word for word 'I'm allowed to do' is 'They let me do' in Spanish.

all right adjective & adverb
1 (*good, well*) **bien**
 to be all right estar bien
 How are you? – All right. ¿Cómo estás? – Bien.

2 (*not so bad*); **no mal**
 to be all right no estar mal
 Do you like your teacher? – He's all right. ¿Te gusta tu maestro? – No está mal.
3 (*with verbs starting with 'to'*)
 Is it all right to open the window? ¿Se puede abrir la ventana?

🔑 **LANGUAGE**
Use **poder** (can) in this meaning (Can I open the window?).

all right exclamation
1 **¡bueno!**
 All right, I'm coming! ¡Bueno, ya voy!
 All right, let's begin. ¡Bueno! Vamos a empezar.
2 (*saying yes*) **¡vale!**
 Do you want to come with us? – All right! ¿Quieres venir con nosotros? – ¡Vale!

almost adverb
 casi
 It's almost finished. Está casi terminado.

alone adjective
1 **solo** *masc.*, **sola** *fem.*
 Don't go out alone. No salgas sola.
 We're all alone. Estamos completamente solos.
2 **Leave me alone!** ¡Déjame en paz!
 Leave my bike alone! ¡No toques mi bici!

along preposition & adverb
1 **por**
 Let's run along the beach. Vamos a correr por la playa.
2 (*from one end to the other*) **a lo largo de**
 There are trees along the street. Hay árboles a lo largo de la calle.

aloud adverb
 en voz alta
 Read these words aloud. Lee estas palabras en voz alta.

• Languages and nationalities do not take a capital letter in Spanish.

alphabet noun
el alfabeto *masc.*

alphabetical adjective
Put them in alphabetical order.
Ponlos en orden alfabético.

already adverb
ya
Vicky has already left. Vicky ya se
ha ido.

also adverb
también
I also have a sister. También tengo
una hermana.

although conjunction
aunque
**Although I'm tired, I will help
you.** Aunque estoy cansado, te voy
a ayudar.

altogether adverb
en total
That's fifteen euros altogether.
Son quince euros en total.

always adverb
siempre
I always win! ¡Siempre gano!

am verb SEE **be**
I'm in the garden. Estoy en el
jardín.
I'm English. Soy inglés.

a.m. abbreviation
de la mañana
at six a.m. a las seis de la mañana

amazing adjective
1 (*really good or unusual*)
extraordinario *masc.*,
extraordinaria *fem.*
She's an amazing pupil. Es una
alumna extraordinaria.
2 (*really surprising*) increíble
Amazing! ¡Increíble!

ambulance noun
la ambulancia *fem.*

America noun
1 los Estados Unidos *masc. plural*
My grandparents live in America.
Mis abuelos viven en los Estados
Unidos.
2 (*continent*) América *fem.*

LANGUAGE
Be careful: América can mean the United
States but it usually means either the
continent of America or Latin America.

American adjective
norteamericano *masc.*,
norteamericana *fem.*
an American film una película
norteamericana
He's American. Es
norteamericano.

American noun
el norteamericano *masc.*,
la norteamericana *fem.*
We have an American in our class.
Tenemos un norteamericano en
nuestra clase .

among preposition
entre
She's the only girl among six boys.
Es la única chica entre seis chicos.

amount noun
la cantidad *fem.*
a large amount of money una
gran cantidad de dinero

amusement arcade noun
el salón de juegos *masc.*

an determiner
un *masc.*, una *fem.*
an egg un huevo
an orange una naranja

LANGUAGE
Use un before a masculine noun (like
huevo), and una before a feminine noun
(like naranja).

• *The months of the year and days of the week do not take a capital letter in Spanish.*

English Spanish

and conjunction
1 y
the tables and chairs las mesas y las sillas
Arthur and Martin Arthur y Martin
2 e
I speak Spanish and English. Hablo español e inglés.

> 🔑 **LANGUAGE**
> Use e instead of y before words beginning with the 'i' sound (pronounced 'ee').

angel noun
el ángel *masc.*

angry adjective
enfadado *masc.*, enfadada *fem.*
I'm angry with you. Estoy enfadado contigo.
to get angry enfadarse
I get angry with my brother. Me enfado con mi hermano.

animal noun
el animal *masc.*

ankle noun
el tobillo *masc.*

anniversary noun
el aniversario *masc.*
It's their wedding anniversary. Es su aniversario de boda.

to **annoy** verb
molestar
My cousin annoys me. Mi primo me molesta.

annoyed adjective
enfadado *masc.*, enfadada *fem.*
I'm annoyed with you. Estoy enfadado contigo.

annoying adjective
to be annoying molestar
This noise is very annoying. Este ruido me molesta mucho.

anorak noun
el anorak *masc.* (plural los **anoraks**)

• *See the centre section for verb tables.*

another adjective
otro *masc.*, otra *fem.*
another day otro día
Another juice? ¿Otro zumo?
I want another one. Quiero otro.
another ten kilometres diez kilómetros más

answer noun
la respuesta *fem.*
The answer is right. La respuesta es correcta.
The answer is wrong. La respuesta está mal.

to **answer** verb
1 contestar
He doesn't answer. No contesta.
2 contestar a
I can't answer the question. No puedo contestar a la pregunta.

ant noun
la hormiga *fem.*

anthem noun
the national anthem el himno nacional *masc.*

antibiotic noun
el antibiótico *masc.*
He's on antibiotics. Está tomando antibióticos.

any adjective
(*no translation*)
Do you have any bread? ¿Tienes pan?
Tell me if you have any problems. Dime si tienes problemas.
Would you like any water? ¿Quieres agua?
I don't have any time. No tengo tiempo.
She doesn't have any money. No tiene dinero.

> 🔑 **LANGUAGE**
> When 'any' is used in questions, with negatives ('not', 'never', etc.), and after 'if', there is usually no translation.

a
b
c
d
e
f
g
h
i
j
k
l
m
n
o
p
q
r
s
t
u
v
w
x
y
z

a
b
c
d
e
f
g
h
i
j
k
l
m
n
o
p
q
r
s
t
u
v
w
x
y
z

any pronoun
(*no translation*)
We need to buy some fish but there isn't any. Necesitamos comprar pescado pero no hay.

> **LANGUAGE**
> When 'any' refers to singular nouns like 'fish', it is usually not translated.

any adverb
She doesn't come here any more. Ya no viene aquí.
I'm not hungry any more. No tengo más hambre.

> **LANGUAGE**
> To mean 'not any more' use **ya no** or **no … más**

anybody pronoun
1 (*in questions and with 'if'*) **alguién**
Has anybody seen my glasses? ¿Alguién ha visto mis gafas?
2 (*with negatives and 'if'*) **nadie**
I don't know anybody. No conozco a nadie.

anyone pronoun SEE **anybody**

anything pronoun
1 (*in questions and with 'if'*) **algo**
Are you looking for anything? ¿Buscas algo?
Tell me if you want anything. Dime si quieres algo.
2 (*with negatives and 'if'*) **nada**
He doesn't do anything. No hace nada.
I don't have anything to do. No tengo nada que hacer.
There isn't anything to eat. No hay nada de comer.

anywhere adverb
1 (*in questions and with 'if'*) **en alguna parte**
Have you seen my gloves anywhere? ¿Has visto mis guantes en alguna parte?
2 (*with negatives and 'if'*) **en ninguna parte**
I can't find them anywhere. No los encuentro en ninguna parte.
We're not going anywhere. No vamos a ninguna parte.

> **LANGUAGE**
> When 'anywhere' means 'to' a place use **a** with **parte** instead of **en**.

apart adverb
apart from menos
They're all here apart from him. Todos están aquí menos él.

to apologize verb
pedir perdón
He apologized to me. Me pidió perdón.
I apologize! ¡Lo siento!

apostrophe noun
el **apóstrofo** *masc.*

apple noun
la **manzana** *fem.*
apple juice el zumo de manzana
an apple tree un manzano

appointment noun
(*with a doctor, hairdresser, etc.*)
la **hora** *fem.*
I have a doctor's appointment. Tengo hora en el médico.
My mum has to make an appointment. Mi madre tiene que pedir hora.

April noun
1 **abril** *masc.*
in April en abril
They arrive on the tenth of April. Llegan el diez de abril.
2 **April Fools' Day** el día de los Santos Inocentes

> **CULTURE**
> **El día de los Santos Inocentes** (the Feast of the Holy Innocents) is similar to April Fools' Day and is celebrated on 28 December. There's a tradition of sticking a paper doll on somebody's back as a joke.

• Use **el** and **uno** for masculine words and **la** and **una** for feminine words.

apron noun
el delantal *masc.*

Arab adjective
árabe *masc. & fem.*
the Arab countries los países
árabes

Arab noun
el or la árabe *masc. & fem.*

are verb SEE **be**
We're in the kitchen. Estamos en
la cocina.
Where are you? ¿Dónde estás?
They're English. Son ingleses.

area noun
(*of a country, town, etc.*) la zona *fem.*
a play area una zona para juegos
infantiles

Argentina noun
Argentina *fem.*

Argentinian adjective
argentino *masc.*, argentina *fem.*

Argentinian noun
el argentino *masc.*,
la argentina *fem.*

to **argue** verb
discutir
They're always arguing. Siempre
están discutiendo.

argument noun
la discusión *fem.*
We had an argument. Tuvimos
una discusión.

arm noun
el brazo *masc.*

armchair noun
el sillón *masc.* (plural los **sillones**)

army noun
el ejército *masc.*
He's in the army. Está en el
ejército.

around preposition & adverb
1 alrededor de
We sit around the fire. Nos
sentamos alrededor del fuego.
I get up around seven. Me levanto
alrededor de las siete.
My mum's around forty. Mi madre
tiene unos cuarenta años.
2 (*with places or countries*) por
They travel around Europe. Viajan
por Europa.
around here por aquí
My dad's somewhere around.
Mi padre está por ahí.

to **arrive** verb
llegar
I arrive at nine. Llego a las
nueve.

arrow noun
la flecha *fem.*

art noun
1 (*in school*) el dibujo *masc.*
an art class una clase de
dibujo
2 el arte *masc.*
Spanish art el arte español
an art gallery un museo

LANGUAGE
Museo also means 'museum'.

artist noun
el or la artista *masc. & fem.*
He's an artist. Es artista.

as conjunction & preposition
1 como
as you know como sabes
**My teacher treats me as a
friend.** Mi maestro me trata como
amigo.
2 **as well** también
Is Juan coming as well? ¿Viene
Juan también?
3 (*when comparing*)
as ... as tan ... como
I'm as tall as my mother. Soy tan
alta como mi madre.

• Languages and nationalities do not take a capital letter in Spanish.

4 as much tanto *masc.*, tanta *fem.*
I have as much money as you.
Tengo tanto dinero como tú.

5 as many tantos *masc. plural*, tantas *fem. plural*
Paul has as many apples as me.
Paul tiene tantas manzanas como yo.

🔑 **LANGUAGE**
Tanto … como means 'as much as' in the singular and 'as many as' in the plural.

ashamed adjective
I'm ashamed. Me da vergüenza.
Aren't you ashamed? ¿No te da vergüenza?
She's ashamed of her sister. Le da vergüenza su hermana.

🔑 **LANGUAGE**
Vergüenza means 'shame' so word for word Me da vergüenza is 'It gives me shame'.

Asia noun
Asia *fem.*

Asian adjective
1 (*from India*) indio *masc.*, india *fem.*
2 (*from Pakistan*) paquistaní *masc. & fem.*
3 (*from Asia*) asiático *masc.*, asiática *fem.*

Asian noun
1 (*from India*) el indio *masc.*, la india *fem.*
2 (*from Pakistan*) el or la paquistaní *masc. & fem.*
3 (*from Asia*) el asiático *masc.*, la asiática *fem.*

to **ask** verb
1 preguntar
I'm going to ask. Voy a preguntar.
to ask somebody something preguntar algo a alguien
Ask your teacher. Pregúntale a tu maestra.

2 to ask a question hacer una pregunta
Can I ask you a question? ¿Puedo hacerte una pregunta?

3 to ask for something pedir algo
Sophie asked me for a pen. Sophie me pidió un bolígrafo.

4 (*invite*) invitar
Jim has asked me to the party. Jim me ha invitado a la fiesta.

asleep adjective
dormido *masc.*,
dormida *fem.*, durmiendo
She's asleep. Está dormida or durmiendo.

assembly noun
la reunión de maestros y alumnos *fem.*

🌍 **CULTURE**
Spanish schools do not have assemblies.

assistant noun
1 (*in a shop*) el dependiente *masc.*, la dependienta *fem.*
2 (*in the classroom*) el profesor auxiliar *masc.*, la profesora auxiliar *fem.*
3 (*for languages*) el or la ayudante *masc. & fem.*

asthma noun
el asma *fem.*
I have asthma. Tengo asma.

🔑 **LANGUAGE**
Be careful: you use el with asma but it is not a masculine noun.

astronaut noun
el or la astronauta *masc. & fem.*

at preposition
1 en
at school en la escuela
at home en casa
We're at Jason's. Estamos en casa de Jason.
at the station en la estación

• *The months of the year and days of the week do not take a capital letter in Spanish.*

2 (*with time, ages*) **a**
I go to bed at eight. Me acuesto a las ocho.
at midnight a medianoche
3 at night por la noche
at last por fin

athlete noun
el or la **atleta** *masc. & fem.*

Atlantic noun
el **Atlántico** *masc.*

atlas noun
el **atlas** *masc.* (plural los **atlas**)

attack noun
el **ataque** *masc.*
an asthma attack un ataque de asma

to **attack** verb
atacar

to **attend** verb
to attend school ir a la escuela

attention noun
la **atención** *fem.*
Pay attention! ¡Prestad atención!
Pay attention to what you're doing! ¡Pon or Presta atención en lo que estás haciendo!

attractive adjective
guapo *masc.*, **guapa** *fem.*
a very attractive girl una niña muy guapa

audience noun
el **público** *masc.*

August noun
agosto *masc.*
We're going on holiday in August. Nos vamos de vacaciones en agosto.
The plane leaves on the tenth of August. El avión sale el diez de agosto.

aunt, **aunty** noun
la **tía** *fem.*
She's my aunt. Es mi tía.
my aunt and uncle mis tíos
We've invited Aunty Ruth. Hemos invitado a la tía Ruth.

au pair noun
el or la **au pair** *masc. & fem.*

Australia noun
Australia *fem.*
My cousins live in Australia. Mis primos viven en Australia.

Australian adjective
australiano *masc.*, **australiana** *fem.*
She's Australian. Es australiana.

Australian noun
el **australiano** *masc.*, la **australiana** *fem.*

Austria noun
Austria *fem.*

Austrian noun
el **austriaco** *masc.*, la **austriaca** *fem.*

author noun
el **escritor** *masc.*, la **escritora** *fem.*
He's a well-known author. Es un escritor muy conocido.
the author of the book el autor *or* la autora del libro

autumn noun
el **otoño** *masc.*
in the autumn en otoño

average adjective
1 medio *masc.*, **media** *fem.*
I'm average height. Soy de estatura media.
2 (*not good or bad*) **regular** *masc. & fem.*
What's the food like? – Average. ¿Qué tal la comida? – Regular.

• *See the centre section for verb tables.*

average noun
1 la **media** *fem.*
an average of four a day una media de cuatro al día
2 el **promedio** *masc.*
twice a week, on average dos veces a la semana, como promedio
Work out the average. Encuentra el promedio.

to **avoid** verb
evitar

awake adjective
despierto *masc.*, **despierta** *fem.*
Are you awake? ¿Estás despierto?

away adverb
1 (*absent*)
The teacher is away today. La maestra no está hoy.
She's away in Spain. Está en España.

My parents are away until tomorrow. Mis padres están fuera hasta mañana.
2 **far away** lejos
I live far away from school. Vivo lejos de la escuela.
It's five kilometres away. Está a cinco kilómetros.

🔑 **LANGUAGE**
When you talk about how far something is from something else, use **a** in front of the number.

awful adjective
1 **horrible** *masc. & fem.*
I don't like this awful weather. No me gusta este tiempo horrible.
How awful! ¡Qué horror!
2 (*film, book, concert, etc.*)
malísimo *masc.*, **malísima** *fem.*
This book is awful. Este libro es malísimo.

Bb

baby noun
1 el **bebé** *masc.*
2 el **niño** *masc.*, la **niña** *fem.*
a baby boy un niño
a baby girl una niña
Don't be a baby! ¡No seas niño!

🔑 **LANGUAGE**
In Spanish **niño** can also mean 'child'.

to **babysit** verb
hacer de canguro
We babysit for our neighbours. Hacemos de canguro para los vecinos.

babysitter noun
el or la **canguro** *masc. & fem.*

back noun
1 (*of a person*) la **espalda** *fem.*

My back hurts. Me duele la espalda.
I sleep on my back. Duermo boca arriba.

🔑 **LANGUAGE**
Word for word **boca arriba** means 'with your mouth up'!

2 (*of an animal*) el **lomo** *masc.*
3 (*of a house or car*) la **parte de atrás** *fem.*
They're playing at the back of the house. Están jugando en la parte de atrás de la casa.
I'll sit in the back. Yo me siento atrás.
4 (*of a room, drawer, cupboard*) el **fondo** *masc.*
I always sit at the back of the class. Siempre me siento al fondo de la clase.

• *Use* **el** *and* **uno** *for masculine words and* **la** *and* **una** *for feminine words.*

back adjective
1 **de atrás**
 the back seat el asiento de atrás
 the back door la puerta de atrás
2 (*page, row*) **último** *masc.*,
 última *fem.*
 the back row la última fila

back adverb
1 (*using 'volver' for saying that somebody comes back*)
 I'll be back in ten minutes. Volveré dentro de diez minutos.
 When are you back from Madrid? ¿Cuándo vuelves de Madrid?
 to come back volver
2 (*to look, move, lean*) **hacia atrás**
 Take two steps back. Dad dos pasos hacia atrás.
3 **back to front** al revés
 You've put your sweater on back to front. Te has puesto el jersey al revés.

backpack noun
 la **mochila** *fem.*

backwards adverb
1 **hacia atrás**
 Don't lean backwards. No te eches hacia atrás.
2 **al revés**
 Your T-shirt's on backwards. Llevas la camiseta al revés.

bacon noun
 el **bacon** *masc.*
 bacon and eggs los huevos con bacon

bad adjective
1 **malo** *masc.*, **mala** *fem.*
 a bad book un libro malo
 a very bad idea una idea muy mala

> 🗝 **LANGUAGE**
> You can also use **malo** and **mala** before the noun, but then the masculine singular **malo** becomes **mal**.

 It's bad weather. Hace mal tiempo.
 I have bad news. Tengo malas noticias.
 Rick is bad at drawing. A Rick se le da mal el dibujo.
2 (*serious*) **grave** *masc. & fem.*
 a bad accident un accidente grave
3 **fuerte** *masc. & fem.*
 a bad pain un dolor fuerte
 I have a bad cough. Tengo mucha tos.
4 **Do you like the film? – It's not bad.** ¿Te gusta la película? – No está mal.
 How are you? – Not bad! ¿Cómo estás? – ¡Bien!

badge noun
1 (*made of plastic or metal*) la **chapa** *fem.*
2 (*made of cloth*) la **insignia** *fem.*

badly adverb
1 **mal**
 The team is playing very badly. El equipo juega muy mal.
2 **badly hurt** malherido

badminton noun
 el **bádminton** *masc.*
 Miguel plays badminton. Miguel juega al bádminton.

bag noun
1 la **bolsa** *fem.*
 a carrier bag una bolsa de plástico
2 el **bolso**
 The lady has lost her bag. La señora ha perdido el bolso.

> 🗝 **LANGUAGE**
> When you mean a woman's handbag, use **bolso**, not **bolsa**.

bagpipes plural noun
 la **gaita** *fem.*
 Alistair plays the bagpipes. Alistair toca la gaita.

• *Languages and nationalities do not take a capital letter in Spanish.*

a
b
c
d
e
f
g
h
i
j
k
l
m
n
o
p
q
r
s
t
u
v
w
x
y
z

to **bake** verb
to bake something hacer algo al horno
to bake a cake hacer un pastel
a baked potato una patata asada

baked beans plural noun
las **judías con salsa de tomate** fem. plural

🌍 **CULTURE**
Baked beans are not eaten in Spain.

baker noun
el **panadero** masc.,
la **panadera** fem.
He's a baker. Es panadero.
the baker's shop la panadería
I'm going to the baker's. Voy a la panadería.

balance noun
el **equilibrio** masc.
I lost my balance. Perdí el equilibrio.

balcony noun
el **balcón** masc. (plural los **balcones**)

bald adjective
calvo masc., **calva** fem.
He's bald. Es calvo.

ball noun
1 (for tennis, rugby, golf, etc.) la **pelota** fem.
a tennis ball una pelota de tenis
2 (for football) el **balón** masc. (plural los **balones**)

ballet dancing noun
el **ballet** masc.

balloon noun
el **globo** masc.
There are lots of balloons for the party. Hay muchos globos para la fiesta.

⚠ **FALSE FRIEND**
a balloon = un globo (not un balón)

ballpoint pen noun
el **bolígrafo** masc.

banana noun
el **plátano** masc.

band noun
1 (playing rock or pop music) el **grupo** masc.
a rock band un grupo de rock
They've formed a band. Han formado un grupo.
2 (playing music with trumpets, saxophones) la **orquesta** fem.

bandage noun
la **venda** fem.

bang noun
1 (noise, knock) el **golpe** masc.
Did you hear a bang on the door? ¿Oíste un golpe en la puerta?
2 (of a bomb etc.) la **explosión** fem.

to **bang** verb
1 (to knock)
Jack banged his knee. Jack se dio un golpe en la rodilla.
2 (to slam)
to bang the door dar un portazo
She always bangs the door. Siempre da portazos.

bank noun
1 (for money) el **banco** masc.
Dad's going to the bank. Papá va a ir al banco.
2 (at the side of a river) la **orilla** fem.
I sat down on the river bank. Me senté a la orilla del río.

bar noun
1 (made of metal) la **barra** fem.
an iron bar una barra de hierro
2 (place selling drinks) el **bar** masc.; (counter for buying drinks) la **barra** fem.
3 **a bar of chocolate** una tableta de chocolate
a bar of soap una pastilla de jabón

barbecue noun
la **barbacoa** fem.

• The months of the year and days of the week do not take a capital letter in Spanish.

bare adjective
(*arms, walls, etc.*) desnudo *masc.*,
desnuda *fem.*
with bare feet descalzo *masc.*,
descalza *fem.*

to **bark** verb
ladrar
Mi perro ladra mucho. My dog
barks a lot.

baseball noun
el béisbol *masc.*
Ahmed is playing baseball.
Ahmed juega al béisbol.
a baseball cap una gorra de
béisbol

basement noun
el sótano *masc.*

to **bash** verb
William bashed his knee. William
se dio un golpe en la rodilla.

basin noun
(*for washing*) el lavabo *masc.*

basket noun
la cesta *fem.*
a shopping basket una cesta de la
compra

basketball noun
el baloncesto *masc.*
Do you play basketball? ¿Juegas
al baloncesto?

bat noun
1 (*for cricket or baseball*) el bate *masc.*
2 (*for table tennis*) la pala *fem.*
3 (*flying animal*) el murciélago *masc.*

bath noun
1 (*wash*) el baño *masc.*
a hot bath un baño caliente
I want to have a bath. Quiero
bañarme., Quiero darme un baño.
2 (*container you sit in*) la bañera *fem.*
**There's too much water in the
bath.** Hay demasiada agua en la
bañera.

• *See the centre section for verb tables.*

bathroom noun
el cuarto de baño *masc.*

battery noun
(*for a torch, radio, camera, toy*) la pila *fem.*

⚠ **FALSE FRIEND**
a battery = una pila (*not* una batería)

battle noun
la batalla *fem.*

to **be** verb

⚟ **LANGUAGE**
Be careful: in Spanish there are two main
verbs for translating 'be': **ser** and **estar**.

1 **ser**
I'm English. Soy inglés.
Are you my friend? ¿Eres mi
amigo?
She's tall. Es alta.
It's not a problem. No es
problema.
It's six o'clock. Son las seis.
It's the fifth of June. Es el cinco de
junio.
When is it? ¿Cuándo es?
We're Spanish. Somos españoles.
You're my friends. Sois mis
amigos.
Are you Mrs Sanders? ¿Es usted la
señora Sanders?
They're friendly. Son simpáticos.
Two and two are four. Dos y dos
son cuatro.

⚟ **LANGUAGE**
Use **ser** when you're talking about
something permanent or saying what
something is, and with time and dates.

2 **estar**
I'm in the garden. Estoy en el
jardín.
I'm playing the clarinet. Estoy
tocando el clarinete.
How are you, Pete? ¿Cómo estás,
Pete?
Are you sad? ¿Estás triste?
He's in London. Está en Londres.

We're very tired. Estamos muy cansados.
Are you ready? ¿Estáis listos?
What are they doing? ¿Qué están haciendo?
My father has been ill. Mi padre ha estado enfermo.

> **⚷ LANGUAGE**
> Use **estar** when you're talking about where something is, or about something that normally lasts only a short time, and when translating English verbs made up of 'be' and a verb ending in '-ing' (e.g. 'I'm doing' is **estoy haciendo**).

3 tener
I'm hot. Tengo calor.
Are you sleepy? ¿Tienes sueño?
We're hungry. Tenemos hambre.
I'm eleven. Tengo once años.
She's nine. Tiene nueve años.

> **⚷ LANGUAGE**
> English = **I am** hot/cold/hungry/thirsty/scared/6 years old.
> Spanish = **Tengo** calor/frío/hambre/sed/miedo/6 años.

4 (when talking about the weather) **hacer**
It's hot. Hace calor.
It's very sunny. Hace mucho sol.

> **⚷ LANGUAGE**
> With the weather 'it is' = **hacer**

> **⚷ LANGUAGE**
> To translate questions such as 'isn't it?' or 'aren't you?', you can use either ¿**no?** or ¿**verdad?**, e.g. 'She's English, isn't she?' is **Es inglesa, ¿no?** or **Es inglesa, ¿verdad?**

beach noun
la **playa** fem.

bean noun
la **judía** fem.
baked beans las judías con salsa de tomate
green beans las judías verdes

bear noun
el **oso** masc.

beard noun
la **barba** fem.
My dad has a beard. Mi padre tiene barba.

to **beat** verb
1 ganar
to beat somebody ganarle a alguien
I beat my sister at chess. Le gané a mi hermana al ajedrez.
Their team has beaten us. Su equipo nos ha ganado.
2 to beat somebody up golpear a alguien
They beat me up. Me golpearon.

beautiful adjective
1 (very attractive) **precioso** masc., **preciosa** fem.
What a beautiful dress! ¡Qué vestido más precioso!
2 (pretty) **bonito** masc., **bonita** fem.
What a beautiful skirt! ¡Qué falda tan bonita!
3 (baby, girl, woman) **muy guapo** masc., **muy guapa** fem.
a beautiful girl una chica muy guapa

> **⚷ LANGUAGE**
> You can also say **hermoso** in Spanish, e.g. **una mujer hermosa** (a beautiful woman).

4 (very good) **muy bueno** masc., **muy buena** fem.
The weather's beautiful. Hace muy buen tiempo.

because conjunction
1 porque
I can't go out because I'm ill. No puedo salir porque estoy enfermo.
2 because of (when blaming somebody) por culpa de
I was late because of my brother. Llegué tarde por culpa de mi hermano.
because of you por tu culpa

• Use **el** and **uno** for masculine words and **la** and **una** for feminine words.

to **become** verb
1 hacerse
We became friends. Nos hicimos amigos.
She became famous. Se hizo famosa.
2 ponerse
to become very angry ponerse furioso
She became ill. Se puso enferma.
3 llegar a ser
He later became king. Más tarde llegó a ser rey.

bed noun
1 la **cama** fem.
I'm in bed. Estoy en la cama.
2 to go to bed acostarse
Claire goes to bed at nine. Claire se acuesta a las nueve.
I'm going to bed. Me voy a la cama.

bedroom noun
el **dormitorio** masc.
She's in her bedroom. Está en su dormitorio.

bedtime noun
It's bedtime. Ya es hora de irse a la cama.
Bedtime! ¡A la cama!

bee noun
la **abeja** fem.

beef noun
la **carne de vaca** fem.

been verb SEE **be**
I've never been to Spain. No he estado nunca en España.
It's been an exciting game. Ha sido un partido emocionante.

beer noun
la **cerveza** fem.

beetle noun
el **escarabajo** masc.

beetroot noun
la **remolacha** fem.

before preposition & conjunction
antes de
before Sunday antes del domingo
before doing something antes de hacer algo
We want to watch TV before doing our homework. Queremos ver la tele antes de hacer los deberes.

before adverb
1 antes
I saw her two weeks before. La vi dos semanas antes.
2 (already) **ya**
Have you read this book before? ¿Ya has leído este libro?

to **begin** verb
empezar
My classes begin at nine. Mi clases empiezan a las nueve.
It's beginning to rain. Está empezando a llover.

beginner noun
el or la **principiante** masc. & fem.
I'm a beginner. Soy principiante.

beginning noun
el **principio** masc.
At the beginning it's very easy. Al principio es muy fácil.

to **behave** verb
portarse
Simon behaves badly in class. Simon se porta mal en clase.

behaviour noun
el **comportamiento** masc.

behind preposition & adverb
1 detrás de
behind the door detrás de la puerta
2 detrás
The tallest children behind! ¡Los niños más altos detrás!

being verb SEE **be**
She likes being an only child. Le gusta ser hija única.

• Languages and nationalities do not take a capital letter in Spanish.

English Spanish

a
b
c
d
e
f
g
h
i
j
k
l
m
n
o
p
q
r
s
t
u
v
w
x
y
z

being noun
a human being un ser humano

Belgian adjective
belga *masc. & fem.*
He's Belgian. Es belga.

Belgian noun
el or la belga *masc. & fem.*

Belgium noun
Bélgica *fem.*

to **believe** verb
creer
I believe you. Te creo.
Do you believe it? ¿Lo crees?
They don't believe in ghosts.
No creen en fantasmas.

bell noun
1 (*on a door or bicycle*) el timbre *masc.*
to ring the bell tocar el timbre
2 (*electric bell in school*) el timbre *masc.*
The bell's gone. Ha sonado el
timbre.
3 (*of a church*) la campana *fem.*
The church bells are ringing.
Suenan las campanas.

to **belong** verb
1 (*to somebody*) ser de
This bike belongs to David. Esta
bici es de David.
Who does this pen belong to?
¿De quién es este bolígrafo?
It belongs to me. Es mío.
2 (*to be part of a group*) ser socio or socia
de
Does she belong to any club?
¿Es socia de algún club?

below preposition
debajo de
the flat below ours el piso debajo
del nuestro

below adverb
abajo
down below in the street abajo en
la calle

It's on the shelf below. Está en el
estante de abajo.

belt noun
1 el cinturón *masc.* (plural los
cinturones)
2 (*seatbelt in a car*) el cinturón de
seguridad *masc.*

bench noun
el banco *masc.*

bend noun
(*in the road*) la curva *fem.*
a dangerous bend una curva
peligrosa

to **bend** verb
1 doblar
You have to bend your knees.
Tienes que doblar las rodillas.
Do not bend. No doblar.
2 **to bend your head** inclinar la
cabeza
to bend over inclinarse
to bend down agacharse

beneath preposition
debajo de

beside preposition
al lado de
beside the table al lado de la mesa
Sit down beside me. Siéntate a mi
lado.

besides preposition & adverb
1 además de
**Besides maths I have to study
science.** Además de matemáticas
tengo que estudiar ciencias.
2 además
Besides, you're too young.
Además, eres demasiado joven.

best adjective
mejor *masc. & fem.*
She's my best friend. Es mi mejor
amiga.
Which are the best ones? ¿Cuáles
son los mejores?
It's best to wait. Lo mejor es
esperar.

• *The months of the year and days of the week do not take a capital letter in Spanish.*

best noun
el or la **mejor** *masc. & fem.*
This book is the best. Este libro es
el mejor.
She's the best in the class. Es la
mejor de la clase.

best adverb
mejor
Liam is the one who plays best.
Liam es el que juega mejor.
I like this dress best. Éste es el
vestido que más me gusta.

> **LANGUAGE**
> Say **más** (more) instead of **mejor** when
> using **gustar** to translate 'like'.

better adjective
mejor *masc. & fem.*
Your idea is better than mine.
Tu idea es mejor que la mía.
Yes, that's better. Sí, eso es mejor.
I'm better now. Ya estoy mejor.
Are you feeling better? ¿Te
encuentras mejor?

better adverb
mejor
I play better than you. Juego
mejor que tú.
to get better mejorar
Your Spanish has got better. Tu
español ha mejorado.
Get better soon! ¡Que te mejores!

between preposition & adverb
1 **entre**
between seven and ten o'clock
entre las siete y las diez
2 **in between** en medio
Put it down in between. Ponlo en
medio.

Bible noun
la **Biblia** *fem.*

bicycle noun
la **bicicleta** *fem.*
I go to school by bicycle. Voy a la
escuela en bicicleta.

Can you ride a bicycle? ¿Sabes
montar en bicicleta?

big adjective
1 **grande** *masc. & fem.*
a big garden un jardín grande
Our house is big. Nuestra casa es
grande.

> **LANGUAGE**
> You can use **grande** before the noun, but
> before a singular noun it becomes **gran**.

a big surprise una gran sorpresa
her big blue eyes sus grandes ojos
azules
2 (*older*) **mayor** *masc. & fem.*
She's my big sister. Es mi hermana
mayor.

bike noun
la **bici** *fem.*
by bike en bici

> **LANGUAGE**
> **Bici** is short for **bicicleta**.

bikini noun
el **bikini** *masc.*

bilingual adjective
bilingüe *masc. & fem.*

bill noun
1 (*in a restaurant*) la **cuenta** *fem.*
The bill, please! ¡La cuenta, por
favor!
2 (*for gas, electricity, etc.*) el **recibo** *masc.*
the phone bill el recibo del
teléfono

bin noun
1 (*for rubbish*) el **cubo de basura** *masc.*
Throw this apple in the bin. Tira
esta manzana a la basura.
2 (*wastepaper basket*) la **papelera** *fem.*

binoculars plural noun
los **gemelos** *masc. plural*

biology noun
la **biología** *fem.*

• *See the centre section for verb tables.*

bird noun
 el **pájaro** *masc.*

Biro® noun
 el **boli** *masc.*

🔑 **LANGUAGE**
Boli is short for **bolígrafo.**

birth noun
 el **nacimiento** *masc.*
 What's your date of birth? ¿Cuál es su fecha de nacimiento?

birthday noun
 el **cumpleaños** *masc.*
 My birthday is the fifth of October. Mi cumpleaños es el cinco de octubre.
 It's my tenth birthday tomorrow. Mañana cumplo diez años.
 a birthday card una tarjeta de cumpleaños
 a birthday cake una tarta de cumpleaños
 a birthday party una fiesta de cumpleaños
 Happy birthday! ¡Feliz cumpleaños!

🔑 **LANGUAGE**
Cumpleaños comes from **cumplir años** ('to complete years').

biscuit noun
 la **galleta** *fem.*

bit noun
 1 (*a piece*) el **trozo** *masc.*
 Would you like that bit of bread? ¿Quieres ese trozo de pan?
 Mum cut the apple into little bits. Mamá cortó la manzana en trocitos.
 2 (*not very much of something*)
 a bit un poco
 I'm a bit tired. Estoy un poco cansado.

to **bite** verb
 1 morder
 My dog doesn't bite. Mi perro no muerde.
 2 (*talking about an insect*) **picar**
 I've been bitten by a mosquito. Me ha picado un mosquito.

bitter adjective
 amargo *masc.*, **amarga** *fem.*
 It has a bitter taste. Tiene un sabor amargo.

black adjective
 negro *masc.*, **negra** *fem.*
 a black car un coche negro
 She's black. Es negra.
 a black coffee un café solo

black noun
 el **negro** *masc.*
 Carol likes black. A Carol le gusta el negro.

blackberry noun
 la **mora** *fem.*

blackboard noun
 la **pizarra** *fem.*
 on the blackboard en la pizarra

to **blame** verb
 I'm not to blame. Yo no tengo la culpa.
 I blame my sister. Mi hermana tiene la culpa.
 Don't blame me! ¡No me eches la culpa a mí!
 You're to blame for the accident. El accidente es culpa tuya.

blanket noun
 la **manta** *fem.*

blazer noun
 (*of school uniform*) la **chaqueta** *fem.*

to **bleed** verb
 My nose is bleeding. Me sale sangre de la nariz.
 I'm bleeding. Me sale sangre.

• Use **el** and **uno** for masculine words and **la** and **una** for feminine words.

to **bless** verb
Bless you! ¡Jesús!

CULTURE
In Spain people say the name of Jesus when somebody sneezes.

blind adjective
ciego *masc.*, **ciega** *fem.*
He's blind. Es ciego.

blind noun
(*on a window*) la **persiana** *fem.*
Pull down the blinds. Baja las persianas.

block noun
a block of flats un bloque de pisos

blond, or **blonde** adjective
rubio *masc.*, **rubia** *fem.*
Jack has blond hair. Jack tiene el pelo rubio.
Sarah is blonde. Sarah es rubia.

blood noun
la **sangre** *fem.*

blouse noun
la **blusa** *fem.*

to **blow** verb
1 **soplar**
Blow hard. Sopla fuerte.
Blow out the candles. Sopla las velas.
2 **to blow a whistle** tocar un silbato
The referee blew his whistle. El árbitro tocó el silbato.
3 **to blow up a balloon** inflar un globo
4 **to blow your nose** sonarse la nariz
Blow your nose. Suénate la nariz.

blue adjective
azul *masc. & fem.*
a blue shirt una camisa azul

blue noun
el **azul** *masc.*
I prefer blue. Prefiero el azul.

to **blush** verb
ponerse colorado *masc.*, **ponerse colorada** *fem.*
You're blushing! ¡Te estás poniendo colorado!

LANGUAGE
Word for word this means 'to go red'.

board noun
1 la **pizarra** *fem.*
Write on the board. Escribe en la pizarra.
2 (*piece of wood*) la **tabla** *fem.*
an ironing board una tabla de planchar
3 **a board game** un juego de mesa

boarding school noun
el **internado** *masc.*

boat noun
1 el **barco** *masc.*
to go by boat ir en barco
2 (*small boat*) la **barca** *fem.*

body noun
el **cuerpo** *masc.*
a dead body un cadáver

to **boil** verb
hervir
The water is boiling. El agua está hirviendo.
to boil the water hervir el agua
a boiled egg un huevo pasado por agua

boiling adjective
boiling water agua hirviendo
This tea is boiling hot. Este té está hirviendo.
It's a boiling hot day today. Hoy hace muchísimo calor.

bone noun
el **hueso** *masc.*
The dog is looking for a bone. El perro está buscando un hueso.

a
b
c
d
e
f
g
h
i
j
k
l
m
n
o
p
q
r
s
t
u
v
w
x
y
z

• *Languages and nationalities do not take a capital letter in Spanish.*

English Spanish

a
b
c
d
e
f
g
h
i
j
k
l
m
n
o
p
q
r
s
t
u
v
w
x
y
z

bonfire noun
la **hoguera** fem.
My parents lit a bonfire in the garden. Mis padres encendieron una hoguera en el jardín.

 CULTURE
Bonfire Night is not celebrated in Spain but there are many festivals where bonfires and fireworks are lit, such as the Fallas in Valencia every year in March.

book noun
1 el **libro** masc.
2 (exercise book) el **cuaderno** masc.
Close your books. Cerrad los cuadernos.
3 **an address book** una libreta de direcciones

to **book** verb
reservar
I'd like to book a ticket. Quiero reservar un billete.

bookcase noun
la **estantería** fem.

bookshelf noun
el **estante** masc.

bookshop noun
la **librería** fem.

🔑 **LANGUAGE**
Librería and 'library' are both related to **libro** (book) but a **librería** is where you buy books, not where you borrow them. Library is **la biblioteca**.

boot noun
1 **la bota** fem.
football boots las botas de fútbol
2 (of a car) el **maletero** masc.
Put it in the boot. Ponlo en el maletero.

border noun
la **frontera** fem.

bored adjective
aburrido masc., **aburrida** fem.
I'm bored. Estoy aburrido.
to get bored aburrirse
I'm getting bored. Me aburro.

boring adjective
aburrido masc., **aburrida** fem.
It's boring. Es aburrido.

born adjective
to be born nacer
I was born in London. Nací en Londres.

to **borrow** verb
pedir prestado
I borrowed a pen. Pedí prestado un boli.
Can I borrow the bike? ¿Me prestas la bici?, ¿Me dejas la bici?

🔑 **LANGUAGE**
Spanish doesn't have a word for 'to borrow'. **Prestar** means means 'to lend' and **dejar** means 'to leave' so if you want to borrow something you say ¿Me **prestas ... ?** (Can you lend me ... ?) or ¿Me **dejas ... ?** (Can you leave me ... ?).

bossy adjective
mandón masc., **mandona** fem.
He's very bossy. Es muy mandón.

🔑 **LANGUAGE**
The plural of the masculine **mandón** is **mandones**.

both pronoun & adjective
los **dos** masc. plural, las **dos** fem. plural
Hassan and James are both tired. Hassan y James están cansados los dos.
both my sisters mis dos hermanas
both hands las dos manos

• *The months of the year and days of the week do not take a capital letter in Spanish.*

to **bother** verb
1 (*to disturb, pester*) molestar
 I'm sorry to bother you. Siento molestarle.
2 **Don't bother, I'm leaving!** ¡No te molestes, me voy!
 I can't be bothered to go. No tengo ganas de ir.

bottle noun
 la botella *fem.*

bottom noun
1 (*of a glass, bag, river, street, etc.*) el fondo *masc.*
 at the bottom of the garden al fondo del jardín
2 (*of a wall, mountain, etc.*) el pie *masc.*
 at the bottom of the stairs al pie de las escaleras
3 (*of a list, page*) el final *masc.*
 at the bottom of the page al final de la página
4 (*a part of the body*) el trasero *masc.*, el culo *masc.*

bottom adjective
 de abajo
 the bottom shelf el estante de abajo
 the bottom part la parte de abajo
 He got the bottom mark. Sacó la nota más baja.
 You're bottom of the class. Eres el último de la clase.

to **bounce** verb
 botar
 This ball doesn't bounce. Esta pelota no bota.

bow noun
1 (*in a ribbon or shoelaces*) el lazo *masc.*
 to tie a bow hacer un lazo
2 el arco *masc.*
 bow and arrow arco y flecha

• *See the centre section for verb tables.*

bowl noun
 el tazón *masc.* (plural los **tazones**)
 a bowl of cereal un tazón de cereales

bowling noun
 los bolos *masc. plural*
 We go bowling every Friday. Jugamos a los bolos todos los viernes.
 a bowling alley una bolera

box noun
1 la caja *fem.*
 a box of chocolates una caja de bombones
 a cardboard box una caja de cartón
2 (*on forms, worksheets, etc.*) la casilla *fem.*
 Tick the box. Marca la casilla.

boxer shorts plural noun
 los calzoncillos *masc. plural*

boxing noun
 el boxeo *masc.*

Boxing Day noun
 el día después de Navidad *masc.*

> **CULTURE**
> **Boxing Day** is translated simply as 'the day after Christmas', and is not a holiday in Spain.

boy noun
1 (*young child*) el niño *masc.*
 a little boy of five un niño de cinco años
2 (*older child or teenager*) el chico *masc.*
 a boy of seventeen un chico de diecisiete años

boyfriend noun
 el novio *masc.*

bra noun
 el sujetador *masc.*

brace noun
(for teeth) el aparato masc.
I wear a brace. Llevo un aparato.

bracelet noun
la pulsera fem.

brain noun
el cerebro masc.

brainy adjective
inteligente masc. & fem.

brake noun
el freno masc.
to put on the brakes frenar

branch noun
la rama fem.

brand-new adjective
nuevo masc., nueva fem.
I have a brand-new bike. Tengo
una bicicleta nueva.

brave adjective
valiente masc. & fem.

bread noun
el pan masc.
I'm eating some bread. Estoy
comiendo pan.
a piece of bread un trozo de pan

break noun
(playtime in school) el recreo masc.
We go out for break at eleven.
Salimos al recreo a las once.

to **break** verb
1 **to break something** romper algo
Shaun has broken a glass. Shaun
ha roto un vaso.
I've broken my arm. Me he roto el
brazo.
2 romperse
The plate broke. Se rompió el
plato.
3 **to break down** estropearse
The car has broken down. Se ha
estropeado el coche.
4 **We break up tomorrow.**
Terminamos las clases mañana.

breakfast noun
el desayuno masc.
to have breakfast desayunar
I have breakfast at seven.
Desayuno a las siete.

breath noun
el aliento masc.
He arrived out of breath. Llegó sin
aliento.

to **breathe** verb
respirar

breeze noun
la brisa fem.

brick noun
el ladrillo masc.
a brick wall una pared de
ladrillo

bride noun
la novia fem.
the bride and groom los novios
masc. plural

bridegroom noun
el novio masc.

bridesmaid noun
la dama de honor fem.

bridge noun
el puente masc.

bright adjective
1 (colour) vivo masc., viva fem.
bright colours colores vivos
2 (light, sun) brillante masc. & fem.
a bright light una luz brillante
a very bright room una habitación
con mucha luz
3 (clever) inteligente masc. & fem.
He's very bright. Es muy
inteligente.
a bright idea una brillante
idea

• Use el and uno for masculine words and la and una for feminine words.

brilliant adjective
1 (*really good*) **estupendo** *masc.*, **estupenda** *fem.*
The weather was brilliant. Hizo un tiempo estupendo.
a brilliant idea una idea genial
2 (*very clever*) **brillante** *masc. & fem.*
She's a brilliant student. Es una alumna brillante.

to **bring** verb
1 (*to bring with you*) **traer**
Have you brought your umbrella? ¿Has traído el paraguas?
Bring your best friend. Trae a tu mejor amigo.
2 (*to bring to a place*) **llevar**
Bring this book to your teacher. Lleva este libro al maestro.
3 **to bring something back** devolver algo
I'll bring back your bike tomorrow. Te devolveré la bici mañana.
to bring somebody back to ... llevar a alguien a ...
Granddad brought me back home by car. Mi abuelo me llevó a casa en coche.

Britain noun
Gran Bretaña *fem.*
We live in Britain. Vivimos en Gran Bretaña.

British adjective
británico *masc.*, **británica** *fem.*
Emma is British. Emma es británica.
the British Isles las Islas Británicas

British noun
the British los británicos *masc. plural*

broccoli noun
el **brécol** *masc.*, el **brócoli** *masc.*

broken adjective
roto *masc.*, **rota** *fem.*
It's broken. Está roto.
She has a broken leg. Tiene la pierna rota.

bronze noun
el **bronce** *masc.*
a bronze medal una medalla de bronce

broom noun
la **escoba** *fem.*

brother noun
el **hermano** *masc.*
Bring your brother. Trae a tu hermano.
Do you have any brothers or sisters? ¿Tienes hermanos?

brown adjective
1 **marrón** *masc. & fem.*
a brown blouse una blusa marrón
brown shoes zapatos marrones

> **⚷ LANGUAGE**
> The singular form **marrón** is the same in the masculine and feminine, and the plural is **marrones**. 'Maroon' is related to **marrón** but it means a dark red colour.

2 (*hair*) **castaño** *masc.*, **castaña** *fem.*
Liz has brown hair. Liz tiene el pelo castaño.
3 (*from the sun*) **moreno** *masc.*, **morena** *fem.*
You're getting brown. Te pones moreno.

brown noun
el **marrón** *masc.*
I prefer brown to blue. Prefiero el marrón al azul.

brown bread noun
el **pan integral** *masc.*

a
b
c
d
e
f
g
h
i
j
k
l
m
n
o
p
q
r
s
t
u
v
w
x
y
z

• Languages and nationalities do not take a capital letter in Spanish.

English Spanish

a
b
c
d
e
f
g
h
i
j
k
l
m
n
o
p
q
r
s
t
u
v
w
x
y
z

Brownie noun
la alita *fem.*
She's in the Brownies. Pertenece a
las alitas.

bruise noun
el moretón *masc.* (plural los
moretones)
I have a bruise on my knee. Tengo
un moretón en la rodilla.

brush noun
1 (*for hair, cleaning, etc.*) el cepillo *masc.*
2 (*for painting walls etc.*) la brocha *fem.*

to **brush** verb
1 (*hair, clothes, etc.*) cepillar
I'm brushing my hair. Me estoy
cepillando el pelo.
2 **to brush your teeth** lavarse los
dientes

Brussels sprouts plural noun
las coles de Bruselas *fem. plural*

bubble noun
1 (*in water*) la burbuja *fem.*
2 (*in the air*) la pompa *fem.*
soap bubbles pompas de jabón

bucket noun
el cubo *masc.*
a bucket and spade un cubo y una
pala

Buddhist adjective
budista *masc. & fem.*

bug noun
1 (*insect*) el insecto *masc.*
2 (*germ*) el microbio *masc.*;
(*virus*) el virus *masc.* (plural los **virus**)

buggy noun
(*for a baby*)
la sillita *fem.*, el cochecito *masc.*

to **build** verb
construir

builder noun
1 (*working man*) el albañil *masc.*
2 (*somebody who people work for*)
el constructor *masc.*,
la constructora *fem.*

building noun
el edificio *masc.*

bulb noun
la bombilla *fem.*
Mum changed the light bulb.
Mamá cambió la bombilla.

bull noun
el toro *masc.*

bully noun
el matón *masc.*, la matona *fem.*

⚷ **LANGUAGE**
The plural of **matón** is **matones**.

bump noun
1 (*on your head*) el chichón *masc.*
2 (*in the road*) el bache *masc.*
3 (*noise*) el golpe *masc.*

to **bump** verb
1 (*to knock*) **I bumped my head.** Me di
un golpe en la cabeza.
2 (*to hit*) **to bump into something**
tropezar contra algo
I bumped into the table. Tropecé
contra la mesa.
3 (*to meet*) **to bump into somebody**
encontrarse con alguien
**We bumped into her in the
supermarket.** Nos encontramos
con ella en el supermercado.

bumpy adjective
(*road, street*) lleno de baches *masc.*,
llena de baches *fem.*

bun noun
1 (*sweet*) el bollo *masc.*
2 (*for a hamburger*) el panecillo *masc.*

bunch noun
1 **a bunch of flowers** un ramo de
flores
2 **a bunch of friends** un grupo de
amigos

• *The months of the year and days of the week do not take a capital letter in Spanish.*

bunk beds plural noun
la **litera** *fem.*

> 🔑 **LANGUAGE**
> You can also use **litera** to mean one bunk bed.

burger noun
la **hamburguesa** *fem.*

burglar noun
el **ladrón** *masc.*, la **ladrona** *fem.*
a burglar alarm una alarma antirrobo

> 🔑 **LANGUAGE**
> The plural of **ladrón** is **ladrones**.

to burn verb
1 to burn something quemar algo
He burned the rubbish. Quemó la basura.
I've burnt my finger. Me he quemado el dedo.
2 (*talking about something that burns*)
quemarse
The house burned down. Se quemó la casa.

burnt adjective
quemado *masc.*, **quemada** *fem.*
The toast is burnt. La tostada está quemada.

to burst verb
reventarse
The balloon burst. El globo se reventó.

bus noun
el **autobús** *masc.* (plural los **autobuses**)
We go to school by bus. Vamos a la escuela en autobús.
a bus stop una parada de autobús
the bus station la estación de autobuses
a school bus un autobús escolar

• See the centre section for verb tables.

bush noun
el **arbusto** *masc.*

business noun
los **negocios** *masc. plural*
a business trip un viaje de negocios

busy adjective
1 ocupado *masc.*, **ocupada** *fem.*
I'm busy. Estoy ocupado.
2 (*shops, streets, etc.*)
The shops are busy. Hay mucha gente en las tiendas.

but conjunction
1 pero
I want to go but my parents won't let me. Quiero ir pero mis padres no me dejan.
2 sino
It's not blue but green. No es azul sino verde.

butcher noun
el **carnicero** *masc.*, la **carnicera** *fem.*
He's a butcher. Es carnicero.
the butcher's shop la carnicería
Dad went to the butcher's. Papá fue a la carnicería.

butter noun
la **mantequilla** *fem.*

butterfly noun
la **mariposa** *fem.*

button noun
el **botón** *masc.* (plural los **botones**)

to buy verb
comprar
We're going to buy a computer. Vamos a comprar un ordenador.
He bought me some sweets. Me compró caramelos.

by preposition
1 por
a book written by Cervantes un libro escrito por Cervantes
one by one uno por uno
by chance por casualidad

a
b
c
d
e
f
g
h
i
j
k
l
m
n
o
p
q
r
s
t
u
v
w
x
y
z

English Spanish

a
b
c
d
e
f
g
h
i
j
k
l
m
n
o
p
q
r
s
t
u
v
w
x
y
z

2 de
 a painting by Goya un cuadro de
 Goya
 a book by Roald Dahl un libro de
 Roald Dahl
3 *(with car, bike, plane, etc.)* en
 by train en tren
 by boat en barco
4 *(near to)* al lado de

The restaurant is by the station.
El restaurante está al lado de la
estación.
5 *(not later than)* antes de
 I'll come back by nine. Volveré
 antes de las nueve.

bye exclamation
 ¡adiós!

Cc

cab noun
 el taxi *masc.*
 to go by cab ir en taxi

cabbage noun
 la col *fem.*
 Do you like cabbage? ¿Te gusta la
 col?

cable noun
 el cable *masc.*
 cable television la televisión por
 cable

cafe noun
 la cafetería *fem.*

🌐 **CULTURE**
British cafes do not sell drinks with
alcohol in them.

cafeteria noun
 la cafetería *fem.*

cage noun
 la jaula *fem.*

cake noun
 el pastel *masc.*
 Amy's eating some cake. Amy está
 comiendo pastel.
 a cake shop una pastelería

to **calculate** verb
 calcular

calculator noun
 la calculadora *fem.*

calendar noun
 el calendario *masc.*

calf noun
 (baby cow) el ternero *masc.*

call noun
 (phone call) la llamada *fem.*
 I have to make a phone call. Voy
 tiene que hacer una llamada.

to **call** verb
1 llamar
 I'm going to call the doctor. Voy a
 llamar al médico.
 to call the register pasar lista
2 to be called llamarse
 What's your cat called? ¿Cómo se
 llama tu gato?
3 *(to visit somebody)* pasar
 I'll call round at your house.
 Pasaré por tu casa.

to **call back** verb
 volver a llamar
 Dad's busy – he'll call back later.
 Papá está ocupado – volverá a
 llamar más tarde.

to **call off** verb
 suspender
 They called off the party.
 Suspendieron la fiesta.

• *Use* el *and* uno *for masculine words and* la *and* una *for feminine words.*

calm adjective
tranquilo *masc.*, tranquila *fem.*
Keep calm! ¡Tranquilo!

to **calm** verb
to calm down calmarse
Calm down, Bob! ¡Cálmate, Bob!

camcorder noun
la videocámara *fem.*

came verb SEE **come**
I came with her. Vine con ella.
He came by bike. Vino en bici.

camel noun
el camello *masc.*

camera noun
la cámara *fem.*
a digital camera una cámara digital

camp noun
el campamento *masc.*
a summer camp un campamento de verano

to **camp** verb
acampar
We camped by the river.
Acampamos cerca del río.

camping noun
el camping *masc.*
I like camping. Me gusta ir de camping.
to go camping ir de camping
We went camping in Spain Fuimos de camping a España.

campsite noun
el camping *masc.* (plural los **campings**)

can noun
la lata *fem.*
a can of sardines una lata de sardinas

can verb
1 poder
I can help you. Puedo ayudarte.

**Can you turn the volume down? –
Yes, I can.** ¿Puedes bajar el
volumen? – Sí, puedo.
Can she come tomorrow? ¿Puede
venir mañana?

> **LANGUAGE**
> Translate 'can' using **poder** but when it
> means 'know how to do something' use
> **saber**.

2 saber
Can you swim? ¿Sabes nadar?
I can't read yet. Aún no sé leer.
3 (*sometimes not translated*)
Can you hear? ¿Oyes?
I can see you. Te veo.
I can't remember. No me acuerdo.

Canada noun
Canadá *masc.*
We're going to Canada. Vamos a
Canadá.

Canadian adjective
canadiense *masc. & fem.*
She's Canadian. Es canadiense.

Canadian noun
el or la canadiense *masc. & fem.*

canal noun
el canal *masc.*

canary noun
el canario *masc.*

cancel verb
cancelar
The flight has been cancelled.
El vuelo ha sido cancelado.

cancer noun
el cáncer *masc.*
He has cancer. Tiene cáncer.

candle noun
la vela *fem.*
Blow out the candles. Sopla las
velas.

candyfloss noun
el algodón de azúcar *masc.*

a
b
c
d
e
f
g
h
i
j
k
l
m
n
o
p
q
r
s
t
u
v
w
x
y
z

• *Languages and nationalities do not take a capital letter in Spanish.*

cannot verb SEE **can**
I cannot do it. No lo puedo hacer.
He cannot read. No sabe leer.

canoe noun
la **canoa** *fem.*

can't verb SEE **can**
I can't come. No puedo venir.
She can't swim. No sabe nadar.

canteen noun
(*in a school, factory, etc.*) el **comedor** *masc.*

cap noun
la **gorra** *fem.*
Put your cap on. Ponte la gorra.

capital noun
1 (*capital city*) la **capital** *fem.*
Madrid is the capital of Spain.
Madrid es la capital de España.
2 (*capital letter*) la **mayúscula** *fem.*
in capitals en mayúsculas

capital adjective
a capital letter una mayúscula
It's written with a capital D. Se escribe con D mayúscula.

captain noun
el **capitán** *masc.*, la **capitana** *fem.*
the captain of our team el capitán de nuestro equipo

🔑 **LANGUAGE**
The plural of **capitán** is **capitanes**.

car noun
el **coche** *masc.*,
(*Latin America*) el **carro** *masc.*
We will go by car. Iremos en coche.
a car park un aparcamiento

caravan noun
la **caravana** *fem.*

card noun
1 la **tarjeta** *fem.*
a birthday card una tarjeta de cumpleaños

a greetings card la tarjeta de felicitación
2 la **carta** *fem.*
to play cards jugar a las cartas

🔑 **LANGUAGE**
Be careful: **carta** only means card when talking about a playing card.

cardboard noun
el **cartón** *masc.*
a cardboard box una caja de cartón

cardigan noun
la **chaqueta** *fem.*

care noun
el **cuidado** *masc.*
with care con cuidado
Take care crossing the road.
Cuidado al cruzar la calle.
to take care of cuidar
Rachel takes care of the children.
Rachel cuida a los niños.

to **care** verb
I don't care. No me importa.

careful adjective
to be careful tener cuidado
Be careful crossing the road. Ten cuidado al cruzar la calle.
Careful! ¡Cuidado!

carefully adverb
con cuidado
Close the door carefully. Cierra la puerta con cuidado.
We listened carefully.
Escuchamos con atención.

caretaker noun
1 (*in a building*) el **portero** *masc.*, la **portera** *fem.*
2 (*in a school*) el or la **conserje** *masc. & fem.*

Caribbean adjective
caribeño *masc.*, **caribeña** *fem.*

Caribbean noun
the Caribbean el Caribe

• *The months of the year and days of the week do not take a capital letter in Spanish.*

carnival noun
el **carnaval** *masc.*

 CULTURE
Spanish people celebrate the festival known as **carnaval** in the middle of February just before Christian Lent. They put on fancy dress, play music, and dance. Two famous **carnavales** are those of Tenerife and Cadiz.

carol noun
a Christmas carol un villancico

carpenter noun
el **carpintero** *masc.*,
la **carpintera** *fem.*
My dad's a carpenter. Mi padre es carpintero.

carpet noun
1 (*wall-to-wall*) la **moqueta** *fem.*
2 (*rug*) la **alfombra** *fem.*

carriage noun
(*on a train*) el **vagón** *masc.* (plural los **vagones**)

carrier bag noun
la **bolsa de plástico** *fem.*

carrot noun
la **zanahoria** *fem.*

to carry verb
llevar
Ruth is carrying a bag. Ruth lleva una bolsa.

to carry on verb
seguir
Carry on! ¡Sigue!
to carry on doing something seguir haciendo algo
Do you want to carry on reading? ¿Quieres seguir leyendo?

carton noun
(*of milk or juice*) el **cartón** *masc.* (plural los **cartones**)

cartoon noun
1 (*film*)
a cartoon una película de dibujos animados
Do you like cartoons? ¿Te gustan los dibujos animados?
2 (*funny drawing*) el **chiste** *masc.*

case noun
1 (*luggage*) la **maleta** *fem.*
Have you packed your case? ¿Has hecho la maleta?
2 (*soft cover for glasses, guitar, etc.*) la **funda** *fem.*
Where is my glasses case? ¿Dónde está la funda de mis gafas?
3 (*cover for pencils, make-up, etc.*) el **estuche** *masc.*
4 **just in case** por si acaso
Take your umbrella just in case. Llévate el paraguas por si acaso.

cash noun
el **dinero** *masc.*
Do you have any cash? ¿Tienes dinero?
a cash machine un cajero automático

cashier noun
el **cajero** *masc.*, **la cajera** *fem.*

cassette noun
el **casete** *masc.*

castle noun
el **castillo** *masc.*

cat noun
el **gato** *masc.*, **la gata** *fem.*
I have three cats. Tengo tres gatos.

catch verb
1 (*a ball, bus, thief, fish, etc.*) **coger**
We'll catch the bus. Cogeremos el autobús.
I caught a cold. Cogí un resfriado.
Catch! ¡Coge!
2 **to catch up with somebody** alcanzar a alguien

• *See the centre section for verb tables.*

a
b
c
d
e
f
g
h
i
j
k
l
m
n
o
p
q
r
s
t
u
v
w
x
y
z

247

English Spanish

a
b
c
d
e
f
g
h
i
j
k
l
m
n
o
p
q
r
s
t
u
v
w
x
y
z

catching adjective
contagioso *masc.*, contagiosa *fem.*
It's not catching. No es contagioso.

caterpillar noun
la oruga *fem.*

cathedral noun
la catedral *fem.*

Catholic adjective
católico *masc.*, católica *fem.*

cauliflower noun
la coliflor *fem.*

cause noun
la causa *fem.*

cave noun
la cueva *fem.*

CD noun
el CD *masc.* (plural los **CDs**)
a CD player un reproductor CD

ceiling noun
el techo *masc.*

celebrate verb
celebrar
How are you going to celebrate your birthday? ¿Cómo vas a celebrar tu cumpleaños?
Let's celebrate! ¡Vamos a celebrarlo!

celery noun
el apio *masc.*

cello noun
el violonchelo *masc.*
Ambika plays the cello. Ambika toca el violonchelo.

cemetery noun
el cementerio *masc.*

cent noun
1 (*part of a euro*) el céntimo *masc.*
It costs fifty cents. Cuesta cincuenta céntimos.
2 (*part of a dollar etc.*) el centavo *masc.*

centigrade adjective
centígrado *masc.*, centígrada *fem.*
fifteen degrees centigrade quince grados centígrados

centimetre noun
el centímetro *masc.*

central adjective
1 central *masc. & fem.*
central heating la calefacción central
2 (*near the town centre*) céntrico *masc.*, céntrica *fem.*

centre noun
el centro *masc.*
in the centre of the room en el centro de la habitación
a shopping centre un centro comercial
I live in the town centre. Vivo en el centro de la ciudad.

century noun
el siglo *masc.*
in the twenty-first century en el siglo veintiuno

cereal noun
los cereales *masc. plural*
We always have cereal for breakfast. Siempre desayunamos cereales.

> **LANGUAGE**
> English = **cereal** is singular
> Spanish = **los cereales** is plural

certain adjective
seguro *masc.*, segura *fem.*
Are you certain? ¿Estás seguro?

certainly adverb
(*of course*) por supuesto
Certainly not! ¡Por supuesto que no!

certificate noun
el certificado *masc.*

chain noun
la cadena *fem.*
a gold chain una cadena de oro

• *Use* el *and* uno *for masculine words and* la *and* una *for feminine words.*

chair noun
1 la **silla** *fem.*
I sat down on the chair. Me senté en la silla.
2 (*armchair*) el **sillón** *masc.* (plural los **sillones**)

chalk noun
la **tiza** *fem.*
a piece of chalk una tiza

champion noun
el **campeón** *masc.*,
la **campeona** *fem.*
He's a cycling champion.
Es campeón de ciclismo.

> **LANGUAGE**
> The plural of **campeón** is **campeones**.

chance noun
1 (*something that might happen*)
la **posibilidad** *fem.*
We have no chance of winning.
No tenemos ninguna posibilidad de ganar.
2 (*opportunity*) la **oportunidad** *fem.*
Now you have a chance to ask questions. Ahora tenéis la oportunidad de hacer preguntas.
3 (*risk*) el **riesgo** *masc.*
You're taking a big chance. Corres un gran riesgo.
4 **by chance** por casualidad
I bumped into Jamal by chance.
Me encontré a Jamal por casualidad.

change verb
1 **cambiar**
Can I change this book? ¿Puedo cambiar este libro?
He hasn't changed much. No ha cambiado mucho.
2 **cambiar de**

> **LANGUAGE**
> You use **cambiar** de when you mean to change one thing for another.

Do you want to change places?
¿Quieres cambiar de sitio?

I'm going to change my socks.
Me voy a cambiar de calcetines.
I've changed my mind. He cambiado de idea.
3 (*to put on different clothes*) **cambiarse**
Go and change. Ve a cambiarte.

change noun
el **cambio** *masc.*
I don't have any change for the bus. No tengo cambio para el autobús.
There have been lots of changes.
Ha habido muchos cambios.

changing room noun
1 (*for sports*) el **vestuario** *masc.*
2 (*for trying on clothes*) el **probador** *masc.*

channel noun
(*on TV*) el **canal** *masc.*
What channel is the film on?
¿En qué canal dan la película?
Can I change channels? ¿Puedo cambiar de canal?

Channel noun
el **Canal de la Mancha** *masc.*
the Channel Tunnel el túnel del Canal de la Mancha, el Eurotúnel
the Channel Islands las Islas del Canal de la Mancha

chapter noun
el **capítulo** *masc.*

character noun
1 (*in a book, play, or film*) el **personaje** *masc.*
the character of Harry Potter
el personaje de Harry Potter
the main character in the novel
el protagonista de la novela
2 (*somebody's personality*) el **carácter** *masc.*

charge noun
1 (*money you pay*)
There's no charge. Es gratuito.
There's an extra charge. Hay un suplemento.

a
b
c
d
e
f
g
h
i
j
k
l
m
n
o
p
q
r
s
t
u
v
w
x
y
z

• *Languages and nationalities do not take a capital letter in Spanish.*

a
b
c
d
e
f
g
h
i
j
k
l
m
n
o
p
q
r
s
t
u
v
w
x
y
z

2 the person in charge el or la responsable
Who's in charge? ¿Quién es el responsable?
In this house mum's in charge! ¡En esta casa manda mamá!

⚷ **LANGUAGE**
When 'be in charge' means 'be the boss' then use the verb **mandar**, e.g. 'Who's in charge here?' is **¿Quién manda aquí?**

to **charge** verb
cobrar
They charged us ten euros for breakfast. Nos cobraron diez euros por el desayuno.

chart noun
(*diagram*) el gráfico *masc.*

to **chase** verb
perseguir
They chased the thief. Persiguieron al ladrón.

chat noun
la charla *fem.*
to have a chat with somebody charlar con alguien

to **chat** verb
charlar
Stop chatting! ¡Deja de charlar!

chatroom noun
el chat *masc.*
The chatroom is empty. El chat está vacío.

cheap adjective
barato *masc.*, barata *fem.*
a cheap T-shirt una camiseta barata

cheat noun
el tramposo *masc.*,
la tramposa *fem.*
You're a cheat! ¡Eres un tramposo!

to **cheat** verb
hacer trampa
He always cheats. Siempre hace trampa.
That's cheating. Eso es trampa.

to **check** verb
1 (*to make sure*) comprobar
Check the date of the concert. Comprueba la fecha del concierto.
2 (*passports or tickets*) controlar
3 to check in (*at an airport*) facturar

check noun
1 el control *masc.*
passport check el control de pasaportes
2 (*pattern*) los cuadros *masc. plural*
a check skirt una falda de cuadros

checkout noun
(*at a supermarket*) la caja *fem.*
There's a queue at the checkout. Hay cola en la caja.

cheek noun
la mejilla *fem.*
She kissed me on the cheek. Me dio un beso en la mejilla.

cheeky adjective
descarado *masc.*, descarada *fem.*

cheer verb
aplaudir

cheerful adjective
alegre *masc. & fem.*

cheers exclamation
1 (*thanking somebody*) ¡gracias!
2 (*saying goodbye*) ¡hasta luego!

cheese noun
el queso *masc.*
He's eating some cheese. Está comiendo queso.
a cheese sandwich un sandwich de queso

chef noun
el chef *masc.* (plural los **chefs**)
My father's a chef. Mi padre es chef.

chemist noun
el farmacéutico *masc.*,
la farmacéutica *fem.*
She's a chemist. Es farmacéutica.
the chemist's la farmacia

• *The months of the year and days of the week do not take a capital letter in Spanish.*

He went to the chemist's Fue a la farmacia.

cheque noun
el **cheque** *masc.*

cherry noun
la **cereza** *fem.*

chess noun
el **ajedrez** *masc.*
We play chess. Jugamos al ajedrez.

chest noun
1 el **pecho** *masc.*
My chest hurts. Me duele el pecho.
2 **a chest of drawers** una cómoda

chestnut noun
la **castaña** *fem.*

chew verb
masticar

chewing gum noun
el **chicle** *masc.*

chick noun
el **pollito** *masc.*

chicken noun
1 (*food*) el **pollo** *masc.*
They're eating chicken. Están comiendo pollo.
a chicken leg un muslo de pollo
2 (*animal*) la **gallina** *fem.*
John's going to feed the chickens. John va a darles de comer a las gallinas.

chickenpox noun
la **varicela** *fem.*
I have chickenpox. Tengo la varicela.

child noun
1 (*boy*) el **niño** *masc.*; (*girl*) la **niña** *fem.*
a child of five un niño de cinco años
2 (*son*) el **hijo** *masc.*; (*daughter*) la **hija** *fem.*
I'm the oldest child. Soy la hija mayor.

• *See the centre section for verb tables.*

childminder noun
la **niñera** *fem.*

children plural noun
1 (*boys and girls*) los **niños** *masc. plural*
There are lots of children. Hay muchos niños.
2 (*sons and daughters*) los **hijos** *masc. plural*
They have four children. Tienen cuatro hijos.

Chile noun
Chile *masc.*

chilly adjective
frío *masc.*, **fría** *fem.*
The weather's chilly. Hace frío.
I'm chilly. Tengo frío.

> ☞ **LANGUAGE**
> English = **to be chilly** **I'm chilly.**
> Spanish = **tener frío** **Tengo frío.**

chimney noun
la **chimenea** *fem.*

chin noun
la **barbilla** *fem.*

> ☞ **LANGUAGE**
> Note the relation between **la barbilla** (chin) and **la barba** (beard).

China noun
China *fem.*

Chinese adjective
chino *masc.*, **china** *fem.*
a Chinese town una ciudad china
a Chinese man un chino
a Chinese woman una china

Chinese noun
1 (*language*) el **chino** *masc.*
Do you speak Chinese? ¿Hablas chino?
2 **the Chinese** los chinos *masc. plural*

chip noun
la **patata frita** *fem.*
Do you like fish and chips? ¿Te gusta el pescado con patatas fritas?

a
b
c
d
e
f
g
h
i
j
k
l
m
n
o
p
q
r
s
t
u
v
w
x
y
z

choc-ice noun
el **bombón helado** *masc.*

chocolate noun
1 el **chocolate** *masc.*
I love chocolate. Me encanta el chocolate.
a chocolate cake un pastel de chocolate
2 el **bombón** *masc.* (plural los **bombones**)
Would you like a chocolate? ¿Quieres un bombón?

> **LANGUAGE**
> Be careful! When you mean one chocolate sweet use **bombón**, not **chocolate**.

choice noun
la **elección** *fem.* (plural las **elecciones**)
a good choice una buena elección

choir noun
el **coro** *masc.*
We sing in the choir. Cantamos en el coro.

choose verb
elegir
Choose a card. Elige una carta.

chop noun
la **chuleta** *fem.*
a pork chop una chuleta de cerdo

chopsticks plural noun
los **palillos** *masc. plural*

Christian adjective
cristiano *masc.*, **cristiana** *fem.*

Christmas noun
la **Navidad** *fem.*
at Christmas en Navidad
Where are you spending Christmas? ¿Dónde vas a pasar la Navidad?
Happy Christmas! ¡Feliz Navidad!
a Christmas card una tarjeta de Navidad
Christmas Day el día de Navidad

Christmas dinner la comida de Navidad

> **CULTURE**
> In Spain the main Christmas meal is on Christmas Eve, and it is eaten before Midnight Mass.

Christmas Eve la Nochebuena
a Christmas present un regalo de Navidad

> **CULTURE**
> Spanish children usually receive their Christmas presents on 6th January, known as **el día de Reyes** (the day of the Three Wise Men). Children put out their shoes for the Wise Men to leave the presents in!

a Christmas tree un árbol de Navidad

church noun
la **iglesia** *fem.*
to go to church ir a la iglesia

cinema noun
el **cine** *masc.*
We're going to the cinema. Vamos al cine.

circle noun
el **círculo** *masc.*
The children sat down in a circle. Los niños se sentaron en círculo.

circus noun
el **circo** *masc.*
Do you like the circus? ¿Os gusta el circo?

city noun
la **ciudad** *fem.*
the city centre el centro de la ciudad

clap verb
1 (*when you like something*) **aplaudir**
Everyone clapped. Todos aplaudieron.
2 (*with the music*) **dar palmas**
You sing and I clap. Tú cantas y yo doy palmas.

• *Use* **el** *and* **uno** *for masculine words and* **la** *and* **una** *for feminine words.*

clarinet noun
el clarinete *masc.*
Yasmina plays the clarinet.
Yasmina toca el clarinete.

class noun
la clase *fem.*
He's in my class. Está en mi clase.
Today we have a Spanish class.
Hoy tenemos clase de español.

classroom noun
el aula *fem.*, la clase *fem.*
a classroom assistant un or una
auxiliar de aula

🔑 **LANGUAGE**
Be careful: you use **el** with **aula** but it is
not a masculine noun.

clean adjective
limpio *masc.*, limpia *fem.*
The room is clean. La habitación
está limpia.

to **clean** verb
limpiar
Dad's cleaning the house. Papá
está limpiando la casa.
I'm going to clean my teeth. Voy a
lavarme los dientes.

cleaner noun
(*man*) el hombre de la limpieza
masc.; (*woman*) la mujer de la
limpieza *fem.*

cleaning noun
la limpieza *fem.*
I don't like doing the cleaning.
No me gusta hacer la limpieza.

clear adjective
claro *masc.*, clara *fem.*
Your explanation is very clear. Tu
explicación es muy clara.

to **clear** verb
1 **to clear the table** quitar la mesa
2 **to clear up** recoger
Clear up your toys! ¡Recoge los
juguetes!

clearly adverb
claramente

clementine noun
la clementina *fem.*

clever adjective
inteligente *masc. & fem.*

to **click** verb
hacer clic
Click on the icon. Haz clic en el
icono.

cliff noun
el acantilado *masc.*

climate noun
el clima *masc.*

🔑 **LANGUAGE**
Be careful: **clima** ends in an -**a** but it is not
a feminine noun.

to **climb** verb
subir
to climb the stairs subir las
escaleras
to climb a tree subir a un árbol

cloakroom
1 (*for coats*) el guardarropa *masc.*
2 (*toilet*) los servicios *masc. plural*

🔑 **LANGUAGE**
Be careful: **guardarropa** ends in an -**a** but
it is not a feminine noun.

clock noun
el reloj *masc.*
The kitchen clock is broken.
El reloj de la cocina está roto.
an alarm clock un despertador

close adverb
(*nearby*) cerca
We live close by. Vivimos muy
cerca.
close to cerca de
The school is close to the library.
El colegio está cerca de la
biblioteca.

• *Languages and nationalities do not take a capital letter in Spanish.*

English Spanish

a
b
c
d
e
f
g
h
i
j
k
l
m
n
o
p
q
r
s
t
u
v
w
x
y
z

to **close** verb
cerrar
Close the door. Cierra la puerta.
The supermarket closes at ten.
El supermercado cierra a las diez.

closed adjective
cerrado masc., **cerrada** fem.
The shops are closed. Las tiendas
están cerradas.

cloth noun
1 (for cleaning) el **trapo** masc.
2 (material) la **tela** fem.
Is it made of cloth? ¿Es de tela?

clothes plural noun
la **ropa** fem.
Your clothes are dirty. Tu ropa
está sucia.

🔑 **LANGUAGE**
English = **clothes** is plural
Spanish = **la ropa** is singular

cloud noun
la **nube** fem.

cloudy adjective
nublado masc., **nublada** fem.
It's cloudy today. Hoy está
nublado.

clown noun
el **payaso** masc., la **payasa** fem.

club noun
1 el **club** masc. (plural los **clubs**)
a football club un club de fútbol
2 (for dancing) la **discoteca** fem.
My sister went to a club.
Mi hermana fue a una discoteca.

🔑 **LANGUAGE**
The Spanish word **club** is pronounced
'cloob'.

clumsy adjective
torpe masc. & fem.
You're so clumsy today! ¡Qué
torpe estás hoy!

coach noun
el **autocar** masc.
by coach en autocar
the coach station la estación de
autobuses

coal noun
el **carbón** masc.

coast noun
la **costa** fem.
**We spend our holidays on the
coast.** Pasamos las vacaciones en
la costa.

coat noun
el **abrigo** masc.

cocoa noun
el **cacao** masc.

cobweb noun
la **telaraña** fem.
full of cobwebs lleno de telarañas

coconut noun
el **coco** masc.

cod noun
el **bacalao** masc.

code noun
la **clave** fem.
a secret code una clave secreta
The message is in code. El mensaje
está en clave.

coffee noun
el **café** masc.
a cup of coffee una taza de café
Shall we have a coffee? ¿Tomamos
un café?
a black coffee un café solo
a white coffee un café con leche

coin noun
la **moneda** fem.
a one euro coin una moneda de un
euro

coincidence noun
la **casualidad** fem.
What a coincidence! ¡Qué
casualidad!

• The months of the year and days of the week do not take a capital letter in Spanish.

Coke® noun
la **Coca-Cola®** *fem.*
a can of Coke una lata de
Coca-Cola®

cold adjective
frío *masc.*, **fría** *fem.*
The water's cold. El agua está
fría.
The weather's cold. Hace frío.
It's cold today. Hoy hace frío.
I'm cold. Tengo frío.
He's very cold. Tiene mucho frío.

> ⚷ **LANGUAGE**
> English = **to be** cold **I'm cold.**
> Spanish = **tener** frío **Tengo frío.**

cold noun
1 (*the cold weather*) el **frío** *masc.*
I don't like the cold. No me gusta
el frío.
2 (*illness*) el **resfriado** *masc.*
to catch a cold coger un resfriado
to have a cold estar resfriado
masc., estar resfriada *fem.*
Jenny has a cold. Jenny está
resfriada.

collar noun
1 el **cuello** *masc.*
my shirt collar el cuello de mi
camisa
2 (*on a dog*) el **collar** *masc.*

to **collect** verb
1 (*to pick up*) **recoger**
Can I collect the exercise books?
¿Puedo recoger los cuadernos?
2 (*as a hobby*) **coleccionar**
Do you collect stamps?
¿Coleccionas sellos?

collection noun
la **colección** *fem.* (plural las
colecciones)
a CD collection una colección de
CDs

college noun
la **institución de educación
superior** *fem.*

colour noun
el **color** *masc.*
What colour is her hair? ¿De qué
color es su pelo?

to **colour** verb
colorear
to colour in a picture colorear un
dibujo
a colouring book un cuaderno
para colorear

column noun
la **columna** *fem.*

comb noun
el **peine** *masc.*
Do you have a comb? ¿Tienes un
peine?

to **comb** verb
to comb your hair peinarse
I haven't combed my hair. No me
he peinado.

to **come** verb
venir
Come and see me tomorrow. Ven a
verme mañana.
I want to come with you. Quiero
venir contigo.
Come with me. Ven conmigo.
The bus is coming. Ya viene el
autobús.
I come from Madrid. Soy de
Madrid.
Wait for me, I'm coming!
¡Espérame, ya voy!
Come on! ¡Venga!
Has the post come yet? ¿Ya ha
llegado el correo?

to **come back** verb
volver
Come back later. Vuelve más
tarde.

to **come down** verb
bajar
I'm coming down! ¡Ya bajo!
He came down the stairs. Bajó las
escaleras.

a
b
c
d
e
f
g
h
i
j
k
l
m
n
o
p
q
r
s
t
u
v
w
x
y
z

• *See the centre section for verb tables.*

to **come in** verb
entrar
She came into the dining room.
Entró en el comedor.
Come in! ¡Pase!, ¡Adelante!

to **come out** verb
salir
When are you coming out of your room? ¿Cuándo vas a salir de tu cuarto?

to **come up** verb
subir
I'm coming up now. Ahora subo.
They came up the stairs. Subieron las escaleras.

comfortable adjective
(*chair, shoes, etc.*) cómodo *masc.*, cómoda *fem.*
These shoes are very comfortable.
Estos zapatos son muy cómodos.

comic noun
el cómic *masc.*
Malcolm loves reading comics.
A Malcolm le encanta leer cómics.

comma noun
la coma *fem.*

comments plural noun
(*by teacher on homework etc.*)
los comentarios *masc. plural*

common adjective
1 corriente *masc. & fem.*
John is a very common name. John es un nombre muy corriente.
2 **in common** en común
We have nothing in common.
No tenemos nada en común.

company noun
la compañía *fem.*
My mum works in an insurance company. Mi madre trabaja en una compañía de seguros.

to **compare** verb
comparar

compass noun
la brújula *fem.*

compasses plural noun
a pair of compasses un compás
(plural los **compases**)

competition noun
1 el concurso *masc.*
a fancy dress competition
un concurso de disfraces
2 (*for sports*) la competición *fem.*
a swimming competition una competición de natación

competitor noun
el or la participiante *masc. & fem.*
the competitors in the race los participiantes en la carrera

to **complain** verb
quejarse
You're always complaining about something! ¡Siempre te estás quejando de algo!

complete adjective
1 (*sentence, list, etc.*) completo *masc.*, completa *fem.*
2 (*change, disaster, etc.*) total *masc. & fem.*
complete silence un silencio total

to **complete** verb
1 terminar
Have you completed your work?
¿Has terminado tu trabajo?
2 (*to add something missing*) completar
Complete this sentence with the right word. Completa esta frase con la palabra adecuada.

completely adverb
completamente

complicated adjective
complicado *masc.*, complicada *fem.*

comprehension noun
(*an exercise in school*) el ejercicio de comprensión *masc.*

comprehensive noun
(*school*) el instituto de enseñanza secundaria *masc.*
My sister goes to a comprehensive.
Mi hermana va al instituto.

• *Use* el *and* uno *for masculine words and* la *and* una *for feminine words.*

XXX

computer noun
el ordenador *masc.*,
(*Latin America*) el computador *masc.*,
la computadora *fem.*
My parents have bought me a new computer. Mis padres me han comprado un ordenador nuevo.
a computer game un videojuego
a computer program un programa informático
a computer room una sala de ordenadores

to **concentrate** verb
concentrarse
Be quiet, I can't concentrate! ¡Cállate, que no me puedo concentrar!

concert noun
el concierto *masc.*
My brother went to a rock concert. Mi hermano fue a un concierto de rock.

condition noun
in good condition en buen estado

conductor noun
(*of an orchestra*) el director *masc.*,
la directora *fem.*

cone noun
an ice-cream cone un cucurucho

confused adjective
confundido *masc.*,
confundida *fem.*
I'm still confused. Todavía estoy confundido.
to get confused confundirse
I got confused. Me confundí.

congratulations plural noun
la enhorabuena *fem.*
Congratulations! ¡Enhorabuena!

conjunction noun
la conjunción *fem.* (plural las conjunciones)

to **connect** verb

to connect to the Internet conectarse a Internet
I connect every day. Me conecto a Internet todos los días.
We're connected to the Internet. Estamos conectados a Internet.

conservatory noun
(*room made of glass*) la galería *fem.*

console noun
a games console una videoconsola

consonant noun
la consonante *fem.*

to **contact** verb
ponerse en contacto con

container noun
el recipiente *masc.*

contest noun
el concurso *masc.*

continent noun
1 el continente *masc.*
How many continents are there? ¿Cuántos continentes hay?
2 (*Europe*)
on the Continent en Europa

to **continue** verb
continuar, seguir
I continued reading. Continué leyendo., Seguí leyendo.
Continue with what you're doing. Sigue con lo que estás haciendo.

to **control** verb
controlar
Control yourself! ¡Contrólate!

convenient adjective
1 (*time, place*) conveniente *masc. & fem.*
2 cómodo *masc.*, cómoda *fem.*
It's convenient living near the school. Es cómodo vivir cerca de la escuela.

conversation noun
la conversación *fem.* (plural las conversaciones)

a b c d e f g h i j k l m n o p q r s t u v w x y z

• Languages and nationalities do not take a capital letter in Spanish.

a
b
c
d
e
f
g
h
i
j
k
l
m
n
o
p
q
r
s
t
u
v
w
x
y
z

to **cook** verb
1 cocinar
Do you like cooking? ¿Te gusta cocinar?
What are you cooking? ¿Qué estás cocinando?
2 to cook a meal hacer una comida
Granddad is cooking dinner. El abuelo está haciendo la cena.
3 hacerse
The potatoes are cooking. Las patatas se están haciendo.

cook noun
el cocinero *masc.*, la cocinera *fem.*
Mum's a good cook. Mamá es muy buena cocinera.

cookbook noun
el libro de cocina *masc.*

cooked adjective
(*cake, chicken, etc.*) hecho *masc.*, hecha *fem.*
The meat is well cooked. La carne está bien hecha.

cooker noun
la cocina *fem.*
a gas cooker una cocina de gas

cookie noun
la galleta *fem.*

cooking noun
la cocina *fem.*
Spanish cooking la cocina española
to do the cooking cocinar

cool adjective
1 fresco *masc.*, fresca *fem.*
a cool drink una bebida fresca
The weather is cool. Hace fresco.
2 (*good or great*) guay *masc. & fem.*
He's a really cool guy! ¡Qué chico más guay!
You look cool in that jacket. Esa chaqueta te queda guay.

to **cool down** verb
enfriar
Let the soup cool down. Deja enfriar la sopa.

copy noun
la copia *fem.*
I need two copies. Necesito dos copias.

to **copy** verb
copiar
Can I copy your notes? ¿Puedo copiar tus apuntes?

corn noun
(*wheat*) el trigo *masc.*

corner noun
1 (*of a street, table, page, etc.*) la esquina *fem.*
the corner of the table la esquina de la mesa
There's a post office on the corner. Hay una oficina de correos en la esquina.
2 (*of a room, drawer, cupboard, etc.*) el rincón *masc.*
There's a cupboard in the corner. Hay un armario en el rincón.

LANGUAGE
Be careful: there are two words for corner. Use esquina when you mean the corner from the *outside*, and rincón when you mean the corner from the *inside*.

cornflakes plural noun
los copos de maíz *masc. plural*, los cereales *masc. plural*

Cornwall noun
Cornualles *masc.*

correct adjective
(*amount, number, sentence, etc.*) correcto *masc.*, correcta *fem.*
Your answer is correct. Tu respuesta es correcta.
Correct! ¡Correcto!

• The months of the year and days of the week do not take a capital letter in Spanish.

258

to **correct** verb
 corregir
 You have to correct the mistakes.
 Tienes que corregir las faltas.

correction noun
 la corrección *fem.* (plural las **correcciones**)

correctly adverb
 correctamente, bien

corridor noun
 el pasillo *masc.*
 It's at the end of the corridor. Está al final del pasillo.

to **cost** verb
 costar
 How much does it cost? ¿Cuánto cuesta?
 It cost me ten euros. Me costó diez euros.

costume noun
 1 el traje *masc.*
 a swimming costume un traje de baño
 2 (*fancy dress*) el disfraz *masc.* (plural los **disfraces**)

cot noun
 la cuna *fem.*

cottage noun
 la casita *fem.*

🔑 **LANGUAGE**
Casita is the Spanish for 'little house'.

cotton noun
 el algodón *masc.*
 a cotton shirt una camisa de algodón
 cotton wool el algodón

couch noun
 el sofá *masc.*

cough noun
 la tos *fem.*
 a cough medicine un jarabe para la tos
 I have a cough. Tengo tos.

Alice has a bad cough. Alice tiene mucha tos.

to **cough** verb
 toser
 Smoke makes me cough. El humo me hace toser.

could verb
 poder
 Could I ask you a question? ¿Puedo hacerte una pregunta?
 Could you open the window? ¿Puedes abrir la ventana?

to **count** verb
 contar
 Count up to twenty. Cuenta hasta veinte.
 The teacher counted his pupils. El maestro contó a sus alumnos.

counter noun
 1 (*in a shop*) el mostrador *masc.*
 2 (*in a bank or post office*) la ventanilla *fem.*
 3 (*in a game*) la ficha *fem.*

country noun
 1 (*Britain, Spain, etc.*) el país *masc.*
 a foreign country un país extranjero
 Have you visited many countries? ¿Has visitado muchos países?
 2 (*not the town*) el campo *masc.*
 Maite lives in the country. Maite vive en el campo.

countryside noun
 el campo *masc.*
 in the countryside en el campo

couple noun
 1 **a couple of** un par de
 a couple of hours un par de horas
 2 (*two people*) la pareja *fem.*
 a young couple una pareja joven
 a married couple una pareja de casados

• See the centre section for verb tables.

a b c d e f g h i j k l m n o p q r s t u v w x y z

courgette noun
el calabacín *masc.* (plural los **calabacines**)

course noun
1 (*lessons*) el curso *masc.*
a Spanish course un curso de español
My sister's going on a course.
Mi hermana va a hacer un curso.
2 (*part of a meal*) el plato *masc.*
the main course el plato principal
3 of course claro
Can you help me? – Of course I can!
¿Puedes ayudarme? – ¡Claro que sí!
of course not claro que no

court noun
(*for sports*) la pista *fem.*
a tennis court una pista de tenis

cousin noun
el primo *masc.*, la prima *fem.*

cover noun
(*of a book or magazine*) la tapa *fem.*
the covers (*on a bed*) las mantas

to **cover** verb
cubrir
I covered myself with a sheet.
Me cubrí con una sábana.
You're covered in mud! ¡Estás cubierta de barro!

cow noun
la vaca *fem.*

cowboy noun
el vaquero *masc.*

crab noun
el cangrejo *masc.*

cracker noun
(*biscuit*) la galleta salada *fem.*

CULTURE
Christmas crackers do not exist in Spain so there is no word for them in Spanish.

crash noun
el accidente *masc.*, el choque *masc.*
a car crash un accidente de coche
a crash helmet un casco

to **crash** verb
to crash into something chocar con algo
The lorry crashed into a lamp-post. El camión chocó con una farola.

to **crawl** verb
1 (*talking about babies*) gatear
2 (*talking about insects*) andar

crayon noun
el lápiz de color *masc.*, la crayola® *fem.*

crazy adjective
loco *masc.*, loca *fem.*
You're crazy! ¡Estás loco!
My brother's crazy about football.
A mi hermano le encanta el fútbol.

cream noun
1 (*from milk*) la nata *fem.*
strawberries and cream fresas con nata
2 (*for your skin*) la crema *fem.*

to **create** verb
crear

crèche noun
la guardería *fem.*

crew noun
(*on a plane or ship*) la tripulación *fem.* (plural las **tripulaciones**)

cricket noun
el críquet *masc.*
Do you like playing cricket?
¿Te gusta jugar al críquet?
a cricket bat un bate de críquet

 CULTURE
Spanish people do not play cricket.

• *Use el and uno for masculine words and la and una for feminine words.*

260

crime noun
1 el delito *masc.*
2 (*serious crime, such as murder*) el crimen *masc.* (plural los **crímenes**)

criminal noun
1 el or la delincuente *masc. & fem.*
2 (*murderer*) el or la criminal *masc. & fem.*

crisps plural noun
las patatas fritas *fem. plural*
a bag of crisps una bolsa de patatas fritas

> **LANGUAGE**
> Word for word **patatas fritas** means 'fried potatoes'. The Spanish can also mean 'chips'.

to criticize verb
criticar

crocodile noun
el cocodrilo *masc.*

> **LANGUAGE**
> English = **crocodile**
> Spanish = **cocodrilo**

crooked adjective
torcido *masc.*, torcida *fem.*
The picture is crooked. El cuadro está torcido.

to cross verb
1 cruzar
Let's cross the road. Vamos a cruzar la calle.
Cross your arms. Cruzad los brazos.
2 **to cross something out** tachar algo

cross noun
la cruz *fem.* (plural las **cruces**)
Put a cross in the box. Pon una cruz en la casilla.

cross adjective
(*angry*) enfadado *masc.*, enfadada *fem.*
Are you cross with me? ¿Estás enfadado conmigo?
to get cross enfadarse

I got cross with my sister. Me enfadé con mi hermana.

crossing
1 (*safe place to cross the road*) el paso de peatones *masc.*
2 (*by boat*) la travesía *fem.*

crossroads noun
el cruce *masc.*
at the crossroads en el cruce

crossword noun
el crucigrama *masc.*
I like doing crosswords. Me gusta hacer crucigramas.

> **LANGUAGE**
> Be careful: **crucigrama** ends in an -**a** but it is not a feminine noun.

crowd noun
a crowd mucha gente *fem.*
There are crowds of people in the shops. Hay mucha gente en las tiendas.

> **LANGUAGE**
> Word for word **mucha gente** means 'lots of people'. In Spanish you normally say this for a crowd.

crowded adjective
It's crowded. Hay mucha gente.

crown noun
la corona *fem.*

cruel adjective
cruel *masc. & fem.*
a cruel man un hombre cruel

crumbs plural noun
las migas *fem. plural*

to crush verb
aplastar

crust noun
la corteza *fem.*

• *Languages and nationalities do not take a capital letter in Spanish.*

crutch noun
la **muleta** *fem.*
She's on crutches. Anda con muletas.

to **cry** verb
llorar
Don't cry! ¡No llores!

cub noun
(*young lion, bear, or wolf*) el **cachorro** *masc.*

Cub noun
(*Scout*) el **lobato** *masc.*
He's in the Cubs. Pertenece a los lobatos.

Cuba noun
Cuba *fem.*

cube noun
el **cubo** *masc.*
an ice cube un cubito de hielo

cucumber noun
el **pepino** *masc.*

cup
1 la **taza** *fem.*
a cup of tea una taza de té
2 (*prize*) la **copa** *fem.*
the World Cup la Copa del Mundo

cupboard noun
el **armario** *masc.*

curious adjective
curioso *masc.*, **curiosa** *fem.*

curly adjective
rizado *masc.*, **rizada** *fem.*
I have curly hair. Tengo el pelo rizado.

curriculum noun
the curriculum el plan de estudios

curry noun
el **curry** *masc.* (plural los **currys**)
chicken curry el pollo al curry

cursor noun
el **cursor** *masc.*

curtain noun
la **cortina** *fem.*

curve noun
la **curva** *fem.*

curved adjective
curvo *masc.*, **curva** *fem.*
a curved line una línea curva

cushion noun
el **cojín** *masc.* (plural los **cojines**)

custard noun
las **natillas** *fem. plural*

custom noun
la **costumbre** *fem.*

customer noun
el **cliente** *masc.*, **la clienta** *fem.*

to **cut** verb
1 **cortar**
Cut the cake. Corta el pastel.
I've cut my finger. Me he cortado el dedo.
I've cut my hair. Me he cortado el pelo
2 **to cut something out** recortar algo
Cut this picture out of the paper. Recorta esta foto del periódico.

cut noun
(*on your finger etc.*) el **corte** *masc.*

cutlery noun
los **cubiertos** *masc. plural*

to **cycle** verb
ir en bicicleta
My brother cycles to school. Mi hermano va al colegio en bicicleta.
to go cycling ir en bicicleta
a cycle path un carril bici

cycling noun
(*sport*) el **ciclismo** *masc.*

cyclist noun
el or la **ciclista** *masc. & fem.*

• *The months of the year and days of the week do not take a capital letter in Spanish.*

a b **c** d e f g h i j k l m n o p q r s t u v w x y z

Dd

dad noun
el **papá** *masc.*, el **padre** *masc.*
Good night, dad. Buenas noches, papá.
My dad works in an office. Mi padre trabaja en una oficina.
my mum and dad mis papás

daddy noun
el **papá** *masc.*
Bye, daddy! ¡Adiós, papá!

daily adjective
diario *masc.*, **diaria** *fem.*

damage noun
los **daños** *masc. plural*

LANGUAGE
English = **damage** is singular
Spanish = **los daños** is plural

damp adjective
húmedo *masc.*, **húmeda** *fem.*

dance noun
el **baile** *masc.*
She goes to dance classes. Va a clase de baile.

to **dance** verb
bailar
I love dancing. Me encanta bailar.

dancer noun
el **bailarín** *masc.*, la **bailarina** *fem.*

LANGUAGE
The Spanish words are related to the English word 'ballerina'.

danger noun
el **peligro** *masc.*
We're in danger. Estamos en peligro.

dangerous adjective
peligroso *masc.*, **peligrosa** *fem.*

• *See the centre section for verb tables.*

to **dare** verb
atreverse
I don't dare to go out. No me atrevo a salir.

dark adjective
1 (*room, colours, hair, etc.*) **oscuro** *masc.*, **oscura** *fem.*
It's dark here. Está oscuro aquí.
I have dark eyes. Tengo los ojos oscuros.
dark blue dresses vestidos azul oscuro

LANGUAGE
With colours use **oscuro** and the colour word in the masculine singular form only.

2 (*describing night-time*)
It's dark. Es de noche.
It's getting dark. Se está haciendo de noche.

dark noun
la **oscuridad** *fem.*
I'm afraid of the dark. Me da miedo la oscuridad.

darling exclamation
¡cariño!
Yes, darling! ¡Sí, cariño!

database noun
el **banco de datos** *masc.*

date noun
la **fecha** *fem.*
What's your date of birth? ¿Cuál es tu fecha de nacimiento?
What's the date today? ¿A qué fecha estamos hoy?

daughter noun
la **hija** *fem.*

day noun
1 el **día** *masc.*
two days later dos días más tarde
every day todos los días

What day is it today? ¿Qué día es hoy?
It rained all day. Llovió todo el día.
2 **the day before yesterday** anteayer
the day after tomorrow pasado mañana

> **LANGUAGE**
> Be careful: **día** ends in an **-a** but it is not a feminine noun.

daytime noun
el **día** masc.

dead adjective
muerto masc., **muerta** fem.
He's dead. Está muerto.

> **LANGUAGE**
> Be careful: translate 'be dead' by **estar muerto**, not **ser muerto**, even though you normally use **estar** for something that lasts a short time.

deaf adjective
sordo masc., **sorda** fem.
He's deaf. Es sordo.

dear adjective
1 (person) **querido** masc., **querida** fem.
Dear Tina ... Querida Tina ...
2 (expensive) **caro** masc., **cara** fem.
This blouse is too dear. Esta blusa es demasiado cara.

dear exclamation
Oh dear! ¡Oh, no!

death noun
la **muerte** fem.

December noun
diciembre masc.
I was born in December. Nací en diciembre.
We're going to Valencia on the fifth of December. Vamos a Valencia el cinco de diciembre.

to **decide** verb
decidir
I've decided to learn Spanish. He decidido aprender español.
I can't decide. No puedo decidir.

decision noun
la **decisión** fem. (plural las **decisiones**)
I've made a decision. He tomado una decisión.

> **LANGUAGE**
> Use **tomar** (to take) with **decisión**, not **hacer** (to make).

deckchair noun
la **hamaca** fem.

to **decorate** verb
1 (with pictures, balloons, etc.) **decorar**
We've decorated the classroom. Hemos decorado la clase.
2 **to decorate the Christmas tree** adornar el árbol de Navidad
3 (to paint) **pintar**
We're decorating the dining room. Estamos pintando el comedor.

decorations plural noun
los **adornos** masc. plural
I'm putting up the Christmas decorations. Estoy poniendo los adornos de Navidad.

deep adjective
profundo masc., **profunda** fem.
a deep river un río profundo

deer noun
el **ciervo** masc.

to **defend** verb
defender

definite
(certain) **seguro** masc., **segura** fem.
I can come but it's not definite. Puedo venir pero no es seguro.
a definite date una fecha segura

definitely adverb
yes, definitely sí, claro
Are you coming? – Yes, definitely. ¿Vienes tú? – Sí, claro.
definitely not claro que no

• Use **el** and **uno** for masculine words and **la** and **una** for feminine words.

degree noun
1 (*of temperature*) el **grado** *masc.*
 It's twenty-five degrees. Estamos a veinticinco grados.
2 (*university certificate*) el **título universitario** *masc.*

delay noun
el **retraso** *masc.*

to delay verb
retrasar
Our flight has been delayed. Nuestro vuelo se ha retrasado.

delete verb
(*a file, word, etc.*) **borrar**
Delete that file. Borra ese fichero.

delicious adjective
delicioso *masc.*, **deliciosa** *fem.*
This cake is delicious. Este pastel está delicioso.

> ⚷ **LANGUAGE**
> In Spanish you can also say **rico/rica**, e.g. **Este pastel está muy rico.**

deliver verb
(*milk, newspapers, pizzas, etc.*) **traer**
Have they delivered the pizzas? ¿Han traído las pizzas?
to deliver a parcel entregar un paquete

denim adjective
vaquero *masc.*, **vaquera** *fem.*
a denim skirt una falda vaquera

dentist noun
el or la **dentista** *masc. & fem.*
I'm going to the dentist. Voy al dentista.

department noun
1 (*in a store*) la **sección** *fem.* (plural las **secciones**)
 the toy department la sección de juguetes

> ⚷ **LANGUAGE**
> **Sección** is similar to 'section' in English.

2 (*in a university*) el **departamento** *masc.*
3 **a department store** unos grandes almacenes

departure noun
la **salida** *fem.*

to depend verb
depender
That depends on you. Depende de ti.
It all depends. Depende.

deputy head noun
el **subdirector** *masc.*, la **subdirectora** *fem.*

to describe verb
describir
Describe your family. Describe a tu familia.

description noun
la **descripción** *fem.* (plural las **descripciones**)

desert noun
el **desierto** *masc.*

to deserve verb
merecer
You deserve the prize. Te mereces el premio.

design noun
el **diseño** *masc.*
a flower design un diseño de flores

to design verb
diseñar
My mother designs dresses. Mi madre diseña vestidos.

desk noun
1 (*for a pupil*) la **mesa** *fem.*
2 (*in an office, and for a teacher*) el **escritorio** *masc.*

dessert noun
el **postre** *masc.*
What's for dessert? ¿Qué hay de postre?

English Spanish

a
b
c
d
e
f
g
h
i
j
k
l
m
n
o
p
q
r
s
t
u
v
w
x
y
z

• *Languages and nationalities do not take a capital letter in Spanish.*

English Spanish

a
b
c
d
e
f
g
h
i
j
k
l
m
n
o
p
q
r
s
t
u
v
w
x
y
z

destination noun
el **destino** *masc.*

to **destroy** verb
destruir

detail noun
el **detalle** *masc.*
in detail con todo detalle

detective noun
el or la **detective** *masc. & fem.*
a private detective un detective
privado *masc.*, una detective
privada *fem.*
a detective story una novela
policíaca

detention noun
to be in detention estar castigado
masc., estar castigada *fem.*
The teacher gave her a detention.
La maestra la dejó castigada
después de clase.

> **LANGUAGE**
> **Castigar** means 'to punish'; there is no
> word for **detention** in Spanish.

devil noun
el **diablo** *masc.*

diagram noun
el **diagrama** *masc.*
to draw a diagram hacer un
diagrama

> **LANGUAGE**
> Be careful: **diagrama** ends in an -a but it
> is not a feminine noun.

to **dial** verb
marcar
to dial a number marcar un
número

diamond noun
el **diamante** *masc.*
a diamond ring un anillo de
diamantes

diary noun
1 (*for writing appointments in*) la **agenda**
fem.

2 (*for writing private things in*) el **diario**
masc.
I keep a diary. Escribo un diario.

> **LANGUAGE**
> The Spanish **diario** also means 'daily'
> because you write in it every day.

dice noun
el **dado** *masc.*
Throw the dice. Tira el dado.

> **LANGUAGE**
> The plural of dice is also 'dice' so 'Throw
> the dice' can also be **Tira los dados**.

dictionary noun
el **diccionario** *masc.*
**I'm looking up a word in the
dictionary.** Estoy buscando una
palabra en el diccionario.

did verb SEE **do**
I didn't do it. No lo hice.
He did nothing. No hizo nada.

to **die** verb
morir
My cat died last week. Mi gato
murió la semana pasada.

diet noun
(*food*) la **dieta** *fem.*
I have a healthy diet. Llevo una
dieta sana.

difference noun
la **diferencia** *fem.*
**What's the difference between the
two?** ¿Qué diferencia hay entre los
dos?

different adjective
distinto *masc.*, **distinta** *fem.*
I'm very different from my sister.
Soy muy distinta a mi hermana.

> **LANGUAGE**
> You can also say **diferente** in Spanish.

difficult adjective
difícil *masc. & fem.*
It's very difficult. Es muy difícil.

• *The months of the year and days of the week do not take a capital letter in Spanish.*

to **dig** verb
cavar
to dig a hole cavar un agujero

digital adjective
(camera, television, watch) digital masc. & fem.

dining room noun
el comedor masc.

dinner noun
1 (in the evening) la cena fem.
What's for dinner? ¿Qué hay de cena?
to have dinner cenar
It's dinner time. Es la hora de cenar.
2 (at midday) la comida fem.
to have dinner comer
It's dinner time. Es la hora de comer.
Do you like school dinners? ¿Te gusta comer en el colegio?

dinosaur noun
el dinosaurio masc.

direct adjective
directo masc., directa fem.

direction noun
la dirección fem. (plural las **direcciones**)
We're going in the opposite direction. Vamos en dirección contraria.
Are we going in the right direction? ¿Vamos bien?
I asked for directions to the station. Pregunté el camino a la estación.

directory noun
(phone book) la guía telefónica fem.

dirty adjective
sucio masc., sucia fem.
The table is dirty. La mesa está sucia.
My hands are dirty. Tengo las manos sucias.

• See the centre section for verb tables.

disabled adjective
minusválido masc.,
minusválida fem.

to **disagree** verb
I disagree. No estoy de acuerdo.

to **disappear** verb
desaparecer
My pen has disappeared. Mi bolígrafo ha desaparecido.

to **disappoint** verb
decepcionar
I'm disappointed. Estoy decepcionada.

disaster noun
el desastre masc.

disco noun
1 (party where you dance) el baile masc.
2 (place where you dance) la discoteca fem.

to **discover** verb
descubrir

discovery noun
el descubrimiento masc.

to **discuss** verb
to discuss something hablar de algo

disease noun
la enfermedad fem.

disguise noun
el disfraz masc. (plural los **disfraces**)

to **disguise** verb
disfrazar
I disguised myself as a pirate. Me disfracé de pirata.

disguised adjective
disfrazado masc., disfrazada fem.
I'm disguised as a pirate. Estoy disfrazada de pirata.

disgusting adjective
asqueroso masc., asquerosa fem.
This food's disgusting. Esta comida está asquerosa.

dish noun
el **plato** *masc.*
I'm doing the dishes. Estoy
lavando los platos.

dishwasher noun
el **lavaplatos** *masc.* (plural los
lavaplatos)

disk noun
el **disco** *masc.*
I copied the files onto a disk.
He copiado los archivos en un disco.

to **dislike** verb
I dislike this music. No me gusta
esta música.

LANGUAGE
Gustar means 'to please' so the order of
the words in the Spanish sentence is
different, e.g. 'I dislike this music' is, word
for word, 'This music does not please me'.

to **disobey** verb
desobedecer

to **display** verb
exponer
**We're going to display the
pictures in the classroom.** Vamos a
exponer los dibujos en la clase.

distance noun
la **distancia** *fem.*
**What's the distance between
London and Madrid?** ¿Qué
distancia hay entre Londres y
Madrid?
in the distance a lo lejos

district noun
1 (*in a town*) el **barrio** *masc.*
2 (*in a country*) la **región** *fem.* (plural las
regiones)

to **disturb** verb
molestar
Sorry to disturb you. Siento
molestarle.

to **dive** verb
1 (*into the water*) **tirarse de cabeza**
I dived into the swimming pool.
Me tiré de cabeza a la piscina.

2 (*under the water*) **bucear**
I want to go diving. Quiero ir a
bucear.

diver noun
el or la **submarinista** *masc. & fem.*

to **divide** verb
dividir
Eight divided by two is four. Ocho
dividido por dos son cuatro.

divorced adjective
divorciado *masc.*, **divorciada** *fem.*
My parents are divorced. Mis
padres están divorciados.

dizzy adjective
mareado *masc.*, **mareada** *fem.*
I feel dizzy Estoy mareado

DJ noun
el or la **disc-jockey** *masc. & fem.*

to **do** verb
1 hacer
I do my homework. Hago mis
deberes.
What are you doing? ¿Qué estás
haciendo?
What have you done with my pen?
¿Qué has hecho con mi boli?
Who did that? ¿Quién hizo eso?
2 (*in questions 'do' and 'does' are not
translated*)
Do you want some bread?
¿Quieres pan?
Where do you live? ¿Dónde vives?
How much does it cost? ¿Cuánto
cuesta?
3 (*in negative sentences use 'no' before the
verb*)
I don't know. No sé.
He doesn't like tomatoes. No le
gustan los tomates.

LANGUAGE
To translate questions such as 'doesn't
she?' or 'don't you?', you can use ¿**no?** in
Spanish, e.g. 'You play football, don't
you?' is **Juegas al fútbol, ¿no?**

• *Use* **el** *and* **uno** *for masculine words and* **la** *and* **una** *for feminine words.*

to **do up** verb
1 (*a coat, jacket, etc.*) abrochar
Do up your shirt. Abróchate la camisa.
2 (*shoes*) atar
Do up your shoes. Átate los zapatos.
3 (*a room, house, etc.*) arreglar

doctor noun
el médico *masc.*, la médica *fem.*
He's a doctor. Es médico.
I'm going to the doctor. Voy al médico.

dodgems plural noun
los autos or los coches de choque *masc. plural*

does verb SEE **do**
Dad does the shopping. Papá hace la compra.
She doesn't know. No sabe.

dog noun
el perro *masc.*, la perra *fem.*
I like dogs. Me gustan los perros.

doll noun
la muñeca *fem.*
a doll's house una casa de muñecas

dollar noun
el dólar *masc.*

dolphin noun
el delfín *masc.* (plural los **delfines**)

dominoes plural noun
el dominó *masc.*
to play dominoes jugar al dominó

done verb SEE **do**
I've done my homework. He hecho mis deberes.
Have you done it? ¿Lo has hecho?

donkey noun
el burro *masc.*

door noun
la puerta *fem.*
Close the door. Cierra la puerta.

doorbell noun
el timbre *masc.*
Ring the doorbell. Toca el timbre.

dormitory noun
el dormitorio *masc.*

> **LANGUAGE**
> Both 'dormitory' and dormitorio are related to the Spanish word dormir (to sleep) because you sleep there.

dot noun
el punto *masc.*

double adjective
doble *masc. & fem.*
a double room una habitación doble
a double bed una cama de matrimonio

double-decker noun
el autobús de dos pisos *masc.*

> **LANGUAGE**
> The plural of autobús is autobuses.

doubt noun
la duda *fem.*

to **doubt** verb
dudar
I doubt it. Lo dudo.

dough noun
la masa *fem.*

doughnut noun
la rosquilla *fem.*, el donut *masc.*

down adverb & preposition
abajo
It's down there. Está allí abajo.
I looked down. Miré hacia abajo.
Helen lives just down the road. Helen vive muy cerca.

> **LANGUAGE**
> 'Down' is often translated as part of a verb such as 'to go down' (bajar) or 'to sit down' (sentarse).

• *Languages and nationalities do not take a capital letter in Spanish.*

down adjective
(*not working*)
The computers are down. Los ordenadores no funcionan.

to **download** verb
descargar
I downloaded the program. Descargé el programa.

downstairs adverb
abajo
I'm downstairs in the kitchen. Estoy abajo en la cocina.
Come downstairs! ¡Baja!

LANGUAGE
Use **bajar** to translate 'to come downstairs' or 'to go downstairs'.

dozen noun
la docena *fem.*
two dozen dos docenas
a dozen eggs una docena de huevos

LANGUAGE
When 'dozen' is followed by a noun use **de** before the noun in Spanish.

dragon noun
el dragón *masc.* (plural los **dragones**)

draught noun
la corriente *fem.*
There's a draught here. Aquí hay corriente.

draughts plural noun
las damas *fem. plural*
We're playing draughts. Estamos jugando a la damas.

to **draw** verb
1 dibujar
I'm drawing a dog. Dibujo un perro.
to draw a picture hacer un dibujo
2 **to draw the curtains** correr las cortinas
3 (*in a match*) empatar

The two teams drew. Los dos equipos empataron.

draw noun
el empate *masc.*
The match ended in a draw. El partido acabó en empate.

drawer noun
el cajón *masc.* (plural los **cajones**)

LANGUAGE
Cajón comes from **caja** (box) and **-ón** (meaning big) – it's a big box.

drawing noun
el dibujo *masc.*
I love your drawing. Me encanta tu dibujo.

drawing pin noun
la chincheta *fem.*

dreadful adjective
(*weather, accident, etc.*) horrible *masc. & fem.*

dream noun
el sueño *masc.*
I've had a strange dream. He tenido un sueño extraño.

to **dream** verb
soñar
I dreamt about you! ¡Soñé contigo!

dress noun
el vestido *masc.*
I like your dress. Me gusta tu vestido .

to **dress** verb
1 **to get dressed** vestirse
I'll get dressed. Me voy a vestir.
2 **to dress up** disfrazarse
I want to dress up as a pirate. Quiero disfrazarme de pirata.

dressed adjective
1 vestido *masc.*, vestida *fem.*
Are you dressed? ¿Estás vestido?
2 **to get dressed** vestirse
She's getting dressed. Se está vistiendo.

• *The months of the year and days of the week do not take a capital letter in Spanish.*

dressing gown noun
la **bata** *fem.*

drink noun
la **bebida** *fem.*
a hot drink una bebida caliente
Do you want a drink? ¿Quieres beber algo?

to **drink** verb
beber
I drank a glass of water. Bebí un vaso de agua.

drive noun
1 la **vuelta en coche** *fem.*
Do you want to go for a drive? ¿Quieres ir a dar una vuelta en coche?
2 (*place in front of the house*) la **entrada** *fem.*
They've parked the car in the drive. Han aparcado el coche en la entrada.

to **drive** verb
1 **conducir**
to drive a car conducir un coche
Can you drive? ¿Sabes conducir?
2 (*to go somewhere by car*) **ir en coche**
We drove to Spain. Fuimos a España en coche.
3 (*to take somebody by car*) **llevar en coche**
My dad drives me to school. Mi padre me lleva a la escuela en coche.

driver noun
el **conductor** *masc.*,
la **conductora** *fem.*
a taxi driver un or una taxista

driving licence noun
el **permiso de conducir** *masc.*

drop noun
la **gota** *fem.*
a drop of water una gota de agua

to **drop** verb
1 **I dropped the plate.** Tiré el plato.
Don't drop it! ¡No lo tires!

🔑 **LANGUAGE**
You can also use the verb **caerse** (to fall down) in Spanish, so 'I dropped the plate' can be **El plato se me cayó**. Word for word this means 'The plate fell down from me'.

2 (*to let somebody out of a car*) **dejar**
Can you drop me at the school? ¿Me puedes dejar delante del colegio?

to **drown** verb
ahogarse
He fell into the river and drowned. Se cayó al río y se ahogó.

drum noun
el **tambor** *masc.*
the drums la batería *fem.*
My brother plays the drums. Mi hermano toca la batería.

drunk adjective
borracho *masc.*, **borracha** *fem.*
He's drunk. Está borracho.

dry adjective
seco *masc.*, **seca** *fem.*
The towels are dry. Las toallas están secas.

to **dry** verb
secar
I'm drying the dishes. Estoy secando los platos.
She's drying her hair. Se está secando el pelo.

duck noun
el **pato** *masc.*

dull adjective
1 (*boring*) **aburrido** *masc.*,
aburrida *fem.*
2 (*weather*) **gris** *masc. & fem.*
It's very dull today. Es un día muy gris.

• *See the centre section for verb tables.*

dumb adjective
(*stupid*) tonto *masc.*, tonta *fem.*

dummy noun
el chupete *masc.*

during preposition
durante
during the class durante la clase

dust noun
el polvo *masc.*

dustbin noun
el cubo de basura *masc.*

dusty adjective
lleno de polvo *masc.*, llena de polvo *fem.*

Dutch adjective
holandés *masc.*, holandesa *fem.*
She's Dutch. Es holandesa.

LANGUAGE
The plural of **holandés** is **holandeses**.

Dutch noun
1 (*language*) el holandés *masc.*
2 the Dutch los holandeses *masc. plural*

duvet noun
el edredón *masc.* (plural los **edredones**)

DVD noun
el DVD *masc.* (plural los **DVDs**)
a DVD player un reproductor DVD

dwarf noun
el enano *masc.*, la enana *fem.*

dyslexic adjective
disléxico *masc.*, disléxica *fem.*
I'm dyslexic. Soy disléxico.

Ee

each adjective
cada *masc. & fem.*
each time cada vez

each pronoun
cada uno *masc.*, cada una *fem.*
The pupils have a computer each. Los alumnos tienen un ordenador cada uno.

each other pronoun
We hate each other! ¡Nos odiamos!
Do you know each other? ¿Os conocéis?
They write to each other. Se escriben.

LANGUAGE
Use **nos, os,** or **se** to translate **each other**; they are the pronouns that go with reflexive verbs in Spanish.

eagle noun
el águila *fem.*

LANGUAGE
Be careful: you use **el** with **águila** but it is not a masculine noun.

ear noun
la oreja *fem.*, el oído *masc.*
The elephant has big ears. El elefante tiene orejas grandes.
My ear hurts. Me duele el oído.

LANGUAGE
La oreja is the part of the ear you can see; **el oído** is the inside part of the ear that you hear with.

earache noun
el dolor de oídos *masc.*
I have an earache. Tengo dolor de oídos.

• *Use* el *and* uno *for masculine words and* la *and* una *for feminine words.*

earlier adverb
más temprano
Wake up earlier tomorrow.
Despiértate más temprano mañana.

early adjective
I'm having an early night. Me voy a la cama temprano.

early adverb
temprano, pronto
I get up early. Me levanto temprano.
It's too early. Es demasiado temprano.
to arrive early llegar pronto
You're early. Has llegado pronto.

to **earn** verb
ganar
My mum earns a lot of money.
Mi madre gana mucho dinero.

earring noun
el pendiente masc.

earth noun
la tierra fem.

earthquake noun
el terremoto masc.

easily adverb
fácilmente

east noun & adjective
el este masc.
in the east en el este
the east coast la costa este

Easter noun
la Semana Santa fem.
I'm going to Madrid at Easter.
Voy a Madrid en Semana Santa.
Easter Day el Domingo de Pascua
an Easter egg un huevo de Pascua

CULTURE
Word for word **Semana Santa** is Holy Week: it means the whole Easter period. **Pascua** is Easter Sunday or Monday. Spanish people take part in religious processions, such as the famous one in Seville.

easy adjective
fácil masc. & fem.
It's easy to speak Spanish. Es fácil hablar español.

to **eat** verb
comer
I'm eating an apple. Estoy comiendo una manzana.
I want something to eat. Quiero comer algo.

edge noun
el borde masc.
the edge of the table el borde de la mesa

Edinburgh noun
Edimburgo masc.

education noun
la educación fem.
primary education la enseñanza primaria

educational adjective
(game, toy, etc.) educativo masc., educativa fem.

effort noun
el esfuerzo masc.
Make an effort. Haz un esfuerzo.

e.g. abbreviation
p. ej.

LANGUAGE
e.g. stands for Latin exempli gratia, and **p. ej.** is short for Spanish por ejemplo (for example).

egg noun
el huevo masc.
a boiled egg un huevo pasado por agua
a hard-boiled egg un huevo duro
a fried egg un huevo frito
scrambled eggs los huevos revueltos

eggcup noun
la huevera fem.

• Languages and nationalities do not take a capital letter in Spanish.

eight number
ocho
I go to bed at eight. Me acuesto a las ocho.
Luke is eight. Luke tiene ocho años.

🔑 **LANGUAGE**
In English you can say 'eight o'clock' or just 'eight', 'eight years old' or just 'eight'. In Spanish you must add **las** (for time) and **años** (for age).

eighteen number
dieciocho
My brother is eighteen. Mi hermano tiene dieciocho años.

eighth adjective
octavo masc., octava fem.
on the eighth floor en el octavo piso
the eighth of June el ocho de junio

🔑 **LANGUAGE**
With dates you use **ocho** (eight).

eighty number
ochenta

either adverb
tampoco
You can't swim and I can't either. Tú no sabes nadar y yo tampoco.
I don't have any friends either. Yo tampoco tengo amigos.

either pronoun
1 cualquiera
Take either of them. Toma cualquiera de los dos.
2 (with negatives) ninguno masc., ninguna fem.
I don't want either of them. No quiero ninguno.

either conjunction
either ... or o ... o
You can have either meat or fish. Puedes comer o carne o pescado.
I don't like either tea or coffee. No me gusta el té ni el café.

🔑 **LANGUAGE**
With negatives use **ni** instead of **o**.

elastic band noun
la goma fem.

elbow noun
el codo masc.

eldest adjective
mayor masc. & fem.
my eldest sister mi hermana mayor

electric adjective
eléctrico masc., eléctrica fem.

electrician noun
el or la electricista masc. & fem.
My dad's an electrician. Mi padre es electricista.

🔑 **LANGUAGE**
Be careful: **electricista** ends in an -**a** but it can be a masculine or feminine noun.

electricity noun
la electricidad fem.

elephant noun
el elefante masc.

eleven number
once
I woke up at eleven. Me desperté a las once.
My friend is eleven. Mi amiga tiene once años.

🔑 **LANGUAGE**
In English you can say 'eleven o'clock' or just 'eleven', 'eleven years old' or just 'eleven'. In Spanish you must add **las** (for time) and **años** (for age).

eleventh adjective
the eleventh floor el piso once
the eleventh of December el once de diciembre

🔑 **LANGUAGE**
In Spanish, you usually use **once** (eleven).

else adverb
1 (using más)
nobody else nadie más
nothing else nada más

• *The months of the year and days of the week do not take a capital letter in Spanish.*

274

What else? ¿Qué más?
Anything else? ¿Algo más?
2 (*using* otra)
somebody else otra persona
something else otra cosa
somewhere else en otra parte
3 (*using* demás)
everybody else todos los demás
everything else todo lo demás

> 🔑 **LANGUAGE**
> Remember the three main ways to say 'else' in Spanish: **más** means 'more', **otra** means 'other', and **lo demás** means 'the rest'.

email noun
el email *masc.*, el correo electrónico *masc.*
I've sent an email. He enviado un email.
an email address una dirección de email

to **email** verb
to email somebody enviar un email a alguien

emergency noun
la emergencia *fem.*
in an emergency en caso de emergencia
an emergency exit una salida de emergencia

empty adjective
vacío *masc.*, vacía *fem.*
The bottle is empty. La botella está vacía.

to **empty** verb
vaciar

encyclopedia noun
la enciclopedia *fem.*

end noun
1 (*the last part*) el final *masc.*
at the end of the book al final del libro
at the end of July a finales de julio

• *See the centre section for verb tables.*

2 (*of a place*) el final *masc.*, el fondo *masc.*
at the end of the street al final de la calle
at the end of the corridor al fondo del pasillo
at the other end of town al otro extremo de la ciudad

to **end** verb
terminar
The film ends at two. La película termina a las dos.

ending noun
(*of a book, film, or play*) el final *masc.*
a happy ending un final feliz

enemy noun
el enemigo *masc.*, la enemiga *fem.*

energy noun
la energía *fem.*

engaged adjective
1 (*going to be married*) prometido *masc.*, prometida *fem.*
They're engaged. Están prometidos.
2 (*talking about a phone*) comunicando
It's engaged. Está comunicando.
3 (*talking about a toilet*) ocupado *masc.*, ocupada *fem.*

engine noun
1 (*in a car*) el motor *masc.*
2 (*of a train*) la locomotora *fem.*

> 🔑 **LANGUAGE**
> **Locomotora** is related to 'locomotive'.

engineer noun
1 (*who designs things*) el ingeniero *masc.*, la ingeniera *fem.*
2 (*who fixes things*) el técnico *masc.*, la técnica *fem.*

England noun
Inglaterra *fem.*
We live in England. Vivimos en Inglaterra.
They want to go to England. Quieren ir a Inglaterra.

a b c d e f g h i j k l m n o p q r s t u v w x y z

275

English adjective
inglés *masc.*, **inglesa** *fem.*
an English town una ciudad inglesa
I'm English. Soy inglés.
She's English. Es inglesa.
my English lesson mi clase de inglés
English people los ingleses

🗝 **LANGUAGE**
The masculine plural of **inglés** is **ingleses**.

English noun
1 (*language*) el inglés *masc.*
Do you speak English? ¿Habla usted inglés?
2 **the English** los ingleses *masc. plural*

Englishman,
Englishwoman noun
el inglés *masc.* (plural los **ingleses**);
la inglesa *fem.*

to **enjoy** verb
1 **I enjoy reading.** Me gusta leer.

🗝 **LANGUAGE**
Gustar means 'to please' so the order of the words in the Spanish sentence is different, e.g. 'I enjoy reading' is, word for word, 'It pleases me to read'.

2 **to enjoy yourself** divertirse
I enjoyed myself. Me divertí mucho.

enjoyable adjective
1 agradable *masc. & fem.*
enjoyable holidays unas vacaciones agradables
2 divertido *masc.*, divertida *fem.*
The film is very enjoyable. La película es muy divertida.

enormous adjective
enorme *masc. & fem.*

enough adverb & pronoun
bastante
I've eaten enough. He comido bastante.
Is there enough? ¿Hay bastante?
That's enough! ¡Basta!

enough adjective
bastante *masc. & fem.*, suficiente *masc. & fem.*
I have enough money. Tengo bastante dinero.
I don't have enough money. No tengo suficiente dinero.

to **enter** verb
(*a competition, an exam*) presentarse a
I'm entering the competition. Me presento al concurso.

entrance noun
la entrada *fem.*
Where's the entrance? ¿Dónde está la entrada?
an entrance exam un examen de ingreso

entry noun
'No entry' (*on a door*) 'Prohibida la entrada'

envelope noun
el sobre *masc.*

environment noun
el medio ambiente *masc.*

episode noun
el episodio *masc.*

equal adjective
igual *masc. & fem.*
two equal groups dos grupos iguales

to **equal** verb
ser igual a
Four plus two equals six. Cuatro más dos es igual a seis.

equipment noun
el equipo *masc.*

error noun
el error *masc.*

escalator noun
la escalera mecánica *fem.*

to **escape** verb
escaparse
The rabbit has escaped. Se ha escapado el conejo.

• Use **el** and **uno** for masculine words and **la** and **una** for feminine words.

especially adverb
especialmente, sobre todo
I like Madrid, especially the people. Me gusta Madrid, especialmente la gente.

essay noun
la redacción *fem.*

essential adjective
esencial *masc. & fem.*
It's essential to know Spanish. Es esencial saber español.

estate noun
(*housing estate*) la urbanización *fem.* (plural las **urbanizaciones**)
I live on an estate. Vivo en una urbanización.

EU noun
la UE *fem.*

⚷ **LANGUAGE**
The Spanish is short for **Unión Europea**, and is pronounced 'oo-ay'.

euro noun
el euro *masc.*
It costs five euros. Cuesta cinco euros.

Europe noun
Europa *fem.*

European adjective
europeo *masc.*, europea *fem.*
the European Union la Unión Europea

European noun
el europeo *masc.*, la europea *fem.*

Eve noun
Christmas Eve la Nochebuena
New Year's Eve la Nochevieja

even adverb
1 incluso
Everyone's coming, even my sister. Todos vienen, incluso mi hermana.
2 (*when comparing things*) aún, todavía
even more difficult aún más difícil, todavía mas difícil

even adjective
an even number un número par

evening noun
1 (*before it gets dark*) la tarde *fem.*
In the evening I watch TV. Por la tarde veo la tele.
at six in the evening a la seis de la tarde
this evening esta tarde
tomorrow evening mañana por la tarde
Good evening! ¡Buenas tardes!
2 (*when it's dark*) la noche *fem.*
at nine in the evening a las nueve de la noche
Good evening! ¡Buenas noches!
an evening class una clase nocturna

⚷ **LANGUAGE**
Remember that Spanish has two words for 'evening': **tarde** (when it's light) also means 'afternoon', and **noche** (when it's dark) also means 'night'.

ever adverb
1 alguna vez
Have you ever been to Madrid? ¿Has estado alguna vez en Madrid?
2 nunca
The cat's fatter than ever. El gato está más gordo que nunca.
I hardly ever eat fish. Casi nunca como pescado.

⚷ **LANGUAGE**
Nunca means 'never' so, word for word, **casi nunca** means 'almost never'.

3 (*always*) siempre
for ever para siempre
4 **ever since, ever since then** desde entonces

• *Languages and nationalities do not take a capital letter in Spanish.*

every adjective
1 todos *masc. plural*, todas *fem. plural*
every day todos los días
every week todas las semanas
every Saturday todos los sábados

🔑 **LANGUAGE**
Todos is always followed by **los** and **todas** by **las**.

2 cada *masc. & fem.*
Every pupil has an exercise book. Cada alumno tiene un cuaderno.
every time cada vez

everybody pronoun
todo el mundo, todos *masc. plural*
Everybody has seen this film. Todo el mundo ha visto esta película.
Everybody has come. Todos han venido.
everybody else todos los demás

everyone pronoun
todo el mundo, todos *masc. plural*

everything pronoun
todo
That's everything. Eso es todo.
Everything's ready. Todo está listo.
everything else todo lo demás

everywhere adverb
1 por todas partes
I looked everywhere. Busqué por todas partes.
2 (*with 'go'*) a todas partes
I go everywhere by bike. Voy en bici a todas partes.

evil adjective
malo *masc.*, mala *fem.*

exact adjective
exacto *masc.*, exacta *fem.*

exactly adverb
exactamente
at exactly the same time exactamente a la misma hora
It's exactly ten o'clock. Son las diez en punto.

to **exaggerate** verb
exagerar

exam noun
el examen *masc.* (plural los exámenes)
a Spanish exam un examen de español

example noun
el ejemplo *masc.*
for example por ejemplo

excellent adjective
excelente *masc. & fem.*

except preposition
excepto, menos
all the boys except me todos los chicos excepto yo, todos los chicos menos yo

to **exchange** verb
cambiar
Can I exchange this book for another one? ¿Puedo cambiar este libro por otro?

excited adjective
entusiasmado *masc.*, entusiasmada *fem.*

exciting adjective
(*book, film, etc.*) emocionante *masc. & fem.*
an exciting match un partido emocionante

exclamation mark noun
el signo de admiración *masc.*

excuse noun
la excusa *fem.*

to **excuse** verb
Excuse me! ¡Perdón!

• *The months of the year and days of the week do not take a capital letter in Spanish.*

exercise noun
el ejercicio *masc.*
a Spanish exercise un ejercicio de español
Do you do exercise? ¿Haces ejercicio?
an exercise book un cuaderno

exhausted adjective
agotado *masc.*, agotada *fem.*
I'm exhausted. Estoy agotado.

exhibition noun
la exposición *fem.* (plural las exposiciones)

to **exist** verb
existir

exit noun
la salida *fem.*

to **expect** verb
1 (*to wait for*) esperar
I'm expecting my dad. Estoy esperando a mi padre.
She's expecting a baby. Está esperando un niño.
2 (*to suppose*) suponer
I expect so. Supongo que sí.

expensive adjective
caro *masc.*, cara *fem.*
It's too expensive. Es demasiado caro.

experience noun
la experiencia *fem.*

experiment noun
el experimento *masc.*
to do an experiment hacer un experimento

expert noun
el experto *masc.*, la experta *fem.*

to **explain** verb
explicar
I'll explain. Te explico.

explanation noun
la explicación *fem.* (plural las explicaciones)

to **explode** verb
estallar

to **explore** verb
explorar

explosion noun
la explosión *fem.* (plural las explosiones)

expression noun
(*sentence, look*) la expresión *fem.* (plural las expresiones)

extra adjective & adverb
1 (*more*) más
We need extra exercise books. Necesitamos más cuadernos.
to pay extra pagar más
2 (*left over*) de más
There are three extra sweets. Hay tres caramelos de más.
3 (*in a restaurant*)
Breakfast is extra. El desayuno no está incluido.

extraterrestrial noun
el or la extraterrestre *masc. & fem.*

extremely adverb

🔑 **LANGUAGE**
Add **-ísimo** (masculine) or **-ísima** (feminine) to the adjective in Spanish.

extremely difficult dificilísimo
extremely tired cansadísimo

eye noun
el ojo *masc.*
I have blue eyes. Tengo los ojos azules.

eyebrow noun
la ceja *fem.*

eyelid noun
el párpado *masc.*

eyesight noun
la vista *fem.*

• See the centre section for verb tables.

279

Ff

fabulous adjective
fabuloso *masc.*, fabulosa *fem.*

face noun
la cara *fem.*

facing preposition
(*opposite*) enfrente de
I sat down facing the teacher.
Me senté enfrente de la maestra.

fact noun
el hecho *masc.*

factory noun
la fábrica *fem.*
My dad works in a factory.
Mi padre trabaja en una fábrica.

to **fail** verb
suspender
My sister has failed her exam. Mi hermana ha suspendido el examen.

to **faint** verb
desmayarse
Amy fainted. Amy se desmayó.

fair adjective
1 (*right*) justo *masc.*, justa *fem.*
It's not fair! ¡No es justo!
2 (*hair*) rubio *masc.*, rubia *fem.*
I have fair hair. Tengo el pelo rubio.

fair noun
la feria *fem.*
Can I go to the fair ¿Puedo ir a la feria?

fair-haired adjective
I'm fair-haired. Tengo el pelo rubio.

fairly adverb
bastante
It's fairly expensive. Es bastante caro.

fairy noun
el hada *fem.*
a fairy tale un cuento de hadas

> 🔑 **LANGUAGE**
> Be careful: you use **el** with **hada** but it is not a masculine noun.

to **fall** verb
1 caerse
Be careful, you'll fall! ¡Cuidado, te vas a caer!
I fell down the stairs. Me caí por la escalera.
She fell off the chair. Se cayó de la silla.
2 (*talking about snow, rain, bombs, etc.*) caer
The snow is falling. Cae la nieve.

> 🔑 **LANGUAGE**
> When 'fall' means 'fall down accidentally' use **caerse**; otherwise use **caer**.

false adjective
falso *masc.*, falsa *fem.*
True or false? ¿Verdadero o falso?

family noun
la familia *fem.*
the Turner family la familia Turner
a big family una familia numerosa

famous adjective
famoso *masc.*, famosa *fem.*

fan noun
1 (*of a person*) el or la fan *masc. & fem.*
(plural los or las **fans**)
I'm a great Harry Potter fan.
Soy un gran fan de Harry Potter.
2 (*of a team*) el or la hincha *masc. & fem.*
He's a Manchester United fan.
Es hincha del Manchester United.
3 (*machine for keeping cool*) el ventilador *masc.*

• *Use* el *and* uno *for masculine words and* la *and* una *for feminine words.*

to fancy verb
apetecer
I fancy an ice cream. Me apetece un helado.

> **LANGUAGE**
> The order of the words in the Spanish sentence is different, so 'I fancy an ice cream' is, word for word, 'An ice cream takes my fancy'.

fancy dress noun
el disfraz *masc.* (plural los **disfraces**)
a fancy dress party una fiesta de disfraces
She's in fancy dress. Está disfrazada.

fantastic adjective
estupendo *masc.*, estupenda *fem.*

> **LANGUAGE**
> You can also say **fantástico/fantástica**.

far adjective & adverb
1 lejos
Is it far? ¿Está lejos?
It's not very far away. No está muy lejos.
How far is it to York? ¿A qué distancia está York?
2 **as far as** hasta
I went as far as the bridge. Fui hasta el puente.
so far hasta ahora

farm noun
la granja *fem.*
I live on a farm. Vivo en una granja.

farmer noun
(*man*) el agricultor *masc.*, el granjero *masc.*;
(*woman*) la agricultora *fem.*, la granjera *fem.*

fashion noun
la moda *fem.*
a fashion show un desfile de modas

fashionable adjective
de moda
Black shoes are fashionable. Los zapatos negros están de moda.

fast adverb
1 rápido
I read very fast. Leo muy rápido.
Can you go faster? ¿Puedes ir más rápido?
2 **She's fast asleep.** Está profundamente dormida.

fast adjective
rápido *masc.*, rápida *fem.*
a fast car un coche rápido

to fast-forward verb
avanzar
to fast-forward the tape avanzar la cinta

fat adjective
gordo *masc.*, gorda *fem.*
He's very fat. Está muy gordo.

father noun
el padre *masc.*
My father works in a factory. Mi padre trabaja en una fábrica.
my father and mother mis padres
Father Christmas Papá Noel
Father's Day el día del Padre

fault noun
la culpa *fem.*
It's not my fault. No es mi culpa.

favourite adjective
favorito *masc.*, favorita *fem.*
Spanish is my favourite subject. El español es mi asignatura favorita.

fear noun
el miedo *masc.*

feather noun
la pluma *fem.*

a b c d e f g h i j k l m n o p q r s t u v w x y z

• *Languages and nationalities do not take a capital letter in Spanish.*

February noun
febrero *masc.*
Come to my house in February.
Ven a mi casa en febrero.
It's my birthday on the sixth of February. Es mi cumpleaños el seis de febrero.

fed up adjective
I'm fed up! ¡Estoy harto!
We're fed up with him! ¡Estamos hartos de él!

to **feed** verb
dar de comer a
I've fed the dog. Le he dado de comer al perro.

to **feel** verb
1 *(happy, tired, etc.)* sentirse
I don't feel well. No me siento bien.
I feel cold. Tengo frío.

> **LANGUAGE**
> English = to feel cold I feel cold.
> Spanish = tener frío Tengo frío.

2 *(talking about feeling something in your body)* sentir
I didn't feel a thing. No sentí nada.
3 *(talking about touching something)* tocar
Feel my hands - they're cold. Tócame las manos - las tengo frías.
4 **to feel like doing something** tener ganas de hacer algo
I feel like going out. Tengo ganas de salir.

> **LANGUAGE**
> To say you feel like something, use apetece in the singular and apetecen in the plural.

I feel like an ice cream. Me apetece un helado.

feet plural noun
los pies *masc. plural*
I have cold feet. Tengo los pies fríos.

felt-tip pen noun
el rotulador *masc.*

female noun
la hembra *fem.*

female adjective
hembra *masc. & fem.*
a female elephant un elefante hembra

feminine adjective
femenino *masc.*, femenina *fem.*

> **LANGUAGE**
> English = feminine
> Spanish = femenino

fence noun
la valla *fem.*

ferry noun
el ferry *masc.* (plural los **ferries**)

to **fetch** verb
traer
Fetch my glasses. Tráeme las gafas.

few adjective & pronoun
a few algunos *masc. plural*, algunas *fem. plural*
a few books algunos libros
a few of the books algunos de los libros
quite a few bastantes
quite a few mistakes bastantes faltas

fewer adjective & pronoun
menos
fewer dogs menos perros
fewer than ten menos de diez

field noun
(for wheat, playing football, etc.) el campo *masc.*

fierce adjective
feroz *masc. & fem.* (plural **feroces**)

• *The months of the year and days of the week do not take a capital letter in Spanish.*

fifteen number
quince
My sister is fifteen. Mi hermana tiene quince años.

> **LANGUAGE**
> In English you can say just 'fifteen'. In Spanish you must add **años**.

fifth adjective
quinto *masc.*, quinta *fem.*
on the fifth floor en el quinto piso
the fifth of June el cinco de junio

> **LANGUAGE**
> With dates you use **cinco** (five).

fifty number
cincuenta
My dad is fifty. Mi padre tiene cincuenta años.

> **LANGUAGE**
> In English you can say just 'fifty'. In Spanish you must add **años**.

fight noun
la pelea *fem.*

to **fight** verb
pelearse
Jake and Ben are fighting in the playground. Jake y Ben se están peleando en el patio.

figure noun
(*number*) la cifra *fem.*
Write the amount in figures. Escribe la suma en cifras.

file
1 (*cover for papers*) la carpeta *fem.*
I keep my drawings in a file. Guardo mis dibujos en una carpeta.
2 (*on a computer*) el archivo *masc.*
I've created a file. He creado un archivo.
3 **in single file** en fila india

• *See the centre section for verb tables.*

to **fill** verb
llenar
Fill the bucket with water. Llena el cubo de agua.
to fill in a form rellenar un formulario

film noun
1 (*in the cinema or on TV*) la película *fem.*
Do you like films? ¿Te gustan las películas?
a film star una estrella de cine
2 (*in a camera*) el carrete *masc.*

final adjective
(*last*) último *masc.*, última *fem.*
the final week la última semana

final noun
la final *fem.*
Our team has won the final. Nuestro equipo ha ganado la final.

to **find** verb
1 encontrar
Have you found my pen? ¿Has encontrado mi boli?
I can't find my glasses. No encuentro mis gafas.

> **LANGUAGE**
> The word 'can't' is not translated into Spanish. Word for word this Spanish sentence means 'I don't find my glasses'.

2 (*to look for*) buscar
Find page 10. Busca la página diez.
3 (*when you want to discover what happened*)
to find out descubrir
I've found out who did it. He descubierto quién lo hizo.

fine adjective & adverb
(*good, well*) bien
How are you? – Fine. ¿Qué tal estás? – Bien.
Can I come tomorrow? – That's fine. ¿Puedo venir mañana? – Está bien.
It's working fine. Funciona bien.
The weather's fine. Hace buen tiempo.

English Spanish

a
b
c
d
e
f
g
h
i
j
k
l
m
n
o
p
q
r
s
t
u
v
w
x
y
z

finger noun
el **dedo** masc.
I wear a ring on my finger.
Llevo un anillo en el dedo.

fingerprint noun
la **huella dactilar** fem.

to **finish** verb
terminar
I've finished my homework.
He terminado mis deberes.
School finishes at three. El colegio termina a las tres.
Have you finished eating? ¿Has terminado de comer?

finish noun
(in a race) la **llegada** fem.

fire noun
1 el **fuego** masc.
Dad lit the fire. Papá encendió el fuego.
It's on fire. Está ardiendo.
2 (fire that destroys things) el **incendio** masc.
The firemen have put out the fire.
Los bomberos han apagado el incendio.
a fire alarm una alarma contra incendios
a fire engine un camión de bomberos
a fire station un parque de bomberos

firefighter noun
el **bombero** masc., la **bombera** fem.

fireplace noun
la **chimenea** fem.

fireworks plural noun
(display) los **fuegos artificiales** masc. plural

firm noun
la **empresa** fem.

first adjective & pronoun
primero masc., **primera** fem.
for the first time por primera vez

I'm the first. Soy el primero.
Bradley came first. (in the race)
Bradley quedó primero.

LANGUAGE
Before a masculine singular noun
primero becomes **primer**.

the first year el primer año
first aid los primeros auxilios
my first name mi nombre

LANGUAGE
With dates you use **uno** (one).

on the first of March el uno de marzo

first adverb
1 (before doing anything else) **primero**
First I'm going to eat. Primero voy a comer.
first of all en primer lugar
2 **at first** al principio

fish noun
1 (eaten as food) el **pescado** masc.
I like fish. Me gusta el pescado.
fish and chips el pescado frito con patatas fritas
2 (alive in the sea or river) el **pez** masc.
(plural los **peces**)
There are lots of fish in the river.
Hay muchos peces en el río.
3 **fish fingers** los palitos de pescado
a fish shop una pescadería
a fish tank una pecera

to **fish** verb
pescar
Do you like fishing? ¿Te gusta pescar?
to go fishing ir a pescar

fisherman noun
el **pescador** masc.

fishing rod noun
la **caña de pescar** fem.

fishmonger noun
el **pescadero** masc., la **pescadera** fem.

• Use **el** and **uno** for masculine words and **la** and **una** for feminine words.

fist noun
el puño *masc.*

fit adjective
en forma
to be fit estar en forma

to **fit** verb
1 estar bien
These shoes don't fit me. Estos zapatos no me están bien.
2 to fit into something caber en algo
My books don't fit into this box. Mis libros no caben en esta caja.

five number
cinco
We're going to the cinema at five. Vamos al cine a las cinco.
It's five to eight. Son las ocho menos cinco.
It's five past seven. Son las siete y cinco.
I'm five. Tengo cinco años.

🔑 **LANGUAGE**
In English you can say 'five o'clock' or just 'five', 'five years old' or just 'five'. In Spanish you must add **las** (for time) and **años** (for age).

to **fix** verb
(*to repair*) arreglar
Dad has fixed my bike. Papá me ha arreglado la bici.

fizzy adjective
con gas
fizzy water agua con gas

flag noun
la bandera *fem.*

flame noun
la llama *fem.*

flan noun
la tarta *fem.*

flash noun
a flash of lightning un relámpago

flat adjective
1 plano *masc.*, plana *fem.*
a flat screen una pantalla plana
flat shoes zapatos planos
2 (*when describing land or ground*)
llano *masc.*, llana *fem.*
a flat country un país llano
3 to have a flat tyre tener un pinchazo

flat noun
el piso *masc.*
They have a flat in London. Tienen un piso en Londres.

flavour noun
el sabor *masc.*
It has a chocolate flavour. Tiene sabor a chocolate.

flight noun
el vuelo *masc.*
the next flight to Madrid el próximo vuelo para Madrid

flip-flop noun
la chancleta *fem.*

to **float** verb
flotar

flood noun
la inundación *fem.* (plural las inundaciones)

floor noun
1 el suelo *masc.*
on the floor en el suelo
2 (*a level in a building*) el piso *masc.*
on the second floor en el segundo piso
on the ground floor en la planta baja

florist noun
el or la florista *masc. & fem.*

flour noun
la harina *fem.*

to **flow** verb
(*talking about water or rivers*) correr

a b c d e **f** g h i j k l m n o p q r s t u v w x y z

• *Languages and nationalities do not take a capital letter in Spanish.*

flower noun
la flor *fem.*
a bunch of flowers un ramo de flores

flowerpot noun
la maceta *fem.*

flu noun
la gripe *fem.*
I have the flu. Tengo gripe.

fluently adverb
con fluidez
I speak Spanish fluently. Hablo español con fluidez.

flute noun
la flauta *fem.*
Jacob plays the flute. Jacob toca la flauta.

to **fly** verb
1 (*talking about birds, planes, balloons, etc.*) volar
The birds are flying. Los pájaros están volando.
2 (*to go somewhere by plane*) ir en avión
We flew to Malaga. Fuimos a Málaga en avión.

fly noun
la mosca *fem.*
I hate flies. Odio las moscas.

flying saucer noun
el platillo volante *masc.*

fog noun
la niebla *fem.*

foggy adjective
It's foggy. Hay niebla.

> **LANGUAGE**
> Word for word the Spanish means 'there is fog'.

to **fold** verb
1 doblar
to fold something in half doblar algo por la mitad
2 **to fold your arms** cruzar los brazos

folder noun
(*for papers, and on a computer*)
la carpeta *fem.*

to **follow** verb
seguir
Follow me. Sígueme.
I'll follow. Yo te sigo.

following adjective
siguiente *masc. & fem.*
the following week la semana siguiente

food noun
la comida *fem.*
to buy food comprar comida
English food la comida inglesa
I want some food. Quiero comer algo.

> **LANGUAGE**
> Word for word **Quiero comer algo** means 'I want to eat something'.

fool noun
el or la idiota *masc. & fem.*

foot noun
el pie *masc.*
My foot hurts. Me duele el pie.
on foot a pie
I'm five foot tall. Mido un metro cincuenta.

> **CULTURE**
> Spanish measurements are in metres and centimetres; a **foot** is about 30 centimetres.

football noun
1 (*game*) el fútbol *masc.*
I love playing football. Me encanta jugar al fútbol.
football boots las botas de fútbol
2 (*ball*) el balón de fútbol *masc.*
(plural los **balones de fútbol**)

footballer noun
el or la futbolista *masc. & fem.*
He's a footballer. Es futbolista.

• The months of the year and days of the week do not take a capital letter in Spanish.

footprint noun
la **huella** *fem.*

for preposition
1 **para**
It's for you. Es para ti.
I need it for tomorrow. Lo necesito para mañana.
What's this for? ¿Para qué es?
2 *(when giving reasons, or talking about buying or selling)* **por**
They punished me for that. Me han castigado por eso.
I bought it for six euros. Lo compré por seis euros.
3 *(for showing something still going on)*
I've been living here for a year. Hace un año que vivo aquí.

> 🔑 **LANGUAGE**
> You can use the verb **hacer** (to make) to say you are still doing something, like living somewhere or waiting, so word for word **Hace un año que vivo aquí** means 'It makes a year that I live here'.

4 *(for showing something that happened in the past)* **durante**
I lived in Toledo for six months. Viví en Toledo durante seis meses.

to **forbid** verb
prohibir
My parents have forbidden me to go out. Mis padres me han prohibido salir.
Smoking is forbidden. Está prohibido fumar.

forecast noun
(weather forecast) el **pronóstico** *masc.*

forehead noun
la **frente** *fem.*

foreign adjective
extranjero *masc.*, **extranjera** *fem.*
foreign languages las lenguas extranjeras

foreigner noun
el **extranjero** *masc.*,
la **extranjera** *fem.*
I'm a foreigner. Soy extranjero.

forest noun
el **bosque** *masc.*
a tropical forest una selva tropical

to **forget** verb
1 **olvidarse de**
You always forget my birthday. Siempre te olvidas de mi cumpleaños.
I forget everything. Me olvido de todo.
2 **olvidarse**
I've forgotten your name. Se me ha olvidado tu nombre.
I forgot! ¡Se me olvidó!

to **forgive** verb
perdonar
I forgive you. Te perdono.

fork noun
el **tenedor** *masc.*

form noun
1 *(paper)* el **formulario** *masc.*
to fill in a form rellenar un formulario
2 *(in school)* **la clase** *fem.*

to **form** verb
formar
Form a circle! ¡Formad un círculo!

fortnight noun
quince días *masc. plural*
in a fortnight dentro de quince días

> 🔑 **LANGUAGE**
> Word for word **quince días** is fifteen days although a **fortnight** is fourteen.

• *See the centre section for verb tables.*

287

a
b
c
d
e
f
g
h
i
j
k
l
m
n
o
p
q
r
s
t
u
v
w
x
y
z

forty number
cuarenta
My mum is forty. Mi madre tiene cuarenta años.

> 🔑 **LANGUAGE**
> In English you can say just 'forty'. In Spanish you must add **años**.

forward adverb
adelante
I took one step forward. Di un paso adelante.
to move forward avanzar

fountain noun
la fuente *fem.*

four number
cuatro
The party starts at four. La fiesta empieza a las cuatro.
Catherine is four. Catherine tiene cuatro años.

> 🔑 **LANGUAGE**
> In English you can say 'four o'clock' or just 'four', 'four years old' or just 'four'. In Spanish you must add **las** (for time) and **años** (for age).

fourteen number
catorce
My brother is fourteen. Mi hermano tiene catorce años.

fourth adjective
cuarto *masc.*, cuarta *fem.*
on the fourth floor en el cuarto piso
the fourth of December el cuatro de diciembre

> 🔑 **LANGUAGE**
> With dates you use **cuatro** (four).

fox noun
el zorro *masc.*

France noun
Francia *fem.*
Alain lives in France. Alain vive en Francia.
I'm going to France. Me voy a Francia.

freckles plural noun
las pecas *fem. plural*
I have freckles. Tengo pecas.

free adjective
1 libre *masc. & fem.*
Are you free tomorrow? ¿Estás libre mañana?
This seat is free. Este asiento está libre.
2 (*when you don't pay*) gratis *masc. & fem.*
It's free. Es gratis.
a free ticket una entrada gratis

freedom noun
la libertad *fem.*

to freeze verb
1 (*in the cold weather*) helarse
The water has frozen. El agua se ha helado.
2 (*in a freezer*) congelar
frozen fish pescado congelado

freezer noun
el congelador *masc.*

freezing adjective
I'm freezing! ¡Estoy helado!
It's freezing today. Hoy hace muchísimo frío.

French adjective
francés *masc.*, francesa *fem.*
French food la comida francesa
Fabrice is French. Fabrice es francés.
French people los franceses
French fries las patatas fritas

> 🔑 **LANGUAGE**
> The masculine plural of **francés** is **franceses**.

• *Use* el *and* uno *for masculine words and* la *and* una *for feminine words.*

French noun
1 (*language*) el **francés** *masc.*
Do you speak French? ¿Habla usted francés?
2 **the French** los franceses *masc. plural*

Frenchman, Frenchwoman noun
el **francés** *masc.* (plural los **franceses**); la **francesa** *fem.*

fresh adjective
fresco *masc.*, **fresca** *fem.*
fresh eggs huevos frescos

Friday noun
el **viernes** *masc.*
Today is Friday. Hoy es viernes.
on Friday el viernes
I'll see you on Friday. Te veo el viernes.
on Fridays los viernes
It's closed on Fridays. Está cerrado los viernes.

> **LANGUAGE**
> Remember the difference in Spanish between **el viernes** (one Friday only) and **los viernes** (every Friday).

fridge noun
el **frigorífico** *masc.*

fried adjective
frito *masc.*, **frita** *fem.*
a fried egg un huevo frito

friend noun
el **amigo** *masc.*, la **amiga** *fem.*
She's my best friend. Es mi mejor amiga.
I'm a friend of his. Soy uno de sus amigos.
I'm friends with him. Somos amigos.

friendly adjective
simpático *masc.*, **simpática** *fem.*
Anne is very friendly. Anne es muy simpática.
I'm friendly with her. Somos amigas.

fries plural noun
las **patatas fritas** *fem. plural*

fright noun
el **susto** *masc.*
You gave me a fright. Me has dado un susto.
What a fright! ¡Qué susto!

to frighten verb
asustar
You frightened me Me has asustado

frightened adjective
I'm frightened. Tengo miedo.
She's frightened of the dark. Tiene miedo a la oscuridad.
I'm frightened to go by plane. Tengo miedo de ir en avión.

> **LANGUAGE**
> English = **I am** frightened.
> Spanish = **Tengo** miedo = I have fear

fringe noun
el **flequillo** *masc.*
I have a fringe. Llevo flequillo.

frisbee® noun
el **frisbee®** *masc.*

frog noun
la **rana** *fem.*

from
1 **de**
a present from your brother un regalo de tu hermano
It's not far from the airport. No está lejos del aeropuerto.

> **LANGUAGE**
> de + el = del

2 (*starting from a particular time etc.*) **desde**
from today desde hoy
from now on desde ahora
books from five euros libros desde cinco euros

a b c d e f g h i j k l m n o p q r s t u v w x y z

• *Languages and nationalities do not take a capital letter in Spanish.*

English Spanish

a
b
c
d
e
f
g
h
i
j
k
l
m
n
o
p
q
r
s
t
u
v
w
x
y
z

front noun

1 (*the front part of something*) la **parte de delante** *fem.*
There's a light at the front. Hay una luz en la parte de delante.
Sit in the front of the car. Siéntate delante.

2 (*of a classroom, theatre, etc.*) la **primera fila** *fem.*
I always sit at the front. Siempre me siento en primera fila.

3 **in front of** delante de
in front of my house delante de mi casa

front adjective

1 (*seat, wheel, leg, etc.*) **delantero** *masc.*, **delantera** *fem.*
the front seat el asiento delantero
the front door la puerta de la calle

2 (*page, row*) **primero** *masc.*, **primera** *fem.*
the front row la primera fila

frost noun

la **helada** *fem.*
There's a frost. Ha caído una helada.

frosty adjective

It's frosty. Ha helado.

frozen adjective

1 **helado** *masc.*, **helada** *fem.*
I'm frozen. Estoy helado.

2 (*vegetables, fish, etc.*) **congelado** *masc.*, **congelada** *fem.*

fruit noun

la **fruta** *fem.*
I like fruit. Me gusta la fruta.
a fruit juice un zumo de fruta
a fruit salad una macedonia de frutas

frying pan noun

la **sartén** *fem.* (plural las **sartenes**)

full adjective

1 **lleno** *masc.*, **llena** *fem.*
The glass is full of water. El vaso está lleno de agua.
I'm full. Estoy lleno.

2 **a full stop** un punto

fun noun

to have fun divertirse
I had a lot of fun. Me divertí mucho.
Have fun! ¡Qué te diviertas!
It's fun! ¡Es divertido!

funeral noun

el **entierro** *masc.*

funfair noun

la **feria** *fem.*

funny adjective

1 (*making you laugh*) **gracioso** *masc.*, **graciosa** *fem.*

2 (*strange*) **raro** *masc.*, **rara** *fem.*

fur noun

(*of an animal*) el **pelo** *masc.*
the cat's fur el pelo del gato

furious adjective

furioso *masc.*, **furiosa** *fem.*
My dad is furious with me. Mi padre está furioso conmigo., Mi padre está muy enfadado conmigo.

> 🔑 **LANGUAGE**
> Word for word **muy enfadado** means 'very angry'.

furniture noun

los **muebles** *masc. plural*
a piece of furniture un mueble

further adverb

1 (*talking about places*) **más lejos**
Madrid is a bit further. Madrid está un poco más lejos.

2 (*more*) **más**
further down más abajo

future noun

el **futuro** *masc.*
in the future en el futuro

• *The months of the year and days of the week do not take a capital letter in Spanish.*

Gg

game noun
1 el **juego** *masc.*
 a board game un juego de mesa
 the Olympic Games los Juegos
 Olímpicos
 Do you want to play a game?
 ¿Quieres jugar?
2 (*of chess, hide-and-seek, etc.*) la **partida**
 fem.
 Let's play a game of chess. Vamos
 a jugar una partida de ajedrez.
3 (*of football, tennis*) el **partido** *masc.*
 a football game un partido de
 fútbol
4 (*sport when it's a school subject*) **games**
 el deporte *masc.*
 We have games on Monday.
 Tenemos deporte los lunes.

gang noun
 la **pandilla** *fem.*
 There's a gang in my
 neighbourhood. Hay una pandilla
 en mi barrio.

gap noun
 (*in a fence, wall, etc.*) el **hueco** *masc.*

garage noun
 el **garaje** *masc.*

> **LANGUAGE**
> English = garage
> Spanish = garaje

garden noun
 el **jardín** *masc.* (plural los **jardines**)

gardener noun
 el **jardinero** *masc.*,
 la **jardinera** *fem.*
 My dad's a gardener. Mi padre es
 jardinero.

gardening noun
 la **jardinería** *fem.*

garlic noun
 el **ajo** *masc.*

gas noun
 el **gas** *masc.*
 a gas cooker una cocina de gas

gate noun
 la **puerta** *fem.*

to **gather** verb
1 (*to get together*) **reunirse**
 The children gather in the
 playground. Los niños se reúnen
 en el patio.
2 (*to come closer*) **acercarse**
 Gather round! ¡Acercaos!

GCSE noun
 el **certificado de estudios** *masc.*

> 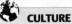 **CULTURE**
> In Spain, children do not do special exams
> at sixteen as they do in the UK.

geese noun
 los **gansos** *masc. plural*

gender noun
 el **género** *masc.*
 What gender is 'ventana'? ¿De qué
 género es 'ventana'?

general adjective
 general *masc. & fem.*

generally adverb
 generalmente

generous adjective
 generoso *masc.*, **generosa** *fem.*

genius noun
 el **genio** *masc.*
 You're a genius! ¡Eres un genio!

gentle adjective
1 **dulce** *masc. & fem.*
 Rebecca is very gentle. Rebecca es
 muy dulce.
2 **to be gentle with something** tener
 cuidado con algo
 Be gentle with that cup. Ten
 cuidado con esa taza.

a
b
c
d
e
f
g
h
i
j
k
l
m
n
o
p
q
r
s
t
u
v
w
x
y
z

• *The months of the year and days of the week do not take a capital letter in Spanish.*

gently adverb
(*carefully*) con cuidado
Put it down gently on the table.
Ponlo con cuidado en la mesa.

gents noun
(*toilets*) los servicios de caballeros
masc. plural

geography noun
la geografía *fem.*

gerbil noun
el jerbo *masc.*

German adjective
1 alemán *masc.*, alemana *fem.*
She's German Es alemana
2 **German measles** la rubeola *fem.*

German noun
1 (*language*) el alemán *masc.*
Can you speak German? ¿Hablas alemán?
2 (*person*) el alemán *masc.*,
la alemana *fem.*

> **LANGUAGE**
> The plural of alemán is alemanes.

Germany noun
Alemania *fem.*

germs plural noun
los microbios *masc. plural*

to get verb

> **LANGUAGE**
> Be careful in choosing the correct translation of 'get'. Look at the English signpost words until you find the meaning you want.

1 (*to receive*) recibir
I got your letter. Recibí tu carta.
He got a knock on his head. Ha recibido un golpe en la cabeza.
2 (*a prize, mark, idea*) sacar
I got good marks. Saqué buenas notas.
3 (*a job, some information, money*) conseguir

My dad got a job. Mi padre ha conseguido un trabajo.
4 (*as a present*)
I got a computer for my birthday. Me regalaron un ordenador para mi cumpleaños.
5 (*when translating 'have got' or 'has got'*) tener
I've got fair hair. Tengo el pelo rubio.
Have you got a bike? ¿Tienes una bici?
They've got a big house. Tienen una casa grande.
6 (*to buy*) comprar
Dad got me a CD. Papá me ha comprado un CD.
7 (*a bus, train, cold, thief, etc.*) coger
I don't like getting the bus. No me gusta coger el autobús.
Did they get the thief? ¿Han cogido al ladrón?
8 (*to fetch*) buscar
Go and get my glasses. Vete a buscar mis gafas.
9 (*to arrive somewhere*) llegar
We get to Glasgow at four. Llegamos a Glasgow a las cuatro.
How do you get to the station? ¿Cómo se llega a la estación?
10 (*when translating 'have got' or 'has got to do something'*) tener que
I've got to go to the doctor. Tengo que ir al médico.
You've got to open the window. Tienes que abrir la ventana.
11 (*to become*)
to get angry enfadarse
to get tired cansarse
I'm getting hungry. Me está entrando hambre.

> **LANGUAGE**
> When 'get' is followed by an adjective, the translation depends on the adjective, e.g. 'dark', 'late', 'old'.

• *See the centre section for verb tables.*

to **get away** verb
escaparse
The thief has got away. Se ha escapado el ladrón.

to **get back** verb
volver
Mum gets back at seven. Mamá vuelve a las siete.

to **get down** verb
bajar
Get down from there! ¡Baja de allí!

to **get in** verb
subir
Get in the car. Sube al coche.
Get in, Jack. Sube, Jack.

to **get off** verb
bajarse
I got off the bus at Richmond. Me bajé del autobús en Richmond.
Get off the bike. Bájate de la bici.

to **get on** verb
1 **subir, subirse**
We've got on the bus. Hemos subido al autobús., Nos hemos subido al autobús.
I got on my bike. Subí a mi bici.
2 **to get on with somebody** llevarse bien con alguien
I get on with my mum. Me llevo bien con mi madre.
3 **How are you getting on?** ¿Qué tal te va?
I'm getting on well. Voy bien.

to **get out** verb
1 **salir**
Get out! ¡Sal!
to get out of a car bajarse de un coche
2 **to get something out** sacar algo
Get out your exercise books. Sacad los cuadernos.

to **get up** verb
levantarse
I get up at six. Me levanto a las seis.

ghost noun
el **fantasma** masc.

> 🔑 **LANGUAGE**
> Be careful: **fantasma** ends in an **-a** but it is not a feminine noun.

giant noun
el **gigante** masc., la **giganta** fem.

gift noun
el **regalo** masc.
a gift shop una tienda de regalos

gigantic adjective
gigantesco masc., **gigantesca** fem.

ginger adjective
to have ginger hair ser pelirrojo or pelirroja
I've got ginger hair. Soy pelirrojo.

> 🔑 **LANGUAGE**
> Be careful: don't use the word **pelo** (hair) with **pelirrojo**.

giraffe noun
la **jirafa** fem.

> 🔑 **LANGUAGE**
> English = **giraffe**
> Spanish = **jirafa**

girl noun
1 (young child) la **niña** fem.
a little girl of five una niña de cinco años
It's a baby girl. Es una niña.
2 (older child or teenager) la **chica** fem.
a girl of sixteen una chica de dieciséis años

girlfriend noun
la **novia** fem.
My brother has a girlfriend. Mi hermano tiene novia.

to **give** verb
dar
Give me a pen. Dame un boli.
He gave me the book. Me dio el libro.

• Use **el** and **uno** for masculine words and **la** and **una** for feminine words.

to **give back** verb
devolver
I'll give it back to you tomorrow.
Te lo devuelvo mañana.

to **give in** verb
entregar
I've given in my homework.
He entregado mis deberes.

to **give out** verb
repartir
The teacher gave out the books.
La maestra repartió los cuadernos.

to **give up** verb
rendirse
I give up! ¡Me rindo!

glad adjective
to be glad alegrarse
I'm glad to see you. Me alegro de verte.
Yes, I'm glad. Sí, me alegro.

glass noun
1 (for drinking) el **vaso** masc.
a glass of milk un vaso de leche
2 el **cristal** masc.
It's made of glass. Es de cristal.
a glass door una puerta de cristal
Careful, there's broken glass.
Cuidado, hay cristales rotos.

glasses plural noun
las **gafas** fem. plural,
(Latin America) los **anteojas** masc. plural
I wear glasses. Llevo gafas.

globe noun
el **globo** masc.

glove noun
el **guante** masc.

glue noun
el **pegamento** masc.

go noun
It's your go. Te toca a ti.
Whose go is it? ¿A quién le toca?

> **LANGUAGE**
> Use **tocar** (to be somebody's turn). It also means 'to touch'.

to **go** verb
1 **ir**
I want to go to the cinema. Quiero ir al cine.
I'm going to school. Voy a la escuela.
Where are you going? ¿Adónde vas?
She's gone to the doctor. Ha ido al médico.
Let's go! ¡Vamos!
2 (to leave) **irse**
I'm going. Ya me voy.
I went at six. Me fui a las seis.
3 (talking about trains, planes, etc.) **salir**
What time does the train go?
¿A qué hora sale el tren?
4 (used with another verb when talking about the future) **ir**
What are you going to do? ¿Qué vas a hacer?
I'm going to play in the garden.
Voy a jugar en el jardín.

to **go away** verb
irse
Go away, Philip! ¡Vete, Philip!

to **go back** verb
volver
I'm going back home. Vuelvo a casa.

to **go down** verb
bajar
I'm going down to the basement.
Bajo al sótano.
She went down the stairs. Bajó las escaleras.
The sun is going down. Se pone el sol.

to **go in** verb
entrar
Go in. Entra.
I went into the room. Entré en la habitación.

to **go off** verb
1 (to explode) **estallar**
A bomb has gone off. Una bomba ha estallado.

• Languages and nationalities do not take a capital letter in Spanish.

2 (*to sound*) **sonar**
Has the alarm clock gone off?
¿Ha sonado el despertador?

to **go on** verb
1 (*to continue*) **seguir**
to go on doing something seguir
haciendo algo
Go on reading. Sigue leyendo.
2 (*to happen*)
What's going on? ¿Qué pasa?

to **go out** verb
salir
I don't go out much. No salgo
mucho.
Go out! ¡Sal!
Ben's going out with my sister.
Ben sale con mi hermana.

to **go up** verb
subir
I'm going up to my room. Subo a
mi habitación.
She went up the stairs. Subió las
escaleras.

goal noun
1 el **gol** *masc.*
They scored two goals. Marcaron
dos goles.
2 (*the goalposts*) la **portería** *fem.*

goalkeeper noun
el **portero** *masc.*, la **portera** *fem.*

goat noun
la **cabra** *fem.*

God noun
Dios *masc.*

goddaughter noun
la **ahijada** *fem.*

godfather noun
el **padrino** *masc.*

godmother noun
la **madrina** *fem.*

godson noun
el **ahijado** *masc.*

goggles plural noun
(*for swimming*) las **gafas (de
natación)** *fem. plural*

gold noun
el **oro** *masc.*
a gold ring un anillo de oro

goldfish noun
el **pez de colores** *masc.* (plural los
peces de colores)

> **LANGUAGE**
> Word for word the Spanish means 'fish of
> colours'.

golf noun
el **golf** *masc.*
My uncle plays golf. Mi tío juega
al golf.
a golf course un campo de golf

gone verb SEE **go**
They've gone to the cinema. Han
ido al cine.
Amanda has gone. Amanda se ha
ido.

good adjective
1 **bueno** *masc.*, **buena** *fem.*
Be good! ¡Sé bueno!
Apples are good for you. Las
manzanas son buenas para la
salud.

> **LANGUAGE**
> The masculine singular **bueno** becomes
> **buen** when it is used before a noun.

a good example un buen ejemplo
Good! ¡Muy bien!
2 **I'm good at Spanish.** Se me da bien
el español.
Cheryl is no good at numbers.
Cheryl no es buena para los
números.
3 (*when wishing somebody something*)
Good morning! ¡Buenos días!
Good afternoon! ¡Buenas tardes!
Good night! ¡Buenas noches!
Have a good trip! ¡Buen viaje!

• The months of the year and days of the week do not take a capital letter in Spanish.

goodbye exclamation
¡adiós!

Good Friday noun
el Viernes Santo *masc.*

good-looking adjective
guapo *masc.*, guapa *fem.*
He's very good-looking. Es muy
guapo.

goodnight exclamation
¡buenas noches!

goose noun
el ganso *masc.*

gorilla noun
el gorila *masc.*

🔑 **LANGUAGE**
Be careful: **gorila** ends in an **-a** but it is not
a feminine noun.

got verb SEE **get, have**
I got your postcard. Recibí tu postal.
I've got black hair. Tengo el pelo
negro.
We've got to go to the dentist.
Tenemos que ir al dentista.

grade noun
(*in school subjects*) la nota *fem.*
**My brother always gets good
grades.** Mi hermano siempre saca
buenas notas.

graffiti noun
los graffiti *masc. plural*

gram noun
el gramo *masc.*

grammar noun
la gramática *fem.*

grandchildren plural noun
los nietos *masc. plural*

granddad, **grandpa** noun
el abuelito *masc.*

granddaughter noun
la nieta *fem.*

grandfather noun
el abuelo *masc.*

grandma noun
la abuelita *fem.*

grandmother noun
la abuela *fem.*

grandparents plural noun
los abuelos *masc. plural*

grandson noun
el nieto *masc.*

granny noun
la abuelita *fem.*

grape noun
la uva *fem.*

grapefruit noun
el pomelo *masc.*

grass noun
la hierba *fem.*
I'm sitting on the grass. Estoy
sentada en la hierba.

gravy noun
la salsa de carne *fem.*
Do you want some gravy?
¿Quieres salsa?

greasy adjective
(*hair, skin, food*) graso *masc.*,
grasa *fem.*

great adjective
estupendo *masc.*, estupenda *fem.*
That's great! ¡Estupendo!

Great Britain noun
Gran Bretaña *fem.*
We live in Gret Britain. Vivimos en
Gran Bretaña.

Greece noun
Grecia *fem.*

greedy adjective
glotón *masc.*, glotona *fem.*
You're very greedy! ¡Eres muy
glotón!

🔑 **LANGUAGE**
The masculine plural of **glotón** is
glotones.

• *See the centre section for verb tables.*

Greek adjective
griego *masc.*, griega *fem.*

Greek noun
1 (*language*) el griego *masc.*
He speaks Greek. Hablar griego.
2 (*person*) el griego *masc.*,
la griega *fem.*

green adjective
verde *masc. & fem.*
I have green eyes. Tengo los ojos
verdes.

green noun
1 el verde *masc.*
I love green. Me encanta el verde.
2 **greens** las verduras *fem. plural*
Eat your greens! ¡Cómete las
verduras!

greengrocer's noun
la verdulería *fem.*

grey adjective
gris *masc. & fem.*
a grey shirt una camisa gris

grey noun
el gris *masc.*
Grey is my favourite colour. El gris
es mi color favorito.

grocer's noun
the grocer's la tienda de
comestibles *fem.*

groom noun
el novio *masc.*
the bride and groom los novios

ground noun
1 el suelo *masc.*
I'm sitting on the ground. Estoy
sentado en el suelo.
2 (*for football etc.*) el campo *masc.*
a sports ground un campo de
deportes
3 **the ground floor** la planta baja
I live on the ground floor. Vivo en
la planta baja.

group noun
el grupo *masc.*

grow
(*to get bigger*) crecer
You've grown a lot! ¡Has crecido
mucho!
My plants are growing well.
Mis plantas crecen muy bien.
**I want to be a teacher when I grow
up.** Quiero ser profesor cuando sea
mayor.

grown-up noun
el adulto *masc.*, la adulta *fem.*

grumpy adjective
gruñón *masc.*, gruñona *fem.*

LANGUAGE
The masculine plural of **gruñón** is
gruñones.

to **guess** verb
adivinar
Guess what I saw. Adivina lo que
he visto.

guest noun
el invitado *masc.*, la invitada *fem.*
You're my guest. Eres mi
invitado.

LANGUAGE
The Spanish means 'person who has been
invited'.

guide noun
1 (*book*) la guía *fem.*
2 (*person*) el or la guía *masc. & fem.*

Guide noun
(*Scout*) la guía *fem.*
She's in the Guides. Pertenece a las
guías.

guidebook noun
la guía *fem.*

guinea pig noun
el or la cobaya *masc. & fem.*

a
b
c
d
e
f
g
h
i
j
k
l
m
n
o
p
q
r
s
t
u
v
w
x
y
z

• *Use* **el** *and* **uno** *for masculine words and* **la** *and* **una** *for feminine words.*

a
b
c
d
e
f
g
h
i
j
k
l
m
n
o
p
q
r
s
t
u
v
w
x
y
z

guitar noun
la guitarra *fem.*
Daniel plays the guitar. Daniel toca la guitarra.

gum noun
(*chewing gum*) el chicle *masc.*

gun noun
la pistola *fem.*

guy noun
el tío *masc.*
He's a nice guy. Es un tío simpático.

gym noun
1 (*PE*) la gimnasia *fem.*
We have gym on Tuesdays. Los martes tenemos clase de gimnasia.
2 (*room in a school, health club*) el gimnasio *masc.*
My dad goes to the gym. Mi padre va al gimnasio.

gymnastics noun
la gimnasia *fem.*
to do gymnastics hacer gimnasia

Hh

habit noun
la costumbre *fem.*
a bad habit una mala costumbre

had verb SEE **have**
I've had an accident. He tenido un accidente.
He had a problem. Tuvo un problema.

hail noun
el granizo *masc.*

to **hail** verb
granizar
It's hailing. Está granizando.

hair
el pelo *masc.*
I've got black hair. Tengo el pelo negro.
cat hairs pelos de gato

haircut noun
el corte de pelo *masc.*
I'm going to have a haircut. Voy a cortarme el pelo.

hairdresser noun
el peluquero *masc.*,
la peluquera *fem.*
She's a hairdresser. Es peluquera.

I'm going to the hairdresser's. Voy a la peluquería.

hairdryer noun
el secador de pelo *masc.*

hairstyle noun
el peinado *masc.*

hairy adjective
peludo *masc.*, peluda *fem.*

half noun
1 la mitad *fem.*
half my apple la mitad de mi manzana
to cut something in half cortar algo por la mitad
2 (*use medio after numbers*)
six and a half seis y medio
3 (*use media with times*)
an hour and a half una hora y media
It's half past nine. Son las nueve y media.

half adjective
medio *masc.*, media *fem.*
half an hour media hora
half a kilo medio kilo

• *Languages and nationalities do not take a capital letter in Spanish.*

half adverb
medio
She's half asleep. Está medio dormida.

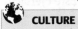

🔑 **LANGUAGE**
Be careful: the adverb **medio** does not change when it is in front of a feminine or plural adjective.

half-brother noun
el *hermanastro* masc.

half-sister noun
la *hermanastra* fem.

half-term noun
las *vacaciones de mitad de trimestre* fem. plural

🌎 **CULTURE**
There are no half-term holidays in Spanish schools but summer holidays are longer.

half-time noun
el *descanso* masc.
at half-time en el descanso

halfway adverb
a mitad de camino
It's halfway between Manchester and Leeds. Está a mitad de camino entre Manchester y Leeds.

hall noun
1 (big room) la *sala* fem.
a concert hall una sala de conciertos
2 (in a school) el *salón de actos* masc.
3 (in a house) la *entrada* fem.

Hallowe'en noun
la *víspera del día de Todos los Santos* fem.

 CULTURE
The Spanish means 'the Eve of All Saints' Day'. In Spain people do not usually celebrate **Hallowe'en**, but **el día de Todos los Santos** is a public holiday.

ham noun
el *jamón* masc. (plural los **jamones**)
a ham sandwich un sándwich de jamón

hamburger noun
la *hamburguesa* fem.

hammer noun
el *martillo* masc.

hamster noun
el *hámster* masc. (plural los **hámsters**)

hand noun
1 la *mano* fem.
Put your hand up. Levantad la mano.
Can you give me a hand? ¿Me puedes echar una mano?
2 (on a clock or watch) la *manecilla* fem.
the hands of the clock las manecillas del reloj

to **hand** verb
1 *pasar*
Hand me the pencil. Pásame el lápiz.
2 **to hand in** entregar
I've handed in my homework. He entregado mis deberes.
3 **to hand out** repartir
Edward handed out the exercise books. Edward repartió los cuadernos.

handbag noun
el *bolso* masc.

handkerchief noun
el *pañuelo* masc.

handle noun
1 (on a door) el *picaporte* masc.
2 (on a knife, broom, frying pan) el *mango* masc.
3 (on a cup, bag) el *asa* fem.

🔑 **LANGUAGE**
Be careful: you use **el** with **asa** but it is not a masculine noun

• *The months of the year and days of the week do not take a capital letter in Spanish.*

handlebars plural noun
el **manillar** *masc.*

> **LANGUAGE**
> English = **handlebars** is plural
> Spanish = **el manillar** is singular

handsome adjective
guapo *masc.*, **guapa** *fem.*
Dylan is very handsome. Dylan es muy guapo.

handwriting noun
la **letra** *fem.*
You have very good handwriting. Tienes muy buena letra.

> **LANGUAGE**
> In Spanish **letra** is also 'letter of the alphabet': 'handwriting' is how we write **letras**.

handy adjective
1 (*useful*) **práctico** *masc.*, **práctica** *fem.*
My mobile phone is very handy. Mi móvil es muy práctico.
2 (*easy to get at*) **a mano**
I always keep a pen handy. Siempre tengo un bolígrafo a mano.

to hang verb
1 **colgar**
I hung the picture on the wall. Colgué el cuadro en la pared.
The picture is hanging on the wall. El cuadro está colgado en la pared.
2 **Hang on!** ¡Espera!

hangman noun
el **ahorcado** *masc.*
We're playing hangman. Estamos jugando al ahorcado.

happen verb
pasar
What's happened? ¿Qué ha pasado?
What happened to dad? ¿Qué le pasó a papá?

happiness noun
la **felicidad** *fem.*

happy adjective
feliz *masc. & fem.* (plural **felices**)
Hassan is very happy. Hassan es muy feliz.
Happy birthday! ¡Feliz cumpleaños!
Happy Christmas! ¡Feliz Navidad!
Happy New Year! ¡Feliz Año Nuevo!

harbour noun
el **puerto** *masc.*

hard adjective
1 (*not soft*) **duro** *masc.*, **dura** *fem.*
This bread is very hard. Este pan está muy duro.
a hard-boiled egg un huevo duro
2 (*not easy*) **difícil** *masc. & fem.*
This exercise is hard. Este ejercicio es difícil.

hard adverb
mucho
I work hard. Trabajo mucho.

hardly adverb
casi
I hardly ever eat meat. Casi nunca como carne.
hardly anybody casi nadie

> **LANGUAGE**
> **Casi** is the Spanish word for 'almost'.

hard-working adjective
trabajador *masc.*, **trabajadora** *fem.*

has verb SEE have
She has blue eyes. Tiene los ojos azules.
He has seen the film. Ha visto la película.

hat noun
1 el **sombrero** *masc.*
2 (*soft hat, e.g. worn by children*) el **gorro** *masc.*
a woolly hat un gorro de lana

to hate verb
odiar
I hate swimming. Odio la natación.

• *See the centre section for verb tables.*

a b c d e f g h i j k l m n o p q r s t u v w x y z

to **have** verb
1 tener
I have two brothers. Tengo dos hermanos.
I don't have any time. No tengo tiempo.
Do you have a bike? ¿Tienes una bici?
He has a blue shirt. Tiene una camisa azul.
They have a problem. Tienen un problema.

> **LANGUAGE**
> 'Have' and 'have got' mean the same, and have the same translation in Spanish.

She's got fair hair. Tiene el pelo rubio.
We've got lots of friends. Tenemos muchos amigos.
2 (*to eat or drink*) **tomar**
I'm going to have an omelette. Voy a tomar una tortilla.
3 (*used for making past tenses*) **haber**
I've finished. He terminado.
He has read the book. Ha leído el libro.
4 (*when translating 'have to do something' or 'have got to do something'*) **tener que**
I have to go to the doctor. Tengo que ir al médico.
You've got to help me. Tienes que ayudarme.
5 (*when translating questions such as 'hasn't he?' or 'haven't you?'*) **He's arrived, hasn't he?** Ha llegado, ¿no?
You've finished, haven't you? Has terminado, ¿no?

> **LANGUAGE**
> When talking about activities (like having a shower) there are many ways of translating 'have' + noun into Spanish. These expressions are usually given in the dictionary under the noun.

to have a shower ducharse
to have lunch comer

hay noun
el **heno** *masc.*
hay fever la fiebre del heno

he pronoun
1 (*not usually translated*)
He's tall. Es alto.
He lives in London. Vive en Londres.
2 él
He's tall but his sister is short. Él es alto pero su hermana es baja.

> **LANGUAGE**
> Use **él** when you want to give special importance to the word **he**.

head
1 la cabeza *fem.*
He banged his head. Se dio un golpe en la cabeza.
2 (*headteacher*) el **director** *masc.*, la **directora** *fem.*
3 (*when throwing a coin*) **heads!** ¡cara!
Heads or tails? ¿Cara o cruz?

headache noun
I have a headache. Me duele la cabeza.

> **LANGUAGE**
> Word for word the Spanish means 'my head hurts'.

headmistress, headmaster noun
el **director** *masc.*; la **directora** *fem.*

headphones noun
los **auriculares** *masc. plural*

headteacher noun
el **director** *masc.*, la **directora** *fem.*

health noun
la **salud** *fem.*

healthy adjective
sano *masc.*, **sana** *fem.*
I'm healthy. Estoy sano.

to **hear** verb
oír
I hear a noise Oigo un ruido
Can you hear me? ¿Me oyes?

• Use **el** and **uno** for masculine words and **la** and **una** for feminine words.

301

a
b
c
d
e
f
g
h
i
j
k
l
m
n
o
p
q
r
s
t
u
v
w
x
y
z

heart noun
1 el corazón masc. (plural los corazones)
It's good for your heart Es bueno para el corazón
2 to learn something by heart aprender algo de memoria

heat noun
el calor masc.

heater noun
la estufa fem.
an electric heater una estufa eléctrica

heating noun
la calefacción fem.

heavy adjective
pesado masc., pesada fem.
It's very heavy. Es muy pesado.

hedge noun
el seto masc.

heel noun
el talón masc. (plural los **talones**)

height noun
1 (of a person) la estatura fem.
2 (of a wall, building, etc.) la altura fem.

helicopter noun
el helicóptero masc.

hello exclamation
1 ¡hola!
Hello, mum! ¡Hola, mamá!
2 (when answering the phone) ¡diga!, ¡dígame!

helmet noun
el casco masc.

help noun
la ayuda fem.
I need help. Necesito ayuda.

to **help** verb
1 ayudar
Help me make the bed. Ayúdame a hacer la cama.
Help! ¡Socorro!

2 to help yourself to something (food or drinks) servirse algo
Help yourself! ¡Sírvete!

hen noun
la gallina fem.

her adjective
1 (before a singular noun) su
her father su padre
2 (before a plural noun) sus
her books sus libros
3 (with parts of the body, clothes, etc.)
She's washing her hands. Se está lavando las manos.
She put her coat on. Se puso el abrigo.

LANGUAGE
Use se with el, la, los, or las instead of su and sus in these examples.

her pronoun
1 (after a verb) la
I know her. La conozco.
Have you seen her? ¿La has visto?

LANGUAGE
With commands and infinitives la is joined with the verb to make one word.

Help her. Ayúdala.
I want to see her. Quiero verla.
2 (to her) le
I have sent a letter to her. Le he mandado una carta.
Give her the pen. Dale el bolígrafo.

LANGUAGE
When le is used with lo or la you use se instead of le.

I've given it to her. Se lo he dado.
Give it to her. Dáselo.
3 (after a preposition etc.) ella
with her con ella
You're taller than her. Eres más alto que ella.
It's her. Es ella.

• Languages and nationalities do not take a capital letter in Spanish.

here adverb
1 aquí
I live here. Vivo aquí.
Come here! ¡Ven aquí!
Here he is. Aquí está.
2 (when you're giving something)
Here's the book. Aquí tienes el libro.
Here are the pens. Aquí tienes los bolis.

> 🗝 **LANGUAGE**
> In Spanish aquí tienes (word for word 'here you have') can be used for 'here is' and 'here are'.

hero noun
el héroe masc.

heroine noun
la heroína fem.

hers pronoun
1 (with a singular noun) el suyo masc., la suya fem.
My house is bigger than hers. Mi casa es más grande que la suya.
2 (with a plural noun) los suyos masc. plural, las suyas fem. plural
my friends and hers mis amigos y los suyos
3 (following 'is') suyo masc., suya fem.
This book is hers. Este libro es suyo.
This apple is hers. Esta manzana es suya.
4 (following 'are') suyos masc. plural, suyas fem. plural
These books are hers. Estos libros son suyos.

herself pronoun
1 ella misma
She has done it herself. Lo ha hecho ella misma.
2 (with a reflexive verb) se
María is washing herself. María se está lavando.
3 by herself sola
She's sitting by herself. Está sentada sola.

hi exclamation
¡hola!

hiccups plural noun
to have hiccups tener hipo

to **hide**
1 esconderse
I hid behind a tree. Me escondí detrás de un árbol.
2 to hide something esconder algo
Hide the book. Esconde el libro.

hide-and-seek noun
el escondite masc.
to play hide-and-seek jugar al escondite

hiding place noun
el escondite masc.

high adjective
alto masc., alta fem.
This building is very high. Este edificio es muy alto.

high school noun
el instituto masc.

hill noun
1 (in the countryside) la colina fem.
2 (in the town) la cuesta fem.

him pronoun
1 (after a verb) lo
I know him. Lo conozco.
Have you seen him? ¿Lo has visto?

> 🗝 **LANGUAGE**
> With commands and infinitives lo is joined with the verb to make one word.

Call him. Llámalo.
Can you help him? ¿Puedes ayudarlo?
2 (to him) le
I have sent a present to him. Le he mandado un regalo.
Give him the CD. Dale el CD.

> 🗝 **LANGUAGE**
> When le is used with lo or la you use se instead of le.

I've given it to him. Se lo he dado.
Give it to him. Dáselo.

• The months of the year and days of the week do not take a capital letter in Spanish.

3 (after a preposition etc.) **él**
with him con él
I'm younger than him. Soy más joven que él.
It's him. Es él.

himself pronoun
1 **él mismo**
He has done it himself. Lo ha hecho él mismo.
2 (with a reflexive verb) **se**
He's washing himself. Se está lavando.
3 **by himself** solo
He doesn't go out by himself. No sale solo.

Hindu adjective
hindú masc. & fem. (plural **hindúes**)

hip noun
la **cadera** fem.

hip hip hurrah exclamation
¡viva!

hippopotamus noun
el **hipopótamo** masc.

to hire verb
(a bike, car, etc.) **alquilar**

his adjective
1 (before a singular noun) **su**
his dog su perro
2 (before a plural noun) **sus**
his parents sus padres
3 (with parts of the body, clothes, etc.)
He's washing his hands. Se está lavando las manos.
He took his coat off. Se quitó el abrigo.

> **LANGUAGE**
> Use **se** with **el**, **la**, **los**, or **las** instead of **su** and **sus** in these examples.

his pronoun
1 (with a singular noun) el **suyo** masc., la **suya** fem.
My house is smaller than his. Mi casa es más pequeña que la suya.

• See the centre section for verb tables.

2 (with a plural noun) los **suyos** masc. plural, las **suyas** fem. plural
my toys and his mis juguetes y los suyos
3 (following 'is') **suyo** masc., **suya** fem.
This pen is his. Este bolígrafo es suyo.
This magazine is his. Esta revista es suya.
4 (following 'are') **suyos** masc. plural, **suyas** fem. plural
These pens are his. Estos bolígrafos son suyos.

history noun
la **historia** fem.

hit noun
(song) el **éxito** masc.
It's his latest hit. Es su último éxito.

to hit verb
1 **golpear**
They've hit me! ¡Me han golpeado!
2 **darse un golpe en**
I hit my head. Me di un golpe en la cabeza.
3 (to bump into) **chocar con**
My bike hit a tree. Mi bici chocó con un árbol.

hobby noun
el **pasatiempo** masc., el **hobby** masc. (plural los **hobbies**)

hockey noun
el **hockey** masc.
I play hockey. Juego al hockey.

to hold verb
1 **tener**
What are you holding in your hand? ¿Qué tienes en la mano?

> **LANGUAGE**
> Use **tener** when you describe what you've got in your hand, otherwise **sostener**.

2 **sostener**
Can you hold this box, please? ¿Me sostienes esta caja, por favor?

3 to hold on (*to wait*) esperar
Hold on a moment! ¡Espera un momento!
4 to hold up (*to lift up*) levantar
Hold up your hands! ¡Levantad la mano!

hold-up noun
(*traffic jam*) el atasco *masc.*

hole noun
el agujero *masc.*

holiday noun
1 las vacaciones *fem. plural*
I'm on holiday. Estoy de vacaciones.
When are you going on holiday? ¿Cuándo te vas de vacaciones?
the Christmas holidays las vacaciones de Navidad
the school holidays las vacaciones escolares
2 (*public holiday*) la fiesta *fem.*
Tomorrow is a holiday. Mañana es fiesta.

Holland noun
Holanda *fem.*

holly noun
el acebo *masc.*

holy adjective
santo *masc.*, santa *fem.*

home noun
1 la casa *fem.*
at home en casa
My dad is at home. Mi papá está en casa.
2 (*on web page*) el inicio *masc.*
the home page la página de inicio

home adverb
a casa
I'm going home. Me voy a casa.
Mum gets home at six. Mamá llega a casa a las seis.

homeless adjective
a homeless person una persona sin hogar

homework noun
los deberes *masc. plural*
my Spanish homework mis deberes de español

⚷ **LANGUAGE**
English = **homework** is singular
Spanish = **los deberes** is plural

honest adjective
(*telling the truth*) sincero *masc.*, sincera *fem.*

honey noun
la miel *fem.*

hood noun
(*on a coat*) la capucha *fem.*

hook noun
(*for a picture or clothes*) el gancho *masc.*

hooray exclamation
¡hurra!

Hoover® noun
la aspiradora *fem.*

to **hoover** verb
pasar la aspiradora
I've hoovered my room. He pasado la aspiradora por mi habitación.

to **hop** verb
(*on one leg*) saltar a la pata coja

to **hope** verb
esperar
I hope to see you tomorrow. Espero verte mañana.
I hope so. Espero que sí.
I hope not. Espero que no.

hopeless adjective
muy malo *masc.*, muy mala *fem.*
I'm hopeless at maths. Soy muy malo para las matemáticas.

horn noun
1 (*on a bull etc.*) el cuerno *masc.*
2 (*on a car*) la bocina *fem.*

horrible adjective
horrible *masc. & fem.*

a
b
c
d
e
f
g
h
i
j
k
l
m
n
o
p
q
r
s
t
u
v
w
x
y
z

• *Use* el *and* uno *for masculine words and* la *and* una *for feminine words.*

horror film noun
la **película de terror** *fem.*

horse noun
el **caballo** *masc.*

hospital noun
el **hospital** *masc.*
My grandfather's in hospital.
Mi abuelo está en el hospital.

hot adjective
caliente *masc. & fem.*
The water's hot. El agua está
caliente.
The weather's hot. Hace calor.
It's hot today. Hoy hace calor.
I'm hot. Tengo calor.
He's very hot. Tiene mucho calor.

🔑 **LANGUAGE**
English = **to be** hot **I'm hot.**
Spanish = **tener** calor **Tengo calor.**

hot dog noun
el **perrito caliente** *masc.*

hotel noun
el **hotel** *masc.*

hour noun
la **hora** *fem.*
half an hour media hora
a quarter of an hour un cuarto de
hora
two and a half hours dos horas y
media

house noun
la **casa** *fem.*
at my house en mi casa
I'm at Parminder's house. Estoy en
casa de Parminder.
I'm going to Tom's house. Voy a
casa de Tom.

housework noun
la **limpieza** *fem.*
to do the housework hacer la
limpieza

how adverb
1 cómo
How are you? ¿Cómo estás?
2 how much? ¿cuánto?
How much is it? ¿Cuánto es?
How much money do you have?
¿Cuánto dinero tienes?
3 how many? ¿cuántos?
How many books do you want?
¿Cuántos libros quieres?
4 how often? ¿cada cuánto?
How often do you see your uncle?
¿Cada cuánto ves a tu tío?
5 How old are you? ¿Cuántos años
tienes?

huge adjective
enorme *masc. & fem.*

human adjective
humano *masc.*, **humana** *fem.*
a human being un ser humano

humour noun
to have a sense of humour tener
sentido del humor

hundred number
1 cien
a hundred children cien niños
about a hundred children unos
cien niños
2 ciento
a hundred and five ciento cinco
hundreds of children cientos de
niños
two hundred doscientos or
doscientas
two hundred and ten euros
doscientos diez euros
five hundred quinientos or
quinientas

🔑 **LANGUAGE**
Use **cien** in front of nouns and **ciento** for
numbers 101 to 199. For numbers 200 to
999 join **dos, tres**, etc. to **cientos** to make
one word (e.g. **doscientos**); sometimes
the first number has a different form
(e.g. **quinientos**, not **cincocientos**).

• *Languages and nationalities do not take a capital letter in Spanish.*

hungry adjective
I'm hungry. Tengo hambre.
He's very hungry. Tiene mucha
hambre.

LANGUAGE
English = **to be** hungry **I'm** hungry.
Spanish = **tener** hambre **Tengo**
 hambre.

hurricane noun
el **huracán** masc. (plural los
huracanes)

hurry noun
to be in a hurry tener prisa
I'm in a hurry. Tengo prisa.

to **hurry** verb
darse prisa
Hurry up, granddad! ¡Date prisa,
abuelo!

to **hurt** verb
1 **My arm hurts.** Me duele el
brazo.
It hurts a lot. Me duele mucho.
My feet hurt. Me duelen los pies.
2 **to hurt somebody** hacer daño a
alguien
You're hurting me! ¡Me estás
haciendo daño!
Have you hurt yourself? ¿Te has
hecho daño?

hurt adjective
(in an accident) **herido** masc.,
herida fem.
He's hurt. Está herido.

husband noun
el **marido** masc.

hyphen noun
el **guión** masc. (plural los **guiones**)

Ii

I pronoun
1 (not usually translated in Spanish)
I'm English. Soy inglés.
I have a dog. Tengo un perro.
2 **yo**
I'm reading a book and my
brother's playing. Yo estoy
leyendo un libro y mi hermano está
jugando.
my father and I mi padre y yo

LANGUAGE
Use **yo** when you want to give special
importance to the word 'I'.

ice noun
el **hielo** masc.

ice-cold adjective
(water, hands, etc.) **helado** masc.,
helada fem.

ice cream noun
el **helado** masc.
a strawberry ice cream un helado
de fresa

ice cube noun
el **cubito de hielo** masc.

ice lolly noun
el **polo** masc.

ice rink noun
la **pista de hielo** fem.

ice-skating noun
el **patinaje sobre hielo** masc.
I go ice-skating. Voy a patinar.

icon noun
el **icono** masc.
Click on the icon. Haz clic en el
icono.

a
b
c
d
e
f
g
h
i
j
k
l
m
n
o
p
q
r
s
t
u
v
w
x
y
z

• *The months of the year and days of the week do not take a capital letter in Spanish.*

ICT noun
las **TIC** *fem. plural*,
la **informática** *fem.*

🔑 **LANGUAGE**
TIC is short for **Tecnologías de la información y de la comunicación.**

icy adjective
1 *(wind, hands, etc.)* **helado** *masc.*, **helada** *fem.*
2 **The roads are icy.** Hay hielo en la carretera.

idea noun
la **idea** *fem.*
I have an idea. Tengo una idea.

identical adjective
idéntico *masc.*, **idéntica** *fem.*

idiot noun
el or la **idiota** *masc. & fem.*

if conjunction
si
if you can si puedes
Tell me if you want to come. Dime si quieres venir.
if not si no

🔑 **LANGUAGE**
si = if
sí = yes

ill adjective
enfermo *masc.*, **enferma** *fem.*
I'm ill. Estoy enfermo.

illness noun
la **enfermedad** *fem.*

imaginary adjective
imaginario *masc.*, **imaginaria** *fem.*
an imaginary friend un amigo imaginario

imagination noun
la **imaginación** *fem.*

to imagine verb
imaginar
Imagine you have lots of money. Imagina que tienes mucho dinero.

· *See the centre section for verb tables.*

to imitate verb
imitar

immediately adverb
inmediatamente

🔑 **LANGUAGE**
English = **immediately**
Spanish = **inmediatamente**

important adjective
importante *masc. & fem.*

impossible adjective
imposible *masc. & fem.*

to improve verb
mejorar
Your Spanish has improved.
Tu español ha mejorado.
I want to improve my Spanish.
Quiero mejorar mi español.

🔑 **LANGUAGE**
Mejorar comes from **mejor** (better).

in preposition & adverb
1 **en**
I'm in the garden. Estoy en el jardín.
in Spain en España
in Spanish en español
in April en abril
in here aquí dentro
2 *(with 'most' + adjective, or words like 'best', 'biggest')* **de**
the most intelligent girl in the class la chica más inteligente de la clase
the best school in Madrid el mejor colegio de Madrid
3 *(talking about time in the future)* **dentro de**
I'm coming back in two days.
Vuelvo dentro de dos días.
4 *(talking about being at home)* **to be in** estar
Is Nicole in? ¿Está Nicole?
She's not in. No está.

a b c d e f g h **i** j k l m n o p q r s t u v w x y z

inch noun
I'm two inches taller than you.
Soy cinco centímetros más alto que tú.

 CULTURE
Spanish measurements are in metres and centimetres; an inch is about 2.5 centimetres.

included adjective
incluido *masc.*, incluida *fem.*
The service is included El servicio está incluido

incorrect adjective
incorrecto *masc.*, incorrecta *fem.*

to **increase** verb
aumentar

incredible adjective
increíble *masc. & fem.*

indeed adverb
realmente
I'm very tired indeed. Estoy realmente cansado.
Thanks very much indeed! ¡Muchísimas gracias!

independent adjective
independiente *masc. & fem.*

India noun
la India *fem.*

Indian adjective
indio *masc.*, india *fem.*
an Indian town una ciudad india

Indian noun
el indio *masc.*, la india *fem.*

indoor adjective
(*swimming pool, tennis court, etc.*)
cubierto *masc.*, cubierta *fem.*
an indoor pool una piscina cubierta

indoors adverb
dentro
They're eating indoors. Están comiendo dentro.
to go indoors entrar

infant school noun
la guardería *fem.*

 CULTURE
In Spain the **guardería** is a nursery school for children before they start primary school at the age of 6. In Britain the **infant school** is for children from 4 to 7 years.

infection noun
la infección *fem.* (plural las **infecciones**)
a throat infection una infección de garganta

infinitive noun
el infinitivo *masc.*

information noun
la información *fem.*

ingredient noun
el ingrediente *masc.*

initials plural noun
las iniciales *fem. plural*
My initials are BTN. Mis iniciales son BTN.

injection noun
la inyección *fem.* (plural las **inyecciones**)
The doctor gave me an injection. El médico me puso una inyección.

injured adjective
1 (*in an accident etc.*) herido *masc.*, herida *fem.*
There are many injured people. Hay muchos heridos.
2 (*in sports*) lesionado *masc.*, lesionada *fem.*
The player is injured. El jugador está lesionado.

injury noun
1 (*in an accident etc.*) la herida *fem.*
2 (*in sports*) la lesión *fem.*

ink noun
la tinta *fem.*
an ink mark una mancha de tinta

• *Use* el *and* uno *for masculine words and* la *and* una *for feminine words.*

insect noun
el insecto *masc.*

inside preposition
dentro de
inside the box dentro de la caja

inside adverb
dentro
What's inside? ¿Qué hay dentro?
Your socks are inside out. Tus calcetines están al revés.

to **install** verb
instalar
Have you installed the program? ¿Has instalado el programa?

instead adverb
1 (*not translated*)
Ali's not well so I went instead. Ali está enfermo así que fui yo.
2 **instead of** en vez de
I went to the cinema instead of going to school. Fui al cine en vez de ir al colegio.

instructions plural noun
las instrucciones *fem. plural*

instructor noun
el monitor *masc.*, la monitora *fem.*
a ski instructor un monitor de esquí

instrument noun
el instrumento *masc.*
I play an instrument. Toco un instrumento.

intelligent adjective
inteligente *masc. & fem.*

to **intend** verb
to intend to do something pensar hacer algo

interest noun
(*hobby*) la afición *fem.*
My interests are football and swimming. Mis aficiones son el fútbol y la natación.

to **interest** verb
interesar
I'm not interested. No me interesa.
I'm interested in music. Me interesa la música.

LANGUAGE
To say 'you're interested in something' in Spanish, you say 'something interests you'.

interesting adjective
interesante *masc. & fem.*

international adjective
internacional *masc. & fem.*

Internet noun
Internet *masc. & fem.*
on the Internet en Internet
an Internet cafe un cibercafé

LANGUAGE
El or la are not used with 'Internet'.

to **interrupt** verb
interrumpir
Don't interrupt me! ¡No me interrumpas!

interval noun
(*in the cinema or theatre*) el intermedio *masc.*

into
1 en
I went into the classroom. Entré en la clase.
2 a
Get into the car. Sube al coche.
to translate something into Spanish traducir algo al español

to **introduce** verb
presentar
Are you going to introduce me to your friend? ¿Me presentas a tu amiga?

to **invent** verb
inventar

invention noun
el invento *masc.*

• *Languages and nationalities do not take a capital letter in Spanish.*

invisible adjective
invisible *masc. & fem.*

invitation noun
la invitación *fem.* (plural las **invitaciones**)

to invite verb
invitar

Ireland noun
Irlanda *fem.*
I live in Ireland. Vivo en Irlanda.

Irish adjective
irlandés *masc.*, irlandesa *fem.*
an Irish town una ciudad irlandesa
He's Irish. Es irlandés.
Irish people los irlandeses

Irish noun
1 (*language*) el irlandés *masc.*
She speaks Irish. Habla irlandés.
2 **the Irish** los irlandeses *masc. plural*

Irishman noun
el irlandés *masc.* (plural los **irlandeses**)

Irishwoman noun
la irlandesa *fem.*

iron noun
1 (*metal*) el hierro *masc.*
an iron bar una barra de hierro
2 (*for clothes*) la plancha *fem.*

to iron verb
planchar
I like ironing. Me gusta planchar.

ironing noun
to do the ironing planchar
an ironing board una tabla de planchar

is verb SEE be
He's in the kitchen. Está en la cocina.
She's tall. Es alta.

Islamic adjective
islámico *masc.*, islámica *fem.*

island noun
la isla *fem.*

isle noun
la isla *fem.*
the Isle of Man la Isla de Man
the Isle of Wight la Isla de Wight

it pronoun

1 (*not usually translated in Spanish*)
Do you like my shirt? It's red. ¿Te gusta mi camisa? Es roja.
Where's the umbrella? – It's in the car. ¿Dónde está el paraguas? – Está en el coche.
Who is it? – It's me. ¿Quién es? – Soy yo.
It's raining. Está lloviendo.
It's cold. Hace frío.
There's a book behind it. Hay un libro detrás.
2 (*after a verb, standing for a masculine noun*) lo
I have a pen. Do you want it? Tengo un bolígrafo. ¿Lo quieres?
It's my book. Bring it to me. Es mi libro. Tráemelo.

3 (*after a verb, standing for a feminine noun*) la
Here's the letter. I have read it. Aquí está la carta. La he leído.
The film is interesting. I want to see it. La película es interesante. Quiero verla.

• *The months of the year and days of the week do not take a capital letter in Spanish.*

4 (to it) **le**
The dog is hungry. I gave it a bone.
El perro tiene hambre. Le di un
hueso.
Give it a bone. Dale un hueso.
5 (talking about the time)
It's one o'clock. Es la una.
It's four o'clock. Son las cuatro.

> **LANGUAGE**
> With the time translate 'it is' by **es** for 'one
> o'clock' and by **son** for all other times.

IT noun
la **informática** fem.

Italian adjective
italiano masc., **italiana** fem.
She's Italian. Es italiana.

Italian noun
1 (language) el **italiano** masc.
He speaks Italian. Habla italiano.
2 (person) el **italiano** masc.,
la **italiana** fem.

Jj

jacket noun
1 la **chaqueta** fem.
2 a jacket potato una patata asada
(con la piel)

> **LANGUAGE**
> Word for word this means 'potato baked
> with the skin'.

jail noun
la **cárcel** fem.
in jail en la cárcel

jam noun
1 la **mermelada** fem.
strawberry jam la mermelada de
fresa

> **LANGUAGE**
> In Spanish **mermelada** is the same word
> for 'jam' and 'marmalade'.

2 a traffic jam un atasco

Italy noun
Italia fem.

to **itch** verb
picar
My arm itches. Me pica el brazo.

itchy adjective
This T-shirt is itchy. Esta camiseta
me pica.

its adjective
1 (before a singular noun) **su**
a dog with its bone un perro con su
hueso
2 (before a plural noun) **sus**
the town and its inhabitants
la ciudad y sus habitantes

itself pronoun
1 (with a reflexive verb) **se**
The cat's washing itself. El gato se
está lavando.
2 by itself solo masc., sola fem.

jammed adjective
(drawer, window, etc.) **atascado** masc.,
atascada fem.

January noun
enero masc.
I'm going to Spain in January.
Voy a España en enero.
**The plane leaves on Monday, the
ninth of January.** El avión sale el
lunes nueve de enero.

Japan noun
Japón masc.

Japanese adjective
japonés masc., **japonesa** fem.
Japanese food la comida japonesa

> **LANGUAGE**
> The masculine plural of **japonés** is
> **japoneses**.

• See the centre section for verb tables.

Japanese noun
1 (*language*) el japonés *masc.*
My sister speaks Japanese.
Mi hermana habla japonés.
2 **the Japanese** los japoneses *masc.*
plural

jar noun
el bote *masc.*
a jar of jam un bote de
mermelada

jealous adjective
celoso *masc.*, celosa *fem.*
My sister is jealous of me.
Mi hermana está celosa de mí.

jeans plural noun
los vaqueros *masc. plural*
I'm wearing jeans. Llevo
vaqueros.
a pair of jeans unos vaqueros

> **LANGUAGE**
> The Spanish word comes from **vaquero**,
> meaning 'cowboy'.

jelly noun
la gelatina *fem.*
There's jelly for dessert. De postre
hay gelatina.

jersey noun
1 el jersey *masc.* (plural los **jerseys** or
jerséis)
2 (*for football*) la camiseta *fem.*
a football jersey una camiseta de
fútbol

jewel noun
la joya *fem.*

jewellery noun
las joyas *fem. plural*
a jewellery shop una joyería

Jewish adjective
judío *masc.*, judía *fem.*

jigsaw puzzle noun
el rompecabezas *masc.* (plural los
rompecabezas)
I'm doing a jigsaw puzzle.
Estoy haciendo un
rompecabezas.

job
el trabajo *masc.*
My sister has found a job.
Mi hermana ha encontrado un
trabajo.
**Cleaning the house is a difficult
job.** Limpiar la casa es un trabajo
difícil.

jogging noun
el footing *masc.*
to go jogging hacer footing

join verb
1 (*a club etc.*) hacerse socio or socia
de
2 **to join in** participar

joke noun
1 (*something silly or funny*)
la broma *fem.*
It's a joke! ¡Es una broma!
2 (*a funny story*) el chiste *masc.*
I like telling jokes. Me gusta
contar chistes.

to joke verb
bromear
I'm joking! ¡Estoy bromeando!

journey noun
el viaje *masc.*
the bus journey el viaje en
autobús
Have a good journey! ¡Buen
viaje!

joy noun
la alegría *fem.*

a b c d e f g h i j k l m n o p q r s t u v w x y z

• *Use* el *and* uno *for masculine words and* la *and* una *for feminine words.*

a
b
c
d
e
f
g
h
i
j
k
l
m
n
o
p
q
r
s
t
u
v
w
x
y
z

joystick noun
(*for computer games*) el **mando** *masc.*

judge noun
el or la **juez** *masc. & fem.*

judo noun
el **judo** *masc.*
Do you do judo? ¿Haces judo?

🗝 **LANGUAGE**
The Spanish **judo** is pronounced with a 'j'
sound as in English.

jug noun
(*for water, wine, etc.*) la **jarra** *fem.*

to **juggle** verb
hacer malabarismos

juice noun
el **zumo** *masc.*
Do you want an orange juice?
¿Quieres zumo de naranja?

July noun
julio *masc.*
They're going to come in July. Van
a venir en julio.
It's the tenth of July. Es el diez de
julio.

to **jump** verb
saltar
Jump! ¡Salta!
to jump over a fence saltar una valla

jumper noun
el **jersey** *masc.* (plural los **jerseys** or
jerséis)

June noun
junio *masc.*

Kk

kangaroo noun
el **canguro** *masc.*

karate noun
el **kárate** *masc.*

My birthday is in June.
Mi cumpleaños es en junio.
I was born on the fifth of June.
Nací el cinco de junio,

jungle noun
la **selva** *fem.*

junior school noun
la **escuela primaria** *fem.*

 CULTURE
Spanish children go to the **escuela
primaria** from age 6 to 11.

just adverb
1 **justo**
just after my birthday justo
después de mi cumpleaños
just in time justo a tiempo
2 (*only*) **sólo**
I just have ten euros. Sólo tengo
diez euros.
3 **to have just done something**
acabar de hacer algo
I've just eaten. Acabo de
comer.

🗝 **LANGUAGE**
English = **to have just** eaten
I've just eaten.
Spanish = **acabar de** comer
Acabo de comer.

4 (*no translation*)
I'm just coming!
¡Ya voy!
Wait just a moment. Espera un
momento.

My brother does karate.
Mi hermano hace kárate.

keen adjective
entusiasmado *masc.*,
entusiasmada *fem.*

• *Languages and nationalities do not take a capital letter in Spanish.*

to **keep** verb
1 (a secret, something for somebody, etc.)
 guardar
 Can you keep my seat?
 ¿Me guardas el sitio?
 I keep my toys in a box. Guardo los
 juguetes en una caja.
2 (talking about something you don't have to
 give back) quedarse con
 You can keep this CD. Puedes
 quedarte con este CD.
3 (to carry on) seguir
 to keep doing something seguir
 haciendo algo
 I kept working. Seguí trabajando.
4 (to stay)
 Keep still! ¡Estate quieto!
 Keep quiet! (to one person) ¡Cállate!;
 (to more than one person) ¡Callaos!
 to keep fit mantenerse en
 forma

kennel noun
 la caseta fem.

kettle noun
 la tetera fem.

CULTURE
Electric kettles are not common in
Spain. Water is normally boiled in a
pan. The Spanish **tetera** also means
'teapot'.

key noun
1 la llave fem.
2 (on a computer or piano) la tecla fem.

keyboard noun
 el teclado masc.

kick noun
 la patada fem.

to **kick** verb
 dar una patada a
 He kicked me. Me ha dado una
 patada.

kid noun
1 (child) el niño masc., la niña fem.
 There are twenty kids in the class.
 Hay veinte niños en la clase.
2 (son or daughter) el hijo masc.,
 la hija fem.
 They have three kids. Tienen tres
 hijos.

to **kill** verb
 matar

kilo noun
 el kilo masc.
 four euros a kilo cuatro euros el
 kilo

kilometre noun
 el kilómetro masc.
 at fifty kilometres an hour
 a cincuenta kilómetros por hora

kind noun
 el tipo masc.
 What kind of bike do you have?
 ¿Qué tipo de bici tienes?
 all kinds of people todo tipo de
 personas

kind adjective
 amable masc. & fem.
 Ahmed is very kind to me. Ahmed
 es muy amable conmigo.

king noun
 el rey masc.

kingdom noun
 el reino masc.
 the United Kingdom el Reino
 Unido

kiss noun
 el beso masc.
 Give me a kiss. Dame un beso.

to **kiss** verb
1 besar
 She kissed me. Me besó.
2 (to kiss each other) besarse
 They're kissing. Se están besando.

a
b
c
d
e
f
g
h
i
j
k
l
m
n
o
p
q
r
s
t
u
v
w
x
y
z

• The months of the year and days of the week do not take a capital letter in Spanish.

kit noun
(*clothes etc.*) el **equipo** *masc.*
my PE kit mi equipo de gimnasia
my football kit mi ropa de fútbol

kitchen noun
la **cocina** *fem.*

kite noun
la **cometa** *fem.*
to fly a kite hacer volar una cometa

LANGUAGE
Do you think a kite looks like a comet? The Spanish words for both are the same but the genders are different – 'comet' is masculine: **el cometa**.

kitten noun
el **gatito** *masc.*, la **gatita** *fem.*

knee noun
la **rodilla** *fem.*

to **kneel** verb
ponerse de rodillas
Kneel down! ¡Ponte de rodillas!
I'm kneeling. Estoy de rodillas.

knickers plural noun
las **bragas** *fem. plural*

knife noun
el **cuchillo** *masc.*

to **knit** verb
hacer punto
I like knitting. Me gusta hacer punto.

knob noun
1 (*on a door etc.*) el **pomo** *masc.*
2 (*on a radio etc.*) el **botón** *masc.* (plural los **botones**)

knock noun
el **golpe** *masc.*
a knock on the door un golpe en la puerta
I got a knock on my head. Me di un golpe en la cabeza.

to **knock** verb
1 (*to hit*) **dar se un golpe en**
I knocked my head. Me di un golpe en la cabeza.
2 (*on a door*) **llamar**
Somebody's knocking on the door. Alguien está llamando a la puerta.
3 **to knock somebody down** (*in a road accident*) atropellar a alguien
to knock something over (*a bottle, glass, ink, etc.*) tirar algo

knot noun
el **nudo** *masc.*
to tie a knot in something hacer un nudo en algo

to **know** verb
1 **saber**
Do you know where she is? ¿Sabes dónde está?
I know. Ya lo sé.
I don't know. No lo sé.
to know how to do something saber hacer algo
Do you know how to swim? ¿Sabes nadar?
2 **conocer**
I know your brother. Conozco a tu hermano.
Andrew knows Barcelona well. Andrew conoce bien Barcelona.

LANGUAGE
As a general guide use **saber** when it is followed by words like 'that', 'if', 'where', or 'how to'. Use **conocer** when you are talking about a person or place, or things like a book, film, or name.

knowledge noun
(*of a subject*) los **conocimientos** *masc. plural*

Koran noun
el **Corán** *masc.*

• *See the centre section for verb tables.*

Ll

label noun
la **etiqueta** *fem.*

lace noun
(*for a shoe*) el **cordón** *masc.* (plural los **cordones**)
to do up your laces atarse los cordones

ladder noun
la **escalera (de mano)** *fem.*
to climb a ladder subirse a una escalera

> **LANGUAGE**
> Word for word **escalera de mano** means 'hand stairs'.

ladies noun
(*toilets*) los **servicios de señoras** *masc. plural*

lady noun
la **señora** *fem.*
a young lady una señorita

ladybird noun
la **mariquita** *fem.*

lake noun
el **lago** *masc.*

lamb noun
el **cordero** *masc.*
a lamb chop una chuleta de cordero

lamp noun
la **lámpara** *fem.*

lamp-post noun
la **farola** *fem.*

land noun
la **tierra** *fem.*

to **land** verb
aterrizar
The plane has landed. El avión ha aterrizado.

lane noun
1 (*in the countryside*) el **camino** *masc.*
2 (*part of a road*) el **carril** *masc.*

language noun
el **idioma** *masc.*
a foreign language un idioma extranjero

> **LANGUAGE**
> Be careful: **idioma** ends in an **-a** but it is not a feminine noun.

lap noun
las **rodillas** *fem. plural*
Sit on my lap. Siéntate en mis rodillas.

laptop noun
el **ordenador portátil** *masc.*

large adjective
grande *masc. & fem.*
a large house una casa grande

> **LANGUAGE**
> You can also use **grande** before the noun, but before a singular noun it becomes **gran**.

a large number of ... un gran número de ...

> ⚠ **FALSE FRIEND**
> **large = grande** (*not* largo)

last adjective & pronoun
1 **último** *masc.*, **última** *fem.*
the last time la última vez
I came last. (*in the race*) Llegué el último.
Are you the last? ¿Eres la última?
2 **pasado** *masc.*, **pasada** *fem.*
last week la semana pasada
last Monday el lunes pasado
last night anoche

a
b
c
d
e
f
g
h
i
j
k
l
m
n
o
p
q
r
s
t
u
v
w
x
y
z

• *Use* el *and* uno *for masculine words and* la *and* una *for feminine words.*

last → least

last adverb
1 (last of all) **por último**
I did my homework last. Por último hice los deberes.
2 (talking about the last time) **por última vez**
When did you see Jon last? ¿Cuándo viste a Jon por última vez?
3 **at last!** ¡por fin!

to **last** verb
durar
The holidays last three weeks. Las vacaciones duran tres semanas.

late adjective & adverb
tarde
You're late. Llegas tarde.
I'm late. Voy a llegar tarde.
I'm going to be late for school. Voy a llegar tarde al colegio.
We arrived late. Llegamos tarde.
It's late. Es tarde.
It's getting late. Se está haciendo tarde.

lately adverb
últimamente

later adverb
más tarde
He's coming later. Va a llegar más tarde.
See you later! ¡Hasta luego!

latest adjective
último masc., **última** fem.
the latest Disney film la última película de Disney

to **laugh** verb
1 **reírse**
I laughed a lot. Me reí mucho.
Don't laugh. No te rías.
2 **reír**
She makes me laugh. Me hace reír.

lawyer noun
el **abogado** masc., la **abogada** fem.
My mum's a lawyer. Mi madre es abogada.

to **lay** verb
to lay the table poner la mesa

lazy adjective
perezoso masc., **perezosa** fem.
I'm very lazy. Soy muy perezoso.

lead noun
to be in the lead (in a race or game) ir en cabeza

to **lead** verb
to be leading (in a match etc.) ir ganando
Our team is leading by two goals. Nuestro equipo va ganando por dos goles.

leader noun
1 (of a group or gang) el **jefe** masc., la **jefa** fem.
2 (in a race etc.) el or la **líder** masc. & fem.

leaf noun
la **hoja** fem.

to **lean** verb
1 **apoyar**
Lean your bike against the wall. Apoya la bici en la pared.
I'm leaning against the wall. Estoy apoyado en la pared.
2 **to lean out of the window** asomarse por la ventana
to lean over inclinarse

to **learn** verb
aprender
I'm learning Spanish. Estoy aprendiendo español.
Samuel is learning to swim. Samuel está aprendiendo a nadar.

least adverb, adjective & pronoun
1 **menos**
It's the colour I like least. Es el color que menos me gusta.
the least interesting book el libro menos interesante
It's Jill who has the least ice cream. Jill es la que menos helado tiene.
I have the least. Yo soy el que menos tengo.

• Languages and nationalities do not take a capital letter in Spanish.

318

2 at least por lo menos
I have at least ten books. Tengo por lo menos diez libros.

leather noun
el **cuero** *masc.*
a leather jacket una chaqueta de cuero

to **leave** verb
1 (*to go away*) **irse**
I'm leaving tomorrow. Me voy mañana.
We left Scotland on Saturday. Nos fuimos de Escocia el sábado.
2 (*to go out*) **salir**
The train leaves at five. El tren sale a las cinco.
I leave the house at eight. Salgo de casa a las ocho.
3 dejar
Leave the book on the table. Deja el libro en la mesa.
Leave me alone! ¡Déjame en paz!
4 (*to forget*) **dejarse**
I left my pen at your house. Me dejé el bolígrafo en tu casa.

left adjective
1 izquierdo *masc.*, **izquierda** *fem.*
my left hand mi mano izquierda
2 (*left over*) **to be left** quedar
I have two chocolates left. Me quedan dos bombones.
There's nothing left. No queda nada.

left noun & adverb
on the left a la izquierda
Our school is on the left. Nuestro colegio está a la izquierda.
We drive on the left. Se conduce por la izquierda.
Turn left. Gira a la izquierda.

left-handed adjective
zurdo *masc.*, **zurda** *fem.*
Daniel is left-handed. Daniel es zurdo.

left-luggage office noun
la **consigna** *fem.*

leg noun
1 (*of a person*) la **pierna** *fem.*
2 (*of an animal*) la **pata** *fem.*
3 (*in cooking*) **a chicken leg** un muslo de pollo

leisure centre noun
el **polideportivo** *masc.*

lemon noun
el **limón** *masc.* (plural los **limones**)
a lemon tea un té con limón

lemonade noun
la **gaseosa** *fem.*

to **lend** verb
dejar
I lent a book to my friend. Le dejé un libro a mi amiga.
Can you lend me your pen? ¿Puedes dejarme el boli?

length noun
la **longitud** *fem.*

leopard noun
el **leopardo** *masc.*

less adverb, adjective & pronoun
1 menos
I eat less than you. Como menos que tú.
My book is less interesting than yours. Mi libro es menos interesante que el tuyo.
Less milk, please. Menos leche, por favor.
2 less than (*with numbers*) menos de
less than three hours menos de tres horas

lesson noun
1 la **clase** *fem.*
We have a Spanish lesson at ten. Tenemos clase de español a las diez.
2 (*in a book*) la **lección** *fem.* (plural las **lecciones**)
Lesson two is hard. La lección dos es difícil.

• *The months of the year and days of the week do not take a capital letter in Spanish.*

to let verb
1 dejar
Let me speak. Déjame hablar.
They don't let me watch TV. No me dejan ver la tele.
Can you let me in? ¿Me dejas entrar?
Let go of me! ¡Suéltame!
2 (*making suggestions*)
Let's ... Vamos a ...
Let's play. Vamos a jugar.
Let's go! ¡Vámonos!

letter noun
1 la **carta** *fem.*
I'm writing a letter. Estoy escribiendo una carta.
2 (*of the alphabet*) la **letra** *fem.*
the letter D la letra D

letter box noun
el **buzón** *masc.* (plural los **buzones**)

lettuce noun
la **lechuga** *fem.*

level noun
el **nivel** *masc.*

liar noun
el **mentiroso** *masc.*,
la **mentirosa** *fem.*

library noun
la **biblioteca** *fem.*

⚠ **FALSE FRIEND**
a library = una biblioteca (*not* una librería)

licence noun
el **permiso** *masc.*
a driving licence un permiso de conducir

to lick verb
lamer

lid noun
la **tapa** *fem.*

lie noun
la **mentira** *fem.*
Don't tell lies! ¡No digas mentiras!

to lie verb
1 (*to tell lies*) **mentir**
Ana never lies. Ana nunca miente.
2 (*to be flat*) **echarse**
Lie down on the sofa. Échate en el sofá.

life noun
la **vida** *fem.*
all my life toda mi vida

lifebelt noun
el **salvavidas** *masc.* (plural los **salvavidas**)

lift noun
el **ascensor** *masc.*
Let's get the lift. Vamos a coger el ascensor.

to lift verb
levantar
I can't lift this case. No puedo levantar esta maleta.

light noun
la **luz** *fem.*
Turn on the light. Enciende la luz.
Turn off the light Apaga la luz

light adjective
1 (*not heavy*) **ligero** *masc.*, **ligera** *fem.*
a light backpack una mochila ligera
2 (*describing colours*) **claro** *masc.*, **clara** *fem.*
a light brown skirt una falda marrón claro

🔑 **LANGUAGE**
When **claro** follows the name of a colour (e.g. **verde**, **rojo**), use **claro** and the colour word in the masculine singular form only.

3 (*talking about daylight*)
It's light. Es de día.
It gets light at five. Se hace de día a las cinco.

to light verb
(*the oven, a match, a candle, etc.*)
encender
to light a fire encender un fuego

• *See the centre section for verb tables.*

light bulb noun
la **bombilla** fem.

lighthouse noun
el **faro** masc.

lightning noun
los **relámpagos** masc. plural
a flash of lightning un relámpago

to like verb
1 I like jam. Me gusta la mermelada.
I like it. Me gusta.
I don't like cats. No me gustan los gatos.
David likes Emma. A David le gusta Emma.
Do you like reading? ¿Te gusta leer?

> **LANGUAGE**
> In Spanish **gustar** means 'to please' so the order of the words in the Spanish sentence is different, e.g. 'I like jam' is, word for word, 'Jam pleases me'.

2 (to want) **querer**
I would like ... Quiero ...
I'd like a glass of water, please. Quiero un vaso de agua, por favor.
Would you like ...? ¿Quiere usted ...?, ¿Quieres ...?
What would you like, sir? ¿Qué quiere usted, señor?
What would you like to drink, dad? ¿Qué quieres beber, papá?
if you like si quieres

like preposition
1 **como**
a bike like this una bici como ésta
2 What's it like? ¿Cómo es?
What's your house like? ¿Cómo es tu casa?
What's the weather like? ¿Qué tiempo hace?

> **LANGUAGE**
> When **como** is used in questions you put an accent on it: **cómo**.

likely adjective
probable masc. & fem.

• See the centre section for verb tables.

line noun
1 la **línea** fem.
a straight line una línea recta
2 (of people or things) la **fila** fem.
to get into line ponerse en fila

to line up verb
(in the playground etc.) **ponerse en fila**

link noun
el **enlace** masc.
Click on the link. Haz clic en el enlace.

lion noun
el **león** masc. (plural los **leones**)

lip noun
el **labio** masc.

lipstick noun
el **pintalabios** masc. (plural los **pintalabios**)
My sister wears lipstick. Mi hermana se pinta los labios.

> **LANGUAGE**
> Word for word **pintalabios** means 'paints lips'.

liquid noun
el **líquido** masc.

list noun
la **lista** fem.

to listen verb
escuchar
Listen! ¡Escucha!
I like to listen to the radio. Me gusta escuchar la radio.
Listen to me. Escúchame.

> **LANGUAGE**
> English = to listen to something/ somebody
> Spanish = **escuchar** algo/a alguien

literature noun
la **literatura** fem.

litre noun
el **litro** masc.

a b c d e f g h i j k l m n o p q r s t u v w x y z

litter noun
(*papers, rubbish*) la basura *fem.*
a litter bin una papelera

little adjective, pronoun & adverb
1 (*not big*) pequeño *masc.*,
pequeña *fem.*
a little house una casa pequeña
my little sister mi hermana
pequeña
2 (*not much*) poco *masc.*, poca *fem.*
very little money muy poco dinero
I eat very little. Como muy poco.
3 **a little** un poco
**Do you speak Spanish? – Just a
little.** ¿Hablas español? – Un poco.
Would you like a little more?
¿Quieres un poco más?

to **live** verb
vivir
I live in Birmingham. Vivo en
Birmingham.
Where do you live? ¿Dónde vives?
**'... and they lived happily ever
after'.** (*in stories*) '... y fueron felices y
comieron perdices'.

> 🔑 **LANGUAGE**
> Word for word the Spanish means 'they
> were happy and ate partridges'.

lively adjective
(*party, street, person, etc.*)
animado *masc.*, animada *fem.*

living room noun
el salón *masc.* (plural los **salones**)

lizard noun
1 (*big*) el lagarto *masc.*
2 (*small*) la lagartija *fem.*

load noun
loads of un montón de
I have loads of things to do. Tengo
un montón de cosas que hacer.

loaf noun
el pan *masc.*
a loaf of bread un pan

lock noun
la cerradura *fem.*

to **lock** verb
cerrar con llave
The door is locked. La puerta está
cerrada con llave.

locker noun
el armario *masc.*

to **log off** verb
1 (*from a computer program*) salir
2 (*from the Internet*) desconectar

to **log on** verb
1 (*to a computer program*) entrar
2 (*to the Internet*) conectarse a
Internet

lollipop noun
el chupachups® *masc.*,
la piruleta *fem.*

lolly noun
(*ice lolly*) el polo *masc.*

London noun
Londres *masc.*
I was born in London. Nací en
Londres.

lonely adjective
solo *masc.*, sola *fem.*
I feel lonely. Me siento solo.

long adjective & adverb
1 largo *masc.*, larga *fem.*
I have long hair. Tengo el pelo
largo.
2 **a long time** mucho tiempo
I've been waiting a long time.
Llevo mucho tiempo esperando.
I didn't stay long. No me quedé
mucho tiempo.
I won't be long. No tardo mucho.
3 **a long way** lejos
Is it a long way? ¿Está lejos?
4 **how long?** ¿cuánto tiempo?
How long have you been waiting?
¿Cuánto tiempo llevas esperando?
The journey is three hours long.
El viaje dura tres horas.

> 🔑 **LANGUAGE**
> Word for word this means 'The journey
> lasts three hours'.

• Use el and uno for masculine words and la and una for feminine words.

English Spanish

a
b
c
d
e
f
g
h
i
j
k
l
m
n
o
p
q
r
s
t
u
v
w
x
y
z

loo noun
el **baño** *masc.*

look noun
to have a look mirar
Have a look at this picture. Mira
este dibujo.

to **look** verb
1 mirar
Look! ¡Mira!
I'm looking at the photos. Estoy
mirando las fotos.
Look at me! ¡Mírame!

> **LANGUAGE**
> English = **to look at** something/
> somebody
> Spanish = **mirar** algo/a alguien

2 (*followed by an adjective*) **parecer**
It looks easy. Parece fácil.
3 to look like parecerse a
You look like your dad. Te pareces
a tu padre.

to **look after** cuidar
**My sister looks after the
children.** Mi hermana cuida a los
niños.

to **look for** buscar
I'm looking for my book. Estoy
buscando mi libro.

to **look out** tener cuidado
Look out! ¡Cuidado!

to **look up** buscar
Look it up in the dictionary.
Búscalo en el diccionario.

loose adjective
1 (*clothes*) **ancho** *masc.*, **ancha** *fem.*
These jeans are loose on me. Estos
vaqueros me están anchos.
2 I have a loose tooth. Se me mueve
un diente.

> **LANGUAGE**
> Word for word the Spanish means 'A tooth
> is moving'!

lorry noun
el **camión** *masc.* (plural los
camiones)
a lorry driver un camionero
masc., una camionera *fem.*
My dad's a lorry driver. Mi padre
es camionero.

to **lose** verb
perder
I've lost my pen. He perdido el
boli.

lost adjective
perdido *masc.*, **perdida** *fem.*
I'm lost. Estoy perdido.
to get lost perderse
I got lost. Me perdí.
lost property los objetos
perdidos

lot noun
1 a lot mucho
I read a lot. Leo mucho.
a lot of mucho *masc.*, mucha *fem.*
a lot of people mucha gente
I have a lot of CDs. Tengo muchos
CDs.
2 quite a lot bastante
I eat quite a lot. Como bastante.
quite a lot of bastante *masc. & fem.*
I have quite a lot of books. Tengo
bastantes libros.

lottery noun
la **lotería** *fem.*
to play the lottery jugar a la
lotería
I've won the lottery. Me ha tocado
la lotería.

loud adjective & adverb
fuerte *masc. & fem.*
a loud noise un ruido fuerte
The radio's too loud. La radio está
muy fuerte.
Speak louder. Habla más fuerte.
in a loud voice en voz alta

a
b
c
d
e
f
g
h
i
j
k
l
m
n
o
p
q
r
s
t
u
v
w
x
y
z

• *Languages and nationalities do not take a capital letter in Spanish.*

a
b
c
d
e
f
g
h
i
j
k
l
m
n
o
p
q
r
s
t
u
v
w
x
y
z

lounge noun
el salón *masc.* (plural los **salones**)

love noun
el amor *masc.*
a love story una historia de amor
to be in love with somebody estar enamorado de alguien
They're in love. Están enamorados.
Love, Carol. (*in a letter*) Con mucho cariño, Carol., Un abrazo, Carol.

to **love** verb
1 (*talking about being in love with somebody*) querer
He loves her. La quiere.
2 (*talking about liking something very much*) **I love Madrid.** Me encanta Madrid.
I love apples. Me encantan las manzanas.
Sally loves chocolate. A Sally le encanta el chocolate.
I love to read. Me encanta leer.

> 🔑 **LANGUAGE**
> **Encantar** means 'to please very much' so the order of the words in the Spanish sentence is different, e.g. 'I love Madrid' is, word for word, 'Madrid pleases me very much'.

lovely adjective
1 (*beautiful*) precioso *masc.*, preciosa *fem.*
a lovely dress un vestido precioso
2 (*very good*) buenísimo *masc.*, buenísima *fem.*
The weather's lovely. Hace un tiempo buenísimo.
I had a lovely time. Lo pasé muy bien.

3 (*adorable*) encantador *masc.*, encantadora *fem.*
They are lovely girls. Son unas niñas encantadoras.

low adjective
bajo *masc.*, baja *fem.*
a low ceiling un techo bajo

luck noun
la suerte *fem.*
Good luck! ¡Buena suerte!
Bad luck! ¡Qué mala suerte!
It brings me luck. Me trae suerte.

lucky adjective
1 (*talking about people*)
to be lucky tener suerte
I'm always lucky. Siempre tengo suerte.
2 (*talking about things or numbers*)
The number seven is lucky. El número siete trae suerte.
my lucky number mi número de la suerte

luggage noun
el equipaje *masc.*
I have lots of luggage. Tengo mucho equipaje.

lunch noun
la comida *fem.*
My dad prepares lunch. Mi padre prepara la comida.
What's for lunch? ¿Qué hay para comer?
to have lunch comer
a lunch box una fiambrera

lunchtime noun
la hora de comer *fem.*

luxury noun
el lujo *masc.*
a luxury car un coche de lujo

• *The months of the year and days of the week do not take a capital letter in Spanish.*

324

Mm

macaroni noun
los **macarrones** *masc. plural*

> ⚷ **LANGUAGE**
> English = **macaroni** is singular
> Spanish = **los macarrones** is plural

machine noun
la **máquina** *fem.*

mad adjective
1 (*crazy*) **loco** *masc.*, **loca** *fem.*
You're mad! ¡Estás loco!
2 (*angry*) **enfadado** *masc.*,
enfadada *fem.*
I'm mad at you. Estoy enfadada
contigo.
3 **I'm mad about bikes.** Me chiflan
las bicis.
He's mad about football. Le chifla
el fútbol.

> ⚷ **LANGUAGE**
> **Chiflar** means 'to please very much' so
> the order of the words in the Spanish
> sentence is different.

madam noun
señora *fem.*
Yes, madam. Sí, señora.

made verb SEE **make**
I made a lot of noise. Hice mucho
ruido.
She has made a cake. Ha hecho un
pastel.

magazine noun
la **revista** *fem.*

magic adjective
mágico *masc.*, **mágica** *fem.*
a magic wand una varita mágica
a magic trick un truco de magia

magic noun
la **magia** *fem.*

• *See the centre section for verb tables.*

magician noun
el **mago** *masc.*, la **maga** *fem.*

magnet noun
el **imán** *masc.* (plural los **imanes**)

magnifying glass noun
la **lupa** *fem.*

mail noun
el **correo** *masc.*
Is there any mail? ¿Hay correo?

to **mail** verb
mandar por correo
Mail the parcel to me. Mándame el
paquete por correo.

mailbox noun
(*for getting email*) el **buzón** *masc.*
(plural los **buzones**)

main adjective
principal *masc. & fem.*
the main road la carretera
principal
That's the main thing. Eso es lo
principal.

make noun
la **marca** *fem.*
What make is your computer?
¿De qué marca es tu ordenador?

to **make** verb
1 **hacer**
I always make the bed. Siempre
hago la cama.
You make me happy. Tú me haces
feliz.
He makes me laugh. Me hace reír.
I've made some sandwiches. He
hecho bocadillos.
2 (*to build*) **fabricar**
to make cars fabricar coches
'Made in Spain.' 'Fabricado en
España.'

a b c d e f g h i j k l **m** n o p q r s t u v w x y z

325

make-up → map

3 (*to get ready*) **preparar**
My mum's making lunch. Mi madre está preparando la comida.
4 (*to earn*) **ganar**
My uncle makes a lot of money. Mi tío gana mucho dinero.
5 (*with some adjectives: nervous, sad, furious, etc.*) **poner**
It makes me sad. Eso me pone triste.
6 (*with hungry, thirsty, sleepy*) **dar**
It makes me hungry. Me da hambre.
It makes me sleepy. Me da sueño.
7 **ser**
Two and three make five. Dos y tres son cinco.
8 to make up inventarse
You've made up the story! ¡Te has inventado la historia!

make-up noun
el **maquillaje** *masc.*
She doesn't wear make-up. No lleva maquillaje.

male noun
el **macho** *masc.*

male adjective
macho *masc. & fem.*
a male hamster un hámster macho

mall noun
shopping mall el centro comercial *masc.*

man noun
el **hombre** *masc.*
a man and a woman un hombre y una mujer
a young man un joven
an old man un anciano, un viejo

LANGUAGE
Anciano is a polite word for 'old man'.

manage verb
to manage to do something poder hacer algo
I've managed to open the window. He podido abrir la ventana.

manager noun
1 (*of a company*) el **director** *masc.*, la **directora** *fem.*
2 (*of a shop or restaurant*) el **encargado** *masc.*, la **encargada** *fem.*

manners plural noun
los **modales** *masc. plural*
to have good manners tener buenos modales
bad manners malos modales

many adjective & pronoun
1 **muchos** *masc. plural*, **muchas** *fem. plural*
I don't have many books. No tengo muchos libros.
many people mucha gente
Do you have many? ¿Tienes muchos?
2 how many? ¿cuántos? *masc. plural*, ¿cuántas? *fem. plural*
How many times have you seen the film? ¿Cuántas veces has visto la película?
3 so many tantos *masc. plural*, tantas *fem. plural*
I've read so many books! ¡He leído tantos libros!
4 too many demasiados *masc. plural*, demasiadas *fem. plural*
There are too many apples. Hay demasiadas manzanas.
too many people demasiada gente
That's too many. Son demasiados.

map noun
1 (*of a country*) el **mapa** *masc.*
a map of Spain un mapa de España
2 (*of a town*) el **plano** *masc.*
a map of Madrid un plano de Madrid

LANGUAGE
Be careful: **mapa** ends in an -a but it is not a feminine noun.

• Use **el** and **uno** for masculine words and **la** and **una** for feminine words.

326

marathon noun
el or la maratón *masc. & fem.* (plural
los **maratones**)
to run in a marathon correr una
maratón

marble noun
la canica *fem.*
to play marbles jugar a las
canicas

March noun
marzo *masc.*
**My grandparents are coming in
March.** Los abuelos llegan en
marzo.
**We leave on Sunday, the fourth of
March.** Salimos el domingo cuatro
de marzo.

margarine noun
la margarina *fem.*

margin noun
el margen *masc.*
Don't write in the margin.
No escribas en el margen.

mark noun
1 (*in school subjects*) la nota *fem.*
I always get good marks. Siempre
saco buenas notas.
2 (*stain*) la mancha *fem.*
an ink mark una mancha de
tinta
3 (*from fingers, on the body, etc.*) la marca
fem.

to **mark** verb
1 (*homework etc.*) corregir
Have they marked the exercises?
¿Han corregido los ejercicios?
2 (*to show*) señalar
Mark with a cross. Señala con una
cruz.

market noun
el mercado *masc.*

marmalade noun
la mermelada (de naranja) *fem.*

marriage noun
el matrimonio *masc.*

married adjective
casado *masc.*, casada *fem.*
Are they married? ¿Están casados?
to get married casarse
**They're getting married
tomorrow.** Se casan mañana.

to **marry** verb
casarse con
She has married an Englishman.
Se ha casado con un inglés.

Martian noun
el marciano *masc.*,
la marciana *fem.*

masculine adjective
masculino *masc.*, masculina *fem.*

mashed potatoes plural noun
el puré de patatas *masc.*

mask noun
la máscara *fem.*

mass noun
1 (*church service*) la misa *fem.*
to go to mass ir a misa
2 **masses of** un montón de
Angela has masses of friends.
Angela tiene un montón de
amigas.

massive adjective
enorme *masc. & fem.*

mat noun
1 la alfombrilla *fem.*
2 (*doormat*) el felpudo *masc.*

match noun
1 la cerilla *fem.*
a box of matches una caja de
cerillas
2 (*a team game*) el partido *masc.*
a football match un partido de
fútbol

a
b
c
d
e
f
g
h
i
j
k
l
m
n
o
p
q
r
s
t
u
v
w
x
y
z

• *Languages and nationalities do not take a capital letter in Spanish.*

English Spanish

a
b
c
d
e
f
g
h
i
j
k
l
m
n
o
p
q
r
s
t
u
v
w
x
y
z

to **match** verb
1 (*talking about clothes etc.*) **pegar con**
This blouse doesn't match the skirt. Esta blusa no pega con la falda.
These colours don't match. Estos colores no pegan.
2 (*to find similar things*)
Match the words and the pictures. Encuentra la palabra que corresponda a cada dibujo.

mate noun
el **amigo** *masc.*, la **amiga** *fem.*

material noun
(*cloth*) la **tela** *fem.*

mathematics noun
las **matemáticas** *fem. plural*

maths noun
las **matemáticas** *fem. plural*

matter noun
What's the matter? ¿Qué pasa?
What's the matter with you? ¿Qué te pasa?
There's something the matter with this bike. A esta bici le pasa algo.

to **matter** verb
It doesn't matter. No importa.

mattress noun
el **colchón** *masc.* (plural los **colchones**)

maximum noun
el **máximo** *masc.*

maximum adjective
máximo *masc.*, **máxima** *fem.*

may verb
(*asking for permission*) **poder**
May I open the window? ¿Puedo abrir la ventana?

May noun
mayo *masc.*
We're going on holiday in May. Nos vamos de vacaciones en mayo.

Come to my house on the tenth of May. Ven a mi casa el diez de mayo.
May Day el uno de mayo

 CULTURE
El uno de mayo is a public holiday.

maybe adverb
quizás, **a lo mejor**
Maybe he's left. Quizás se ha ido., A lo mejor se ha ido.
Maybe not. Quizás no.

mayonnaise noun
la **mayonesa** *fem.*

mayor noun
el **alcalde** *masc.*, la **alcaldesa** *fem.*

maze noun
el **laberinto** *masc.*

me pronoun
1 (*after a verb*) **me**
She knows me. Me conoce.
Are they looking for me? ¿Me están buscando?

⚷ **LANGUAGE**
With commands and infinitives **me** is joined with the verb to make one word.

Call me. Llámame.
Can you see me? ¿Puedes verme?
2 (*to me*) **me**
Hassan has sent a letter to me. Hassan me ha mandado una carta.
Give me the pen. Dame el bolígrafo.
Give it to me. Dámelo.
3 (*after a preposition*) **mí**
without me sin mí
behind me detrás de mí
with me conmigo

⚷ **LANGUAGE**
Remember the special word **conmigo** to translate 'with me'; never say **con mí**.

4 (*after 'than' and the verb 'to be'*) **yo**
She's taller than me. Es más alta que yo.
It's me. Soy yo.

• *The months of the year and days of the week do not take a capital letter in Spanish.*

meal noun
la comida *fem.*
I have three meals a day. Hago tres comidas al día.
I've had a good meal. He comido bien.

to **mean** verb
1 querer decir
What does 'lápiz' mean? ¿Qué quiere decir 'lápiz'?
What do you mean? ¿Qué quieres decir?

⚷ **LANGUAGE**
Word for word **querer decir** means 'want to say'.

2 to mean to do something querer hacer algo
I didn't mean to break it. No quería romperlo.

⚷ **LANGUAGE**
Word for word **querer hacer** means 'want to do'.

mean adjective
1 (*with money*) tacaño *masc.*, tacaña *fem.*
He's very mean. Es muy tacaño.
2 (*nasty*) malo *masc.*, mala *fem.*
Norman is mean to his sister. Norman es malo con su hermana.

meaning noun
el significado *masc.*

measles noun
el sarampión *masc.*

to **measure** verb
medir

meat noun
la carne *fem.*
Do you eat meat? ¿Comes carne?

mechanic noun
el mecánico *masc.*, la mecánica *fem.*
My dad's a mechanic. Mi padre es mecánico.

• *See the centre section for verb tables.*

medal noun
la medalla *fem.*
a gold medal una medalla de oro

medical room noun
la enfermería *fem.*

medicine noun
el medicamento *masc.*, la medicina *fem.*
Take the medicine. Toma la medicina., Toma el medicamento.

Mediterranean noun
the Mediterranean el Mediterráneo

medium adjective
mediano *masc.*, mediana *fem.*
of medium height de estatura mediana

to **meet** verb
1 (*by chance*) encontrarse con
I met her in the street. Me encontré con ella en la calle.
We met in the supermarket. Nos encontramos en el supermercado.
2 (*to plan to meet*) quedar con
I'm meeting my friends in the library. He quedado con mis amigos en la biblioteca.
Where shall we meet? ¿Dónde quedamos?
3 (*to go and get*) recoger
My dad's meeting me at the airport. Mi padre va a recogerme al aeropuerto.
4 (*to meet for the first time*) conocer
I met Juan two years ago. Conocí a Juan hace dos años.

meeting noun
la reunión *fem.* (plural las **reuniones**)

melon noun
el melón *masc.* (plural los **melones**)

to **melt** verb
derretirse
My ice cream is melting. Mi helado se derrite.

a b c d e f g h i j k l m n o p q r s t u v w x y z

member noun
1 el miembro masc.
2 (of a club) el socio masc., la socia fem.

to **memorize** verb
aprender de memoria

memory noun
1 la memoria fem.
I have a good memory. Tengo buena memoria.
2 (something you remember) el recuerdo masc.
I have good memories of my school. Tengo buenos recuerdos de mi colegio.

men plural noun
los hombres masc. plural

to **mend** verb
arreglar

menu noun
el menú masc. (plural los **menús**)

mermaid noun
la sirena fem.

merry adjective
Merry Christmas! ¡Feliz Navidad!

merry-go-round noun
el tiovivo masc.

mess noun
el desorden masc.
Tidy up this mess! ¡Arregla este desorden!
The house is in a mess. La casa está desordenada.

to **mess up** verb
(papers, books, house, etc.) desordenar
You've messed up the room! ¡Has desordenado la habitación!

message noun
el mensaje masc.
a text message un mensaje de texto

messy adjective
(room, house, etc.)
desordenado masc.,
desordenada fem.

metal noun
el metal masc.
a metal box una caja de metal

metre noun
el metro masc.

mice plural noun
los ratones masc. plural

microphone noun
el micrófono masc.

microscope noun
el microscopio masc.

microwave noun
el microondas masc. (plural los **microondas**)

midday noun
el mediodía masc.
at midday a mediodía

middle noun
1 el medio masc.
in the middle of the room en medio de la habitación
the middle drawer el cajón de en medio
a middle name un segundo nombre
2 (talking about when something happens) la mitad fem.
in the middle of the night en mitad de la noche

midnight noun
la medianoche fem.
at midnight a medianoche

might verb
She might have gone out. Quizás ha salido.
Can you come? – I might. ¿Puedes venir? – Quizás.

mild adjective
The weather's mild. No hace frío.

• Use el and uno for masculine words and la and una for feminine words.

mile noun
I live three miles away. Vivo a cinco kilómetros de aquí.
We've walked for miles. Hemos andado muchos kilómetros.

 CULTURE
In Spain they use kilometres for distances: one mile is just over one and a half kilometres.

milk noun
la leche *fem.*
a glass of milk un vaso de leche
a milk shake un batido

milkman noun
el lechero *masc.*

million noun
el millón *masc.*
two million dos millones
a million people un millón de personas

🔑 **LANGUAGE**
English = **a million** + noun
Spanish = **un millón de** + noun

millionaire noun
el millonario *masc.*,
la millonaria *fem.*
He's a millionaire. Es millonario.

mind noun
I've changed my mind. He cambiado de opinión.
to make up your mind decidirse
Make up your mind! ¡Decídete!

to **mind** verb
1 (*to look after*) cuidar
Can you mind the baby? ¿Puedes cuidar al niño?
2 **do you mind ...?** ¿le importa ...?
Do you mind if I close the window? ¿Le importa si cierro la ventana?
I don't mind. No me importa.
Never mind! ¡No importa!
3 (*to watch out*)
Mind your head! ¡Cuidado con la cabeza!

mine pronoun
1 (*with a singular noun*) el mío *masc.*,
la mía *fem.*
Your mum is younger than mine. Tu madre es más joven que la mía.
2 (*with a plural noun*) los míos *masc. plural*,
las mías *fem. plural*
her toys and mine sus juguetes y los míos
3 (*following 'is'*) mío *masc.*, mía *fem.*
This CD is mine. Este CD es mío.
This bike is mine. Esta bici es mía.
4 (*following 'are'*) míos *masc. plural*,
mías *fem. plural*
These books are mine. Estos libros son míos.

mine noun
la mina *fem.*
My dad works in a mine. Mi padre trabaja en una mina.

mineral water noun
el agua mineral *fem.*

🔑 **LANGUAGE**
Be careful: you use **el** with **agua** but it is not a masculine noun.

minibus noun
el microbús *masc.* (plural los microbuses)

minimum noun
el mínimo *masc.*

minimum adjective
mínimo *masc.*, mínima *fem.*

miniskirt noun
la minifalda *fem.*

mint noun
1 (*sweet*) el caramelo de menta *masc.*
2 (*plant*) la menta *fem.*

minus preposition
menos
Five minus two is three. Cinco menos dos son tres.
It's minus three today. Hoy hace tres grados bajo cero.

a b c d e f g h i j k l m n o p q r s t u v w x y z

• *Languages and nationalities do not take a capital letter in Spanish.*

a
b
c
d
e
f
g
h
i
j
k
l
m
n
o
p
q
r
s
t
u
v
w
x
y
z

minute noun
el minuto masc.
Wait a minute. Espera un minuto.
I'll be back in a minute. Enseguida vuelvo.

miracle noun
el milagro masc.

mirror noun
el espejo masc.

to **misbehave** verb
portarse mal
Holly misbehaves in class. Holly se porta muy mal en clase.

mischief noun
to get up to mischief hacer travesuras

miserable adjective
1 (sad) triste masc. & fem.
Why are you miserable? ¿Por qué estás triste?
2 **The weather's miserable.** Hace un tiempo fatal.

to **miss** verb
1 (the bus, train, etc.) perder
I don't want to miss the bus. No quiero perder el autobús.
2 (the party, film, etc.) perderse
I've missed the film. Me he perdido la película.

> 🔑 **LANGUAGE**
> Use **perder** when you mean you don't catch the bus etc., and **perderse** when you're too late to go somewhere.

3 (to feel sad)
I miss you. Te echo de menos.
I miss her. La echo de menos.
I miss my parents. Echo de menos a mis padres.

miss noun
(talking about your teacher etc.)
la señorita fem.
Miss is very nice. La señorita es muy simpática.
Please, miss! ¡Por favor, señorita!
Yes, miss. Sí, señorita.

Miss noun
la señorita fem.
Good afternoon, Miss Price.
Buenas tardes, señorita Price.

> 🔑 **LANGUAGE**
> **Señorita** is usually written on an envelope as **Srta.**, e.g. **Srta. Price.**

missing adjective
1 **to be missing** faltar
There's a page missing. Falta una página.
the missing page la página que falta
2 **to go missing** desaparecer

mist noun
la neblina fem.

mistake noun
1 el error masc.
I've made a mistake. He cometido un error.
by mistake por error
2 (in your writing, spelling, or typing) la falta fem.
to make a spelling mistake cometer una falta de ortografía

mistletoe noun
el muérdago masc.

> 🌍 **CULTURE**
> In Spain it isn't a tradition to kiss under the mistletoe at Christmas.

misty adjective
It's misty. Hay neblina.

> 🔑 **LANGUAGE**
> Word for word the Spanish means 'there is mist'.

to **mix** verb
1 mezclar
Mix these colours together.
Mezcla estos colores.
You've mixed up all the photos!
¡Has mezclado todas las fotos!
2 (to confuse) confundir
I get her and her sister mixed up.
La confundo con su hermana.

• *The months of the year and days of the week do not take a capital letter in Spanish.*

mixture noun
la mezcla *fem.*

to **moan** verb
(*to complain*) quejarse

mobile noun
el móvil *masc.*
You can call me on the mobile.
Puedes llamarme al móvil.
a mobile phone un móvil

model noun
1 (*a copy of a bigger thing*) la maqueta *fem.*
a model plane una maqueta de avión
2 (*a type of thing*) el modelo *masc.*
It's the latest model. Es el último modelo.
3 (*a person*) el or la modelo *masc. & fem.*
She's a model. Es modelo.

modern adjective
moderno *masc.*, moderna *fem.*

moment noun
el momento *masc.*
Just a moment! ¡Un momento!
at the moment en este momento
I'll be back in a moment.
Enseguida vuelvo.

Monday noun
el lunes *masc.*
Today is Monday. Hoy es lunes.
on Monday el lunes
We're going to the cinema on Monday. Vamos al cine el lunes.
on Mondays los lunes
We have games on Mondays.
Tenemos deporte los lunes.

> 🔑 **LANGUAGE**
> Remember the difference in Spanish between **el lunes** (one Monday only) and **los lunes** (every Monday).

money noun
el dinero *masc.*
It costs a lot of money. Cuesta mucho dinero.
a money box una hucha

• *See the centre section for verb tables.*

monitor noun
(*computer screen*) el monitor *masc.*

monkey noun
el mono *masc.*, la mona *fem.*

monster noun
el monstruo *masc.*

month noun
el mes *masc.*
I'm leaving in a month. Me voy dentro de un mes.
this month este mes
last month el mes pasado
next month el mes que viene

mood noun
el humor *masc.*
Are you in a good or bad mood?
¿Estás de buen o de mal humor?

moon noun
la luna *fem.*

more adverb, adjective & pronoun
1 más
more interesting más interesante
I read more than you. Leo más que tú.
More water, please. Más agua, por favor.
a bit more un poco más
I don't want any more. No quiero más.
ten more days diez días más
2 **more than** (*with numbers*) más de
more than ten books más de diez libros
3 (*talking about something you did but don't do now*)
I don't come here any more. Ya no vengo aquí.
I'm not playing with you any more. No juego más contigo.

> 🔑 **LANGUAGE**
> To mean 'not any more' use **ya no** or **no ... más**.

English Spanish

a
b
c
d
e
f
g
h
i
j
k
l
m
n
o
p
q
r
s
t
u
v
w
x
y
z

morning noun
la mañana *fem.*
In the morning I go to school. Por la mañana voy al colegio.
at eight o'clock in the morning a las ocho de la mañana
this morning esta mañana
tomorrow morning mañana por la mañana
Good morning! ¡Buenos días!

mosque noun
la mezquita *fem.*

mosquito noun
el mosquito *masc.*
a mosquito bite una picadura de mosquito

most adverb, adjective & pronoun
1 más
I like Spanish most. Lo que más me gusta es el español.
the most boring book el libro más aburrido
the most expensive ones los más caros
It's Andrew who has the most cake. Andrew es el que más pastel tiene.
I have the most. Yo soy la que más tengo.
2 (*over half*) la mayoría de
most children la mayoría de los niños
most people la mayoría de la gente
most of my friends la mayoría de mis amigos
3 (*almost all*) casi todo *masc.*, casi toda *fem.*
I've eaten most of the ice cream. He comido casi todo el helado.
I've eaten most of it. He comido casi todo.
most of the time la mayor parte del tiempo

moth noun
la mariposa de la luz *fem.*

mother noun
la madre *fem.*
My mother is a dentist. Mi madre es dentista.
my mother and father mis padres
Mother's Day el día de la Madre

CULTURE
In Spain Mother's Day is the first Sunday in May; it's in March in Britain.

motorbike noun
la moto *fem.*

motorcycle noun
la motocicleta *fem.*

motorcyclist noun
el or la motorista *masc. & fem.*

motorist noun
el or la automovilista *masc. & fem.*

⚠ **FALSE FRIEND**
motorist = automovilista (*not* motorista)

motorway noun
la autopista *fem.*

mountain noun
la montaña *fem.*
a mountain bike una bicicleta de montaña

mouse noun
el ratón *masc.* (plural los **ratones**)
a mouse mat una alfombrilla de ratón

LANGUAGE
As in English, a ratón is an animal and a part of your computer.

moustache noun
el bigote *masc.*
He has a moustache. Tiene bigote.

mouth noun
la boca *fem.*

move noun
1 (*in a game*)
It's your move. Te toca a ti.
2 **Get a move on!** ¡Date prisa!

• *Use* el *and* uno *for masculine words and* la *and* una *for feminine words.*

to move verb

1 mover
Can you move your hand? ¿Puedes mover la mano?

2 (to move your body) moverse
Don't move. No te muevas.
I can't move. No puedo moverme.

3 (to put out of the way) quitar
Move your things off the table. Quita tus cosas de la mesa.
Move your bag. Quita tu bolso de aquí.

4 (to move house) mudarse
We're moving tomorrow. Nos mudamos mañana.

to move forward verb
avanzar

to move over verb
correrse
Move over a bit. Córrete un poco.

movement noun
el movimiento masc.

movie noun
la película fem.
Do you like movies? ¿Te gustan las películas?
to go to the movies ir al cine
a movie star una estrella de cine

Mr noun
el señor masc.
Good morning, Mr Short. Buenos días, señor Short.

> **LANGUAGE**
> Señor is usually written on an envelope as Sr., e.g. Sr. Short.

Mrs noun
la señora fem.
Goodbye, Mrs Patel. Adiós, señora Patel.

> **LANGUAGE**
> Señora is usually written on an envelope as Sra., e.g. Sra. Patel.

Ms noun
la señora fem.
Good morning, Ms Solomon. Buenos días, señora Solomon.

> **CULTURE**
> You use 'Ms' when you don't want to say whether a woman is married or not. There is no special word in Spanish for this, but señora can always be used.

much adverb, adjective & pronoun

1 mucho
I don't read much. No leo mucho.
much bigger mucho más grande
very much mucho

2 mucho masc., mucha fem.
I don't have much chocolate. No tengo mucho chocolate.
There's not much snow. No hay mucha nieve.
Thank you very much! ¡Muchas gracias!

3 how much? ¿cuánto? masc., ¿cuánta? fem.
How much is it? ¿Cuánto es?
How much milk? ¿Cuánta leche?

4 so much tanto masc., tanta fem.
Not so much milk! ¡No tanta leche!

5 too much demasiado masc., demasiada fem.
too much work demasiado trabajo
I eat too much. Como demasiado.

mud noun
el barro masc.

muddy adjective
(hands, shoes, etc.) lleno de barro masc., llena de barro fem.

mug noun
(of tea or coffee) la taza fem.

to multiply verb
multiplicar
Four multiplied by two is eight. Cuatro multiplicado por dos son ocho.

• Languages and nationalities do not take a capital letter in Spanish.

English Spanish

a
b
c
d
e
f
g
h
i
j
k
l
m
n
o
p
q
r
s
t
u
v
w
x
y
z

mum noun
la mamá *fem.*, la madre *fem.*
Yes, mum. Sí, mamá.
My mum works in an office.
Mi madre trabaja en una oficina.,
Mi mamá trabaja en una oficina.
my mum and dad mis papás

mummy noun
la mamá *fem.*
Hello, mummy! ¡Hola, mamá!

mumps noun
las paperas *fem. plural*

murder noun
el asesinato *masc.*

to **murder** verb
asesinar

> **LANGUAGE**
> The English word assassinate is like
> asesinar and means 'to murder
> somebody important or famous'.

murderer noun
el asesino *masc.*, la asesina *fem.*

muscle noun
el músculo *masc.*

museum noun
el museo *masc.*

mushroom noun
el champiñón *masc.* (plural los
champiñones)

music noun
la música *fem.*
I'm listening to music. Estoy
escuchando música.

musical adjective
a musical instrument un
instrumento musical

musician noun
el músico *masc.*, la música *fem.*

Muslim adjective
musulmán *masc.*,
musulmana *fem.*

mussels plural noun
los mejillones *masc. plural*

must verb
1 tener que
I must leave. Tengo que irme.
You must do it. Tienes que hacerlo.
2 deber
He must not tell lies. No debe
mentir.
I must leave right away. Debo
irme enseguida.

> **LANGUAGE**
> Use deber when the sentence is negative,
> or as a stronger way of saying 'must'.

3 (*for saying something is probably true*)
deber de, deber
You must be tired. Debes de estar
cansado., Debes estar cansado.

mustard noun
la mostaza *fem.*

my adjective
1 (*before a singular noun*) mi
my brother mi hermano
2 (*before a plural noun*) mis
my toys mis juguetes
3 (*with parts of the body, clothes, etc.*)
I'm washing my hands. Me estoy
lavando las manos.
I put my coat on. Me puse el
abrigo.

> **LANGUAGE**
> Use me with el, la, los, or las instead of
> mi and mis in these examples.

myself pronoun
1 yo mismo *masc.*, yo misma *fem.*
I wrote it myself. Lo escribí yo
mismo.
2 (*with a reflexive verb*) me
I'm washing myself. Me estoy
lavando.
3 **by myself** solo *masc.*, sola *fem.*
I'm at home by myself. Estoy solo
en casa.

mysterious adjective
misterioso *masc.*, misteriosa *fem.*

mystery noun
el misterio *masc.*

• *The months of the year and days of the week do not take a capital letter in Spanish.*

Nn

nail noun
1 la **uña** *fem.*
I bite my nails. Me muerdo las uñas.
nail varnish el esmalte de uñas
2 el **lavo** *masc.*
with a hammer and nails con un martillo y unos clavos

naked adjective
desnudo *masc.*, **desnuda** *fem.*

name noun
el **nombre** *masc.*
I don't remember your name. No me acuerdo de tu nombre.
What's your name? ¿Cómo te llamas?
My name's Karim. Me llamo Karim.
What's his name? ¿Cómo se llama?

nanny noun
(*who looks after children*) la **niñera** *fem.*

nap noun
la **siesta** *fem.*
to have a nap echarse una siesta

napkin noun
la **servilleta** *fem.*

nappy noun
el **pañal** *masc.*

narrow adjective
estrecho *masc.*, **estrecha** *fem.*

nasty adjective
1 (*bad, cruel*) **malo** *masc.*, **mala** *fem.*
It's nasty weather. Hace un tiempo muy malo.
He's nasty to his sister. Es malo con su hermana.
2 (*horrible*) **horrible** *masc. & fem.*
a nasty accident un accidente horrible

national adjective
nacional *masc. & fem.*
the national anthem el himno nacional

nationality noun
la **nacionalidad** *fem.*
What nationality are you? ¿De qué nacionalidad eres?

natural adjective
natural *masc. & fem.*

nature noun
la **naturaleza** *fem.*

naughty adjective
malo *masc.*, **mala** *fem.*
Naughty boy! ¡Malo!

navy blue adjective
azul marino *masc. & fem.*
navy blue socks calcetines azul marino

🔑 **LANGUAGE**
Azul marino is the same in the masculine, feminine, and plural.

near adjective
cercano *masc.*, **cercana** *fem.*
the nearest supermarket el supermercado más cercano

near adverb & preposition
1 **cerca**
I live very near. Vivo muy cerca.
2 (*with nouns and pronouns*) **cerca de**
near the school cerca del colegio
near me cerca de mí

nearby adverb
cerca
The station is nearby. La estación está cerca.

• *See the centre section for verb tables.*

nearly adverb
casi
It's nearly five o'clock. Son casi las cinco.

neat adjective
1 (room, person) **ordenado** masc., **ordenada** fem.
2 (clothes, hair) **arreglado** masc., **arreglada** fem.

necessary adjective
necesario masc., **necesaria** fem.

neck noun
el **cuello** masc.

necklace noun
el **collar** masc.

nectarine noun
la **nectarina** fem.

to need verb
1 **necesitar**
I need some money. Necesito dinero.
2 (talking about something you must do) **tener que**
I need to go home. Tengo que irme a casa.

needle noun
la **aguja** fem.

negative noun
(in grammar) el **negativo** masc.

neighbour noun
el **vecino** masc., la **vecina** fem.

neighbourhood noun
el **barrio** masc.

neither pronoun & conjunction
1 **ninguno** masc., **ninguna** fem.
Do you want the red dress or the green one? – Neither. ¿Quieres el vestido rojo o el verde? – Ninguno.
2 **neither … nor** ni … ni
Neither one nor the other. Ni el uno ni el otro.
3 (in replies) **tampoco**

I don't want to go. – Neither do I. No quiero ir. – Yo tampoco.
I don't like cheese. – Neither do I. No me gusta el queso. – A mí tampoco.

nephew noun
el **sobrino** masc.

nerve noun
1 el **nervio** masc.
She gets on my nerves. Me pone los nervios de punta.
2 (being rude) la **cara** fem.
You've got a nerve! ¡Qué cara tienes!

> **LANGUAGE**
> Word for word this means 'What a face you have!'

nervous adjective
nervioso masc., **nerviosa** fem.
Are you nervous? ¿Estás nervioso?

nest noun
el **nido** masc.

net noun
1 (for fishing, tennis, etc.) la **red** fem.
2 **the Net** la Red
to surf the Net navegar por la Red

netball noun

> **CULTURE**
> Girls do not play netball in Spain; instead girls – and boys – play basketball (**el baloncesto**).

Netherlands noun
the Netherlands los Países Bajos

never adverb
nunca
I never go out alone. No salgo nunca sola.
Never again! ¡Nunca más!
Never mind! ¡No importa!

> **LANGUAGE**
> no + verb + nunca, for example: **No** salgo **nunca**

• Use **el** and **uno** for masculine words and **la** and **una** for feminine words.

new adjective
1 **nuevo** *masc.*, **nueva** *fem.*
 my new friends mis nuevos amigos
 I have a new bike. Tengo una bici nueva.
2 **the New Year** el Año Nuevo
 Happy New Year! ¡Feliz Año Nuevo!
 New Year's Day el día de Año Nuevo
 New Year's Eve la Nochevieja

 CULTURE
On New Year's Eve Spanish people eat twelve grapes (one for each month of the year) just as the clock strikes twelve.

news noun
1 la **noticia** *fem.*
 That's good news. Es una buena noticia.
 I have bad news. Tengo malas noticias.

🔑 **LANGUAGE**
las noticias = more than one piece of news

2 (*on TV or the radio*) **las noticias** *fem. plural*
 I watch the news. Veo las noticias.

newsagent's noun
 la **tienda de periódicos** *fem.*

newspaper noun
 el **periódico** *masc.*

news-stand noun
 el **kiosco de periódicos** *masc.*

New Zealand noun
 Nueva Zelanda *fem.*

next adjective
1 (*in time*) **próximo** *masc.*, **próxima** *fem.*
 next time la próxima vez
 the next stop la próxima parada
2 (*week, month, year, Monday, etc.*) **que viene**, **próximo** *masc.*, **próxima** *fem.*

next week la semana que viene, la próxima semana

🔑 **LANGUAGE**
Word for word **la semana que viene** means 'the week that comes'.

3 (*following on*) **siguiente** *masc. & fem.*
 on the next page en la página siguiente
 the next day el día siguiente
 Next, please! ¡El siguiente!
 Who's next? ¿Quién es el siguiente?

next adverb
1 (*after this*) **luego**
 What did you do next? ¿Qué hiciste luego?
2 (*now*) **ahora**
 What shall we do next? ¿Qué hacemos ahora?
3 **next to** al lado de
 Sit next to your brother. Siéntate al lado de tu hermano.
 next to me a mi lado
 next door al lado
 He lives next door. Vive al lado.

nice adjective
1 (*good*) **bueno** *masc.*, **buena** *fem.*
 The soup's very nice. La sopa está muy buena.
 It's nice weather. Hace buen tiempo.
 He's very nice to me. Es muy bueno conmigo.
2 (*pretty*) **bonito** *masc.*, **bonita** *fem.*
 a very nice dress un vestido muy bonito
3 (*friendly*) **simpático** *masc.*, **simpática** *fem.*
 My teacher is very nice. La maestra es muy simpática.

nickname noun
 el **apodo** *masc.*

a
b
c
d
e
f
g
h
i
j
k
l
m
n
o
p
q
r
s
t
u
v
w
x
y
z

• *Languages and nationalities do not take a capital letter in Spanish.*

English Spanish

a
b
c
d
e
f
g
h
i
j
k
l
m
n
o
p
q
r
s
t
u
v
w
x
y
z

niece noun
la **sobrina** *fem.*

night noun
la **noche** *fem.*
all night toda la noche
at night por la noche
at nine o'clock at night a las nueve de la noche
last night anoche
Good night! ¡Buenas noches!

nightdress, **nightie** noun
el **camisón** *masc.* (plural los **camisones**)

nightmare noun
la **pesadilla** *fem.*
to have a nightmare tener una pesadilla

night-time noun
la **noche** *fem.*

nil noun
el **cero** *masc.*
We've won two nil. Hemos ganado dos a cero.

nine number
nueve
We ate at nine. Comimos a las nueve.
Ben is nine. Ben tiene nueve años.

> 🔑 **LANGUAGE**
> In English you can say 'nine o'clock' or just 'nine', 'nine years old' or just 'nine'. In Spanish you must add **las** (for time) and **años** (for age).

nineteen number
diecinueve
My cousin is nineteen. Mi primo tiene diecinueve años.

ninety number
noventa

ninth adjective
noveno *masc.*, **novena** *fem.*
on the ninth floor en el noveno piso
the ninth of January el nueve de enero

> 🔑 **LANGUAGE**
> With dates you use **nueve** (nine).

no adverb
no
Do you live in London? – No. ¿Vives en Londres? – No.
No thanks. No, gracias.

no adjective
1 (*not any*) **no**
I have no time. No tengo tiempo.
There's no more milk. No hay más leche.
No problem! ¡Sin problema!
2 (*on signs*)
'No smoking.' 'Prohibido fumar.'

nobody pronoun
nadie
Who wants to play? – Nobody! ¿Quién quiere jugar? – ¡Nadie!
There's nobody in the garden. No hay nadie en el jardín.
Nobody knows me. Nadie me conoce.

> 🔑 **LANGUAGE**
> **no** + *verb* + **nadie**, for example: **No veo a nadie**

noise noun
el **ruido** *masc.*
to make a noise hacer ruido

noisy adjective
It's noisy here. Hay mucho ruido aquí.
My computer is very noisy. Mi ordenador hace mucho ruido.

none pronoun
1 **ninguno** *masc.*, **ninguna** *fem.*
How many CDs do you have? – None. ¿Cuántos CDs tienes? – Ninguno.

• *The months of the year and days of the week do not take a capital letter in Spanish.*

There are none left. No queda ninguno.
none of the children ninguno de los niños
2 nada
How much bread is left? – None. ¿Cuánto pan queda? – Nada.

> **LANGUAGE**
> Use **ninguno** when talking about plural nouns, and **nada** with singular nouns such as 'bread', 'money', or 'chocolate'.

nonsense noun
las tonterías *fem. plural*, la tontería *fem.*
You're talking a lot of nonsense! ¡Dices muchas tonterías!
What nonsense! ¡Qué tontería!

noodles plural noun
los fideos *masc. plural*

noon noun
el mediodía *masc.*
at noon a mediodía
It's noon. Es mediodía.

no-one, **no one** pronoun
nadie
Who wants to help me? – No-one! ¿Quién quiere ayudarme? – ¡Nadie!
There's no-one in the shop. No hay nadie en la tienda.
No-one knows me. Nadie me conoce.

> **LANGUAGE**
> no + *verb* + **nadie**, for example: **No veo a nadie.**

nor conjunction
1 neither … nor ni … ni
Neither Yasmina nor her sister are at home. Ni Yasmina ni su hermana están en casa.
2 tampoco
I don't want to do it. – Nor do I. No quiero hacerlo. – Yo tampoco.
I don't like fish. – Nor do I. No me gusta el pescado. – A mí tampoco.

• See the centre section for verb tables.

normal adjective
1 normal *masc. & fem.*
That's not normal. No es normal.
2 (*time or place*) de siempre
at the normal time a la hora de siempre

north noun & adjective
1 el norte *masc.*
in the north en el norte
the north coast la costa norte
2 North America Norteamérica *fem.*
the North Pole el Polo Norte
the North Sea el Mar del Norte

Northern Ireland noun
Irlanda del Norte *fem.*
I live in Northern Ireland. Vivo en Irlanda del Norte.

nose noun
la nariz *fem.* (plural las **narices**)

nosy adjective
curioso *masc.*, curiosa *fem.*

not adverb
no
I'm not tired. No estoy cansado.
He hasn't come. No ha venido.
It's not big. No es grande.
Do you want some ice cream or not? ¿Quieres helado o no?
not yet todavía no
not much no mucho

> **LANGUAGE**
> When you use a verb remember to put **no** in front of the verb in Spanish.

note noun
1 (*message*) la nota *fem.*
Dad has left you a note. Papá te ha dejado una nota.
2 notes los apuntes *masc. plural*
The students are taking notes. Los alumnos toman apuntes.
3 (*paper money*) el billete *masc.*
a five-pound note un billete de cinco libras

notebook noun
el cuaderno *masc.*

notepad noun
el bloc *masc.* (plural los **blocs**)

nothing pronoun
nada
What do you want? – Nothing.
¿Qué quieres? – Nada.
There's nothing in the box. No hay
nada en la caja.
It's nothing. No es nada.
Nothing has changed. Nada ha
cambiado.
nothing much no mucho

> 🔑 **LANGUAGE**
> no + *verb* + **nada**, for example: **No** hay
> **nada**.

to **notice** verb
notar
Do you notice the difference?
¿Notas la diferencia?

notice noun
(*on a wall, door, etc.*) el letrero *masc.*
notice board el tablón de
anuncios (plural los **tablones de
anuncios**)

noun noun
el nombre *masc.*

novel noun
la novela *fem.*

November noun
noviembre *masc.*
in November en noviembre
**My grandparents are arriving in
November** Mis abuelos llegan en
noviembre.
**I'm going to Valencia on the ninth
of November.** Voy a Valencia el
nueve de noviembre.

now adverb
ahora
Where are you now? ¿Dónde estás
ahora?
from now on de ahora en
adelante
now and again de vez en cuando
She left just now. Acaba de irse.

nowhere adverb
a or en ninguna parte
Where are you going? – Nowhere.
¿Adónde vas? – A ninguna parte.
The book is nowhere in the house.
El libro no está en ninguna parte de
la casa.

number noun
(*of a house, page, etc.*) el número *masc.*
my phone number mi número de
teléfono
I live at number twenty-five. Vivo
en el número veinticinco.
a large number of un gran número
de

nun noun
la monja *fem.*

nurse noun
el enfermero *masc.*,
la enfermera *fem.*
My mother's a nurse. Mi madre es
enfermera.

nursery noun
la guardería *fem.*
a nursery rhyme una canción
infantil
nursery school la guardería

nut noun
el fruto seco *masc.*

> 🔑 **LANGUAGE**
> Word for word the Spanish means 'dried
> fruit'.

• *Use* el *and* uno *for masculine words and* la *and* una *for feminine words.*

Oo

oats plural noun
la **avena** *fem.*

🔑 **LANGUAGE**
English = **oats** is plural
Spanish = **la avena** is singular

to **obey** verb
1 **obedecer**
My dog obeys me. Mi perro me obedece.
2 **to obey the rules** respetar las reglas

object noun
el **objeto** *masc.*

obvious adjective
evidente *masc. & fem.*

obviously adverb
claro
Do you want to come? – Obviously!
¿Quieres venir? – ¡Claro!

occasion noun
la **ocasión** *fem.*
a very special occasion una ocasión muy especial

occasionally adverb
de vez en cuando

occupation noun
(*job*) el **empleo** *masc.*

ocean noun
el **océano** *masc.*

o'clock adverb
at eight o'clock a las ocho
It's one o'clock. Es la una.
It's four o'clock. Son las cuatro.

October noun
octubre *masc.*
I'm going camping in October.
Me voy de camping en octubre.

It's my birthday on Tuesday, the tenth of October. Es mi cumpleaños el martes diez de octubre.

octopus noun
el **pulpo** *masc.*

odd adjective
1 (*strange*) **raro** *masc.*, **rara** *fem.*
2 **an odd number** un número impar

of preposition

🔑 **LANGUAGE**
de + el = del

1 **de**
a glass of water un vaso de agua
a boy of six un niño de seis años
a page of the book una página del libro
the door of the house la puerta de la casa
2 (*no translation when 'of' is followed by 'it' or 'them'*)
Give me some of it. Dame un poco.
I've eaten a lot of it. He comido mucho.
There are ten of them. Hay diez.

of course adverb
claro
Do you have lots of friends? – Of course I do! ¿Tienes muchos amigos? – ¡Claro que sí!
of course not claro que no

off adjective
1 (*light, TV, radio, etc.*) **apagado** *masc.*, **apagada** *fem.*
The TV is off. La tele está apagada.
2 (*tap, gas*) **cerrado** *masc.*, **cerrada** *fem.*
The tap is off. El grifo está cerrado .
3 (*cancelled*)
The match is off. El partido se ha suspendido.

• *Languages and nationalities do not take a capital letter in Spanish.*

English Spanish

a
b
c
d
e
f
g
h
i
j
k
l
m
n
o
p
q
r
s
t
u
v
w
x
y
z

343

English Spanish

a
b
c
d
e
f
g
h
i
j
k
l
m
n
o
p
q
r
s
t
u
v
w
x
y
z

off adverb & preposition
1 (*going somewhere*) **to be off** irse
I'm off now. Ahora me voy.
2 (*away from school or work*) **a day off**
un día libre
I'm off school. No he ido al colegio.
We have a week off. Tenemos una
semana de vacaciones.
3 (*from*) **de**
I fell off the chair. Me caí de la
silla.
I got off the bus. Me bajé del
autobús.

> **LANGUAGE**
> 'Off' is often translated as part of a verb
> such as 'to switch off' (**apagar**) or 'to take
> off' (**quitar**).

to **offer** verb
ofrecer
to offer somebody something
ofrecer algo a alguien

office noun
la **oficina** *fem.*
My mum works in an office. Mi
madre trabaja en una oficina.

often adverb
a menudo
I often go to the cinema. Voy al
cine a menudo.
**How often do you see your
grandfather?** ¿Cada cuánto ves a
tu abuelo?

ogre noun
el **ogro** *masc.*

oil noun
el **aceite** *masc.*

okay adjective & adverb
1 (*good, well*) **bien**
to be okay estar bien
How are you? – Okay. ¿Cómo
estás? – Bien.
I sing okay. Canto bien.
2 (*not so bad*); **no mal**
to be okay no estar mal

Do you like the film? – It's okay.
¿Te gusta la película? – No está mal.
3 (*with verbs starting with 'to'*)
Is it okay to close the window? ¿Se
puede cerrar la ventana?

> **LANGUAGE**
> Use **poder** (can) in this meaning (Can I
> close the window?).

okay exclamation
1 **¡bueno!**
Okay, I'm coming! ¡Bueno, ya voy!
2 (*saying yes*) **¡vale!**
**Do you want to come with us? –
Okay!** ¿Quieres venir con
nosotros? – ¡Vale!

old adjective
1 **viejo** *masc.*, **vieja** *fem.*
an old bicycle una bicicleta vieja
an old man un hombre viejo
2 (*when being polite about people*) **mayor**
masc. & fem.
My grandfather is very old.
El abuelo es muy mayor.
an old lady una anciana
old people los ancianos
3 (*talking about ages*) **How old are you?**
¿Cuántos años tienes?
Hakim is six years old. Hakim
tiene seis años.
4 (*from your past*) **antiguo** *masc.*,
antigua *fem.*
my old school mi antiguo colegio

older adjective
(*talking about people*) **mayor** *masc. &
fem.*
I'm older than you. Soy mayor que
tú.
She's two years older than me.
Es dos años mayor que yo.

oldest noun
el or la **mayor** *masc. & fem.*
I'm the oldest in the class. Soy el
mayor de la clase.

• *The months of the year and days of the week do not take a capital letter in Spanish.*

old-fashioned adjective
(*clothes, person, etc.*) anticuado *masc.*,
anticuada *fem.*

olive noun
la aceituna *fem.*

Olympic adjective
the Olympic Games los Juegos
Olímpicos *masc. plural*

omelette noun
la tortilla *fem.*

on preposition
1 en
Write it on the board. Escríbelo en
la pizarra.
on the beach en la playa
on TV en la tele
2 a

> **LANGUAGE**
> a + el = al

I got on the bus. Subí al autobús.
on foot a pie
on a horse a caballo
3 (*talking about books, films, etc.*) sobre
a film on dinosaurs una película
sobre los dinosaurios
4 on Sunday el domingo
on Sundays los domingos
on the ninth of December el nueve
de diciembre
on Christmas Day el día de
Navidad

> **LANGUAGE**
> With days and dates you don't translate
> 'on' in Spanish but the determiner **el**
> (plural **los**) is used instead.

on adjective & adverb
1 (*light, TV, computer, etc.*)
encendido *masc.*, encendida *fem.*
The TV is on. La tele está encendida.
2 (*tap, gas*) abierto *masc.*, abierta *fem.*
The tap is on. El grifo está abierto.
3 (*wearing something*) **I've got my
glasses on.** Llevo mis gafas.
I don't have a watch on. No llevo
reloj.

• *See the centre section for verb tables.*

He has nothing on! ¡Está desnudo!

> **LANGUAGE**
> 'On' is often translated as part of a verb
> such as 'to switch on' (**encender**) or 'to
> put on' (**poner**).

once adverb
1 una vez
once a day una vez al día
once again otra vez
2 at once enseguida
Come at once. Ven enseguida.
3 (*a long time ago*) antes
'Once upon a time there was ...'
(*in stories*) 'Érase una vez ...'

one number & pronoun
uno *masc.*, una *fem.*

> **LANGUAGE**
> Uno becomes **un** in front of a masculine
> noun.

One and one are two. Uno y uno
son dos.
one euro un euro
It's one o'clock. Es la una.
The baby is one. El niño tiene un
año.
one of my friends uno de mis
amigos
Do you want one? ¿Quieres uno?
Take the blue one. Coge el azul.

onion noun
la cebolla *fem.*

online adjective
en línea, conectado or
conectada a Internet *masc. & fem.*

online adverb
en línea
to buy online comprar en línea

only adjective
único *masc.*, única *fem.*
the only book el único libro
It's the only one I have. Es el único
que tengo.
He's an only child. Es hijo único.
She's an only child. Es hija única.

only adverb
sólo
I only have one pen. Sólo tengo un boli.

onto preposition
1 **a**
It's fallen onto the floor. Se ha caído al suelo.
2 **en**
Put it onto the table. Ponlo en la mesa.

open adjective
abierto masc., **abierta** fem.
The museum is open. El museo está abierto.

to **open** verb
abrir
Open the window. Abre la ventana.
The shops open at nine. Las tiendas abren a las nueve.

operation noun
I'm going to have an operation. Van a operarme.

opinion noun
la **opinión** fem. (plural las **opiniones**)
in my opinion en mi opinión

opportunity noun
la **oportunidad** fem.

opposite adjective
1 (page, wall, etc.) **de enfrente**
the opposite house la casa de enfrente
on the opposite side of the road al otro lado de la calle
2 (different) **opuesto** masc., **opuesta** fem.
in the opposite direction en la dirección opuesta
3 **the opposite of** lo contrario de
'Big' is the opposite of 'small'. 'Big' es lo contrario de 'small'.

opposite adverb & preposition
1 **enfrente**
We live opposite. Vivimos enfrente.
2 (with nouns and pronouns) **enfrente de**
opposite the school enfrente del colegio
She's sitting opposite me. Está sentada enfrente de mí.

optician noun
el or la **oculista** masc. & fem.
to go to the optician's ir a la óptica

or conjunction
1 **o**
yes or no sí o no

> **LANGUAGE**
> O becomes **u** in front of a word starting with **o** or **ho**.

ten or eleven diez u once
2 (in sentences with 'not', 'never', etc.) **ni ... ni**
I don't have any brothers or sisters. No tengo ni hermanos ni hermanas.

orange noun
1 (fruit) la **naranja** fem.
an orange juice un zumo de naranja
2 (colour) el **naranja** masc.
I don't like orange. No me gusta el naranja.

orange adjective
naranja masc. & fem.
orange shirts camisas naranja

> **LANGUAGE**
> **Naranja** is the same in the masculine, feminine, and plural.

orchestra noun
la **orquesta** fem.

order noun
1 el **orden** masc.

• Use **el** and **uno** for masculine words and **la** and **una** for feminine words.

Put the names in alphabetical order. Pon los nombres en orden alfabético.
They're in the right order. Están ordenados.
They're in the wrong order. Están desordenados.
2 (*talking about a machine, lift, etc.*)
It's out of order. No funciona.

to **order** verb
(*in a restaurant*) **pedir**
We ordered fish. Pedimos pescado.

ordinary adjective
normal *masc. & fem.*

organize verb
organizar

original adjective
(*idea, version, etc.*) **original** *masc. & fem.*

orphan noun
el **huérfano** *masc.*, la **huérfana** *fem.*

other adjective & pronoun
otro *masc.*, **otra** *fem.*
the other day el otro día
other countries otros países
the other one el otro *masc.*, la otra *fem.*
the others los otros *masc. plural*, las otras *fem. plural*

otherwise conjunction
si no
Hurry, otherwise you'll be late. Date prisa, si no vas a llegar tarde.

ouch exclamation
¡ay!

ought verb
deber
You ought to work harder. Deberías trabajar más.

our adjective
1 (*before a singular noun*) **nuestro** *masc.*, **nuestra** *fem.*
our school nuestro colegio
2 (*before a plural noun*) **nuestros** *masc. plural*, **nuestras** *fem. plural*

our friends nuestros amigos
3 (*with parts of the body, clothes, etc.*)
We're washing our hands. Nos estamos lavando las manos.
We put our coats on. Nos pusimos el abrigo.

LANGUAGE
Use **nos** with **el, la, los,** or **las** in these examples instead of **nuestro** and **nuestros**.

ours pronoun
1 (*with a singular noun*) el **nuestro** *masc.*, la **nuestra** *fem.*
Their house is bigger than ours. Su casa es más grande que la nuestra.
2 (*with a plural noun*) los **nuestros** *masc. plural*, las **nuestras** *fem. plural*
your parents and ours tus padres y los nuestros
3 (*following 'is'*) **nuestro** *masc.*, **nuestra** *fem.*
This bike is ours. Esta bici es nuestra.
4 (*following 'are'*) **nuestros** *masc. plural*, **nuestras** *fem. plural*
These books are ours. Estos libros son nuestros.

ourselves pronoun
1 nosotros mismos *masc. plural*, **nosotras mismas** *fem. plural*
We've made it ourselves. Lo hemos hecho nosotros mismos.
2 (*with a reflexive verb*) **nos**
We're washing ourselves. Nos estamos lavando.
3 by ourselves solos *masc. plural*, solas *fem. plural*
We're at home by ourselves. Estamos solas en casa.

out adverb
1 (*outside*) **fuera**
I'm out here. Estoy aquí fuera.
It's cold out. Fuera hace frío.
I go out. Salgo.
I'm looking out of the window. Estoy mirando por la ventana.

• *Languages and nationalities do not take a capital letter in Spanish.*

English Spanish

2 (*from*)
It's made out of wood. Es de madera.
Take the letter out of my pocket. Saca la carta de mi bolsillo.
I've got fifteen out of twenty. He sacado quince sobre veinte.

> 🔑 **LANGUAGE**
> 'Out' is often translated as part of a verb such as 'to go out' (**salir**) or 'to take out' (**sacar**).

out adjective
1 (*talking about not being at home*) **to be out** no estar
Karim is out. Karim no está.
2 (*light, fire*) apagado *masc.*, apagada *fem.*
The lights are out. Las luces están apagadas.
3 (*in games*) **You're out!** ¡Fuera!

outdoor adjective
(*swimming pool etc.*) al aire libre
outdoor games juegos al aire libre

outdoors adverb
fuera

outer space noun
el espacio *masc.*

outing noun
la excursión *fem.* (plural las **excursiones**)
to go on an outing ir de excursión

outside adverb & preposition
1 fuera
Wait outside. Espera fuera.
2 (*in front of*) delante de
Wait for me outside the school. Espérame delante del colegio.

outside noun
el exterior *masc.*
The outside is dirty. El exterior está sucio.

oval adjective
ovalado *masc.*, ovalada *fem.*

oven noun
el horno *masc.*

over preposition & adverb
1 sobre
a bridge over the river un puente sobre el río
The helicopter flew over the town. El helicóptero voló sobre la ciudad.
2 por encima de
The ball has gone over the wall. La pelota ha pasado por encima del muro.
I looked over the wall. Miré por encima del muro.

> 🔑 **LANGUAGE**
> Use **por encima de** with verbs of movement like 'go' or 'jump'.

3 (*more than*) más de
I'm over ten. Tengo más de diez años.
4 (*during*) durante
over the summer durante el verano
5 (*everywhere*)
all over por todas partes
all over the house por toda la casa
6 over here aquí
over there allí
7 (*talking about somebody's house*)
Come over tomorrow. Ven a mi casa mañana.

> 🔑 **LANGUAGE**
> 'Over' is often translated as part of a verb such as 'to be left over' (**quedar**) or 'to come over' (**venir**).

over adjective
(*finished*)
to be over terminar
The film's over. Ha terminado la película.
The holidays are over. Han terminado las vacaciones.

to **overtake** verb
(*in a car*) adelantar

• *The months of the year and days of the week do not take a capital letter in Spanish.*

to **owe** verb
deber
I owe you two euros. Te debo dos euros.

owl noun
el **búho** *masc.*

own adjective
propio *masc.*, **propia** *fem.*
Do you have your own computer?
¿Tienes tu propio ordenador?

own pronoun
1 **I've got a room of my own.** Tengo mi propia habitación.

2 **on your own** solo *masc.*, sola *fem.*
They've left me on my own. Me han dejado solo.

to **own** verb
tener
He owns three bikes. Tiene tres bicis.

owner noun
el **dueño** *masc.*, la **dueña** *fem.*

oxygen noun
el **oxígeno** *masc.*

Pp

Pacific noun
el **Pacífico** *masc.*

to **pack** verb
1 (*one case only*) **hacer la maleta**
I'm going to pack. Voy a hacer la maleta.
2 (*more than one case*) **hacer las maletas**

pack noun
a pack of cards una baraja *fem.*

package noun
el **paquete** *masc.*

packed lunch noun
la **comida** *fem.*
Do you take a packed lunch?
¿Te llevas la comida al colegio?

🌎 CULTURE
In Spain children do not have packed lunches in school; **comida** is the Spanish word for 'lunch'.

packet noun
el **paquete** *masc.*
a packet of biscuits un paquete de galletas

a packet of crisps una bolsa de patatas fritas

page noun
la **página** *fem.*
on page five en la página cinco

pain noun
el **dolor** *masc.*
I'm in a lot of pain. Tengo mucho dolor.
I have a pain in my arm. Me duele el brazo.

painful adjective
My leg is painful. Me duele la pierna.
Is it very painful? ¿Te duele mucho?
My shoes are painful. Me hacen daño los zapatos.

paint noun
1 la **pintura** *fem.*
a tin of paint un bote de pintura
2 **paints** las pinturas *fem. plural*;
(*watercolours*) las acuarelas *fem. plural*
a box of paints una caja de acuarelas

• *See the centre section for verb tables.*

English Spanish

to **paint** verb
 pintar
 I love to paint. Me encanta pintar.
 I want to paint it blue. Quiero
 pintarlo en azul.

paintbrush noun
 1 (for pictures) el pincel masc.
 2 (for painting walls etc.) la brocha fem.

painter noun
 el pintor masc., la pintora fem.
 My dad's a painter. Mi padre es
 pintor.

painting noun
 1 (picture) el cuadro masc.
 a painting by Dalí un cuadro de
 Dalí
 2 (hobby)
 I like painting. Me gusta pintar.

pair noun
 1 (of shoes, gloves, etc.) el par masc.
 a pair of socks un par de calcetines
 2 (two people) la pareja fem.
 to work in pairs trabajar en
 parejas
 3 a pair of jeans unos vaqueros
 a pair of trousers unos pantalones

Pakistan noun
 Paquistán masc.

Pakistani adjective
 paquistaní masc. & fem.

Pakistani noun
 el or la paquistaní masc. & fem.

palace noun
 el palacio masc.

pale adjective
 pálido masc., pálida fem.
 You look very pale. Estás muy
 pálida.

palm tree noun
 la palmera fem.

pan noun
 1 (saucepan) la cacerola fem.
 2 (frying pan) la sartén fem. (plural las
 sartenes)

pancake noun
 el crepe masc.
 Pancake Day el martes de
 Carnaval

🌏 **CULTURE**

El martes de Carnaval is Shrove
Tuesday, when children in Britain eat
pancakes. In Spain children dress up for
Carnaval, dance, and play music but
they don't eat pancakes!

panda noun
 el panda masc., el oso panda masc.

🔑 **LANGUAGE**

Be careful: **panda** ends in an **-a** but it is
not a feminine noun.

to **panic** verb
 Don't panic! ¡Calma!

pantomime noun
 la comedia para niños fem.

pants plural noun
 los calzoncillos masc. plural

paper noun
 1 el papel masc.
 a sheet of paper una hoja de papel
 a piece of paper un papel
 a paper bag una bolsa de papel
 paper chains las cadenetas
 2 (newspaper) el periódico masc.
 a paper boy un repartidor de
 periódicos
 I do a paper round. Reparto
 periódicos.
 a paper shop una tienda de
 periódicos

paperback noun
 el libro de bolsillo masc.

paperclip noun
 el clip masc. (plural los **clips**)

parachute noun
 el paracaídas masc. (plural los
 paracaídas)

parade noun
 el desfile masc.

• Use **el** and **uno** for masculine words and **la** and **una** for feminine words.

paragraph noun
el **párrafo** *masc.*

parcel noun
el **paquete** *masc.*

pardon noun
Pardon? ¿Perdón?

> 🔑 **LANGUAGE**
> Use **perdón** when you want somebody to say something again.

parents plural noun
los **padres** *masc. plural*
my parents mis padres

> ⚠ **FALSE FRIEND**
> parents = **los padres** (*not* los parientes)

> 🔑 **LANGUAGE**
> In the singular **padre** means 'father'.

park noun
1 el **parque** *masc.*
Let's go to the park. Vamos al parque.
2 **a car park** un aparcamiento *masc.*

to **park** verb
aparcar
to park the car aparcar el coche
You can park here. Puedes aparcar aquí.

parking noun
'No parking' 'Prohibido aparcar'
a parking space un aparcamiento

parrot noun
el **loro** *masc.*

part noun
1 la **parte** *fem.*
the last part of the book la última parte del libro
2 (*in a play or film*) el **papel** *masc.*
I play the part of the witch. Hago el papel de la bruja.
3 **to take part in something** participar en algo

parting noun
(*in hair*) la **raya** *fem.*

partly adverb
en parte

partner noun
(*in a game, school play, etc.*) la **pareja** *fem.*

party noun
la **fiesta** *fem.*
I'm having a party. Voy a dar una fiesta.
a birthday party una fiesta de cumpleaños
a Christmas party una fiesta de Navidad

to **pass** verb
1 (*to go past*) **pasar por**
I passed your house. Pasé por tu casa.
2 (*to give*) **pasar**
Pass me the chocolates, please. ¿Me pasas los bombones, por favor?
3 **to pass an exam** aprobar un examen

passenger noun
el **pasajero** *masc.*, la **pasajera** *fem.*

passport noun
el **pasaporte** *masc.*

password noun
la **contraseña** *fem.*

past preposition & adverb
1 (*in front of*) **por delante de**
The bus goes past the school. El autobús pasa por delante del colegio.
I went past on my bike. Pasé en bici.
2 (*after*) **después de**
My house is just past the library. Mi casa está justo después de la biblioteca.
3 (*talking about the time*)
It's ten past nine. Son las nueve y diez.

a
b
c
d
e
f
g
h
i
j
k
l
m
n
o
p
q
r
s
t
u
v
w
x
y
z

• *Languages and nationalities do not take a capital letter in Spanish.*

It's a quarter past one. Es la una y cuarto.
It's half past six. Son las seis y media.

past adjective
1 **último** masc., **última** fem.
 the past two weeks las últimas dos semanas
2 **the past tense** el pasado masc.

past noun
 the past el pasado masc.
 in the past en el pasado

pasta noun
 la **pasta** fem.
 I like pasta. Me gusta la pasta.

pastry noun
 el **pastel** masc.
 Would you like a pastry? ¿Quieres un pastel?

path noun
 el **camino** masc.

patient adjective
 paciente masc. & fem.
 My sister's very patient. Mi hermana es muy paciente.

patient noun
 (of a doctor) el or la **paciente** masc. & fem.

pattern noun
 el **dibujo** masc.

pavement noun
 la **acera** fem.

paw noun
 la **pata** fem.

pay noun
 el **sueldo** masc.

to **pay** verb
1 **pagar**
 Pay at the checkout. Paga en caja.
 to pay for something pagar algo
 I've paid for the ticket. He pagado el billete.
2 **to pay attention** poner atención

Pay attention to what you're doing! ¡Pon atención en lo que estás haciendo!

PC noun
 el **ordenador** masc., el **PC** masc.
 (plural los **PCs**)

PE noun
 la **gimnasia** fem.
 to do PE hacer gimnasia
 We have PE on Thursdays. Los jueves tenemos clase de gimnasia.

pea noun
 el **guisante** masc.

peace noun
 la **paz** fem.
 Let me have some peace! ¡Déjame en paz!
 I want some peace and quiet. Quiero estar tranquilo.

peaceful adjective
 tranquilo masc., **tranquila** fem.
 a very peaceful spot un sitio muy tranquilo

peach noun
 el **melocotón** masc. (plural los **melocotones**)

peanut noun
 el **cacahuete** masc.
 peanut butter la mantequilla de cacahuete

pear noun
 la **pera** fem.

pearl noun
 la **perla** fem.
 a pearl necklace un collar de perlas

pedal noun
 el **pedal** masc.

pedestrian noun
 el **peatón** masc. (plural los **peatones**)

to **peel** verb
 (apple, banana, etc.) **pelar**

• The months of the year and days of the week do not take a capital letter in Spanish.

peel noun
la piel *fem.*

peg noun
(*hook for coats*) la percha *fem.*

pen noun
1 (*ballpoint*) el bolígrafo *masc.*, el boli *masc.*
2 (*fountain pen*) la pluma *fem.*

pence plural noun
los peniques *masc. plural*
fifty pence cincuenta peniques

pencil noun
el lápiz *masc.* (plural los **lápices**)
in pencil a lápiz
a coloured pencil un lápiz de colores
a pencil case un estuche
a pencil sharpener un sacapuntas (plural **sacapuntas**)

penfriend noun
el amigo por correspondencia or por correo *masc.*, la amiga por correspondencia or por correo *fem.*

penguin noun
el pingüino *masc.*

penknife noun
la navaja *fem.*

penny noun
el penique *masc.*

people plural noun
1 la gente *fem.*
a lot of people mucha gente
most people la mayoría de la gente

LANGUAGE
Gente is a singular noun in Spanish.

2 (*talking about numbers of people*) las personas *fem. plural*
how many people? ¿cuántas personas?
five people cinco personas

• *See the centre section for verb tables.*

pepper noun
1 la pimienta *fem.*
Would you like salt or pepper? ¿Quieres sal o pimienta?
2 (*vegetable*) el pimiento *masc.*
a green pepper un pimiento verde

per cent adverb
por ciento
ten per cent diez por ciento

perfect adjective
perfecto *masc.*, perfecta *fem.*
Vincent speaks perfect Spanish. Vincent habla un español perfecto.

perfectly adverb
perfectamente

performance noun
1 (*of a film*) la sesión *fem.* (plural las sesiones)
2 (*of a play*) la representación *fem.* (plural las representaciones)

perfume noun
el perfume *masc.*

perhaps adverb
quizás, a lo mejor
Perhaps she's missed the bus. Quizás ha perdido el autobús., A lo mejor ha perdido el autobús.

period noun
1 el periodo *masc.*
a period of six months un periodo de seis meses
the holiday period la época de vacaciones
2 (*school lesson*) la clase *fem.*
We have a Spanish period now. Ahora tenemos clase de español.

permission noun
el permiso *masc.*
I don't have permission to go out. No tengo permiso para salir.

person noun
la persona *fem.*
a friendly person una persona simpática

personality noun
la **personalidad** *fem.*

pest noun
el **pesado** *masc.*, la **pesada** *fem.*
She's a real pest. Es muy pesada.

pet noun
1 el **animal** *masc.*
Do you have any pets at home?
¿Tienes animales en casa?
2 la **mascota** *fem.*
I have a hamster as a pet. Tengo
un hámster como mascota.
3 **the teacher's pet** el favorito *masc.*
de la maestra, la favorita *fem.* de la
maestra

petrol noun
la **gasolina** *fem.*
to get petrol echar gasolina
a petrol station una gasolinera

pharmacy noun
la **farmacia** *fem.*

phone noun
1 el **teléfono** *masc.*
The phone's ringing. Suena el
teléfono.
I'm on the phone. Estoy hablando
por teléfono.
2 **the phone book** la guía telefónica
a phone box una cabina telefónica
a phone call una llamada
telefónica
to make a phone call hacer una
llamada
a phone number un número de
teléfono

to **phone** verb
llamar (por teléfono)
Phone me. Llámame por teléfono.
I'll phone you later. Te llamo más
tarde.

photo noun
la **foto** *fem.*
to take photos hacer fotos
I've taken a photo of my bike.
He hecho una foto de mi bici.

I've taken a photo of my teacher.
Le he hecho una foto a mi maestra.

⚷ **LANGUAGE**
You can also use **sacar** instead of **hacer**,
e.g. **He sacado una foto.**

photocopier noun
la **fotocopiadora** *fem.*

photocopy noun
la **fotocopia** *fem.*

to **photocopy** verb
fotocopiar

photograph noun
la **fotografía** *fem.*
to take a photograph hacer una
fotografía
**I've taken a photograph of my
teacher.** Le he hecho una
fotografía a mi maestra.

⚷ **LANGUAGE**
You can also use **sacar** instead of **hacer**,
e.g. **Le he sacado una fotografía.**

photographer noun
el **fotógrafo** *masc.*,
la **fotógrafa** *fem.*

phrase noun
la **frase** *fem.*
a useful Spanish phrase una frase
útil en español
a phrase book un libro de frases

physical adjective
físico *masc.*, **física** *fem.*

pianist noun
el or la **pianista** *masc. & fem.*

piano noun
el **piano** *masc.*
I play the piano. Toco el piano.

pick noun
Take your pick! ¡Elige!, ¡Escoge!

• *Use* **el** *and* **uno** *for masculine words and* **la** *and* **una** *for feminine words.*

to **pick** verb
1 (to choose) elegir, escoger
I've picked the green one. He elegido el verde., He escogido el verde.
2 (apples, flowers, etc.) recoger

to **pick up** verb
1 recoger
Pick up your toys! ¡Recoge tus juguetes!
I'm going to pick up Daniel from school. Voy a recoger a Daniel al colegio.
2 coger
I picked up my books and left. Cogí mis libros y salí.
3 (something heavy) levantar
I can't pick it up! ¡No lo puedo levantar!

picnic noun
el picnic masc. (plural los **picnics**)
to have a picnic hacer un picnic
to go for a picnic ir de picnic

picture noun
1 (drawing) el dibujo masc.
I've drawn a picture of my dog. He hecho un dibujo de mi perro.
2 (by a painter) el cuadro masc.
a picture by Dali un cuadro de Dalí
3 (photo) la foto fem.
to take pictures hacer fotos
4 (on TV screen) la imagen fem.
5 (in a book) la ilustración fem. (plural las **ilustraciones**)

pie noun
el pastel masc.
an apple pie un pastel de manzana

piece noun
1 (bit of something) el trozo masc.
a piece of bread un trozo de pan
2 (in a jigsaw puzzle) la pieza fem.
a puzzle of one hundred pieces un rompecabezas de cien piezas

pierced adjective
She has her ears pierced. Tiene agujeros en las orejas.

LANGUAGE
Word for word the Spanish means 'She has holes in her ears'.

pig noun
el cerdo masc.

pigeon noun
la paloma fem.

piggy bank noun
la hucha fem.

pigtails plural noun
las coletas fem. plural
She has pigtails. Lleva coletas.

pile noun
el montón masc. (plural los **montones**)
a pile of books un montón de libros

pill noun
la pastilla fem.
to take pills tomar pastillas

pillow noun
la almohada fem.

pilot noun
el or la piloto masc. & fem.

pimple noun
el grano masc.

pin noun
(for sewing) el alfiler masc.

to **pinch** verb
(to steal) quitar
Who pinched my book? ¿Quién me ha quitado el libro?

pineapple noun
la piña fem.

ping-pong noun
el ping-pong masc.
to play ping-pong jugar al ping-pong

a b c d e f g h i j k l m n o **p** q r s t u v w x y z

• Languages and nationalities do not take a capital letter in Spanish.

pink adjective
rosa *masc. & fem.*
pink dresses vestidos rosa

🔑 **LANGUAGE**
Rosa is the same in the masculine, feminine, and plural.

pink noun
el rosa *masc.*
I like pink. Me gusta el rosa.

🔑 **LANGUAGE**
Don't confuse el rosa with la rosa (rose): it's the same word in Spanish for the colour and the flower.

pint noun
la pinta *fem.*

🌍 **CULTURE**
In Spain litres and centilitres are used instead of pints. A pint is just over half a litre.

pirate noun
el or la pirata *masc. & fem.*

pitch noun
el campo *masc.*
a football pitch un campo de fútbol

pity noun
What a pity! ¡Qué lástima!

pizza noun
la pizza *fem.*

place noun
1 el sitio *masc.*
Can you keep my place? ¿Me guardas el sitio?
I've changed places. Me he cambiado de sitio.
2 el lugar *masc.*
I finished in second place. Terminé en segundo lugar.
It's a beautiful place. Es un lugar precioso.

plain adjective
1 sencillo *masc.*, sencilla *fem.*
She's wearing a very plain dress. Lleva un vestido muy sencillo.
2 (*with no special flavour*) natural *masc. & fem.*
a plain yoghurt un yogur natural

plaits plural noun
las trenzas *fem. plural*
She has plaits. Lleva trenzas.

plan noun
1 el plan *masc.*
Do you have any plans for tomorrow? ¿Tienes planes para mañana?
2 (*map of a building*) el plano *masc.*
the plan of a house el plano de la casa

to **plan** verb
1 (*a journey, party, etc.*) planear
My parents are planning a trip to Spain. Mis padres están planeando un viaje a España.
2 **to plan to do something** pensar hacer algo
Are you planning to go? ¿Piensas ir?

plane noun
el avión *masc.* (plural los **aviones**)
to go by plane ir en avión
a plane crash un accidente de avión

planet noun
el planeta *masc.*

🔑 **LANGUAGE**
Be careful: planeta ends in an -a but it is not a feminine noun.

plant noun
la planta *fem.*

to **plant** verb
plantar

plaster noun
1 (*for a cut, burn, etc.*) la tirita *fem.*
2 la escayola *fem.*
in plaster escayolado *masc.*, escayolada *fem.*

• *The months of the year and days of the week do not take a capital letter in Spanish.*

I've got my arm in plaster. Tengo el brazo escayolado.

plastic noun
el **plástico** masc.
It's made of plastic. Es de plástico.
a plastic bag una bolsa de plástico

Plasticine® noun
la **plastilina®** fem.

plate noun
el **plato** masc.

platform noun
(at a train station) el **andén** masc.
(plural los **andenes**)

play noun
(for acting in) la **obra** fem.
to put on a play hacer una obra

to **play** verb
1 **jugar**
I play with my friends on Saturdays. Juego con mis amigas los sábados.
2 (games and sports) **jugar a**
We play football. Jugamos al fútbol.
3 (an instrument) **tocar**
Daniel plays the guitar. Daniel toca la guitarra.
to play a tune tocar una melodía

🔑 **LANGUAGE**
Tocar also means 'to touch'.

4 (a CD, DVD, or tape) **poner**
Can you play me your new CD? ¿Me puedes poner tu nuevo CD?

player noun
1 el **jugador** masc., la **jugadora** fem.
a football player un jugador de fútbol
2 el **reproductor** masc.
an MP3 player un reproductor MP3, un MP3 masc.

• See the centre section for verb tables.

playground noun
1 (in school) el **patio de recreo** masc.
The children are playing in the playground. Los niños están jugando en el patio.
2 (in the park) los **columpios** masc. plural
I want to go to the playground. Quiero ir a los columpios.

🔑 **LANGUAGE**
Columpios means 'swings' and is often used to mean the whole playground.

playgroup noun
la **guardería** fem.

playing field noun
el **campo de deportes** masc.

playtime noun
el **recreo** masc.

pleasant adjective
agradable masc. & fem.

please exclamation
por favor
Two ice creams, please. Dos helados, por favor.

pleased adjective
contento masc., **contenta** fem.
I'm very pleased with the presents. Estoy muy contento con los regalos.

plenty pronoun
1 (a lot)
plenty of mucho masc., mucha fem.
You have plenty of books. Tienes muchos libros.
You've given me plenty. Me has dado mucho or muchos.
2 (enough)
plenty of bastante masc. & fem.
There are plenty of chocolates for everybody. Hay bastantes bombones para todos.
That's plenty. Eso es suficiente.

to **plug in** verb
enchufar
Is the TV plugged in? ¿Está enchufada la tele?

plum noun
la **ciruela** *fem.*

plumber noun
el **fontanero** *masc.*,
la **fontanera** *fem.*
My dad's a plumber. Mi padre es
fontanero.

plural noun
el **plural** *masc.*
The sentence is in the plural. La
frase está en plural.

plus preposition
más
Three plus five is eight. Tres más
cinco son ocho.

p.m. abbreviation
1 (*from midday until evening*) **de la tarde**
at 2 p.m. a las dos de la tarde
2 (*from evening until midnight*) **de la noche**
at 9 p.m. a las nueve de la noche

pocket noun
el **bolsillo** *masc.*
Keep your pen in your pocket.
Guarda el bolígrafo en el bolsillo.
pocket money la paga

poem noun
el **poema** *masc.*

> **LANGUAGE**
> Be careful: **poema** ends in an **-a** but it is
> not a feminine noun.

poet noun
el or la **poeta** *masc. & fem.*

point noun
1 (*in a game*) el **punto** *masc.*
I've scored three points. He sacado
tres puntos.
2 (*of a pencil, knife, etc.*) la **punta** *fem.*
3 (*decimal point*) la **coma** *fem.*
four point five cuatro coma cinco

> **LANGUAGE**
> In Spanish you use a comma in decimal
> numbers, e.g. 4.5 is **4,5**.

4 (*the reason for something*) el **sentido**
masc.
There's no point. No tiene sentido.

to **point** verb
(*with your finger*) **señalar**
Point to the picture. Señala el
cuadro.

to **point out** verb
señalar
Can you point out your school?
¿Me puedes señalar tu escuela?

poison noun
el **veneno** *masc.*

poisonous adjective
(*snake, plant, etc.*) **venenoso** *masc.*,
venenosa *fem.*
a poisonous mushroom una seta
venenosa

Poland noun
Polonia *fem.*

polar bear noun
el **oso polar** *masc.*

Pole noun
1 **the North Pole** el Polo Norte
the South Pole el Polo Sur
2 (*Polish person*) el **polaco** *masc.*,
la **polaca** *fem.*

police noun
la **policía** *fem.*
to call the police llamar a la
policía
The police have come. La policía
ya ha llegado.
a police car un coche de policía
a police station una comisaría

> **LANGUAGE**
> Use the verb in the singular with **policía**.

policeman noun
el **policía** *masc.*
My dad's a policeman. Mi padre es
policía.

• *Use* **el** *and* **uno** *for masculine words and* **la** *and* **una** *for feminine words.*

policewoman noun
la **policía** fem.
My mum's a policewoman.
Mi madre es policía.

Polish adjective
polaco masc., **polaca** fem.
She's Polish. Es polaca.

Polish noun
(the language) el **polaco** masc.

polite adjective
educado masc., **educada** fem.
She's very polite. Es muy educada.

polluted adjective
contaminado masc.,
contaminada fem.

pollution noun
la **contaminación** fem.

pond noun
(in a garden or park) el **estanque** masc.

pony noun
el **poni** masc.

ponytail noun
la **cola de caballo** fem.,
la **coleta** fem.
She has a ponytail. Lleva una cola
de caballo., Lleva coleta.

> **LANGUAGE**
> Word for word **cola de caballo** means
> 'horse's tail'.

pool noun
la **piscina** fem.
an indoor swimming pool una
piscina cubierta

poor adjective
1 **pobre** masc. & fem.
They're poor. Son pobres.
a poor family una familia pobre
Your poor mum! ¡Tu pobre madre!

> **LANGUAGE**
> Use **pobre** after the noun when it means
> the opposite of 'rich', and before the noun
> when you feel sad about somebody.

2 (bad) **malo** masc., **mala** fem.
I always get poor marks. Siempre
saco malas notas.
The weather's poor. Hace mal
tiempo.

> **LANGUAGE**
> Before a masculine singular nouns **malo**
> becomes **mal**.

pop noun
(music) el **pop** masc.
My sister likes pop. A mi hermana
le gusta el pop.

pop adjective
(song, singer, music, etc.) **pop** masc. & fem.
pop music la música pop
a pop group un grupo de
pop
a pop star una estrella del
pop

> **LANGUAGE**
> The Spanish adjective **pop** is the same in
> the masculine, feminine, and plural.

popcorn noun
las **palomitas** fem. plural

> **LANGUAGE**
> English = **popcorn** is singular
> Spanish = **las palomitas** is plural

Pope noun
el **Papa** masc.

> **LANGUAGE**
> Be careful: **Papa** ends in an -a but it is not
> a feminine noun.

popular adjective
popular masc. & fem.

porch noun
el **porche** masc.

pork noun
el **cerdo** masc.
a pork chop una chuleta de
cerdo

• Languages and nationalities do not take a capital letter in Spanish.

porridge noun
los copos de avena *masc. plural*

🔑 **LANGUAGE**
English = **porridge** is singular
Spanish = **los copos de avena** is plural

port noun
el puerto *masc.*

portable adjective
(*television etc.*) portátil *masc. & fem.*

portion noun
(*of food*) la ración *fem.* (plural las **raciones**)

a portion of potatoes una ración de patatas

portrait noun
el retrato *masc.*

Portugal noun
Portugal *masc.*

Portuguese adjective
portugués *masc.*, portuguesa *fem.*
Portuguese food la comida portuguesa

🔑 **LANGUAGE**
The masculine plural of **portugués** is **portugueses**.

Portuguese noun
1 (*language*) el portugués *masc.*
Do you speak Portuguese? ¿Hablas portugués?
2 **the Portuguese** los portugueses *masc. plural*

posh adjective
(*hotel, restaurant, etc.*) elegante *masc. & fem.*

position noun
la posición *fem.* (plural las **posiciones**)

positive adjective
(*certain*) seguro *masc.*, segura *fem.*
Are you positive? ¿Estás seguro?

possible adjective
posible *masc. & fem.*
It's possible. Es posible.
as soon as possible lo más pronto posible

possibly adverb
(*maybe*) quizás

post noun
1 (*letters*) el correo *masc.*
The post has come. Ha llegado el correo.
2 **to send something by post** mandar algo por correo

to post verb
1 (*to put into the postbox etc.*) echar al correo
Can you post this for me? ¿Me puedes echar esto al correo?
2 (*to send by post*) mandar por correo
Can you post the parcel to me? ¿Me puedes mandar el paquete por correo?

postbox noun
el buzón *masc.* (plural los **buzones**)

🌍 **CULTURE**
In Spain postboxes are usually yellow.

postcard noun
la postal *fem.*

postcode noun
el código postal *masc.*

poster noun
el póster *masc.* (plural los **pósters**); el cartel *masc.*

postman noun
el cartero *masc.*
Has the postman been? ¿Ha venido el cartero?

🔑 **LANGUAGE**
Cartero is related to carta (letter).

• *The months of the year and days of the week do not take a capital letter in Spanish.*

post office *noun*
Correos *masc.*, la oficina de correos *fem.*
to go to the post office ir a Correos, ir a la oficina de correos

> **LANGUAGE**
> Be careful: Correos is spelt with a capital C and ends with an s. Never use el with it.

postwoman *noun*
la cartera *fem.*
My mum's a postwoman. Mi madre es cartera.

> **LANGUAGE**
> Cartera is related to carta (letter).

pot *noun*
1 (*teapot*) la tetera *fem.*
to make a pot of tea hacer té en una tetera
2 (*for flowers*) la maceta *fem.*
3 (*for cooking*) la cacerola *fem.*
the pots and pans los cacharros *masc. plural*

potato *noun*
la patata *fem.*, (*Latin America*) la papa *fem.*
baked potatoes patatas asadas
boiled potatoes patatas hervidas

pound *noun*
1 (*money*) la libra *fem.*
ten pounds diez libras
2 (*weight*)
a pound of apples medio kilo de manzanas

> **CULTURE**
> Spanish weights are in kilos and grams; a pound is just under half a kilo.

to pour *verb*
1 echar
Pour the milk into the glass. Echa la leche en el vaso.
2 (*to serve*) servir
Pour the soup. Sirve la sopa.

• See the centre section for verb tables.

3 **It's pouring with rain.** Está lloviendo a cántaros., Llueve mucho.

power cut *noun*
el apagón *masc.* (plural los apagones)

powerful *adjective*
poderoso *masc.*, poderosa *fem.*

practically *adverb*
(*almost*) casi

practice *noun*
1 (*sports training*) el entrenamiento *masc.*
I have football practice today. Hoy tengo entrenamiento de fútbol.
2 (*on an instrument*) los ejercicios *masc. plural*
to do piano practice hacer los ejercicios de piano

to practise *verb*
1 (*a language or instrument*) practicar
I have to practise my Spanish. Tengo que practicar mi español.
2 (*to do a sport*) entrenar
Our team practises every day. Nuestro equipo entrena cada día.

prawn *noun*
la gamba *fem.*

to pray *verb*
rezar

prayer *noun*
la oración *fem.* (plural las oraciones)

to prefer *verb*
preferir
I prefer apples to oranges. Prefiero las manzanas a la naranjas.
I prefer to read. Prefiero leer.

pregnant *adjective*
embarazada *fem.*
She's five months pregnant. Está embarazada de cinco meses.

English Spanish

a b c d e f g h i j k l m n o **p** q r s t u v w x y z

prehistoric adjective
prehistórico *masc.*,
prehistórica *fem.*

to **prepare** verb
preparar
Dad's preparing lunch. Papá está preparando la comida.

preposition noun
la preposición *fem.* (plural las **preposiciones**)

present adjective
1 presente *masc. & fem.*
Is Zafir present? ¿Está presente Zafir?
2 **the present tense** el presente *masc.*

present noun
1 (*gift*) el regalo *masc.*
What a lovely present! ¡Qué regalo tan bonito!
a birthday present un regalo de cumpleaños
2 (*the time now*) el presente *masc.*
the present and the past el presente y el pasado

president noun
el presidente *masc.*,
la presidenta *fem.*

to **press** verb
1 (*a button, doorbell, etc.*) pulsar
Press the button. Pulsa el botón.
2 empujar
Press here to open the door. Empuja aquí para abrir la puerta.

to **pretend** verb
1 fingir
He's pretending to be asleep. Finge dormir.
2 (*to imagine*) imaginar
Pretend you are a lion. Imagina que eres un león.

pretty adjective
1 (*thing, town, animal, etc.*) bonito *masc.*,
bonita *fem.*
a pretty skirt una falda bonita
2 (*girl, woman*) guapo *masc.*,
guapa *fem.*
a very pretty girl una niña muy guapa

pretty adverb
(*fairly*) bastante
a pretty good book un libro bastante bueno

to **prevent** verb
(*an accident, a problem, etc.*) evitar

price noun
el precio *masc.*
a price list una lista de precios

priest noun
el sacerdote *masc.*

primary school noun
la escuela primaria *fem.*

CULTURE
Spanish children go to the **escuela primaria** from the ages of 6 to 12. In Britain children go to primary school at around the age of 4 until they are 11.

Prime Minister noun
el primer ministro *masc.*,
la primera ministra *fem.*

prince noun
el príncipe *masc.*

princess noun
la princesa *fem.*

to **print** verb
1 (*on a computer etc.*) imprimir
Can you print out this page? ¿Me puedes imprimir esta página?
2 (*to write in big letters*) escribir en mayúsculas
Print your name. Escribe tu nombre en mayúsculas.

• *Use* el *and* uno *for masculine words and* la *and* una *for feminine words.*

printer noun
la impresora *fem.*
The printer isn't working.
La impresora no funciona.

prison noun
la cárcel *fem.*
He's in prison. Está en la cárcel.

prisoner noun
(*in prison*) el preso *masc.*,
la presa *fem.*

private adjective
1 privado *masc.*, privada *fem.*
a private school una escuela
privada
2 (*lesson, teacher*) particular *masc. & fem.*
private lessons clases particulares

prize noun
el premio *masc.*
to win a prize ganar un premio
the prize-giving la entrega de
premios

prizewinner noun
el ganador *masc.*, la ganadora *fem.*

probably adverb
probablemente

problem noun
el problema *masc.*
No problem! ¡No hay problema!

LANGUAGE
Be careful: problema ends in an -a but it
is not a feminine noun.

to **produce** verb
(*to make, create*) producir

profession noun
la profesión *fem.* (plural las
profesiones)

program noun
(*on a computer*) el programa *masc.*
a computer program un programa
informático

LANGUAGE
Be careful: programa ends in an -a but it
is not a feminine noun.

programme noun
(*on TV or radio, for concert etc.*)
el programa *masc.*
a TV programme un programa de
televisión

LANGUAGE
Be careful: programa ends in an -a but it
is not a feminine noun.

progress noun
to make progress mejorar
I'm making progress in Spanish.
Mi español está mejorando.

promise noun
la promesa *fem.*
You made a promise! ¡Me has
hecho una promesa!
I've kept my promise. He
cumplido mi promesa.
That's a promise. Te lo prometo.

to **promise** verb
prometer
You promised to come tomorrow.
Has prometido venir mañana.
I promise. Te lo prometo.

pronoun noun
el pronombre *masc.*

to **pronounce** verb
pronunciar
**How do you pronounce it in
Spanish?** ¿Cómo se pronuncia en
español?

pronunciation noun
la pronunciación *fem.*

properly adverb
(*well*) bien
I read properly. Leo bien.

to **protect** verb
proteger

Protestant adjective
protestante *masc. & fem.*

• *Languages and nationalities do not take a capital letter in Spanish.*

proud adjective
orgulloso *masc.*, orgullosa *fem.*
We're proud of you. Estamos orgullosos de ti.

proverb noun
el proverbio *masc.*

prune noun
la ciruela pasa *fem.*

🔑 **LANGUAGE**
Word for word the Spanish means 'dried plum'.

pub noun
el bar *masc.*, el pub *masc.*

public noun
el público *masc.*
It's open to the public. Está abierto al público.

public adjective
1 público *masc.*, pública *fem.*
a public library una biblioteca pública
public transport el transporte público
2 **a public holiday** un día de fiesta
Tomorrow is a public holiday. Mañana es fiesta.
3 **a public school** un colegio privado

⚠️ **FALSE FRIEND**
a public school = un colegio privado (*not* una escuela pública)

pudding noun
1 el pudín *masc.* (plural los **pudines**)
2 (*dessert*) el postre *masc.*

puddle noun
el charco *masc.*

to **pull** verb
tirar
Don't pull so hard. No tires tan fuerte.
to pull something tirar de algo
I pulled her hair. Le tiré del pelo.

to **pull down** verb
bajar
Pull down the blinds. Baja las persianas.

to **pull off** verb
(*a lid, cover, etc.*) quitar
I pulled off my socks. Me quité los calcetines.

to **pull out** verb
(*a plug, tooth, etc.*) sacar
What did you pull out of your pocket? ¿Qué has sacado del bolsillo?

pullover noun
el jersey *masc.* (plural los **jerseys** or **jerséis**)

pump noun
la bomba *fem.*
a bicycle pump una bomba de bicicleta

to **pump** verb
to pump up a tyre inflar una rueda

pumpkin noun
la calabaza *fem.*

punch noun
el puñetazo *masc.*

to **punch** verb
to punch somebody dar un puñetazo a alguien
She punched me. Me ha dado un puñetazo.

punctual adjective
puntual *masc. & fem.*
I'm very punctual. Soy muy puntual.

🔑 **LANGUAGE**
English = **punctual**
Spanish = **puntual**

• *The months of the year and days of the week do not take a capital letter in Spanish.*

punctuation noun
la **puntuación** fem.

🔑 **LANGUAGE**
English = **punctuation**
Spanish = **puntuación**

to **punish** verb
castigar
I've been punished. Me han castigado.

punishment noun
el **castigo** masc.

pupil noun
el **alumno** masc., la **alumna** fem.
all the pupils in my class todos los alumnos de mi clase

puppet noun
el **títere** masc., la **marioneta** fem.

puppy noun
el **cachorro** masc., la **cachorra** fem.

pure adjective
puro masc., **pura** fem.

purple adjective
morado masc., **morada** fem.
a purple skirt una falda morada

purple noun
el **morado** masc.
I love purple. Me encanta el morado.

purpose noun
on purpose a propósito
I didn't do it on purpose. No lo he hecho a propósito.

purse noun
el **monedero** masc.
I have ten euros in my purse. Tengo diez euros en el monedero.

to **push** verb
1 **empujar**
Don't push me! ¡No me empujes!
Push the door. Empuja la puerta.
2 (a button, doorbell, etc.) **pulsar**
Push the button. Pulsa el botón.

pushchair noun
la **sillita** fem.

to **put** verb
poner
Put your book on the table. Pon tu libro en la mesa.
Where have you put it? ¿Dónde lo has puesto?

to **put away** verb
guardar
Put your toys away. Guarda los juguetes.

to **put back** verb
volver a poner
Put the CD back in the box. Vuelve a poner el CD en la caja.

to **put down** verb
1 **poner**
Put it down on the floor. Ponlo en el suelo.
2 (your hand, the blind, etc.) **bajar**
Put the window down. Baja la ventanilla.

to **put off** verb
1 **apagar**
I've put the light off. He apagado la luz.
2 **aplazar**
They've put off the game. Han aplazado el partido.

to **put on** verb
1 (clothes, music, a CD, etc.) **poner**
Put the TV on. Pon la tele.
I'm putting my socks on. Me pongo los calcetines.
2 to put the light on encender la luz
3 to put on a play hacer una obra

to **put out** verb
(a light etc.) **apagar**
They've put out the fire. Han apagado el incendio.

• See the centre section for verb tables.

to **put up** verb
(*a picture, decorations, etc.*) **poner**
I've put up photos in my room.
He puesto fotos en mi habitación.
to put your hand up levantar la mano
to put up the price subir el precio

puzzle noun
el **rompecabezas** *masc.* (plural los **rompecabezas**)

puzzled adjective
confuso *masc.*, **confusa** *fem.*

pyjamas plural noun
el **pijama** *masc.*
I'm in pyjamas. Estoy en pijama.
a pair of pyjamas un pijama

> **LANGUAGE**
> English = **pyjamas** is plural
> Spanish = **el pijama** is singular

> **LANGUAGE**
> Be careful: **pijama** ends in an -**a** but it is not a feminine noun.

pyramid noun
la **pirámide** *fem.*

Qq

quality noun
la **calidad** *fem.*

quantity noun
la **cantidad** *fem.*

to **quarrel** verb
discutir
They're always quarrelling. Siempre están discutiendo.

quarter noun
1 la **cuarta parte** *fem.*
a quarter of the pupils una cuarta parte de los alumnos
2 (*talking about time, weights, etc.*) el **cuarto** *masc.*
a quarter of an hour un cuarto de hora
It's a quarter past seven. Son las siete y cuarto.
at a quarter to seven a las siete menos cuarto
an hour and a quarter una hora y cuarto

queen noun
la **reina** *fem.*

question noun
la **pregunta** *fem.*

to ask a question hacer una pregunta
Can I ask you a question? ¿Puedo hacerte una pregunta?
a question mark un signo de interrogación

queue noun
la **cola** *fem.*
We're standing in the queue. Estamos haciendo cola.

> **LANGUAGE**
> The Spanish word **cola** also means 'tail': queues can be long or short like tails.

to **queue** verb
hacer cola
You have to queue up. Tienes que hacer cola.

quick adjective
rápido *masc.*, **rápida** *fem.*
It's quicker by bike. Es más rápido en bici.
Quick! ¡Rápido!
Be quick! ¡Date prisa!

quickly adverb
rápido, **rápidamente**

• *Use* **el** *and* **uno** *for masculine words and* **la** *and* **una** *for feminine words.*

quiet adjective
1 (*peaceful*) tranquilo *masc.*, tranquila *fem.*
a quiet street una calle tranquila
2 (*not noisy*) silencioso *masc.*, silenciosa *fem.*
a quiet car un coche silencioso
Quiet, please! ¡Silencio, por favor!
Be quiet!, Keep quiet! (*to one person*) ¡Cállate!; (*to more than one person*) ¡Callaos!

quietly adverb
1 (*without noise*) sin hacer ruido, en silencio
2 (*to talk, say, etc.*) en voz baja

quite adverb
1 (*fairly*) bastante
quite often bastante a menudo
quite a good film una película bastante buena
2 (*completely*) totalmente
quite different totalmente distinto
3 quite a lot bastante
I read quite a lot. Leo bastante.
quite a lot of bastante *masc. & fem.*
I have quite a lot of friends. Tengo bastantes amigas.

quiz noun
(*on TV etc.*) el concurso *masc.*
a quiz show un programa concurso

Rr

rabbi noun
el rabino *masc.*, la rabina *fem.*

rabbit noun
el conejo *masc.*

race noun
1 la carrera *fem.*
Let's have a race to the house.
Te echo una carrera hasta la casa.
2 (*people*) la raza *fem.*
the human race la raza humana

racing car noun
el coche de carreras *masc.*

racket noun
la raqueta *fem.*
a tennis racket una raqueta de tenis

radiator noun
el radiador *masc.*

> **LANGUAGE**
> English = radiator
> Spanish = radiador

radio noun
la radio *fem.*
Put on the radio. Pon la radio.
on the radio en la radio
I heard it on the radio. Lo oí por la radio.
a radio station una emisora de radio

rail noun
to go by rail ir en tren

railway carriage noun
el vagón *masc.* (plural los **vagones**)

railway line noun
1 (*between two places*) la línea de ferrocarril *fem.*
2 (*the metal bars*) la vía *fem.*
You're not allowed to play on the line. Está prohibido jugar en la vía.

railway station noun
la estación de trenes *fem.* (plural las **estaciones de trenes**)

rain noun
la lluvia *fem.*
Don't go out in the rain. No salgas, que está lloviendo.
a rain forest una selva tropical

a b c d e f g h i j k l m n o p q r s t u v w x y z

• *Languages and nationalities do not take a capital letter in Spanish.*

English Spanish

a
b
c
d
e
f
g
h
i
j
k
l
m
n
o
p
q
r
s
t
u
v
w
x
y
z

to **rain** verb
llover
It's raining. Está lloviendo.

rainbow noun
el arco iris masc.

raincoat noun
el impermeable masc.

rainy adjective
lluvioso masc., lluviosa fem.
a rainy day un día lluvioso
It's always rainy in Norwich.
Siempre llueve en Norwich.

to **raise**
levantar
Raise your hand. Levanta la mano.

raisin noun
la pasa fem.

ramp noun
(for a wheelchair) la rampa fem.

rap noun
el rap masc.

rare adjective
poco común masc. & fem.
These animals are rare. Estos
animales son poco comunes.

rarely adverb
casi nunca
I rarely see my uncle. Casi nunca
veo a mi tío.

rash noun
el sarpullido masc.
I've got a rash. Me ha salido un
sarpullido.

raspberry noun
la frambuesa fem.
raspberry jam la mermelada de
frambuesa

rat noun
la rata fem.

rather adverb
1 (talking about preferring something)
I would rather wait. Prefiero
esperar.
**I don't want the red dress. I'd
rather have the green one.** No
quiero el vestido rojo. Prefiero el
verde.

🔑 **LANGUAGE**
Use the verb **preferir** for this meaning.

2 (instead)
rather than en vez de
**Choose the jeans rather than the
skirt.** Elige los vaqueros en vez de
la falda.
3 (fairly) bastante
a rather good book un libro
bastante bueno
rather a lot of bastante masc. & fem.
rather a lot of presents bastantes
regalos

raw adjective
crudo masc., cruda fem.
a raw carrot una zanahoria cruda

razor noun
la máquina de afeitar fem.

to **reach** verb
1 (to get to) llegar a
We reached Madrid at two.
Llegamos a Madrid a las dos.
2 (by stretching your arm)
alcanzar, llegar a
I can't reach the shelf. No alcanzo
al estante., No llego al estante.

to **read** verb
leer
I read a lot. Leo mucho.
What are you reading? ¿Qué estás
leyendo?

reading noun
la lectura fem.
a reading book un libro de lectura
I like reading. Me gusta leer.

• The months of the year and days of the week do not take a capital letter in Spanish.

ready adjective
1 listo *masc.*,
lista *fem.*, preparado *masc.*,
preparada *fem.*
I'm ready. Estoy listo or
preparado.
We're ready to leave. Estamos
listas or preparadas para salir.
2 (*food*) preparado *masc.*,
preparada *fem.*
Lunch is ready. La comida está
preparada.
3 **to get ready** prepararse
Get ready! ¡Prepárate!
to get something ready preparar
algo

real adjective
verdadero *masc.*, verdadera *fem.*
my real name mi verdadero
nombre

really adverb
(*with adjectives and adverbs*) muy
My bike is really old. Mi bici es
muy vieja.
really well muy bien
Are you tired? - Not really. ¿Estás
cansado? – No mucho.

reason noun
la razón *fem.* (plural las **razones**)
For what reason? ¿Por qué razón?

reasonable adjective
1 (*person, price, idea, etc.*) razonable
masc. & fem.
Zafir's very reasonable. Zafir es
muy razonable.
2 (*meal, work, etc.*) bastante
bueno *masc.*, bastante buena *fem.*
reasonable weather un tiempo
bastante bueno

> **LANGUAGE**
> Use razonable when you mean
> 'sensible', and bastante bueno when you
> mean 'fairly good'.

to receive verb
recibir
I've received your letter. He
recibido tu carta.

recent adjective
reciente *masc. & fem.*

recently adverb
recientemente

reception noun
(*desk in a hotel*) la recepción *fem.*
I'm waiting at reception. Estoy
esperando en recepción.

receptionist noun
el or la recepcionista *masc. & fem.*

recipe noun
la receta *fem.*

to recognize verb
reconocer
I don't recognize you. No te
reconozco.

to recommend verb
recomendar

record noun
1 (*for music*) el disco *masc.*
My granddad has lots of records.
Mi abuelo tiene muchos discos.
2 (*in sport*) el récord *masc.* (plural los
récords)
to beat the world record batir el
récord mundial

to record verb
(*pictures, sounds, etc.*) grabar
Shall we record the film?
¿Grabamos la película?
It's recording. Está grabando.

recorder noun
la flauta dulce *fem.*
to play the recorder tocar la flauta
dulce

> **LANGUAGE**
> Word for word flauta dulce means
> 'sweet flute'.

• *See the centre section for verb tables.*

a b c d e f g h i j k l m n o p q r s t u v w x y z

369

a
b
c
d
e
f
g
h
i
j
k
l
m
n
o
p
q
r
s
t
u
v
w
x
y
z

rectangle noun
el **rectángulo** *masc.*

red adjective
1 **rojo** *masc.*, **roja** *fem.*
 red socks calcetines rojos
2 (*in the face*) **colorado** *masc.*,
 colorada *fem.*
 You're going red! (*blushing*) ¡Te estás
 poniendo colorado!
3 **a red wine** un vino tinto
4 **to have red hair** ser pelirrojo *masc.*;
 ser pelirroja *fem.*

red noun
el **rojo** *masc.*
 I prefer red. Prefiero el rojo.

redhead noun
el **pelirrojo** *masc.*, la **pelirroja** *fem.*

to **redo** verb
 volver a hacer
 You have to redo it. Tienes que
 volver a hacerlo.

to **reduce** verb
 (*price, number, etc.*) **reducir**

referee noun
el **árbitro** *masc.*, la **árbitra** *fem.*

reflexive adjective
 (*in grammar*)
 a reflexive verb un verbo reflexivo

> 🔑 **LANGUAGE**
> In Spanish a reflexive verb is a verb that is
> used with a pronoun, e.g. **levantarse** (to
> get up): me **levanto** is 'I get up', te
> **levantas** is 'you get up', etc.

refrigerator noun
el **frigorífico** *masc.*

to **refuse** verb
 to refuse to do something no
 querer hacer algo
 He refuses to eat. No quiere comer.

region noun
la **región** *fem.* (plural las **regiones**)

register noun
la **lista** *fem.*
 to take the register pasar lista

registration noun
 (*in school*)
 Registration is at eight o'clock.
 Pasan lista a las ocho.

> 🔑 **LANGUAGE**
> There is no word in Spanish for
> registration. Use **pasar lista** (to take the
> register) instead.

regular adjective
1 **regular** *masc. & fem.*
 at regular intervals a intervalos
 regulares
2 (*customer, time*) **habitual** *masc. & fem.*
3 (*size, model*) **normal** *masc. & fem.*
 One regular fries, please. Una
 porción normal de patatas fritas,
 por favor.

rehearsal noun
el **ensayo** *masc.*

reindeer noun
el **reno** *masc.*

related adjective
1 (*ideas, problems, etc.*)
 relacionado *masc.*,
 relacionada *fem.*
2 (*people*)
 to be related ser parientes
 David and Daniel are related.
 David y Daniel son parientes.
3 (*words*) **de la misma familia**
 'Rainbow' and 'rainy' are related.
 'Rainbow' y 'rainy' son de la misma
 familia.

relation noun
el or la **pariente** *masc. & fem.*
 my relations mis parientes

relative noun
el or la **pariente** *masc. & fem.*
 my relatives mis parientes

• *Use* **el** *and* **uno** *for masculine words and* **la** *and* **una** *for feminine words.*

to **relax** verb
relajarse, descansar
I watch TV to relax. Veo la tele para relajarme., Veo la tele para descansar.
Relax! (*don't worry*) ¡Tranquilo!
Music is relaxing. La música me relaja.

relaxed adjective
relajado *masc.*, relajada *fem.*
I feel relaxed. Estoy relajado.

religion noun
la religión *fem.* (plural las religiones)

religious adjective
religioso *masc.*, religiosa *fem.*

to **remain** verb
1 (*to stay*) quedarse
Remain in the classroom. Quédate en la clase.
2 (*to be left*) quedar
It's all that remains. Esto es todo lo que queda.

to **remember** verb
1 acordarse
I don't remember. No me acuerdo.
Do you remember? ¿Te acuerdas?
2 **to remember something** acordarse de algo
I remember your name. Me acuerdo de tu nombre.

to **remind** verb
recordar
You remind me of my brother. Me recuerdas a mi hermano.
This reminds me of the summer. Esto me recuerda el verano.

remote control noun
el mando (a distancia) *masc.*

to **remove** verb
quitar
Remove your toys from the table! ¡Quita tus juguetes de la mesa!

to **rent** verb
(*a flat, car, etc.*) alquilar

to **repair** verb
arreglar, reparar
They've repaired the TV. Han arreglado la tele., Han reparado la tele.

to **repeat** verb
repetir
Can you repeat the question? ¿Puede repetir la pregunta?

to **replace** verb
1 (*to change*) cambiar
Have you replaced the batteries? ¿Has cambiado las pilas?
2 (*to put back*) volver a poner

reply noun
la respuesta *fem.*
I haven't got a reply. No he tenido respuesta.

to **reply** verb
responder
She's replied to my letter. Ha respondido a mi carta.

report noun
a school report un boletín de notas
I've got a good report. He sacado buenas notas.

reptile noun
el reptil *masc.*

to **rescue** verb
salvar
The firemen rescued her from the fire. Los bomberos la salvaron del incendio.

to **reserve** verb
reservar
This seat is reserved. Este asiento está reservado.

resort noun
(*for holidays*) el centro turístico *masc.*
a ski resort una estación de esquí

respect noun
el respeto *masc.*

a
b
c
d
e
f
g
h
i
j
k
l
m
n
o
p
q
r
s
t
u
v
w
x
y
z

• *Languages and nationalities do not take a capital letter in Spanish.*

a
b
c
d
e
f
g
h
i
j
k
l
m
n
o
p
q
r
s
t
u
v
w
x
y
z

to **respect** verb
respetar

responsibility noun
la responsabilidad *fem.*

responsible adjective
responsable *masc. & fem.*
She's a very responsible girl.
Es una niña muy responsable.
Who's responsible? ¿Quién es el responsable?

⚷ **LANGUAGE**
English = responsible
Spanish = responsable

rest noun
1 (*talking about something left over*)
the rest el resto *masc.*
the rest of the week el resto de la semana
2 (*talking about other people*)
the rest los otros *masc. plural*, las otras *fem. plural*
The rest have left. Los otros se han ido.
the rest of the boys los otros niños
3 (*time to relax*) el descanso *masc.*
I need some rest. Necesito descanso.
to have a rest descansar

to **rest** verb
descansar
I rested for an hour. Descansé una hora.

restaurant noun
el restaurante *masc.*

result noun
el resultado *masc.*
the exam results los resultados de los exámenes

to **retire** verb
jubilarse
My granddad retires in May.
Mi abuelo se jubila en mayo.
My grandma is retired. Mi abuela está jubilada.

return noun
1 la vuelta *fem.*
the return to school la vuelta al colegio
the return journey el viaje de vuelta
2 (*ticket*) el billete de ida y vuelta *masc.*
A return to York, please. Un billete de ida y vuelta a York, por favor.
a return ticket un billete de ida y vuelta
3 **Many happy returns!** ¡Feliz cumpleaños!

to **return** verb
1 (*to come or go back*) volver
When do you return to Barcelona?
¿Cuándo vuelves a Barcelona?
She hasn't returned. No ha vuelto.
2 (*to give back*) devolver
Return the book to the library.
Devuelve el libro a la biblioteca.

to **reverse** verb
(*in a car*) dar marcha atrás

reverse adjective
in reverse order en orden inverso

to **revise** verb
repasar
My sister's revising for her exams.
Mi hermana está repasando para los exámenes.

revision noun
el repaso *masc.*
a revision exercise un ejercicio de repaso
to do revision repasar

reward noun
la recompensa *fem.*
a fifty-euro reward una recompensa de cincuenta euros

to **rewind** verb
rebobinar
Rewind the video. Rebobina el vídeo.

• *The months of the year and days of the week do not take a capital letter in Spanish.*

rhinoceros noun
el **rinoceronte** masc.

rhyme noun
la **rima** fem.

to **rhyme** verb
rimar
'House' rhymes with 'mouse'.
'House' rima con 'mouse'.

rhythm noun
el **ritmo** masc.

rib noun
la **costilla** fem.

ribbon noun
la **cinta** fem.

rice noun
el **arroz** masc.
Would you like some rice?
¿Quieres arroz?
rice pudding el arroz con leche

rich adjective
rico masc., **rica** fem.
They're very rich. Son muy ricos.

rid adjective
1 **to get rid of** (to throw away) tirar
I've got rid of my old magazines.
He tirado las revistas viejas.
2 **to get rid of** (to take away) quitar
to get rid of a stain quitar una
mancha

riddle noun
la **adivinanza** fem.

ride noun
1 (in a car, on a horse, etc.) la **vuelta** fem.
to go for a ride dar una vuelta
I went for a ride on my bike. Fui a
dar una vuelta en bici.
2 (at a funfair)
We went on lots of rides. Nos
subimos a muchos aparatos.

to **ride** verb
1 **to ride a bike** montar en bici
Can you ride a bike? ¿Sabes
montar en bici?
to ride a horse montar a caballo

2 (to travel somewhere on a bicycle, horse, etc.)
ir
I ride my bike to school. Voy a la
escuela en bici.

ridiculous adjective
ridículo masc., **ridícula** fem.

riding noun
la **equitación** fem.
to go riding hacer equitación

right adjective
1 (correct) **correcto** masc.,
correcta fem.
the right answer la respuesta
correcta
2 (not translated)
This is the right house. Ésta es la
casa.
Do you have the right time?
¿Tienes hora?
3 (true)
That's right. Es verdad.
4 (at the beginning of a sentence) **¡bueno!**
Right! I'm leaving. ¡Bueno! Me voy.
5 (talking about people) **to be right** tener
razón
You're right, Emma. Tienes razón,
Emma.
6 (the opposite of left) **derecho** masc.,
derecha fem.
my right hand mi mano derecha

right adverb
1 (correctly) **bien**
Am I doing it right? ¿Lo estoy
haciendo bien?
2 (in time or place) **justo**
right before my birthday justo
antes de mi cumpleaños
right away ahora mismo
3 (the opposite of left) **a la derecha**
Turn right. Gira a la derecha.

right noun
on the right a la derecha
The school is on the right.
La escuela está a la derecha.
We drive on the right. Se conduce
por la derecha.

a b c d e f g h i j k l m n o p q r s t u v w x y z

• See the centre section for verb tables.

a
b
c
d
e
f
g
h
i
j
k
l
m
n
o
p
q
r
s
t
u
v
w
x
y
z

right-handed adjective
to be right-handed escribir con la mano derecha

ring noun
1 (*for your finger*) el **anillo** *masc.*
a gold ring un anillo de oro
2 (*phone call*)
to give somebody a ring llamar a alguien

to **ring** verb
1 (*to call on the phone*) **llamar**
Ring me tomorrow. Llámame mañana.
2 (*talking about a phone, bell, etc.*) **sonar**
The phone's ringing. El teléfono está sonando.
The bell rang. Ha sonado el timbre.
to ring the bell tocar el timbre
Somebody's ringing the doorbell. Llaman a la puerta.

rink noun
an ice rink una pista de hielo

ripe adjective
maduro *masc.*, **madura** *fem.*

to **rise** verb
salir
The sun is rising. Está saliendo el sol.

river noun
el **río** *masc.*
the River Severn el río Severn

road noun
1 (*between towns etc.*) la **carretera** *fem.*
the road to Bilbao la carretera de Bilbao
a road accident un accidente de tráfico
a road map un mapa de carreteras
a road sign una señal de tráfico
2 (*a street in a town or village*) la **calle** *fem.*
They live across the road. Viven al otro lado de la calle.

roadworks plural noun
las **obras** *fem. plural*

to **roar** verb
rugir
The lion is roaring. El león ruge.

to **rob** verb
1 (*a person*) **robar**
We've been robbed. Nos han robado.
2 (*a bank, shop, etc.*) **asaltar**, **robar**

robber noun
el **ladrón** *masc.*, la **ladrona** *fem.*

⚷ **LANGUAGE**
The plural of **ladrón** is **ladrones**.

robbery noun
el **robo** *masc.*

robot noun
el **robot** *masc.* (plural los **robots**)

rock noun
1 (*big stone*) la **roca** *fem.*
2 (*music*) el **rock** *masc.*
a rock group un grupo de rock
rock music la música rock
a rock star una estrella del rock

rocket noun
el **cohete** *masc.*

rocking horse noun
el **caballito de balancín** *masc.*

rod noun
a fishing rod una caña de pescar

role-play noun
el **juego de roles** *masc.*

roll noun
1 (*of paper etc.*) el **rollo** *masc.*
2 (*bread roll*) el **panecillo** *masc.*

to **roll** verb
rodar
Roll the ball. Rueda la pelota.
The ball has rolled under the bed. La pelota ha rodado por debajo de la cama.

Rollerblades® plural noun
los **patines en línea** *masc. plural*

• Use **el** and **uno** for masculine words and **la** and **una** for feminine words.

roller coaster noun
la **montaña rusa** *fem.*

> 🔑 **LANGUAGE**
> Word for word the Spanish means
> 'Russian mountain': there are plenty of
> ups and downs.

roller skates plural noun
los **patines de ruedas** *masc. plural*

roller-skating noun
el **patinaje sobre ruedas** *masc.*
to go roller-skating ir a patinar

Roman adjective
romano *masc.*, **romana** *fem.*
a Roman road una calzada romana

Roman noun
the Romans los romanos *masc. plural*

roof noun
el **tejado** *masc.*

room noun
1 (*in a house*) la **habitación** *fem.* (plural las **habitaciones**)
I'm in my room. Estoy en mi habitación.
2 (*in school*) la **sala** *fem.*
the computer room la sala de ordenadores
3 (*space*) el **sitio** *masc.*
There's no room. No hay sitio.
to make room hacer sitio

root noun
la **raíz** *fem.* (plural las **raíces**)

rope noun
la **cuerda** *fem.*

rose noun
la **rosa** *fem.*

rotten adjective
1 (*apple, pear, etc.*) **podrido** *masc.*, **podrida** *fem.*
2 (*film, food, weather, etc.*) **malísimo** *masc.*, **malísima** *fem.*

rough adjective
1 (*person, behaviour, game*) **violento** *masc.*, **violenta** *fem.*
2 (*hands, towel*) **áspero** *masc.*, **áspera** *fem.*
3 (*life, voice*) **duro** *masc.*, **dura** *fem.*
4 (*area of town*) **peligroso** *masc.*, **peligrosa** *fem.*

roughly adverb
más o menos
It weighs roughly ten kilos. Pesa diez kilos más o menos.

round adjective
redondo *masc.*, **redonda** *fem.*
He has a round face. Tiene la cara redonda.

round preposition & adverb
1 **alrededor de**
a trip round the world un viaje alrededor del mundo
They live round the corner. Viven muy cerca.
round here por aquí
round about ten o'clock alrededor de la diez
2 (*talking about somebody's house*)
Come round tomorrow. Ven a mi casa mañana.

roundabout noun
1 (*merry-go-round*) el **tiovivo** *masc.*
2 (*for traffic*) la **rotonda** *fem.*

row noun
1 (*of people in the cinema etc.*) la **fila** *fem.*
in the front row en la primera fila
in the back row en la última fila
2 (*of chairs, houses, trees, etc.*) la **hilera** *fem.*

to **row** verb
(*in a boat*) **remar**

rowing boat noun
el **bote de remos** *masc.*

a b c d e f g h i j k l m n o p q r s t u v w x y z

• *Languages and nationalities do not take a capital letter in Spanish.*

a
b
c
d
e
f
g
h
i
j
k
l
m
n
o
p
q
r
s
t
u
v
w
x
y
z

royal adjective
real *masc. & fem.*
the royal family la familia real

rubber noun
la goma *fem.*
Do you have a rubber? ¿Tienes una goma?
It's made of rubber. Es de goma.
a rubber band una goma elástica

rubbish noun
1 (*food, papers, etc. thrown out*) la basura *fem.*
to put out the rubbish sacar la basura
a rubbish bin un cubo de basura
2 (*nonsense*) las tonterías *fem. plural*, la tontería *fem.*
to talk rubbish decir tonterías
What rubbish! ¡Qué tontería!

rubbish adjective
(*very bad*) **to be rubbish** ser una porquería
The book is rubbish. El libro es una porquería.

to **rub out** verb
borrar
Rub this word out with your rubber. Borra esta palabra con tu goma.

rude adjective
maleducado *masc.*, maleducada *fem.*
to be rude to somebody ser maleducado con alguien
That's rude. Eso es de mala educación.
a rude word una palabrota

rug noun
(*carpet*) la alfombra *fem.*

rugby noun
el rugby *masc.*
to play rugby jugar al rugby

to **ruin** verb
(*a dress, toy, etc.*) estropear
You're going to ruin that shirt. Vas a estropear esa camisa.

ruins plural noun
(*of a castle etc.*) las ruinas *fem. plural*

rule noun
1 (*in grammar etc.*) la regla *fem.*
the rules of the game las reglas del juego
2 (*in a school, office, etc.*)
the rules el reglamento
the school rules el reglamento del colegio
It's against the rules. Está prohibido.

ruler noun
la regla *fem.*

run noun
to go for a run ir a correr

to **run** verb
1 correr
Jamal runs very fast. Jamal corre muy rápido.
I ran down the hill. Bajé la cuesta corriendo.

> ⚷ **LANGUAGE**
> Word for word the Spanish means 'I went down the hill running'.

2 (*activities, classes, etc.*) organizar

to **run away** verb
escaparse
The children have run away. Los niños se han escapado.

to **run into** verb
chocar con
The car ran into a tree. El coche chocó con un árbol.

to **run over** verb
atropellar
Be careful, you'll get run over! ¡Cuidado, te van a atropellar!

• *The months of the year and days of the week do not take a capital letter in Spanish.*

runner noun
el corredor *masc.*,
la corredora *fem.*

running noun
el footing *masc.*
to go running hacer footing

runny adjective
to have a runny nose tener mocos

runway noun
(*for planes*) la pista *fem.*

to **rush** verb
correr
Don't rush! ¡No corras!
You're always rushing. Siempre
estás corriendo.

rush noun
1 to be in a rush tener prisa
2 in the rush hour a la hora punta

Russia noun
Rusia *fem.*

Russian adjective
ruso *masc.*, rusa *fem.*
She's Russian. Es rusa.

Russian noun
1 (*language*) el ruso *masc.*
2 (*person*) el ruso *masc.*, la rusa *fem.*

rusty adjective
(*bike, wire, etc.*) oxidado *masc.*,
oxidada *fem.*

Ss

sack noun
el saco *masc.*

sad adjective
triste *masc. & fem.*
I'm sad. Estoy triste.

saddle noun
1 (*on a horse*) la silla de montar *fem.*
2 (*on a bicycle*) el sillín *masc.* (plural los
sillines)

sadness noun
la tristeza *fem.*

safe adjective
1 (*not dangerous, not in danger*)
seguro *masc.*, segura *fem.*
His car isn't very safe. Su coche no
es muy seguro.
You're safe here. Estás segura
aquí.
It's not safe to go out. Es peligroso
salir.
2 (*not hurt*) sano y salvo *masc.*, sana y
salva *fem.*
Mum came back safe. Mamá
volvió sana y salva.

safe noun
(*for money*) la caja fuerte *fem.*

safely adverb
1 (*without danger*)
They've arrived safely. Han
llegado sin problemas.
to drive safely conducir con
cuidado
2 (*in a safe place*) en un sitio seguro

safety noun
la seguridad *fem.*

sailing noun
la vela *fem.*
to go sailing hacer vela
a sailing boat un barco de vela

sailor noun
el marinero *masc.*

saint noun
el santo *masc.*, la santa *fem.*

salad noun
la ensalada *fem.*
a chicken salad una ensalada de
pollo

• *See the centre section for verb tables.*

a
b
c
d
e
f
g
h
i
j
k
l
m
n
o
p
q
r
s
t
u
v
w
x
y
z

a
b
c
d
e
f
g
h
i
j
k
l
m
n
o
p
q
r
s
t
u
v
w
x
y
z

sale noun
1 'For sale'. 'Se vende'.
'Bicycle for sale'. 'Se vende
bicicleta'.
2 the sales las rebajas *fem. plural*
to buy something in the sales
comprar algo en las rebajas

salt noun
la sal *fem.*
Put on some salt. Echa un poco de
sal.

salty adjective
salado *masc.*, salada *fem.*
The food is salty. La comida está
salada.

same adjective & pronoun
1 mismo *masc.*, misma *fem.*
I've got the same dress as you.
Tengo el mismo vestido que tú.
I've got the same one. Tengo el
mismo.
at the same time al mismo tiempo
It's not the same. No es lo mismo.
2 (*describing things that look the same*)
igual *masc. & fem.*
They look the same. Parecen
iguales.
You're the same as your dad.
Eres igual a tu padre.

sand noun
la arena *fem.*
a sand castle un castillo de arena

sandal noun
la sandalia *fem.*
a pair of sandals un par de
sandalias

sandwich noun
el sándwich *masc.* (plural los
sándwiches)
a cheese sandwich un sándwich de
queso

Santa Claus noun
Papá Noel *masc.*

satellite noun
el satélite *masc.*
satellite television la televisión
vía satélite
a satellite dish una antena
parabólica *fem.*

Saturday noun
el sábado *masc.*
Today is Saturday. Hoy es sábado.
on Saturday el sábado
They come back on Saturday.
Vuelven el sábado.
on Saturdays los sábados
It's closed on Saturdays. Está
cerrado los sábados.

LANGUAGE
Remember the difference in Spanish
between el sábado (one Saturday only)
and los sábados (every Saturday).

sauce noun
la salsa *fem.*

saucepan noun
la cacerola *fem.*

saucer noun
el platillo *masc.*
a flying saucer un platillo volante

sausage noun
la salchicha *fem.*

to **save** verb
1 (*from danger*) salvar
They saved the dog from the fire.
Han salvado al perro del incendio.
2 (*to keep*) guardar
Save me a place. Guárdame un
sitio.
3 (*money, time*) ahorrar
I've saved twenty pounds.
He ahorrado veinte libras.
... to save time ... para ahorrar
tiempo
4 (*a computer file etc.*) grabar
I've saved the file onto a disk.
He grabado el archivo en un disco.
I've saved my work. He guardado
mi trabajo.

• Use el and uno for masculine words and la and una for feminine words.

to **save up** verb
ahorrar
I'm saving up for a computer.
Estoy ahorrando para un
ordenador.

to **say** verb
1 decir
He says it's raining. Dice que está
lloviendo.
I didn't say anything. No he dicho
nada.
How do you say 'boy' in Spanish?
¿Cómo se dice 'boy' en español?
2 (*to repeat*) **repetir**
Say these words after me. Repetid
estas palabras después de mí.

saying noun
el **refrán** *masc.* (plural los **refranes**)

scales noun
la **báscula** *fem.*
I weighed myself on the scales.
Me he pesado en la báscula.

scanner noun
el **escáner** *masc.*

scar noun
la **cicatriz** *fem.* (plural las **cicatrices**)

scared adjective
I'm scared. Tengo miedo.
I'm scared of the dark. Tengo
miedo a la oscuridad.
She's scared of her teacher.
Le tiene miedo a su maestra.
He's scared to go out by himself.
Le da miedo salir solo.

> **LANGUAGE**
> English = **I am** scared.
> Spanish = **Tengo** miedo = I have fear

scarf noun
1 (*long and warm*) la **bufanda** *fem.*
a woolly scarf una bufanda de
lana
2 (*thin headscarf*) el **pañuelo** *masc.*
a silk scarf un pañuelo de seda

scary adjective
(*story, monster, etc.*) **que da miedo**
Spiders are very scary. Las arañas
me dan mucho miedo.
a scary film una película de miedo

scenery noun
(*in the countryside*) el **paisaje** *masc.*

school noun
la **escuela** *fem.*
at school en la escuela
to go to school ir a la escuela
a school bus un autobús escolar
the school holidays las vacaciones
escolares
the school year el año escolar
a school uniform un uniforme
escolar

> **LANGUAGE**
> You can also say **el colegio**, e.g. 'at
> school' is **en el colegio**.

schoolbag noun
1 (*carried on your back*) la **mochila** *fem.*
2 (*carried in your hand*) la **cartera** *fem.*

schoolbook noun
el **libro de texto** *masc.*

schoolboy noun
el **colegial** *masc.*

schoolchildren noun
los **colegiales** *masc. plural*

schoolgirl noun
la **colegiala** *fem.*

science noun
la **ciencia** *fem.*
I like science. Me gustan las
ciencias.

> **LANGUAGE**
> When science is a school subject, use the
> plural in Spanish.

scientist noun
el **científico** *masc.*, la **científica** *fem.*
She's a scientist. Es científica.

a
b
c
d
e
f
g
h
i
j
k
l
m
n
o
p
q
r
s
t
u
v
w
x
y
z

• *Languages and nationalities do not take a capital letter in Spanish.*

scissors plural noun
las **tijeras** *fem. plural*
a pair of scissors unas tijeras

scooter noun
1 (*for children*) el **patinete** *masc.*
2 (*motorcycle*) el **scooter** *masc.* (plural
los **scooters**)

score noun
(*in sports*) el **resultado** *masc.*
The score was four two. El
resultado fue cuatro a dos.
What's the score? ¿Cómo van?

to **score** verb
1 (*in football etc.*) **marcar**
Mohammed has scored a goal.
Mohammed ha marcado un gol.
2 (*in a competition etc.*) **sacar**
I've scored ten points. He sacado
diez puntos.

Scot noun
el **escocés** *masc.*, la **escocesa** *fem.*

> **LANGUAGE**
> The plural of **escocés** is **escoceses**.

Scotland noun
Escocia *fem.*
We live in Scotland. Vivimos en
Escocia.

Scotsman noun
el **escocés** *masc.* (plural los
escoceses)

Scotswoman noun
la **escocesa** *fem.*

Scottish adjective
escocés *masc.*, **escocesa** *fem.*
a Scottish footballer un futbolista
escocés
She's Scottish. Es escocesa.
Scottish people los escoceses

> **LANGUAGE**
> The masculine plural of **escocés** is
> **escoceses**.

Scout noun
el **scout** *masc.*
I'm a Scout. Soy scout.

scrapbook noun
el **álbum de recortes** *masc.*

to **scratch** verb
1 (*an arm, leg, etc. that itches*) **rascarse**
I'm scratching my back. Me rasco
la espalda.
2 (*to hurt*) **arañar**
The cat scratched me. El gato me
arañó.

to **scream** verb
gritar, **chillar**

screen noun
la **pantalla** *fem.*
on the screen en la pantalla

sea noun
el **mar** *masc.*
at the bottom of the sea en el
fondo del mar
to travel by sea viajar en barco

seafood noun
el **marisco** *masc.*

seagull noun
la **gaviota** *fem.*

seal noun
(*animal*) la **foca** *fem.*

to **search** verb
buscar
I'm searching for my glasses.
Estoy buscando mis gafas.
I've searched everywhere.
He buscado por todas partes.

seashore noun
la **orilla del mar** *fem.*

seashell noun
la **concha** *fem.*

seasick adjective
mareado *masc.*, **mareada** *fem.*
I'm seasick. Estoy mareado.
I get seasick. Me mareo.

• *The months of the year and days of the week do not take a capital letter in Spanish.*

seaside noun
 la **playa** *fem.*
 to go to the seaside ir a la playa

season noun
 1 *(of the year)* la **estación** *fem.* (plural
 las **estaciones**)
 2 *(for sports etc.)* la **temporada** *fem.*
 the football season la temporada
 de fútbol

seat noun
 el **asiento** *masc.*
 the front seat el asiento delantero
 This seat is taken. Este asiento está
 ocupado.
 Save me a seat. Guárdame un
 asiento.

seatbelt noun
 el **cinturón de seguridad** *masc.*
 (plural los **cinturones de seguridad**)

second adjective
 segundo *masc.*, **segunda** *fem.*
 for the second time por segunda vez
 I came second. *(in the race)* Quedé
 segunda.
 I'm the second one. Soy el
 segundo.
 on the second of August el dos de
 agosto

> **LANGUAGE**
> With dates you use **dos** (two).

second noun
 el **segundo** *masc.*
 two minutes and ten seconds dos
 minutos y diez segundos

secondary school noun
 el **instituto de enseñanza
 secundaria** *masc.*

secret noun
 el **secreto** *masc.*
 Shall I tell you a secret?
 ¿Te cuento un secreto?

secret adjective
 secreto *masc.*, **secreta** *fem.*
 a secret door una puerta secreta

secretary noun
 el **secretario** *masc.*,
 la **secretaria** *fem.*
 My mum's a secretary. Mi madre
 es secretaria.

section noun
 1 *(in a big store etc.)* la **sección** *fem.*
 the toy section la sección de
 juguetes
 2 *(part of something)* la **parte** *fem.*
 the first section of the book
 la primera parte del libro

to **see** verb
 1 **ver**
 I can see the sea. Veo el mar.
 Have you seen the film? ¿Has visto
 la película?
 I saw her yesterday. La vi ayer.
 2 **See you!** ¡Hasta luego!
 See you soon! ¡Hasta pronto!
 See you on Monday! ¡Hasta el
 lunes!

> **LANGUAGE**
> Use **hasta** in Spanish to translate 'See
> you ...!'. It means 'until'.

seed noun
 la **semilla** *fem.*

to **seem** verb
 parecer
 It seems a good idea to me.
 Me parece una buena idea.

seesaw noun
 el **balancín** *masc.* (plural los
 balancines)

to **select** verb
 seleccionar

selfish adjective
 egoísta *masc. & fem.*
 He's selfish. Es egoísta.

to **sell** verb
 vender
 They sell bicycles. Venden
 bicicletas.

a
b
c
d
e
f
g
h
i
j
k
l
m
n
o
p
q
r
s
t
u
v
w
x
y
z

• See the centre section for verb tables.

I've sold my computer to my cousin. He vendido mi ordenador a mi primo.
The tickets are sold out. No hay billetes.

Sellotape® noun
el celo masc.
Stick down the photo with Sellotape. Pega la foto con celo.

semicircle noun
el semicírculo masc.
in a semicircle en semicírculo

semifinal noun
la semifinal fem.

to send verb
mandar
Send me a photo. Mándame una foto.
to send something back devolver algo

sense noun
el sentido masc.
It doesn't make sense. No tiene sentido.
My mum has a sense of humour. Mi madre tiene sentido del humor.

sensible adjective
sensato masc., sensata fem.
Anne is very sensible. Anne es muy sensata.

⚠️ **FALSE FRIEND**
sensible = sensato (not sensible)

sensitive adjective
sensible masc. & fem.
Chen is very sensitive. Chen es muy sensible.

sentence noun
la frase fem., la oración fem.
(plural las **oraciones**)

separate adjective
1 (different) distinto masc., distinta fem.
Put them in separate piles. Ponlos en montones distintos.

2 (another) otro masc., otra fem.
It's in a separate building. Está en otro edificio.

to separate verb
separar
The teacher separated the two boys. La maestra ha separado a los dos niños.

separated adjective
separado masc., separada fem.
Her parents are separated. Sus padres están separados.

September noun
septiembre masc.
I'm going in September. Voy en septiembre.
It's my birthday on Saturday, the tenth of September. Mi cumpleaños es el sábado diez de septiembre.

series noun
la serie fem.
a TV series une serie de televisión

serious adjective
1 serio masc., seria fem.
a serious man un hombre serio
I'm serious. Estoy hablando en serio.
2 (accident, problem, etc.) grave masc. & fem.
a serious illness una enfermedad grave
a serious mistake un error grave

seriously adverb
gravemente
to be seriously ill estar gravemente enfermo

to serve verb
servir
Can I serve the food? ¿Puedo servir la comida?

serviette noun
la servilleta fem.

• Use **el** and **uno** for masculine words and **la** and **una** for feminine words.

set noun
 a chess set un ajedrez
 a train set un tren de juguete
 a TV set una televisión (plural
 las **televisiones**)

to **set** verb
 1 poner
 to set the table poner la mesa
 Have you set the alarm? ¿Has
 puesto el despertador?
 to set fire to something prender
 fuego a algo
 2 ponerse
 The sun is setting. Se está poniendo
 el sol.

to **set off** salir
 We set off for Madrid. Salimos
 para Madrid.

to **set out** verb
 salir

settee noun
 el sofá *masc.*

to **settle down** verb
 Settle down, boys! ¡Niños!
 ¡Tranquilos!

seven number
 siete
 **We're going to the library at
 seven.** Vamos a la biblioteca a las
 siete.
 I'm seven. Tengo siete años.

🔑 **LANGUAGE**
In English you can say 'seven o'clock' or
just 'seven', 'seven years old' or just
'seven'. In Spanish you must add **las** (for
time) and **años** (for age).

seventeen number
 diecisiete
 My sister is seventeen. Mi
 hermana tiene diecisiete años.

seventh adjective
 séptimo *masc.*, séptima *fem.*
 on the seventh floor en el séptimo
 piso
 the seventh of November el siete
 de noviembre

🔑 **LANGUAGE**
With dates you use **siete** (seven).

seventy number
 setenta
 My grandmother is seventy.
 Mi abuela tiene setenta años.

🔑 **LANGUAGE**
In English you can say just 'seventy'. In
Spanish you must add **años**.

several adjective & pronoun
 varios *masc. plural*, varias *fem. plural*
 several times varias veces
 several of the books varios libros

to **sew** verb
 coser
 I like to sew. Me gusta coser.

shade noun
 la sombra *fem.*
 to sit in the shade sentarse a la
 sombra

shadow noun
 la sombra *fem.*

shady adjective
 It's shady here. Aquí hay sombra.

to **shake** verb
 1 (*a person, tree, towel, etc.*) sacudir
 He shook the carpet. Sacudió la
 alfombra.
 2 to shake hands with somebody
 dar la mano a alguien
 I shake hands with him. Le doy la
 mano.
 They shake hands. Se dan la mano.
 3 (*talking about a building, your hand, etc. that
 shakes*) temblar
 You're shaking! ¡Estás temblando!

• *Languages and nationalities do not take a capital letter in Spanish.*

shall verb
Shall I close the door? ¿Cierro la puerta?
Shall we go for a walk? ¿Vamos a dar un paseo?

> **LANGUAGE**
> When you ask a question using 'Shall I?', just use the verb in the present tense in Spanish, e.g. 'Shall I close ...?' is ¿**Cierro ...?** When you ask a question using 'Shall we?', you can often use **vamos** (= 'let's go').

shallow adjective
poco profundo *masc.*, poco profunda *fem.*

shame noun
What a shame! ¡Qué pena!

shampoo noun
el champú *masc.*

shape noun
la forma *fem.*
What shape is it? ¿Qué forma tiene?
in the shape of a star en forma de estrella

to share verb
compartir
I share the sweets with my friends. Comparto los caramelos con mis amigas.

shark noun
el tiburón *masc.* (plural los tiburones)

sharp adjective
These scissors are very sharp. Estas tijeras cortan muy bien.
This knife isn't sharp. Este cuchillo no corta.
This pencil is sharp. Este lápiz tiene mucha punta.

> **LANGUAGE**
> In Spanish you often use **cortar** (to cut) to translate sharp.

to sharpen verb
to sharpen a pencil sacarle punta a un lápiz

sharpener noun
el sacapuntas *masc.* (plural los sacapuntas)

she pronoun
1 (*not usually translated in Spanish*) **She's tired.** Está cansada.
She has lots of books. Tiene muchos libros.
2 ella
She's tall but her brother is small. Ella es alta pero su hermano es pequeño.

> **LANGUAGE**
> Use **ella** when you want to give special importance to the word 'she'.

shed noun
(*in the garden*) la caseta *fem.*

sheep noun
la oveja *fem.*

sheet noun
1 (*on a bed*) la sábana *fem.*
2 **a sheet of paper** una hoja de papel

shelf noun
el estante *masc.*

shell noun
1 (*of an egg or nut*) la cáscara *fem.*
2 (*on the beach, of a snail, etc.*) la concha *fem.*

shield noun
el escudo *masc.*

to shine verb
brillar
The sun is shining. Brilla el sol.

shiny adjective
(*metal, hair, etc.*) brillante *masc. & fem.*

ship noun
el barco *masc.*
by ship en barco

• *The months of the year and days of the week do not take a capital letter in Spanish.*

shirt noun
1 la **camisa** *fem.*
 a clean shirt una camisa limpia
2 (*for football, rugby*) la **camiseta** *fem.*
 a football shirt una camiseta de
 fútbol

to **shiver** verb
 temblar, temblar de frío

shoe noun
 el **zapato** *masc.*
 a pair of shoes un par de zapatos
 a shoe shop una zapatería

shoelace noun
 el **cordón de zapato** *masc.*
 Can you do up your shoelaces?
 ¿Sabes atarte los cordones?

shop noun
 la **tienda** *fem.*
 a clothes shop una tienda de ropa
 a shop assistant un
 dependiente *masc.*, una
 dependienta *fem.*
 a shop window un escaparate

shopkeeper noun
 el or la **comerciante** *masc. & fem.*
 My dad's a shopkeeper. Mi padre
 es comerciante.

shopping noun
 la **compra** *fem.*
 to do the shopping hacer la
 compra, hacer las compras
 to go shopping ir de compras
 a shopping bag una bolsa de la
 compra
 a shopping centre un centro
 comercial
 a shopping list una lista de la
 compra

short adjective
1 (*dress, visit, grass, etc.*) **corto** *masc.*,
 corta *fem.*
 to have short hair tener el pelo corto
 a short time ago hace poco tiempo
 Mike is short for Michael. Mike es
 el diminutivo de Michael.

2 (*person*) **bajo** *masc.*, **baja** *fem.*
 I'm quite short. Soy bastante bajo.

short cut noun
 el **atajo** *masc.*

shorts plural noun
 los **shorts** *masc. plural*
 I'm wearing blue shorts. Llevo
 unos shorts azules.
 a pair of shorts unos shorts

short-sighted adjective
 miope *masc. & fem.*
 I'm short-sighted. Soy miope.

should verb
 deber
 You should go. Deberías ir.

shoulder noun
 el **hombro** *masc.*

to **shout** verb
 gritar
 Stop shouting! ¡Deja de gritar!
 Don't shout! ¡No grites!

to **show** verb
 enseñar
 Show me the dress. Enséñame el
 vestido.
 Show me how to do it Enséñame
 cómo se hace

show noun
1 (*with actors, musicians, etc.*)
 el **espectáculo** *masc.*
 a children's show un espectáculo
 para niños
2 (*on TV*) el **programa** *masc.*
 a quiz show un programa concurso

🔑 **LANGUAGE**
Be careful: **programa** ends in an -**a** but it
is not a feminine noun.

shower noun
1 la **ducha** *fem.*
 I want to have a shower. Quiero
 ducharme.
 I'm in the shower. Me estoy
 duchando.

• *See the centre section for verb tables.*

a b c d e f g h i j k l m n o p q r s t u v w x y z

2 (*rain*) el chaparrón *masc.* (plural los **chaparrones**)
It's only a shower. Sólo es un chaparrón.

Shrove Tuesday noun
el martes de Carnaval *masc.*

CULTURE
This is the last day before Christian Lent and in Spain children celebrate by dressing up, dancing, and playing music.

to **shut** verb
cerrar
Shut your eyes. Cierra los ojos.
The museum shuts at six. El museo cierra a las seis.

shut adjective
cerrado *masc.*, cerrada *fem.*
The door's shut. La puerta está cerrada.

to **shut up** verb
callarse
Shut up! ¡Cállate!

shuttle noun
the space shuttle el transbordador espacial

shy adjective
tímido *masc.*, tímida *fem.*

sick adjective
1 (*ill*) enfermo *masc.*, enferma *fem.*
I'm sick. Estoy enferma.
2 to feel sick tener ganas de devolver
I'm going to be sick. Voy a devolver.

side noun
1 el lado *masc.*
on this side of the road a este lado de la calle
on the other side al otro lado
2 (*edge*) el borde *masc.*
by the side of the road al borde de la carretera
3 (*team*) el equipo *masc.*
He's on our side. Está en nuestro equipo.

sightseeing noun
el turismo *masc.*
to go sightseeing hacer turismo

sign noun
1 (*on a door, wall, etc.*) el letrero *masc.*
2 (*on a road*) la señal *fem.*
a road sign una señal de tráfico
The policeman made a sign. El guardia hizo una señal.

to **sign** verb
firmar
Your parents sign here. Tus padres firman aquí.

signal noun
la señal *fem.*

signature noun
la firma *fem.*

sign language noun
el lenguaje de signos *masc.*
to talk in sign language hablar por señas

Sikh adjective
sij *masc. & fem.*

silence noun
el silencio *masc.*

silent adjective
silencioso *masc.*, silenciosa *fem.*

silk noun
la seda *fem.*
a silk blouse una blusa de seda

silly adjective
tonto *masc.*, tonta *fem.*
You're so silly! ¡Tú eres tonto!

silver noun
la plata *fem.*
a silver bracelet una pulsera de plata

similar adjective
parecido *masc.*, parecida *fem.*
Your bike is similar to mine. Tu bici es parecida a la mía.

• *Use* el *and* uno *for masculine words and* la *and* una *for feminine words.*

simple adjective
1 (*dress, problem, etc.*) sencillo *masc.*, sencilla *fem.*
2 (*easy*) fácil

since preposition & adverb
desde
I haven't seen her since Sunday. No la he visto desde el domingo.
since then, ever since desde entonces
I've been waiting since three o'clock. Estoy esperando desde las tres.

> 🔑 **LANGUAGE**
> For showing something still going on, use the present tense in Spanish, not the past.

to sing verb
cantar
I like to sing. Me gusta cantar.
singing lessons clases de canto

singer noun
el or la cantante *masc. & fem.*

single adjective
1 solo *masc.*, sola *fem.*
He hasn't got a single friend. No tiene ni un solo amigo.
2 (*bed, portion, etc.*) individual *masc. & fem.*
a single room una habitación individual
3 **in single file** en fila india
a single ticket un billete de ida

single noun
(*ticket*) el billete de ida *masc.*
a single to Cambridge un billete de ida para Cambridge

singular noun
el singular *masc.*
'Mouse' is in the singular. 'Mouse' está en singular.

sink noun
1 (*in the kitchen*) el fregadero *masc.*
2 (*in the bathroom*) el lavabo *masc.*

to sink verb
hundirse
The boat sank. El barco se hundió.

sir noun
(*talking about your teacher etc.*) señor *masc.*
Please, sir! ¡Por favor, señor!
Yes, sir. Sí, señor.

sister noun
la hermana *fem.*
my big sister mi hermana mayor

to sit verb
1 sentarse
Sit next to your sister. Siéntate al lado de tu hermana.
2 **to be sitting** estar sentado *masc.*, estar sentada *fem.*
She's sitting on the sofa. Está sentada en el sofá.

to sit down verb
sentarse
I sat down on the floor. Me senté en el suelo.
Sit down, Dylan. Siéntate, Dylan.
Sit down, children. Niños, sentaos.

site noun
1 (*website*) el sitio web *masc.*
I like this site. Me gusta este sitio.
2 **a camping site** un camping (plural los **campings**)

sitting room noun
el salón *masc.* (plural los **salones**)

situation noun
la situación *fem.* (plural las **situaciones**)

six number
seis
I went out at six. Salí a las seis.
I'm six. Tengo seis años.

> 🔑 **LANGUAGE**
> In English you can say 'six o'clock' or just 'six', 'six years old' or just 'six'. In Spanish you must add **las** (for time) and **años** (for age).

• *Languages and nationalities do not take a capital letter in Spanish.*

a
b
c
d
e
f
g
h
i
j
k
l
m
n
o
p
q
r
s
t
u
v
w
x
y
z

a
b
c
d
e
f
g
h
i
j
k
l
m
n
o
p
q
r
s
t
u
v
w
x
y
z

sixteen number
dieciséis
My cousin is sixteen. Mi prima tiene dieciséis años.

sixth adjective
sexto masc., **sexta** fem.
on the sixth floor en el sexto piso
the sixth of March el seis de marzo

🔑 **LANGUAGE**
With dates you use **seis** (six).

sixty number
sesenta
My uncle is sixty. Mi tío tiene sesenta años.

🔑 **LANGUAGE**
In English you can say just 'sixty'. In Spanish you must add **años**.

size noun
1 el **tamaño** masc.
What size is it? ¿De qué tamaño es?
2 (of clothes) la **talla** fem.
What size do you take? ¿Qué talla usas?
3 (of shoes) el **número** masc.
What size do you take? ¿Qué número usas?

to **skate** verb
(on ice) **patinar**

skateboard noun
el **monopatín** masc. (plural los **monopatines**)

skateboarding noun
to go skateboarding montar en monopatín

skating noun
(on ice) el **patinaje sobre hielo** masc.
to go skating ir a patinar
a skating rink una pista de hielo

skeleton noun
el **esqueleto** masc.

ski noun
el **esquí** masc.
a pair of skis un par de esquís

ski boots las botas de esquí
a ski slope una pista de esquí

to **ski** verb
esquiar

skiing noun
el **esquí** masc.
I like skiing. Me gusta el esquí.
to go skiing ir a esquiar

skin noun
la **piel** fem.

to **skip** verb
(with a rope) **saltar a la cuerda**, **jugar a la comba**
a skipping rope una cuerda, una comba

skirt noun
la **falda** fem.

sky noun
el **cielo** masc.

skyscraper noun
el **rascacielos** masc. (plural los **rascacielos**)

to **slam** verb
to slam the door dar un portazo

🔑 **LANGUAGE**
Word for word the Spanish means 'to give a bang with the door' (**puerta** is 'door').

sledge noun
el **trineo** masc.

to **sleep** verb
dormir
He's sleeping. Está durmiendo.
a sleeping bag un saco de dormir

🔑 **LANGUAGE**
The verb **dormir** is related to the English word 'dormitory' (a room where lots of people sleep).

sleep noun
el **sueño** masc.
eight hours' sleep ocho horas de sueño
to go to sleep dormirse
Go to sleep! ¡Duérmete!

• *The months of the year and days of the week do not take a capital letter in Spanish.*

sleepover noun
I went for a sleepover at Jessica's.
Me quedé a dormir en casa de
Jessica.

sleepy adjective
to be sleepy tener sueño

> **LANGUAGE**
> English = **to be** sleepy **I'm sleepy.**
> Spanish = **tener** sueño **Tengo sueño.**

sleeve noun
la **manga** *fem.*
a shirt with short sleeves una
camisa de manga corta

slice noun
1 la **rebanada** *fem.*
a slice of bread una rebanada de
pan
2 (*of cake, cheese*) el **trozo** *masc.*

to **slide** verb
deslizarse
They're sliding down the slide.
Se deslizan por el tobogán.

slide noun
(*in a playground*) el **tobogán** *masc.*
(plural los **toboganes**)

slight adjective
1 (*pain, accent, taste*) **ligero** *masc.*,
ligera *fem.*
2 (*problem, change, chance*)
pequeño *masc.*, **pequeña** *fem.*

slightly adverb
un poco
slightly bigger un poco más
grande

slim adjective
delgado *masc.*, **delgada** *fem.*

to **slip** verb
resbalarse
I slipped on the floor. Me resbalé
en el suelo.

• *See the centre section for verb tables.*

slipper noun
la **zapatilla** *fem.*
a pair of slippers un par de
zapatillas

> **LANGUAGE**
> In Spanish **zapato** means 'shoe', so
> **zapatilla** is a 'little shoe'.

slippery adjective
to be slippery resbalar
This floor's slippery. Este suelo
resbala.

slope noun
la **cuesta** *fem.*

slow adjective
lento *masc.*, **lenta** *fem.*

slowly adverb
despacio
Speak more slowly. Habla más
despacio.

smack noun
1 (*on the backside*) el **azote** *masc.*
2 (*on the face*) la **bofetada** *fem.*

small adjective
pequeño *masc.*, **pequeña** *fem.*
You're smaller than me. Eres más
pequeña que yo.

smart adjective
1 (*clothes, shop, etc.*) **elegante** *masc. &
fem.*
You're very smart today. Estás
muy elegante hoy.
2 (*clever*) **listo** *masc.*, **lista** *fem.*
She's a very smart girl. Es una
chica muy lista.

to **smash** verb
romper

smell noun
el **olor** *masc.*
a nasty smell un mal olor

to **smell** verb
1 oler
I can't smell anything. No huelo nada.
I can smell fish. Huele a pescado.
It smells lovely! ¡Qué bien huele!
It smells bad here. Aquí huele mal.
2 **to smell of something** oler a algo
It smells of fish. Huele a pescado.

LANGUAGE
The Spanish for 'I can smell fish' is, word for word, 'It smells of fish'.

smelly adjective
Your socks are smelly. Tus calcetines huelen mal.

to **smile** verb
sonreír
He smiled at me. Me sonrió.

smile noun
la sonrisa fem.

smoke noun
el humo masc.

to **smoke** verb
fumar
My parents don't smoke. Mis padres no fuman.
'No smoking.' 'Prohibido fumar.'

smooth adjective
liso masc., lisa fem., suave masc. & fem.

snack noun
to have a snack comer algo
a snack bar una cafetería fem.

CULTURE
Spanish people sometimes have a snack in mid-morning (el almuerzo) or late afternoon (la merienda).

snail noun
el caracol masc.

snake noun
la serpiente fem.

to **sneeze** verb
estornudar

CULTURE
In Spain people say ¡Jesús! (Jesus) when somebody sneezes.

to **snore** verb
roncar

snow noun
la nieve fem.

to **snow** verb
nevar
It's snowing. Está nevando.

snowball noun
la bola de nieve fem.

snowflakes plural noun
los copos de nieve masc. plural

snowman noun
el muñeco de nieve masc.

so conjunction
(giving a reason) así que
I'm ill, so I can't come. Estoy enfermo, así que no puedo venir.

so adverb
1 (so very much) tan
I'm so tired! ¡Estoy tan cansado!
2 (also) también
Miguel is Spanish and so am I. Miguel es español y yo también.
I like football and so does she. A mi me gusta el fútbol y a ella también.

LANGUAGE
Word for word yo también means 'me too' and ella también means 'she too'. To translate words like 'so am I', 'so does she', use también with the correct pronoun.

3 (after 'think', 'hope', etc.)
I think so. Creo que sí.
4 **so much** (with nouns) tanto masc., tanta fem.
He has so much money. Tiene tanto dinero.

• Use el and uno for masculine words and la and una for feminine words.

5 so much (*with verbs*) tanto
 I like it so much. Me gusta tanto.
6 so many tantos *masc. plural*,
 tantas *fem. plural*
 I have so many friends. Tengo
 tantas amigas.

soaking wet adjective
 empapado *masc.*, empapada *fem.*

soap noun
1 el jabón *masc.*
 a bar of soap una pastilla de jabón
2 (*TV programme*) la telenovela *fem.*

soccer noun
 el fútbol *masc.*
 to play soccer jugar al fútbol

sock noun
 el calcetín *masc.* (plural los
 calcetines)

sofa noun
 el sofá *masc.*

soft adjective
1 (*cushion, butter, bed, etc.*) blando *masc.*,
 blanda *fem.*
 a soft mattress un colchón blando
2 (*cloth, music, voice, etc.*) suave *masc. &
 fem.*
 soft skin la piel suave
3 a soft drink un refresco *masc.*

software noun
 el software *masc.*

solar adjective
 solar *masc. & fem.*
 the solar system el sistema solar

sold verb SEE **sell**
 I've sold my bike. He vendido mi
 bici.

soldier noun
 el or la soldado *masc. & fem.*
 He's a soldier. Es soldado.

solicitor noun
 el abogado *masc.*, la abogada *fem.*
 My mum's a solicitor. Mi madre es
 abogada.

to **solve** verb
 resolver

some adjective & pronoun
1 (*usually not translated*)
 I'm eating some fish. Estoy
 comiendo pescado.
 I've bought some sweets. He
 comprado caramelos.
 **Do you want some water? – No, I
 have some.** ¿Quieres agua? – No,
 ya tengo.
 I've eaten some of it. He comido un
 poco.
2 (*compared to others*) algunos *masc.
 plural*, algunas *fem. plural*
 Some books are very expensive.
 Algunos libros son muy caros.
 I like some of my teachers. Me
 gustan algunos de mis maestros.
 Some of them have come. Han
 venido algunos.

somebody pronoun
 alguien
 There's somebody at the door.
 Hay alguien en la puerta.
 somebody else otra persona

someone pronoun SEE **somebody**

something pronoun
 algo
 I've eaten something. He comido
 algo.
 something else otra cosa

sometimes adverb
 a veces

somewhere adverb
 en or a alguna parte
 to be somewhere estar en alguna
 parte
 to go somewhere ir a alguna parte
 somewhere else en otra parte
 I want to go somewhere else.
 Quiero ir a otra parte.

> ⚷ **LANGUAGE**
> When 'somewhere' means 'in' a place use
> **en** with **parte** and when it means 'to' use
> **a** instead.

• *Languages and nationalities do not take a capital letter in Spanish.*

a
b
c
d
e
f
g
h
i
j
k
l
m
n
o
p
q
r
s
t
u
v
w
x
y
z

son noun
el **hijo** *masc.*

song noun
la **canción** *fem.* (plural las **canciones**)
to sing a song cantar una canción

soon adverb
pronto
See you soon! ¡Hasta pronto!
as soon as possible lo más pronto posible
soon after poco después

sore adjective
I have a sore throat. Me duele la garganta.
It's sore. Me duele.

⚷ **LANGUAGE**
Word for word **me duele** means 'It hurts me'.

sorry adjective
1 **I'm sorry.** Lo siento.
I'm very sorry, I can't come. Lo siento mucho, no puedo venir.
2 (*meaning 'excuse me!' when being polite or not hearing*)
Sorry! Did I hurt you? ¡Perdón! ¿Te he hecho daño?
Sorry, what did you say? ¿Perdón, cómo has dicho?

sort noun
1 el **tipo** *masc.*
What sort of book is it? ¿Qué tipo de libro es?
2 **a sort of** una especie de
It's a sort of hat. Es una especie de sombrero.

to **sort out** verb
(*to fix or to tidy*) **arreglar**
to sort out a problem arreglar un problema
Sort out your room! ¡Arregla tu habitación!
Sort out your toys! ¡Guarda los juguetes!

sound noun
1 (*noise*) el **ruido** *masc.*
the sound of traffic el ruido del tráfico
2 (*from the TV, music, etc.*) el **sonido** *masc.*
the sound of a guitar el sonido de una guitarra
3 (*volume*) el **volumen** *masc.*
Turn down the sound. Baja el volumen.

to **sound** verb
1 (*to seem*) **parecer**
That sounds a good idea to me. Me parece una buena idea.
It sounds good. Me parece bien.
2 (*to make a sound*) **sonar**
His name sounds French. Su nombre suena francés.

soup noun
la **sopa** *fem.*
vegetable soup la sopa de verduras

sour adjective
agrio *masc.*, **agria** *fem.*

south noun & adjective
1 el **sur** *masc.*
in the south en el sur
the south coast la costa sur
2 **South Africa** Sudáfrica *fem.*
the South Pole el Polo Sur

South America noun
Sudamérica *fem.*

South American adjective
sudamericano *masc.*, **sudamericana** *fem.*

South American noun
el **sudamericano** *masc.*, la **sudamericana** *fem.*

souvenir noun
el **recuerdo** *masc.*
a souvenir shop una tienda de recuerdos

• *The months of the year and days of the week do not take a capital letter in Spanish.*

a b c d e f g h i j k l m n o p q r s t u v w x y z

space noun
el **espacio** *masc.*
Leave a space. Deja un espacio.
There's enough space. Hay suficiente espacio.
a journey into space un viaje en el espacio

spaceship noun
la **nave espacial** *fem.*

spade noun
la **pala** *fem.*
a bucket and spade un cubo y una pala

spaghetti noun
los **espaguetis** *masc. plural*
I like spaghetti. Me gustan los espaguetis.

🔑 **LANGUAGE**
English = **spaghetti** is singular
Spanish = **los espaguetis** is plural

Spain noun
España *fem.*
They live in Spain. Viven en España.
I'm going to Spain. Voy a España.

Spaniard noun
el **español** *masc.*, la **española** *fem.*

Spanish adjective
español *masc.*, **española** *fem.*
Spanish cooking la comida española
He's Spanish. Es español.
my Spanish lesson mi clase de español
Spanish people los españoles

Spanish noun
1 (*language*) el **español** *masc.*
I speak Spanish. Hablo español.
2 the Spanish los españoles *masc. plural*

spare adjective
1 a spare room un cuarto de invitados
spare time el tiempo libre

2 (*extra*) **de más**
Do you have a spare ticket?
¿Tienes una entrada de más?

to speak verb
hablar
I speak Spanish. Hablo español.
'English spoken.' 'Se habla inglés.'
to speak to somebody hablar con alguien
to speak about something hablar de algo

speaker noun
(*for sound and music*) el **altavoz** *masc.*
(plural los **altavoces**)

special adjective
especial *masc. & fem.*

specially adverb
especialmente

speech noun
el **discurso** *masc.*
to make a speech dar un discurso
the parts of speech las partes de la oración

speed noun
la **velocidad** *fem.*
What speed are you doing? ¿A qué velocidad vas?

to speed up verb
ir más rápido

to spell verb
1 (*to write*) **escribir**
You've spelled my name wrong.
Has escrito mal mi nombre.
How do you spell 'enough'?
¿Cómo se escribe 'enough'?
2 (*to say out loud*) **deletrear**
Can you spell it? ¿Me lo deletreas?

spell noun
a magic spell un hechizo

spelling noun
la **ortografía** *fem.*
a spelling mistake una falta de ortografía

• *See the centre section for verb tables.*

a
b
c
d
e
f
g
h
i
j
k
l
m
n
o
p
q
r
s
t
u
v
w
x
y
z

to **spend** verb
1 (money) gastar
How much have you spent?
¿Cuánto has gastado?
2 (time) pasar
I spent two weeks in Valencia.
Pasé dos semanas en Valencia.

spicy adjective
(curry, sauce, etc.) picante masc. & fem.

spider noun
la araña fem.

to **spill** verb
tirar
I've spilled water on the floor. He
tirado agua en el suelo.

spinach noun
las espinacas fem.plural

> 🔑 **LANGUAGE**
> English = **spinach** is singular
> French = **las espinacas** is plural

to **spit** verb
escupir

spite noun
in spite of a pesar de

to **split** verb
dividir
They've split us into two groups.
Nos han dividido en dos grupos.

to **spoil** verb
1 (plans, holidays, shirt, etc.) estropear
2 (a child) mimar
spoilt children niños mimados

spoilsport noun
el or la aguafiestas masc. & fem.
(plural los or las **aguafiestas**)

sponge noun
la esponja fem.

spooky adjective
(place, house, etc.) que da miedo
It's spooky here! ¡Da miedo estar
aquí!

spoon noun
la cuchara fem.

sport noun
1 el deporte masc.
I play a lot of sport. Hago mucho
deporte.
2 **a sports bag** una bolsa de deporte
a sports car un coche deportivo
a sports centre un polideportivo
a sports club un club deportivo
sports day el día de competiciones
deportivas
a sports ground un campo de
deportes

sportsman, **sportswoman**
noun
el deportista masc.;
la deportista fem.

sporty adjective
deportista masc. & fem.

spot noun
1 (pimple) el grano masc.
I'm full of spots. Estoy lleno de
granos.
2 (dot) el lunar masc.
a green blouse with black spots
una blusa verde con lunares negros
3 (place) el sitio masc.
a quiet spot un sitio tranquilo

to **spot** verb
1 (to find) encontrar
2 (to see) ver

to **sprain** verb
I've sprained my ankle. Tengo un
esguince en el tobillo.

to **spread** verb
(butter, glue, a towel, etc.) extender

spring noun
la primavera fem.
in the spring en primavera

sprouts plural noun
las coles de Bruselas fem. plural

spy noun
1 el or la espía masc. & fem.
2 **I spy** el veo veo masc.
to play I spy jugar al veo veo

• Use **el** and **uno** for masculine words and **la** and **una** for feminine words.

square adjective
cuadrado *masc.*, cuadrada *fem.*
a square room una habitación cuadrada

square noun
1 (*shape*) el cuadrado *masc.*
2 (*in a town or village*) la plaza *fem.*
the village square la plaza del pueblo
3 (*in crosswords etc.*) la casilla *fem.*

squash noun
1 (*sport*) el squash *masc.*
to play squash jugar al squash
2 (*drink*)
an orange squash una naranjada *fem.*

squirrel noun
la ardilla *fem.*

stable noun
la cuadra *fem.*

stack noun
el montón *masc.* (plural los **montones**)
a stack of books un montón de libros

stadium noun
el estadio *masc.*

staff room noun
la sala de profesores *fem.*

stain noun
la mancha *fem.*

staircase noun
la escalera *fem.*

stairs plural noun
las escaleras *fem. plural*, la escalera *fem.*
I went down the stairs. Bajé las escaleras., Bajé la escalera.

stamp noun
el sello *masc.*
a stamp album un álbum de sellos
a stamp collection una colección de sellos

to **stamp** verb
to stamp your foot dar una patada en el suelo

to **stand** verb
1 estar de pie, estar
I'm sitting but my sister's standing. Estoy sentada pero mi hermana está de pie.
I'm standing outside the school. Estoy delante del colegio.
2 (*to get up*) levantarse
Stand up! ¡Levántate!
3 (*to go and stand somewhere*) ponerse
Stand by the board, Amy. Ponte delante de la pizarra, Amy.
Go and stand in line. Poneos en fila.
4 (*to hate something*) soportar
I can't stand that music. No soporto esta música.

to **stand for** verb
significar
What does 'PE' stand for? ¿Qué significa 'PE'?

staple noun
la grapa *fem.*

stapler noun
la grapadora *fem.*

star noun
(*in the sky, shape, person*) la estrella *fem.*
a film star una estrella de cine

start noun
1 el principio *masc.*
at the start of the film al principio de la película
at the start of the year a principios del año
2 (*of a race*) la salida *fem.*

to **start** verb
1 empezar
Shall we start? ¿Empezamos?
The holidays start tomorrow. Las vacaciones empiezan mañana.
I've started to learn Spanish. He empezado a aprender español.

• *Languages and nationalities do not take a capital letter in Spanish.*

English Spanish

a
b
c
d
e
f
g
h
i
j
k
l
m
n
o
p
q
r
s
t
u
v
w
x
y
z

2 *(talking about a car)* **arrancar**
The car won't start. El coche no
arranca.
3 *(a group, club, etc.)* **formar**

to **starve** verb
I'm starving! ¡Me muero de
hambre!

⚬━ **LANGUAGE**
Word for word the Spanish means 'I'm
dying of hunger'.

States plural noun
the States Estados Unidos *masc.*
They live in the States. Viven en
Estados Unidos.

station noun
1 *(for trains etc.)* la **estación** *fem.* (plural
las **estaciones**)
at the station en la estación
a tube station una estación de
metro
a bus station una estación de
autobuses
2 a radio station una emisora *fem.*
a police station una comisaría *fem.*

stationery noun
(paper) el **papel** *masc.*

statue noun
la **estatua** *fem.*

stay noun
la **estancia** *fem.*
my stay in Madrid mi estancia en
Madrid

to **stay** verb
1 quedarse
Stay five more minutes. Quédate
cinco minutos más.
I stayed with my brother.
Me quedé en casa de mi
hermano.
Stay still. *(don't move)* No te
muevas.
2 *(in a hotel etc.)* **alojarse**
We stayed in a hotel. Nos
alojamos en un hotel.

3 *(to spend time)* **pasar**
**We're going to stay a week in
Toledo.** Vamos a pasar una
semana en Toledo.

to **stay in** verb
(in the house) **quedarse en casa**

to **stay up** verb
(not to go to bed) **no acostarse**
I want to stay up late. Quiero
acostarme tarde.

steak noun
el **bistec** *masc.*
steak and chips el bistec con
patatas fritas

to **steal** verb
robar
He stole a bike. Robó una bici.

steam noun
el **vapor** *masc.*

steep adjective
(slope, stairs, etc.) **empinado** *masc.*,
empinada *fem.*
This hill is steep. Esta cuesta es
empinada.

steering wheel noun
el **volante** *masc.*

step noun
1 *(with your foot)* el **paso** *masc.*
Take two steps forward. Da dos
pasos hacia adelante.
2 *(of stairs)* el **escalón** *masc.* (plural los
escalones)
Mind the step! ¡Cuidado con el
escalón!

stepbrother noun
el **hermanastro** *masc.*

stepdaughter noun
la **hijastra** *fem.*

stepfather noun
el **padrastro** *masc.*

stepmother noun
la **madrastra** *fem.*

• *The months of the year and days of the week do not take a capital letter in Spanish.*

stepsister noun
la **hermanastra** *fem.*

stepson noun
el **hijastro** *masc.*

stereo noun
el **equipo de música** *masc.*

stew noun
el **estofado** *masc.*

stick noun
1 (*for hitting etc.*) el **palo** *masc.*
2 (*walking stick*) el **bastón** *masc.* (plural los **bastones**)

to **stick** verb
(*with glue etc.*) **pegar**
Stick the stamps on the envelope.
Pega los sellos en el sobre.

to **stick out** verb
to stick out your tongue sacar la lengua

sticker noun
la **pegatina** *fem.*

sticky adjective
1 (*dirty*) **pegajoso** *masc.*, **pegajosa** *fem.*
My hands are sticky. Tengo las manos pegajosas.
2 (*paper, label, etc.*) **adhesivo** *masc.*, **adhesiva** *fem.*
sticky tape la cinta adhesiva

stiff adjective
(*leg, arm, etc.*) **agarrotado** *masc.*, **agarrotada** *fem.*
I'm stiff. (*after doing sport*) Tengo agujetas.

still adverb
todavía
She's still eating. Todavía está comiendo.
That's better still. Es todavía mejor.

still adjective
quieto *masc.*, **quieta** *fem.*
Keep still!, Sit still! ¡Estate quieto!

• See the centre section for verb tables.

to **sting** verb
picar
I've been stung by a wasp. Me ha picado una avispa.

sting noun
la **picadura** *fem.*
a wasp sting una picadura de avispa

to **stink** verb
apestar
It stinks of fish. Apesta a pescado.

stink noun
el **mal olor** *masc.*
What a stink! ¡Qué mal olor!

stitch noun
el **punto** *masc.*
I had three stitches. Me dieron tres puntos.

stomach noun
el **estómago** *masc.*

stomach ache noun
I have a stomach ache. Me duele el estómago.

🔑 **LANGUAGE**
Word for word the Spanish means 'my stomach hurts'.

stone noun
1 la **piedra** *fem.*
He's throwing stones at me.
Me está tirando piedras.
2 (*when weighing people*)
I weigh four stone. Peso unos veinticinco kilos.

🌐 **CULTURE**
In Spain they use kilos for weighing. A stone is about 6.3 kilos.

stool noun
el **taburete** *masc.*

stop noun
la **parada** *fem.*
a bus stop una parada de autobús

stop verb
1 parar
I stopped in front of the school. Paré delante del colegio.
The bus stops here. El autobús para aquí.
It's stopped raining. Ha parado de llover.
2 (to stop working) **pararse**
The clock has stopped. Se ha parado el reloj.
3 to stop something parar algo
Stop the car. Para el coche.
Stop it! ¡Basta!, ¡Para!
4 to stop doing something dejar de hacer algo
Stop annoying your sister. Deja de molestar a tu hermana.

store noun
(big shop) la **tienda** fem.
a department store unos grandes almacenes

> **LANGUAGE**
> English = **a department store** is singular
> Spanish = **unos grandes almacenes** is plural

storey noun
el **piso** masc., la **planta** fem.
a five-storey building un edificio de cinco pisos, un edificio de cinco plantas

storm noun
la **tormenta** fem.

stormy adjective
It's stormy. Hay tormenta.

story noun
1 la **historia** fem.
a true story una historia verdadera

> **LANGUAGE**
> In Spanish **historia** also means 'history'.

2 (for children) el **cuento** masc.
Tell me a story. Cuéntame un cuento.

straight adjective
1 (road, nose, etc.) **recto** masc., **recta** fem.
a straight line una línea recta
2 (talking about pictures, hats, etc.) **derecho** masc., **derecha** fem.
The picture isn't straight. El cuadro no está derecho.
3 to have straight hair tener el pelo liso

straight adverb
1 (without stopping) **directamente**
I went straight to school. Fui directamente al colegio.
2 (immediately) **enseguida**
I'm coming straight back. Vuelvo en seguida.
straight away en seguida
3 Go straight ahead. Sigue todo recto.

strange adjective
raro masc., **rara** fem.

> **LANGUAGE**
> You can also say **extraño/extraña** in Spanish.

stranger noun
el **desconocido** masc., la **desconocida** fem.
Don't talk to strangers. No hables con desconocidos.

strap noun
1 (on a watch, handbag, etc.) la **correa** fem.
2 (on a dress, swimsuit, etc.) el **tirante** masc.

straw noun
1 la **paja** fem.
a straw hat un sombrero de paja
2 (for drinking) la **pajita** fem.
to drink with a straw beber con una pajita

strawberry noun
la **fresa** fem.
strawberry jam la mermelada de fresa

• Use **el** and **uno** for masculine words and **la** and **una** for feminine words.

stream noun
el **arroyo** *masc.*

street noun
la **calle** *fem.*
in the street en la calle

strength noun
la **fuerza** *fem.*

to **stretch** verb
1 (*after waking up etc.*) **estirarse**
I stretched. Me estiré.
2 (*arm, hand*) **extender**
She stretched out her hand.
Extendió la mano.

strict adjective
estricto *masc.*, **estricta** *fem.*

string noun
(*for tying things, and for a guitar etc.*)
la **cuerda** *fem.*

stripe noun
la **raya** *fem.*
a skirt with green stripes una
falda con rayas verdes

striped adjective
de rayas
a striped shirt una camisa de rayas

to **stroke** verb
(*a cat, dog, etc.*) **acariciar**

strong adjective
fuerte *masc. & fem.*
My brother is very strong. Mi
hermano es muy fuerte.

stubborn adjective
terco *masc.*, **terca** *fem.*

stuck adjective
(*drawer, window, etc.*) **atascado** *masc.*,
atascada *fem.*

student noun
el or la **estudiante** *masc. & fem.*
My sister's a student. Mi hermana
es estudiante.

to **study** verb
estudiar
My cousin is studying Spanish.
Mi primo estudia español.

stuff noun
1 (*things*) las **cosas** *fem. plural*
I've left my stuff on the floor.
He dejado mis cosas en el suelo.
2 (*thing*) la **cosa** *fem.*
What's this green stuff called?
¿Cómo se llama esta cosa verde?

stupid adjective
tonto *masc.*, **tonta** *fem.*
to do something stupid hacer una
tontería

> 🔑 **LANGUAGE**
> You can also say **estúpido/estúpida** but
> it is much stronger than 'stupid' in English.

subject noun
1 (*in school*) la **asignatura** *fem.*
My favourite subject is Spanish. Mi
asignatura favorita es el español.
2 (*of a book etc.*) el **tema** *masc.*

> 🔑 **LANGUAGE**
> Be careful: **tema** ends in an -**a** but it is not
> a feminine noun.

submarine noun
el **submarino** *masc.*

subtitles plural noun
los **subtítulos** *masc. plural*

to **subtract** verb
restar
Subtract five from ten. Resta cinco
de diez.

suburbs plural noun
las **afueras** *fem. plural*
I live in the suburbs. Vivo en las
afueras.

subway noun
el **paso subterráneo** *masc.*

success noun
el **éxito** *masc.*
a great success un gran éxito

• *Languages and nationalities do not take a capital letter in Spanish.*

English Spanish

a
b
c
d
e
f
g
h
i
j
k
l
m
n
o
p
q
r
s
t
u
v
w
x
y
z

successful adjective
to be successful tener éxito
The book is very successful. El libro tiene mucho éxito.

such adverb & adjective
1 tan
She's such a pretty girl! ¡Es una niña tan guapa!
They're such pretty girls! ¡Son niñas tan guapas!
2 **such a lot** (*with nouns*) tanto *masc.*, tanta *fem.*
such a lot of money tanto dinero
3 **such a lot** (*with verbs*) tanto
I have to study such a lot. Tengo que estudiar tanto.
4 **such as** como
sports such as football deportes como el fútbol

sudden noun
all of a sudden de repente

suddenly adverb
de repente

to **suffer** verb
sufrir

sugar noun
el azúcar *masc.*
I don't take sugar. No tomo azúcar.

suggestion noun
la sugerencia *fem.*

suit noun
1 (*for a man*) el traje *masc.*
2 (*for a woman*) el traje de chaqueta *masc.*

to **suit** verb
(*when talking about clothes etc.*)
to suit somebody quedar bien a alguien
Green suits you. El verde te queda bien.

suitcase noun
la maleta *fem.*

sum noun
la suma *fem.*
to do sums hacer sumas
I'm good at sums. Soy bueno en aritmética.

summer noun
el verano *masc.*
in the summer en verano
the summer holidays las vacaciones de verano

sun noun
el sol *masc.*
in the sun al sol
The sun's out. Hace sol.

to **sunbathe** verb
tomar el sol

sunburnt adjective
quemado por el sol *masc.*, quemada por el sol *fem.*
I don't want to get sunburnt. No quiero quemarme con el sol.

Sunday noun
el domingo *masc.*
Today is Sunday. Hoy es domingo.
on Sunday el domingo
I come back on Sunday. Vuelvo el domingo.
on Sundays los domingos
I play football on Sundays. Juego al fútbol los domingos.

🔑 LANGUAGE
Remember the difference in Spanish between **el domingo** (one Sunday only) and **los domingos** (every Sunday).

sunflower noun
el girasol *masc.*

sunglasses plural noun
las gafas de sol *fem. plural*

sunny adjective
(*room, beach, etc.*) soleado *masc.*, soleada *fem.*
a sunny day un día de sol
It's sunny. Hace sol.

• *The months of the year and days of the week do not take a capital letter in Spanish.*

sunshade noun
la **sombrilla** *fem.*

sunshine noun
el **sol** *masc.*
in the sunshine al sol

suntan noun
el **bronceado** *masc.*
to get a suntan ponerse
moreno *masc.*, ponerse morena *fem.*

super adjective
genial *masc. & fem.*
That's a super idea! ¡Es una idea
genial!

supermarket noun
el **supermercado** *masc.*

superstar noun
la **gran estrella** *fem.*

superstore noun
el **hipermercado** *masc.*

supper noun
la **cena** *fem.*
to have supper cenar

to support verb
(*a team*) **ser hincha de**
Alex supports Liverpool. Alex es
hincha del Liverpool.

to suppose verb
1 suponer
I suppose you're right. Supongo
que tienes razón.
I suppose so. Supongo que sí.
2 (*using 'deber'*)
You're supposed to be at school.
Deberías estar en la escuela.
I'm not supposed to do that. No
debería hacer eso.
3 (*using 'decir'*)
It's supposed to be a good film.
Dicen que es una buena película.

sure adjective
seguro *masc.*, **segura** *fem.*
Are you sure? ¿Estás seguro?
I'm not sure. No estoy seguro.
Sure! ¡Claro!

to surf verb
to surf the Internet navegar en
Internet

surface noun
la **superficie** *fem.*

surname noun
el **apellido** *masc.*

surprise noun
la **sorpresa** *fem.*
What a surprise! ¡Qué sorpresa!

to surprise verb
sorprender

surprised adjective
sorprendido *masc.*,
sorprendida *fem.*
I'm surprised. Estoy sorprendido.

to surround verb
rodear
surrounded by trees rodeado de
árboles
surrounded by a wall rodeado por
un muro

to swallow verb
tragar

swan noun
el **cisne** *masc.*

to swap verb
cambiar
**I want to swap my book for your
CD.** Quiero cambiar mi libro por tu
CD.
I've swapped places. Me he
cambiado de sitio.

to swear verb
decir palabrotas

to sweat verb
sudar

sweater noun
el **jersey** *masc.* (plural los **jerseys** or
jerséis)

sweatshirt noun
la **sudadera** *fem.*

a
b
c
d
e
f
g
h
i
j
k
l
m
n
o
p
q
r
s
t
u
v
w
x
y
z

• *The months of the year and days of the week do not take a capital letter in Spanish.*

English Spanish

a b c d e f g h i j k l m n o p q r s t u v w x y z

sweet noun
1 el caramelo *masc.*
I like sweets. Me gustan los caramelos.
a sweet shop una tienda de golosinas
2 (*part of a meal*) el postre *masc.*

sweet adjective
1 (*like sugar*) dulce *masc. & fem.*
This cake's very sweet. Este pastel es muy dulce.
2 (*nice, kind*) encantador *masc.*, encantadora *fem.*
She's a very sweet girl. Es una niña encantadora.

sweetcorn noun
el maíz *masc.*

swim noun
to go for a swim ir a nadar

swim verb
nadar
I can swim. Yo sé nadar.

swimmer noun
el nadador *masc.*, la nadadora *fem.*
He's a good swimmer. Es buen nadador.

swimming noun
1 la natación *fem.*
I love swimming. Me encanta la natación.
to go swimming ir a nadar
2 **a swimming costume** un traje de baño, un bañador
a swimming pool una piscina
swimming trunks un bañador, un traje de baño

swimsuit noun
el traje de baño *masc.*

swing noun
el columpio *masc.*

Swiss adjective
suizo *masc.*, suiza *fem.*

Swiss noun
the Swiss los suizos *masc. plural*

switch noun
1 (*for turning or pressing*) el botón *masc.* (plural los **botones**)
Press the switch. Pulsa el botón.
2 (*up-down type*) el interruptor *masc.*

to **switch** verb
1 (*to change*) cambiar
to switch channels cambiar de canal
I've switched to the other channel. He cambiado al otro canal.
2 (*a TV, computer, etc.*) **to switch off** apagar
Switch the light off. Apaga la luz.
3 (*a TV, computer, etc.*) **to switch on** encender
I've switched the light on. He encendido la luz.

Switzerland noun
Suiza *fem.*

swollen adjective
(*leg, arm, etc.*) hinchado *masc.*, hinchada *fem.*

sword noun
la espada *fem.*

syllable noun
la sílaba *fem.*

symbol noun
el símbolo *masc.*

synagogue noun
la sinagoga *fem.*

system noun
el sistema *masc.*

LANGUAGE
Be careful: **sistema** ends in an -**a** but it is not a feminine noun.

• *See the centre section for verb tables.*

402

Tt

table noun
1 la **mesa** *fem.*
 on the table en la mesa
 table tennis el tenis de mesa
 to play table tennis jugar al tenis de mesa
2 **the times tables** las tablas de multiplicar
 the five-times table la tabla del cinco

tablecloth noun
el **mantel** *masc.*

tablespoon noun
la **cuchara de servir** *fem.*

tablet noun
la **pastilla** *fem.*
to take a tablet tomar una pastilla

tadpole noun
el **renacuajo** *masc.*

tail noun
1 (*of an animal*) la **cola** *fem.*
2 (*when throwing a coin*) **tails!** ¡cruz!
 Heads or tails? ¿Cara o cruz?

to take verb
1 (*with your hand, go by car, etc.*) **coger**, **tomar**
 Take a chocolate. Coge un bombón., Toma un bombón.
 I took the bus. Cogí el autobús., Tomé el autobús.
2 (*a medicine, photo, course, etc.*) **tomar**
 Do you take sugar? ¿Tomas azúcar?
 I've taken the antibiotics. He tomado los antibióticos.
3 (*to take to another place*) **llevar**
 Take this book to Yasmina. Lleva este libro a Yasmina.
 My dad takes me to school. Mi padre me lleva al colegio.
 Who's taken my bike? ¿Quién se ha llevado mi bici?

4 **to take an exam** hacer un examen
 What size do you take? ¿Qué talla usas?

to take away verb
1 **quitar**
 Take your toys away. Quita tus juguetes de aquí.
2 **llevar**
 Eat here or take away? ¿Para comer aquí o para llevar?

to take back verb
devolver
I took the book back to the library. Devolví el libro a la biblioteca.

to take down verb
1 **bajar**
 Can you take down that book for me? ¿Me puedes bajar ese libro?
2 (*from a wall*) **quitar**
 Take down the picture. Quita el cuadro.

to take off verb
1 **quitar**
 I've taken my coat off. Me he quitado el abrigo.
2 **despegar**
 The plane has taken off. El avión ha despegado.

to take out verb
sacar
I took the toys out of the box. Saqué los juguetes de la caja.

to take up verb
(*from downstairs etc.*) **subir**
Can you take up the suitcase? ¿Puedes subir la maleta?

takeaway noun
(*meal*) la **comida para llevar** *fem.*

take-off noun
(*of a plane*) el **despegue** *masc.*

a
b
c
d
e
f
g
h
i
j
k
l
m
n
o
p
q
r
s
t
u
v
w
x
y
z

• Use **el** and **uno** for masculine words and **la** and **una** for feminine words.

English Spanish

tale noun
el **cuento** masc.
a fairy tale un cuento de hadas

talk noun
la **charla** fem.
to give a talk dar una charla

to **talk** verb
hablar
to talk to somebody hablar con alguien
to talk about something hablar de algo

talkative adjective
hablador masc., **habladora** fem.

tall adjective
alto masc., **alta** fem.
I'm tall. Soy alta.
How tall are you? ¿Cuánto mides?
I'm five feet tall. Mido un metro cincuenta.

tan noun
el **bronceado** masc.
to get a tan ponerse moreno masc., ponerse morena fem.

tangerine noun
la **mandarina** fem.

tank noun
1 (used in war) el **tanque** masc.
2 **a fish tank** una pecera

tanned adjective
moreno masc., **morena** fem.
I'm tanned. Estoy moreno.

tap noun
el **grifo** masc.
The tap is off. El grifo está cerrado.

tape noun
la **cinta** fem.
Do you have a tape to record the film? ¿Tienes una cinta para grabar la película?
sticky tape la cinta adhesiva
I've got it on tape. Lo tengo grabado.

a tape measure un metro
a tape recorder un magnetófono

to **tape** verb
grabar
Can you tape the film? ¿Puedes grabar la película?
It's taping. Está grabando.

tart noun
la **tarta** fem.
an apple tart une tarta de manzana

taste noun
el **sabor** masc.
It has a lovely taste. Tiene muy buen sabor.
Can I have a taste? ¿Puedo probarlo?

to **taste** verb
1 (to eat or drink) **probar**
Taste this. Prueba esto.
2 (to have a flavour) **tener sabor**
It tastes bitter. Tiene un sabor amargo.
It tastes of strawberry. Tiene sabor a fresa.
It tastes nice. Está delicioso.

tasty adjective
delicioso masc., **deliciosa** fem.

tattoo noun
el **tatuaje** masc.
He's got a tattoo on his arm. Tiene un tatuaje en el brazo.

taxi noun
el **taxi** masc.
by taxi en taxi
a taxi driver un or una taxista

tea noun
1 el **té** masc.
to have a cup of tea tomar una taza de té
a tea with milk un té con leche
a lemon tea un té con limón
2 (afternoon snack) la **merienda** fem.
to have tea merendar

• Languages and nationalities do not take a capital letter in Spanish.

3 (*evening meal*) la **cena** *fem.*
to have tea cenar

 CULTURE
In Spain people usually have lemon rather than milk in their tea.

teabag noun
la **bolsita de té** *fem.*

to **teach** verb
enseñar
Mr Delgado teaches Spanish. El señor Delgado enseña español.
They've taught me to swim. Me han enseñado a nadar.

teacher noun
1 (*in a primary or nursery school*)
el **maestro** *masc.*, la **maestra** *fem.*
My dad's a teacher. Mi padre es maestro.
2 (*in a secondary school*)
el **profesor** *masc.*, la **profesora** *fem.*
My mum's a teacher. Mi madre es profesora.
a Spanish teacher un profesor de español

teacup noun
la **taza de té** *fem.*

team noun
el **equipo** *masc.*
a football team un equipo de fútbol

teapot noun
la **tetera** *fem.*

tear noun
(*when you cry*) la **lágrima** *fem.*

to **tear** verb
romper
I've torn my shirt! ¡Me he roto la camisa!
She tore up the letter. Rompió la carta.

teaspoon noun
la **cucharita** *fem.*

teatime noun
1 (*afternoon snack*) la **hora de merendar** *fem.*
2 (*evening meal*) la **hora de cenar** *fem.*

teddy bear noun
el **osito de peluche** *masc.*

LANGUAGE
Word for word the Spanish means 'little bear made out of plush' (plush is a soft material).

teenager noun
el or la **adolescente** *masc. & fem.*

teens plural noun
to be in your teens ser adolescente

tee-shirt noun
la **camiseta** *fem.*

teeth plural noun
los **dientes** *masc. plural*
I'm brushing my teeth. Me estoy lavando los dientes.

telephone noun
el **teléfono** *masc.*
I'm on the telephone to mum. Estoy hablando por teléfono con mamá.
a telephone call una llamada telefónica
the telephone directory la guía telefónica
a telephone number un número de teléfono

telescope noun
el **telescopio** *masc.*
to look through the telescope mirar por el telescopio

television noun
la **televisión** *fem.* (plural las **televisiones**)
to watch television ver la televisión
on television en televisión
a television set una televisión

a
b
c
d
e
f
g
h
i
j
k
l
m
n
o
p
q
r
s
t
u
v
w
x
y
z

• *The months of the year and days of the week do not take a capital letter in Spanish.*

a
b
c
d
e
f
g
h
i
j
k
l
m
n
o
p
q
r
s
t
u
v
w
x
y
z

to **tell** verb
1 decir
I'm telling the truth. Digo la verdad.
He's telling lies. Dice mentiras.
What did he tell you? ¿Qué te ha dicho?
Can you tell the time? ¿Sabes decir la hora?
2 (*to talk about*) hablar
Tell me about your family. Háblame de tu familia.
3 (*a story, secret, joke*) contar
Tell me a story. Cuéntame un cuento.
4 to tell off regañar

telly noun
la tele *fem.*
to watch telly ver la tele

temper noun
to lose your temper enfadarse mucho
He lost his temper. Se enfadó mucho.

temperature noun
1 la temperatura *fem.*
the temperature of the water la temperatura del agua
2 to have a temperature tener fiebre

temple noun
el templo *masc.*
a Sikh temple un templo sij

ten number
diez
It starts at ten. Empieza a las diez.
It's ten to nine. Son las nueve menos diez.
It's ten past six. Son las seis y diez.
I'm ten. Tengo diez años.

> 🔑 **LANGUAGE**
> In English you can say 'ten o'clock' or just 'ten', 'ten years old' or just 'ten'. In Spanish you must add **las** (for time) and **años** (for age).

• *See the centre section for verb tables.*

tennis noun
el tenis *masc.*
I play tennis. Juego al tenis.
a tennis ball una pelota de tenis
a tennis court una pista de tenis
a tennis racket una raqueta de tenis

tense noun
the present tense el presente *masc.*
the past tense el pasado *masc.*
the future tense el futuro *masc.*

tent noun
la tienda *fem.*
to put up a tent montar una tienda

tenth adjective
décimo *masc.*, décima *fem.*
on the tenth floor en el décimo piso
the tenth of May el diez de mayo

> 🔑 **LANGUAGE**
> With dates you use **diez** (ten).

term noun
el trimestre *masc.*
the last day of term el último día del trimestre

terrible adjective
terrible *masc. & fem.*

> 🔑 **LANGUAGE**
> You can also say **espantoso/espantosa**.

terrific adjective
estupendo *masc.*, estupenda *fem.*

terrified adjective
aterrorizado *masc.*, aterrorizada *fem.*
to be terrified of tener mucho miedo a
She's terrified of her teacher. Le tiene mucho miedo a su maestra.

test noun
(*in school*) la prueba *fem.*, el examen *masc.* (plural los exámens)

text noun
(*text message*) el **SMS** *masc.*,
el **mensaje (de texto)** *masc.*
to send a text enviar un
SMS, enviar un mensaje

to **text** verb
to text somebody enviar un SMS a
alguien, enviar un mensaje a
alguien

textbook noun
el **libro de texto** *masc.*

Thames noun
the Thames el Támesis *masc.*

than conjunction
1 **que**
I'm taller than you. Soy más alto
que tú.
2 (*with numbers*) **de**
more than twenty más de v
einte

to **thank** verb
to thank somebody dar las gracias
a alguien
Thank you! ¡Gracias!
Thank you very much! ¡Muchas
gracias!
Thank you for the present. Gracias
por el regalo.

thanks exclamation
¡gracias!
Thanks for the ice cream. Gracias
por el helado.
No thanks. No, gracias.

that conjunction
que
I think that it's a good film. Creo
que es una buena película.

that adjective
1 **ese** *masc.*, **esa** *fem.*
that cat ese gato
that house esa casa
that one ése *masc.*, ésa *fem.*
Take that one. Toma ése.

2 (*talking about something further away*)
aquel *masc.*, **aquella** *fem.*
that book over there aquel libro
that lady aquella señorita
that one aquél *masc.*, aquélla *fem.*

that pronoun
1 **ése** *masc.*, **ésa** *fem.*
That's not my book. Ése no es mi
libro.
That's my bike. Ésa es mi bici.
2 **eso**
What's that? ¿Qué es eso?
That's true. Eso es cierto.
Don't do that. No hagas eso.
3 (*talking about something further away*)
aquél *masc.*, **aquélla** *fem.*
That's my brother over there.
Aquél es mi hermano.
That's my house. Aquélla es mi
casa.
4 **aquello**
What's that over there? ¿Qué es
aquello?
5 **que**
the boy that I met el niño que
conocí
the toys that are in the box los
juguetes que están en la caja

the determiner
1 (*before a masculine noun*) **el** (plural **los**)

🔑 **LANGUAGE**
de + el = de
la + el = al

the car el coche
the cars los coches
a page of the book una página del
libro
to go to the cinema ir al cine
at the end of the film al final de la
película
2 (*before a feminine noun*) **la** (plural **las**)
the window la ventana
the windows las ventanas

theatre noun
el **teatro** *masc.*

• Use el and uno for masculine words and la and una for feminine words.

their adjective
1 (before a singular noun) su
 their school su colegio
2 (before a plural noun) sus
 their friends sus amigos
3 (with parts of the body, clothes, etc.)
 They're washing their hands. Se
 están lavando las manos.
 They put their shoes on. Se
 pusieron los zapatos.

🔑 **LANGUAGE**
Use se with el, la, los, or las in these
examples instead of su and sus.

theirs pronoun
1 (with a singular noun) el suyo masc.,
 la suya fem.
 our dog and theirs nuestro perro y
 el suyo
 Our house is bigger than theirs.
 Nuestra casa es más grande que la
 suya.
2 (with a plural noun) los suyos masc.
 plural, las suyas fem. plural
 **Our parents are Spanish and theirs
 too.** Nuestros padres son españoles
 y los suyos también.
 our photos and theirs nuestras
 fotos y las suyas
3 (following 'is') suyo masc., suya fem.
 This house is theirs. Esta casa es
 suya.
4 (following 'are') suyos masc. plural,
 suyas fem. plural
 These pens are theirs. Estos
 bolígrafos son suyos.

them pronoun
1 (after a verb) los masc., las fem.
 **Do you know my brothers? – Yes, I
 know them.** ¿Conoces a mis
 hermanos? – Sí, los conozco.
 My glasses, have you seen them?
 ¿Mis gafas, las has visto?

🔑 **LANGUAGE**
With commands and infinitives los and
las are joined with the verb to make one
word.

Call them. Llámalos.
I want to help them. Quiero
ayudarlas.
2 (to them) les
 I've sent a letter to them. Les he
 mandado una carta.
 Give them the book. Dales el
 libro.

🔑 **LANGUAGE**
When les is used with lo or la you use se
instead of les.

 I've given it to them. Se lo he dado.
 Give it to them. Dáselo.
3 (after a preposition etc.) ellos masc.,
 ellas fem.
 with them con ellos
 **Hazel and Claire? I'm taller than
 them.** ¿Hazel y Claire? Yo soy más
 alta que ellas.
 It's them. Son ellos.

theme park noun
 el parque temático masc.

themselves pronoun
1 ellos mismos masc., ellas
 mismas fem.
 They've done it themselves.
 Lo han hecho ellos mismos.
2 (with a reflexive verb) se
 They're washing themselves.
 Se están lavando.
3 by themselves solos masc.,
 solas fem.
 They don't go out by themselves.
 No salen solos.

then adverb
1 (next) luego
 **I went to school and then to the
 cinema.** Fui al colegio y luego al
 cine.
2 (at that time) entonces
 I was in Madrid then. Entonces
 estaba en Madrid.
3 (so) entonces
 What shall we do then? Entonces,
 ¿qué hacemos?

• Languages and nationalities do not take a capital letter in Spanish.

there adverb
1 *(fairly close to you)* **ahí**
 Sit there. Siéntate ahí.
 over there ahí
 up there ahí arriba
2 *(further away)* **allí**
 Sit there. Siéntate allí.
 over there allí
 up there allí arriba
3 **there is** hay
 There's a book on the table.
 Hay un libro en la mesa.
 There isn't any sugar. No hay
 azúcar.
4 **there are** hay
 **There are thirty children in my
 class.** Hay treinta niños en mi
 clase.

> 🔑 **LANGUAGE**
> **Hay** is used for 'there is' and 'there
> are'.

5 *(when shouting, or pointing to something)*
 ¡ahí!
 There he is! ¡Ahí está!

thermometer noun
 el **termómetro** *masc.*

these adjective
 estos *masc.*, **estas** *fem.*
 these CDs estos CDs
 these pages estas páginas
 these ones éstos *masc.*, éstas *fem.*
 I want these ones. Quiero
 éstos.

these pronoun
 éstos *masc.*, **éstas** *fem.*
 **Which dresses do you want? –
 These.** ¿Qué vestidos quieres? –
 Éstos
 These are my photos. Éstas son mis
 fotos.

they pronoun
1 *(not usually translated in Spanish)*
 **Have you seen my glasses? –
 They're here.** ¿Has visto mis gafas?
 – Están aquí.

2 **ellos** *masc.*, **ellas** *fem.*
 **They're going to the cinema but
 I'm going swimming.** Ellos van al
 cine pero yo voy a la piscina.

> 🔑 **LANGUAGE**
> Use **ellos** and **ellas** when you want to
> give special importance to the word
> 'they'.

thick adjective
1 *(wall, slice, etc.)* **grueso** *masc.*,
 gruesa *fem.*
2 *(soup, fog, smoke)* **espeso** *masc.*,
 espesa *fem.*

thief noun
 el **ladrón** *masc.*, la **ladrona** *fem.*

> 🔑 **LANGUAGE**
> The plural of **ladrón** is **ladrones**.

thin adjective
1 **delgado** *masc.*, **delgada** *fem.*
 I'm thin. Soy delgado.
2 *(slice, paper, line)* **fino** *masc.*, **fina** *fem.*
 a thin slice una rebanada fina

thing noun
 la **cosa** *fem.*
 I have lots of things to do. Tengo
 muchas cosas que hacer.
 Put your things on the table. Pon
 tus cosas en la mesa.

to **think** verb
1 **pensar**
 What are you thinking? ¿Qué
 piensas?
 I'm thinking about the holidays.
 Pienso en las vacaciones.
2 *(to believe)* **creer**
 I think you're tired. Creo que estás
 cansada.
 I think so. Creo que sí.
 I don't think so. Creo que no.

• *The months of the year and days of the week do not take a capital letter in Spanish.*

a
b
c
d
e
f
g
h
i
j
k
l
m
n
o
p
q
r
s
t
u
v
w
x
y
z

English Spanish

a
b
c
d
e
f
g
h
i
j
k
l
m
n
o
p
q
r
s
t
u
v
w
x
y
z

third adjective
tercero *masc.*, tercera *fem.*
for the third time por tercera vez
I came third. (*in the race*) Quedé tercero.
on the third floor en el tercer piso
on the third of November el tres de noviembre

> **LANGUAGE**
> Use **tercer** instead of **tercero** before a masculine singular noun.

> **LANGUAGE**
> With dates you use **tres** (three).

third noun
la tercera parte *fem.*
a third of the class una tercera parte de la clase

thirsty adjective
I'm thirsty. Tengo sed.
She's very thirsty. Tiene mucha sed.

> **LANGUAGE**
> English = **to be thirsty** **I'm thirsty.**
> Spanish = **tener sed** **Tengo sed.**

thirteen number
trece
My cousin is thirteen. Mi prima tiene trece años.

> **LANGUAGE**
> In English you can say just 'thirteen'. In Spanish you must add **años**.

thirty number
treinta
My dad is thirty. Mi padre tiene treinta años.

> **LANGUAGE**
> In English you can say just 'thirty'. In Spanish you must add **años**.

this adjective
este *masc.*, esta *fem.*
this dog este perro
this chair esta silla
this one éste *masc.*, ésta *fem.*
I want this one. Quiero éste.

this pronoun
1 éste *masc.*, ésta *fem.*
This is not my pen. Éste no es mi boli.
This is my bike. Ésta es mi bici.
2 esto
What's this? ¿Qué es esto?
Don't do this. No hagas esto.

those adjective
1 esos *masc.*, esas *fem.*
those children esos niños
those tables esas mesas
those ones ésos *masc.*, ésas *fem.*
Take those ones. Toma ésos.
2 (*talking about something further away*) aquellos *masc.*, aquellas *fem.*
those men over there aquellos hombres
those houses aquellas casas
those ones aquéllos *masc.*, aquéllas *fem.*

those pronoun
1 ésos *masc.*, ésas *fem.*
Which dresses do you want? – Those. ¿Qué vestidos quieres? – Ésos.
Those are my photos. Ésas son mis fotos.
2 (*talking about something further away*) aquéllos *masc.*, aquéllas *fem.*
Which jeans? – Those. ¿Qué vaqueros? – Aquéllos
Those are the girls. Aquéllas son las niñas.

though conjunction
aunque
though I'm tired aunque estoy cansado

though adverb
pero
It's cold, though. Pero hace frío.

• *See the centre section for verb tables.*

thousand number
mil
a thousand euros mil euros
two thousand euros dos mil euros
thousands of people miles de personas

three number
tres
I'll come back at three. Vuelvo a las tres.
I'm three. Tengo tres años.

> **⚟ LANGUAGE**
> In English you can say 'three o'clock' or just 'three', 'three years old' or just 'three'. In Spanish you must add **las** (for time) and **años** (for age).

throat noun
la *garganta* *fem.*
I have a sore throat Me duele la garganta

> **⚟ LANGUAGE**
> Word for word the Spanish means 'my throat hurts'.

throne noun
el *trono* *masc.*

through preposition
por
to look through the window mirar por la ventana
to go through the park ir por el parque

through adverb
to get through pasar
Let me through! ¡Déjame pasar!
Go through! ¡Pasa!

to **throw** verb
tirar
Throw the ball to me. Tírame la pelota.
She's throwing stones at me. Me está tirando piedras.

to **throw away** verb
tirar (a la basura)
Throw this newspaper away. Tira este periódico.

to **throw out** verb
tirar (a la basura)

to **throw up** verb
devolver
I feel like throwing up. Tengo ganas de devolver.

thumb noun
el *pulgar* *masc.*

thunder noun
los *truenos* *masc. plural*
There's thunder and lightning. Hay truenos y relámpagos.

thunderstorm noun
la *tormenta* *fem.*

Thursday noun
el *jueves* *masc.*
Today is Thursday. Hoy es jueves.
on Thursday el jueves
Come to my house on Thursday. Ven a mi casa el jueves.
on Thursdays los jueves
It's open on Thursdays. Está abierto los jueves.

> **⚟ LANGUAGE**
> Remember the difference in Spanish between **el jueves** (one Thursday only) and **los jueves** (every Thursday).

tick noun
la *cruz* *fem.*

to **tick** verb
(an answer, name, etc.) *marcar con una cruz*

ticket noun
1 *(for train, plane, bus, etc.)* el *billete* *masc.*
a bus ticket un billete de autobús
2 *(for cinema, museum, etc.)* la *entrada* *fem.*
3 **a ticket office** una taquilla *fem.*

*• Use **el** and **uno** for masculine words and **la** and **una** for feminine words.*

to **tickle** verb
to tickle somebody hacer cosquillas a alguien

ticklish adjective
I'm ticklish. Tengo cosquillas.

tide noun
la **marea** fem.
The tide's in. La marea está alta.
The tide's out. La marea está baja.

tidy adjective
(room or house) **ordenado** masc., **ordenada** fem.
a tidy bedroom una habitación ordenada

to **tidy** verb
(a room, toys, etc.) **recoger**
to tidy up recoger las cosas

tie noun
1 la **corbata** fem.
to wear a tie llevar corbata
2 (in a match) el **empate** masc.
It was a tie. Terminó en empate.

to **tie** verb
(a parcel, an animal, etc.) **atar**
Tie your laces. Átate los cordones.
to tie a knot hacer un nudo

tiger noun
el **tigre** masc.

tight adjective
ajustado masc., **ajustada** fem.
tight jeans unos vaqueros ajustados

tights plural noun
las **medias** fem. plural
a pair of tights unas medias

till noun
la **caja** fem.
There's a queue at the till. Hay cola en la caja.

till preposition
hasta
Wait till Tuesday. Espera hasta el martes.

time noun
1 (an amount of time) el **tiempo** masc.
I don't have time. No tengo tiempo.
at the same time al mismo tiempo
a long time mucho tiempo
a very long time ago hace mucho tiempo
to have a nice time divertirse
I had a nice time. Me divertí mucho.
2 (on the clock) la **hora** fem.
What time is it? ¿Qué hora es?
Do you have the right time? ¿Tienes hora?
What time do you go to school? ¿A qué hora vas a la escuela?
It's time to eat. Es hora de comer.
to arrive on time llegar puntual
3 (a point in time) el **momento** masc.
at this time en este momento
4 (an occasion) la **vez** fem.
for the first time por primera vez
how many times? ¿cuántas veces?
three times tres veces
this time esta vez
Two times five is ten. Dos por cinco son diez.

timetable noun
el **horario** masc.

tin noun
la **lata** fem.
a tin of tomatoes una lata de tomates
a tin of paint un bote de pintura

tinfoil noun
el **papel de aluminio** masc.

tiny adjective
muy pequeño masc., **muy pequeña** fem.

tip noun
(end) la **punta** fem.
the tip of my nose la punta de la nariz

tiptoe noun
on tiptoe de puntillas

• Languages and nationalities do not take a capital letter in Spanish.

tired adjective
cansado *masc.*, cansada *fem.*
I'm tired. Estoy cansada.

tissue noun
el pañuelo de papel *masc.*
Do you have a tissue? ¿Tienes un pañuelo?

title noun
el título *masc.*

to preposition
1 a
to the station a la estación
to Spain a España
I'm going to the doctor. Voy al médico.
It's started to rain. Ha empezado a llover.
2 (*to a person, when giving, sending, etc.*) a
I've given the pencil to Dave. Le he dado el lápiz a Dave.
Give the book to me. Dame el libro.

> ⚷ **LANGUAGE**
> a + el = al

3 (*with 'road'*) de
the road to Burgos la carretera de Burgos
4 (*often not translated with infinitives*)
I want to eat. Quiero comer.
It's difficult to do it. Es difícil hacerlo.
5 (*showing a reason*) para
Give me some money to buy sweets. Dame dinero para comprar caramelos.
6 (*with 'have' and infinitive*) que
I have nothing to do. No tengo nada que hacer.
I have a lot to do. Tengo mucho que hacer.
I have to study. Tengo que estudiar.
7 (*following adjectives like 'kind', 'nasty', 'cruel'*) con
She's very nice to me. Es muy buena conmigo.

8 (*talking about the time*)
It's ten to eight. Son las ocho menos diez.

toad noun
el sapo *masc.*

toast noun
el pan tostado *masc.*
a slice of toast una tostada *fem.*

today adverb
hoy
Today is my birthday. Hoy es mi cumpleaños.
What's the date today? ¿A qué fecha estamos hoy?

toe noun
el dedo del pie *masc.*
my big toe el dedo gordo del pie

> ⚷ **LANGUAGE**
> Word for word **dedo del pie** means 'finger of the foot'!

together adverb
juntos *masc. plural*, juntas *fem. plural*
We always play together. Siempre jugamos juntos.

toilet noun
1 el baño *masc.*
to go to the toilet ir al baño
toilet paper el papel higiénico
2 (*in a hotel, restaurant, etc.*) el servicio *masc.*
Where are the toilets? ¿Dónde están los servicios?

tomato noun
el tomate *masc.*
tomato sauce la salsa de tomate

tomorrow adverb
mañana
See you tomorrow! ¡Hasta mañana!
tomorrow morning mañana por la mañana
tomorrow night mañana por la noche
the day after tomorrow pasado mañana

a b c d e f g h i j k l m n o p q r s **t** u v w x y z

• *The months of the year and days of the week do not take a capital letter in Spanish.*

a
b
c
d
e
f
g
h
i
j
k
l
m
n
o
p
q
r
s
t
u
v
w
x
y
z

tongue noun
la **lengua** *fem.*

tonight adverb
esta noche

tonsillitis noun
las **anginas** *fem. plural*
I've got tonsillitis. Tengo anginas.

too adverb
1 (*as well*) **también**
I'm going too. Yo también voy.
You too? – Yes, me too. ¿Tú también? – Sí, yo también.
2 (*more than something*) **demasiado**
It's too big. Es demasiado grande.
3 **too much** (*with nouns*)
demasiado *masc.*, demasiada *fem.*
too much milk demasiada leche
4 **too much** (*with verbs*) demasiado
I eat too much. Como demasiado.
5 **too many** demasiados *masc. plural*,
demasiadas *fem. plural*
too many cars demasiados coches
There are too many. Hay demasiados.

tools plural noun
las **herramientas** *fem. plural*

tooth noun
el **diente** *masc.*
the tooth fairy el ratoncito Pérez

🔑 **LANGUAGE**
Diente is related to the English word 'dentist' (somebody who looks after teeth).

 CULTURE
Spanish children just like British ones leave their tooth under the pillow at bedtime and in the morning find some money or a present there instead. The difference is it's not the tooth fairy but a little mouse (**ratoncito**) whose name is Pérez that comes and takes the tooth away.

• *See the centre section for verb tables.*

toothache noun
I have a toothache. Tengo dolor de muelas.

toothbrush noun
el **cepillo de dientes** *masc.*

toothpaste noun
la **pasta de dientes** *fem.*

top noun
1 (*of a hill, tree, ladder, etc.*) lo **alto** *masc.*
to get to the top of the hill llegar a lo alto de la colina
the top of the mountain la cima de la montaña
2 (*of a box, page, swimsuit, etc.*) la **parte de arriba** *fem.*
on the top of the cupboard en la parte de arriba del armario
3 (*blouse*) la **blusa** *fem.*
4 (*jacket*) **la chaqueta** *fem.*
5 **on top of** encima de
It's on top of the bed. Está encima de la cama.

top adjective
de arriba
the top shelf el estante de arriba
the top floor el último piso
I've got the top mark. He sacado la nota más alta.
You're top of the class. Eres la mejor de la clase.

torch noun
la **linterna** *fem.*

tortoise noun
la **tortuga** *fem.*

total noun
el **total** *masc.*

touch verb
tocar
Don't touch the glass. No toques el cristal.

tough adjective
1 (*not soft*) **duro** *masc.*, **dura** *fem.*
This meat's tough. Esta carne está dura.
2 (*not easy*) **difícil** *masc. & fem.*

tour noun
1 (of a town, museum, etc.) la **visita** fem.
2 (of a country) el **viaje** masc.

tourist noun
el or la **turista** masc. & fem.
a tourist office una oficina de turismo

towards preposition
hacia
He ran towards me. Corrió hacia mí.

towel noun
la **toalla** fem.

tower noun
la **torre** fem.
a tower block un bloque de pisos

town noun
la **ciudad** fem.
to go into town ir a la ciudad
the town centre el centro de la ciudad

toy noun
el **juguete** masc.
a toy shop una juguetería fem.

to **trace** verb
(with tracing paper) **calcar**
to trace a picture calcar un dibujo
tracing paper el papel de calco

track noun
1 (for races) la **pista** fem.
2 (railway line) la **vía** fem.

tracksuit noun
el **chándal** masc.

tractor noun
el **tractor** masc.

traffic noun
el **tráfico** masc.
There's a lot of traffic. Hay mucho tráfico.
a traffic jam un atasco
the traffic lights el semáforo
The traffic lights are green. El semáforo está verde.

train noun
el **tren** masc.
by train en tren
the train to ... el tren para ...
a train set un tren de juguete

to **train** verb
(for football, running, etc.) **entrenar**
He trains every day. Entrena todos los días.

trainers plural noun
las **zapatillas de deporte** fem. plural

> **LANGUAGE**
> In Spanish **zapato** means 'shoe', so word for word this means 'little sports shoes'.

training noun
(for football etc.) el **entrenamiento** masc.

tram noun
el **tranvía** masc.

> **LANGUAGE**
> Be careful: **tranvía** ends in an -a but it is not a feminine noun.

trampoline noun
el **trampolín** masc. (plural los **trampolines**)

to **translate** verb
traducir
Translate this sentence into Spanish. Traduce esta frase al español.

translation noun
la **traducción** fem. (plural las **traducciones**)

transport noun
public transport el transporte público masc.

trap noun
la **trampa** fem.

a b c d e f g h i j k l m n o p q r s t u v w x y z

• Use el and uno for masculine words and la and una for feminine words.

a
b
c
d
e
f
g
h
i
j
k
l
m
n
o
p
q
r
s
t
u
v
w
x
y
z

to **travel** verb
viajar
I like to travel. Me gusta viajar.

travel agent's noun
la agencia de viajes *fem.*

tray noun
la bandeja

to **tread** verb
to tread on something pisar algo
to tread on somebody's foot pisar
a alguien

treasure noun
el tesoro *masc.*

🔑 **LANGUAGE**
English = treasure
Spanish = tesoro

treat noun
a treat algo especial
It's a birthday treat. Es algo
especial para mi cumpleaños.

tree noun
el árbol *masc.*

triangle noun
el triángulo *masc.*

trick noun
1 (*using magic etc.*) el truco *masc.*
a magic trick un truco de magia
2 (*a joke*) la broma *fem.*
to play a trick on somebody gastar
una broma a alguien

tricky adjective
(*difficult*) difícil *masc. & fem.*

trip noun
1 (*by plane, boat, etc.*) el viaje *masc.*
to go on a trip hacer un viaje
Have a good trip! ¡Buen viaje!
2 (*short trip by bus etc.*) la excursión *fem.*
(plural las **excursiones**)
**We're going on a trip to the
seaside.** Vamos de excursión a la
playa.

to **trip** verb
tropezar

trolley noun
(*for shopping*) el carro *masc.*

trouble noun
los problemas *masc. plural*
I'm in trouble. Tengo problemas.
I have trouble walking. Tengo
problemas para andar.

trousers plural noun
los pantalones *masc. plural*
I'm wearing trousers. Llevo
pantalones.
a pair of trousers unos pantalones

truck noun
el camión *masc.* (plural los
camiones)
a truck driver un camionero *masc.*,
una camionera *fem.*

true adjective
verdadero *masc.*, verdadera *fem.*
a true story una historia verdadera
That's true. Es verdad.

trumpet noun
la trompeta *fem.*
to play the trumpet tocar la
trompeta

trunk noun
1 el tronco *masc.*
a tree trunk un tronco
2 la trompa *fem.*
the elephant's trunk la trompa del
elefante

trunks plural noun
el bañador *masc.*
a pair of trunks un bañador

🔑 **LANGUAGE**
English = trunks is plural
Spanish = el bañador is singular

truth noun
la verdad *fem.*
It's the truth. Es la verdad.

• *Languages and nationalities do not take a capital letter in Spanish.*

to **try** verb
1 intentar
 to try to do something intentar hacer algo
 Try again. Inténtalo otra vez.
2 (*food, machine, etc.*) probar
 Try this soup. Prueba esta sopa.

to **try on** verb
 probarse
 Try these jeans on. Pruébate estos vaqueros.

T-shirt noun
 la camiseta *fem.*

tube noun
1 el tubo *masc.*
2 (*underground*) el metro *masc.*
 to go by tube ir en metro

Tuesday noun
 el martes *masc.*
 Today is Tuesday. Hoy es martes.
 on Tuesday el martes
 Can I go to the cinema on Tuesday? ¿Puedo ir al cine el martes?
 on Tuesdays los martes
 I play tennis on Tuesdays. Juego al tenis los martes.

⚷ **LANGUAGE**
Remember the difference in Spanish between **el martes** (one Tuesday only) and **los martes** (every Tuesday).

tumble-dryer noun
 la secadora *fem.*

tummy noun
 el estómago *masc.*,
 la barriga *fem.*, el vientre *masc.*

tummy ache noun
 I have a tummy ache. Me duele el estómago.

tuna noun
 el atún *masc.*
 a tuna sandwich un sándwich de atún

tune noun
 la melodía *masc.*

tunnel noun
 el túnel *masc.*
 to go through a tunnel pasar por un túnel

turkey noun
 el pavo *masc.*

turn noun
 el turno *masc.*
 It's my turn. Es mi turno.
 It's Jamal's turn. Es el turno de Jamal.
 Whose turn is it? ¿A quién le toca?

to **turn** verb
1 girar
 Turn right. Gira a la derecha.
 She turned the steering wheel. Giró el volante.
2 (*a page, corner*) dar la vuelta a
 Turn the page. Da la vuelta a la página.
3 (*to become*) ponerse
 He turned red. Se puso rojo.
 The prince turned into a frog! ¡El príncipe se convirtió en rana!

to **turn back** verb
 volver
 We have to turn back. Tenemos que volver.

to **turn down** verb
 (*a TV, the heating, etc.*) bajar
 Turn down the sound. Baja el volumen.

to **turn off** verb
1 (*a TV, computer, etc.*) apagar
 Turn the light off. Apaga la luz.
2 **to turn off the tap** cerrar el grifo

to **turn on** verb
1 (*a light, computer, etc.*) encender
 Turn the TV on. Enciende la tele.
2 **to turn on the tap** abrir el grifo

a
b
c
d
e
f
g
h
i
j
k
l
m
n
o
p
q
r
s
t
u
v
w
x
y
z

• *The months of the year and days of the week do not take a capital letter in Spanish.*

to **turn out** verb
to turn out the light apagar la luz

to **turn over** verb
(*a page, mattress, etc.*) **dar la vuelta a**

to **turn round** verb
darse la vuelta
I turned round. Me di la vuelta.

to **turn up** verb
(*a radio, the heating, etc.*) **subir**
Turn up the sound. Sube el volumen.

turning noun
la **calle** *fem.*

turtle noun
la **tortuga (de mar)** *fem.*

TV noun
la **tele** *fem.*
on TV en la tele
a TV set una tele

twelfth adjective
the twelfth floor el piso doce
the twelfth of February el doce de febrero

> 🔑 **LANGUAGE**
> In Spanish you usually use **doce** (twelve).

twelve number
doce
I eat at twelve. Como a las doce.
I'm twelve. Tengo doce años.

> 🔑 **LANGUAGE**
> In English you can say 'twelve o'clock' or just 'twelve', 'twelve years old' or just 'twelve'. In Spanish you must add **las** (for time) and **años** (for age).

twentieth adjective
the twentieth floor el piso veinte
the twentieth of July el veinte de julio

> 🔑 **LANGUAGE**
> In Spanish you usually use **veinte** (twenty).

twenty number
veinte
It's twenty to seven. Son las siete menos veinte.
It's twenty past eight. Son las ocho y veinte.
My sister is twenty. Mi hermana tiene veinte años.

> 🔑 **LANGUAGE**
> In English you can say just 'twenty'. In Spanish you must add **años**.

twice adverb
dos veces
twice a week dos veces a la semana

twin noun
el **mellizo** *masc.*, la **melliza** *fem.*
They're twins. Son mellizos.
identical twins los gemelos *masc. plural*, las gemelas *fem. plural*
my twin sister mi hermana melliza

to **twist** verb
torcer
I've twisted my ankle. Me he torcido el tobillo.

two number
dos
The film begins at two. La película empieza a las dos.
Harry's two. Harry tiene dos años.

> 🔑 **LANGUAGE**
> In English you can say 'two o'clock' or just 'two', 'two years old' or just 'two'. In Spanish you must add **las** (for time) and **años** (for age).

type noun
el **tipo** *masc.*
What type of bike do you have? ¿Qué tipo de bici tienes?

to **type** verb
(*a letter etc. on a computer*) **escribir**
to type in (*a password etc.*) teclear

tyre noun
el **neumático** *masc.*

• *See the centre section for verb tables.*

Uu

UFO noun
el **OVNI** *masc.*

> **⚷ LANGUAGE**
> The Spanish stands for **objeto volador no identificado**, matching the English 'unidentified flying object'.

ugly adjective
feo *masc.*, **fea** *fem.*
The dog is very ugly. El perro es muy feo.

UK noun
el **Reino Unido** *masc.*
I live in the UK. Vivo en el Reino Unido.

Ulster noun
el **Ulster** *masc.*
I live in Ulster. Vivo en el Ulster.

umbrella noun
el **paraguas** *masc.* (plural los **paraguas**)

> **⚷ LANGUAGE**
> The Spanish **paraguas** comes from **parar** (to stop) and **agua** (water) – to stop the water!

umpire noun
(*in cricket, tennis, etc.*) el **árbitro** *masc.*, la **árbitra** *fem.*

unable adjective
to be unable to do something no poder hacer algo
Sally's unable to come. Sally no puede venir.

unbelievable adjective
increíble *masc. & fem.*

uncle noun
el **tío** *masc.*
He's my uncle. Es mi tío.
my uncle and aunt mis tíos

uncomfortable adjective
(*chair, shoes, etc.*) **incómodo** *masc.*, **incómoda** *fem.*
I'm uncomfortable in this armchair. Estoy incómodo en este sillón.

under preposition
1 **debajo de**
under the table debajo de la mesa
2 **por debajo de**
I went under a ladder. Pasé por debajo de una escalera.

> **⚷ LANGUAGE**
> Use **por debajo de** with verbs of movement like 'go', 'walk', or 'jump'.

underground noun
el **metro** *masc.*
to go by underground ir en metro

underground adjective
subterráneo *masc.*, **subterránea** *fem.*
an underground car park un aparcamiento subterráneo

underline verb
subrayar

underneath preposition
1 **debajo de**
underneath the bed debajo de la cama
2 **por debajo de**
The train goes underneath the bridge. El tren pasa por debajo del puente.

> **⚷ LANGUAGE**
> Use **por debajo de** with verbs of movement like 'go', 'walk', or 'jump'.

underneath adverb
debajo
Look underneath. Mira debajo.

a
b
c
d
e
f
g
h
i
j
k
l
m
n
o
p
q
r
s
t
u
v
w
x
y
z

• *Use* **el** *and* **uno** *for masculine words and* **la** *and* **una** *for feminine words.*

understand verb
entender
I don't understand. No entiendo.
Do you understand Spanish?
¿Entiendes el español?

underwater adverb
(*to swim etc.*) debajo del agua

underwear noun
la ropa interior *fem.*

> 🔑 **LANGUAGE**
> Word for word the Spanish means 'inside clothes'.

to undo verb
1 (*shoelaces, parcel, etc.*) desatar
Your laces are undone. Tienes los cordones desatados.
2 (*a coat, jacket, etc.*) desabrochar
Undo your shirt. Desabróchate la camisa.
3 (*to cancel on a computer*) cancelar

to undress verb
desnudarse
to get undressed desnudarse

unemployed adjective
parado *masc.*, parada *fem.*
My dad's unemployed. Mi padre está parado.

unexpected adjective
inesperado *masc.*,
inesperada *fem.*

unfair adjective
injusto *masc.*, injusta *fem.*
That's unfair. Es injusto.

to unfold verb
(*a map, newspaper*) desplegar

unfriendly adjective
antipático *masc.*, antipática *fem.*
He's very unfriendly. Es muy antipático.

unhappy adjective
(*sad*) triste *masc. & fem.*
I'm unhappy. Estoy triste.

unhealthy adjective
(*food, person, etc.*) no muy sano *masc.*, no muy sana *fem.*
This diet is unhealthy. Esta dieta no es muy sana.

uniform noun
el uniforme *masc.*
I'm wearing my school uniform.
Llevo el uniforme del colegio.

> 🌍 **CULTURE**
> In Spain schoolchildren don't usually wear uniforms.

Union Jack noun
la bandera del Reino Unido *fem.*

United Kingdom noun
el Reino Unido *masc.*
We live in the United Kingdom.
Vivimos en el Reino Unido.

United States plural noun
Estados Unidos *masc.*
I'm going to the United States.
Voy a Estados Unidos.

> 🔑 **LANGUAGE**
> Estados Unidos is usually singular, and los (the) is not usually given.

universe noun
el universo *masc.*

university noun
la universidad *fem.*
My brother goes to university.
Mi hermano va a la universidad.

unless conjunction
si no
I'm going to the cinema unless it rains. Voy al cine si no llueve.

• *Languages and nationalities do not take a capital letter in Spanish.*

a b c d e f g h i j k l m n o p q r s t u v w x y z

unlikely adjective
poco probable *masc. & fem.*

to **unlock** verb
(*a door, car, etc.*) abrir

unlucky adjective
1 (*talking about people*)
to be unlucky tener mala suerte
He's unlucky. Tiene mala suerte.
2 (*talking about things or numbers*)
The number thirteen is unlucky.
El número trece trae mala suerte.

to **unpack** verb
1 (*one case only*) deshacer la maleta
I've unpacked my case.
He deshecho mi maleta.
2 (*more than one case*) deshacer las maletas

unpleasant adjective
desagradable *masc. & fem.*

to **unplug** verb
desenchufar
Can you unplug the computer?
¿Puedes desenchufar el ordenador?

unsafe adjective
(*dangerous*) peligroso *masc.*,
peligrosa *fem.*
an unsafe place un sitio peligroso

untidy adjective
(*room or house*) desordenado *masc.*,
desordenada *fem.*
My bedroom's untidy. Mi
habitación está desordenada.

to **untie** verb
(*parcel, knot, etc.*) desatar
Untie your laces. Desátate los
cordones.

until preposition
hasta
Wait until tomorrow. Espera
hasta mañana.

untrue adjective
falso *masc.*, falsa *fem.*

unusual adjective
1 (*word, name, etc.*) poco corriente
masc. & fem.
2 (*strange*) raro *masc.*, rara *fem.*

🔑 **LANGUAGE**
You can also say **extraño/extraña.**

to **unwrap** verb
(*presents etc.*) abrir

up adverb & preposition
1 arriba
I looked up. Miré hacia arriba.
up here aquí arriba
Hands up, children! ¡Niños,
levantad la mano!
It's up the hill. Está en lo alto de la
colina.
2 **up to** hasta
to count up to twenty contar hasta
veinte
up to now hasta ahora
That's up to you. Depende de ti.
What are you up to? ¿Qué estás
haciendo?

🔑 **LANGUAGE**
'Up' is often translated as part of a verb
such as 'to go up' (**subir**) or 'to get up'
(**levantarse**).

up adjective
(*out of bed*) levantado *masc.*,
levantada *fem.*
Are you up? ¿Estás levantada?

upset adjective
1 (*sad*) triste *masc. & fem.*
2 (*angry*) enfadado *masc.*,
enfadada *fem.*
3 **I have an upset stomach.** Tengo
mal el estómago.

to **upset** verb
1 **to upset somebody** enfadar a
alguien
2 (*water, tea, etc.*) tirar
I've upset the milk. He tirado la
leche.

a
b
c
d
e
f
g
h
i
j
k
l
m
n
o
p
q
r
s
t
u
v
w
x
y
z

• *The months of the year and days of the week do not take a capital letter in Spanish.*

upside down adjective
al revés
The picture is upside down. El cuadro está al revés.

upstairs adverb
arriba
I'm upstairs. Estoy arriba.
Go upstairs! ¡Sube!

> **⚷ LANGUAGE**
> Use **subir** to translate 'to come upstairs' or 'to go upstairs'.

up-to-date adjective
(*computer, camcorder, etc.*)
moderno *masc.*, moderna *fem.*

urgent adjective
urgente *masc. & fem.*

us pronoun
1 (*after a verb*) nos
They know us. Nos conocen.
Has he seen us? ¿Nos ha visto?

> **⚷ LANGUAGE**
> With commands and infinitives **nos** is joined with the verb to make one word.

Call us. Llámanos.
Can you help us? ¿Puedes ayudarnos?
2 (*to us*) nos
She has sent a present to us. Nos ha mandado un regalo.
Give us the book. Danos el libro.
Give it to us. Dánoslo.
3 (*after a preposition etc.*) nosotros *masc.*, nosotras *fem.*
with us con nosotros
They're taller than us. Son más altos que nosotros.
It's us. Somos nosotros.

US plural noun
Estados Unidos *masc.*
I'm going to the US. Voy a Estados Unidos.

> **⚷ LANGUAGE**
> **Estados Unidos** is usually singular, and **los** (the) is not usually given.

USA noun
Estados Unidos *masc.*

to use verb
usar
Use a hammer. Usa un martillo.
Can I use the toilet? ¿Puedo ir al baño?

use noun
It's no use ... Es inútil ...
It's no use shouting. Es inútil gritar.

used adjective
1 (*bicycle, clothes, etc.*) usado *masc.*, usada *fem.*
a used car un coche usado
2 **to be used to something** estar acostumbrado or acostumbrada a algo
I'm used to taking the bus. Estoy acostumbrado a coger el autobús.

useful adjective
útil *masc. & fem.*
It's very useful. Es muy útil.

useless adjective
1 (*ideas, effort, etc.*) inútil *masc. & fem.*
useless things cosas inútiles
2 (*knife, book, etc.*) que no sirve para nada
Those scissors are useless. Esas tijeras no sirven para nada.
3 (*really bad*) muy malo *masc.*, muy mala *fem.*
He's a useless player. Es un jugador muy malo.

usual adjective
1 normal *masc. & fem.*
the usual price el precio normal
2 (*time, place, etc.*) de siempre
at the usual time a la hora de siempre
as usual como siempre

usually adverb
normalmente

• *See the centre section for verb tables.*

a b c d e f g h i j k l m n o p q r s t u v w x y z

Vv

to **vacuum** verb
pasar la aspiradora
I've vacuumed the carpet. He pasado la aspiradora por la alfombra.
a vacuum cleaner una aspiradora

valley noun
el **valle** masc.

valuable adjective
valioso masc., **valiosa** fem.
This picture is very valuable. Este cuadro es muy valioso.

van noun
la **furgoneta** fem.

vanilla noun
la **vainilla** fem.
a vanilla ice cream un helado de vainilla

> 🔑 **LANGUAGE**
> English = vanilla
> Spanish = vainilla

to **vanish** verb
desaparecer

various adjective
varios masc. plural, **varias** fem. plural
I've seen him in various films. Lo he visto en varias películas.

varnish noun
el **barniz** masc.
nail varnish el esmalte de uñas

vase noun
el **jarrón** masc. (plural los **jarrones**)

vegetable noun
la **verdura** fem.
vegetable soup sopa de verduras

vegetarian adjective
vegetariano masc., **vegetariana** fem.

vegetarian noun
el **vegetariano** masc.,
la **vegetariana** fem.
I'm a vegetarian. Soy vegetariana.

vending machine noun
la máquina expendedora fem.

verb noun
el **verbo** masc.

very adverb
1 **muy**
very tired muy cansado
very well muy bien
very much mucho
I like it very much. Me gusta mucho.
2 **mucho** masc., **mucha** fem.
I'm very hungry. Tengo mucha hambre.
It's very hot. Hace mucho calor.

> 🔑 **LANGUAGE**
> English = to be **very** hungry
> Spanish = tener **mucha** hambre
> English = to be **very** hot
> Spanish = hacer **mucho** calor

vest noun
la **camiseta** fem.

vet noun
el **veterinario** masc.,
la **veterinaria** fem.

vicar noun
el **párroco** masc.

video noun
1 el **vídeo** masc.
to watch a video ver un vídeo
on video en vídeo
a video game un videojuego
a video recorder un vídeo
2 (music video) el **clip** masc.

> 🔑 **LANGUAGE**
> **Video** means the film you watch, the cassette you buy, and the machine you watch the film on, just as in English.

a
b
c
d
e
f
g
h
i
j
k
l
m
n
o
p
q
r
s
t
u
v
w
x
y
z

• Use **el** and **uno** for masculine words and **la** and **una** for feminine words.

a
b
c
d
e
f
g
h
i
j
k
l
m
n
o
p
q
r
s
t
u
v
w
x
y
z

view noun
la vista *fem.*

village noun
el pueblo *masc.*

vinegar noun
el vinagre *masc.*

violin noun
el violín *masc.* (plural los **violines**)
to play the violin tocar el violín

virus noun
el virus *masc.* (plural los **virus**)
a computer virus un virus
informático

visit noun
la visita *fem.*
a visit to the museum una visita al
museo

to **visit** verb
visitar
I'm going to visit my cousins.
Voy a visitar a mis primos.

visitor noun
la visita *fem.*
We have visitors. Tenemos visitas.

vocabulary noun
el vocabulario *masc.*

voice noun
la voz *fem.* (plural las **voces**)
to speak in a loud voice hablar en
voz alta
Can you keep your voice down?
¿Puedes bajar la voz?

volcano noun
el volcán *masc.* (plural los **volcanes**)

volleyball noun
el voleibol *masc.*
to play volleyball jugar al
voleibol

volume noun
el volumen *masc.*
Turn down the volume. Baja el
volumen.

volunteer noun
el voluntario *masc.*,
la voluntaria *fem.*

to **vote** verb
votar

voucher noun
a gift voucher un vale de regalo

vowel noun
la vocal *fem.*

Ww

to **wag** verb
mover
It's wagging its tail. Mueve la cola.

waist noun
la cintura *fem.*

waistcoat noun
el chaleco *masc.*

to **wait** verb
esperar
Wait a minute! ¡Espera un
momento!

I'm waiting for you. Te estoy
esperando.
Wait for me. Espérame.
a waiting room una sala de espera

LANGUAGE
English = **to wait for** somebody
Spanish = **esperar** a alguien

waiter noun
el camarero *masc.*

waitress noun
la camarera *fem.*

• *Languages and nationalities do not take a capital letter in Spanish.*

to wake up verb
1 despertarse
 I wake up at seven. Me despierto a las siete.
 Wake up! ¡Despiértate!
2 despertar
 Wake me up at nine. Despiértame a las nueve.

Wales noun
 Gales masc.
 I live in Wales. Vivo en Gales.

walk noun
 el paseo masc.
 to go for a walk ir de paseo, ir a dar un paseo
 to take the dog out for a walk sacar a pasear al perro

to walk verb
1 andar
 You walk too fast. Andas demasiado rápido.
2 (to go on foot, not by bike, bus, etc.) ir a pie
 I walk to school. Voy al colegio a pie.
3 to walk with somebody acompañar a alguien
 to walk in entrar
 to walk out salir
 to walk across the road cruzar la calle

walking noun
 Walking is good for you. Andar es muy sano.
 I like walking. Me gusta andar.
 a walking stick un bastón (plural bastones)

wall noun
1 (of a house or room) la pared fem.
 There's a picture on the wall. Hay un cuadro en la pared.
2 (in a garden, field, etc.) el muro masc.
 Jump off the wall. Salta del muro.

wallet noun
 la cartera fem.

wallpaper noun
 el papel pintado masc.

walnut noun
 la nuez fem. (plural las nueces)

wand noun
 la varita fem.
 a magic wand una varita mágica

to want verb
 querer
 I want an ice cream. Quiero un helado.
 Do you want some water? ¿Quieres agua?
 I want to watch TV. Quiero ver la tele.
 What do you want to do, children? Niños, ¿qué queréis hacer?

war noun
 la guerra fem.

wardrobe noun
 el armario masc.

warm adjective
 caliente masc. & fem.
 My room is warm. Mi habitación está caliente.
 These gloves are very warm. Estos guantes son muy calientes.
 It's warm today. Hoy hace calor.
 I'm warm. Tengo calor.

> **LANGUAGE**
> English = to be warm I'm warm.
> Spanish = tener calor Tengo calor.

to warn verb
 advertir
 I'm warning you! ¡Te lo advierto!

• The months of the year and days of the week do not take a capital letter in Spanish.

425

English Spanish

a
b
c
d
e
f
g
h
i
j
k
l
m
n
o
p
q
r
s
t
u
v
w
x
y
z

was verb SEE **be**
I was tired. Estaba cansado.
Yesterday was my birthday. Ayer fue mi cumpleaños.

wash noun
to have a wash lavarse

to **wash** verb
1 (clothes, a floor, car, etc.) **lavar**
Have you washed the blouse? ¿Has lavado la blusa?
2 (your hands etc.) **lavarse**
I get up and wash. Me levanto y me lavo.
I've washed my hands. Me he lavado las manos.
He's washing his face. Se está lavando la cara.

to **wash up** verb
fregar los platos, **lavar los platos**

washbasin noun
el **lavabo** masc.

washing noun
(clothes) la **ropa** fem.
the dirty washing la ropa sucia
to do the washing lavar la ropa
a washing machine una lavadora
washing powder el detergente

washing-up noun
los **platos sucios** masc. plural
to do the washing-up fregar los platos

wasp noun
la **avispa** fem.

waste noun
It's a waste of time. Es una pérdida de tiempo.

to **waste** verb
perder
You're wasting your time. Estás perdiendo el tiempo.

watch noun
el **reloj** masc.
I don't have a watch. No tengo reloj.

to **watch** verb
1 (to look at) **mirar**
Watch me. Mírame.
2 (a film, programme, etc.) **ver**
I'm watching TV. Estoy viendo la tele.
3 (to look after) **cuidar**
Can you watch the children? ¿Puedes cuidar a los niños?

to **watch out** verb
tener cuidado
Watch out for flies! ¡Cuidado con las moscas!

water noun
el **agua** fem.
Do you want some water? ¿Quieres agua?

🔑 **LANGUAGE**
Be careful: you use **el** with **agua** but it is not a masculine noun.

to **water** verb
regar
I'm watering the plants. Estoy regando las plantas.

watermelon noun
la **sandía** fem.

wave noun
(in the sea) la **ola** fem.

to **wave** verb
(to say hello) **saludar con la mano**
She waved goodbye to me. Me hizo adiós con la mano.

wavy adjective
to have wavy hair tener el pelo ondulado

• See the centre section for verb tables.

way noun

1 (*to a place*) el **camino** *masc.*
I know the way. Yo sé el camino.
to ask the way to ... preguntar el camino a ...
Do you know the way to the library? ¿Sabes cómo se llega a la biblioteca?
It's a long way. Está muy lejos.
You're in my way! ¡No me dejas pasar!
the way in la entrada
the way out la salida

2 (*direction*)
We're going the opposite way. Vamos en dirección contraria.
Which way is it? ¿Por dónde es?
this way por aquí
that way por ahí

3 (*a way of doing something*) la **manera** *fem.*
which way? ¿de qué manera?
Do it this way. Hazlo de esta manera.
You're doing it the wrong way. Lo estás haciendo mal.
You've done it the right way. Lo has hecho bien.

we pronoun

1 (*not usually translated in Spanish*)
We're English. Somos ingleses.
We want an ice cream. Queremos un helado.

2 **nosotros** *masc.*, **nosotras** *fem.*
They watch TV but we read books. Ellos ven la tele, pero nosotros leemos libros.

> 🔑 **LANGUAGE**
> Use **nosotros/nosotras** when you want to give special importance to the word 'we'.

weak adjective
débil *masc. & fem.*
I feel weak. Me siento débil.

to **wear** verb

1 **llevar**
I'm wearing a blue dress. Llevo un vestido azul.

2 **ponerse**
What are you going to wear? ¿Qué te vas a poner?

> 🔑 **LANGUAGE**
> Use **ponerse** (to put on) rather than **llevar** when you talk about the clothes you are going to put on.

weather noun
el **tiempo** *masc.*
What's the weather like? ¿Qué tiempo hace?
The weather's nice. Hace buen tiempo.
The weather's cold. Hace frío.
the weather forecast el tiempo, el pronóstico del tiempo

web noun

1 (*spider's web*) la **telaraña** *fem.*
2 (*the Internet*) la **web** *fem.*
a web page una página web

website noun
el **sitio web** *masc.*
to visit a website visitar un sitio web

wedding noun
la **boda** *fem.*
a wedding anniversary un aniversario de boda
a wedding dress un vestido de novia

Wednesday noun
el **miércoles** *masc.*
Today is Wednesday. Hoy es miércoles.
on Wednesday el miércoles

a b c d e f g h i j k l m n o p q r s t u v w x y z

• *Use* **el** *and* **uno** *for masculine words and* **la** *and* **una** *for feminine words.*

I'm going swimming on Wednesday. Voy a la piscina el miércoles.
on Wednesdays los miércoles
We play football on Wednesdays. Jugamos al fútbol los miércoles.

> **LANGUAGE**
> Remember the difference in Spanish between **el miércoles** (one Wednesday only) and **los miércoles** (every Wednesday).

weed noun
la **mala hierba** fem.

> **LANGUAGE**
> Word for word the Spanish means 'bad grass'.

week noun
la **semana** fem.
We're leaving in a week. Nos vamos dentro de una semana.
this week esta semana
last week la semana pasada
next week la semana que viene
during the week entre semana

weekday noun
on weekdays entre semana

weekend noun
el **fin de semana** masc.
last weekend el fin de semana pasado
next weekend el fin de semana que viene

to **weigh** verb
pesar
I weigh thirty kilos. Peso treinta kilos.

weight noun
el **peso** masc.
to put on weight engordar
to lose weight adelgazar

welcome adjective
bienvenido masc.,
bienvenida fem.
Welcome! ¡Bienvenido!
Welcome to Madrid! ¡Bienvenidos a Madrid!
Thank you! – You're welcome! ¡Gracias! – ¡De nada!

> **LANGUAGE**
> Remember to use **¡Bienvenida!** if you're talking to a girl or woman, and **¡Bienvenidos!** if you're talking to two people or more.

well adverb & adjective
1 bien
You draw well. Dibujas bien.
Well done! ¡Muy bien!, ¡Bien hecho!
2 (in good health)
I'm well. Estoy bien.
I don't feel well. No me encuentro bien.
Get well soon! ¡Que te mejores!
3 as well también
I'm going as well. Yo voy también.

well exclamation
¡bueno!
Well, I'm going! ¡Bueno, me voy!

well noun
el **pozo** masc.
to get water from the well sacar agua del pozo

well-behaved adjective
He's well-behaved. Se porta bien.

wellingtons plural noun
las **botas de goma** fem. plural

well-known adjective
conocido masc., **conocida** fem.

Welsh adjective
galés masc., **galesa** fem.
a Welsh actor un actor galés
She's Welsh. Es galesa.
Welsh people los galeses

> **LANGUAGE**
> The masculine plural of **galés** is **galeses**.

• Languages and nationalities do not take a capital letter in Spanish.

Welsh noun

1 (*language*) el galés *masc.*
 Rhys speaks Welsh. Rhys habla galés.
2 **the Welsh** los galeses *masc. plural*

Welshman noun
 el galés *masc.* (plural los **galeses**)

Welshwoman noun
 la galesa *fem.*

went verb SEE **go**
 I went to school. Fui al colegio.
 She went to Spain. Fue a España.

were verb SEE **be**
 We were at home. Estábamos en casa.
 You were ill. Estabas enfermo.
 They were kind to me. Fueron amables conmigo.

west noun & adjective
 el oeste *masc.*
 in the west en el oeste
 the west coast la costa oeste

western noun
 la película del oeste *fem.*

West Indies plural noun
 las Antillas *fem. plural*

wet adjective

1 mojado *masc.*, mojada *fem.*
 The towel is wet. La toalla está mojada.
 to get wet mojarse
2 (*rainy*) lluvioso *masc.*, lluviosa *fem.*
 a wet day un día lluvioso
 I don't go out when it's wet. No salgo cuando llueve.

whale noun
 la ballena *fem.*

what pronoun & adjective

1 (*in questions*) qué
 What are you doing? ¿Qué estás haciendo?
 What is it? ¿Qué es?
 What time is it? ¿Qué hora es?
 What chocolates do you want? ¿Qué bombones quieres?
 What? ¿Qué?
 What for? ¿Para qué?
 What are you talking about? ¿De qué hablas?
2 cuál (plural **cuáles**)
 what is ...? ¿cuál es ...?
 what are ...? ¿cuáles son ...?
 What's your address? ¿Cuál es tu dirección?
 What's the problem? ¿Cuál es el problema?
 What's the Spanish for 'house'? ¿Cómo se dice 'house' en español?
3 (*when there isn't a question*) lo que
 I don't know what you want. No sé lo que quieres.
 Tell me what happened. Dime lo que ha pasado.
4 (*in exclamations*) qué
 What a pity! ¡Qué lástima!
 What a pretty girl! ¡Qué niña tan guapa!

wheat noun
 el trigo *masc.*

wheel noun
 la rueda *fem.*
 the front wheel la rueda delantera
 the steering wheel el volante

wheelchair noun
 la silla de ruedas *fem.*

• *The months of the year and days of the week do not take a capital letter in Spanish.*

when adverb & conjunction

1 (*in questions*) cuándo
When are you leaving? ¿Cuándo te vas?
2 (*when there isn't a question*) cuando
I don't go out when it rains No salgo cuando llueve

> **LANGUAGE**
> Remember to put the accent on **cuándo** in questions.

where adverb

1 (*in questions*) dónde
Where are you? ¿Dónde estás?
Where are you going? ¿Adónde vas?, ¿Dónde vas?
I don't know where it is. No sé dónde está.
2 (*when there isn't a question*) donde
This is the street where I live. Ésta es la calle donde vivo.

> **LANGUAGE**
> Remember to put the accent on **dónde** in questions.

whether adverb

si
I don't know whether it's possible. No sé si es posible.

which adjective

1 qué
Which book are you reading? ¿Qué libro lees?
Which house is it? ¿Qué casa es?
2 cuál (plural **cuáles**)
I have two CDs. Which of them do you want? Tengo dos CDs. ¿Cuál quieres?
which one? ¿cuál?
Which one do you want? ¿Cuál quieres?
which ones? ¿cuáles?
Which ones do you like best? ¿Cuáles te gustan más?

which pronoun

que
the book which is on the table el libro que está en la mesa
the bike which I want la bici que quiero

while conjunction

mientras
Wait here while I wash my hands. Espérame aquí mientras me lavo las manos.

while noun

a short while un momento
a long while mucho tiempo
I lived in Spain for a while. Viví una temporada en España.

whiskers plural noun

(*of a cat*) los bigotes *masc. plural*

to whisper verb

susurrar

whistle noun

el silbato *masc.*
to blow a whistle tocar un silbato

to whistle verb

silbar

white adjective

blanco *masc.*, blanca *fem.*
a white dress un vestido blanco
a white coffee un café con leche

white noun

el blanco *masc.*
I like white. Me gusta el blanco.

whiteboard noun

la pizarra blanca *fem.*
on the whiteboard en la pizarra

who pronoun

1 quién (plural **quiénes**)
Who wants an ice cream? ¿Quién quiere un helado?
Who's that? ¿Quién es?
I don't know who they are. No sé quiénes son.
2 que

• See the centre section for verb tables.

English Spanish

my uncle who lives in Sheffield mi tío que vive en Sheffield

whole adjective
todo *masc.*, **toda** *fem.*
the whole village todo el pueblo
my whole family toda mi familia

> 🔑 **LANGUAGE**
> **Todo** is the usual Spanish word for 'all' so, word for word, **todo el pueblo** is 'all the village'.

whose pronoun
de quién (plural **de quiénes**)
Whose bike is this? ¿De quién es esta bici?
Whose is it? ¿De quién es?
Whose are they? ¿De quiénes son?

why adverb
por qué
Why are you sad? ¿Por qué estás triste?
Why not? ¿Por qué no?

wicked adjective
1 (*evil*) malo *masc.*, mala *fem.*
He's very wicked. Es muy malo.
2 (*very good*) genial *masc. & fem.*
Wicked! ¡Genial!

wide adjective
1 ancho *masc.*, ancha *fem.*
This road is very wide. Esta calle es muy ancha.
2 **wide awake** completamente despierto *masc.*, completamente despierta *fem.*

wife noun
la mujer *fem.*
my brother's wife la mujer de mi hermano

wild adjective
salvaje *masc. & fem.*
wild animals animales salvajes

will verb
1 (*for talking about the very near future*) ir
I'll be late. Voy a llegar tarde.
What will you do? ¿Qué vas a hacer?
2 (*translated by the future tense in Spanish*)
I'll see you tomorrow. Te veré mañana.
It won't rain. No lloverá.
3 (*when asking*) querer
Will you have a Coke? ¿Quieres una Coca-Cola?
Will you behave yourself? ¿Quieres portarte bien?
4 (*when you mean 'does not or do not want to'*) no querer
She won't help me. No quiere ayudarme.

to **win** verb
ganar
Have you won? ¿Has ganado?

wind noun
el viento *masc.*

windmill noun
el molino de viento *masc.*

window noun
1 la ventana *fem.*
Open the window. Abre la ventana.
2 (*the glass of a window*) el cristal *masc.*
to break a window romper un cristal
3 (*of a car*) la ventanilla *fem.*
4 (*shop window*) el escaparate *masc.*

windy adjective
It's windy. Hace viento.

wine noun
el vino *masc.*
red wine el vino tinto

wing noun
el ala *fem.*

> 🔑 **LANGUAGE**
> Be careful: you use **el** with **ala** but it is not a masculine noun.

• *See the centre section for verb tables.*

a
b
c
d
e
f
g
h
i
j
k
l
m
n
o
p
q
r
s
t
u
v
w
x
y
z

English Spanish

a
b
c
d
e
f
g
h
i
j
k
l
m
n
o
p
q
r
s
t
u
v
w
x
y
z

winner noun
el **ganador** *masc.*, la **ganadora** *fem.*

winter noun
el **invierno** *masc.*
in the winter en invierno

to **wipe** verb
(*a table, your hands, etc.*) **limpiar**

wire noun
1 (*of TV, phone, etc.*) el **cable** *masc.*
an electric wire un cable eléctrico
2 (*of a cage, fence, etc.*) el **alambre** *masc.*

wise adjective
sabio *masc.*, **sabia** *fem.*

wish noun
el **deseo** *masc.*
to make a wish pedir un deseo
Best wishes on your birthday! ¡Felicidades!
With best wishes, Jenny. (*in a letter*) Saludos de Jenny.

to **wish** verb
desear
I wish you a happy birthday. Te deseo un feliz cumpleaños.

witch noun
la **bruja** *fem.*

with preposition
1 **con**
with a knife con un cuchillo
Come with me. Ven conmigo.
He went with you. Fue contigo.
2 (*at somebody's house*) **en casa de**
I stayed with my sister. Me quedé en casa de mi hermana.

without preposition
sin
without me sin mi
without an umbrella sin paraguas
without looking sin mirar

wizard noun
el **mago** *masc.*

wolf noun
el **lobo** *masc.*
the big bad wolf el lobo feroz

🔑 **LANGUAGE**
Little Red Riding Hood is the same in Spain but the 'big bad wolf' is the 'fierce wolf'.

woman noun
la **mujer** *fem.*
men and women los hombres y las mujeres
a young woman una joven
an old woman una anciana, una vieja

🔑 **LANGUAGE**
Anciana is a polite word for 'old woman'.

wonderful adjective
maravilloso *masc.*, **maravillosa** *fem.*

wood noun
1 la **madera** *fem.*
It's made of wood. Es de madera.
2 (*little forest*)
the woods el bosque *masc.*
I walked through the woods. Fui de paseo por el bosque.

wooden adjective
de madera
a wooden chair una silla de madera

wool noun
la **lana** *fem.*

woolly adjective
de lana
a woolly jumper un jersey de lana

word noun
la **palabra** *fem.*
What does this word mean? ¿Qué quiere decir esta palabra?
What's the Spanish word for 'tree'? ¿Cómo se dice 'tree' en español?
the words of a song la letra de una canción

work noun
el **trabajo** *masc.*

• *Use* **el** *and* **uno** *for masculine words and* **la** *and* **una** *for feminine words.*

lots of work mucho trabajo
Mum's at work. Mamá está en el trabajo.
to go to work by car ir al trabajo en coche

to **work** verb
1 **trabajar**
I work hard. Trabajo mucho.
2 (*talking about machines*) **funcionar**
The TV isn't working. La tele no funciona.

to **work out** verb
1 (*to calculate*) **calcular**
Have you worked it out? ¿Lo has calculado?
2 (*in the gym*) **hacer ejercicio**

worker noun
1 (*in a factory etc.*) el **trabajador** *masc.*, la **trabajadora** *fem.*
2 (*in an office*) el **empleado** *masc.*, la **empleada** *fem.*
3 (*on a building site*) el **obrero** *masc.*, la **obrera** *fem.*

worksheet noun
la **hoja de ejercicios** *fem.*

workshop noun
(*for learning, doing repairs, etc.*) el **taller** *masc.*

world noun
el **mundo** *masc.*
the best in the world el mejor del mundo
to travel all over the world viajar por todo el mundo

worm noun
el **gusano** *masc.*

worried adjective
preocupado *masc.*, **preocupada** *fem.*
to be worried about estar preocupado por
Mum's worried about her. Mamá está preocupada por ella.

to **worry** verb
preocuparse

Don't worry! ¡No te preocupes!

worse adjective
peor *masc. & fem.*
Your Spanish is worse than mine. Tu español es peor que el mío.
I'm feeling worse. Me encuentro peor.

worse adverb
peor
They sing worse than us. Cantan peor que nosotros.

worst adjective
peor *masc. & fem.*
He's the worst pupil in the class. Es el peor alumno de la clase.
the worst one el or la peor

worst noun
el or la **peor** *masc. & fem.*
This book is the worst. Este libro es el peor.

worth adjective
to be worth valer
It's worth a lot of money. Vale mucho dinero.
It's worth doing it. Vale la pena hacerlo.
It's not worth it. No vale la pena.

would verb
1 (*when asking for something*)
I would like ... Quiero ..., Quisiera ...
I'd like to say something. Quiero decir algo., Quisiera decir algo.
2 (*in questions*)
Would you like ...? ¿Quieres ...?, ¿Quiere ...?
Would you like some Coke®? ¿Quieres Coca-Cola®?
Would you like something to eat? ¿Quieres comer algo?
Would you like anything else, sir? ¿Quiere usted algo más, señor?
3 (*when telling somebody politely*)
Would you help me, dad? ¿Puedes ayudarme, papá?

a
b
c
d
e
f
g
h
i
j
k
l
m
n
o
p
q
r
s
t
u
v
w
x
y
z

• *Languages and nationalities do not take a capital letter in Spanish.*

433

a
b
c
d
e
f
g
h
i
j
k
l
m
n
o
p
q
r
s
t
u
v
w
x
y
z

Would you wait here, please?
¿Puede usted esperar aquí, por favor?

⚲ **LANGUAGE**
Use the verb **querer** for meanings 1 and 2,
and **poder** for meaning 3.

to **wrap** verb
envolver
to wrap up a present envolver un
regalo
wrapping paper el papel de regalo

wrist noun
la **muñeca** fem.

to **write** verb
escribir
She's written me an email.
Me ha escrito un email.
We write to each other.
Nos escribimos.

to **write back** verb
contestar
He didn't write back. No me
contestó.

to **write down** verb
apuntar
I've written down the date.
He apuntado la fecha.

writer noun
el **escritor** masc., la **escritora** fem.

writing noun
la **letra** fem.

Xx

Xmas noun
la **Navidad** fem.

X-ray noun
la **radiografía** fem.
I've had an X-ray. Me han hecho
una radiografía.

to **X-ray** verb
(an arm, leg, etc.) **hacer una
radiografía de**

I can't read your writing.
No entiendo tu letra.
a writing pad un bloc (plural
los **blocs**)

wrong adjective
1 (not correct) **equivocado** masc.,
equivocada fem.
the wrong answer la respuesta
equivocada
2 (not true) **falso** masc., **falsa** fem.
That's wrong! ¡Eso es falso!
3 (no translation)
This is the wrong house. Ésta no es
la casa.
The book's in the wrong place.
El libro no está en su sitio.
4 (talking about people) **to be wrong**
estar equivocado masc., estar
equivocada fem.
You're wrong, Carol. Estás
equivocada, Carol.
5 What's wrong? ¿Qué pasa?
What's wrong with you? ¿Qué te
pasa?
**There's something wrong with the
computer.** El ordenador no
funciona bien.

wrong adverb
(not correctly) **mal**
I've done it wrong. Lo he hecho
mal.

They've X-rayed my leg. Me
han hecho una radiografía de la
pierna.

xylophone noun
el **xilófono** masc.
to play the xylophone tocar el
xilófono

• The months of the year and days of the week do not take a capital letter in Spanish.

Yy

yard noun
It's a hundred yards away. Está a unos cien metros de aquí.

 CULTURE
Spanish measurements are in metres and centimetres; a yard is about 90 centimetres.

to **yawn** verb
bostezar

year noun
el **año** masc.
this year este año
last year el año pasado
next year el año que viene
the New Year el Año Nuevo
Happy New Year! ¡Feliz Año Nuevo!
I'm in year five. Estoy en quinto de primaria.
I'm eight. Tengo ocho años.

LANGUAGE
English = **to be** eight years old
 I'm eight years old.
Spanish = **tener** ocho años
 Tengo ocho años.

yellow adjective
amarillo masc., **amarilla** fem.
a yellow blouse una blusa amarilla

yellow noun
el **amarillo** masc.
Yellow suits you. El amarillo te queda bien.

yes adverb
sí

yesterday adverb
ayer
yesterday morning ayer por la mañana
yesterday night ayer por la noche
the day before yesterday anteayer

yet adverb
1 not yet todavía no
I haven't seen her yet. Todavía no la he visto.
2 (in questions) **ya**
Are you ready yet? ¿Ya estás listo?

yoghurt noun
el **yogur** masc.
a plain yoghurt un yogur natural

yolk noun
la **yema** fem.

you pronoun

LANGUAGE
There are different ways of saying 'you' in Spanish: there's a familiar way (for talking to friends, people in your family, and people your own age) and a polite way (for grown-ups and strangers). There are also singular and plural words in Spanish – if you're talking to one person or more than one.

1 (not usually translated when it's the subject of the sentence)
You're my friend. Eres mi amigo.
Do you want some cake, children? ¿Niños, queréis un poco de tarta?
Would you like anything else, sir? ¿Quiere algo más, señor?
2 (familiar form) **tú**, (after preposition) **ti** (plural **vosotros** masc., **vosotras** fem.)
I'm ten. How old are you? Yo tengo diez años. ¿Cuántos años tienes tú?
I'm taller than you. Soy más alta que tú.
We're going to the cinema, and you? Nosotras vamos al cine, ¿y vosotras?

a
b
c
d
e
f
g
h
i
j
k
l
m
n
o
p
q
r
s
t
u
v
w
x
y
z

• See the centre section for verb tables.

a
b
c
d
e
f
g
h
i
j
k
l
m
n
o
p
q
r
s
t
u
v
w
x
y
z

Can we play with you? ¿Podemos jugar con vosotros?

A present for you, mum. Un regalo para ti, mamá.

Can I go with you, dad? ¿Puedo ir contigo, papa?

> 🔑 **LANGUAGE**
> Use **tú** and **vosotros/vosotras** when you want to give special importance to the word 'you'; use **ti** and **vosotros/vosotras** after a preposition ('with', 'for, etc.); use **tú** and **vosotros/vosotras** after the word 'than'. Remember the special word **contigo** to translate 'with you'.

3 (*polite form*) usted (plural **ustedes**)

What would you like? ¿Qué quiere usted?

What would you like? (*plural*) ¿Qué quieren ustedes?

for you para usted

for you (*plural*) para ustedes

4 (*familiar form: after a verb*) te (plural **os**)

I know you. Te conozco.

I want to help you. Quiero ayudarte.

I know you. (*plural*) Os conozco.

I want to help you. (*plural*) Quiero ayudaros.

> 🔑 **LANGUAGE**
> With infinitives **te** and **os** are joined with the verb to make one word.

5 (*familiar form: to you*) te (plural **os**)

I've written to you. Te he escrito.

I've written to you. (*plural*) Os he escrito.

6 (*polite form: after a verb*) lo *masc.* (plural **los**); la *fem.* (plural **las**)

I saw you, Mr Brown. Lo vi, señor Brown.

I saw you, Mrs Patel. La vi, señora Patel.

I saw you both. Los vi.

I want to help you both. Quiero ayudarlos.

> 🔑 **LANGUAGE**
> With infinitives, **lo/los** and **la/las** are joined with the verb to make one word.

> 🔑 **LANGUAGE**
> You can also use **le** and **les** in Spanish instead of **lo** and **los**, e.g. 'I saw you' can be **Lo vi** or **Le vi**.

7 (*polite form: to you*) le (plural **les**)

They've sent a letter to you. Le han mandado una carta.

They've sent a letter to you. (*plural*) Les han mandado una carta.

They want to send a letter to you. Quieren mandarle una carta.

They've sent it to you. Se la han mandado.

> 🔑 **LANGUAGE**
> When **le** or **les** are used with **lo/los** or **la/las** you use **se** instead.

young adjective

joven *masc. & fem.*

My sister's very young. Mi hermana es muy joven.

a young man un joven

a young woman una joven

young people los jóvenes

younger adjective

más joven *masc. & fem.*

I'm younger than you. Soy más joven que tú.

You're a year younger than me. Tienes un año menos que yo.

youngest adjective

menor *masc. & fem.*

I'm the youngest daughter. Soy la hija menor.

youngest noun

el or la menor *masc. & fem.*

I'm the youngest in the family. Soy el menor de la familia.

• *Use **el** and **uno** for masculine words and **la** and **una** for feminine words.*

your adjective
1 (*familiar form: talking to one person*) **tu** (plural **tus**)
your book tu libro
your sisters tus hermanas
2 (*familiar form: talking to more than one person*) **vuestro** *masc.*, **vuestra** *fem.*
your house vuestra casa
your toys vuestros juguetes
3 (*polite form*) **su** (plural **sus**)
Mr Clarke, here is your coat. Señor Clarke, aquí está su abrigo.
Where are your suitcases, miss? ¿Dónde están sus maletas, señorita?
4 (*with parts of the body, clothes, etc.*)
Have you washed your hands, David? ¿Te has lavado las manos, David?
Wash your hands, children. Niños, lavaos las manos.
Would you like to take your coat off, sir? ¿Quiere quitarse el abrigo, señor?

🔑 **LANGUAGE**
Use **te**, **os**, and **se** with **el**, **la**, **los**, or **las** in these examples.

yours pronoun
1 (*familiar form: talking to one person*) el **tuyo** *masc.*, la **tuya** *fem.*
my book and yours mi libro y el tuyo
My bike is older than yours. Mi bici es más vieja que la tuya.
That's yours. Eso es tuyo.
2 (*familiar form: talking to more than one person*) el **vuestro** *masc.*, la **vuestra** *fem.*
our CD and yours nuestro CD y el vuestro
our friends and yours nuestras amigas y las vuestras
These pens are yours. Estos bolis son vuestros.
3 (*polite form*) el **suyo** *masc.*, la **suya** *fem.*

my house and yours mi casa y la suya
These are yours, miss. Éstos son suyos, señorita.

yourself pronoun
1 (*familiar form*) **tú mismo** *masc.*, **tú misma** *fem.*
Do it yourself. Hazlo tú mismo.
2 (*familiar form: with a reflexive verb*) **te**
Go and wash yourself. Lávate.
3 (*polite form*) **usted mismo** *masc.*, **usted misma** *fem.*
Have you done it yourself, sir? ¿Lo ha hecho usted mismo, señor?
4 (*polite form: with a reflexive verb*) **se**
Have your hurt yourself, miss? ¿Se ha hecho daño, señorita?
5 **by yourself** solo *masc.*, sola *fem.*
Do you go out by yourself? ¿Sales sola?

yourselves pronoun
1 (*familiar form*) **vosotros mismos** *masc. plural*, **vosotras mismas** *fem. plural*
Have you written it yourselves? ¿Lo habéis escrito vosotros mismos?
2 (*familiar form: with a reflexive verb*) **os**
Go and wash yourselves. Lavaos.
3 (*polite form*) **ustedes mismos** *masc. plural*, **ustedes mismas** *fem. plural*
Have you seen it yourselves, ladies? ¿Lo han visto ustedes mismas, señoras?
4 (*polite form: with a reflexive verb*) **se**
Have you enjoyed yourselves? ¿Se han divertido?
5 **by yourselves** solos *masc. plural*, solas *fem. plural*
Do you go out by yourselves? ¿Salís solos?

youth hostel noun
el **albergue juvenil** *masc.*

yo-yo noun
el **yoyó** *masc.*

a b c d e f g h i j k l m n o p q r s t u v w x y z

• *Languages and nationalities do not take a capital letter in Spanish.*

Zz

zebra noun
la **cebra** *fem.*

zero noun
el **cero** *masc.*

zip noun
la **cremallera** *fem.*
to undo the zip abrir la cremallera

zoo noun
el **zoo** *masc.*, el **zoológico** *masc.*
I'm going to the zoo. Voy al zoo.

• *The months of the year and days of the week do not take a capital letter in Spanish.*

Age 4+

Oxford Very First Dictionary
9780199115419 HB / 9780199115426 PB

Age 5+

Oxford First Dictionary
9780199115198 HB / 9780199115204 PB

Oxford First Thesaurus
9780199115433 HB / 9780199115457 PB

Age 7+

Oxford Junior Illustrated Dictionary
NEW edition
9780199115211 HB / 9780199115228 PB

Oxford Junior Illustrated Thesaurus
NEW edition
9780199113194 HB / 9780199113200 PB

Oxford Junior Dictionary
NEW edition
9780199115129 HB

Oxford Junior Thesaurus
NEW edition
9780199115136 HB

Age 8+

Oxford Primary Dictionary
9780199115334 HB

Oxford Primary Thesaurus
9780199115167 HB

Oxford Primary Dictionary
9780199116931 HB / 9780199113088 PB

Oxford Primary Spanish Dictionary
9780199115242 HB

Age 10+

Oxford School Dictionary
NEW edition
9780199115341 HB

Oxford School Thesaurus
NEW edition
9780199115358 HB

Oxford Dictionary & Thesaurus
9780199115365 HB / 9780199115372 PB

Oxford Pocket School Dictionary
9780199115389 PB

Oxford Pocket School Thesaurus
9780199115396 PB

Oxford Mini School Dictionary
9780199115174 PB

Oxford Mini School Thesaurus
9780199115181 PB

Oxford Mini School Dictionary & Thesaurus

Oxford School Dictionary
9780199115280 PB

Oxford School Spanish Dictionary
9780199115297 PB

Oxford School German Dictionary
9780199115303 PB

Oxford Mini School Dictionary
9780199115273 PB

Oxford Mini School Spanish Dictionary
9780199115259 PB

Oxford Mini School German Dictionary
9780199115266 PB

Age 14+

Oxford Student's Dictionary
9780199115327 HB / 9780199115310 PB

Oxford Student's Thesaurus
9780199116522 PB

Oxford Children's Dictionaries
Think Dictionaries. Think Oxford.
www.oup.com